THE OXFORD HANDBOOK OF

# THE EGYPTIAN BOOK OF THE DEAD

# THE OXFORD HANDBOOK OF

# THE EGYPTIAN BOOK OF THE DEAD

*Edited by*
RITA LUCARELLI
*and*
MARTIN ANDREAS STADLER

Oxford University Press is a department of the University of Oxford. It furthers
the University's objective of excellence in research, scholarship, and education
by publishing worldwide. Oxford is a registered trade mark of Oxford University
Press in the UK and certain other countries.

Published in the United States of America by Oxford University Press
198 Madison Avenue, New York, NY 10016, United States of America.

© Oxford University Press 2023

All rights reserved. No part of this publication may be reproduced, stored in
a retrieval system, or transmitted, in any form or by any means, without the
prior permission in writing of Oxford University Press, or as expressly permitted
by law, by license, or under terms agreed with the appropriate reproduction
rights organization. Inquiries concerning reproduction outside the scope of the
above should be sent to the Rights Department, Oxford University Press, at the
address above.

You must not circulate this work in any other form
and you must impose this same condition on any acquirer.

CIP data is on file at the Library of Congress
ISBN 978–0–19–021000–7

DOI: 10.1093/oxfordhb/9780190210007.001.0001

Printed by Sheridan Books, Inc., United States of America

# Contents

*Acknowledgments* ix
*List of Contributors* xi

Introduction 1
RITA LUCARELLI AND MARTIN ANDREAS STADLER

## PART I  THE TEXTUAL HISTORY OF THE BOOK OF THE DEAD

1. The Transition from the Coffin Texts to the Book of the Dead 9
   LOUISE GESTERMANN

2. The Book of the Dead in the Eighteenth Dynasty 36
   IRMTRAUT MUNRO

3. The Ramesside Book of the Dead and the Deir el-Medina Tradition 61
   BARBARA LÜSCHER

4. The Book of the Dead in the Third Intermediate Period 76
   GIUSEPPINA LENZO

5. The Book of the Dead Papyri in the Twenty-Sixth Dynasty 116
   SVENJA A. GÜLDEN

6. The Last Books of the Dead 141
   FLORENCE ALBERT

## PART II  TYPES OF SOURCES: THE MATERIAL ASPECT OF THE BOOK OF THE DEAD

7. Writing Book of the Dead Manuscripts: Tasks and Traditions 161
   URSULA VERHOEVEN

8. Production and Layout of New Kingdom Book of the Dead Papyri  180
   Ogden Goelet

9. Female Owners of Book of the Dead Papyri  197
   Susanne Töpfer

10. Book of the Dead on Tissues: Shrouds and Mummy Bandages  218
    Annie Gasse

11. The Book of the Dead in Tombs  231
    Silvia Einaudi

12. The Book of the Dead in Temples  245
    Holger Kockelmann

# PART III  THE BOOK OF THE DEAD'S POSITION IN ANCIENT EGYPTIAN RELIGION

13. The Book of the Dead as a Source for the Study of Ancient Egyptian Religion: Methodology, Problems, Prospects  263
    Martin Andreas Stadler

14. The Funerary Literature Related to the Book of the Dead  279
    Foy Scalf

15. The Book of the Dead in the Ptolemaic and Roman Periods and the Contemporary Funerary Texts  295
    Andrea Kucharek

16. The Book of the *Ba*  321
    Andrea Kucharek

# PART IV  PARTICULAR ASPECTS OF THE BOOK OF THE DEAD'S CONTENTS

17. Thematic Groups and Sequences of Spells  341
    Felicitas Weber

18. Spell 1 of the Book of the Dead and Its Vignette  357
    Tarek Sayed Tawfik

19. The Field of Offerings or Field of Reeds  373
    Milagros Álvarez Sosa

20. The Judgment — JIŘÍ JANÁK — 393

21. Gods and Demons in the Book of the Dead — RITA LUCARELLI — 421

22. The So-Called *Chapitres supplémentaires* — ANNIK WÜTHRICH — 433

23. Illustrations in Saite through Ptolemaic Books of the Dead — MALCOLM MOSHER — 445

# PART V THE BOOK OF THE DEAD IN MODERN TIMES

24. The Time of the Pioneers (Seventeenth to Nineteenth Centuries) — BARBARA LÜSCHER — 487

25. Just a Catchy Title? On the History of Reception of the Egyptian Book of the Dead — ARIS LEGOWSKI — 504

26. Translating the Book of the Dead — BURKHARD BACKES — 521

27. The Conservation of Book of the Dead Papyri — MYRIAM KRUTZSCH — 542

28. The Art of Forgery in the Manuscript Culture in Antiquity — RITA LUCARELLI AND MALCOLM CHOAT — 556

*Index* — 569

# Acknowledgments

The idea for this volume came from a conversation with Stefan Vranka of Oxford University Press, whom we wish to thank for supporting the editing work through its various stages. Moreover, we are grateful to the publisher and its staff at Oxford University Press, in the United Kingdom and the United States, and in particular to Sarah Green, publishing editor of OUP's service provider Newgen Publishing UK Ltd., and our copy-editor Jennifer McIntyre. We would also like to thank Ms. Allister Humphrey (research assistant at the University of Würzburg) who assisted us with reviewing the English of the non-native speaker authors, and Ms. Veronika Appel (student assistant at the University of Würzburg) who assisted us with the index.

Rita Lucarelli                                                                     Martin Andreas Stadler

# List of Contributors

**Florence Albert**, Institut français d'archéologie orientale, Cairo

**Milagros Álvarez Sosa**, curator, Casa Museo Cayetano Gómez Felipe, La Laguna (Tenerife)

**Burkhard Backes**, Adjunct Professor of Egyptology and Research Associate, Eberhard Karl University Tübingen

**Malcolm Choat**, Professor of History and Head of Department of History, Macquarie University

**Silvia Einaudi**, Research Associate, École Pratique des Hautes Études de Paris, Section des sciences religieuses, équipe Égypte ancienne : archéologie, langue, religion

**Annie Gasse**, Directeur de Recherche, Centre nationale de la Recherche Scientifique, affiliated to the UMR 5140 – University of Montpellier II

**Louise Gestermann**, Adjunct Professor of Egyptology, Georg August University Göttingen

**Ogden Goelet**, Research Associate at the Institute for the Study of the Ancient World, New York University

**Svenja A. Gülden**, Research Associate of "Altägyptische Kursivschriften", Academy of Sciences and Literature Mainz

**Jiří Janák**, Associate Professor of Egyptology, Charles University Prague

**Holger Kockelmann**, Professor of Egyptology, University of Leipzig

**Myriam Krutzsch**, Former Papyrus Conservator, Egyptian Museum Berlin

**Andrea Kucharek**, Research Associate, Ruprecht Karl University Heidelberg

**Aris Legowski**, University of Bonn

**Giuseppina Lenzo**, Senior Lecturer of Egyptology, Institute of Archeology and Classical Studies, University of Lausanne

**Rita Lucarelli**, Associate Professor of Egyptology, University of California, Berkeley

**Barbara Lüscher**, University of Basel

**Malcolm Mosher**, Independent Scholar

**Irmtraut Munro**, former senior research associate of the Bonn Totenbuchprojekt, North Rhine-Westphalian Academy of Sciences, Humanities and the Arts Düsseldorf

**Foy Scalf**, Research Associate, Head of Research Archives, and Head of the Integrated Database Project at the Oriental Institute, University of Chicago

**Martin Andreas Stadler**, Professor of Egyptology, Julius Maximilian University Würzburg

**Tarek Sayed Tawfik**, Associate Professor of Egyptology, University of Cairo

**Susanne Töpfer**, curator responsible for the papyrus collection in the Museo Egizio of Turin

**Ursula Verhoeven**, Professor of Egyptology, Johannes Gutenberg University Mainz

**Felicitas Weber**, University of Bonn

**Annik Wüthrich**, Research Associate, University of Vienna

# INTRODUCTION

## RITA LUCARELLI AND MARTIN ANDREAS STADLER

An overwhelming and often bewildering plethora of sources has been passed down from ancient Egypt. Some can be grouped as corpora of which many attestations have survived; others are unique but may quote from well-known sources. The ancient Egyptian Book of the Dead is certainly one of these famous corpora that any student of Egyptian religion will come across sooner or later because the Book of the Dead (BD) is the most representative textual evidence of the Egyptian mortuary religion and of the magical and ritual practices belonging to it.

Of course, we, the present *Oxford Handbook*'s two editors, were no exception: both of us came across it during our studies. The Book of the Dead enthralled us so much that we even chose subjects from the field of the Book of the Dead for our theses and thus devoted a considerable time at crucial points in our careers to the Book of the Dead. Our previous work on this fascinating corpus shows the great diversity of approaches that the Book of the Dead allows: one can use it either to study a single manuscript, or as a guideline through the thicket of Egyptian religious texts and traditions while studying a wider issue of ancient Egyptian religion such as a particular deity (Stadler, 2009) or a category of netherworld inhabitants (Lucarelli, 2006a). For the latter way of studying the sources, the two editors again provide two different examples conditioned by the evidence that the Egyptians themselves provided. Thus, Stadler (2003) even conducted research on a very small selection of spells surviving in a manuscript from the very end of the tradition, rendering the papyrus a complex product of textual tradition, while Rita Lucarelli (2006b) chose an almost full set of spells on one single scroll a beautifully written (hieratic) and illustrated 18-meter-long papyrus dated to the Twenty-first Dynasty. Her case study focussed on the patterns of selection and distribution of texts and vignettes within a document.

When texts and vignettes were chosen to be copied on a medium, be that a papyrus, coffin, tomb wall, or other magical object, the funerary beliefs and practices of the time and where the papyrus was produced played a role, and such an influence can be seen in the final product. Lucarelli's study shows that each Book of the Dead scroll is unique in the way it originates from a wider textual tradition that reiterates and at the same time renews the contents through a creative process of innovation within the tradition. Each papyrus or other medium of the Book of the Dead is a unique artifact that expresses a world view and a set of magical and mortuary rituals of whom knowledge is necessary for the modern readers to fully appreciate the Book of the Dead even if only in translation.

Martin Stadler believes that those translations, even if addressed to a wider public, are not particularly accessible to non-specialists because many spells remain esoteric even to Egyptologists and require some exegetical effort. That was his approach when he took the Book of the Dead as the starting point for an investigation on a general issue of Egyptian religious history (Stadler, 2009). However, he identified three problems that prevent the Book of the Dead from being an easy source, as it superficially might seem, and that called for careful methodological reflections: (i) the variation of text witnesses—almost every manuscript deviates from the next one in more or less crucial and in more or less numerous aspects, which leads to (ii) a wide range of more or less deviating Egyptological translations, i.e., interpretations that require (iii) one's own positioning when reading the Book of the Dead. To put it polemically, everybody has her or his own understanding of the Book of the Dead.

Thus, coming from different angles, we both encountered issues that center around the texts and images providing unique information not only on mortuary traditions but also on myths and priestly rituals as well as the scribal practices in ancient Egypt from the second millennium BCE to the Hellenistic Period. This combination of thematic richness and potential approaches to the corpus sparked the idea of a handbook on the Book of the Dead in each of us individually until we exchanged our ideas and then decided to act together. Our main motivation was the realization that specialists who have researched a specific topic for years tend to have information that newcomers do not share. Because of this, obstacles arise, usually inadvertently. We felt a handbook could help to tear down those hurdles for students as well as colleagues from neighboring fields. The *Handbook* aims to do this in five sections.

"Book of the Dead" is the conventional name coined by Carl Richard Lepsius when he published the funerary papyrus inscribed for a certain Iufankh who dwelled in Thebes during the Ptolemaic Period (Lepsius, 1842). Egyptologists subsequently realized that this scroll was not unique in terms of its contents and, by taking over Lepsius's nomenclature for similar manuscripts (*Todtenbuch* in nineteenth-century German orthography, *Book of the Dead* in English, *Livre des Morts* in French, *Libro dei Morti* in Italian), they gave this title to a collection of magical compositions the ancient Egyptians actually called "Book for Coming Forth by Day." This title refers to the main wish of the deceased, who hoped to be able to leave their tomb and move freely between this world and the next. The Book of the Dead corpus includes about 200 spells (although only selections of them are found on each papyrus) supplemented by illustrations, the so-called vignettes. All provided the equipment thought to be helpful to achieve this goal. However, each Book of the Dead manuscript is unique: none contains the entire corpus of spells but rather only a certain selection, possibly the result of the ancient owner's choice and taste. We do know, however, of the existence of workshops where the papyri were bought, and therefore a few common stylistic features can be recognized according to different regional traditions of writing and manufacture.

The first section is devoted to the textual history. The Book of the Dead is a historically changing corpus of spells, the core of which emerges from the Coffin Texts (CT) at the transition from the Middle to the New Kingdom (Gestermann, this volume) and which finally continues into the Roman Period (Albert, this volume). In other words, it was an actual corpus for at least 1,700 years, although the majority of the spells are at least 400 years older due to their use in the CT and a few of them go back as far as the Pyramid Texts (PT) and thus at least to the twenty-fourth century BCE. In view of this long textual tradition, a considerable variance in the understanding of the text by the Egyptians themselves is hardly surprising. At best, the Book of the Dead offers somewhat uniform readings for certain epochs of Egyptian religious history (Munro, Lüscher, Lenzo, Gülden, all this volume). However, even within specific epochs, the individual manuscripts show variations among themselves. The historical change, which caused even greater differences in readings and deviations, influenced not only the choice of words in the individual text witnesses, which can be traced back to the continuous development of the Egyptian language during the long period of transmission, but also—partly brought about by this—the meaning of the text. Furthermore, issues of textual history transgress the boundaries of the Book of the Dead in the narrow sense and thus of Section One. Therefore, some contributions in Section Three, *The Book of the Dead's Position in Ancient Egyptian Religion*, on later funerary corpora are related to chapters in the first section. While Scalf contextualizes the Book of the Dead within a wider framework of Egyptian funerary literature as it is attested in different periods, Kucharek focuses on the tradition in the Ptolemaic and Roman Periods and shows how, in particular, the Book of the Dead may be perceived as a reservoir of religious texts. Spells from it are also found in various other contexts of use, which may even be the primary ones, showing that the Book of the Dead occupies a central position within the religious texts of Egypt as a whole. It can thus serve as a guide through a good part of Egyptian religious history, whose developments it follows (Stadler, this volume). However, each spell of the Book of the Dead is embedded in a sequence of spells, thus providing a context that might be relevant for the interpretation of the spell's context. Each period had its own preferred sequence—an issue that Weber treats in her chapter, which serves as an introduction to Section Four, *Particular Aspects of the Book of the Dead's Contents*. Addressing the question of how certain spells gain a special place in the corpus, seen from a chronological perspective, she explains that spells are generally grouped in thematic clusters. This changing of the grouping raises the question of whether the spells' messages changed over time. An intensive exegetical study of all the BD spells cannot be done before a thematic structure of a text witness can be soundly assessed. Manuscripts with sequences of spells exemplary for certain epochs treated as a closed system have been examined, for example, the CT (Willems, 1996; Meyer-Dietrich, 2001, 2006), but rarely the Book of the Dead itself (e.g., Lucarelli, 2006b).

In Stadler's aforementioned exegetical approach, a crucial element of the Book of the Dead manuscripts is mostly left aside, namely the visual aspect of the text witnesses: Book of the Dead manuscripts are not just texts but also materializations of a text, or rather of texts. Those materializations again experience a formal change throughout the almost one and a half millennia of their tradition. The variants among the spells and vignettes, as well as in the papyrus layout, are important to analyze in order to understand how the Book of the Dead has never been a canonical composition but rather has changed throughout time and adapted to the religious and socio-cultural issues of each period of ancient Egyptian history and according to the local workshop where it was produced. Additionally, paratextual features (the vignettes) are in fact an integral element of any Book of the Dead scroll. The numerous illustrations in this handbook—particularly those in Section Two, *Types of Sources: The Material Aspect of the Book of the Dead*, which are untypical for a handbook—show how important both the material and the paratextual aspects of these papyrus scrolls are. These vignettes also make the papyri attractive objects for a wider audience, particularly for visitors to any museum that owns one or more of those several-meters-long scrolls, which are impressive because of their sheer size.

The corpus of the Book of the Dead spells can be found written on a wide variety of media, not just on papyrus: mummy bandages, shrouds, and other funerary items that accompanied the deceased in the grave have all been used as text media for this corpus. Verhoeven prepares the ground by generally explaining the production process and basic scribal practices. On this builds Goelet's chapter, which goes into greater detail and presents a case study, which focuses on the New Kingdom, of how we can reconstruct the production process by having a closer look at the papyri. By discussing the papyri's layout and scribal features, one can compare the Book of the Dead on papyrus with copies on tissue and mummy bandages (Gasse, this volume) to understand how the scribes and artists working on each version selected and adapted the text and the images to the specific medium on which they were being copied. How gender of those for whom the scrolls were made affects the material aspects is still a largely ill-studied subject (Töpfer, this volume). While the occurrence of inscriptions on tomb walls, i.e., in a funerary context, is to be expected (Einaudi, this volume), the manifold parallels in other magical and ritual texts attested to in temple inscriptions (Kockelmann, this volume) and on magical objects and amulets raise the important question of the mortuary literature in fact being strongly linked with the daily religious life and beliefs of the ancient Egyptians.

Again, material aspects also play an important role in chapters in other sections, more precisely when it comes to important individual spells that stand out in terms of both their length and their large-scale vignettes, which can occur on their own, without the accompanying text. These are treated in Section Four, *Particular Aspects of the Book of the Dead's Contents*. After Weber has given an overview on how the spells were grouped thematically (something that changed over time), the next chapter starts with a detailed discussion of some outstandingly significant spells, beginning with the very first spell (Tawfik, this volume), goes on to the Field of Offerings as described in BD spell 110 (Alvarez Sosa, this volume), and leads to the judgment of the dead, for which BD spell 125 provides the necessary knowledge (Janák, this volume). The role of the vignettes in general is central to the magical function of the corpus and for providing the deceased with a visual résumé of the text (Mosher, this volume); moreover, some compositions are only attested in certain late papyri and deserve a study of their own (Wüthrich, this volume). And if the Book of the Dead is perceived as a magical handbook for the deceased's journey to the netherworld and her or his existence there, with all the dangers that one might encounter in this mysterious, unknown, and therefore daunting place, then the major role played by gods and demons in the spells is not surprising. Gods and demons are pivotal for the understanding of the corpus itself and of how ancient Egyptian magical and ritual practices are mirrored in it (Lucarelli, this volume).

The fifth and last section of this book, *The Book of the Dead in Modern Times*, illustrates the history of the study and reception of the Book of the Dead since the eighteenth century, the first papyrus facsimiles and editions that appeared in the nineteenth century (Lüscher, this volume) to the more modern reception of the corpus in the arts, literature, and music, as filtered through the so-called phenomenon of "Egyptomania" (Legowski, this volume). The methodology and interpretations of its various translators have had a great influence on the modern reception of the Book of the Dead (Backes, this volume). However, this brings us back to the issue of the variant, differing, sometimes even contradicting translations as far as details are concerned, and how to deal with them. Stemmatics as a form of textual criticism appears to be a method of avoiding this confusion, but it has also its disadvantages under the specific circumstances of the Egyptian forms of textual tradition. One possible methodology that attempts to achieve a sensible access to the corpus is offered here (Stadler, this volume), but it is just one option among many. The work of conservators in museums is yet another modern form of dealing with the papyri—and this brings us back again to the materiality of the Book of the Dead papyri. Modern conservation technologies have made it possible to read papyri containing peculiar variants of spells and vignettes that would have otherwise been lost and remained undocumented (Krutzsch, this volume). Finally, the popularity of the Book of the Dead since the time of the first discoveries of papyrus scrolls has also brought about the production of forgeries that were (and occasionally still are) sold to private collectors but that can also unfortunately be found in museums and libraries (Choat/Lucarelli, this volume).

This handbook aims to shed light on all the aspects and topics of research mentioned above, in relation both to the Book of the Dead itself and to broader research on ancient Egyptian religion and magic. Certain issues run like a red thread through the entire *Handbook*, such as the historical perspective, the materiality and visuality, and the question of how to understand the Book of the Dead. Thus, there are different ways of reading the present *Handbook*, and this introduction has attempted to provide an extensive overview of the following sequence of chapters. It is hoped that the essays included in this volume will refresh and stimulate the study of the Book of the Dead in multiple directions, as summarized in the book sections presented above, and lay the foundations for further studies of a "book" that was made about 3,500 years ago for the dead by the living, and which today speaks to the living about the ancient Egyptian conception of death and rebirth, in assimilation to the daily cycle of the sun god and of his "coming forth by day."

## Bibliography

Lepsius, C. R. (1842). *Das Todtenbuch der Ägypter nach dem hieroglyphischen Papyrus in Turin mit einem Vorworte zum Ersten Male hrsg. von R. Lepsius* (Leipzig: Georg Wigand).

Lucarelli, R. (2006a). "Demons in the Book of the Dead." In *Totenbuch-Forschungen. Gesammelte Beiträge des 2. Internationalen Symposiums 2005*. Studien zum altägyptischen Totenbuch, 11, edited by B. Backes, I. Munro, and S. Stöhr, 203–12 (Wiesbaden).

Lucarelli, R. (2006b). *The Book of the Dead of Gatseshen: Ancient Egyptian Funerary Religion in the Tenth Century BC*. Egyptologische Uitgaven, 21 (Leiden: Nederlands Inst. voor het Nabije Oosten).

Meyer-Dietrich, E. (2001). *Nechet und Nil: Ein ägyptischer Frauensarg des Mittleren Reiches aus religionsökologischer Sicht*. Acta Universitatis Upsaliensis, 18 (Uppsala: Uppsala University Library).

Meyer-Dietrich, E. (2006). *Senebi und Selbst: Personenkonstituenten zur rituellen Wiedergeburt in einem Frauensarg des Mittleren Reiches*. Orbis Biblicus et Orientalis, 216. (Freiburg, Schweiz; Göttingen: Academic Press; Vandenhoeck & Ruprecht).

Stadler, M. A. (2003). *Der Totenpapyrus des Pa-Month (P. Bibl. nat. 149)*. Studien zum altägyptischen Totenbuch, 6 (Wiesbaden: Harrassowitz).

Stadler, M. A. (2009). *Weiser und Wesir: Studien zu Vorkommen, Rolle und Wesen des Gottes Thot im ägyptischen Totenbuch*. Orientalische Religionen in der Antike, 1 (Tübingen: Mohr Siebeck).

Willems, H. (1996). *The Coffin of Heqata (Cairo JdE 36481): A Case Study of Egyptian Funerary Culture of the Early Middle Kingdom*. Orientalia Lovaniensia Analecta, 70 (Leuven: Peeters).

# PART I

# THE TEXTUAL HISTORY OF THE BOOK OF THE DEAD

# CHAPTER 1

# THE TRANSITION FROM THE COFFIN TEXTS TO THE BOOK OF THE DEAD

LOUISE GESTERMANN

## First Appearance and Most Extensive Distribution: The Coffin Texts in the Eleventh and the First Half of the Twelfth Dynasty

At the beginning of the Middle Kingdom, during the Eleventh Dynasty, a new corpus of funerary texts appears, designated as CT, to set them apart from the PT (Jürgens, 1995: 5–6). The earliest sources of the CT originate from Thebes, the newly established capital at the beginning of the Middle Kingdom in the south of Egypt and away from the cultural center of the Old Kingdom at Memphis (Willems, 2008: 178–81): a sarcophagus (T3C; for an explanation of the sigla here and in the following, see de Buck, 1935–1961; Willems, 1988: 19–34; and Willems, 2014: 230–315) and a burial chamber (TT 319) belonging to two royal wives of Mentuhotep II, unifier and founder of the Middle Kingdom. Both women were entombed in his funerary temple (Willems, 1988: 110; Jürgens, 1995: 5–6; Lapp, 1993: 252 § 600, 307–8; Backes, 2020). In addition, the high and the highest officials of the Theban administration, including a vizier, had their burial chambers (TT 240, belonging to the overseer of sealers, Meru), their limestone burial chamber and coffin (T1C, belonging to the follower, Horhetep), their limestone coffin (T2C, belonging to the vizier, Dagi) and wooden coffins (T9C, belonging to the overseer of the house, Buau, T2NY, belonging to the high administrator and overseer of the sealed goods, Meketre, and T1L, belonging to the king's acquaintance, Imau) decorated with CT (Willems, 1988: 32 and 34; Lapp, 1993: 306–11; Grajetzki, 2000). The burials of these officials are situated in the basin of Deir el-Bahri, close to Mentuhotep's funerary temple. The perception of the CT as "new" texts is evident, since they are mostly attested en bloc on the aforementioned monuments and coffins and are kept apart from the PT on the same monuments, although the latter may also have been used in the south during the Eleventh Dynasty for the first time (Mathieu, 2004: 247–62). In fact, the spells of the so-called CT must be considered newly added. They have not been attested for the Old Kingdom yet, for the most part, but they may have already been part of the pool of funerary texts and therefore added to those spells with which coffins and so forth could be inscribed.

As early as the Eleventh Dynasty, the distribution of the CT is evident outside Thebes, especially in Deir el-Bersheh in Middle Egypt (Willems, 1988: 20–21 and 68–81; Willems, 2008, 2014; Lapp, 1993: 71–76, §§ 169–80; for the text program of the sources see Lesko, 1979). In this necropolis, the nomarchs, including some even carrying the title of vizier, had their coffins inscribed with CT, as well as a few of their wives (see, among others, the coffins B3–4Bo and B6–7Bo). The reasons for the expansion of the CT's usage in this area in particular might have to do with events occurring in the course of Egypt's reunification under Mentuhotep II.

During the following generations, the CT spread almost explosively all over the country; their appearance primarily on coffins and sarcophagi is eponymous (Lapp, 1993; Willems, 1988). Many new cemeteries were opened for this new corpus of funerary texts. But, as the Deir el-Bersheh evidence shows, the CT texts were used exclusively for a small group of burials (Willems, 2014: 140–54). This tradition is mainly supported by the nomarchs of Middle Egypt, with the centers of this tradition being at Deir el-Bersheh and Assiut. Apart from that, with the relocation of the residence to Itjitawy under Amenemhat I, the necropolis of Lisht evolved into a royal cemetery (Allen, 1996: 1–15; Willems, 2014: 172–76; Grajetzki, 2010: 28–31). His officials followed him and were also buried there. This early stage of the first appearance of the CT and of their most extensive distribution ends in the second half of the Twelfth Dynasty, when the nomarchs lost their powerful position due to the centralization of the administrative structure that began in the reign of Senwosret II.

During this time in the early Middle Kingdom the number of CT, as documented on the coffins of the aforementioned elite officials, increased to almost 1,200 spells (de Buck, 1935–1961). They became an integral component of the decoration on the inner sides of these box-shaped coffins. The CT are probably of different origins; the content of the spells varies greatly, and it is not easy to understand and interpret the individual spells. Moreover, the great number of spells provided an opportunity to create varying decoration programs: each coffin shows only a selection of the corpus. Nevertheless, some observations can be made in regard to the use of the CT and their importance for the deceased, even though only a small number of coffins have been studied in further detail concerning their decorations and the function of these (Willems, 1996; Backes, 2020). Texts, as well as representations, perform a specific function that seems to be very similar for most of the coffins of this time. This would change during later use and obviously differs from the application of the BD.

The deceased, lying in his coffin on his left side and facing the east, is surrounded by his own cosmos, which is created both by the box-shaped coffin and by the decoration of the individual sides. As can be pointed out for these early coffins, the decoration of each inner side is connected with a particular theme that refers to both the position and the orientation of the side (Willems, 1988: 175ff; 2014: 182–92; 1996: 363–88; 1997: 343–72). For the relationship between hymns addressed to goddesses that act as guardians of parts of the deceased's body and the position of these spells on the coffin see Nyord, 2007: 5–34). Spells from the CT on these earlier coffins of the Middle Kingdom normally refer to the deceased's journey through the night and, within this journey, to the last phase before sunrise. The sunrise itself, along with the hope for one's own rebirth and renewal, is present only as an event in the future, expressed in the texts by the use of wish clauses. The deceased reaches the point of sunrise, but is not taking part in it.

The direction of the sunset and the western or back side of the coffin represents the world the deceased enters after his death and the sphere he lives in now. Corresponding CT highlight this movement and this specific situation. The CT on the bottom of the coffin reflect an understanding of this part of the coffin as the underworld. The decoration with the Book of Two Ways, indicating a kind of landscape of the western sphere, shows this reference very clearly. Other CT on the bottom, which focus on the passing of gates or on the crossing to the netherworld in a ferry boat, often include an examination of the deceased. Here, he needs to prove his profound knowledge, for instance of gatekeepers who guard the doors and gates to the "House of Osiris," or give mythological explanations for the individual parts of the ferry boat. The decoration on the eastern or front side of the coffin has two themes that are closely connected. One of them is the sunrise the deceased witnesses while looking through the pair of eyes (*udjat(wḏꜣt)*-eyes) with which the panel is adorned, representing his own hope for rebirth as well. The second issue is in regard to the provisioning of the deceased and can be illustrated by the representations of a false door and an offering table as offering places. The accompanying CT underline these two functions—for example, with spells ensuring the continuing provisioning. The two panels at the head and feet of the deceased are connected with ritual acts that refer to these parts of the body. The decoration of the lid portrays the night sky.

There are different ways to approach the themes of a side. Cosmological events like the sunrise can be described in a CT; mythological interpretations can be given and may explain special situations or acts; or else the CT can refer to ritual ceremonies like the mummification of the deceased or the *Schutzwache* in the embalming hall. The reference to a ritual event depends on the central idea that the son acts as ritualist for his deceased father. The main, but not the only model is that of the son Horus and his (dead) father Osiris. The CT can also present the deceased acting for the god Osiris.

The decoration on the exterior sides of a coffin shows *udjat*-eyes corresponding with the eyes on the inner side, as well as palace facades and false doors presenting the coffin as the habitat of the deceased and these special locations as places of worship and offering. The texts written on these sides offer formulae ("A royal offering of Anubis, who is on his mountain, ..., i.e., his [i.e., the deceased's] beautiful burial in the western desert...") and short texts that place the deceased under the protection of special gods, such as the members of the ennead of Heliopolis and the sons of Horus (e.g., "the revered one near Anubis"). At the same time, these texts clarify that the deceased is now a member of the realm of gods.

Therefore, a coffin with its texts, among them CT, and its representations has to be understood as a coherent and complex composition. It illustrates and explains the coffin as a cosmos in which the deceased is now—and forever—living.

# The Decline of the Coffin Texts: Second Half of the Twelfth and Thirteenth Dynasties

The time between the late Twelfth Dynasty and the first half of the Second Intermediate Period is marked by numerous changes in historical, political, social, and cultural conditions. Likewise, the appearance of the CT in this period is influenced to a certain extent by this situation. The change of ruling families, the location of their residences, and the use of different royal cemeteries and burial places for the high officials constitute the first framework in which the appearance of the CT can be embedded (Ryholt, 1997: 5–6 and 293–311). More so than during other periods, the time between the later Middle Kingdom and the Second Intermediate Period involved the demarcation of cultural areas, each one of them with its own special features. Separate developments within the locally characterized dynasties (XIII, XVI, and XVII) are clearly distinguishable and set them apart from the two Cananaean dynasties (XIV and XV) in the Delta (Ryholt, 1997: 5, 94–150 and passim). The Fourteenth and Fifteenth dynasties seem to be of no importance for the history of the CT (for the occurrence of sources with CT in the Delta, see later in this chapter). This situation, as well as the accessibility and, respectively, the lack of accessibility to cultural heritage, is also responsible for the occurrence of the CT or the lack of sources with CT.

After the reign of Amenemhat II, several necropolises emerged in the region between Memphis and the entrance to the Fayum, where burials of the royal family and high officials are attested (Gestermann, 1995: 37–41). Their distribution is based on the position of the royal pyramids (Hölzl, 2004: 117–37). At Dahshur, around the pyramids of Amenemhat II, Senwosret III, and Amenemhat III, associated cemeteries were developed for the members of the royal family and officials (Grajetzki, 2010: 24–28). Additional necropolises are attested in el-Lahun and el-Hagara, on the periphery of the pyramid of Senwosret II, and in Hawara, where Amenemhat III built his second pyramid (Grajetzki, 2010: 32–39). The cemetery of Saqqara does not display the changeover to the northerly necropolis (like Dahshur, for instance), since the area was used as a burial ground throughout all of pharaonic history (Lapp, 1993: 41–55, §§ 113–39;

Willems, 1988: 105–7; Grajetzki, 2010: 23). A monument like the tomb of Khesuwer in Kom el-Hisn (KH1KH) on the western edge of the Nile delta, the dating of which is uncertain, might have been affected by the situation at Saqqara (Silvermann, 1988; 1996: 136–37; Backes, 2005: 159–62).

The second framework in which the occurrence of the CT during the end of the Middle Kingdom can be seen is defined by the disappearance of the nomarchs both as a social group and as local seats of power (Willems, 2014: 222, 229 and passim). This development was caused by the centralization of the administration under Senwosret II, and had a considerable impact on the local distribution of elite burials and on the occurrence of CT. Before the end of the Twelfth Dynasty, starting in the reigns of Senwosret II and III, the number of richly equipped burials clearly decreases in provincial cemeteries, which were used up until that point by the nomarchs, their families, and their subordinates. These social groups were no longer bearers of the CT tradition, a situation only partly compensated for by the royal cemeteries.

The political situation and changes brought to an end the CT tradition as it was known from the earlier Middle Kingdom. This happened either at some point during the reign of Senwosret III or somewhat later in the reign of Amenemhat III. A disparate occurrence and use of CT replaced the quite clearly defined appearance of the CT and their meaning for the deceased in the former time. More detailed information about this new situation is affected to some degree by uncertainties concerning above all the date of the sources, but also by the fragmentary condition of some objects. Nevertheless, the sources show a new understanding of the CT and give an insight into the transition from the CT to the BD.

For the first time since the Eleventh Dynasty, objects in royal burials of the late Twelfth and Thirteenth Dynasties were now inscribed once again with CT. Most of these sources come from the cemetery of Dahshur. By the end of the Twelfth Dynasty, possibly in the reign of Amenemhat III (Grajetzki, 2010: 24), some coffins were being produced for princesses. These are the coffins of Sathathormeret (Da1C), Khenmet (Da3X), and Itweret (Da4X), as well as coffin Da2X of It (Grajetzki, 2010: 24 and 96–97; Willems, 1988: 22–23; Lapp, 1993: 280–81). The coffins are associated with the canopic boxes of Sathathormeret, Khenmet, and Itweret (Lüscher, 1990: 75–76 and 98 (nr. 17), 104 (nr. 50), and 105 (nr. 56)). Chronologically, these burials date to before the (single) royal burial of Awibre Hor, from which parts of a coffin (Da4C) originate (Grajetzki, 2010: 24 and 25; Lapp, 1993: 280–81; Willems, 1988: 22; Lesko, 1979: 54), and the burials of the princess Nubheteptikhered (with the coffin Da2C) and Satsobek (with the coffin Da3C) (Grajetzki, 2010: 26–27; Lapp, 1993: 280–281; Willems, 1988: 22; Lesko, 1979: 54). The coffins display similarities to each other and can be dated, since Awibre Hor can be identified as a king of the Thirteenth Dynasty (Ryholt, 1997: 208, 216, 318, and passim). The coffin of Queen Keminub (Da5X) likely also stems from the Thirteenth Dynasty (Grajetzki, 2010: 27–28).

Even though they are of different kinds, in various conditions, and from slightly different times, these sources allow some general remarks concerning the occurrence of CT. In a first approach, it must be pointed out that the shape of the coffins as text media for the CT remains the same as before, meaning box-shaped. However, the decoration of canopic boxes with CT constitutes an innovation, even though some objects other than coffins were also inscribed with CT in earlier times. It is also a new development in that the sources are now decorated with only a few spells and their text program shows a high degree of repetition.

Besides the typological similarities, the coffins of the princesses from the Twelfth Dynasty also display a strikingly analogue text program. It contains several PT, a formula for "opening the face" of the deceased (*wn-ḥr*) to provide him with offerings (CT 788), in other words, a so-called pyramidion-spell (de Buck, 1961 (1); Vernus, 1976: 119–28; Grajetzki, 2010: 61; Willems, 1988: 168–69), as well as individual spells of funerary content that had not occurred in the corpus of CT so far. These spells were provided with "temporary numbers" (Lesko, 1979: 54 and 55). They include a text shaped as a divine speech of Geb (CT temp. 361), which also appears together with CT 788 on the canopic boxes of the women (Lüscher, 1990: 75–76).

In regard to the text program of the three coffins, Da2–4C, from the Thirteenth Dynasty (always placed on the outer side), the only completely preserved coffin, that of Nubheteptikhered (Da2C), displays a considerable reduction of the inscriptions. It is not discernible whether the two other coffins, those of Satsobek (Da3C) and Awibre Hor (Da4C), follow this trend because of their fragmentary state of preservation. On all three coffins, once again the *wn-ḥr* formula (CT 788) is preserved, as it is on coffins and some canopic jars from the earlier group (Willems, 1988: 168–69; Grajetzki, 2010: 61–64). The *wn-ḥr* formula also makes it possible to connect the previously mentioned coffins from Dahshur (Da1–4C and Da2–4X) with sources from other sites, since the text is also attested on the coffins from Meir (M2NY), Lisht (L2Li), and Thebes (T3Be). Further examples are additional texts from the outer sides of the coffins from Dahshur (Grajetzki, 2010: 61–64; Lapp, 1993: 226–29 §§ 536–538; Willems, 1988: 168–71).

Only two text fields of Queen Keminub's coffin (Da5X) have survived (Grajetzki, 2010): 27–28). They likely belong to the coffin's external side, between the horizontal and the vertical inscription. This source follows the innovation of writing CT on the outer sides of the coffin. Da5X shares this feature not only with other coffins from the Thirteenth Dynasty mentioned earlier, but also with the coffin of Amenhotep (Da6X) of the same time (Grajetzki, 2010: 26–27). The preserved fragments of Keminub's coffin display BD 151, the spell for the mummy mask, and BD 30B, a spell addressed to the deceased's heart, imploring it to be strong (Grajetzki, 2010: 28; Lüscher, 1998: 52–53). While the coffin of Keminub is the earliest attestation for BD 30B, mask spell BD 151 occurs on coffins from the Middle Kingdom (CT 531) and can therefore be used for comparison. According to Barbara Lüscher, "The fragmentary copy of *Kmj-nwb* is already in the edited version of the evidence of the New Kingdom and hence no longer follows the tradition of the masks from the Middle Kingdom" (Lüscher, 1998: 52). Despite a deviating tradition for masks and coffins being rather unlikely (Lüscher, 1998: 52), it must be pointed out that only sources from Meir are known for CT 531 and that other areas could certainly have developed a different text tradition. A single piece of evidence from Deir-Rifeh is impossible to interpret (Lüscher, 1998: 52 with n. 184). However, these comments do not reject the possibility that the text on the coffin of Keminub already distinctively hints at the text version of the BD. This could certainly be the case. This isolated evidence is, however, barely sufficient to justify the assumption of an accomplished BD revision at this point.

The sources from Dahshur in the Twelfth and Thirteenth Dynasties display several developments and innovations. Coffins, as well as other objects of the burial equipment like canopic boxes, could be used as text media. A reduced use of CT and an occurrence of new spells can be observed. Since most of the sources are preserved in rather poor condition, further remarks as to the sources in Dahshur themselves and with regard to their relationships to sources from other cemeteries are yet to be clarified. However, it is notable that the text material from Dahshur was regionally widespread; for example, CT in a similar layout occur in Mirgissa (Grajetzki, 2010: 54). Several necropolises can be connected through the texts from Dahshur, as can be seen from the occurrence of the pyramidion texts in Lisht and Thebes. The question remains whether this phenomenon can be explained by the relocation of the text material, which could have coincided with the rise of a new royal dynasty.

Developments comparable to that seen in the royal cemeteries can be observed in the occurrence of CT in some private burials: less elaborately decorated coffins, a less extensive collection of spells written on the coffins, a high rate of repetition within the used spells, and the appearance of new texts. Two examples from the cemeteries of Beni Hasan and Meir may illustrate this.

The coffin of Netjeruhotep from Beni Hasan (BH4C) belongs to a group of coffins (BH1Br, BH4C, BH1–2Liv, and BH15) that were produced during the later years of Amenemhat II and the early reign of Senwosret III (Willems, 1988: 66–67 and 22; Lapp, 1993: 61–66, §§ 155–62, and 278–79). Similar to early examples, the coffin BH4C shows that the text material was continuously enlarged by previously unattested spells. From the number of CT found on the back side of the coffin (symbolizing the west)—eleven spells in all—six are found exclusively on BH4C (CT 308, 475, 898–901); three are on coffin L1Li (CT 243, 307, and 340), and CT spells 308 and 475 are the precursors of BD 153, a spell for escaping the net (for CT 308, see BD 153B; for CT 475, see BD 153).

The coffin of Hapiankhtify from Meir (M2NY) can be dated to the reign of Senwosret III or later (Willems, 1988: 26 and 99; Lapp, 1993: §§ 250–9, 108–12 and 288–89). Unique spells are also attested on this coffin; they represent approximately one-third of the text program (CT 786–787 and 794–800). Two of the texts (CT 786 and 787) merge into the BD (BD 44); they are not positioned beside each other on the coffin, which may indicate their affiliation to an earlier text tradition. M2NY could possibly be seen in connection with the Theban tradition of the CT (Jürgens, 1995: 67); the mutual usage of CT 788 indicates a connection to Lisht and Dahshur.

# A Changed Understanding of the Coffin Texts: The Second Intermediate Period

Besides the fact that the number of coffins with a rich (funerary) text program, including the CT, is declining, and that the rich tradition of the CT ends in the reigns of Senwosret III and Amenemhat III, an opposing development can be observed.

This can be illustrated by the two coffins (outer and inner coffin) of the lector priest Sesenebenef from Lisht (L1–2Li) and by the coffin of the overseer of the house, Ameni, from Assiut (S8X). They originate from the cemetery of the old Middle Kingdom capital (L1–2Li) and from one of the largest provincial cemeteries of Middle Egypt (S8X). The exact dating of both coffins is uncertain. The dating of coffin S8X diverges from scholar to scholar. Suggestions range from the time after the Twelfth Dynasty up until the era between the Thirteenth and Seventeenth Dynasties (Willems, 1988: 29 and 103; Lapp, 1993: 144–45; Gestermann, 2005 (1), 215; Grajetzki, 2006: 213). The late dating is mainly based upon the text material that is inscribed on the coffin. Typologically, it fits in more with the Middle Kingdom coffins, making a dating into the (late) Twelfth or Thirteenth Dynasty more preferable. The controversial dating of Sesenebenef's burial has also been discussed (Allen, 1996: 15). The coffins elude dating and assigning them to the "standard class coffins" (Willems, 1988: 24, 49–50, 105). The text display on the coffins offers at least an indication of the chronological classification into the time after Amenemhat III (Willems, 1988: 105; Grajetzki, 2010: 30). This is confirmed by the use of mutilated hieroglyphs that eliminate the lower parts of some signs (Lüscher, 1990: 65 with n. 83 and passim; Willems, 1988: 105, n. 208). The dating into the beginning of the Thirteenth Dynasty could be implied by a depiction on the inner side of the coffin (Grajetzki, 2010: 30; 2006: 207). A study of Sesenebenef's canopic box and other funerary objects from his burial equipment that are still preserved also suggests the date of origin to be in the late Twelfth or early Thirteenth Dynasty (Grajetzki, 2010: 30–31; Lüscher, 1990: 29; Lapp, 1993: 286–87; 1986: 144–45; Buchberger, 1993: 137). Even though the cemeteries do not belong to the earliest places where CT were used at the beginning of the Middle Kingdom, they display an extensive usage of these texts. Lisht occupied a special position, since it was the capital and since it could be perceived as a center of text tradition—aside from Assiut and Deir el-Bersheh (Kahl, 1999: passim).

The two coffins have some general features in common: They are elaborately decorated and display an extensive text program. Furthermore, they exhibit numerous texts that are unique in the repertoire of the CT as well as a large number of texts that were later included in the BD. The text program of the two coffins gives the opportunity to observe and describe the differences in typology and text program in contrast to those of the coffins from the earlier Middle Kingdom, as well as the changed understanding connected with the decoration of the coffins.

In general, the decoration pattern of the coffins is the same as that of earlier coffins: lines and columns by which the outer surface is structured, and *udjat*-eyes corresponding with the eyes on the inner side and palace facades. As a new element, the panels are inscribed with CT or—more generally—with funerary texts. This characteristic feature can also be found on the two coffins of Keminub and Amenhotep (Da5–6X) from Dahshur (see earlier discussion) and on the coffin of Senebhenaf (Aby7) from Assiut (see discussion later in this section), and may be understood as a new and general development. The chronological order of these coffins and whether or not they were a possible influence on each other, however, are uncertain.

The selection of texts on the outer coffin of Sesenebenef is striking in two respects (Lesko, 1979: 58; 1993: 143, 141, and 144; Dorman, 2019: 26). First, a rather large number of spells are attested only once on this coffin, and, second, two-thirds of the spells survived in the BD while the others did not. Nevertheless, the spells express familiar topics as well as new themes. Fixed contents of the text program remain, for example, those that ensure the deceased's provisioning. This could be illustrated by old spells from the CT, like CT 179, but also by a new offering formula attested only on Sesenebenef's coffin (CT 793) and also by two new spells later transmitted in the BD: CT 352/BD 52 ("Spell for not eating excrement in the god's land") on the back of the coffin and CT 222/BD 56 ("Spell for breathing air, beside water, in the god's land") on the front. The titles given here and in the following text refer to later sources, since the spells on Sesenebenef's coffin are mostly attested without titles.

The theme of the deceased's protection by several gods and especially by Nut (on the lid) that is so prominent in the outer decoration of earlier coffins remains important for the decoration of Sesenebenef's coffin, too. This is illustrated by some new Nut-spells not transmitted in the BD, like CT 792 on the inner side of the lid and CT 803 on the head of the inner coffin L2Li ("Words spoken by Nut who enfolds [him] and who puts (her) arms around NN [in] life so that NN will not die.").

At the same time, the texts as they occur on Sesenebenef's outer coffin open up new dimensions for the existence of the deceased. This manifests itself, e.g., in a larger number of spells and the combination of several spells regarding one special feature, the use of a revised version of already known texts, and the appearance of new spells with familiar or new themes. Together, these texts that were collected and composed for the decoration of Sesenebenef's coffin present the deceased in another status and in another existence than is the case in the texts on the coffins from the earlier Middle Kingdom (Willems, 2018: 3–15).

One important new element is the deceased's participation in the solar cycle; see, for example, CT 437/BD 38A on the exterior front side ("Formula for living after dying" and "Formula for not dying again in the god's land" in CT versus "Formula for living on air in the god's land" in the BD). The references to the journey of the deceased together with Re in the sun barque become more visible, at least (Bickel, 1998: 53–56). This feature is also expressed in texts dealing with the freedom of movement the deceased has achieved (Lapp, 2000: XXXI–XXXIII; Assmann, 2001: 285–99). To go out in the daylight no longer remains a future event for the deceased, as in the texts and the text program of earlier coffins. On the contrary, the spells describe the cyclic existence that enables the deceased to move between the worlds of the living and the dead, to leave the netherworld and to enter it again, to go out in the day as it is expressed in the famous *pr.t m hrw.w* of some spells. Also common are spells that include the option to move between different zones, to emerge from one zone and then either enter this zone again or go into another one—as a human being or in the form of a creature, for example, a bird, that enables the deceased to undertake these movements. This can be illustrated through the examples of CT 283/296 resp. BD 86 ("Spell for taking form of a swallow"), CT 340 resp. BD 13 ("Spell for going in and going out from the west"), and the variant BD

121 ("Spell for going in after going out"). The three texts are written on the outer foot side of the coffin. The outer lid, which was reserved for texts referring to the night sky and to the protection of the deceased by Nut in earlier times, is now covered by spells that deal with the free movement of the deceased (CT 691/BD 71) and with his ability to enter the world of the living and to return into the netherworld (see also a second version of CT 340/BD 13 resp. BD 121; also CT 395/BD 122).

The decoration of the inner sides of Sesenebenef's coffin is formed in a special way since outer and inner coffins were assembled without leaving much space between them. The surfaces between the outer and inner coffins are without any decoration, the upper part of the inner decoration is painted on the inner side of the outer coffin (L1Li), and the lower part forms the decoration of the inner coffin (L2Li). Some elements of this inner decoration are well known from the coffins of the earlier Middle Kingdom, and their references are the same. This includes the object friezes on the upper parts of the sides, although they represent only textile symbols or elements and unguent vessels. They can be connected with the mummification of the deceased. The pair of *udjat*-eyes accompanied by CT 607, an old offering spell known from other sources but not from coffins, as well as other symbols on the eastern inner side, focus on the provisioning of the deceased. These are features also present in the inner decoration of the earlier coffins.

The texts on the inner sides also include some spells from the PT and, above all, texts not transmitted in the BD. Most of them occur for the first and only time on Sesenebenef's coffin. Exceptions are CT 306 resp. BD 79, a kind of transformation spell ("Spell for taking the form of the greatest of the tribunal"), CT 552/BD 47 ("Spell for preventing the seat or throne of NN being seized from him in the god's land"), and CT 402/BD 24 ("Spell for bringing the magic power of NN to him in the god's land").

Known texts that had already been transmitted for some centuries occur on the coffin of Sesenebenef in a revised version. Evidence for this can be seen in the case of the sequence CT 30–37 (Willems, 2018: 11–12). These spells can (in their original state) be understood as texts accompanying an offering ritual celebrated in the tomb chapel by the son for his (dead) father. In coffins of the earlier Middle Kingdom, this sequence marks the starting point of the nightly journey of the deceased that leads him from the western to the eastern horizon. There, he expects the sunrise and his own rebirth and regeneration, which the texts do not describe as having been fulfilled. In the revised version on Sesenebenef's coffin, the newly composed texts (mainly based on omissions of text sections) lose the characteristics of texts recited parallel to an offering ritual. What remains are spells describing only the journey the deceased undertakes through the netherworld. Another result of the omissions is that the (newly composed) first spell now underlines the new starting point of this journey in the west or western horizon and, therefore, requires the journey across the sky by day to have already been completed.

The bottom of the inner coffin is dominated by spells of the PT (PT 217–19), which can be classified as transfiguration spells. They describe the deceased as a spirit who is accepted in the world of the gods. These spells for the deceased's transfiguration can be defined not as a new element, but as an element much more prominent than in earlier coffins.

As for the coffin of Ameni (S8X), these results remain to be studied (by Lapp, 1993: 135–47, pls. 11–2 and Faltt. 1; 2013: 205–19). Nevertheless, first parallels can be recognized (Dorman, 2019: 26). Approximately half of the spells on Ameni's coffin became part of the BD corpus. Since fewer than 20 percent of the spells of the BD have precursors in the CT, Ameni's coffin is remarkable because it has got a much higher percentage than the relation between CT and BD spells in total. The CT documented on the coffin, moreover, show large deviations to the versions from earlier times and, until now, no earlier versions have been found in the CT for three of the spells on the coffin (BD 102, 123/139). They refer to the deceased's journey in the barque of the sun god (BD 102) and to freedom of movement also connected with the sun god Re (BD 123/139)— new elements within the decoration of these later coffins. The hymn to Osiris written on Ameni's coffin is probably embedded in the ceremonies celebrated in Abydos for this god (Lapp, 2013: 217). Since both the feast and the deceased's participation in a feast can be seen as one opportunity to leave the netherworld and to return to the living, this text can be connected to the new motif of the *pr.t m hrw.w*, with freedom of movement, a cyclic existence, and participation in the solar cycle (Assmann, 2001: 299–318). It, therefore, seems highly probable that the decoration of Ameni's coffin follows a similar approach and similar ideas to that of Sesenebenef's coffin.

The sources prove that the CT remained in use during the time of the fading Twelfth Dynasty, even after the disappearance of the nomarchs, who were previously considered an integral group concerning this usage and tradition. At the same time, a shift in the main application can be noted, moving from the provinces into the necropolises of the residence(s), as well as a considerable reduction of sources inscribed with CT. Only a few monuments and small assemblages of objects are now decorated with CT or similar texts that apparently served the same function. Common to all these CT sources from the Twelfth and early Thirteenth Dynasties is their tradition among the elite, which includes not only the high officials but also the women of the royal family and—in at least one case—the king himself.

During the Middle Kingdom, objects from the funerary equipment may have been decorated with funerary texts, for instance masks or canopic boxes (Willems, 1988: 19–34). This practice seems to increase as objects like the stela-chapel of Kemez (X4Bas), probably originating from the Thirteenth Dynasty, show (Lapp, 1994: 231–52 and pls. 37–41; Oppenheim, et al., 2015: 265–66, Cat. 201). However, the decline of coffins with inner decoration including CT correlates especially with the appearance of specific objects placed in a burial (Borriau, 1991: 10–14; Quirke, 2015: 218–21). While wooden models of, for example, boats, houses and gardens, bakeries, or slaughterhouses begin to disappear, the number of smaller ritual objects (like figurines and faience objects) provided in a burial increases exponentially. This part of the burial equipment also includes scarabs and shabtis, which can be inscribed with spells from the CT resp. BD (Grimm and Schoske, 1999: 19; Quirke, 2001–2002: 31–40; Lüscher, 2016: IX–XII; Dorman, 2019: 26–27).

Between the Twelfth and Thirteenth Dynasties, first examples of shabtis inscribed with BD 6 occur as part of the burial equipment (Bourriau, 1991: 12–13). The shabtis themselves are first documented in the early Twelfth Dynasty; after the Second Intermediate Period, they become a regular part of both royal and private burials. BD 6 has an earlier history, since it is already attested (as CT 472) in the Middle Kingdom, on two coffins from Deir el-Bersheh (B2L and B1P); both coffins presumably originate from the reign of Senwosret II or III (Willems, 1988: 21 and 75–77; Lapp, 1993: 77–85, §§ 181–95, and 276–77). The text written on the shabti is addressed to this "respondent," urging him to carry out heavy agricultural work like digging irrigation canals or moving sand in the underworld.

At almost the same time, heart scarabs begin to occur as a new media for the BD (Lüscher, 2016: IX–XII and 155–75). It is consistent for this particular item to be labeled with a text ensuring that the deceased's heart will be strong, will not turn and speak against its owner, and will not "stand against me as witness" (BD 30B). The reference to the process in which the heart of the deceased is weighed to document his good character during his lifetime is evident. The heart scarab as part of the burial equipment may therefore illustrate the greater influence of this idea—at the same time as it is an obstacle to be overcome on the way to a happy afterlife—and of the more important role of the heart for existence there.

## A New Tradition of CT and BD in the South: The Advanced Thirteenth Dynasty, and the Sixteenth and Seventeenth Dynasties

Even though the relocation of the residence from Memphis to Thebes cannot be definitively dated, the royal court might have moved to Thebes at some point in the Thirteenth Dynasty (Ryholt, 1997: 5, 69–93 and 295–99). The late Thirteenth Dynasty, together with the Sixteenth and Seventeenth Dynasties, would hence form a chronological unity (Grajetzki, 2006: 213–14; Bourriau, 2001: 3). It appears that another dynasty simultaneously came to power in Abydos, possibly at the same time the Sixteenth Dynasty became the ruling family at Thebes (Ryholt, 1997: 151–66 and passim). At the very least, the legacies of three kings indicate the existence of such a dynasty located at Abydos (see Ryholt, 1997: 163–64). The coffins from the necropolis of Abydos attest to the elite status of this area as well; these coffins see are discussed later in the chapter (Grajetzki, 2010: 39–43).

It can be assumed, aside from these uncertainties, that the south of the country forms its own center of power based in Thebes, and that after the Thirteenth Dynasty up until the early New Kingdom, the tradition of the CT is mainly a Theban one (Gestermann,

1998: 83–99). Apparently, a considerable amount of funerary literature was available in Thebes and was used accordingly. The basis for this was most probably the relocation of material from the archives of Deir el-Bersheh and Assiut to Thebes (Gestermann, 2004: 201–17; Kahl, 1999: passim). Corresponding to the political centers, three different cultural areas can be distinguished concerning the usage of CT (and additional texts). However, these regions are connected by the occurrence of common features again and again.

Regarding the occurrence of CT in Thebes, the situation in this region is characterized by several features that can also be found in sources from other cemeteries already mentioned. Coffins are used, as well as other objects as text media (e.g., canopic boxes), and coffins with a reduced text program stand beside those that are decorated in an elaborate and complex way. The text program includes the older PT, already known CT, and new spells. Since there are still great uncertainties regarding the dates of some objects, their chronological order can be only approximately determined.

A more or less reduced text program and the usage of restricted text material can be found on the coffin of Sobekaa (T3Be), for example, probably originating from the end of the Twelfth Dynasty (Willems, 1988: 32 and 114–15; Lapp, 1993: 169–74 §§ 390–400 and 310–11; Grajetzki, 2010: 43). The outer side of the coffin displays a palace facade, as well as four and two columns, respectively, on the long or narrow sides. With this layout and the text program, the coffin correlates with the decorative pattern of earlier times. T3Be is also decorated on the inside (Lesko, 1979: 99). Among those texts (PT and CT), there are some that occur either exclusively on coffin T3Be (CT 828–30) or only on coffins from Thebes (CT 224 and 831). The number of spells that are attested only on Theban coffins or on those from Deir el-Bersheh (CT 349, 490–91, and 499) is notable. Comparable features can be observed for the two coffins of Mentuhotep, the overseer of the house, T1–2Be (Steindorff, 1896 I: pls. I–IV and pls. IV–V).

In contrast, one coffin, the newly discovered and not yet published coffin T1Lux of Ameni, shows an elaborate decoration and text program (Polz, 2007a; Grajetzki, 2010: 43–44). The text program of this coffin can be explained only by access to a large text reservoir.

Another group of evidence, found in a Theban tomb, also has to be taken into account regarding the situation there. It contains the coffin (T10C) and the canopic box (T2Mos) of a man called Senebni, as well as the coffin (T6C) and the canopic box (T1Mos) of his wife Khensu (Willems, 1988: 117; Lüscher, 1990: 56–57, 75, 103, and 106; Lapp, 1993: 175, §§ 401–3 and 310–11). These objects can be dated to the (later) Thirteenth Dynasty because of a staff also found in the tomb that carries the name of the King Sewahenra (Ryholt, 1997: 70–71). The outer sides of the coffins are decorated with CT Spells 777–785; the outer sides of the canopic boxes, among others, contain the first two texts from this sequence. The Theban sources for CT 777 and 778 can be expanded to include coffin T5Be (Berlin, 1901 I: 253 and 254, no. 1175a/b; Quirke, 2007: 102–9). In this regard, sources from Thebes and those from Abydos have something in common, since coffins from Abydos (Aby2–5) also display parts of CT 777–785 (Grajetzki, 2010: 68–87, 42–43, and 94). The coffins from Thebes and Abydos that pass on this sequence (on the outer side) can clearly be regarded as a collective group (Grajetzki, 2006: 207). The occurrence of these texts in Abydos might indicate the status of the town as a temporary center of power on its own.

Most prominent among the sources from Abydos are findings from tomb D 25, including wooden fragments possibly belonging to a coffin (Aby7). They contain the name of Senebhenaf carrying the title of a "mouth of Hierakonpolis" (Grajetzki, 2010: 40–41; 2006: 206–15, pls. 5–7). It presumably dates from the late Thirteenth Dynasty (or the Sixteenth Dynasty) up until the early Seventeenth Dynasty, based for example on analogies with the coffin of Amenhotep (Da6X), mentioned earlier. The use of mutilated hieroglyphs makes it clear that the earliest possible date would be during the reign of Amenemhat III (Grajetzki, 2006: 211–12; 2010: 40–42; Lüscher, 1998: 103–7; Miniaci, 2010: 113–34). The coffin is inscribed on the outside with divine speeches that are reminiscent of those on Amenhotep's coffin, Da6X. Furthermore, one text field and one field with text and depictions on the outer side of the coffin between the vertical columns have survived. The field on the outer east or front side of the coffin displays a text similar to the later BD 33, in later versions titled "Formula for repelling a snake," and—following immediately thereafter—the beginning of BD 149 (first mound), a composition representing and describing places ("mounds") with which the western world is structured (Grajetzki, 2010: 41–42). Naturally, the question arises whether this is indeed a version of BD 33 or the preceding CT 369, and whether BD 149 has to be considered an earlier version from the Middle Kingdom.

In regard to the first text, BD 33, the version on Senebhenaf's coffin displays a closer formal proximity to the versions of the CT than the BD because it is missing an introductory title. This impression is supported by some particular phrases in the text (Grajetzki, 2006: 211; Lüscher, 2010: XIII). Both versions are, however, quite similar, even if the sources for CT 369 are attested in Deir el-Bersheh (B2L, B1C, and B2P) and Qau el-Kebir (K1T), with the coffin of Mentuhotep (T4L; for this coffin, see discussion later in this chapter) originating from Thebes. The last transcript especially shows (Geisen, 2004a: 42, pl. V, and 104) that the variations between the different copies can be quite large during this time and that neither a finalized edition of the text nor a canonical version of the spell should be presumed. The usage of the postscript from CT 369 (and from CT V 33 in CT 370), for instance, as a caption of the spell on the coffin of Mentuhotep provides evidence for this and leads to the title of BD 33 in the New Kingdom.

The following, mostly destroyed, text (BD 149) on the coffin of Senebhenaf obviously does not have the same structure of the spell from the New Kingdom (Lüscher, 2010: IX). BD 149 starts with the recitation note *ḏd mdw in NN*, "words to be spoken by NN," Osiris is addressed on the coffin in the vocative, and the designation of the mound that represents a place in the western realm of the dead is also different. Moreover, only the text of this first mound is recorded (14 exist in total), and there are no accompanying illustrations, which are common for the New Kingdom (see also the mummy shroud of Hori, mentioned later in this chapter in connection with the transition from the Seventeenth to the Eighteenth Dynasty). Thus far, Middle Kingdom evidence from this chapter for the first mound is also unknown; more occurrences are known from the early Eighteenth Dynasty (Munro, 1987: 348–49 and 274, nr. 2 and 4; Robinson, 2008: 123–40). Therefore, the inscriptions on the coffin of Senebhenaf testify to a tradition that apparently makes use of text material for which Senebhenaf's coffin is the earliest example. Even though there are no inscriptions with the sequence CT 777–85 attested on the coffin of Senebhenaf (possibly due to the fragmentary condition of the coffin), those texts are attested on other coffins from Abydos, as mentioned earlier (Grajetzki, 2010: 68–87).

The coffin of Queen Mentuhotep, from Thebes (T4L), is part of this group as well, since it also displays CT 777–84. Besides this, the coffin contains an additional, considerably larger text program showing in more detail the use of these new CT and a new understanding connected with the decoration of a coffin (Geisen, 2004a; Quirke, 2005: 228–38; Müller, 2011: 343–66; Grajetzki, 2010: 46–47; Gestermann, 2012: 70–74; Dorman, 2019: 27–30). There are several approaches to the dating of Mentuhotep's burial. Dating it to the Thirteenth (or Sixteenth) Dynasty can be considered fairly accurate by now. It is based on the reconstruction of Mentuhotep's family ties, as well as typological analyses of her coffin and the canopic box found together with the coffin belonging to her husband, King Djehuty (Ryholt, 1997: 259–60; Geisen, 2004a: 3; 2004b: 149–57; Quirke, 2005: 229–30). The inscription on the coffin is distributed on the inner and outer sides and, therefore, establishes a typological connection to the coffins of the early Middle Kingdom (inner decoration), as well as to the time immediately before the construction of the coffin (outer decoration). The texts are embedded differently, both formally and in regard to the context of their content (Gestermann, 2012: 70–74). While the spells on the outside (including CT 777–84) follow the concept of earlier coffins and are related to the situation in the embalming hall and the ritual of the Hours of the Night (Willems, 1988: 171; Grajetzki, 2010: 86–87), the texts on the inner sides reveal new approaches. They are not connected with the cardinal direction of the coffin's sides, as was the case with the coffins from the earlier Middle Kingdom, and it also seems that the texts do not describe a kind of journey like the early coffins as well as the coffins L1–2Li from the later Middle Kingdom. On the contrary, the spells on the inner sides are written in one single sequence starting at the head side followed by the texts on the back, foot, and front sides of the coffin (Gestermann, 2012: 71–72).

The sequence is introduced by CT 335/BD 17, the famous composition relating to the *pr.t m hrw.w*, "going out in the day." The following spells can be divided into groups of texts, each concerned with another topic or theme. The first spells mainly relate to the body parts of the deceased and their intactness, like BD 22–6, BD 43, and BD 30A (Lüscher, 2016: IX–XII). Only BD 24, ensuring that Mentuhotep will receive magical power, does not necessarily fit into this context. Indeed, it does not enter the later sequences of these texts (Lapp, 1997: 37; Munro, 1987: 155–56, 219–20; Dorman, 2019: 47–49). Two other groups are spells for repelling dangerous animals like crocodiles (BD 31) and snakes (BD 33) and spells for giving air and water to the deceased (CT 362, 372–3 and BD 55–6 and 62). The text program of T4L requires further study. Nevertheless, there are obvious parallels to the occurrence of the BD in the New Kingdom when spells are organized in sequences and when spells referring to the same or a similar topic are often transmitted together. In the case of Mentuhotep, the medium of the texts is still a coffin of which the decoration of the outer sides reflects the tradition of the Middle Kingdom.

## A New Text Corpus: The Transition from the Seventeenth to the Eighteenth Dynasty

During the Seventeenth Dynasty, at the latest, the royal burials in the region show that Thebes has once again emerged as a center, if not *the* center, of Egypt (Ryholt, 1997: 167–83 and 307–9; Polz, 2007b). After the reunification of the country under Ahmose, Thebes regains its status as a residence, a royal cemetery, and a burial place of the elite (Eighteenth Dynasty); the sources providing insight into the development of the CT and BD at the end of the Seventeenth and the beginning of the Eighteenth Dynasty originate, without exception, from Thebes. One such source is the coffin of the princess and king's sister Satdjehuti, of which the upper part, the section for the head, is preserved (Grimm and Schoske, 1999: 2–18; Dorman, 2019: 31–32). The inner side of this piece is inscribed with BD 124, 83, 84, and 85—a sequence of transformation spells (Grimm and Schoske, 1999: 20–21; Munro, 1994: 15; Lapp, 1997: 39; Lüscher, 2006)—which are written with a mixture of cursive hieroglyphs and hieratic signs, in continuous lines and not in retrograde direction. The titles are rubricized (see Munro, 1987: 190–2, and 1995 for further sources).

A second group of sources for this period in Thebes are mummy linens, found in the Valley of the Queens (for mummy linens as text carriers for the Book of the Dead from the Second Intermediate Period until the reign of Thutmose III: Dorman, 2019: 34–44). Among others, it contains the linen of Princess Iahmesu, today kept in Turin (Munro, 1987: 274; Polz, 2007b: 349, nr. 60; Grimm and Schoske, 1999: 21–22 with Fig. 20). Here, the texts are placed in vertical columns and written mostly in cursive hieroglyphs. Preserved is a longer sequence of BD spells containing, alongside the sequence of transformation spells known from Satdjehuti, additional spells. The fragment of mummy linen from Prince Hori, also found in the Valley of the Queens (Franco, 1988: 72–74 with Fig. 1), attests parts of BD 149 that represents and describes the aforementioned "mounds" of the western realm (Lüscher, 2010: XIV). The text is written in cursive hieroglyphs and single hieratic signs and is arranged in retrograde columns. Two sections with illustrations and captions of the fourth and fifth mound are preserved. Both captions are executed in red ink, as are two short paragraphs in the text. The fragments of a mummy linen of a princess whose name is not preserved (Franco, 1988: 74–76 with Fig. 2) display parts of BD 68 and 69, whereas BD 68 still shows a close connection to the early versions of the precursor CT 225 (Franco, 1988: 76; Jürgens, 1995: 213–15). The text is also written in retrograde columns. Neither vignettes nor rubra are preserved on the fragment. Another find from the Valley of the Queens is the mummy linen of Amenemweskhet (Franco, 1988: 77–80 with Figs. 3 and 4). A direct connection to the royal dynasty is not evident, but the fact that she was found in the Valley of the Queens indicates that she was associated with the royal household and might be the anonymous princess mentioned earlier (Franco, 1988: 80). The preserved fragments display parts of BD 17 (Lapp, 2006: XVIII). In this case, the text is not written retrograde and displays a mixture of hieratic and cursive hieroglyphs with rubrication in some places but shows no vignettes.

Regarding the sources from the transition from the Seventeenth to the Eighteenth Dynasty, it is notable that the BD or text collection that is its basis seems to be an exclusive privilege of the members of the royal household (Parkinson and Quirke, 1992: 47–51; Grimm and Schoske, 1999: 16–23; Gestermann, 2006: 103–11). An exception is the aforementioned Amenemweskhet, whose place of burial in the Valley of the Queens suggests that she was connected to the royal household either personally or by blood. (Nota bene: It remains unclear which texts the king himself was buried with at this time.) Regarding the BD (or preceding texts), royal sources, with the exception of the known mummy shroud of Thutmose III, are not attested (Munro, 1994, text volume, 41–5 and photo pls. 14–9, and plate volume, pls. 32–43). The distribution shows a certain continuity in regard to earlier times. The usage of established text carriers continued as well. A good example is the coffin of Satdjehuti, which is no longer box-shaped, but rather has the anthropoid form and belongs to the early type of Rishi coffins. The mummy linens are added to the text carriers, which had not been used for the inscription of funerary texts until then, and lead to the common New Kingdom usage of papyrus (in regard to text carriers such as shabtis and scarabs, see discussion earlier in this chapter).

Structurally, the texts can be designed differently. The wide columns in which the texts were inscribed on the inner sides of Mentuhotep's coffin are no longer found from the late Seventeenth and early Eighteenth Dynasty onward. Instead, separate lines are found on the coffin of Satdjehuti and on the mummy linen from the Valley of the Queens; the reproduction of texts is in (vertical) individual columns. In general, the texts are written in cursive hieroglyphs, intermingled with single hieratic signs. Neither the retrograde nor the prograde direction is executed continuously. Retrograde texts are found on the mummy linens of Hori and an unknown princess, prograde texts on the coffin of Satdjehuti and the mummy linen of Amenemweskhet. A constant pattern can be recognized neither here nor in regard to the rubra. However, conclusions about the usage of rubra on the mummy linens from the Valley of the Queens are rather difficult to make since they are only fragmentarily preserved. Rubra were used on the mummy linen of Prince Hori, where they highlight the caption to the mound of BD 149 and two sections of the texts, as well as on the mummy linen of Amenemweskhet (BD 17). Vignettes are obviously employed rather rarely, as seen on the isolated example of the mummy linen of Hori (BD 149).

What the coffin of Mentuhotep (T4L) foreshadowed finds consolidation and wide distribution at the end of the Seventeenth Dynasty—the appearance of BD texts now in sequences (Dorman: 2019: 47–51). Even though the phenomenon itself is already found in the CT, it now receives a new dimension with the compilation of texts that share the same or similar thematic references. At the beginning of the development, only a sequence of the transformation spells is identifiable, appearing on the coffin of Satdjehuti and the mummy linen of Ahmose (Lapp, 1997: 36–49, §§ 39–74). This new arrangement of texts in sequences possibly correlates with an altered understanding concerning the contextual approach to the texts and their function. A world of thought annunciates itself that is connected with the concept of a *pr.t m hrw.w*, "going out in the day."

## The Canonization: The Book of the Dead since Hatshepsut/Thutmose III

Since the early New Kingdom, the BD exhibits a certain (and well-known) appearance that changes only a little in the period that follows and does not receive a revision earlier than the so-called Saitic recension in the Late Period. For the time between the late Middle and the early New Kingdom, it is possible to deduce developments on several levels from the sources discussed earlier and from the historical context that has already been described. These circumstances also illustrate the transformation of funerary texts from the CT to the BD. However, until the transition from the Seventeenth to the Eighteenth Dynasty, the BD did not receive the layout so typical for it later on. This development certainly takes place in the early Eighteenth Dynasty—more precisely in the reigns of Hatshepsut and Thutmose III, according to the sources (Grajetzki, 2006: 214; Dorman, 2019: 51–52 and passim). In those years, a formal review of the traditional text repertoires must have taken place. Therefore, only now may one call it a "redaction" of the BD, in other words, a classification of the available material, as well as a selection and formal standardization of the selected texts (Hornung, 1979: 21 and 22). The sources do not allow us to identify a precise moment when the redaction took place within the reigns of Hatshepsut and Thutmose III. The early years of Hatshepsut's reign seem at least partially to be distinctly bound to the tradition of the preceding times during the late Middle Kingdom. Therefore, the appearance of the BD is still heterogeneous. Yet, the transition to a canonized layout of the BD, as it was used for centuries to come, is retraceable.

This development led to BD spells becoming a privately used collection of texts, while in a royal context the Amduat (see Scalf, this volume) now appears as the preferred text. Famous exceptions are the linen shroud of Thutmose III, which (still) displays texts from the BD, together with the sun litany and spells from the PT (Munro, 1994, text volume, 41–4 and photo pls. 14–9, and plate volume, pls. 32–43), and the vizier Usiramun's display of the Amduat (beside the sun litany) in his tomb, TT 61 (Hornung, 1994: 42–47). Papyrus establishes itself as a text carrier. However, linen is also still in use, for instance in the shroud of Hatneferet, mother of Senenmut, dating to the first seven years of the reign of Hatshepsut, decorated with BD 72 and a partial copy of CT 335 (Munro, 1994, text volume, 27–9 and photo pls. 10, and plate volume, pls. 24–5; Lapp, 2006: XVIII; Dorman, 2019: 21–24). As is fitting for papyrus and linen as text carriers, cursive scripts are applied (hieratic and cursive hieroglyphs); coffins and tomb walls may also still be decorated with texts from the BD. An example from the royal context is the sarcophagus of Hatshepsut. Even though it is made from stone, it possesses the box form known from the Middle Kingdom and also displays references to earlier times in the decoration program, in particular to the coffin of Neferuptah, daughter of Amenemhat III (von Falck, 2006: 125–40; Grajetzki, 2005: 55–65). In a private context, the sarcophagus of Senenmut (from TT 71), among others, is also from this time (Dorman, 1991: 70–76 and pls. 30–4). Unlike with Hatshepsut, texts from the BD appear on the inner and outer sides of the sarcophagus. The outer sides are inscribed with BD chapters 34, 45, 8b, 62, and 76, and are sometimes completed with vignettes (Dorman, 1991: 113–38, 168–69 and pls. 57b and 58–9) and divine speeches; the inner sides display BD chapter 125. The walls of his tomb, TT 353 (chamber A), are also decorated with funerary texts and sequences from both the PT and the CT, as well as the BD (funerary liturgies). The burial chamber of Djehuti (TT 11) is extensively decorated with spells from the BD. The chamber dates to the time of Hatshepsut and Thutmose III (Galán, 2013: 21–24).

An important change relates to the number of spells that are used since the early New Kingdom for burials and that do not originate from the collection of the PT or CT. The almost 1,200 CT spells are reduced to less than 200 in the BD. Spells as well as complete sequences disappear from the repertoire. So far, there has been no comprehensive methodical analysis on this subject, just individual observations. Most texts categorized by Jan Assmann as "Totenliturgien" [funerary liturgies; see also Stadler, this volume] are no longer found in the BD (Assmann, 2001: 337). As exceptions, he cites BD 151 (CT 531), BD 169 (CT 20–5), and BD 172 (without a parallel in the CT). Assmann explains the continued usage of these texts in particular with the situation of embalming to which they refer. Other collections that were regularly used in the Middle Kingdom are now missing, for example CT 75–83 (Lapp, 2013: 206), and additional observations are to be connected with the phrases *ꜣḫ-iḳr*, "efficient akh-spirit" and *sꜣḫ iqr*, "to make an akh-spirit efficient" (Demarée, 1983: 253). They appear in the BD, mainly in those texts that are new and that cannot be traced back to earlier versions in the CT. They can also be found in additions of certain texts (in titles, for instance), which are usually not known from the Middle Kingdom and shall therefore be considered (modern) additions to older texts that were included into the BD. The concept of a *pr.t m hrw.w*, a "going out in the day," something the deceased hopes for, clearly becomes stronger and more important, as has already been mentioned (Lapp, 2000: 64–72; Assmann, 2001: 285–99). The idea that the deceased can leave the sphere of the netherworld becomes crucial to the funerary beliefs of the New Kingdom; the phrase itself, used in numerous spell titles, grows to be the collective title of the BD in later times (Backes, 2009: 5–27; Assmann, 2001: 289–90). With this innovation comes the text program's dissociation from the context of embalming and the Ritual of the Hourly Vigils during the day and night before burial. This interrelation, however, was formative for the conception of coffin inscriptions in the Middle Kingdom and at least partially relevant for the decoration of a coffin during the beginning of the Second Intermediate Period.

After an apparent selection process, the remaining almost 200 texts become subject to a formal unification, as it is known (Allen, 1974: 2–3). The spells receive titles, and sometimes a postscript that indicates the benefit and function of the spell, and they are illustrated with vignettes. However, also in regard to these criteria, the sources for the time of Hatshepsut and Thutmose III are not coherent. In text witnesses from this time, both the lack of vignettes (on the shroud of Thutmose III for instance) as well as the appearance of accompanying illustrations (Senenmut) can be observed.

## Résumé and Perspectives

The period from the first occurrence of the CT in the beginning of the Middle Kingdom up to the time in which the BD was successfully established as a collection normally used for the deceased covers more than 500 years. It is marked and characterized by countless small changes. The appearance and disappearance of texts and of objects used as text media and the shift of the contents and meaning of texts with which a coffin or another object is covered can be observed and are also of importance for understanding how the replacement of the CT by the new corpus of the BD took place. These developments—also reflecting changes in society to a certain extent—cannot all be included in one great image. Despite this, two main breaks become visible, the first one in the second half of the Twelfth Dynasty and the second one during the Thirteenth/Seventeenth Dynasties. They allow us to identify three main phases within the development from the first appearance of the CT until the establishment of the BD.

The first phase includes the Eleventh and earlier Twelfth Dynasties. It can be defined as the time in which the CT found their widest distribution. During these generations CT mainly occur on the inner sides of coffins. The spells used show a connection to the deceased's body and to its situation in the place of embalming. At the same time, they refer to the cardinal direction of every side and illustrate the nightly journey of the deceased until sunrise, when he expects to achieve rebirth and regeneration. The spells used in this way can be of cosmological, mythological, and ritual character.

This phase ends with the administrative changes that began in the reign of Senwosret II and especially with the decline of the social class of nomarchs that directly affects the use of the CT. Different features can be observed: The inner sides of the coffins are now decorated less and less with CT, and the number of spells used for the decoration decreases, while the rate of repetition within the used texts increases. Simultaneously, new spells are included into the corpus of texts. In a kind of countermovement, a few coffins from this time are elaborately decorated and include an extensive and complex text program. As can be illustrated by the coffins of Sesenebenef (L1–2Li), they also provide a changed understanding connected with the decoration of a coffin and new components that become important for the deceased, like his "going out in the day" and his participation in the solar cycle with the sun god Re.

After the latter part of the Twelfth Dynasty, further changes come about. New objects like canopic boxes, scarabs, and shabtis become text media for the CT; the outer sides of a coffin receive inscriptions, whereas in earlier times the inner sides of a coffin were used. The sources with CT (or similar texts) mainly come from Dahshur, Thebes, and Abydos, but they show the use of certain texts across local borders. It is also striking (1) that the coffins and other objects are decorated with new spells that later occur in the BD and (2) that royal burial and burials of members of the royal family dominate the evidence.

Although it must be pointed out that new texts were already being consulted for the inscription of coffins in the early Twelfth Dynasty, the number of new texts increases considerably. The same can be said for texts that are attested uniquely. Both phenomena could prove either that the production of texts used for inscribing the coffins continued without interruption or—rather likely—that texts were rededicated, meaning they were newly discovered and used for inscribing coffins. In this manner, texts with contents thus far unknown for CT were also newly incorporated into the text program of coffins.

The tradition of equipping a burial with long religious texts also persists during the time ranging from the end of the Thirteenth Dynasty up until the Seventeenth Dynasty. A corresponding handling of those texts can be inferred, possibly even a broad production (Grajetzki, 2006: 212), although the coffin of Mentuhotep (T4L) might be the only proof supporting that. The text program of this complete coffin is of special significance because it either contains a large number of texts that cannot be assigned to the texts known from the Middle Kingdom (CT) or New Kingdom (BD), or possesses alternating references. To what extent this result might be generalized and understood as the trend of the time is impossible to determine. However, the coffin of Mentuhotep also provides indications relating to the function of the funerary texts: The texts are joined together in one long sequence, written one after the other, on the four inner sides of the coffin. Obviously, they are no longer connected to a specific side of the coffin and to a special cardinal direction, but rather represent a collection of spells that are concerned with the "going out in the day" and the physical integrity of the deceased.

Thereafter, those using CT (and BD) until the beginning of the New Kingdom also continue to be members of the royal family; however, some of those persons possessing coffins with CT (or similar texts) cannot be socially specified. As before, carriers of the texts are the boards of the coffins, as well as other objects of burial equipment. The sources are of a different kind and display different typological references, and the placement of the texts is incoherent. As explained earlier, they are devoid of concrete chronological classifications. The situation changes only with the revision of the available spells in the time of Hatshepsut and Thutmose III and the replacement of the CT by the BD as the largest corpus of funerary texts.

The selected and previously discussed examples can be linked to a net that connects several components, such as the form of the burial, the regional distribution of the sources, and the appearance of certain texts, and recognizes a change in a chronological dimension. Therefore, the transition from the CT to the BD has to be understood as a gradual process, reaching from the end of the Twelfth Dynasty up until the early Eighteenth Dynasty, and as one that was not completed before the reign of Hatshepsut and Thutmose III with the standardized compilation of the texts.

For further studies, the work with the single spells of the CT will remain one important step. The synopsis of CT made available by Adriaan de Buck (de Buck, 1935–1961) offers the basis for studies in this field. It allows the philological analysis of the spells, and of their contents in particular. The repeated occurrence also makes it possible to explore the distribution and the transmission of the texts. For the divine speeches, for example, it must be noted that they appear until the Thirteenth Dynasty in great variations. For instance, different gods are mentioned without distinctly defined speeches assigned to them. This changes in the Thirteenth Dynasty; the repertoire now contains a determined group of gods, each uttering the same or a similar speech. That pattern is widespread throughout large parts of Egypt (Grajetzki, 2006: 207). In contrast, the CT attested in this time are hardly standardized. For the repeatedly attested spells CT 777–85, clear differences can be noted within the copies, and some contain only excerpts (Geisen, 2004a: 22–30; 2010: 68–86). The mentioned spells (among others), therefore, allow one to undertake investigations to analyze the dependences between the individual versions and to reconstruct the manner of dissemination.

Because the synopsis separates the individual spell from its original position on a coffin or on other objects, it is also important not to forget another approach, which is to study the sources themselves. Examination and analysis of the decoration of a coffin as a complex composition can provide insight into and a better understanding of this eternal abode of the deceased. Therefore, the documentation and publication of new sources—coffins as well as other objects—will continue to be an important task, ideally including not only an examination of each coffin or object itself, but also a study of the burial equipment and the place of the burial: the tomb chapel and place of worship, the burial chamber, and the archaeological context including the mortuary and ritual landscape of the site. The study of the decoration of the coffins and the exploration of the world and ideas behind it can also bring about visible shifts concerning the function of a given decoration (and of the coffin). This approach may help to close the gaps in the transmission of CT and BD and to construct a more complete picture of this development.

In this context, one relationship may be helpful and can perhaps be food for thought. The time of the Middle Kingdom and the Second Intermediate Period is characterized by changing mortuary practices and burial customs (Bourriau, 1991: 9–10; Seiler, 2005: passim and 161–62 in particular; Dorman, 2019: 25 and 52–53). These may also have influenced the appearance of the CT as well as the process of transition from the CT to the BD. This is illustrated, for instance, by the typological design of the coffins and its development (Willems, 1988; Lapp, 1993; Grajetzki, 2010: passim and 88–102 in particular; Grajetzki, 2006: 206–7), as well as by the compilation of the burial equipment (Willems, 2008: 142–49; Seiler, 2005: passim) that could and did serve as carriers of both texts. A fundamental change was certainly the replacement of the box-type coffin in favor of the anthropoid shape, even though the latter is already attested in the Twelfth Dynasty (Grimm and Schoske, 1999: 2–16; Miniaci, 2007: 94–99 and pl. 7; Seiler, 2005: passim). An explicit classification of the individual coffin types is difficult, mostly because of the uncertain date of particular coffins, and is possibly not even to be determined a priori. It is more likely that the appearance of different coffin types overlapped regionally as well as temporally. In any case, certain coffin designs might have been used in different necropolises (Grajetzki, 2010: 15–21, 24–25). The coffin typology can also connect across dynasties, as is the case for the (Theban) Rishi coffins used in the Seventeenth and early Eighteenth Dynasties. In addition, the change of the coffins' shape illustrates a new understanding of this eternal habitat. For instance, the deceased no longer lies on his left side in the coffin, as was common practice in earlier times, but on his back (Bourriau, 2001: 1–20). Therefore, special parts of the decoration lost their original meaning, for example the pair of eyes with which the head end of the eastern or front side of the coffin could be decorated and which enabled the deceased to look at the sunrise—a symbol of his own renewal and resurrection—and at the offerings presented to him. It therefore seems that a broader view may also have had an influence on the text development that leads from the CT to the BD. It is, therefore, to be hoped that further analyses will illuminate this development, in addition to facets, and make it more comprehensible.

## Bibliography

de Buck, A. (1935–1961). *The Egyptian Coffin Texts*, I-VII, OIP XXXIV, XLIX, LXIV. LXVII, LXXIII, LXXXI, LXXXVII (Chicago: University of Chicago).

Allen, J. P. (1996). "Coffin Texts from Lisht." In *The World of the Coffin Texts*. Proceedings of the Symposium Held on the Occasion of the 100th Birthday of Adriaan de Buck, Leiden, December 17–19, 1992, Egyptologische Uitgaven IX, edited by H. Willems, 1–15 (Leiden: Nederlands Instituut voor het Nabije Oosten).

Allen, Th. G. (1974). *The Book of the Dead or Going Forth by Day. Ideas of the Ancient Egyptians Concerning the Hereafter as Expressed in Their Own Terms*. Studies in Ancient Oriental Civilisation 37 (Chicago: University of Chicago).

Assmann, J. (2001). *Tod und Jenseits im Alten Ägypten* (München: Beck).

Backes, B. (2005). *Das altägyptische "Zweiwegebuch." Studien zu den Sargtext-Sprüchen 1029–1130*. Ägyptologische Abhandlungen 69 (Wiesbaden: Harrassowitz).

Backes, B. (2009). "'Was zu sagen ist'—zum Gesamtteil des Totenbuchs." In *Ausgestattet mit den Schriften des Thot. Festschrift für Irmtraut Munro zu Ihrem 65. Geburtstag*. Studien zum Altägyptischen Totenbuch 14, edited by B. Backes, M. Müller-Roth, and S. Stöhr, 5–27 (Wiesbaden: Harrassowitz).

Backes, B. (2020). *Sarg und Sarkophag der Aaschyt (Kairo JE 47355 und 47267)*, Studien zu Altägyptischen Totentexten 21 (Wiesbaden: Harrassowitz).

Berlin (1901). *Aegyptische Inschriften aus den Königlichen Museen zu Berlin I Inschriften der ältesten Zeit und des Alten Reichs* (Leipzig: Hinrichs).

Bickel, S. (1998). "Die Jenseitsfahrt des Re nach Zeugen der Sargtexte." In *Ein ägyptisches Glasperlenspiel. Ägyptologische Beiträge für Erik Hornung aus seinem Schülerkreis*, edited by A. Brodbeck, 41–56 (Berlin: Gebr. Mann).

Bourriau, J. (1991). "Patterns of Change in Burial Customs During the Middle Kingdom." In *Middle Kingdom Studies*, edited by St. Quirke, 3–20 (New Malden; Surrey: SIA Publishing).

Bourriau, J. (2001). "Change of Body Position in Egyptian Burials from the Mid-XIIth Dynasty until the early XVIIIth Dynasty." In *Social Aspects of Funerary Culture in the Egyptian Old and Middle Kingdoms. Proceedings of the International Symposium Held at Leiden University 6–7 June, 1996*. Orientalia Lovaniensia Analecta 103, edited by H. Willems, 1–20 (Leuven; Paris; Sterling, VA: Peeters).

Buchberger, H. (1993). *Transformation und Transformat. Sargtextstudien I*. Ägyptologische Abhandlungen 52 (Wiesbaden: Harrassowitz).

Demarée, R. J. (1983). *The ꜣḫ-Iḳr Rꜥ -Stelae on Ancestor Worship in Ancient Egypt*. Egyptologische Uitgaven III (Leiden: Nederlands Instituut voor het Nabije Oosten).

Dorman, P. F. (1991). *The Tombs of Senenmut. The Architecture and Decoration of Tombs 71 And 353*. Publications of the Metropolitan Museum of Art XXIV (New York: Metropolitan Museum of Art).

Dorman, P. F. (2017). "The Origins and Early Development of the Book of the Dead." In *Book of the Dead: Becoming God in Ancient Egypt*. Oriental Institute Museum Publications 39, edited by F. Scalf, 29–40 (Chicago: Oriental Institute).

Dorman, P. F. (2019). "Compositional Format and Spell Sequencing in Early Versions of the Book of the Dead." *Journal of the American Research Center in Egypt* 55: 19–53.

von Falck, M. (2006). "Text- und Bildprogramm ägyptischer Särge und Sarkophage der 18. Dynastie: Genese und Weiterleben." *Studien zur Altägyptischen Kultur* 34: 125–40 and pls. 1–3.

Franco, I. (1988). "Fragments de 'livres des morts'—sur toile—découverts dans la Vallée des Reines." *Bulletin de l'institut français d'archéologie orientale* 88: 71–82.

Galán, J. M. (2013). "The Book of the Dead in Djehuty's Burial Chamber." *Egyptian Archaeology* 42: 21–24.

Geisen, Chr. (2004a). *Die Totentexte des verschollenen Sarges der Königin Mentuhotep aus der 13. Dynastie. Ein Textzeuge aus der Übergangszeit von den Sargtexten zum Totenbuch*. Studien zum Altägyptischen Totenbuch 8 (Wiesbaden: Harrassowitz).

Geisen, Chr. (2004b). "Zur zeitlichen Einordnung des Königs Djehuti an das Ende der 13. Dynastie." *Studien zur Altägyptischen Kultur* 32: 149–57.

Gestermann, L. (1998). "Die 'Textschmiede' Theben—Der thebanische Beitrag zu Konzeption und Tradierung von Sargtexten und Totenbuch." *Studien zur Altägyptischen Kultur* 25: 83–99.

Gestermann, L. (1995). "Der politische und kulturelle Wandel unter Sesostris III—Ein Entwurf." In *Per aspera ad astra. Wolfgang Schenkel zum neunundfünfzigsten Geburtstag*, edited by L. Gestermann and H. Sternberg-El Hotabi, 31–50 (Kassel: Verlagsort Kassel).

Gestermann, L. (2004). "Sargtexte aus Dair al-biršā—Zeugnisse eines historischen Wendepunktes?" In *D'un monde à l'autre. Textes des Pyramides & Textes des Sarcophages. Actes de la table ronde internationale "Textes des Pyramides versus Textes des Sarcophages,"* IFAO—24–26 Septembre 2001, Bibliothèque d'Étude 139, edited by S. Bickel and B. Mathieu, 201–17 (Le Caire: IFAO).

Gestermann, L. (2005). *Die Überlieferungsgeschichte ausgewählter Texte altägyptischer Totenliteratur ("Sargtexte") in spätzeitlichen Grabanlagen*. Ägyptologische Abhandlungen 68 (Wiesbaden: Harrassowitz).

Gestermann, L. (2006). "Aufgelesen: Die Anfänge des altägyptischen Totenbuchs." In *Totenbuch-Forschungen. Gesammelte Beiträge des 2. Internationalen Totenbuch-Symposiums*

Bonn, 25. bis 29. September 2005. Studien zum Altägyptischen Totenbuch 11, edited by B. Backes, I. Munro and S. Stöhr, 101–13 (Wiesbaden: Harrassowitz).

Gestermann, L. (2012). "Auf dem Weg zum Totenbuch: Von Tradition und Neuerung." In *Herausgehen am Tage. Gesammelte Schriften zum altägyptischen Totenbuch*. Studien zum Altägyptischen Totenbuch 17, edited by R. Lucarelli, M. Müller-Roth and A. Wüthrich, 67–78 (Wiesbaden: Harrassowitz).

Grajetzki, W. (2000). *Die höchsten Beamten der ägyptischen Zentralverwaltung zur Zeit des Mittleren Reiches. Prosopographie, Titel und Titelreihen*. Achet A2 (Berlin: Achet Verlag).

Grajetzki, W. (2005). "The Coffin of the 'King's Daughter' Neferuptah and the Sarcophagus of the 'Great King's Wife' Hatshepsut." *Göttinger Miszellen* 205: 55–65.

Grajetzki, W. (2006). "Another Early Source for the Book of the Dead: The Second Intermediate Period Burial D 25 at Abydos." *Studien zur Altägyptischen Kultur* 34: 205–16 and pls. 5–8.

Grajetzki, W. (2010). *The Coffin of Zemathor and Other Rectangular Coffins of the Late Middle Kingdom and Second Intermediate Period*. Golden House Publications Egyptology 15 (London: Golden House Publications).

Grimm, G. and Schoske, S. (1999). *Im Zeichen des Mondes. Ägypten zu Beginn des Neuen Reiches*. Schriften aus der Ägyptischen Sammlung 7 (München: Staatliche Sammlung Ägyptischer Kunst).

Hölzl, Chr. (2004). "Die Königsgräber der 11. bis 13. Dynastie." In *Die Pyramiden Ägyptens. Monumente der Ewigkeit*. Schloß Schallaburg 1. Mai bis 1. November 2004, edited by Chr. Hölzl, 117–37 (Wien: Christian Brandstätter).

Hornung, E. (1979). *Das Totenbuch Der Ägypter* (Zürich; München: Artemis).

Hornung, E. (1994). "Die 'königliche' Dekoration der Sargkammer." In *Die Gräber des Vezirs User-Amun. Theben Nr. 61 und 131*. Archäologische Veröffentlichungen 84, edited by E. Dziobek, 42–47 (Mainz: Philipp von Zabern).

Jürgens, P. (1995). *Grundlinien einer Überlieferungsgeschichte der altägyptischen Sargtexte. Stemmata und Archetypen der Spruchgruppen 30–32 + 33–37, 75(–83), 162 + 164, 225 + 226 Und 343 + 345*. Göttinger Orientforschungen IV/31 (Wiesbaden: Harrassowitz).

Kahl, J. (1999). *Siut-Theben. Zur Wertschätzung von Traditionen im Alten Ägypten*. Probleme der Ägyptologie III (Leiden; Boston; Köln: Brill).

Lapp, G. (1986). "Der Sarg des *Jmnj* mit einem Spruchgut am Übergang von Sargtexten zum Totenbuch." *Studien zur Altägyptischen Kultur* 13: 135–47, pls. 11–2 and folded plate.

Lapp, G. (1993). *Typologie der Särge und Sargkammern von der 6. bis 13. Dynastie*. Studien zur Archäologie und Geschichte Altägyptens 7 (Heidelberg: Orientverlag).

Lapp, G. (1994). "Die Stelenkapelle des *Kmz* aus der 13. Dynastie." *Mitteilungen des Deutschen Archäologischen Instituts, Abteilung Kairo* 50: 231–52 and plates 37–41.

Lapp, G. (1997). *The Papyrus of Nu (BM EA 10477). Catalogue of Books of the Dead in the British Museum I* (London: British Museum).

Lapp, G. (2000). *Die prt-m-hrw-Sprüche (Tb 2, 64–72)*. Totenbuchtexte 7 (Basel: Orientverlag).

Lapp, G. (2006). *Totenbuch Spruch 17*. Totenbuchtexte 1 (Basel: Orientverlag).

Lapp, G. (2013). "Ein ungewöhnlicher Osirishymnus aus der Übergangszeit von Sargtexten zum Totenbuch." *Studien zur Altägyptischen Kultur* 42: 205–19.

Lesko, L. H. (1979). *Index of the Spells on Egyptian Middle Kingdom Coffins and Related Documents* (Berkeley: B.C. Scribe Publications).

Lüscher, B. (1990). *Untersuchungen zu den ägyptischen Kanopenkästen*. Hildesheimer Ägyptologische Beiträge 31 (Hildesheim: Gerstenberg).

Lüscher, B. (1998). *Untersuchungen zu Totenbuch Spruch 151*. Studien zum Altägyptischen Totenbuch 2 (Wiesbaden: Harrassowitz).

Lüscher, B. (2006). *Die Verwandlungssprüche (Tb 76-88)*. Totenbuchtexte 2 (Basel: Orientverlag).

Lüscher, B. (2010). *Totenbuch Spruch 149/150*. Totenbuchtexte 6 (Basel: Orientverlag).

Lüscher, B. (2016). *Die Mund- und Herzsprüche (Tb 21-30)*. Totenbuchtexte 9 (Basel: Orientverlag).

Mathieu, B. (2004). "La distinction entre Textes des Pyramides et Textes des Sarcophages est-elle légitime?" In *D'un monde à lautre. Textes des Pyramides & Textes des Sarcophages*. Actes de la table ronde internationale "Textes des Pyramides versus Textes des Sarcophages," Ifao—24-26 septembre 2001, Bibliothèque d'Étude 139, edited by S. Bickel and B. Mathieu, 247–62 (Le Caire: IFAO).

Miniaci, G. (2007). "Some Remarks on the Development of *Rishi* Coffins." In *Life and Afterlife in Ancient Egypt During the Middle Kingdom and Second Intermediate Period*. Gold House Publications Egyptology 7, edited by S. Grallert and W. Grajetzki, 94–99 and pl. 7 (London: Golden House Publications).

Miniaci, G. (2010). "The Incomplete Hieroglyphs System at the End of the Middle Kingdom." *Revue d'égyptologie* 61: 113–34.

Müller, M. (2011). "Wie historisch ist ein kritischer Text? Zum editionsphilologischen Umgang mit funerären Texten." *Wiener Zeitschrift für die Kunde des Morgenlandes* 101: 343–66.

Munro, I. (1987). *Untersuchungen zu den Totenbuch-Papyri der 18. Dynastie. Kriterien ihrer Datierung*. Studies in Egyptology (London; New York: Paul).

Munro, I. (1994). *Die Totenbuch-Handschriften der 18. Dynastie im Ägyptischen Museum Cairo*. Ägyptologische Abhandlungen 54 (Wiesbaden: Harrassowitz).

Munro, I. (1995). *Das Totenbuch des Jah-Mes (Plouvre E. 11085) aus der frühen 18. Dynastie*. Handschriften des Altägyptischen Totenbuches 1 (Wiesbaden: Harrassowitz).

Nyord, R. (2007). "The Body in the Hymns to the Coffin Sides." *Chronique d'Égypte* 82: 5–34.

Adela Oppenheim, A., Arnold, D., Arnold, D., and Yamamoto, K., eds. (2015). *Ancient Egypt Transformed: The Middle Kingdom* (New York: Metropolitan Museum of Art).

Parkinson, R. and Quirke, St. (1992). "The Coffin of Prince Herunefer and the Early History of the Book of the Dead." In *Studies in Pharaonic Religion and Society in Honour of J. Gwyn Griffiths*. EES Occasional Publications 8, edited by Alan B. Lloyd, 37–51 (London: Egypt Exploration Society).

Polz, D., editor (2007a). *Für die Ewigkeit geschaffen. Die Särge des Imeni und der Geheset* (Mainz: Philipp von Zabern).

Polz, D. (2007b). *Der Beginn des Neuen Reiches. Zur Vorgeschichte einer Zeitenwende*. Schriften des Deutschen Archäologischen Instituts, Abteilung Kairo 31 (Berlin; New York: de Gruyter).

Quirke, St. (2001–2002). "Two Thirteenth Dynasty Heart Scarabs." *Jaarbericht van het Vooraziatisch-Egyptisch Gezelschap* 37: 31–40.

Quirke, St. (2005). "Review of Geisen, Chr. (2004a). Die Totentexte des verschollenen Sarges der Königin Mentuhotep aus der 13. Dynastie. Ein Textzeuge aus der Übergangszeit von den Sargtexten zum Totenbuch. Studien zum Altägyptischen Totenbuch 8 (Wiesbaden: Harrassowitz)." *Journal of Ancient Near Eastern Religions* 5: 228–38.

Quirke, St. (2007). "'Book of the Dead Chapter 178': A Late Middle Kingdom Compilation or Excerpts." In *Life and Afterlife in Ancient Egypt During the Middle Kingdom and Second*

*Intermediate Period.* Golden House Publications Egyptology 7, edited by S. Grallert and W. Grajetzki, 100–122 (London: Golden House Publications).

Quirke, St. (2015). "Understanding Death. A Journey between Worlds." In *Ancient Egypt Transformed: The Middle Kingdom*, edited by A. Adela Oppenheim, D. Arnold, D. Arnold, and K. Yamamoto, 218–21 (New York: Metropolitan Museum of Art).

Robinson, P. (2008). "Book of the Dead Chapters 149 & 150 and Their Coffin Text Origins." In *Current Research in Egyptology 2007. Proceedings of the Eighth Annual Symposium, Swansea University April 2007*, edited by K. Griffin, 123–40 (Oxford: Oxbow).

Seiler, A. (2005). *Tradition & Wandel. Die Keramik als Spiegel der Kulturentwicklung Thebens in der Zweiten Zwischenzeit*. Schriften des Deutschen Archäologischen Instituts, Abteilung Kairo 32 (Mainz: Philipp von Zabern).

Ryholt, K. S. B. (1997). *The Political Situation in Egypt During the Second Intermediate Period C. 1800–1550 B.C.* Carsten Niebuhr Institute Publications 20 (Copenhagen: University of Copenhagen).

Silverman, D. P. (1988). *The Tomb Chamber Of Ḫsw the Elder. The Inscribed Material at Kom Al-Ḥisn 1: Illustrations*. American Research Center in Egypt Reports 10 (Winona Lake: Eisenbrauns).

Silverman, D. P. (1996). "Coffin Texts from Bersheh, Kom el Hisn, and Mendes." In *The World of the Coffin Texts. Proceedings of the Symposium Held on the Occasion of the 100th Birthday of Adriaan De Buck, Leiden, December 17–19, 1992*. Egyptologische Uitgaven IX, edited by H. Willems, 129–41 (Leiden: Nederlands Instituut voor het Nabije Oosten).

Steindorf, G. (1896). *Grabfunde des Mittleren Reichs in den Königlichen Museen zu Berlin I. Das Grab des Mentuhotep* (Berlin: W. Speman).

Vernus, P. (1976). "Deux inscriptions de la XII$^e$ dynastie provenant de Saqqara." *Revue d'Égyptologie* 28: 119–38 and pls. 11–4.

Willems, H. (1988). *Chests Of Life. A Study of the Typology and Conceptual Development of Middle Kingdom Standard Class Coffins*. Mededelingen en Verhandelingen van het Vooraziatisch-Egyptisch Genootschap "Ex Oriente Lux," XXV (Leiden: Ex Oriente Lux).

Willems, H. (1996). *The Coffin of Heqata (Cairo Jde 36418). A Case Study of Egyptian Funerary Culture of the Early Middle Kingdom*. Orientalia Lovaniensia Analecta 70 (Leuven: Peeters).

Willems, H. (1997). "The Embalmer Embalmed. Remarks on the Meaning of the Decoration of Some Middle Kingdom Coffins." In *Essays on Ancient Eygpt in Honour of Herman Te Velde*. Egyptological Memoirs 1, edited by J. van Dijk, 343–72 (Groningen: STYX Publications).

Willems, H. (2008). *Les textes des sarcophages et la démocratie. Éléments d'une histoire culturelle du Moyen Empire égyptien. Quatre conférences présentées à l'École Pratique des Hautes Études. Section des Sciences Religieuses. Mai 2006* (Paris: Éditions Cybèle).

Willems, H. (2014). *Historical and Archaeological Aspects of Egyptian Funerary Culture. Religious Ideas and Ritual Practice in Middle Kingdom Elite Cemeteries*. Culture and History of the Ancient Near East 73 (Leiden; Boston: Brill).

Willems, H. (2018). "The Coffins of the Lector Priest Sesenebenef: A Middle Kingdom Book of the Dead?" In *Ancient Egyptian Coffins. Craft Traditions and Functionality*. British Museum Publications on Egypt and Sudan, edited by J. H. Taylor and M. Vandenbeusch, 3–15 (Leuven; Paris; Bristol, CT: Peeters).

# CHAPTER 2

# THE BOOK OF THE DEAD IN THE EIGHTEENTH DYNASTY

IRMTRAUT MUNRO

## Preliminary Remarks: The Sources

The continuous increase of manuscripts from the Eighteenth Dynasty in the database of the Book of the Dead Project, Bonn, during the last decade enables us to base this study upon more than 160 BD sources including about 40 shrouds and parts of coffins. Smaller fragments of insufficient substance are omitted. Many sources are unpublished but can, nevertheless, be searched online: http://totenbuch.akw.nrw.de/objekt/.

## Provenance

Text external evidence of a sure provenance for a manuscript are when it comes from an identified tomb or when its owner is a well-known official, a courtier, or even a relative of a certain king (Dra Abu-el-Naga A 7/ P. London BM EA 10489 + others, Heerma van Voss, 2014; L.New York MMA without no./TT 71 and TT 252, PM I, 1, 337, Roehrig and Dorman, 1987: 127–34, esp. 131; TT 353 BD texts in the tomb; TT 87/P.Nakht-Min, Guksch, 1995; TT 99/P. Senneferi, and L.Senneferi, Strudwick, 2016; TT 61 and TT 131/ P.Edinburgh 1956.315; TT 65/P.Senneferi; TT 79/P.Men-kheper-Ra-seneb, Guksch, 1995; TT 71/P.Cairo TN 25/1/55/6; Assasif No. 729/P.*Nfr-ḥꜣwt* and P.*Rwiw*; KV 34/L.Cairo CG 40001; KV 36/P.Cairo CG 24095, Munro, 1994 and Lakomy, 2016; Dra Abu-el-Naga A 6/P.Berlin P. 3132; TT 82 BD texts in the tomb; TT 8/P. Turin 8438 and P.Paris BN 826; KV 46/P.Cairo CG 51189, Munro, 1988, 271–73; Munro, 1994). Other manuscripts have their provenance assured by naming the archaeological site in the museum's files (P.Cairo J.E. 95575; P.Cairo IFAO; P.London BM EA 9900).

In many cases, text-internal evidence also allows inferences about the provenance of a manuscript, as they include titles of the BD owner that are especially linked to a certain area or to a temple's clergy (P.Tübingen ÄS 2003 a–k, P.Florence 3660) and confirm the museum's records (P.London BM EA 9900; Lapp, 2004: 22).

Particular features, such as a shared sequence of BD spells (P.London BM EA 10477 and P.Paris Louvre E. 21324), a shared, rarely used BD spell (P.Hannover KM 1970.37 and P.Cairo CG 40002; BD 171 with invocation of gods of the Theban region), or a specific layout (P.London BM EA 9900, P.Florence Museo Archeologico 3660, P.Warsaw Muzeum Narodowe 21884) may be strong arguments for a common origin of manuscripts. On the premise that scribes worked only in regional workshops, manuscripts of identical scripts must be attributed to the same area (P.London BM EA 10009 + 9962, 1; P.London BM EA 9913 + 79431 + P.Bologna KS 3168 + P.Moscow I, 1b, 122), even if one document is a BD manuscript on papyrus and another copy is on linen (L.TT 99 and P.TT 99). A very specific border, attested only in a few documents (L.Cairo CG 40001, P.TT 99, P.New York MMA without no., P.London BM EA 10489 + others, Tomb A 7), also very strongly suggests a common provenance (Heerma van Voss, 2014: 99–101).

Based on this, the majority of the manuscripts in the Eighteenth Dynasty originate from Thebes (ca. 50%). Next to Thebes, the northern cemeteries of Memphis are significant as an origin of BD documents (ca. 25%). Other sites as Rifeh, Akhmim, Sedment, or Abydos, known to be the provenance of some manuscripts are of lower importance.

## Problems of Dating

A manuscript seldom mentions a date that can prove its record (Munro, 1988: 4; 2001, for a date inside a manuscript from the Twenty-First Dynasty). One can almost be certain about the dating of a manuscript, if his owner is related to a certain king because of his career or through kinship. (See, for example, P.Cairo CG 51189: the owner is the father-in-law of King Amenhotep III; L.Cairo J.E. 96805: the owner was the grandmother of Ahmose; L.Turin 63001: the owner was the wife of a king of the late Seventeenth Dynasty; L.Senimen/L.New York MMA without no.: the owner was a contemporary of Senenmut; see Munro, 1988: 5–7; Roehrig and Dorman, 1987.) The same certainty is valid for a manuscript whose owner is linked to a well-known official on prosopographic grounds (TT 61/P.Edinburgh Royal Scottish Museum 1956.315; P.Cairo TN 25/1/55/6). If the professional career or floruit covers the reign of more than one king, the most likely dating must be considered (TT 8/P.Turin 8438 and P.Paris BN 826; TT 87/P.Nakht-Min; TT 61/P.Edinburgh Royal Scottish Museum 1956.315; Munro, 1988: 4–5).

However, most manuscripts do not provide any external argument for an exact dating. Therefore, one must establish text-internal evidence that is characteristic of a specific timespan (Munro, 1988: 7–12).

Édouard Naville and Kurt Sethe considered the use of a hieratic script that was very common during the TIP to be an appropriate criterion for dating hieratic documents no earlier than that period (Munro, 1988: 9–10). However, the BD archive, Bonn, possesses records of eleven manuscripts in hieratic writing, of which at least seven must date from the early NK up until the reign of Thutmose III (P.Brussels MRAH without no., Leather BM EA 10281, P.London BM EA 10738, P.London BM EA 74125, P.Paris Louvre E. 11085, P.Moscow I, 1b, 146+132, P.Los Angeles 83.AI.46.3, P.New York, Br.M. 37.1777E (on the verso), P.Cairo TN 25/1/55/6, P.*Nfr-ḥꜣwt*, P.*Rwiw*.) For a definite classification into the early NK we have contemporary material and various paleographic studies at our disposal (Möller, 1909; Megally, 1971; Shorter, 1934: 33ff.).

A rarely used border, a double line filled with stars, is a common characteristic among these, which may also indicate a specific time frame (L.Cairo CG 40001 + L.Boston MFA 60.1472, P.TT 99, P.New York MMA without no., P.London BM EA 10489 + others; tomb A 7).

A special feature of the layout, which is shown in documents dating predominantly from the early NK up until the reign of Amenhotep II, is the horizontal band below the upper border that contains the heading of a spell. This layout was used for shrouds and papyri as well:

- Shrouds: L.Cairo J.E. 96807 + L.Norwich 1921.37.50, L.Cairo J.E. 66218, L.Cairo IFAO, L.Turin 63001, L.TT 99, L.Munich, L.Cairo J.E. 96806, L.Cairo CG 40001.
- Papyri: P.London BM EA 1048 9+ others, P.London BM EA 9905, P.London BM EA 9950, P.London BM EA 9968, P.Paris Louvre N. 3073, P.Paris Louvre N. 3092, P.St. Petersburg 18586 + others, P.Amenemhet (private collection), P.TT 79, P.TT 87, P.TT 99, P.Cairo CG 40003 (pCd).

The only exception with a later date is P.Paris Louvre N. 3092 (reign of Thutmose IV), in which the horizontal band with its heading is reminiscent of an earlier tradition.

One of the manuscripts, most likely from the reign of Amenhotep II, has the layout of the horizontal band but does not make use of it (P.Paris Louvre N. 3073). A second papyrus uses the horizontal band only at the beginning of the document, suggesting that this layout had become an obsolescent model (P.Cairo CG 40003).

It is generally accepted that the manuscripts represent a great variety concerning the selection and sequence of BD spells throughout the NK. Édouard Naville and Erik Hornung characterize the BD corpus as a loose collection of spells in various combinations (Hornung, 1979: 23), or even as a collection without order or system (Naville, 1886: 21). However, when the Book of the Dead was first being produced, many manuscripts, as well as shrouds and papyri, were more or less congruent in regard to their sequence; this may constitute proof that a manuscript belonged to the early production of the Book of the Dead.

A study of the most representative vignettes can uncover text-internal evidence for narrowing down the dating to within a certain period; one example is the entrance vignette or any other adoration scene in which the tomb owner or the papyrus owner wants to be depicted in his full vigor and clad in the latest fashion.

The stylistic-iconographic study of the human representation, for both men and women (Munro, 1988: 24–63), is based on the research into the evolution of style in well-dated tombs of the Eighteenth Dynasty (Wegner, 1933: 38–164; Dziobek, Schneyer, and Semmelbauer, 1992). On the premise that the same stylistic and iconographic features were dominant, and that the same fashions were worn—a short-term, alterable element, ascertained in tombs and other contemporary categories of monuments—the analysis may allow us to transfer the well-established dating criteria from the tombs to the BD manuscripts. This dating method, established more than 25 years ago, proved to be useful at the time and is still valid today, despite the criticism that it may ignore local influences (Lüscher, 2008: 34). In one case, however, an incongruity between the dating of a tomb owner, based on his tomb equipment, and the dating of the associated Book of the Dead papyrus cannot yet be solved (KV 36 and P.Cairo CG 25095: Lakomy, 2016; contra Munro, 1988: 51; 1994: 143). However, the discrepancy between both dates is no more than 20–30 years.

One of the scientific analytical techniques for determining the dating of a papyrus is the method of radiocarbon dating ($C^{14}$), which has so far been employed on two occasions. The Brooklyn Museum gave a report of a $C^{14}$ analysis for P.New York Brooklyn Museum 37.1777E, when it was undergoing its conservation treatment. The most likely date of the papyrus, as shown in the spectra of the results, is about 1540–1450 BCE, which corresponds to the occurrence of the hieratic script during this period. The analysis of a second papyrus, which should be dated on stylistic-iconographic grounds, among other criteria, to the end of the reign of Thutmose III, seemed problematic. The peak of probability (95%) according to the radiocarbon results was between 1535–1436 BCE, an imprecise dating that conflicted with all other dating criteria. A special software program ultimately adjusted the approximate dating to the most exact timespan, between 1435 and 1395 BCE, in the reigns of Thutmose III or Amenophis II (Munro and Fuchs, 2015). To better classify the exact age of papyri, the $C^{14}$ method still needs to be tested more widely in calibrating the measurements as well as more evidence from well-date material. Unfortunately, the cost of such analysis is high, good labs are rare, and the papyrus material required for the test is destroyed at the end of the process.

# The Emergence of the Book of the Dead and the Formative Phase

After the Pyramid Texts and the Coffin Texts, the two precursors of funerary texts (cf. Gestermann, this volume), the third collection of religious texts, spells from the Book of the Dead corpus, occurred in hieratic script on a coffin of Queen Mentuhotep, wife of King Djehuti, whose reign can be convincingly established at the end of the

Thirteenth Dynasty (Geisen, 2004a: 3; 2004b: 149–57). The coffin itself is now lost, but John Gardner Wilkinson had reproduced the inner and outer walls; his is the only surviving documentation of this important source. The copies of the inner sides are in the British Museum (P.London BM EA 10553; Budge, 1910: pl. XXXIX–XLVIII); the manuscript of copies of the external sides resides in the Bodleian Library, Oxford (Geisen, 2004a: 1 and color plates 1–4). The exact site of its provenance is still open for debate (Geisen, 2004a: 2), but it is doubtless of Theban origin, confirmed by its shape and type, clearly showing the tradition of the Theban style of the Thirteenth Dynasty (Geisen, 2004a: 11–14), as well as by text-internal arguments (Rössler-Köhler, 1979: 340–43). Because of some alterations and developments occurring in CT 335/BD 17, we can suppose that there was a text tradition whose time of redaction was even earlier than the Thirteenth Dynasty (Rössler-Köhler, 1979: 340–43; Geisen, 2004a: 19). On the coffin of Queen Mentuhotep, there are Coffin Text spells that do not survive in the Book of the Dead corpus and, conversely, newly redacted BD spells without precursors in the Coffin Texts. Thus, this represents a source in the transitional phase from the Coffin Texts to the Book of the Dead. While the Coffin Texts had different redaction centers (Gestermann, 2006: 101–13, esp. 110, see also this volume), the Book of the Dead corpus was composed exclusively in Thebes, which developed as the center of the Book of the Dead (Rössler-Köhler, 1979: 340; Gestermann, 1998: 83–99, esp. 91, 98; 2006: 113). The fact that almost all documents originate from the Theban area supports this assessment (Kockelmann, 2008: II 9–11, esp. 10).

A second source from the beginning of the Book of the Dead tradition, which is closely linked with Mentuhotep's coffin by the same Theban version of CT 335/BD 17 and the hieratic script, is a board from the coffin of Prince Herunefer (P.London BM EA 29997; Parkinson and Quirke, 1992: 37–51), the eldest son of a king. Two hieratic records from members of royalty should be considered as dating close together (Parkinson and Quirke, 1992: 47).

The sequence of spells, beginning with BD 17–18, distinctly differs from the sources belonging to members of the royal family from the Seventeenth or Eighteenth Dynasty (Geisen, 2004a: 19), which are headed by BD 124 and followed by the transformation spells BD 83–84–85, which may also be an additional argument for these being an antecedent record of these sources.

The head of a Rishi coffin Munich ÄS 7163 (Grimm and Schoske, 1999), one of the new type of anthropoid coffins in the late Seventeenth and early Eighteenth Dynasties, from the burial of Satdjehuti Satibu, a king's daughter, is inscribed with BD texts on its inner surface. This document appears to be the "missing link" (Grimm and Schoske, 1999: 21). It features a wooden text surface, newly redacted Book of the Dead spells, and royal ownership in common with the coffin of Queen Mentuhotep. However, the coffin of Sat-Djehuti Sat-Ibu bears cursive hieroglyphs, and its sequence of Book of the Dead spells closely links it to the almost homogeneous group of linen shrouds bearing either hieratic characters or cursive hieroglyphs, written for members of the royal family (L.Cairo J.E. 96805, L.Turin 63001, L.Cairo J.E. 96810, L.Cairo O.A.E. 325+343, L.Uppsala without no., L.King Inyotef [?]) and possibly, somewhat later, also for elite members of the royal court (L.Munich, L.Cairo J.E. 96806, L.Turin 63002, L.Cairo J.E. 96807, L.Cairo J.E. 96804). Of particular note is how many documents in this group survived from royal female owners and from the high-ranking elite (L. Cairo J.E. 96805, L.Turin 63001, L.Cairo J.E. 96810, L.Cairo O.A.E.325+343, L.Cairo J.E. 96804, L.Cairo J.E. 96807, L.Berlin 10476 + Hanover Dartmouth College 39-64-6623, L.Moscow 1027, L.London BM EA 73807; Gestermann, 2006: 103).

## Range and Sequence of Spells

Judging from the whole spectrum of BD spells occurring during the Eighteenth Dynasty, the range of spells attested on manuscripts of the Formative Phase from the late Seventeenth to the early Eighteenth Dynasty does not seem fully developed (Gestermann, 2006: 106). It is limited to only about 33 percent of the later fully developed BD text spectrum (see Sequence of Book of the Dead Spells, below). While 177 spells are attested during the Eighteenth Dynasty, only 59 spells occur in the Formative Phase.

We can observe two main strands of spell sequences. The first is attested as early as the late 13th Dynasty and followed by a series of manuscripts from the late Seventeenth to the early Eighteenth Dynasty. This tradition also influences documents dating until at least the reign of Thutmose III (see Table 2.1). The second strand is first attested on the coffin of an Ahmoside princess and seems to be the preferred sequence of this time, also called the "Ahmoside Book of the Dead redaction" (see Table 2.2, Grimm and Schoske, 1999: 18). Although the two traditions are clearly separated, one manuscript, however, L.Cairo J.E. 96810, has two variations within its "Ahmoside text sequence," namely a combination of the two strands of text tradition, and can be traced to some later manuscripts dating to the reign of Thutmose III (see Table 2.3).

As far as we can see from the preserved material, a considerable number of manuscripts end with BD 136B-149, sometimes followed by the vignette of BD 150 after BD 149 (L.Cairo J.E. 96810, L.Cairo J.E. 96807, L.Turin 63001, L.Turin 63003, [L. Turin 63005]). This concluding sequence remains very popular during the entirety of the Eighteenth Dynasty (L.TT 99; Munro, 1988: 222-23; 2016).

## The Scripts

The preferred script during the Formative Phase seems to have been hieroglyphs, more precisely the so-called cursive hieroglyphs (L.Cairo J.E. 96805, L.Turin 63001, L.Cairo J.E. 96806, L.Cairo J.E. 96807 + L.Norwich 1921.37.50, L.Cairo O.A.E.325+343, Cairo O.A.E.325, L.Turin 63003 + 63002 + L.Uppsala without no., L.Turin 63004), copied in

## Table 2.1: Sequence of BD Spells in the Formative Phase of BD Production and its Occurrence on Later Manuscripts, Sequence 1

| Manuscript | Sequence |
|---|---|
| Sarcophagus of Queen Mentuhotep | BD 17 – 18 – 22 – 23 – 24 – 25 – 26 – 43 – 30A – 31 – 33 – 45 – 72 – 122 – 56 + 62 – CT 362 – 55 – CT 372/373 – 64LV – 30B – 64SV – 119 – 144 (2 versions) – CT 154 |
| L.Uppsala without no. | BD 17 – 18 /// |
| L.Cairo J.E. 96810, between BD 82 and 77 | BD 22 – 23 – 24 – 25 – 26 – 28 – 27 – 43 – |
| P.Paris Louvre E. 11085 | BD 17 – 18 – 22 – 23 – 24 – 25 – 26 – 28 – 27 – 43 – 30A – 31 – 33 – 34 – 35 – 74 – 45 – 93 – 91 – 41 – 42 – 14 – 68 – 136A+ 136B – 149 |
| Leather London BM EA 10281 | BD 17 – 18 – 22 – 23 – 24 – 25 – 26 – 28 – 27 – 43 – 30A – 31 /// |
| =========== | =========== |
| P.Edinburgh Royal Scottish Museum 1956.315 | /// 23 – 24 – 25 – 26 – 28 – 27 – 43 – 30A /// |
| LT T 99 | BD 17 – 18 /// 22 – 23 – [24] – 25 – 26 – 28 – 27 – 43 – 30A[-] 31 – 33 – [34] /// /// 42 – [14] – 68 /// |
| P.Cairo TN 25/1/55/6 | BD 22 – 23 – 24 – 25 – 26 – 28 – 27 – 43 – 30A – 31 – 33 – 34 – 35 – 74 – 45 – 93 – 91 – 41 – 42 – 14 – 68 – 69 – 70 – 92 – 72 – 71 – 67 – 9 – 8 – 63A – 62 – 59 – 105 – 95 |
| P.London BM EA 10477 | A. of O. – BD 17 – 18 – 1 – 22 – 23 – 25 – 26 – 28 – 27 – 30A – 43 – 24 – 31 – 33 – 34 – 35 – 74 – 45 – 93 – 91 – 41 – 42 – 14 – 68 – 92 – 63A – 105 – 95 – 72 – 71 …. |
| P.Paris Louvre E. 21324 | /// BD 17 – 18 – 71 – 106 – 22 – 23 – 24 – 25 – 26 – 28 – 27 – 43 – 30A – 31 – 33 – 34 – 35 – 74 – 45 – 93 – 91 – 41 – 42 – 14 – 68 – 69 – 70 – 92 – 63A – 105 – 95 – 72 …. |
| P.New York Brooklyn Museum 37.1777E | rto …. BD 18 – 17 – 23 – 24 – 25 – 26 – 28 – 27 – 43 – 30A – 31 – 33 – 34 – 35 – 74 – 45 – 93 – vso 91 – 41 – 61 – 42 – 14 – 68 – 69 – 70 – 92 – 63A – 105 – 95 – 72 …. |
| L.Sydney R 92 | BD 43 – 30A – 31 – 33 – 35 – 74 – 45 /// |

## Table 2.2: Sequence of BD Spells in the Formative Phase of BD Production and its Occurrence on Later Manuscripts, Sequence 2

| Manuscript | Sequence |
|---|---|
| L.Cairo J.E. 96805 | BD 124 – 83 – 84 – [85] – 82 – 77 – 86 – 99B – 119 – 7 – 102 – 38A – 27 – 14 – 39 – 65 – 116 – 91 – 64 /// |
| coffin Munich SSÄK, ÄS 7163 | BD 124 – 83 – 84 – 85 – 82 – 77 – 86 – 99B – 119 – 7 – 102 – 38A – 27 – 14 – 39 – 65 – 116 – 91 – 64 /// |
| L.Turin 63001 | BD 124 – 83 – 84 – 85 – 82 – 77 – 86 – 99B – 119 – 7 – 102 – 38A – 27 – 14 – 39 /// /// 91 – 64 /// |
| L.Cairo J.E. 96806 | BD 124 – 83 – 84 – 85 [–]82 – 77 – 86 – 99B – 119 – 7 – 102 – 38A – 27 – 14 – 39 – [65] – 116 – 91 [–] 64 |
| L.Cairo J.E. 96807 +L.Norwich | BD 124 – 83 – 84 – 85 – 82 – 77 – 86 – 99B – 119 – 7 – 102 – 38A – 27 – 14 – 39 – 65 – 116 – 91 – 64 – 30B – 100 – 136B – 149 /// |
| L.Cairo J.E. 96810 | /// 85 – 82 – … – 77 – 86 – 99B – 38A – 27 – 14 – 39 – 65 – 116 – 91 – 64 – … – 80 – 132 – 94 – 63B – 8 – 64SV – 64LV – 136B – 149 |
| L.Uppsala, without no. + L.Turin 63002+63003 | BD 124 – 83 – 84 – 85 – 86 – 99B – 102 /// /// 65 /// 64 – 30B /// 71 /// 106 – 14 – 136A – 136B – 149 – 150 |
| L.Turin 63005 | /// 102 – 38A – 27 – 27 – 14 [–]39 /// 144 /// 147 /// 149 /// |
| ============ | ============ |
| L.Berlin 10476+Hanover Dartmouth College 39-64-6623 | A. of O. – BD 1 – 124 /// /// 102 – 38A – 27 – 14 – 39 – 65 – 116 |
| L.New York MMA 22.3.296 | BD 149 – 136A – 124 – 83 – 84 – 85 – 82 – 77 – 86 – 99B |
| L.New York MMA 20.3.201 | BD 124 – 83 – 84 – 85 /// |
| L.Sn-ḥtp/TT 65 | BD 124 – 83 – 84 – 85 /// |
| L.London BM 7036 | BD 124 – 83 – 84 /// |
| P.London BM 73669 | /// BD 99B /// 119 [–] 7 – 102 – 38A – 27 [–] 14 [–] 39 – 65 – 116 [–] 91 – 64 … |
| L.London BM 73807 | A. of O. – BD 124 – 83 – 84 – 85 /// |
| P.Paris Louvre E. 21324, rto. | … BD 124 – 83 – 84 – 85 … |
| vso | BD 82 – 77 – 86 – 99B – 119 – 94 – 7 – 102 – 38A – 27 – 14 – 39 – 65 – 95 – 104 – 116 – 91 – … |
| P.Edinburgh Royal Scottish Museum 1956.315 | /// BD 99B [–] 119 – 7 [–] 102 [–] 38A – [27] – 14 – 39 /// |

**Table 2.3: Sequence of BD Spells in the Formative Phase of BD Production and its Occurrence on Later Manuscripts, Variation combining Sequence 1 + 2**

| | |
|---|---|
| L.Cairo J.E. 96810 | … BD 80 – 132 – 94 – 63B – 8 – 64SV – 64LV |
| ========== | ========================= |
| P.London BM 9964 | ///BD 80 – 132 – 94 – 63B – 8 – 64 /// |
| P.London BM EA 10477 | … BD132 – 94 – 63B – 8 – 64 … |
| P.Tübingen ÄS 2003 a-k | /// BD 132 [-] 94 [-] 63B – 8 [-] 64 /// |
| P.London BM EA 9913 + 79431 + P.Bologna KS 3168 + P.Moscow I, 1b, 122 | … BD 80 – 132 – 63B – 8 – 64 /// |
| P.New York Brooklyn Museum 37.1777E | … BD 80 – 132 – 94 – 63B … |

Legend:
– spell succeeding directly
[-] deduced sequence
+ combination of two spells
/// destroyed
… spell not succeeding directly
LV Long version
SV Short version

vertical columns, either strongly influenced by hieratic forms or mixed with purely hieratic signs (Munich ÄS 7163, L.Cairo J.E. 96810, and others). Only a few manuscripts are inscribed with hieratic script, and even then, these do not feature the usual (vis-à-vis the New Kingdom) hieratic writing, in horizontal lines and oriented to the left, but instead use vertical columns in the same way as the manuscripts with cursive hieroglyphs (L. Cairo J.E. 96804, L.Turin 63005, P.Paris Louvre E. 11085: this manuscript also shows horizontal lines with hieratic signs at the beginning). The retrograde writing does not yet prevail as it does in the later course of the Eighteenth Dynasty (Gestermann, 2006: 105, esp. n. 17; L.Turin 63001, L.Turin 63002 + 63003 + L.Uppsala without no. [in BD 71], Turin 63004, L.Turin 63006, L.Cairo J.E. 96810, L.Cairo J.E. 96805, L.Cairo J.E. 96806], but is used equally (L.Turin 63002 + 63003 + L.Uppsala without no., L.Cairo J.E. 96807 + L.Norwich 1921.37.50).

## THE VIGNETTES

From the very beginning of the Book of the Dead production on linen, illustrations accompanying the texts are attested. However, as far as we can conclude from the surviving records, the set of vignettes was still limited. Only vignettes for BD 136B, 149, and 150 are attested, either drawn in black outlines or filled with color (L.Cairo J.E. 96810, L.Turin 63001, L.Turin 63003, P.Paris Louvre E. 11085, L.Munich, L.Moscow 1027). The limited usage of illustrations was altered shortly afterward in the course of the Eighteenth Dynasty, hand in hand with the development of the BD redaction and production for a broader stratum of users.

## THE DEVELOPMENT OF THE BOOK OF THE DEAD DURING THE EIGHTEENTH DYNASTY

While linen was the dominant material to be inscribed with the newly composed funeral texts, papyrus became the main medium for text carriers of Book of the Dead spells. Though linen shrouds continue to be used and are attested in the reign of Thutmose III (L.TT 99, L.Berlin 10476 + Hanover Dartmouth College 39-64-6623, L.Cairo J.E. 66218, L.New York MMA without no.), which could be considered a transitional period, and can even be traced as far back as the reign of Amenhotep II (L.Cairo 40001, + L.Boston MFA 60.1472, L.Paris Louvre N. 3097, L.Heidelberg Ä.I. 1787 + L.Würzburg H 393; Müller-Roth, 2008: 149–53), the custom of using large linen shrouds decreases[1] and shrouds become a negligible fraction of to the now widespread number of papyrus

---

[1] In TT 99, a linen shroud and three BD manuscripts were part of the burial. Perhaps Senneferi did not want to abstain from the traditional shroud and additionally ordered "modern" BD scrolls.

manuscripts. We do not have fully plausible explanations for this change in funerary customs; one explanation may be that the increase in the Book of the Dead spells repertoire was too large for linen shrouds, but a more concrete reason was certainly that, compared to the bigger dimensions of the linen shrouds, a papyrus roll was easier to handle and store (Kockelmann, 2008: II, 10-11). One manuscript on linen is reduced in its dimensions and matches the height of a papyrus scroll (L.Moscow Pushkin Museum I, 1b, 1027).

Beside BD sources on papyrus, we also know of a few leather manuscripts (Leather London BM 10281, Leather Berlin P. 3131 and from the end of the Eighteenth Dynasty, P.London BM EA 10473), and a number of copies of Book of the Dead texts on the walls of tomb chapels (TT 82; de Garis Davies and Gardiner, 1915: Pl. XXXVI-XLVI; TT 353, Dorman, 1991: 78 (No. 18), Pl. 36-7).

There isn't a single manuscript that can be safely dated between the reign of Ahmose and the joint reign of Hatshepsut/Thutmose III, and there is no evidence for a continuous development. However, in this timespan of approximately 64 years (1554-1490 BCE), the production of manuscripts increased considerably. Additionally, the full development of Book of the Dead spells, still limited in the Formative Phase, had taken place and was expanded in the reign of Hatshepsut/Thutmose III, "a time of great activity in the production and spread of Book of the Dead manuscripts" (Munro, 2010: 57). From then on, the whole spectrum of Book of the Dead spells of the Eighteenth Dynasty was available: P.London BM EA 10477 contains 146 spells in total. While many BD spells were composed from precursory texts in the Coffin Texts or at least showed some allusions or similarities to them, the texts only seldom—when compared to the Coffin Text correlations—reference the spells or passages of the Pyramid Texts (Allen, 1974: 225-41; Gestermann, 2012: 67-78, esp. 75-78). Some Book of the Dead manuscripts have incorporated texts directly from the Coffin Texts amid their Book of the Dead spells (L.Cairo J.E. 66218, P.Cairo CG 40002, P.Cairo TN 25/1/55/6, P.New York Brooklyn Museum 37.1777E, O'Rourke, 2016:108, 109), whereas the linen shroud of Thutmose III includes Pyramid Texts and the Litany of Re (Munro, 1988: 42; Piankoff, 1964: pl. I; Hornung, 1975; 1976, 10-11).

Although the introductory scene, the so-called adoration of Osiris that appears at the beginning of many Eighteenth-Dynasty manuscripts, may be considered an illustration of a hymn to Osiris (Munro, 1988: 167-68), the accompanying legends of the existing examples are still rudimentary in comparison to the elaborated versions known from Nineteenth-Dynasty documents (Allen, 1974: 202-9). The same observation applies to the few manuscripts from the Eighteenth Dynasty, in which illustrations of the sunrise and a related legend evoke a close connection to a hymn (P.London BM EA 10009, P.London BM EA 9988).

Not only is the hymn to Hathor unknown in Eighteenth-Dynasty manuscripts, but there are also a number of Book of the Dead spells that occur no earlier than the Nineteenth-Dynasty records (Munro, 1988: 168 and 223-24).

However, some spells identified only on Eighteenth-Dynasty sources did not survive into the Ramesside era (Munro, 1988: 223-24).

## Layout and Formal Features

The standard height of the BD manuscripts of the Eighteenth Dynasty is about 36 cm; this matches the dimensions of other papyri (Munro, 1988: 198 and 258–59). The only exception is that of P.Cairo CG 51189, which is an unusual ~44 cm high (Munro, 1999: 49).

The text field is always framed by an upper and lower border of different types: plain lines, double/triple lines, or stripes, sometimes filled in with color or even—less commonly—with stars (P.London BM EA 10489 + others, P.TT 99, 3rd roll; Munro, 1988: 199–200 and 259–60).

There is no specific rule for separating one single spell from the next; subdividing double lines may delimit the single spells, but one spell can follow another with its heading in red ink as a separator between the two (Munro, 1988: 201–2). Scribes would emphasize certain passages, such as the headings of spells, the names of hostile entities, the postscripts, as well as the users' instructions, by rubricating them.

A particular layout occurring in some manuscripts shows a continuous horizontal line that contains the headings of a spell beneath the upper border. This was already in use during the Formative Phase (L.Turin 63001, L.Cairo J.E. 96807, L.Cairo J.E. 96806, L.Munich) and continued to be applied afterward, with only one exception, until the reign of Amenhotep II (L.Cairo IFAO without no., L.TT 99, L.Cairo J.E. 66218, L.Cairo CG 40001+ L.Boston MFA 60.1472, P.London BM EA 10489 + al., P.TT 99, P.TT 87, P.TT 79, P.St. Petersburg 18586 and others, P.Paris Louvre N. 3073, P.London BM EA 9905, 9950, 9968, P.Warsaw Muzeum Narodowe 21884, P.Cairo J.E. 95834 (Cd), P.Amenemhet, Munro and Fuchs, 2015, P.Paris Louvre N. 3092 [exception]). As the horizontal band becomes less frequent during the reign of Amenhotep II (P.Paris Louvre N. 3073, P.Cairo J.E. 95834), the late occurrence in the time of Thutmose IV seems to be an archaism following an old tradition (Munro and Fuchs, 2015). Though this feature died out after this time, it was revived in the Saite era and was used until the end of the BD tradition.

Another formal feature occurring on BD manuscripts, first attested on Eighteenth-Dynasty papyri, must be mentioned. A continuous horizontal line appears on the verso for showing invocations or other offering formulas (P.London BM EA 10489 + others, P.London BM EA 9913 and others; P.London UC 71004; Lucarelli, 2010: 264–73, esp. 265; Munro, 1988: 198). In P.New York Br. M. 37.1777E, such bands for offering formulas are attested above and below the vertical columns on the recto (O'Rourke, 2016).

Usually the scribes copied the texts on the recto of the papyrus sheets; however, in a few manuscripts, the verso is also inscribed, continuing the course of the intended sequence (P.Paris Louvre E. 21324, P.New York Brooklyn Museum 37.1777E, O'Rourke, 2016; Munro, 1988: 198). The high price of papyrus material may have been the reason for this custom, which we see attested in many manuscripts (P.Paris Louvre E. 21324, P.New York Brooklyn Museum 37.1777E, P.London BM EA 74125). The reuse of papyrus also occurs (P.Cairo J.E. 95575a–d verso).

# Hieratic and Cursive-Hieroglyphic Scripts

Although the bulk of manuscripts surviving from the Eighteenth Dynasty were written in cursive hieroglyphs, there are some sources that use hieratic script (L.Cairo J.E. 96804, L.Turin 63005, P.Cairo TN 25/1/55/6, P.Brussels MRAH without no., P.London BM EA 10738, Leather London BM EA 10281, P.London BM EA 74125, P.Los Angeles 83.AI.46.3, P.Moscow I, 1b, 146+132, P.New York Brooklyn Museum 31.1777E [vso], P.Paris Louvre E. 11085, P.Paris Louvre E. 21324 in BD 133, P.*Nfr-ḥꜣwt*, P.*Rwiw*, L.Cairo J.E. 96810 [cursive hieroglyphs mixed with hieratic ones]). None of these manuscripts can be dated later than the reign of Thutmose III, which may give us an approximate dating criterion, the *terminus ante quem* for this group of documents (Munro, 1988: 190–92; 1995: 3, Figs. 1–7).

However, the overwhelming majority of sources were written in cursive hieroglyphs, a less elaborate and detailed handwriting than the monumental hieroglyphs. No study on the paleography of the cursive hieroglyphs is known so far, but a few features can be observed (Munro, 1988: 193–97).

Putting aside the many individual handwritings of advanced and skilled scribes (P.Cairo CG 40002, P.London BM EA 9913, 9964, 10009, and others), of which it seems impossible to find superordinate time-bound paleographical features within the Eighteenth Dynasty, a group of documents written in standardized cursive hieroglyphs is better suited for defining a superordinate paleographical system. This scribal tradition using the standardized cursive hieroglyphs is characterized by its precise and almost invariably uniform signs (P.Edinburgh 1956.315, P.London BM EA 10477, P.Paris Louvre E. 21324, P.Amenemhet, Munro and Fuchs, 2015, P.London BM EA 9950, 9968, P.Paris Louvre N. 3073, Cairo J.E. 26203 + L.Boston MFA 60.1472; Munro, 1988: 194–95).

The names of the papyri's scribes have not been preserved anywhere, except for one case in which the scribe states that he has finished the copy by "revising and verifying it sign by sign" (P.Cairo CG 51189; Lucarelli, 2010: 264–73, esp. 270). An anonymous scribe of another papyrus clearly shows a full knowledge of the text by altering the end of a text or text passage into a comprehensible and abbreviated version (Munro and Fuchs, 2015). Although there is a reasonable presumption that the owner of P.London BM EA 9900 could be both the copyist and draftsman of his own Book of the Dead papyrus (Lapp, 2004: 23–24; Taylor (ed.), 2010: 279, no. 148), we do not have any conclusive evidence. However, both the poor understanding of the textual composition and the totally unskilled und unprofessional handwriting on the linen shroud of a certain Si-aa show that in this case the shroud was a "self-made" copy, most probably written by the owner himself; see Fig. 2.1 (Munro, 1994: 31–35).

FIG. 2.1. "Self-made" copy, shroud Cairo J.E. 33984.

# Textual Composition

The tradition of text sequences continued and influenced the individual compositions (see Tables 2.1–2.3). While the retrograde use of writing occurred only occasionally, inverted writing with cursive hieroglyphs became the standard after the reign of Hatshepsut/Thutmose III, with a few exceptions (Munro, 1988: 200–201; 261–62). The texts as well as the vignettes run mostly from left to right, while the signs face the right, opposite to the direction of reading. Perhaps practical reasons, such as copying from hieratic-written model textbooks facing right, prompted the retrograde writing (Lucarelli, 2010: 264–73, esp. 266), but it could also be the manifestation of the idea that the journey of the deceased in the afterlife proceeded from the east, the world of the living, to the west, the world of the dead, where the texts and the accompanying images should be effective in the netherworld as sphere of inverted realities (Munro and Fuchs, 2015). In many cases the manuscripts show the introductory vignette "adoration of Osiris" at the very beginning, followed either by BD 1 and BD 124 or BD 17–18, and end with BD 136A/B–149-V 150 (Munro, 1988: 159–61, 222–23). In between these elements, the sequence and choice of spells were composed individually.

It seems doubtful whether there was a predetermined principle of order for an ideal Book of the Dead manuscript (Munro, 1988: 160–62), as there is no evidence for a fixed canon or any defined arrangement of spells as the content of an ideal Book of the Dead scroll in contrast to the Saite recension of a rather canonized sequence of spells (see Albert, Gülden, this volume). The workshops and their scribes were dependent on the selection of spells available, as well as on the customer's choices and his financial means (Munro, 1988: 160–62). For this reason, the manuscripts can differ greatly in regard to their contents and length.

The scribes were unrestricted when arranging a Book of the Dead scroll, especially when they did not produce manuscripts on the direct order of a customer but rather for the general stock. In the latter case, the scribe would either not know the identity of the buyer (e.g., P.Paris Louvre N. 3073, P.London BM EA 9905, P.London BM EA 9950, P.Florence 3661), or fill in his name and title after the work was completed (e.g., P.Hannover KM 1970.37, P.Wien ÖN Aeg. 10.994–10.997). Nevertheless, they often assembled spells in groups or clusters that expressed similar themes: spells detailing a person's abilities (BD 21–25), heart spells (BD 26–30B), spells to ward off hostile animals (BD 31–40), spells for providing water and air (BD 38, 54–56, 57–63), transformation spells (BD 76–88), spells for knowing the souls of the sacred places (BD 108–109, 111–116), and spells regarding the cyclic daily journey in the sun barque (BD 100, 102, 130–136). In many cases the complex BD 17 is followed by BD 18, and almost invariably BD 150 follows BD 149.

The transformation spells seem to have been the most popular and frequently used group of BD spells (Munro, 1988: 153–54, 341–42). They occur in almost every surviving Eighteenth-Dynasty BD source, but there is no case in which all known transformation spells are united in one document; only selections of them occur.

## The Vignettes

Besides the large-scale illustrations such as the opening entrance vignettes or offering scenes, the vignettes are typically positioned at the top of a document, directly beneath the upper border in clear context to the corresponding spells. However, vignettes placed on the lower border are attested as well, while vignettes positioned amid the text can only rarely be observed (contrary to a popular layout of the Ptolemaic Period such as in P.Paris Louvre L.3079 or P.Paris Louvre L. 3087; see Mosher Jr., 1992: 146, Fig. 1 and 147, Fig. 2). Normally the vignettes are separated from the following ones, except for a few examples, which combine the motifs of two spells in one vignette (Munro, 1988: 64–137, esp. 135).

With the increase of Book of the Dead spells over the course of the Eighteenth Dynasty, the occurrence of vignettes also became more widespread, although it remains difficult to prove a steady development. Contemporary manuscripts can display either a high or low percentage of vignettes (Munro, 1988: 204–5). Likewise, it has not yet been possible to prove the assumption of an absent or poor use of coloring in the early BD tradition and the development of rich and polychrome illustrations in the later Eighteenth Dynasty (Ratié, 1968: 10): some manuscripts produced in the same period include vignettes with only outline drawing juxtaposed with those rendered in color (Munro, 1988: 205–6).

However, the tendency to show more sumptuous and more elaborate polychrome illustrations in Nineteenth-Dynasty manuscripts cannot be denied and often contrasts with a lesser quality of the texts (Munro, 2010: 54–63, esp. 57).

FIG. 2.2. P.Amenemhet, Adoration of Osiris.

FIG. 2.3. P.Amenemhet, BD 63B.

The employment of costly and valuable color pigments for the vignettes must have raised the price of a Book of the Dead scroll considerably and could not have been affordable to anyone other than the social elites (Cooney, 2007: 31–32; Janssen, 1975: 291). The same applies for the rare case of using gold leaf, which occurred only twice over the course of the Eighteenth Dynasty (P.Paris Louvre N. 3074, Amenhotep II; P.Cairo CG 51189, Amenhotep III).

In one manuscript, however, the draftsman or gifted artist involved experimented with innovative painting techniques, such as mixing different pigments or overlaying one layer of paint with another to achieve a highly sophisticated polychrome effect, a three-dimensional impression as attested in, for example, P.Amenemhet; see Fig. 2.2 (Fuchs, 2012: 215–34, esp. 227, 230; Munro and Fuchs, 2015, 116). Astonishingly, this painting technique is not known to have been adopted by any other painter or workshop, until we find it employed in elite tombs of the Nineteenth Dynasty (Bianchi, 1992a: 56–65; 1992b: 66–70).

Most vignettes either show a clear reference to the corresponding text in the choice of motifs, or merely illustrate its heading (Munro, 1988: 64–137, esp. 136). Because many motifs appear as isolated occurrences, it seems that a talented draftsman was not obliged to reproduce vignettes from a model book only—if such a repertoire of vignettes actually existed —but instead felt free to create unique motifs, as attested in a papyrus

FIG. 2.4. P.London BM EA 10009, BD 86.

from the time of Thutmose III (see Fig. 2.3; also see Munro and Fuchs, 2015, 95; Bianchi, 1992a), a period known for being open to a variety of innovations in funerary art and literature (Hornung, 1979: 22).

It is not conceivable that the draftsman of P.Paris Louvre Ae/N 3068+3113 found the model for the vignette of BD 1 in a pattern book. This composite illustration realistically combines the stages of the funerary procession with the mummy being dragged by oxen to the tomb, where the last rites are performed in the presence of his mourning widow. The shifting of the scene to the lower border, marking the underground region, is not known from any other Book of the Dead manuscript. A deep shaft, through which the *ba*-bird is approaching the mummy and supplying it with drinking water and bread, combines these worldly activities with the perception of an otherworldly existence. The rarely attested scene of the empty chair underlines the complexity of the whole illustration (Browarski, 1977: 178; Westendorf, 1988: 221–26). Furthermore, the figure of the deceased represents a third level of connotation because of his emergence from the tomb into the daylight and the sunshine, which is the essence of the general Book of the Dead title *pri.t m hrw*, visualized here in the vignette and expressed by its legend (Taylor, 2010: 100–101).

Sometimes we find very different iconographical motifs of the same spell, a phenomenon that cannot be explained by a different regional tradition (Munro, 1988: 64–137). The complex vignette of BD 17 first appears in manuscripts of the post-Amarna period and consists in total of 24 scenes positioned in a continuous strip above its text. It had only rudimentary precursors (Munro, 1988: 64–137, esp. 67–68) and is not attested in the intensely illustrated Book of the Dead documents of P.Cairo CG 51189 and P.Turin 8438, both dated into the reign of Amenhotep III. The draftsman of the latter would not have missed the opportunity to add this new vignette, if it was attested at the time (Munro, 1988: 68). Thus, the occurrence of the systematic vignette of BD 17 can be used as a valid differentiating criterion in dating manuscripts to the Eighteenth Dynasty or to the post-Amarna period and the Nineteenth Dynasty. It was certainly because of the popularity of the transformation spells and the belief in their effectiveness for a powerful passage through the netherworld that additional new spells and accompanying vignettes within this group were created. In P.London BM EA 10009, an illustration is attested that at first seems to be a variation of the vignette of BD 86: a goose instead of the usual swallow; see Fig. 2.4.[2] However, examining the corresponding text beneath, it is evident that the draftsman depicted the goose in conformity with the scribe, who copied a new transformation spell (Munro, 2017: 50 and Fig. 4.3). This is not an isolated attestation.

P.London UC 71002 shows, among other transformation spells, an illustration of a recumbent lion and the corresponding heading in red ink: *iri.t ḫpr.w mꜣi*, "assuming the form of a lion."

Unfortunately, no further text is preserved; see Fig. 2.5 (Munro, 2017: 50 and Fig. 4.4). These two new compositions did not find their way into the common stock of Book of the Dead spells.

Although the motifs of the entities depicted in the vignettes of the transformation spells essentially remain almost invariable during the whole Book of the Dead tradition—the vignettes differ only in the form of their base line or in the addition of the deceased worshipping each entity—the artist of P.Princeton Pharaonic Roll 5 chose an unusual scene combining the mummy with each entity, either above or beside it (Lüscher, 2008: 29–32, Pl. 3–5).

---

[2] At first, one may also consider it to be an error by confusing the consonantal homophony of *mn.t* (swallow) and *smn* (goose).

FIG. 2.5. Transformation spell, P.London UC 71002.

## SOCIAL STATUS OF THE BD OWNERS AND THEIR GENDER

It is generally agreed that buying a Book of the Dead scroll was beyond the financial means of the majority of Egyptian society. Only high-ranking and wealthy officials, a minority making up less than 10 percent of the population, could afford a Book of the Dead manuscript as funeral equipment (Cooney, 2007: 31–32; Janssen, 1975: 291). The high price of a papyrus scroll depended on its length, the quantity of its vignettes, the expensive color pigments for the illustrations, and the cost of the artistic skill of its draftsmen. Preliminary research on the social status of the Book of the Dead owners has revealed their belonging to the highest social ranks (Albert, 2012: 1–66, esp. 2–3).

The first Book of the Dead sources belonged not only to the royal family, the upmost tier of the ancient Egyptian hierarchy, but also to members of the royal court and high officials of non-royal descent; some of these had Asian names and were therefore obviously immigrants (Gabolde, 2008: 25–42, esp. 33–39). Even some influential officials like the vizier Useramun had parents of foreign origin; Useramun was the owner of two tombs and a Book of the Dead papyrus (TT 131 and TT 61; Munro, 1990: 73–89). Senneferi, mayor of Thebes in the reign of Thutmose III, had a shroud along with three different Book of the Dead scrolls and an elaborately decorated tomb (TT 99; Strudwick, 2016). There are many other papyri whose owners held titles in high administration—as overseers of all works, as scribes in secular and temple administration, or as priests of a different kind.

Except for the Formative Phase of the Book of the Dead tradition, in which female owners of royal descent are attested at the same rate as male owners, the majority of Book of the Dead copies over the course of the Eighteenth Dynasty were produced for men. The proportion is about 10:1. However, in many cases the vignettes and especially the entrance scene included a depiction of the owner's wife, and sometimes even the whole family, so that they could share in the benefits from the owner's Book of the Dead manuscript. A separate Book of the Dead copy did not seem to be necessary. Thus, in P.London BM EA 9964, the whole family is mentioned: wife, father, mother, grandmother, and great-grandmother (Quirke, 1999: 227–35, esp. 230–31). That is why in the Eighteenth Dynasty the Book of the Dead copies of two women are a rarity, those of Hatnefret, mother of Senenmut, consisting of a shroud together with a leather manuscript and a papyrus (Munro, 1994: I 27–29; P.Cairo T.N. 25/1/55/6 and a leather manuscript with BD 100 [inv.no. unknown]), or the Book of the Dead copy of Merit, wife of the architect Kha with several references to her husband, although he had a separate manuscript, in which the depiction of his wife was also included (P.Paris BN 826 [Luynes B], P.Turin 8438; Schiaparelli, 1927: 34–65; Heerma van Voss, 1993: 135–38).

The production of the Book of the Dead papyri was temporarily suspended during the Amarna period. We do not know of any manuscripts created in this time. It seems likely to claim that a change of the afterlife conception in the official solar theology of King Akhenaten is behind this phenomenon. Scholars have proposed a few reasons why the Book of the Dead was not produced during the Amarna Period: the abolition of an Osirian netherworld in contrast to the focus on the solar cult (Assmann, 1975: 534); the new placement of the necropolises on the eastern side of the Nile Valley, where the deceased could easily participate in the daily worshipping of and offerings to Aten (Hesse, 2015: 129–54); the focus of the Amarna religion upon the visible light, the life-spending sun disk (Smith, 2017: 276–99). However, any of these reasons can explain the absence of Book of the Dead manuscripts, while other funeral items for a perfect burial and hymns to Aten for welfare in the underworld continued to exist.

After the short reign of Akhenaten and of his advocating successor, the theology in the reign of Tutankhamun revised the Amarna doctrines and revived the traditional BD concept. In the tomb of Tutankhamun himself, occurrences of several Book of the Dead spells are attested on funerary objects, and many amulets placed inside his mummy wrapping can be interpreted as clear allusions to Book of the Dead spells, while no distinct Book of the Dead manuscript was provided for him. The attestations of Book of the Dead spells in Tutankhamun's funerary objects correspond to those of his royal predecessors of the Eighteenth Dynasty (Beinlich, 1988: 7–18; Žabkar, 1985: 375–88).

After the post-Amarna manuscripts, as in P.Leiden T 2 or /P.London BM EA 10471 + 10473, new spells and especially illustrated solar hymns were integrated into the traditional stock of Book of the Dead spells, due to the predominant influence of solar theology in the Amarna period. It is in this same period that a complex vignette, consisting of multiple scenes, first accompanies BD 17 and remains an inherent part of all later Book of the Dead manuscripts.

## Bibliography

Albert, F. (2012). "Quelques observations sur les titulatures attestées dans les Livres des Morts." In *Herausgehen am Tage. Gesammelte Schriften zum altägyptischen Totenbuch*. Studien zum altägyptischen Totenbuch 17, edited by R. Lucarelli, M. Müller-Roth, and A. Wüthrich, 1–66 (Wiesbaden: Harrassowitz).

Allen, T. G. (1974). *The Book of the Dead, or Going Forth by Day*. Studies in Ancient Oriental Civilizations 37 (Chicago: University of Chicago Press).

Assmann, J. (1975). "Aton." In *LÄ* I, 526–40, esp. 534.

Beinlich, H. (1988). "Das Totenbuch bei Tutanchamun." *Göttinger Miszellen* 102: 7–18.

Bianchi, R. St. (1992a). "An Assessment of the Wall Paintings." In Paul Getty Museum (ed.) *In the Tomb of Nefertari. Conservation of the Wall Paintings*, 66–70 (Malibu: The J. Paul Getty Trust).

Bianchi, R. St. (1992b). "On the Nature of Egyptian Painting." In *In the Tomb of Nefertari. Conservation of the Wall Paintings*, 56–65 (Malibu: The J. Paul Getty Trust).

Browarski, E. (1977). "An Allegory of Death." *Journal of Egyptian Archaeology* 63: 178.

Budge, E. A. W. (1910). *Facsimiles of Egyptian Hieratic Papyri* (London: Longmans).

Cooney, K. M. (2007). *The Cost of Death. The Social and Economic Value of Ancient Egyptian Funerary Art in the Ramesside Period*. EU 22 (Leiden: Nederlands Instituut voor het nabije Oosten).

Dorman, P. F. (1991). *The Tombs of Senenmut. The Architecture and Decoration of Tombs 71 and 353*. Publications of the Metropolitan Museum of Art 24 (New York: Metropolitan Museum of Art).

Dziobek, E., Schneyer, Th., and Semmelbauer, N. (1992). *Eine ikonographische Datierungsmethode für thebanische Wandmalereien der 18. Dynastie*. Studien zur Archäologie und Geschichte Altägyptens 3 (Heidelberg: Heidelberger Orientverlag).

Gabolde, L. (2008). "Les Livres des Morts qu'on cherche sans les trouver et d'autres qu'on trouve sans les chercher." *Kyphi* 6: 25–42.

de Garis Davies, N. and Gardiner, A. (1915). *The Tomb of Amenemhêt*. Theban Tombs Series 1 (London: Egypt Exploration Fund).

Fuchs, R. (2012). "Unrolling a Papyrus: Investigations into an Extraordinary 3500-Year-Old Book of the Dead." In M.J. Driscoll (ed.) *Care and Conservation of Manuscripts 13, Proceedings of the Thirteenth International Seminar Held at the University of Copenhagen, April 13th–15th, 2011*, 215–34 (Copenhagen: Museum Tusculanum Press).

Geisen, Chr. (2004a). *Die Totentexte des verschollenen Sarges der Königin Mentuhotep aus der 13. Dynastie*. Studien zum altägyptischen Totenbuch 8 (Wiesbaden: Harrassowitz).

Geisen, Chr. (2004b). "Zur zeitlichen Einordnung des Königs Djehuti an das Ende der 13. Dynastie." *Studien zur altagyptischen Kultur* 32: 149–57.

Gestermann, L. (1998). "Die 'Textschmiede' Theben—Der thebanische Beitrag zu Konzeption und Tradierung von Sargtexten und Totenbuch." *Studien zur altagyptischen Kultur* 25: 83–99.

Gestermann, L. (2006). "Aufgelesen: Die Anfänge des altägyptischen Totenbuchs." In *Totenbuch-Forschungen. Gesammelte Beiträge des 2. Internationalen Totenbuch-Symposiums 2005*. Studien zum altägyptischen Totenbuch 11, edited by B. Backes, I. Munro, and S. Stöhr, 111–13 (Wiesbaden: Harrassowitz).

Gestermann, L. (2012). "Auf dem Weg zum Totenbuch: Von Tradition und Neuerung *Herausgehen am Tage*." *Gesammelte Schriften zum altägyptischen Totenbuch*. Studien zum altägyptischen Totenbuch 17, edited by R. Lucarelli, M. Müller-Roth, and A. Wüthrich, 67–78 (Wiesbaden: Harrassowitz).

Grimm, A. and Schoske, S. (1999). *Im Zeichen des Mondes. Ägypten zu Beginn des Neuen Reiches*. Schriften aus der Ägyptischen Sammlung 7 (München: Staatliche Sammlung Ägyptischer Kunst).

Guksch, H. (1995). *Die Gräber des Nacht-Min und des Men-cheper-Ra-seneb. Theben Nr. 87 und 79*. Archäologische Veröffentlichungen 34 (Mainz: von Zabern).

Heerma van Voss, M. (1993). "Het andere Dodenboek uit TT 8 (Naville's Pj)." In *Individu, societé et spiritualité dans l'Égypte pharaonique et copte. FS Théodoridès*, edited by Chr. Cannuyer and J.-M. Kruchten, 135–38 (Ath; Bruxelles; Mons).

Heerma van Voss, M. (2014). "Zur Sternstunde für Amenhotep." In *The Workman's Progress. Studies in the Village of Deir el-Medina and Other Documents from Western Thebes in Honour of Rob Demarée*, edited by B. J. J. Haring, O. E. Kaper, and R. van Walsem, 99–101 (Leiden; Leuven: Nederlands Instituut voor het nabije Oosten).

Hesse, M. (2015). "Grabsitten und Jenseitszeugnisse in Amarna." In *Bestattungsbräuche, Totenkult und Jenseitsvorstellungen im Alten Ägypten*, edited by C. Elsas, H. Sternberg-el Hotabi, and O. Witthuhn, 129–54 (Sterben, Tod und Trauer in den Religionen und Kulturen der Welt, 3; 1. Aufl., Berlin: EB-Verlag).

Hornung, E. (1979). *Das Totenbuch der Ägypter*. Die Bibliothek der Alten Welt, Reihe der Alte Orient (Zürich; München: Artemis).

Hornung, E. (1975/1976). *Das Buch der Anbetung des Re im Westen*, Aegyptiaca helvetica 2 and 3 (Basel: Éd. de Belles-Lettres).

Janssen, J.-J. (1975). *Commodity Prices from the Ramesside Period* (Leiden: Brill).

Kockelmann, H. (2008). *Untersuchungen zu den späten Totenbuch-Handschriften auf Mumienbinden*, Studien zum altägyptischen Totenbuch 12 (Wiesbaden: Harrassowitz).

Lakomy, K. (2016). *Der Löwe auf dem Schlachtfeld. Das Grab KV 36 und die Bestattung des Maiherperi im Tal der Könige* (Wiesbaden: Reichert-Verlag).

Lapp, G. (2004). *The Papyrus of Nebseni*. Catalogue of the Books of the Dead in the British Museum III (London: British Museum).

Lucarelli, R. (2010). "Making the Book of the Dead." In *Journey through the Afterlife: Ancient Egyptian Book of the Dead*, edited by J. H. Taylor, 264–73 (London: The British Museum).

Lüscher, B. (2008). *Der Totenbuch-Papyrus Princeton Pharaonic Roll 5*. BAÄ 2 (Basel Orientverlag).

Megally, M. (1971). *Considérations sur les variations et la transformation des formes hiératiques du Papyrus E. 3226 du Louvre*. Bibliothèque d'étude 49 (Paris: Institut Français d'Archéologie Orientale du Caire).

Möller, M. (1909). *Hieratische Paläographie. Die Aegyptische Buchschrift in ihrer Entwicklung von der Fünften Dynastie bis zur römischen Kaiserzeit* (Leipzig: Hinrichs).
Mosher Jr., M. (1992). "Theban and Memphite Book of the Dead Traditions in the Late Period." *Journal of the American Research Center in Egypt* 29: 143–72.
Müller-Roth, M. (2008). "Das Leichentuch des Pa-heri-pedjet." *Zanzibar Archaeological Survey* 135: 149–53.
Munro, I. (1988). *Untersuchungen zu den Totenbuch-Papyri der 18. Dynastie. Kriterien ihrer Datierung*. Studies in Egyptology (London; New York: Paul Kegan).
Munro (1990). "Der Totenbuch-Papyrus des Veziers Wsr-Jmn." *Göttinger Miszellen* 116: 73–89.
Munro, I. (1994). *Die Totenbuch-Handschriften der 18. Dynastie im Ägyptischen Museum Cairo*. Ägyptologische Abhandlungen 54 (Wiesbaden: Harrassowitz).
Munro, I. (1995). *Das Totenbuch des Jah-ms (pLouvre E. 11085) aus der frühen 18. Dynastie*. Handschriften zum altägyptischen Totenbuchs 1 (Wiesbaden: Harrassowitz).
Munro, I. (2001). *Das Totenbuch des pPa-en-nesti-taui aus der Regierungszeit des Amenemope (pLondon BM 10064)*. Handschriften zum altägyptischen Totenbuchs 7 (Wiesbaden: Harrassowitz).
Munro, I. (2010). "The Evolution of the Book of the Dead." In *Journey through the afterlife. Ancient Egyptian Book of the Dead*, edited by J. H. Taylor, 54–63 (London: The British Museum).
Munro, I.; Fuchs, R. (2015). *Papyrus Amenemhet. Ein Totenbuchpapyrus der 18. Dynastie*. Studien zu den Ritualszenen altägyptischer Tempel 28 (Dettelbach: J.H. Röll).
Munro, I. (2016). "Papyri und Leichentuch aus Shaft I." In *The Tomb of Pharaoh's Chancellor Senneferi at Thebes (TT99)*, edited by N. Strudwick, 168–80 (Oxford & Philadelphia: Oxbow Books).
Munro, I. (2017). "The Significance of the Book of the Dead Vignettes." In F. Scalf, ed., *Book of the Dead. Becoming God in Ancient Egypt*, OIMP 39, 49–63 (Chicago: Oriental Institute Press 2017).
Naville, E. (1886). *Das aegyptische Totenbuch der XVIII. bis XX. Dynastie*, 3 vols. (Berlin: Asher; reprint Graz 1971).
O'Rourke, P. F. (2016). *An Ancient Egyptian Book of the Dead. The Papyrus of Sobekmose*. Brooklyn Museum (London: Thames & Hudson).
Parkinson, R. and Quirke, S. (1992). "The Coffin of Prince Herunefer and the Early History of the Book of the Dead." In *Studies in Pharaonic Religion and Society (Fs J.G. Griffiths)*. Occasional Publications 8, edited by A. B. Lloyd, 37–51 (London: Egypt Exploration Society).
Piankoff, A. (1964). *The Litany of Re* (New York: Pantheon Books).
Quirke, S. (1999). "Women in Ancient Egypt: Temple Titles and Funerary Papyri." In A. Leahy and J. Tait, eds., Studies on Ancient Egypt in honour of H. S. Smith. Occasional Publications 13, 227–35 (London: Egypt Exploration Society).
Ratié, S. (1968). *Le papyrus of Neferoubenef (Louvre III93)*. Bibliothèque d'étude 43 (Cairo: Institut Français d'Archéologie Orientale du Caire).
Roehrig, C. and Dorman, D. (1987). "Senimen and Senenmut: A Question of Brothers." *Varia Aegyptiaca* 3: 127–34.
Rössler-Köhler, U. (1979). *Kapitel 17 des Ägyptischen Totenbuches. Untersuchungen zur Textgeschichte und Funktion eines Textes der altägyptischen Totenliteratur*, Göttinger Orientforschungen IV/10 (Wiesbaden: Harrassowitz).
Schiaparelli, E. (1927). *La tomba intatta dell'architetto "Cha" nella necropole di Tebe*. Relazione II (Turin: Ministero della Pubblica Istruzione, Direzione Generale delle Antichità e Belle Arti).
Shorter, A. W. (1934). "A Leather Manuscript of the Book of the Dead." *Journal of Egyptian Archaeology* 20: 33–40.

Smith, M. (2017). *Following Osiris: Perspectives on the Osirian Afterlife from Four Millennia* (Oxford: Oxford University Press).

Strudwick, N. (2016). *The Tomb of Pharaoh's Chancellor Senneferi at Thebes (TT99)*. Part I (Oxford; Philadelphia: Oxbow Books).

Taylor, J. H., ed. (2010). *Journey through the Afterlife: Ancient Egyptian Book of the Dead* (London: The British Museum).

Wegner, M. (1933). "Stilentwicklung der thebanischen Beamtengräber." *Mitteilungen des deutschen archaologischen Instituts, Abt. Kairo* 4: 38–164.

Westendorf, W. (1988). "Das leere Grab und der leere Stuhl." In *Religion im Erbe Ägyptens*. Fs. Alexander Böhlig, Ägypten und Altes Testament 14, edited by M. Görg, 221–26 (Wiesbaden: Harrassowitz).

Žabkar, L. V. (1985). "Correlation of the Transformation Spells of the Book of the Dead and the Amulets of Tutankhamun's Mummy." In *Mélanges offert à Jean Vercoutter*, edited by P. Mauroy, 375–88 (Paris: Ed. Recherche sur les Civilisations).

CHAPTER 3

# THE RAMESSIDE BOOK OF THE DEAD AND THE DEIR EL-MEDINA TRADITION

## BARBARA LÜSCHER

Although our knowledge of the Book of the Dead and the number of published specimens has increased considerably since the days of the first scholarly editions (see the other chapter by Lüscher in this volume), we are still far from having sufficiently reliable and accurate criteria for precisely dating and determining the origin of the heterogeneous Book of the Dead material. The reason for this lies not only in the fact that the majority is still unpublished and that many of the manuscripts and text occurrences are fragmentary, but also because the archaeological context of the finds has very often been lost. Many of the papyri and linen shrouds now scattered in museums and collections throughout the world were either brought out of Egypt by early travelers or acquired through auction sales and therefore rarely came with official excavation records. Thus, this lack of reliable external data still represents a problem for current Book of the Dead studies.

## Problems of Dating and Provenance

While making a general distinction between the so-called Theban Recension of the New Kingdom and the Saite Recension of the Late Period (with its more standardized spell sequences and vignettes) is normally quite easy, the differentiation between Eighteenth and Nineteenth/Twentieth Dynasty traditions is often less obvious and sometimes remains doubtful or controversial. Also, some types of Book of the Dead manuscripts produced after the New Kingdom, during the Third Intermediate Period, can be quite similar to earlier specimens (Niwiński, 1989: 118–28 about type BD.II.1), a fact that has also led to an incorrect dating for certain manuscripts (Niwiński, 1989: 10; Lüscher,

2012: XV on item lC9 u.a.). Obviously, the texts and layout of some manuscripts from the Third Intermediate Period had been copied from older master manuscripts (Niwiński, 1989: 235; Lüscher, 2007: 19–20).

As already mentioned, the lack of a secure archaeological context can also cause problems in distinguishing various local traditions. Although many of those New Kingdom papyri that can be ascribed to a particular region, be it through the owner's name, genealogy, and titles, or through the buyer's records, come from Thebes, one should be cautious about assigning a Theban origin to material with unknown provenance, because findings from places like Abydos (P.Chicago OIM 5750), Akhmim (shroud of Senhotep IFAO: Gasse, 1983; Gasse, 2006: 6–7; Müller and Weber, 2012: 121–24), Rifeh (shroud of Hepi, Wellcome Collection Swansea W 869: Heerma van Voss, 1974), Sedment (shroud of Itenem, Horniman Museum London 26.106, 9260i-ii; papyrus Petrie Museum London, P.UC 71002; papyrus Ramose, Fitzwilliam Museum Cambridge E.2.1922; papyrus Khnumemheb, Petrie Museum London UC 32365), and Elephantine make it clear that Book of the Dead production took also place outside of Thebes. Several papyri are clearly of Memphite origin, like the well-known papyrus of Nebseni (P.London BM EA 9900: Lapp, 2004), the papyrus of Bakai (P.Warschau 237128: Andrzejewski, 1951), and the papyrus of Senemnetjer (P.Florence 3660A; Lüscher, 2010: 110–12 with Figs. 1–6, 8). (For a discussion of the Memphite papyri and their distinct tradition see also Lüscher, 2008: 40–43.) Although it is certainly not the rule, there are rare examples where two manuscripts of different provenance show close similarities in style and composition. One reason for that could be, for example, the transfer of a text or model copy from one part of the country to another (Munro, 2010a). Also, some members of the Theban Book of the Dead workshops obviously exercised their craftsmanship in more than one place in the country (for the Memphite region, see Zivie, 2003, 2013). Therefore, the precise date and provenance of a particular Book of the Dead document can be quite difficult to determine and must be based on a combination of various criteria and data. There have been numerous attempts over the past few decades to find such criteria (for the Eighteenth Dynasty see Munro, 1988; for the Third Intermediate Period see Niwiński, 1989), but so far with rather limited results when trying to ascertain an exact date or obtain absolute validity (Niwiński, 1989: 9–12).

As mentioned earlier in this chapter, we still need a far greater number of well-published source material, ideally with a secure historical and archaeological context, to form a solid basis for detailed studies on the texts, illustrations, paleography, grammar, and so forth. In that respect, two long-term projects have provided solid material for study: the Book of the Dead archive at Bonn (Germany), which has collected the available data on the Book of the Dead material from all over the world (now accessible online: http://totenbuch.awk.nrw.de//), including general information, images, bibliography, and various statistical analyses; and the Book of the Dead project at Basel (Switzerland), which is publishing a new standard synoptic text edition of all the spells of the Theban Recension (see our series "Totenbuchtexte"). The material made available through these projects is making all sorts of new studies on the many aspects of the Book of the Dead possible. At the same time, new translations of the spells, based on a far wider selection of differing versions than the former text corpus provided by Naville's edition from 1886, will shed new light on that very important religious text corpus, including its chronological and local development, and on ancient Egyptian funerary customs and beliefs in general.

# The Ramesside Period

With that said, let us now take a closer look at the situation in the Ramesside Period, followed by a narrow focus on the Theban site of Deir el-Medina. As stated earlier, it can sometimes be difficult to distinguish Ramesside manuscripts from earlier ones; again, precise dating criteria are needed.

Unless the ownership or provenance of a particular Book of the Dead is already known through external data—for example, historical relations, archaeological context, other material belonging to the deceased, his parentage, administrative titles, and so forth—there are several stylistic, formal, and textual features that can, to a certain degree, help make a distinction between earlier and later manuscripts within the New Kingdom tradition. To find criteria for different local traditions, additional factors have to be considered, such as differing versions of the same spell (which may hint at separate local archives, for instance), variations in the iconography of the vignettes, certain selections and sequences of spells, the overall style and layout of the manuscript, and so on. Among the criteria and features commonly used or discussed for dating Book of the Dead material within the New Kingdom, the following can be listed here:

## Historical and archaeological data

Ideally, the owner of a particular Book of the Dead can be identified by their name, title, and parentage, or by a genealogical relationship with other known persons, and perhaps linked to a tomb or other monuments attributable to the same person. This will be explored further later in this chapter in the section on the Deir el-Medina tradition. The ideal case, however, is rare, and thus we normally must rely on other criteria. The exact confinement of a document to the reign of a certain pharaoh within a particular dynasty, for instance on the grounds of the owner having a connection to a named king or a well-dated tomb, is also rather rare (see for example the papyrus of Yuya, CG 51189, father-in-law of King Amenhotep III: Naville, 1908; Munro, 1994: 49–88, photo-pls. 20–21, pls. 46–72).

## Pictorial illustrations and vignettes

It is more a tendency than a general rule that the percentage of space allocated for pictorial illustrations compared to text increased over time. The very early specimens had no or very few vignettes, for example the early linen shrouds from the late Seventeenth and early Eighteenth Dynasties (Ronsecco, 1996; Munro, 1994, with several specimens). Rare examples of early linen shrouds with several illustrations are P.London BM EA 73806 and P.London BM EA 73808 (Taylor, 2010: 67). The very long papyrus of Nu (P.London BM EA 10477, see Lapp, 1997) as well as many other as yet unpublished examples from the first half of the Eighteenth Dynasty, have only a very few vignettes (for example, the papyrus of Mesemnetjer, P.Paris Louvre E.21324, which served, together with the papyrus of Nebseni (P.London BM EA 9900), as one of the role models for Édouard Naville's synoptic edition of 1886). An example with very elaborate and beautifully colored vignettes from later in the Eighteenth Dynasty is the London papyrus of Nakht (P.London BM EA 10471+10473) with its exquisite illustrations in an Amarna-influenced style (Taylor, 2010: 112–13, 152, 168–69, 185–89, 220, 249–51; Faulkner, 1985: 28–29, 53, 58–59, 62–63, 70, 72, 82, 85, 89, 95, 98–99, 112, 126–27, 142, 146–47, 151, 156). The highest-quality vignette drawings can be found in the Ramesside Period, which includes the famous London papyri of Ani (P.London BM EA 10470: Dondelinger, 1978–1979) and Hunefer (P.London BM EA 9901: Budge, 1899), the Berlin papyrus of Nakhtamun (P.Berlin 3002; Munro, 1997), and the unpublished papyrus of Ramose at Cambridge (P.Cambridge, Fitzwilliam Museum E.2a.1922), among others. The vignettes tend to become more prominent, elaborate, and refined in the Nineteenth Dynasty, often at the expense of the quality of the text. But there are too many exceptions to this rule to make it a truly valid criterion because one must consider the possibility of different local traditions as well as the personal preferences of the customers.

If a manuscript is well preserved, the style and iconography of the vignettes, particularly the representation of human beings with their proportions and clothing, often provide good clues for assigning a particular date within the New Kingdom, since one might assume that the pictorial illustrations more or less reflect the contemporary fashion of clothes, hair styles, and types of funerary equipment depicted in tombs of the same period (Munro, 1988: 13–63). However, some of the vignettes might also tend to make use of archaization. For example, the coffin shown in the burial scene on the papyrus of Maiherperi (CG 24095; Lakomy, 2016) differs in color from the actual type found in his tomb (KV 46). With regard to the texts, they might remain more closely oriented to the master papyrus and thereby be less "up-to-date" or modern than the vignettes.

The Amarna Period at the end of the Eighteenth Dynasty, with its radical change in the concept of the hereafter (Hornung, 1995: 105–14; Hari, 1985: 10–12; Williamson, 2017; for a slightly different view see Smith, 2017: 276–85, 295–96, 299–300, 350–55), most likely caused a temporary interruption in the Book of the Dead production. After that break from the religious norm, some new spells or illustrations seem to have been included in the corpus and might therefore serve as a *post quem* criterion, for instance the illustrations accompanying the famous BD spell 17 (Munro, 1988: 68, 136–37; 2010b: 57). Another often-cited example is the vignette to the solar hymn of BD spell 15 (Lapp, 2015), although we should proceed with caution here because some unpublished papyri from the British Museum that show a comparable scene were produced before the Amarna Period (Niwiński, 1989: 11–12 with Fig. 1), such as the papyrus of Shemes (P.London BM

EA 9988), the papyrus of Userhat (P.London BM EA 10009), and perhaps also the papyrus of Paser (P.London BM EA 10466–7; Lapp, 2017). More detailed studies on individual spells and their accompanying vignettes are thus needed.

## Formal elements

Purely formal elements, like the kind of colored border patterns that develop from simple to more elaborate and numerous lines (Munro, 1988: 199–200), or the use of horizontal lines for the rubric headers of a chapter, typical of earlier manuscripts (Munro, 1988: 202), can further facilitate the division between the Eighteenth and the Nineteenth/Twentieth Dynasties. Also, the use of linen instead of papyrus seems to be more or less restricted to the earlier part of the New Kingdom.

A more problematic criterion is the individual handwriting and style of script. While there are a few hieratic specimens in the late Seventeenth and earlier Eighteenth Dynasties (for example, the lost wooden coffin of Queen Mentuhotep—see Budge, 1910 and Geisen, 2004; the unpublished papyri of Senenmut's mother Hatnofret; papyrus Jahmes P.Paris Louvre E.11085: Munro, 1995), and of course again after the New Kingdom, the cursive hieroglyphic script typical for the majority of New Kingdom Books of the Dead often looks quite homogeneous at first sight and shows only slight variations. Therefore, dating based solely on paleography is difficult (Munro, 1988: 190–97), and attempts to find valid criteria have delivered rather limited or negative results that often lead only to a mere statistical tendency. Thus, a comparative paleography for the cursive script (Ali, 2001; Allam, 2007; Goelet, 2010) as well as one for the hieratic of the early Books of the Dead is needed. The project "Ancient Egyptian Cursive Scripts" Scripts (AKU: Altägyptische Kursivschriften, see https://aku.uni-mainz.de/) that was begun in 2015 at the Academy of Sciences and Literature Mainz (Germany) recently added an online digital paleography of hieratic and cursive hieroglyphs (AKU-PAL online) to their aforementioned website.

## Texts and spell sequences

What seems to be a very promising method for categorizing different chronological and/or local traditions is an analysis of the spells and their sequences (Lapp, 1997: 36–49, § 39–74; Niwiński, 1989: 22–26), provided the manuscript is not too fragmentary. Although the Theban Recension has no mandatory order or strictly standardized spell sequence, some structure is still evident (Lapp, 1997: 42–49). While one can observe clearly preferred spell sequences or pairings for the beginning and end of a manuscript (for example, Eighteenth Dynasty papyri often end with BD 149–150, while Ramesside manuscripts preferably conclude with BD 186, 148 or 110; see Munro, 1988: 160), some sequences, sometimes with a lengthy series of spells, point to common standard prototypes on papyrus or leather rolls in the archives and workshops, especially in the beginning of the New Kingdom (in general, these types of longer and coherent spell sequences are more typical of the Eighteenth rather than the Nineteenth/Twentieth Dynasty) and even shortly before.

Those prototypes, the archival master manuscripts on papyrus (Kockelmann, 2017: 73) or on leather (like the specimen P.London BM EA 10281: see Shorter, 1934; Quirke, 2013: 80), were presumably shorter than a normal Book of the Dead and consisted of (mostly, but not exclusively) thematically arranged groups of spells like the transformation spells, spells for mouth and heart, spells for providing water and air, for repelling enemies, spells of knowing the souls of sacred places, and many others. Some of these groups or clusters of spells, which are typical for Book of the Dead manuscripts, were already present in the older corpus of the Coffin Texts. For example, the Louvre ostraca E22394 and AF230 obviously represent a copy of an archival master prototype and include only the CT group of spells 154 and 155. They served—alongside a whole set of additional ostraca—as intermediate templates for decorating the walls of the Theban tomb of Nakhtmin/TT 87 (Lüscher, 2013: 42). So, when a Book of the Dead specimen was being composed, spells from these groupings in master manuscripts seem to have been chosen, and the individual selection and length might have been left to the preferences and budget of the client who commissioned it at the artist's workshop. Those workshops and their archives of templates and prototypes probably differed from place to place and from one period to another, making the selection and sequence of spells an additional, potentially local criterion.

Apart from papyri, linen shrouds, and other items of funerary equipment, tomb walls are another important source of material. The Ramesside Period provides us with a wealth of comparative data, with its many elaborately decorated private tombs, many of which included Book of the Dead vignettes and texts (Saleh, 1984). However, a few Eighteenth-Dynasty tombs also incorporated the Book of the Dead, among them the Theban tombs of Djehuty (TT 11), Amenemhat (TT 82), Senenmut (TT 353), and Sennefer (TT 96B). Contrary to some authors' remarks, the texts in the often-cited example of Nakhtmin's funeral chamber (TT 87; Guksch, 1995) are not excerpts from the Book of the Dead, but rather represent a very interesting selection of Coffin and Pyramid texts, copied from a series of large ostraca (as intermediate templates) onto the walls of the burial chamber (Lüscher, 2013).

Outside Thebes, especially in Saqqara, recent excavations in New Kingdom tombs are also bringing new Book of the Dead material to light. Thus, further study and comparative analysis of such new source material from outside Thebes will hopefully help in identifying specific local traditions.

## THE DEIR EL-MEDINA TRADITION

The question of local traditions now leads us to the famous site of the workmen's village and necropolis of Deir el-Medina which, due to its isolated location and to luck on the diggers' part, allows a unique insight into a distinct regional workshop and tradition.

This rather closed community of artists, who lived on the western bank of Thebes in a little valley separated from the usual rural settlements in the cultivated land, had obviously developed its very own tradition of the Book of the Dead.

Especially during the long reign of Ramesses II, the villagers who worked in the royal tombs in the famous Valley of the Kings and the Valley of the Queens could dedicate their spare time to building and decorating their own and their colleagues' private burial places, including their funerary equipment (Andreu, 2002; Bierbrier, 1982). In contrast to the general decoration scheme of other contemporary Theban tombs, the walls of the subterranean funeral chambers in Deir el-Medina show—in the Ramesside Period—an extensive use of the Book of the Dead (Saleh, 1984), probably also partly influenced by the general religious themes and iconography of their working place, the tombs of the kings and queens. As a special example, the tombs of Nakhtamun (TT 335) and Neferrenpet (TT 336) can be mentioned. They both show a scene of the ram-headed, unified Osiris-Re, which has a close parallel in the scene in Queen Nefertari's tomb (QV 66) in the Valley of the Queens (Lüscher, 2007: 26–27, pl. 37).

Until only recently, very few Book of the Dead papyri could be assigned with certainty to a person from the Deir el-Medina community, the most famous being the chisel-bearer Neferrenpet (Speleers, 1917; Milde, 1991). As the owner of tomb 336 in the nearby necropolis, he lived in the Nineteenth Dynasty during the long reign of Ramesses II. His fragmentary but still extensive and exquisite Book of the Dead papyrus is on display in the Royal Museums of Fine Arts of Belgium in Brussels (P.Brussels E.5043), with some fragments in the University of Pennsylvania Museum, Philadelphia. In his discussion of that manuscript, Henk Milde showed the close similarities and mutual influence between the vignettes on this papyrus and the corresponding wall decoration of several Deir el-Medina tombs; among them notably TT 1, 3, 218, 219, 265, 290, and 335, all belonging to members of the same or successive generations. There is also a close similarity between the illustrations in Neferrenpet's papyrus and those on the wall of Nefertari's royal tomb in the Valley of the Queens, another working place of the Deir el-Medina artisans. Some of the scenes and illustrations in the tombs and on the few papyri from this site are unique and found solely on Deir el-Medina material (see, for example, Fig. 3.1 and Fig. 3.2).

Further, it can be shown that those special versions and variations of Book of the Dead vignettes, typical of the papyri and tomb walls of Deir el-Medina, are found not only on papyri and tomb walls, but on other sorts of funerary equipment originating from Deir el-Medina, such as stelae (see Fig. 3.3a) and sarcophagus shrines (Lüscher, 2007). This means that this special Theban community had its own archives and produced its own local models and master copies ("Vorlagen"). Therefore, we can speak of a distinct Deir el-Medina Book of the Dead tradition that differed from other parts of the Theban necropolis.

But this typical Deir el-Medina "style" was not restricted to the iconography, as a detailed study of the textual material from this site shows (Lüscher, 2007). This fact is actually not too surprising, as the thousands of Deir el-Medina ostraca and other finds clearly prove that these specialized craftsmen had a much higher level of literacy than the average Egyptian population.

A critical comparison of the text versions and orthography of particular spells makes it possible to determine with certainty the provenance of several more papyri (Lüscher, 2007; further papyrus fragments from Deir el-Medina have recently been identified in Turin), some of them being very fragmentary, and funerary items as Deir el-Medina. The similarities in the texts and their variants can be seen for example in the synoptic edition of BD spell 1 (Lüscher, 1986) or BD spell 78 (Lüscher, 2006: 32–171, in which the texts in TT 218 (Amunnakht), TT 1 (Sennedjem), TT 290 (Irynefer), on the sarcophagus shrine of Khonsu (a son of Sennedjem, from TT 1), and on the sarcophagus of Pashed (from TT 3), as well as on the stela of Hui (Museo Archeologico di Torino,

FIG. 3.1. Combined vignettes of BD 151a (funeral mask) and BD 166.

3.1a) Papyrus of Neferrenpet (Brussels E.5043).
3.1b) Papyrus of Ankhesenmut (Cairo SR VII 10255).
3.1c) Tomb of Irynefer (TT 290).
© All line drawings by B. Lüscher.

FIG. 3.2. Vignettes of BD 68.

3.2a) Papyrus of Neferrenpet (Brussels E.5043).
3.2b) Tomb of Sennedjem (TT 1).
© 3.2a: Line drawing by B. Lüscher
© 3.2b: Photo IFAO, J. F. Gout

Suppl. 6148bis). All are from Deir el-Medina, and all display the same text variants and orthography. Additional versions of that spell, for example on the British Museum stela of Neferabu (BM EA 305, probably from TT 5; see Fig. 3.3a; Taylor, 2010: 96), or on the papyrus of Pashed (P.London BM EA 9955, probably from TT 3) (Lüscher, 2007: 30, 40, pl. 38a), confirm this result.

A further striking aspect is the fact that some of the Deir el-Medina papyri look very much like duplicates, regarding not only their text versions, but also their vignettes. Among this special group are the aforementioned papyrus of Neferrenpet (see Fig. 3.4a), P.Princeton Pharaonic Roll 2 (see Fig. 3.4b), P.Neuchâtel Eg. 429, P.Kaunas Tt-12848, and the papyrus of Ramose in Berlin (P.Berlin P. 15778) (on all of these, see Lüscher, 2007).

This is unusual and very rare, because in general, there are hardly two manuscripts among the many hundreds of known examples that have identical vignettes. So, this group of Deir el-Medina papyri in question must have been based on the same master copy, as they are products of the same workshop and some of them may have been produced by the same scribal hand. They not only share the same vignettes, but their texts also show the same paleographical details, textual omissions, and variations in the text. Even scribal errors and special hieroglyphic sign forms were stereotypically copied from the master texts onto the final surface (be it papyrus, tomb wall, stela, or coffin).

Of further interest is the fact that those archival templates were obviously still available and in use after the end of the New Kingdom, as a papyrus for a woman named Ankhesenmut from the Twenty-first Dynasty (P.Cairo SR VII 10255) clearly shows (see Fig. 3.1b). While the painter of the illustrations in the papyrus of Ankhesenmut carefully changed the depiction of the deceased from male to female, the scribe erroneously

FIG. 3.3. Vignettes of BD 1.

3.3 a) Stela of Neferabu (London BM EA 305), owner of TT 5.
3.3b) Wall scene from Sennedjem's tomb (TT 1).
© 3.3a: The Trustees of the British Museum.
© 3.3b: Photo B. Lüscher.

(b)

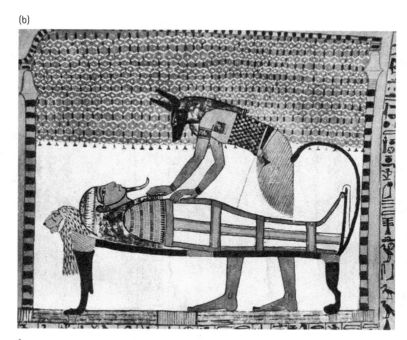

FIG. 3.3. Continued

FIG. 3.4. Comparison of two almost identical papyri from Deir el-Medina.

3.4a) Papyrus of Neferrenpet (P.Brussels E.5043).

3.4b) P.Princeton Pharaonic Roll 2.

© 3.4a: Photo Musées Royaux d'Art et d'Histoire Bruxelles.

© 3.4b: Photo courtesy of Princeton University Library, Manuscripts Division, Department of Rare Books and Special Collections.

(b)

FIG. 3.4. Continued

started copying his template from the wrong end and thus produced a corrupt and partially illegible text (Naville, 1910: 108; Lüscher, 1998: 91–92).

To summarize, the versions of Book of the Dead vignettes and texts found on tomb walls, papyri, and other items of funerary equipment from Deir el-Medina differ significantly in several aspects from versions produced outside these local workshops, even within the Theban necropolis. Those variants clearly point to a specific iconographic and textual tradition for the Book of the Dead in Deir el-Medina during the Nineteenth Dynasty. Such typical regional factors can therefore provide new criteria for more accurately establishing the date and provenance of other New Kingdom Book of the Dead papyri.

## Bibliography

Ali, M. S. (2001). "Die Kursivhieroglyphen. Eine paläographische Betrachtung." *Göttinger Miszellen* 180: 9–21.

Allam, M. (2007). "Die Kursivhieroglyphen. Sind sie Hieroglyphen oder Hieratisch? Zur Stellung der Kursivhieroglyphen innerhalb der ägyptischen Schriftgeschichte." *Annales du Service des Antiquites de l'Egypte* 81: 33–37.

Andreu, G. (2002). *Les artistes de Pharaon. Deir el-Médineh et la Vallée des Rois* (Paris: Editions de la Réunion des musées nationaux).

Andrzejewski, T. (1951). *Ksiega umarłych piastunki Kai. Papirus ze zbiorów Muzeum Narodowego w Warszawie nr. 21884* (Warszawa: Muzeum Narodowe).

Bickel, S. and Díaz-Iglesias, L., eds. (2017). *Studies in Ancient Egyptian Funerary Literature*. Orientalia Lovaniensia Analecta 257 (Leuven: Peeters).

Bierbrier, M. (1982). *The Tomb-builders of the Pharaohs* (London: British Museum Publications).

Budge, E. A. W. (1910). *Facsimiles of Egyptian Hieratic Papyri in the British Museum* (London: Longmans).

Budge, E. A. W. (1899). *The Book of the Dead. Facsimiles of the Papyri of Hunefer, Anhai, Kerasher and Netchemet with Supplementary Text from the Papyrus of Nu* (London: British Museum).

Dondelinger, E. (1978-1979). *Papyrus Ani BM 10.470. Vollständige Faksimile-Ausgabe im Originalformat des Totenbuches aus dem Besitz des British Museum*. Codices Selecti 62. Phototypice Impressi (Graz / Paris: Akademische Druck- und Verlagsanstalt).

Faulkner, R. O. (1985). *The Ancient Egyptian Book of the Dead*, edited by Carol Andrews (London: British Museum Publications).

Gasse, A. (1983). "L'étoffe funéraire de Senhotep." *Bulletin de l'Institut francais d'archeologie orientale* 83: 191-95.

Gasse, A. (2006). "Les livres des morts sur tissu." *Egypte Afrique & Orient* 43: 3-10.

Geisen, C. (2004). *Die Totentexte des verschollenen Sarges der Königin Mentuhotep aus der 13. Dynastie. Ein Textzeuge aus der Übergangszeit von den Sargtexten zum Totenbuch*. Studien zum Altägyptischen Totenbuch 8 (Wiesbaden: Harrassowitz).

Goelet Jr., O. (2010). "Observations on Copying and the Hieroglyphic Tradition in the Production of the Book of the Dead." In *Offerings to the Discerning Eye. An Egyptological Medley in Honor of Jack A. Josephson*. Culture and History of the Ancient Near East 38, edited by S. H. D'Auria, 121-32 (Leiden: Brill).

Grajetzki, W. (2010). *The Coffin of Zemathor and Other Rectangular Coffins of the Late Middle Kingdom and Second Intermediate Period*. Golden House Publications Egyptology 15 (London: Golden House Publications).

Guksch, H. (1995). *Die Gräber des Nacht-Min und des Men-cheper-Ra-seneb. Theben Nr. 87 und 79*. Archäologische Veröffentlichungen 34 (Mainz: von Zabern).

Hari, R. (1985). *New Kingdom Amarna Period: The Great Hymn to Aten*. Iconography of Religions XVI, 6 (Leiden: Brill).

Heerma van Voss, M. (1974). "Een Dodendoek als Dodenboek." *Phoenix* 20: 335-38, figs. 94-95.

Hornung, E. (1995). *Die Religion des Lichtes* (Zürich: Artemis).

Kockelmann, H. (2017). "How a Book of the Dead Manuscript Was Produced." In *Book of the Dead. Becoming God in Ancient Egypt*. Oriental Institute Museum Publications 39, edited by F. Scalf, 67-74 (Chicago: The Oriental Institute).

Lakomy, K. (2016). *"Der Löwe auf dem Schlachtfeld." Das Grab KV 36 und die Bestattung des Maiherperi im Tal der Könige* (Wiesbaden: Reichert Verlag).

Lapp, G. (1997). *The Papyrus of Nu (BM EA 10477)*. Catalogue of Books of the Dead in the British Museum I (London: British Museum).

Lapp, G. (2004). *The Papyrus of Nebseni (BM EA 9900)*. Catalogue of the Books of the Dead in the British Museum III (London: British Museum).

Lapp, G. (2015). *Die Vignetten zu Spruch 15 auf Totenbuch-Papyri des Neuen Reiches*. Beiträge zum Alten Ägypten 6 (Basel: Orientverlag).

Lapp, G. (2017). "Die Vignette zu Tb 15 aus Papyrus London BM EA 10466-7." In *Studies in Ancient Egyptian Funerary Literature*. Orientalia Lovaniensia Analecta 257, edited by S. Bickel and L. Díaz-Iglesias, 331-43 (Leuven: Peeters).

Lepsius, R. (1842). *Das Todtenbuch der Ägypter nach dem hieroglyphischen Papyrus in Turin* (Leipzig: Wigand).

Lüscher, B. (1986). *Totenbuch Spruch 1. Nach Quellen des Neuen Reiches*. Kleine Ägyptische Texte 10 (Wiesbaden: Harrassowitz).

Lüscher, B. (1998). *Untersuchungen zu Totenbuch Spruch 151*. Studien zum Altägyptischen Totenbuch 2 (Wiesbaden: Harrassowitz).

Lüscher, B. (2006). *Die Verwandlungssprüche (Tb 76-88)*. Synoptische Textausgabe nach Quellen des Neuen Reiches. Totenbuchtexte 2 (Basel: Orientverlag).

Lüscher, B. (2007). *Totenbuch-Papyrus Neuchâtel Eg. 429 und Princeton Pharaonic Roll 2. Zur Totenbuch-Tradition von Deir el-Medina*. Beiträge zum Alten Ägypten 1 (Basel: Orientverlag).

Lüscher, B. (2008). *Der Totenbuch-Papyrus Princeton Pharaonic Roll 5*. Beiträge zum Alten Ägypten 2 (Basel: Orientverlag).

Lüscher, B. (2009). *Die Fährmannsprüche (Tb 98-99)*. Synoptische Textausgabe nach Quellen des Neuen Reiches. Totenbuchtexte 4 (Basel: Orientverlag).

Lüscher, B. (2010). "In the footsteps of Edouard Naville (1844-1926)." In *British Museum Studies in Ancient Egypt and Sudan* 15: 103-21.

Lüscher, B. (2012). *Die Sprüche vom Kennen der Seelen (Tb 107-109, 111-116)*. Synoptische Textausgabe nach Quellen des Neuen Reiches. Totenbuchtexte 8 (Basel: Orientverlag).

Lüscher, B. (2013). *Die Vorlagen-Ostraka aus dem Grab des Nachtmin (TT 87)*. Beiträge zum Alten Ägypten 4 (Basel: Orientverlag).

Lüscher, B. (2014). *Auf den Spuren von Edouard Naville. Beiträge und Materialien zur Wissenschaftsgeschichte des Totenbuches*. Totenbuchtexte Supplementa 1 (Basel: Orientverlag).

Milde, H. (1991). *The Vignettes in the Book of the Dead of Neferrenpet*. Egyptologische Uitgaven 7 (Leiden: Nederlands Instituut voor het Nabije Oosten).

Mosher Jr., M. (1989) *The Ancient Egyptian Book of the Dead in the Late Period: A Study of Revisions Evident in Evolving Vignettes and Possible Chronological and Geographical Implications for Differing Versions of Vignettes*. PhD diss., University of Berkeley.

Mosher Jr., M. (1992) "Theban and Memphite Book of the Dead Traditions in the Late Period." *Journal of the American Research Center in Egypt* 29: 143-72.

Mosher Jr., M. (2010). "An Intriguing Theban Book of the Dead Tradition in the Late Period." In *British Museum Studies in Ancient Egypt and Sudan* 15: 123-72.

Müller-Roth, M. and Weber, F. (2012). "Pretty Good Privacy." In *Herausgehen am Tage. Gesammelte Schriften zum altägyptischen Totenbuch*. Studien zum Altägyptischen Totenbuch 17, edited by R. Lucarelli, M. Müller-Roth, and A. Wüthrich, 121-24 (Wiesbaden: Harrassowitz).

Munro, I. (1988). *Untersuchungen zu den Totenbuch-Papyri der 18. Dynastie*. Studies in Egyptology (London: Kegan Paul).

Munro, I. (1994). *Die Totenbuch-Handschriften der 18. Dynastie im Ägyptischen Museum Cairo. Textband und Tafelband*. Ägyptologische Abhandlungen 54 (Wiesbaden: Harrassowitz).

Munro, I. (1995). *Das Totenbuch des Jah-mes (pLouvre E. 11085) aus der frühen 18. Dynastie*. Handschriften des Altägyptischen Totenbuches 1 (Wiesbaden: Harrassowitz).

Munro, I. (1997). *Das Totenbuch des Nacht-Amun aus der Ramessidenzeit (pBerlin P. 3002)*. Handschriften des Altägyptischen Totenbuches 4 (Wiesbaden: Harrassowitz).

Munro, I. (2010a). "Evidence of a Master Copy Transferred from Thebes to the Memphite Area in Dynasty 26." In *British Museum Studies in Ancient Egypt and Sudan* 15: 201–24.

Munro, I. (2010b). "The Evolution of the Book of the Dead." In *Journey Through the Afterlife: Ancient Egyptian Book of the Dead*, edited by J. Taylor, 54–63 (London: British Museum).

Naville, E. (1886). *Das aegyptische Todtenbuch der XVIII. bis XX. Dynastie*. 3 vols. (Berlin: Asher).

Naville, E. (1908). *The Funeral Papyrus of Jouiya* (London: Constable).

Naville, E. (1910). "Les amulettes du chevet et de la tête." *Zeitschrift fur agyptische Sprache und Altertumskunde* 48: 107–11.

Niwiński, A. (1989). *Studies on the Illustrated Theban Funerary Papyri of the 11th and 10th Centuries B.C*. Orbis Biblicus et Orientalis 86 (Freiburg; Schweiz: Universitätsverlag).

Quirke, S. (2013). *Going out in Daylight—prt m hrw. The Ancient Egyptian Book of the Dead: Translation, Sources, Meanings*. GHP Egyptology 20 (London: Golden House Publications).

Ronsecco, P. (1996). *Due Libri dei Morti del principio del nuovo regno. Il lenzuolo funerario della principessa Ahmosi e le tele del sa-nesu Ahmosi*. Catalogo del Museo Egizio di Torino. Seria Prima—Monumenti e Testi VII (Torino: Pozzo).

Saleh, M. (1984). *Das Totenbuch in den thebanischen Beamtengräbern des Neuen Reiches*. Archäologische Veröffentlichungen 46 (Mainz: von Zabern).

Shorter, A. W. (1934). "A Leather Manuscript of the Book of the Dead in the British Museum." *Journal of Egyptian Archaeology* 20: 33–40, Pl. IV–VIII.

Scalf, F., ed. (2017). *Book of the Dead: Becoming God in Ancient Egypt*. Oriental Institute Museum Publications 39 (Chicago: The Oriental Institute).

Smith, M. (2017). *Following Osiris: Perspectives on the Osirian Afterlife from Four Millenia* (Oxford: Oxford University Press).

Speleers, L. (1917). *Le papyrus de Nefer Renpet. Un Livre des Morts de la XVIIIme dynastie aux Musées royaux du Cinquantenaire à Bruxelles* (Bruxelles: Vromant & Co.).

Taylor, J., ed. (2010). *Journey Through the Afterlife. Ancient Egyptian Book of the Dead* (London: British Museum).

Williamson, J. (2017). "Death and the Sun Temple: New Evidence for Private Mortuary Cults at Amarna." *Journal of Egyptian Archaeology* 103: 117–23.

Zivie, A. (2003). "Un détour par Saqqara. Deir el-Médineh et la nécropole memphite." In *Deir el-Médineh et la Vallée des Rois. La vie en Egypte au temps des pharaons du Nouvel Empire*, edited by G. Andreu, 67–82 (Paris: Ed. Khéops).

Zivie, A. (2013). *La tombe de Thoutmes, directeur des peintres dans la Place de Maât (Bub. I.19)*. Les tombes du Bubasteion à Saqqara II (Toulouse: Caracara Ed.).

CHAPTER 4

# THE BOOK OF THE DEAD IN THE THIRD INTERMEDIATE PERIOD

GIUSEPPINA LENZO

DURING the Third Intermediate Period the Book of the Dead tradition consisted mostly of papyri from the Theban area. It was the subject of a number of publications at the beginning of the twentieth century (Budge, 1912; Naville, 1912, 1914; Nagel, 1929). Other funerary papyri of this period have been published, such as the so-called mythological papyri (Piankoff, 1949; Piankoff and Rambova, 1957), the Litany of Re (Piankoff, 1964), and the Amduat (Sadek, 1985). But research on this topic was largely put aside until the funerary papyri of this period were presented by Andrzej Niwiński (1989). In his book, the author distinguishes between different traditions, while grouping together similar papyri based on their content, length, writing, and layout. Niwiński classified texts with extracts of the Amduat, the Litany of Re, "mythological" papyri, and hieroglyphic and hieratic Books of the Dead in different categories based on their features. Other scholars include Matthieu Heerma van Voss (1971, 1974a, 1974b), who especially studied hieroglyphic and "mythological" papyri, and Thomas George Allen (1974), who took versions from this period into account in his translation of the Book of the Dead.

For the past few years, research on the tradition of the Book of the Dead during the Third Intermediate Period has been the subject of a revival among scholars. Indeed, several Book of the Dead papyri have been published, mostly in hieratic script (Kockelmann, 2003; Lenzo, 2007, 2012, 2015a; Lucarelli, 2006; Meeks, 1993; Munro, 1996, 2001; O'Rourke, 2008; Valloggia, 1989, 1991, 1998, 2012). Most recently, in a translation of all the Book of the Dead chapters, Stephen Quirke (2013) incorporated many Third Intermediate Period versions, including new spells.

All the attestations with Book of the Dead spells fall under the principle of *pars pro toto*; in other words, they are a choice of texts or illustrations representing the whole. Thus, the difficulty in studying the Book of the Dead during the Twenty-first to

Twenty-fifth Dynasties is that there are many versions and not only one tradition. For this reason, it is important to study each tradition and also to analyze it as a step between the so-called Theban (Munro, this volume) and Saite redactions (Gülden, this volume).

## Context and Provenance of the Book of the Dead during the Third Intermediate Period

### Thebes

Most of the Books of the Dead of the Third Intermediate Period are from the Theban region and were written on papyri. During the New Kingdom, the walls of royal and private tombs were decorated with a range of various funerary texts; Book of the Dead spells are found in this context as well as on hieroglyphic papyri. The looting of tombs and the social crisis at the end of the New Kingdom had an impact on the burial ensemble. The first consequence thereof was the modification of the tomb itself: most of the time, we can witness the reuse of ancient tombs or the establishment of collective tombs. The walls of Theban tombs are no longer decorated, and, at the same time, a profusion of funerary papyri can be witnessed. Coffins also show innovative vignettes and texts, sometimes also from the Book of the Dead repertoire. So, the decorations missing from the walls were instead elaborated on other text carriers such as coffins, while the number of papyri simultaneously increased. As noticed by Jean-Luc De Cenival (1987), the material in the tombs is specifically more funerary and not taken from daily life as before. Thereby, burial equipment was completely redeveloped in a new way based on a new funerary conception.

The Bab el-Gusus (or Second) Cachette is one of the collective tombs, with more than 150 mummies of priests and priestesses of Karnak having been found there (Daressy, 1907), as well as TT 60 (or MMA 60) and TT 358 (MMA 65) with the mummies of priestesses of Karnak (Winlock, 1942). The best-known one is the Royal Cachette of Deir el-Bahari, with the hidden mummies of the kings of the New Kingdom as well as the High Priests of Amun and their family (Maspero, 1889; regarding the discovery, there is extensive literature on the topic. See most recently Graefe and Belova, 2010). In the same period, the priesthood of Amun and the temple of Karnak grew more and more important and powerful, with the High Priest becoming almost an equal of the Pharaoh. This may explain why the papyri of this time belonged to the family of the High Priest (Table 4.2) as well as members of the lower clergy of Amun. Most of the time, we do not know where the papyri were placed, but a few well-documented examples show mainly two places: on the body of the deceased (for example Daressy, 1907: no. 58, 26; no. 64, 27; nos. 114 and 31), or in an Osiris statuette (Winlock, 1942: 114–15; Raven, 1984).

## Tanis and Memphis

While funerary texts were found on papyri in the Theban area, the walls of tombs were still being decorated in Lower Egypt. The tombs of the Pharaohs of the Twenty-first and Twenty-second Dynasties in Tanis are significantly smaller than in the New Kingdom, but they contain extracts of Book of the Dead spells, as well as other funerary texts such as the Amduat or the Book of the Gates (Roulin, 1998). Concerning private individuals, some traces of tombs have been found in Tanis: some blocks were reused in the tomb of King Sheshonq III in Tanis in the Twenty-second Dynasty (NRT V; Montet, 1960: 81–93, pl. XLVI–LXI; Lull, 2001). Finally, the tomb of Sheshonq, High Priest of Ptah and son of King Osorkon II (Twenty-second Dynasty), situated in Memphis, was also decorated with Book of the Dead spells (Badawi, 1956; Lenzo, 2018; Meffre, Payraudeau, and Lenzo, 2017).

# The "Ensemble" of Papyri in Thebes

In the Theban area the deceased could take two papyri with them for the afterlife. The "ensemble" of papyri has been partly studied (Niwiński, 1989: tables III, XVa; Lenzo, 2004, 52–53; Lenzo, 2021a for the ensemble of papyri of Bab el-Gasus). Taking into account all the available papyri, we have now registered 62 pairs of papyri. In these groups, Book of the Dead extracts are the predominant funerary text. The ensembles are composed in the following way (Table 4.1):

In more than half of the pairs, a Book of the Dead is attested, in hieroglyphic or in hieratic, most of the time accompanied by an Amduat. In other cases, "mythological" papyri can be found with another "mythological" papyrus or a hieroglyphic/hieratic Book of the Dead. An example is the "mythological" papyrus of Gatseshen found together with a hieratic Book of the Dead in TT 60 (or MMA 60), probably from the time of the pontificate of Pinedjem II (Figs. 4.1–4.2). Finally, the Litany of Re is the lesser-used text in pairs.

The Book of the Dead Project database in Bonn registered 118 hieroglyphic papyri for the Third Intermediate Period, plus 227 in hieratic, for a total of 346 papyri for the whole period. "Mythological" papyri (Fig. 4.1), Amduat (Fig. 4.3), and Litany of Re (Fig. 4.4) papyri must be added to this. In addition, papyri of the same ensemble have certainly been dispatched to different museums, and many have yet to be paired. Nevertheless, given that only 52 Book of the Dead papyri out of 346 are part of a pair, it may be inferred that many deceased possessed only one papyrus. Moreover, if we observe the distribution of papyri among the members of the family of the High Priests of Amun (see Table 4.2 at the end of the chapter), we notice that two papyri are frequent but not a prerequisite.

FIG. 4.1. "Mythological" papyrus of Gatsesehn. Pinedjem II/Late Twenty-first Dynasty.

Credit line: P.New York MMA 25.3.31, Metropolitan Museum of Art, New York © www.metmuseum.com.

FIG. 4.2. Book of the Dead of Gatsesehn. Pinedjem II/Late Twenty-first Dynasty.

Credit line: P.New York MMA 25.3.32, Metropolitan Museum of Art, New York © www.metmuseum.com.

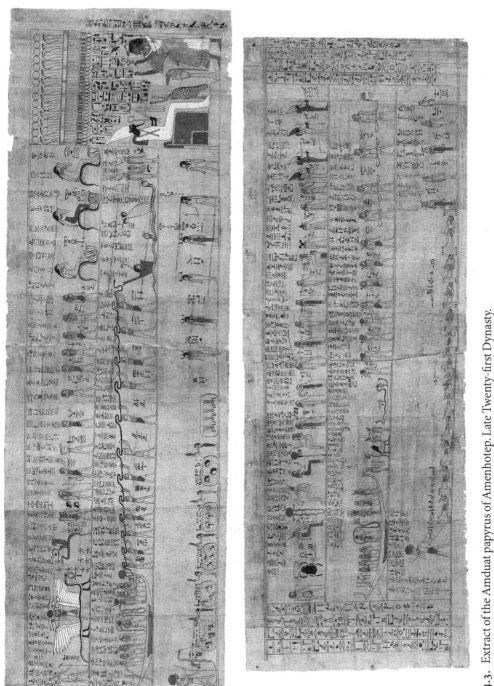

FIG. 4.3. Extract of the Amduat papyrus of Amenhotep. Late Twenty-first Dynasty.

Credit line: P.Berlin P 3005 © Staatliche Museen zu Berlin, Ägyptisches Museum und Papyrussammlung / Sandra Steiß.

FIG. 4.4. Extract of the Litany of Re of Amenmose. Early-middle Twenty-first Dynasty.
Credit line: P.London BM EA 10011, sheet 1, British Museum London ©The Trustees of the British Museum.

## THE INITIAL VIGNETTE ON THEBAN PAPYRI

Many papyri have an initial vignette, the so-called etiquette (Sadek, 1985: 318–22; Niwiński, 1989: 97–104; Lenzo, 2004). The vignette shows the deceased giving offerings or in an adoration position in front of a god (Fig. 4.5). Its use hearkens back to the Book of the Dead of the New Kingdom. During the Third Intermediate Period, this vignette appears not only on Book of the Dead papyri, in either hieroglyphic or hieratic (Figs. 4.2, 4.7), but also in many "mythological" papyri (Fig. 4.1) and several Amduat (Fig. 4.3) or Litany of the Sun papyri. As in the New Kingdom, the god is often Osiris, sometimes accompanied by Isis and/or Nephthys. Osiris is frequently present in papyri that follow the tradition of the New Kingdom or with traditional Book of the Dead spells. Re-Horakhty is attested in the funerary papyri since the High Priest Menkheperre, especially in texts presented in a new way in this period that I call the new tradition of the Book of the Dead, the Amduat, the Litany of Re, and "mythological" papyri (Lenzo, 2004). Later, possibly at the end of the Twenty-first Dynasty, the form of the god Re-Horakhty-Atum also appears. In this case, the god is displayed in an Osirian position, as a substitute of Osiris: this is certainly a way to show the solar concept united with the Osirian one, which gains importance in this period (Niwiński, 1987–1988; Wüthrich, 2010: 32–37). These gods are sometimes associated with other deities such as Osiris or Ptah-Sokar-Osiris, probably after the Twenty-first Dynasty. The etiquettes can be polychrome, bichrome (black/red), or monochrome (black), although they tend to be monochrome in the Twenty-second Dynasty. Finally, two examples have an original vignette

FIG. 4.5. Initial vignette of the Book of the Dead of Padiamenet. Late Twenty-first Dynasty.
Credit line: P.London BM EA 10063, British Museum London © The Trustees of the British Museum.

with the divinized Pharaoh Amenhotep I instead of Osiris or Re-Horakhty (P.Paris BN 59 and P.Turin 1784).

## The Hieroglyphic Book of the Dead Papyri (Twenty-first Dynasty)

Among the 346 Book of the Dead papyri registered by the Book of the Dead Project database in Bonn, 118 are in hieroglyphs. They can be divided into two main groups: papyri following the tradition of the Ramesside Period with some new aspects, and abbreviated papyri with many innovations. According to their content and layout, the abbreviated ones can in turn be catalogued into subgroups.

## Papyri continuing of the tradition of the Ramesside Period

A group of papyri continues the tradition of the Ramesside Period. They are in cursive hieroglyphs and contain Book of the Dead spells with some of the corresponding vignettes that are usually polychrome (Niwiński, 1989: 118–28, pl. 6b–10b), with the texts taking up more space than the illustrations. The general layout and the content are similar to papyri of the Ramesside Period, but they also contain some innovations (for the layout and the position of the spells and vignettes, see Niwiński, 1989: Table VIII).

Among these papyri is a group from the High Priest Pinedjem I's family that originated from the Royal Cachette in Deir el-Bahari: the papyri of Pinedjem I, his mother Nedjmet, and his wife Henuttauy or his daughter Maatkare (for the complete list of papyri and the references, see Table 4.2 at the end of the chapter). They are all quite long, with a length of between 3 and 6 meters (and more than 12 m in the case of P.London BM EA 10541 + P.Paris Louvre E. 6258; Fig. 4.6) and 30–40 centimeters high. Thus, the papyri following the Ramesside tradition are well attested at the beginning of the Twenty-first Dynasty.

Since the mid-Twenty-first Dynasty, the papyri of this group tend to become shorter, usually between 1 and 3 meters in length and 20–25 centimeters high (for example P.London BM EA 9903 or P.Cairo S.R. VII 10222, middle or late Twenty-first Dynasty; Niwiński, 1989: P.London 1 and P.Cairo 59). Longer papyri are attested but are much rarer; for example P.London BM EA 10020, which is 2.74 meters long but 44 centimeters high, from the mid-Twenty-first Dynasty, or P.Cairo S.R. IV 11494 with a length of 5.23 meters but a height of 23 centimeters, from the late Twenty-first Dynasty (Niwiński, 1989: P.London 38 and Cairo 116).

As for the content, the most popular spells are BD 125, 126, 110, 149, 148, and 99, according to Niwiński (1989: 121, Tables IX–X). The judgment of the dead as well as the presentation of offerings are the main themes. Even if the general layout is in the tradition of the Ramesside Period, there are some innovations and new spells (Niwiński, 1989: 122–27; Heerma van Voss, 1971).

In the second part of the Twenty-first Dynasty, the papyri in continuation of the Ramesside tradition became shorter and shorter and seemed to disappear at the end of the dynasty. This category of papyri should be studied in detail in order to find more parallels inside the documents of the group itself, as well as to determine whether there are links between variants and other kinds of Book of the Dead papyri, in both hieroglyphs and hieratic.

## Abbreviated hieroglyphic papyri

### A new tradition in hieroglyphic papyri during the Twenty-first Dynasty

Alongside the Book of the Dead derived from the Ramesside tradition, a new kind of funerary papyrus appears in this period (Niwiński, 1989: 132–51, pl. 21–29). These documents contain original representations with a mix of tradition and innovation.

FIG. 4.6. Book of the Dead of Queen Nedjmet. Early Twenty-first Dynasty.

Credit line: P.London BM EA 10541, British Museum London © The Trustees of the British Museum.

Their main features focus more on the illustrations than on the text, and the vignettes can have multiple colors, be monochrome, or have only a few colors. They are generally of a short length and height (e.g., P.London BM EA 9919; 1.70 m length, 24 cm high; Figs. 4.7–4.9).

Among these, a papyrus in the Louvre (P.Paris Louvre N. 3292; Nagel, 1929) is the best known and stands out from the others because of its length (4.49 m) and height (38 centimeters).

Niwiński (1989: Table XI) has highlighted the arrangement of the spells and the layout, as well as the Book of the Dead spells attested for the sequence (Niwiński, 1989: Table XII). At first sight, the result is that the most frequently used spells are BD 125, or an extract of this spell (such as in P.London BM EA 9918, sheet 2, in which only a few sentences of the negative confession have been selected; see Fig. 4.8); BD 110 on the Field of Offerings (a short extract of the vignette in P.London BM EA 9919, sheet 3; Fig. 4.9); and a few new iconographic compositions such as BD 195 on the ritual of purification, sometimes accompanied by a text (Niwiński, 1989: 134–35; also in P.London BM EA 9919, sheet 2; Fig. 4.8).

Egyptologists have classified some of these papyri as "mythological" papyri (for example, P.Cairo S.R. VII 10256 or P.Cairo S.R. VII 11496, published by Piankoff and Rambova, 1957: nos. 1 and 15). But the presence of innovations combined with Book of the Dead extracts does not prevent one from considering them a full Book of the Dead in use during the Twenty-first Dynasty. According to Niwiński (1989: 150–51), these papyri are attested all throughout the Twenty-first Dynasty—particularly in the

FIG. 4.7. Book of the Dead of Tentosorkon. Late Twenty-first Dynasty.
Credit line: P.London BM EA 9919, sheet 1, British Museum London © The Trustees of the British Museum.

FIG. 4.8. Book of the Dead of Tentosorkon. Late Twenty-first Dynasty.
Credit line: P.London BM EA 9919, sheet 2, British Museum London © The Trustees of the British Museum.

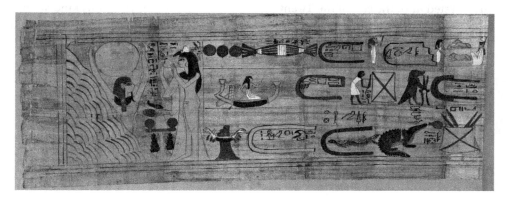

FIG. 4.9. Book of the Dead of Tentosorkon. Late Twenty-first Dynasty.
Credit line: P.London BM EA 9919, sheet 3, British Museum London © The Trustees of the British Museum.

mid-Twenty-first Dynasty—until the pontificate of Pinedjem II. Most of these papyri are unpublished. An edition of them with a full commentary and a comparison with parallels would probably provide more information about this specific Book of the Dead.

## *The so-called mythological papyri*

Like some papyri previously mentioned, other attestations have been called "mythological" papyri because illustrations are present in most parts of them (Piankoff and Rambova, 1957; Refai, 2007). They are short papyri, between 1 and 3 meters in length and 20–25 centimeters in height, and usually polychrome (Fig. 4.1). Some examples are also shorter, for example 14 centimeters, with only one register of illustrations (Fig. 4.10).

FIG. 4.10. "Mythological" papyrus of Pashebmutwebkhet. Late Twenty-first Dynasty.
Credit line: P.London BM EA 10007, sheet 1, British Museum London © The Trustees of the British Museum.

The content of these papyri is a mix of illustrations of different origins: Book of the Dead spells, extracts of the Amduat or other royal funerary texts, and new vignettes (Niwiński, 1989: 192–211, pl. 41–48b). The earliest attestation known is the papyrus of Henuttauy, daughter of the High Priest Pinedjem I, buried under the High Priest Menkheperre in the Theban Tomb 60 (see Table 4.2 at the end of this chapter), and they are attested until the end of the Twenty-first Dynasty. Many papyri of this kind are unpublished; a new study on the illustrations and the new iconographic repertoire would be useful and certainly contribute to a better understanding of this tradition.

## Concluding remarks on the hieroglyphic Books of the Dead

Different traditions of the Book of the Dead on hieroglyphic papyri are attested during the Twenty-first Dynasty. At the beginning of the dynasty, papyri are more strongly linked with the tradition of the Ramesside Period, but at the same time, a new repertoire in the Book of the Dead was created with more of a focus on illustrations. These were used up until the creation of the so-called mythological papyri that could simply be considered new Books of the Dead. The *pars pro toto* (a part for the whole) is the principle adopted during this period. Hieroglyphs are abandoned in Book of the Dead papyri in the Twenty-second Dynasty in favor of hieratic, which was more often used in the second part of the Twenty-first Dynasty. Niwiński (1989) gave a general overview of the characteristics of each kind of tradition, but many hieroglyphic Books of the Dead have yet to be published, and a detailed study of all the attestations in this script remains to be done.

# The Hieratic Book of the Dead Papyri

As indicated earlier in this chapter, most of the Book of the Dead papyri of the Third Intermediate Period were written in hieratic (227 out of 346 papyri), compared to the New Kingdom, for which the database of the Book of the Dead Project registers 15 examples in hieratic, while 336 papyri are attested for that period altogether. The difference between the two periods is important, and the use of hieratic as the script of the Book of the Dead papyri is a significant innovation. The reason for this choice is difficult to determine. This preference for hieratic is more evident during the Libyan rule, not only on papyri but also on stelae, possibly because hieratic was much closer to the spoken language and was easier for non-native speakers such as the Libyans to use (Leahy, 1985: 60; Kaper and Demarée, 2005: 37; Lenzo, 2015b: 277–78). The influence of administrative signs on some papyri may also suggest that the scribes in charge of Book of the Dead papyri were more experienced with hieratic than with hieroglyphs; the script was also quicker to write.

The first dated papyrus in hieratic is that of Queen Nedjmet (P.London BM EA 10490, Fig. 4.11; for references, see Table 4.2 at the end of this chapter). Bought in 1894 by the British Museum, it is certain that it comes from the Royal Cachette of Deir el-Bahari as her coffin was found there. The exact position of the queen in the family of the High Priest of Amun is not clear, but it is possible that she lived until the beginning of the Twenty-first Dynasty (Taylor, 1998; Dodson, 2012, 32–33; Haring, 2012; Thijs, 2013). Nedjmet probably owned two papyri, one in hieroglyphs in the Ramesside tradition (P.London BM EA 10541 + P.Paris Louvre E. 6258; Fig. 4.6) and one in hieratic with several innovations. Although it was unusual for one person to have two Books of the Dead, having two funerary papyri was possible during the Third Intermediate Period (see earlier discussion). To explain the presence of these two papyri, Niwiński (1989: 210) questioned whether the hieratic one was written later, during the pontificate of Pinedjem II, when the mummy of the queen was moved to the Royal Cachette. But there could be another explanation: the papyri of Queen Nedjmet are the first dated examples for two funerary papyri belonging to one person, so these could be the first occurrence of two funerary papyri: a traditional one in hieroglyphs and an attempt at another composition in hieratic and containing an innovative disposition of the spells. Indeed, the papyrus contains some Book of the Dead spells, but also a new spell and a unique version of substantial extracts of the Book of Caverns on papyrus. The sequence of the spells is also new, so the priest made changes in regard not only to the script, but also to the content. Therefore, we can consider it the first Book of the Dead of a new tradition, and probably the first one in hieratic in the Third Intermediate Period (some rare examples are attested during the New Kingdom). In contrast, the members of the family of the High Priest Pinedjem I preferred a hieroglyphic Book of the Dead with another papyrus, but since the pontificate of Menkheperre and especially since Pinedjem II, hieratic came more into use (Table 4.2).

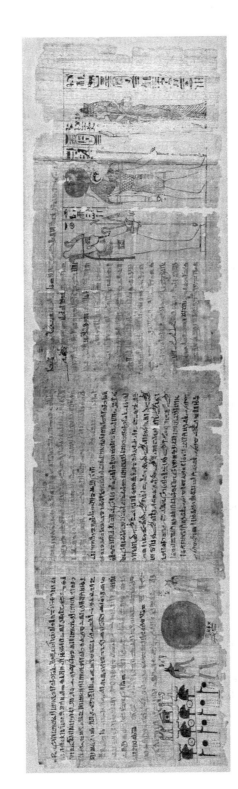

FIG. 4.11. Hieratic Book of the Dead papyrus of Queen Nedjmet. Early Twenty-first Dynasty.

Credit line: P.London BM EA 10490, sheet 1, British Museum London © The Trustees of the British Museum.

## Long hieratic papyri (Twenty-first Dynasty)

Hieratic Books of the Dead can be divided into two main groups: long hieratic papyri and abbreviated versions.

### P.Paennestitauy and P.Gatseshen

During the Twenty-first Dynasty, a group of hieratic papyri seems to have been derived from the tradition of the Ramesside Period. The best-known papyri are those of Paennestitauy, dated in Year 5 of Amenemope (P.London BM EA 10064; Munro, 2001), and Gatseshen, daughter of the High Priest Menkheperre, also buried during the reign of Amenemope (P.Cairo JE 95838; Lucarelli, 2006; Fig. 4.12). The provenance of P.Paennestitauy is unknown, but it is surely from the Theban area, while P.Gatseshen was found in the Second Cachette of Bab el-Gusus. Both papyri are very similar and probably had the same model. Besides the hieratic script, the layout of both papyri is similar to that of the New Kingdom: high pages (about 33 cm high) and a total length of about 14 meters for Paennestitauy and almost 18 meters for Gatseshen. The polychrome vignettes are inserted either in the middle or at the top of the texts, without a separation between illustrations and texts. Lucarelli (2006) has highlighted the different sequences of the Book of the Dead spells on the papyrus; even if some of them were already known during the New Kingdom (for example BD 17–18, BD 23–24–25–26–28–28, BD 130–136A, and 134–130 rubric; Lucarelli, 2006: 66–67, 72), new spells have also been inserted, such as BD 41B (Lucarelli, 2006: 110) or the so-called ritual text (Lucarelli, 2006: 175–81). Other similar papyri were copied from these papyri or from their model during the second half of the Twenty-first Dynasty (Lucarelli, 2006: 237–47; Ragazzoli, 2010: 235). Thus, two kinds of papyri can be related to the two documents from the reign of Amenemope. The first subgroup consists of rather long papyri with vignettes—but shorter than P.Paennestitauy and P.Gatseshen—with a different choice of spells. These are P.London BM EA 10084 (unpublished), P.Paris BN 62–88 (Ragazzoli, 2010), P.Paris BN 138–140 + P.Paris Louvre E. 3661 (unpublished), P.Cairo S.R. IV 549 (unpublished), P.Cairo S.R. IV 981 (unpublished, dated in the period of the High Priest Pinedjem II), and P.Cairo S.R. VII 11573 (= JE 26230 = P.Nesikhonsu, wife of Pinedjem II, buried in Year 5 of Siamon; Naville, 1914). They contain a different selection of spells, which is why they all are shorter than P.Paennestitauy/P.Gatseshen. As two of them are from the second part of the Twenty-first Dynasty, we can suppose that they are mainly from this period; none seem to be from later than the end of the Twenty-first Dynasty. Other abbreviated papyri with different spells have been copied from these two papyri or their model, which constitute the second subgroup (see discussion later in this chapter).

### P.Pinedjem II

The High Priest of Amun at Karnak, Pinedjem II, was buried in Year 10 of Pharaoh Siamon (Munro, 1996: 1), at the end of the Twenty-first Dynasty. His papyrus was found

FIG. 4.12. Extract of the papyrus of Gatseshen. Time of King Amenemope.
Credit line: P.Cairo JE 95838, sheet 26, Egyptian Museum Cairo © Rita Lucarelli (Lucarelli 2006, pl. XXVI).

in the Royal Cachette of Deir el-Bahari (P.London BM EA 10793; Munro, 1996). It is quite a long hieratic papyrus (6.65 m long and about 33 cm high), but shorter than the P.Paennestitauy/P.Gatseshen. The most important difference to the latter lies in the layout of the papyrus: it contains only the vignette at the beginning; no other illustrations were drawn (Fig. 4.13). The content is also different: Some spells are arranged in the same way as in the New Kingdom (for example BD 17–18), but there are also new sequences, and especially new variants for words or sentences. This indicates a new tradition in the Book of the Dead, which stems from the New Kingdom one. From this papyrus or its model, a sequence was selected (BD 23–24–25–26–28–27), which gave way to a new abbreviated papyrus (see discussion later in this chapter).

## *P.Greenfield*

P.Greenfield (P.London BM EA 10554) is without a doubt the most exceptional papyrus of the Third Intermediate Period. It belongs to the priestess of Karnak, Nesitanebetisheru, who was the daughter of the High Priest Pinedjem II and was buried in the Royal Cachette in Deir el-Bahari at the end of the Twenty-first Dynasty (or possibly at the beginning of the Twenty-second Dynasty). Published by Wallis Budge (1912), it was presented during the exhibition on the Book of the Dead at the British Museum (Taylor, 2010: 306–9; the whole papyrus is shown in the Japanese version of the catalogue). A new study of the papyrus by Lenzo is in press (forthcoming).

This papyrus is special in regard to both the layout and the content. It is more than 37 meters long, with sheets of about 44–50 centimeters in height and a total of 96 sheets; it is the longest Book of the Dead papyrus known. Illustrations are drawn only in black and they are often on the upper part of the papyrus, separated from the text by a double line (Fig. 4.14). This method of presenting the vignette is unusual for this period, as vignettes

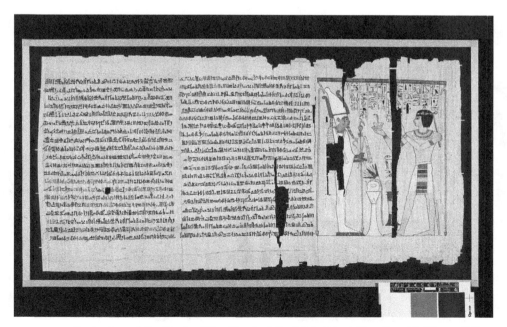

FIG. 4.13. Beginning of the Book of the Dead of the High Priest Pinedjem II. Time of King Siamon.

Credit line: P.London BM EA 10793, sheet 1, British Museum London © The Trustees of the British Museum.

were normally inserted in the middle of the text and not separated from it (Fig. 4.12); this layout is more reminiscent of the later Book of the Dead (Gülden, this volume). Finally, free space is often left void at the end of the page; the fact that this occurs so frequently is also unusual.

The content of P.Greenfield can be divided into several different parts:

- Book of the Dead spells that have almost the same sequence as P.Pinedjem II, but with the presence of many vignettes;

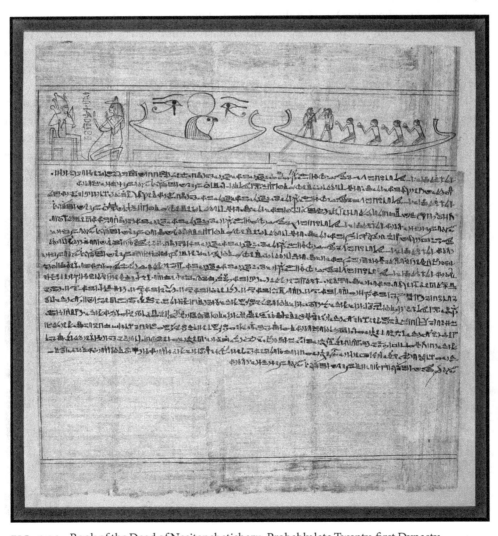

**FIG. 4.14.** Book of the Dead of Nesitanebetisheru. Probably late Twenty-first Dynasty.
Credit line: P.London BM EA 10554, sheet 51, British Museum London © The Trustees of the British Museum.

- other Book of the Dead spells, including new ones;
- several hymns and litanies, sometimes with new texts;
- extracts of the Offering Ritual used as a part of other texts; and
- "mythological" scenes.

The hymns and litanies have already been studied (Zaluskowski, 1996; Quirke, 2013: 564–80), and the sheets with all the parallels have been presented by Lenzo (2021b). Some scenes and texts are also similar to the one in the tombs of Pharaoh Osorkon II in Tanis (Jansen-Winkeln, 1988; Roulin, 1998; Lenzo, 2018) and of his son Sheshonq in Memphis (now in Cairo, Badawi, 1956; Lenzo, 2018; Meffre, Payraudeau, and Lenzo, 2017; Lenzo, Meffre, and Payraudeau, forthcoming).

The presence of new spells or hymns and litanies is not unusual for this period, but what is surprising is their quantity in a sole papyrus. Most of the time one comes across some specific spells but not so many in a single document.

## Abbreviated hieratic papyri (Twenty-first to Twenty-second Dynasty)

The abbreviated—or "miniature"—Book of the Dead is very common during the Third Intermediate Period (Niwiński, 1989: 113–18; Lenzo, 2002; Lenzo Marchese, 2007). The main features of these papyri are the following: short papyri, between 1 and 3 meters, about 25 centimeters high; a unique opening vignette of the adoration of a deity, often Osiris, or no vignette at all; and a limited choice of a small group of spells (Fig. 4.2). The choice of spells is based on the principle of *pars pro toto*, a part for a whole, as if the selection of some specific spell was representative of a complete Book of the Dead for the afterlife. With at least 119 papyri of this kind, they are the most frequently used Book of the Dead type during the Third Intermediate Period. The first dated papyrus of this type is P.New York MMA 25.3.29, found in TT 60 in 1924 and now kept in New York. It belongs to Henuttauy, daughter of the High Priest Menkheperre, and is dated up to the beginning of the pontificate of Pinedjem II. After this, this kind of papyrus appeared no later than Pinedjem II.

The study of this kind of papyri, kept at the Egyptian Museum of Turin by Lenzo Marchese (2007), made it possible to determine different sequences of Book of the Dead spells and their possible model or workshops. Indeed, these abbreviated versions can either be linked to long papyri or contain new spells of the Book of the Dead. Three main groups have been distinguished:

- Papyri derived from the same model as P.Paennestitauy/P.Gatseshen or from the same model as P.Pinedjem II (corresponding to the beginning of P.Greenfield);
- Papyri with an innovative sequence, probably from the time of the High Priest Pinedjem II; and

- Papyri with new spells, often with an extract of BD 23 at the beginning, probably from the Twenty-second Dynasty.

## *Papyri derived from the same model as P.Paennestitauy/P.Gatseshen or P.Pinedjem II*

The study of the sequences, as well as the variants, the writing, and other similarities, seems to indicate that the different papyri are derived from the same tradition stemming from the model used for P.Paennestitauy/P.Gatseshen; one sequence appears to be derived from the model used for P.Pinedjem II and the beginning of P.Greenfield. Different sequences, which were probably already organized by theme in these long papyri, were chosen (see Lucarelli, 2006 and the sequences she highlighted). This choice is interesting, as it indicates which spells were the most important ones in use and reflects the beliefs of the Egyptians in this period.

The sequence of BD 23–24–25–26, often with BD 28 and sometimes BD 27, is the most popular one. The themes of these chapters are all linked with the protection of the body parts (BD 23 for the mouth, BD 26, 28, and 27 for the heart) or the general protection of the deceased (BD 24 in order to benefit from the magic and BD 25 to remind of his name). The group is already known in the Book of the Dead of the New Kingdom and is kept in the Saite redaction (Quirke, 2013: 80).

The sequence as attested in these short papyri is derived mainly from two traditions. The first is linked to the model of P.Paennestitauy/P.Gatseshen (see the comment on the sequence in Lucarelli, 2006: 67–69). The dated papyri (P.Cairo S.R. IV 959, from the time of Psusennes II and P.Paris Louvre E. 31856, probably from the time of Osorkon I) suggest their use in the second half of the Twenty-first Dynasty until the beginning of the Twenty-second Dynasty (for other papyri of this tradition, see Lenzo Marchese, 2007: 104–6).

The second tradition is from the model of P.Pinedjem II, which also gave way to at least six papyri with this sequence (Lenzo Marchese, 2007: 104–6). None is dated with certainty, but they can be placed in the second half of the Twenty-first Dynasty, and they might still have been in use during the Twenty-second Dynasty.

At the end of this sequence (in both traditions), other spells were sometimes added, such as BD 162, which is not attested in the long papyri (Lenzo Marchese, 2007: 104–5; Wüthrich, 2010: 46–47). The title of the spell, "For placing heat under the head of a transfigured state [that is, *akh*-state]," was probably chosen because of the link with the protection of the body from the previous chapter. The spell is probably first attested during the reign of Pinedjem II (Lenzo Marchese, 2007: 105). Thus, shorter papyri were derived from an existing model with a long selection of spells, with other spells such as BD 162 being added from another tradition.

Alongside BD 180, BD 17 is the only one that can be found in short papyri bearing just one spell. The versions used in this case are from the P.Paennestitauy/P.Gatseshen tradition, with some differences (Rössler-Köhler, 1999: 170–77), and they are still in use from the late Twenty-first Dynasty until the beginning of the Twenty-second Dynasty. This spell can be found at the beginning of the Book of the Dead since the New Kingdom, often with BD 18 as in the P.Paennestitauy/P.Gatseshen tradition (Lucarelli, 2006: 64–67). The regular placement of BD 17 with its title, which introduces the whole Book of the Dead, as well as the topic of identification with the sun god and the invocation of different gods, logically contributes to making it the best Book of the Dead example.

As for BD 180, it is attested either on its own or sometimes coupled with other spells such as BD 181 (a complete list of the attestations of the Third Intermediate Period is found in Lenzo, 2015b: 242–43). BD 180 is well known since the New Kingdom, with eleven sources (Lapp, 2002; Lenzo, 2015a). It is a solar spell that includes the theme of the union of Re and Osiris, a very popular motif during the Third Intermediate Period that would explain this choice. The papyri that include only this chapter are of the same tradition as P.Cairo S.R. IV 953 from the late Twenty-first Dynasty (unpublished and containing different spells), which has many features in common with P.Paennestitauy/P.Gatseshen. The shorter papyri are probably from a later period, and they date possibly to the beginning of the Twenty-second Dynasty (P.Berlin P.3120, P.London BM EA 10203, P.London BM EA 10312 and P.Turin CGT 53010). With a total of 24 attestations on hieratic papyri during the Third Intermediate Period, it was clearly an important spell. Nevertheless, the spell was not retained in the Saite redaction.

Three papyri from the time of the High Priest Psusennes III (P.Cairo S.R. IV 525, P.Cairo S.R. IV 961, P.Cairo S.R. IV 967) contain the sequence 1 I–130–136A I–134 I–64–133–136A II–134 II–1 II–72–2–3–65–92–68–69–70–100–136B, with all or part of these spells. Thus, their use is attested at least during the end of the Twenty-first Dynasty. These spells are also found in the P.Paennestitauy/P.Gatseshen tradition. The different themes have been gathered in different sequences by Lucarelli (2006) and follow each other as such:

- BD 130–136A I–134 I–130 (rubric)–64 (short version)–133–136A II–134 II, with the theme of the journey of the deceased in the solar boat (Lucarelli, 2006: 72–75)
- BD 1–72–2–3–65–92–68–69–70, "going out by day" spells (Lucarelli, 2006: 75–80)
- BD 101–100–136B–136A III–98–99B (Lucarelli, 2006: 80–83): in the abbreviated version, only BD 100 and 136B (both linked with the journey in the solar boat) have been retained

The only difference to P.Paennestitauy/P.Gatseshen is the adjunction of BD 1 at the beginning, a practice that is later adopted by the Saite redaction. These spells are focused on the journey, the possibility of going out by day, and the solar boat.

In addition to those that are attested in more than one papyrus, other sequences derived from the P.Paennestitauy/P.Gatseshen tradition have been found on only one papyrus, such as P.Turin CGT 53007 with the sequence BD 33–37–38B–54–55–38A–56–13/121–138–123–187–12/120–58–57–132 (Lenzo Marchese, 2007: 69–90). Further papyri with uniquely attested sequences are P.Cairo S.R. VII 10267 verso, P.Ann Arbor 2725, P.Hamm 2236, and P.London BM EA 10031, most of which are unpublished.

## An innovative Book of the Dead from the time of the High Priest Pinedjem II

At least twelve papyri possess the same features and the sequence BD 190–148–135–1B–15BIII–180–190–133–134–136A–130–166$^{\text{Naville}}$–101–155–156–New spell+137A$^{\text{rubric}}$–100–137B–137A, either complete or abbreviated (Lenzo Marchese, 2007: 35–38). The most comprehensive one is that of P.London BM EA 10988 (unpublished). In addition, these papyri have many errors or variants in common. Three of them date to the pontificate of Pinedjem II (P.Cairo S.R. IV 954, P.Cairo S.R. IV 999/CG 40027, and P.New York MMA 25.3.32), and it is likely that most of them are from the same period. Thus, they were probably copied from the same model in the same workshop.

This selection of spells seems to stem from several groups which were originally different sequences:

- BD 190–148 to provide the provisions for the deceased
- BD 135 (deceased on the solar boat), 1B (formula for going out by day)
- BD 15BIII–180 the solar theme
- BD 190–133–134–136A–130 and 135 "glorifications" spells
- BD 101 and 100 (separated by other chapters) are about the journey in the solar boat
- BD 166$^{\text{Naville}}$, 155–156–New spell+137A$^{\text{rubric}}$, reminiscent of a New Kingdom sequence (Lapp, 1997: 41) are about various amulets, with the adjunction of a new spell, "Formula for the *udjat*-amulet in *bia*-metal," which seems to be known only from this group of papyri (translation in Quirke, 2013: 501; Lenzo, 2019)

Most of these spells are kept in the Saite redaction, while others such as BD 135, 1B, 15BIII, and 180 are no longer in use in the Late Period.

## A new kind of Book of the Dead Papyri during the Twenty-second Dynasty

As indicated earlier, abbreviated Book of the Dead papyri are attested at least until the beginning of the Twenty-second Dynasty. It seems that during the Twenty-second Dynasty, another kind of short papyri appeared, with a new kind of Book of the Dead. The difference between these and the previous papyri can be found in their unusual and often new spells, which are specific to this period.

These papyri often begin with some sentences extracted from BD 23 about the opening of the mouth and then continue with other spells. These sometimes have titles or extracts known from other chapters, but they differ from one papyrus to another. Among them, a group of papyri share these particularities and often contain similar writing (see Table 4.3). At least two papyri can be dated to the second part of the Twenty-second Dynasty (P.Cairo S.R. IV 650 and P.Turin CGT 53012; Lenzo Marchese,

2007: 164–64; Payraudeau, 2014: 159, 428–29), which allows us to place this tradition into this period.

The most prominent spell in this tradition is BD 23 about the opening of the mouth. As during the Twenty-first Dynasty, it was clearly an important element for the deceased. It is highlighted in P.Berlin P. 3010 by the presence of an extract of the Ritual of the Opening of the Mouth (Fig. 4.15). The title of BD 162 is also often used in this context, with a focus on providing a flame—or a variant with offerings—under the head of the deceased. Another frequent title is simply to let the *ba* go out by day, holding on to the general title of the Book of the Dead, so that he can join the stars. Finally, offering formulae are very frequent and hymns are sometimes attested. All these topics are very characteristic of a funerary papyrus; they indicate that a choice had been made on what was probably considered the most important theme for the afterlife. The papyri belong to the clergy of Amun in Karnak. The origins of the new spells or parts of spells are difficult to determine: are they a new creation or adaptations of ritual texts attested in the archives of the temple of Karnak and arranged in another way during this period? Probably both, as proven by the use of an older text such as the Ritual of the Opening of

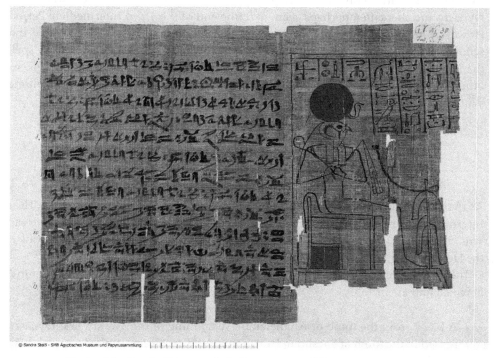

FIG. 4.15. Book of the Dead of Nespaasobek. Twenty-second Dynasty.
Credit line: P.Berlin P 3010 © Staatliche Museen zu Berlin, Ägyptisches Museum und Papyrussammlung / Sandra Steiß.

the Mouth as well as other spells unattested elsewhere (see for example a ritual text in P.London BM EA 10490, and other examples in Lenzo, 2021b). This tradition of short and hieratic Books of the Dead seems to be a special feature of the Libyan Period, and it is up for debate whether this choice and evolution are the results of a Libyan preference. The latest specimens date to the Third Intermediate Period, and the transition to the Saite redaction is not easy to determine. We can observe that the use of abbreviated papyri ceased at a certain time between the end of the Twenty-second and the Twenty-fifth Dynasty.

## Conclusions on the hieratic Books of the Dead

The collection of different traditions in hieratic papyri during the Third Intermediate Period shows that even if they are attested since the beginning of the Twenty-first Dynasty, they became more frequently used as of the pontificate of Pinedjem II. As stressed before, no hieroglyphic papyri are attested for the Twenty-second Dynasty, as they were replaced by the hieratic versions. Likewise, long hieratic papyri seem to be attested exclusively in the mid to late Twenty-first Dynasty, and, except for P.Greenfield, only abbreviated versions are attested during the late Twenty-first Dynasty and thereafter, perhaps even up to the end of the Third Intermediate Period. However, many hieratic papyri still await publication, and it is very probable that scholars will discover other sequences. Finally, we must mention a particular spell, the "chapitre supplémentaire," BD 166, which originates from this period and is another important innovation for the Third Intermediate Period (Wüthrich, this volume, Wüthrich, 2010: 100–102).

# THE BOOK OF THE DEAD IN THE TOMBS

As indicated in the introduction, decorated tomb walls are very rare during the Third Intermediate Period; illustrations in papyri as well as on coffins were preferred instead. This change of burial customs had an impact on the number of occurrences of Book of the Dead spells in tombs.

The database of the Book of the Dead Project lists five tombs (or blocks from tombs), of which four are in Tanis:

- A block from the tomb of Ankhefamun (beginning of the Twenty-first Dynasty) reused in the tomb of Sheshonq III in Tanis (NRT V; Montet, 1960: 86–93, pl. LIV–LXI; Lull, 2001)
- A block from the tomb of Khonsuheb in Tanis (Twenty-first Dynasty), found in the tomb of Sheshonq III (NRT V; Montet, 1960: 81–85, pl. XLVI–LIII)

- Tomb of King Osorkon II in Tanis, Twenty-second Dynasty (NRT I; Montet, 1947; Jansen-Winkeln, 1988; Roulin, 1998: 218–49)
- Tomb of King Sheshonq III in Tanis, Twenty-second Dynasty (NRT V; Montet, 1960; Roulin, 1998: 250–59)
- Tomb of Sheshonq in Memphis, High Priest of Ptah and son of King Osorkon II, Twenty-second Dynasty (now in Cairo JE 88131; Badawi, 1956). A new publication of the texts of the tomb as well as the objects found in it is in press (see Lenzo, Meffre, and Payraudeau, forthcoming and a preliminary presentation in Meffre, Payraudeau, and Lenzo, 2017)

Among the Book of the Dead spells, the most popular are the negative confession (BD 125B) and the scene of the weighing of the heart. The tomb of Osorkon II is the one with the highest number of Book of the Dead spells, together with extracts of other texts dealing with the Underworld such as the Amduat or the Book of the Earth (for details, see Roulin, 1998: 218–49). As noted by Jansen-Winkeln (1988) and Roulin (1998), parts of the Book of the Dead spells or "mythological" scenes are very similar to those in the tombs of Osorkon II in Tanis, Sheshonq in Memphis, and P.Greenfield from the end of the Twenty-first Dynasty in Thebes. They are so similar that they certainly come from the same archetype (compare BD 110 in Osorkon II's tomb and in P.Greenfield; Figs. 4.16–4.17). This observation is further proof for the interconnections between the elite in the north of the country and the Theban leading circles through the exchange of one or more models, probably on papyrus, first used in Thebes and then on the walls of the tombs about 100 years later during the Twenty-second Dynasty (see Lenzo, 2018).

The decoration of these tombs also contains vignettes of a new repertoire, such as the scene of Osiris's enthronement on a podium like the one seen on the blocks from the tombs of Ankhesenamun, Osorkon II in Tanis, and Sheshonq in Memphis. It also appears in the "mythological" papyri and on coffins (Lull, 2001). Moreover, this motif is engraved in the tombs of Osorkon II and Sheshonq in a version very similar to the one of P.Greenfield (sheet 88). Thus, the decoration in the tombs of the Twenty-first and Twenty-second Dynasties in Tanis and Memphis includes funerary texts on the walls that are similar to those on contemporary papyri in Thebes, such as Book of the Dead spells, excerpts from the Amduat, or "mythological" scenes. The only difference is the medium.

## Conclusion

The first impression that the Book of the Dead gives during the Third Intermediate Period is a variety of versions and a great number of innovations. The profusion of papyri in the Theban area replaced decoration in the tombs. Scribes and priests seem to

FIG. 4.16. BD 110 in Tomb of King Osorkon II in Tanis. Twenty-second Dynasty.
Credit line: Nécropole royale de Tanis (NRT I), Room 3, south wall © Montet 1947: pl. XXXVI.

provide up-to-date versions of the Book of the Dead of the so-called Theban redaction, while, at the same time, they create a new repertoire of both Book of the Dead spells and iconographic representations. With inventive compositions in terms of both text and iconography, "we can assume that they are part of a new iconographic repertoire developed by the priests complementary to the Book of the Dead," as Lull (2001: 186) stated with regard to the iconographic innovations. In this respect, the so-called mythological papyri can be interpreted as simply another funerary text in which the iconography is more important than the text.

The innovation also affects the coffins that are richly decorated with Book of the Dead vignettes or new creations similar to the vignettes of the "mythological" papyri (see for example Niwiński, 2006, 2009). One hundred and thirty-nine occurrences of Book of the Dead spells on coffins are registered in the database of the Book of the Dead Project for the Third Intermediate Period and demonstrate the importance for the coffins in that period.

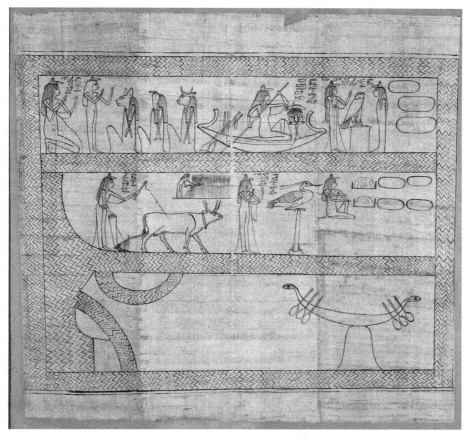

FIG. 4.17. BD 110 in the Book of the Dead of Nesitanebetisheru. Probably late Twenty-first Dynasty.

Credit line: P.London BM EA 10554, sheet 81, British Museum London © The Trustees of the British Museum.

Little by little, hieroglyphic papyri made way for hieratic versions. The evolution of the tradition of the Book of the Dead can be summarized in this list of various observations:

- Two funerary papyri were often taken for the afterlife starting in the beginning of the Twenty-first Dynasty, but it is not a rule, as many deceased persons have only one papyrus. Two papyri can be in use at least until the Twenty-second Dynasty.
- Hieroglyphic papyri are present during the entire Twenty-first Dynasty, but they are mostly drawn up in the Ramesside tradition, with only some innovations, during the beginning of the Twenty-first Dynasty; they also tend to be abbreviated as of the pontificate of Menkheperre, with a new repertoire following the *pars pro toto* principle.

- The Litany of Re seems to be more popular during the first half of the Twenty-first Dynasty and tends to disappear in the second half. It is no longer in use in the Twenty-second Dynasty.
- The so-called mythological papyri are attested from the time of Psusennes I up until the end of the Twenty-first Dynasty. They are probably to be interpreted as a new creation of a kind of "Book of the Dead," i.e., funerary papyri with previously known vignettes and then a new repertoire.
- The Amduat is attested since Menkheperre; it is regularly chosen during the second half of the Twenty-first Dynasty and occasionally during the Twenty-second Dynasty.
- Hieratic papyri are regularly used as of the reign of King Amenemope/High Priest Pinedjem II. Even if they initially follow the New Kingdom tradition in many aspects, they tend to insert new spells. Since Pinedjem II, abbreviated papyri with innovations and no vignettes became preferred; this seems to also be the favored choice during the Twenty-second Dynasty, when hieroglyphic papyri are no longer in use. They also seem to become shorter, except for the remarkable P.Greenfield.
- Hieroglyphic papyri often show polychrome vignettes, but in some cases, there are only few colors, while hieratic papyri have polychrome or bichrome illustrations. However, colors seem to completely disappear during the Twenty-second Dynasty.
- Sequences and the choice of spells differ greatly from papyrus to papyrus. However, a preference for BD 125 can be determined in hieroglyphic script as well as in tombs, while BD 23, 17, and 180 are the most frequently used spells in hieratic. The solar and Osirian union is a prominent theme, particularly in the opening vignette, with the representation of Re-Horakhty(-Atum) in an Osirian stance and the presence of BD 180. This occurs more frequently than in the New Kingdom, and disappears in the Late Period.
- Many priests and especially priestesses of lower rank in the temple of Amun owned a papyrus (Töpfer, this volume).

Table 4.1: Distribution of different funerary papyri type in the ensemble from Thebes

|  | Amduat | Litany of Re | Mythological | HG BD | HT BD |
|---|---|---|---|---|---|
| Amduat | 1 | - | 2 | 12 | 17 |
| Litany of Re | - | - | 1 | 5 | 1 |
| Mythological | 2 | 1 | 10 | 9 | 4 |
| HG BD | 12 | 5 | 9 | - | 1 |
| HT BD | 17 | 1 | 4 | 1 | 2* |
| Total | 32 | 7 | 26 | 27 | 25 |

HG = Hieroglyphs, HT = Hieratic, BD = Book of the Dead
* The second hieratic papyrus is a short one with the "supplementary chapter" 166 (Wüthrich, 2010: 100-103; Wüthrich in this book)

Table 4.2: The funerary papyri of the family of the High Priests of Amun in Karnak

Family of the High Priest Pinedjem I

| | Papyrus 1 | | Papyrus 2 | | | | |
|---|---|---|---|---|---|---|---|
| Inventory No | Writing - Content | Inventory No | Writing - Content | Owner | Datation | Provenance | Bibliography |
| P.London BM EA 10541 + P.Paris Louvre E 6258 | HG – BD | P.London BM EA 10490 | HT – BD + BC | Nedjmet, mother of Pinedjem I | Pinedjem I? | Royal Cachette | Niwiński, 1989: London 59, London 60, Paris 47. Jansen-Winkeln, 2007: no 57, 32-33. Lenzo, 2010. Taylor, 2010: 234-237. |
| P.Cairo S.R. VII 11488 = CG 40006 = P. Pinedjem I | HG – BD | | | Pinedjem I | Psusennes I/ Masaharta | Royal Cachette | Saleh, Sourouzian, 1986: no 235. Niwiński, 1989: Cairo 111 Lesko, 1994. Jansen-Winkeln, 2007: no 39, 23. |
| P.Cairo S.R. IV 955 = JE 95856 = CG 40005 = P.Boulaq 22 | HG – BD | P.Cairo S.R. IV 992 = JE 95887 = P. Boulaq 23 | HG – Litany of Re | Henuttauy, wife of Pinedjem I | Menkheperre | Royal Cachette | Mariette, 1876: pl.12-21. Niwiński, 1989: Cairo 36 and Cairo 47. |
| P.Cairo S.R.IV 980 = JE 26229 = CG 40007 | HG – BD | | | Maatkare, daughter of Pinedjem I | Early or middle 21st Dynasty | Royal Cachette | Naville, 1912. Niwiński, 1989: Cairo 43. |
| P.Cairo S.R. IV 526 = JE 51948 a–c | HG – BD/Myth. | P.Cairo S.R. IV 527 = JE 51949 a–c | HG –BD/Myth. | Henuttauy, daughter of Pinedjem I | Psusennes I | TT 60 | Winlock, 1926: 28. Niwiński, 1989: Cairo 2, Cairo 3. Jansen-Winkeln, 2007: no 20, 192. |
| P.New York MMA 30.3.31 | HG – BD | P.New York MMA 30.3.32 | HG – Litany of Re | Nauny, daughter of Pinedjem I (?) | Psusennes I ? Early 21st Dynasty ? | TT 358/MMA 65 | Winlock, 1942: fig. 78-79. Piankoff, 1964: 114-118, 170-172. Niwiński, 1989: New York 13, New York 14. Jansen-Winkeln, 2007: no 58, 34. |

(continued)

Table 4.2: Continued

Family of the High Priest Menkheperre

| Papyrus 1 | | | Papyrus 2 | | | | |
|---|---|---|---|---|---|---|---|
| Inventory No | Writing - Content | | Inventory No | Writing - Content | Owner | Datation | Provenance | Bibliography |
| P.New York MMA 25.3.29 | HT - BD | | P.New York MMA 25.3.28 | HG - Amduat | Henuttauy, daughter of Menkheperre | Pinedjem II | TT 60 | Winlock, 1942: 96-97, fig.88. Niwiński, 1989: New York 5, New York 6. Jansen-Winkeln, 2007: no 22, 194. |
| P.Cairo S.R. IV 936 = JE HT - BD 95838 = P.Gatseshen | | | P.Cairo S.R. VII 10265 | HG - Amduat | Gatseshen, daughter of Menkheperre | Amenemope / Pinedjem II | Bab el-Gusus | Daressy, 1907: A152. Naville, 1912. Sadek, 1985: C3, 95-98, pl. 7-9. Niwiński, 1989: Cairo 32 and Cairo 94. Lucarelli, 2006. Jansen-Winkeln, 2007: no 46, 108. |
| P.Cairo S.R. VII 10244 = JE 33997 = CG 40014 | HG - BD | | P.Cairo S.R. IV 952 | HG - Litany of Re | Tjaynefer, husband of Gatseshen, daughter of Menkheperre | Pinedjem II | Bab el-Gusus | Daressy, 1907: A151. Piankoff, 1964: 98-109, 158-164. Niwiński, 1989: Cairo 33 and Cairo 81, pl. 22a-b. Jansen-Winkeln, 2007: no 13, 187. |
| | | | P.Cairo S.R. IV 933 = JE 95836 | HG - Amduat | Merytimen, daughter of Menkheperre | Psusennes III | Bab el-Gusus | Daressy, 1907: A.71. Sadek, 1985: C16, 145-150, pl. 26-27. Niwiński, 1989: Cairo 31. Jansen-Winkeln, 2007: no 16, 189. |

## Family of the High Priest Menkheperre

| Papyrus 1 | | | Papyrus 2 | | | | |
|---|---|---|---|---|---|---|---|
| Inventory No | Writing - Content | Inventory No | Writing - Content | Owner | Datation | Provenance | Bibliography |
| P.Cairo S.R. VII 10652 | HG - BD | P.Cairo S.R. VII 10274 | HG - Amduat | Ankhefenmut, son of Menkheperre | Late 21st Dynasty | Bab el-Gusus | Daressy, 1907: A.140. Sadek, 1985: C20, 163-168, pl. 31-32. Niwiński, 1989: Cairo 103, Cairo 105. Jansen-Winkeln, 2007: no 14, 188. BD unpublished. |
| P.Cairo S.R. IV 967 = JE 95866 | HT - BD | P.Cairo S.R. IV 529+ S.R. IV 1004 = JE 95638 | HG - Amduat | Menkheperre, grandson of Menkheperre | Psusennes III | Bab el-Gusus | Daressy, 1907: A.147. Abdelhamid Youssef, 1982. Niwiński, 1989: Cairo 5, Cairo 41. Jansen-Winkeln, 2007: no 18, 190. BD unpublished. |
| P. Cairo S.R. VII 10254 = JE 31986 | HG - BD/ Myth. | P.Cairo S.R. VII 10256 | HG - Myth. | Heruben, granddaughter of Menkheperre | Siamon / Psusennes III | Bab el-Gusus | Daressy, 1907: A.133. Piankoff, 1949. Piankof, Rambova, 1957: no 1, 71-74, no 2, 75-76. Niwiński, 1989: Cairo 89, Cairo 91. Jansen-Winkeln, 2007: no 42, 150. |

*(continued)*

## Table 4.2: Continued

### Family of the High Priest Menkheperre

| | Papyrus 1 | | | Papyrus 2 | | | | |
|---|---|---|---|---|---|---|---|---|
| Inventory No | Writing - Content | | | Inventory No | Writing - Content | Owner | Datation | Provenance | Bibliography |

| Inventory No | Writing - Content | Inventory No | Writing - Content | Owner | Datation | Provenance | Bibliography |
|---|---|---|---|---|---|---|---|
| P.Cairo S.R. IV 1001 = JE 29636 = CG 40013 | HG – BD | (1) P.Cairo S.R. VII 10221 (2) P.Cairo CG 58002 | 1. HG – Amduat 2. HT – BD (BD 166) | Gatseshen, granddaughter of Menkheperre ? | Pinedjem II | Bab el-Gusus | Daressy, 1907: A.139. Golenischeff, 1927: 102-103, pl. 23. Sadek, 1985: C19, 159-162, pl. 30-31. Niwiński, 1989: Cairo 51, Cairo 58, Cairo G. Jansen-Winkeln, 2007: no 19, 191. Wüthrich, 2010: 100. HG BD unpublished. |
| P.Richmond Virginia Museum of Fine Arts 54.10 | HG – BD/ Myth. | P.London BM EA 10018 | HG - BD - Myth | Hennuttauy, granddaughter of Menkheperre | Late 21st Dynasty | Unknown | Niwiński, 1989: London 36, Richmond. Jansen-Winkeln, 2007: no 154, 259. |

# Family of the High Priest Pinedjem II

| Papyrus 1 | | | | Papyrus 2 | | Owner | Datation | Provenance | Bibliography |
|---|---|---|---|---|---|---|---|---|---|
| Inventory No | Writing - Content | Inventory No | Writing - Content | | | | | | |
| P.Cairo S.R. VII 11573 = S.R. VII 11485 = JE 26230 = P. Nesikhonsu | HT - BD | | | | | Nesikhonsu, wife of Pinedjem II, | Buried in year 5 of Siamon | Royal Cachette | Niwiński, 1989: Cairo 109, Cairo A. Jansen-Winkeln, 2007: no 25, 118-119. |
| P.London BM EA 10793 = P. Pinedjem II | HT - BD | P.Cairo S.R. VII 11492 | HG - Amduat | | | Pinedjem II | Buried in year 10 of Siamon | Royal Cachette | Sadek, 1985: C3, 227-228, pl. 48. Niwiński, 1989: Cairo 114, London 63 Munro 1996. Jansen-Winkeln, 2007: no 37-38, 142-143. |
| P.Cairo S.R. IV 525 = JE 26228bis | HT - BD | | | | | Asetemakhbit, wife of Pinedjem II | Buried after year 10 of Siamon, reign of Psusennes II | Royal Cachette | Niwiński, 1989: Cairo 1. |
| P.London BM EA 10554 = P. Greenfield | HT - BD + Myth. | | | | | Nesitanebetisheru, daughter of Pinedjem II and Nesikhonsu | Late 21st Dynasty | Royal Cachette | Budge, 1912. Niwiński, 1989: London 61. Taylor, 2010: 306-309. |
| P.Cairo S.R. 548 = JE 95650 | HT - BD | | | HG - Amduat | | Maatkare, daughter of Pinedjem II and Asetemakhbit | Psusennes III | Bab el-Gusus | Daressy, 1907: A.132. Sadek, 1985: C10, 125-129, pl. 18. Niwiński, 1989: Cairo 13 and Cairo 38, 266. Jansen-Winkeln, 2007: no 17, 189. BD unpublished. |
| P.Brockelhurst I (lost) | HT - BD | P.Cairo S.R. VII 10246 | HG - Amduat | | | Djedptahiuefankh, husband of Nesitanebetisheru | Sheshonq I / Iuput | Royal Cachette | Sadek, 1985: 106-110, pl. 12-13. Niwiński, 1989: Cairo 83, Location unknown 1. |
| P. Paris Louvre E. 31856 | HT - BD | | | | | Nesikhonsupakhered, daughter of Nesitanebeisheru | Osorkon I? | Unknown | Niwiński, 1989: Paris 51. Lenzo, 2002: 102. |

Abbreviations: HG = Hieroglyphs / HT = Hieratic / BD = Book of the Dead / Myth. = "Mythological" papyrus / BC = Book of Caverns

### Table 4.3: Abbreviated Book of the Dead Papyri during the 22$^{nd}$ Dynasty

| Papyrus | Reference |
| --- | --- |
| P.Berlin P 3010 | Lenzo, 2012: 99-104, pl. 1-2; fig. 15 |
| P.Berlin P 3011 + P.Geneva MAH D 190 | Lenzo, 2012: 105-112, pl. 3-4 |
| P.London BM EA 10328 | unpublished |
| P.Paris BN 59 | unpublished |
| P.Paris BN 128 | Yacoub, 2012 |
| P.Cairo S.R. IV 650 (=JE 95716) | unpublished |
| P.Cleveland 1914.733 | Berman, 1999: 377-378 |
| P.Genève Bodmer 103 | Valloggia, 1991 |
| P.Genève Bodmer 106 | Valloggia, 2012 |
| P.Heidelberg 1025 | unpublished |
| P.Paris Louvre N. 3244 | unpublished |
| P.New Haven CtYBR 2755 | unpublished |
| P.Oberlin AMAM 1952.15 | Wilson, 1961-1962 |
| P.Sydney R 402 | Coenen, 2006: 81-82, pl. 13b |
| P.Turin CGT 53011 | Lenzo Marchese, 2007a: 131-139 |
| P.Turin CGT 53012 | Lenzo Marchese, 2007a: 141-165 |
| P.Vatican 38606 | Gasse, 1993: 29-30, pl. XXII |

- Some new spells were added, of which the origins were possibly older and found in the archives of the temples, but there was probably also a redaction of new spells. Quirke (2013: 508–33) gathered many of them in translation.
- There is a link between the tombs and the innovations in papyri: the change of medium does not prevent the choosing of similar texts, also with innovations.

All these points can clearly be observed in the papyri written for the families of the High Priests of Amun (Table 4.2). They constitute a good example of how the different funerary papyri evolved: A clear preponderance of hieroglyphs is notable in Pinedjem I's family, which included the appearance of the Litany of Re and "mythological" papyri. There is also a mix of hieroglyphic and hieratic Books of the Dead in Menkheperre's family, along with a preference for Amduat-papyri. A preponderance of hieratic and Amduat-papyri can clearly be seen in the family of Pinedjem II.

In summary, the first significant changes seem to appear during the pontificates of Menkheperre and especially Pinedjem II. A second change probably takes place at the beginning of the Twenty-second Dynasty, where we see a clear preference for hieratic Books of the Dead, the Amduat, and very short and bichrome papyri. It is difficult to evaluate the impact of the Libyan rulers on the new creations or the use of the new Book of the Dead, but it is a possibility we should take into account. Some of these new features are kept in the Saite redaction: the use of hieratic, some sequences of spells, some variants in sentences, and some new spells (but not many spells; Gülden, this volume). The funerary tradition in the Third Intermediate Period has often been underestimated and should be studied more in detail, as many of these texts serve as a fundamental representation of the funerary conception of their time.

## Bibliography

Abdelhamid Youssef, A. (1982). "The Cairo Imduat Papyri (JE 96638 a, b, c)." *Bulletin de l'Institut Français d'Archéologie Orientale du Caire* 82: 1–17.
Allen, T. G. (1974). *The Book of the Dead or Going forth by Day. Studies in Ancient Oriental Civilization* 37 (Chicago: The University of Chicago Press).
Badawi, A. (1956). "Das Grab des Kronprinzen Scheschonk, Sohnes Osorkon's II. und Hohenpriesters von Memphis." *Annales du Service des Antiquités de l'Égypte* 54(1): 153–77, pl. IX–XI.
Berman, L. M. (1999). *The Cleveland Museum of Art, Catalogue of Egyptian Art* (New York: Hudson Hill Press).
Budge, E. A. W. (1912). *The Greenfield Papyrus in the British Museum* (London: British Museum).
Coenen, M. (2006). "A Preliminary Survey of the Books of the Dead on Papyrus and Linen in the Nicholson Museum." In *Egyptian Art in the Nicholson Museum*, edited by K. N. Sowada and B. G. Ockinga, 81–89 (Sydney: Meditarch).
Daressy, G. (1907). "Les cercueils des prêtres d'Amon (Deuxième trouvaille de Deir el-Bahari)." *Annales du Service des Antiquités de l'Égypte* 8: 3–38.
De Cenival, J.-L. (1987). "Hors catalogue ou, comment les objets ordinaires accumulés peu à peu dans un musée complètent le tableau qu'on déduirait des chefs-d'oeuvre exposés ici." In Ministère des Affaires Étrangères (ed.) *Tanis, L'or des pharaons*, 273–80 (Paris: Association Française d'Action Artistique).
Dodson, A. (2012). *Afterglow of Empire: Egypt from the Fall of the New Kingdom to the Saite Renaissance* (Cairo; New York: American University in Cairo Press).
Gasse, A. (1993). *Les papyrus hiératiques et hiéroglyphiques du Museo Gregoriano Egizio. Aegyptiaca Gregoriana* I (Città del Vaticano: Monumenti, Musei e Gallerie Pontificie).
Haring, B. (2012). "Stela Leiden V 65 and Herihor's Damnatio Memoriae." *Studien zur Altägyptischen Kultur* 41: 139–52.
Graefe, E. and Belova G. (eds.) (2010). *The Royal Cache TT 320: A Re-examination* (Cairo: Supreme Council of Antiquities).
Golénischeff, W. (1927). *Papyrus hiératiques, CG 58001–58036, Catalogue Général du Caire* (Cairo: Imprimerie de l'Institut français d'archéologie orientale).
Heerma van Voss, M. (1971). *Zwischen Grab und Paradies. 30 Faksimilereproduktionen nach dem Totenbuchpapyrus T 3 aus Leiden* (Basel: no publisher).
Heerma van Voss, M. (1974a). "Een mythologische papyrus in Den Haag." *Phoenix* 20: 331–34.
Heerma van Voss, M. (1974b). "Dodenboek 193." *Zeitschrift für ägyptische Sprache und Altertumskunde* 100: 103–4.
Jansen-Winkeln, K. (1988). "Weiteres zum Grab Osorkons II." *Göttinger Miszellen* 102: 31–39.
Jansen-Winkeln, K. (2007). *Inschriften der Spätzeit, Teil I: Die 21. Dynastie* (Wiesbaden: Harrassowitz).

Kaper, O. E. and Demarée, R. J. (2005). "A Donation Stela in the Name of Takeloth III from Amheida, Dakhleh Oasis." *Jaarbericht van het Vooraziatisch-Egyptisch Genootschap Ex Oriente Lux* 39: 19–37.

Kockelmann, H. (2003). "Das hieratische Totenbuch der Iset-em-Achbit im Institut für Papyrologie der Universität Heidelberg (pHeid. Hier. Inv. 2): Totenbuchspruch 136A nach Handschriften der Dritten Zwischenzeit." In *Basel Egyptology Prize 1, Junior Research in Egyptian History, Archaeology and Philology.* Aegyptiaca Helvetica 17, edited by S. Bickel and A. Loprieno, 291–325 (Basel: Schwabe).

Lapp, G. (1997). *The Papyrus of Nu (BM EA 10477).* Catalogue of Books of the Dead in the British Museum 1 (London: British Museum Press).

Lapp, G. (2002). *The Papyrus of Nebseni (BM EA 9900): the Texts of Chapter 180 with New Kingdom Parallels.* British Museum Occasional Paper 139 (London: British Museum).

Leahy, A. (1985). "The Libyan Period in Egypt: An Essay in Interpretation." *Libyan Studies* 16: 51–65.

Lenzo, G. (2002). "Quelques manuscrits hiératiques du Livre des Morts de la Troisième Période Intermédiaire du musée égyptien de Turin." *Bulletin de l'Institut Français d'Archéologie Orientale* 102: 267–83.

Lenzo Marchese, G. (2004). "La vignette initiale dans les papyrus funéraires de la Troisième Période Intermédiaire." *Bulletin de la Société d'Égyptologie, Genève* 26: 43–62.

Lenzo Marchese, G. (2007). *Manuscrits hiératiques du livre des morts de la troisième période intermédiaire (papyrus de Turin CGT 53001-53013).* Cahiers de la Société d'Égyptologie 8; Catalogo del Museo Egizio di Torino, serie seconda—collezioni 11 (Genève: Société d'égyptologie).

Lenzo, G. (2010). "The Two Funerary Papyri of Queen Nedjmet (P.BM EA 10490 and P.BM EA 10541 + Louvre E. 6258)." *British Museum Studies in Ancient Egypt and Sudan* 15: 63–83. http://www.britishmuseum.org/research/online_journals/bmsaes/issue_15/lenzo.aspx

Lenzo, G. (2012). "Deux papyrus hiératiques de la Troisième Période Intermédiaire à Berlin et à Genève." In *Forschung in der Papyrussammlung. Eine Festgabe für das Neue Museum. Ägyptische und Orientalische Papyri und Handschriften des Ägyptischen Museums und Papyrussammlung Berlin 1,* edited by V. M. Lepper, 97–117 (Berlin: Akademie Verlag).

Lenzo, G. (2015a). "Le chapitre 180 du *Livre des Morts* à la Troisième Période Intermédiaire d'après deux papyrus du British Museum (P.BM EA 10203 et P.BM EA 10312)." In *Weitergabe, Festschrift für U. Rössler-Köhler zum 65. Geburtstag.* Göttinger Orientforschungen IV/53, edited by L. D. Morenz and A. El Hawary, 233–53 (Wiesbaden: Harrassowitz).

Lenzo, G. (2015b). "L'écriture hiératique en épigraphie à l'époque napatéenne." In *Neue Forschungen und Methoden der Hieratistik, Ägyptologische "Binsen"-Weisheiten I-II, Akten zweier Tagungen in Mainz im April 2011 und März 2013.* Abhandlungen der Akademie der Wissenschaften und der Literatur Mainz, edited by U. Verhoeven, 273–98 (Stuttgart: Franz Steiner Verlag).

Lenzo, G. (2018). "Comparison of the Texts and Scenes in the Greenfield Papyrus and the Tombs of Osorkon II (Tanis) and Sheshonq (Memphis)." In *Ägyptologische "Binsen"-Weisheiten III. Abhandlungen der Geistes- und sozialwissenschaftlichen Klasse, Einzelveröffentlichungen (AM-GSE).* Abhandlungen der Akademie der Wissenschaften und der Literatur Mainz, edited by U. Verhoeven, 281-300 (Stuttgart: Franz Steiner Verlag).

Lenzo, G. (2019). "Une variante de la formule pour l'amulette-*oudjat* dans deux papyrus hiératiques de la XXI$^e$ dynastie." In *Sur les pistes du désert, Mélanges offerts à Michel Valloggia,* edited by S. Vuilleumier, P. Meyrat, 105-14 (Lausanne: Infolio).]

Lenzo, G. (2021a). "An Overview of the Funerary Papyri from the Cache of Bab el-Gasus." In *Bab El-Gasus in Context, Rediscovering the Tomb of the Priests of Amun*, edited by R. Sousa, A. Amenta, K. M. Cooney, 211-33 (Rome, Bristol: L'Erma di Bretschneider).

Lenzo, G. (2021b). "Les papyrus funéraires des 21$^{\text{ème}}$–22$^{\text{ème}}$ Dynasties et les liens avec les textes gravés sur les parois des tombes et des temples." In *Schrift und Material. Praktische Verwendung religiöser Text- und Bildträger als Artefakte im Alten Ägypten*. Orientalische Religionen in der Antike 41, edited by J. F. Quack and D. Luft, 207-34 (Tübingen: Mohr Siebeck).

Lenzo, G. (forthcoming). *The Greenfield Papyrus. Funerary Papyrus of a Priestess at the Karnak Temple (c. 950 BC)*. British Museum Publications on Egypt and Sudan 15 (Leuven: Peeters).

Lenzo, G., Meffre, R., and Payraudeau F. (forthcoming). *La tombe du Grand Prêtre de Ptah Chéchonq à Memphis et son matériel funéraire*. Mémoires publiés par les membres de l'Institut français d'archéologie orientale 149 (Cairo: Institut français d'archéologie orientale).

Lesko, L. H. (1994). "Some remarks on the Books of the Dead composed for the High Priests Pinedjem I and II." *For His Ka, Essays Offered in Memory of Klaus Baer*. Studies in Ancient Oriental Civilization 55, edited by D. P. Silverman, 179-86 (Chicago: The University of Chicago Press).

Lucarelli, R. (2006). *The Book of the Dead of Gatseshen, Ancient Egyptian Funerary Religion in the 10th Century BC*. Egyptologische Uitgaven 21 (Leiden: Nederlands Instituut voor het Nabije Oosten).

Lull, J. (2001). "A Scene from the Book of the Dead Belonging to a Private Twenty-First Dynasty Tomb in Tanis (Tomb of ʿnḫ.f-n-Jmnw)." *Journal of Egyptian Archaeology* 87: 180-86.

Mariette, A. (1876). *Les papyrus égyptiens du Musée de Boulaq*, vol. 3 (Paris: Franck).

Maspero, G. (1889). *Les momies royales de Deir el-Bahari*, Mémoires publiés par les membres de la Mission Archéologique Française au Caire 1(4): 511-787.

Meeks, D. (1993). "Deux papyrus funéraires de Marseille (Inv. 292 et 5323): à propos de quelques personnages thébains." In *Ancient Egypt and Kush: in memoriam Mikhail A. Korostovtsev*, edited by E. Y. Kormysheva, 290-305 (Moscow: Nauka).

Meffre, R., Payraudeau, F., and Lenzo, G. (2017). "Un nouveau projet de publication sur l'époque libyenne: la tombe du prince Chéchonq, grand prêtre de Ptah." *Bulletin de la Société française d'égyptologie* 197: 46-56.

Montet, P. (1947). *Les constructions et le tombeau d'Osorkon II à Tanis. La nécropole royale de Tanis I* (Paris).

Montet, P. (1960). *Les constructions et le tombeau de Chéchanq III à Tanis. La nécropole royale de Tanis III* (Paris).

Munro, I. (1996). *Der Totenbuch-Papyrus des Hohenpriesters Pa-nedjem II (pLondon BM 10793/pCampbell)*. Handschriften des Altägyptischen Totenbuches 3 (Wiesbaden: Harrassowitz).

Munro, I. (2001). *Das Totenbuch des Pa-en-nesti-taui (pLondon BM 10064) aus der Regierungszeit des Amenemope*. Handschriften des Altägyptischen Totenbuches 7 (Wiesbaden: Harrassowitz).

Nagel, G. (1929). "Un papyrus funéraire de la fin du Nouvel Empire (Louvre 3292)." *Bulletin de l'Institut Français d'Archéologie Orientale du Caire* 29: 1-125, pl. I-VIII.

Naville, E. (1912). *Papyrus funéraires de la XXIe dynastie, I. Le papyrus hiéroglyphique de Kamara, Le papyrus hiératique de Nesikhonsou au Musée du Caire* (Paris: Leroux).

Naville, E. (1914). *Papyrus funéraires de la XXIe dynastie, II. Le papyrus hiératique de Katseshni au Musée du Caire* (Paris: Leroux).

Niwiński, A. (1987–1988). "The Solar-Osirian Unity as Principle of the Theology of the State of Amun in Thebes in the 21st Dynasty." *Jaarbericht van het Vooraziatisch-Egyptisch Genootschap Ex Oriente Lux* 30: 89–106.

Niwiński, A. (1989). *Studies on the Illustrated Theban Funerary Papyri of the 11th and 10th Centuries B.C.*, Orbis Biblicus et Orientalis 86 (Freiburg; Göttingen: Universitätsverlag, Vandenhoeck & Ruprecht).

Niwiński, A. (2006). "The Book of the Dead on the Coffins of the 21st Dynasty." In *Totenbuch-Forschungen: gesammelte Beiträge des 2. Internationalen Totenbuch-Symposiums, Bonn, 25. bis 29. September 2005*. Studien zum Altägyptischen Totenbuch 11, edited by B. Backes, I. Munro, and S. Stöhr, 245–71 (Wiesbaden: Harrassowitz).

Niwiński, A. (2009). "The So-called Chapters BD 141–142 and 148 on the Coffins of the 21st Dynasty from Thebes with Some Remarks Concerning the Funerary Papyri of the Period." In *Ausgestattet mit den Schriften des Thot. Festschrift für Irmtraut Munro zu ihrem 65. Geburtstag*. Studien zum Altägyptischen Totenbuch 14, edited by B. Backes, M. Müller-Roth, and S. Stöhr, 133–62 (Wiesbaden: Harrassowitz)

O'Rourke, P. (2008). "A Funerary Papyrus of [X?] in the Brooklyn Museum." In *Servant of Mut: studies in honor of Richard A. Fazzini*. Probleme der Ägyptologie 28, edited by S. H. D'Auria, 179–84 (Leiden; Boston: Brill).

Payraudeau, F. (2014). *Administration, société et pouvoir à Thèbes sous la XXII$^e$ dynastie bubastite*, Bibliothèque d'étude 160 (Le Caire: Institut français d'archéologie orientale du Caire).

Piankoff, A. (1949). "Les deux papyrus 'mythologiques' der Her-Ouben au Musée du Caire." *Annales du Service des Antiquités de l'Égypte* 49: 129–44.

Piankoff, A. and Rambova, N. (1957). *Mythological Papyri*. Egyptian Religious Texts and Representations 3. Bollingen Series 40(3) (New York: Pantheon Books for the Bollingen Foundation).

Piankoff, A. (1964). *The Litany of Re*. Egyptian Religious Texts and Representations 4. Bollingen Series 40(4) (New York: Pantheon Books for the Bollingen Foundation).

Quirke, S. (2013). *Going out in daylight—prt m hrw: the Ancient Egyptian Book of the Dead; translation, sources, meaning*. GHP Egyptology 20 (London: Golden House Publications).

Ragazzoli, C. (2010). "The Book of the Dead of Ankhesenaset (P.BNF Egyptien 62–88). Traces of workshop production or scribal experiments?" *British Museum Studies in Ancient Egypt and Sudan* 15: 225–48. http://www.britishmuseum.org/research/online_journals/bmsaes/issue_15/ragazzoli.aspx

Raven, M. J. (1984). "Papyrus-sheaths and Ptah-Sokar-Osris Statues." In *Symbols of resurrection: three studies in ancient Egyptian iconography / Symbolen van opstanding: drie studies op het gebied van Oud-Egyptische iconografie*, 251–96 (Leiden: Rijksmuseum van Oudheden).

Refai, H. (2007). "Zu den Schlußszenen in mythologischen Papyri." *Bulletin de l'Institut Français d'Archéologie Orientale* 107: 157–69.

Rössler-Köhler, U. (1999). *Zur Tradierungsgeschichte des Totenbuches zwischen der 17. und 22. Dynastie (Tb 17)*. Studien zum Altägyptischen Totenbuch 3 (Wiesbaden: Harrassowitz).

Roulin, G. (1998). "Les tombes royales de Tanis: analyze du programme decoratif." In *Tanis, Travaux récents sur le Tell Sân el-Hagar, Mission française des fouilles de Tanis, 1897–1997*, edited by P. Brissaud and C. Zivie-Coche, 193–276 (Paris: Noêsis).

Sadek, A.-A. F. (1985). *Contribution à l'étude de l'Amdouat. Les variantes tardives du Livre de l'Amdouat dans les papyrus du Musée du Caire*. Orbis Biblicus et Orientalis 65 (Freiburg; Göttingen: Universitätsverlag, Vandenhoeck & Ruprecht).

Saleh, M. and Sourouzian, H. (1987). *The Egyptian Museum Cairo* (Mainz: Philipp von Zabern).
Taylor, J. H. (1998). "Nodjmet, Payankh and Herihor: The End of the New Kingdom Reconsidered." In *Proceedings of the Seventh International Congress of Egyptologists, Cambridge, 3–9 September 1995*. Orientalia Lovaniensia Analecta 82, edited by C. J. Eyre, 1143–55 (Leuven: Peeters).
Taylor, J. H. (2010). *Journey through the Afterlife: Ancient Egyptian Book of the Dead* (London: British Museum Press).
Thijs, A. (2013). "Nodjmet A, Daughter of Amenhotep, Wife of Piankh and Mother of Herihor." *Zeitschrift für ägyptische Sprache und Altertumskunde* 140: 54–69.
Valloggia, M. (1989). "Le papyrus Bodmer 107 ou les reflets tardifs d'une conception de l'éternité." *Revue d'Egyptologie* 40: 131–44.
Valloggia, M. (1991). "Le papyrus Bodmer 103: un abrégé du Livre des Morts de la Troisième Période Intermédiaire." *Cahiers de Recherches de l'Institut de Papyrologie et d'Égyptologie de Lille* 13: 129–36.
Valloggia, M. (1998). "Le papyrus Bodmer 108: Un 'passeport d'éternité' du début de la Troisième Période Intermédiaire." In W. Clarysse, A. Schoors, and H. Willems (eds.), *Egyptian Religion, The Last Thousand Years: Studies Dedicated to the Memory of Jan Quaegebeur*. Orientalia Lovaniensia Analecta 84, 441–53 (Leuven: Peeters).
Valloggia, M. (2012). "Le papyrus Bodmer 106: contribution à l'histoire d'une concession funéraire de la Troisième Période Intermédiaire située dans l'enceinte du Ramesseum." In *"Parcourir l'éternité": hommages à Jean Yoyotte*. Histoire et prosopographie 8. Bibliothèque de l'École des hautes études, sciences religieuses 156, edited by C. Zivie-Coche and I. Guermeur, 1045–57 (Turnhout: Brepols).
Weber, F. (2012). *Der Totenbuchpapyrus des Anch-ef-en-Amun aus Dresden (Aeg. 775)*. Master thesis, University Bonn.
Wilson, J. A. (1961–1962). "A Late Egyptian Book of the Dead." *Allen Memorial Art Museum Bulletin* 19(2): 90–96.
Winlock, H. E. (1942). *Excavations at Deir el Bahri 1911–1931* (New York: Macmillan).
Wüthrich, A. (2010). *Eléments de théologie thébaine: les chapitres supplémentaires du Livre des Morts*. Studien zum Altägyptischen Totenbuch 16 (Wiesbaden: Harrassowitz).
Yacoub, M. (2012). "Papyrus Bibliothèque Nationale 128 in Paris: Übersetzung und Kommentar." In *Herausgehen am Tage: gesammelte Schriften zum altägyptischen Totenbuch*. Studien zum Altägyptischen Totenbuch 19, edited by R. Lucarelli, M. Müller-Roth, and A. Wüthrich, 229–37 (Wiesbaden: Harrassowitz).
Yoyotte, J. (1977). "Contribution à l'histoire du chapitre 162 du Livre des Morts." *Revue d'Egyptologie* 29: 194–202.
Zaluskowski, C. (1996). *Texte ausserhalb der Totenbuch-Tradierung in PaP.Greenfield*. Master thesis, University of Bonn.
Internet website (2012): *Totenbuch Projekt* database in Bonn: http://totenbuch.awk.nrw.de//

# CHAPTER 5

# THE BOOK OF THE DEAD PAPYRI IN THE TWENTY-SIXTH DYNASTY

SVENJA A. GÜLDEN

COMPARED with the Book of the Dead papyri of other periods, the number of surviving copies dating from the Twenty-sixth Dynasty is relatively low. However, over the last few years, more manuscripts of the Book of the Dead that can be securely dated into the Twenty-sixth Dynasty have been identified (Quirke, 1993: 21; Verhoeven, 2001: 16–19; Munro, 2010: 210).

The online database of the Totenbucharchiv [http://totenbuch.awk.nrw.de] has nearly 40 entries of those copies, and another 15–20 possibly dating into the Twenty-sixth Dynasty. Unfortunately, only a few of these papyri are (more or less) completely preserved; most of them are very fragmentary. Sometimes fragments of a single Book of the Dead papyrus are scattered among museums all over the world or housed in private collections, and it is only in some cases that these fragments can be identified and virtually joined (Verhoeven, 1998; Munro, 2006). The manuscripts listed in Table 5.1, which describe the Twenty-sixth Dynasty Book of the Dead papyri, may illustrate this.

Table 5.1: An overview of the Twenty-sixth Dynasty Book of the Dead papyri discussed in this chapter.

| | |
|---|---|
| **BD of Ankhwahibre [www.trismegistos.org/text/57267]** | |
| Collection and Inventory number | P.London BM EA 10558 |
| Publication | to be published by the author of this chapter |
| This papyrus is one of the few examples that are almost entirely preserved. | |
| **BD of Arptahhep, Maanwahibre [www.trismegistos.org/text/56602]** | |
| Collection and Inventory number | P.Paris Louvre N.3091 |
| Publications (parts of the papyrus) | Mosher, 1992: Fig. 5, Verhoeven, 2001: pl. 3 |
| This Book of the Dead papyrus was written for Arptahhep. But his name was erased later—at least in the first columns of the text. In the following columns his name was crossed out and the name of Maanwahibre was inserted. | |
| **BD of Djedkhi [www.trismegistos.org/text/57724]** | |
| Collections and Inventory numbers | P.Budapest, National Library, Cod. Afr. 2a-b |
| | Heidelberg, Völkerkundemuseum der J. & E. von Portheim-Stiftung, B |
| | Kairo, Ägyptisches Museum, JE 95685 (S.R. IV 615); JE 95690 (S.R. IV 619); JE 95745 (S.R. IV 692); JE 95840 (S.R. IV 938); JE 95841 (S.R. IV 939); S.R. IV 996 |
| | Uppsala, University Museum Gustavianum, VBM 160 |
| Publication | Munro, 2011 |
| This papyrus is one of the very fragmentary preserved papyri (1150 fragments) that was inventoried together with the fragments of the BD of his wife Tasheretenaset (1500 fragments). | |
| **BD of Iahtesnakht [www.trismegistos.org/text/57143]** | |
| Collection and Inventory number | P.Cologne Aeg. 10207 University of Cologne, Institut für Afrikanistik und Ägyptologie |
| Publication | Verhoeven, 1993 |
| The BD of Iahtesnakht is the longest preserved Book of the Dead papyrus of the Twenty-sixth Dynasty (compare Table 5.2), it was produced in advance and individualized afterward in a second step (see "Stock Production or Individual Copy?" in this chapter). | |
| **BD of Khamhor C [www.trismegistos.org/text/57072]** | |
| Collections and Inventory numbers | P.Ann Arbor, Kelsey Museum of Archaeology, 81.4.25 |
| | Florence, Museo Egizio, 11912a-b |
| | New York, Metropolitan Museum of Art, 25.3.212A-G |
| | Providence, John Hay Library, A 18077 |
| | Toronto, Royal Ontario Museum, 910.85.222 |
| | Unknown, private collection of H. Carter (lost) |
| Publication | Verhoeven, 2017 |
| The owner of this Book of the Dead papyrus is well known from other sources. The design and layout of the text are similar to that of the BD of Nespasefy. | |

*(continued)*

## Table 5.1: Continued

| | |
|---|---|
| **BD of Nesikhonsu [www.trismegistos.org/text/112169]** | |
| Collection and Inventory number | P.London, Petrie Museum, University College UC71075 |
| Publication | Gülden, 2010 |
| There are only a few fragments preserved of this Book of the Dead, but the design of the vignettes is similar to that of the BD of Iahtesnakht. | |
| **BD of Nespasefy [www.trismegistos.org/text/57694]** | |
| Collections and Inventory numbers | Albany, Albany Institute of History and Art, 1900.3.1 Cairo, Egyptian Museum, JE 95714 (S.R. IV 647); JE 95649 (S.R. IV 547) Marseille-Vieille Charité, Musée d'Archéologie Mediterranéenne, Collection Egyptienne, Marseille-Vieille Charité, 91/2/1 (former: private collection Brunner) and 291 |
| Publication | Brunner-Traut and Brunner, 1981: 239, pl. 126–127 (part of scroll D), Verhoeven, 1999 |
| The BD of Nespasefy is unique. It consists of individual papyrus scrolls. Scrolls A, B, and D are preserved, whereas scroll C is lost (Verhoeven, 1999: 2 and 10). | |
| **BD of 'Men' [www.trismegistos.org/text/57489]** | |
| Collection and Inventory number | Lille, Université Charles de Gaulle, 139 ("P. Vandier") |
| Publication (col. 1) | Posener, 1985: pl. 9 |
| This Book of the Dead manuscript was written on the verso of the so-called papyrus Vandier and differs significantly in manuscript design and layout from the other Book of the Dead papyri discussed here. | |
| **BD of Pasherientaihet [www.trismegistos.org/text/56970]** | |
| Collection and Inventory number | P.Vatican 48832, Museo Gregoriano Egizio |
| Publication | Gasse, 2001 |
| This Book of the Dead papyrus is incomplete. Nevertheless, it can be stated that it was compiled in two steps: the width of the papyrus sheets used for the first part of the scroll (col. 1–50) is about 24 to 25 cm, whereas the width of sheets beginning with column 51 is about 30 cm. | |
| **BD of Tasheretenaset [www.trismegistos.org/text/57043]** | |
| Collections and Inventory numbers | P.Assisi, Biblioteca Comunale 351 Budapest, National Library, Cod. Afr. 2a-b P.Heidelberg, Sammlung des Ägyptologischen Instituts der Universität, P. Hier. 566 P. Heidelberg, Völkerkundemuseum der J. & E. von Portheim-Stiftung, insert: A P.Jerusalem, Bible Lands Museum, H 376 P.Kairo, Ägyptisches Museum, inv. no. JE 95685 (S.R. IV 615); JE 95745 (S.R. IV 692); JE 95840 (S.R. IV 938); JE 95841 (S.R. IV 939); JE 95864 (S.R. IV 964) P. New York, Institute of Fine Arts, New York University, without number |
| Publication | Munro, 2011 |

## Table 5.1: Continued

| | |
|---|---|
| This papyrus is very fragmentary (1500 fragments) and was inventoried together with the fragments of the BD of Djedkhi (1150 fragments). | |
| **BD of Pefiuiu [www.trismegistos.org/text/57041]** | |
| Collections and Inventory numbers | P.Berlin P.3161, Staatliche Museen zu Berlin–Preußischer Kulturbesitz Ägyptisches Museum und Papyrussammlung<br>P.Kopenhagen Aae 5, Nationalmuseet<br>P.Sydney R346a, Nicholson Museum<br>P.Tübingen 2000, Ägyptische Sammlung der Universität |
| Publications | P.Berlin P. 3161: Gülden, 2007; Verhoeven, 1991; Verhoeven, 2001: pl. 1<br>P.Kopenhagen Aae 5: Munro, 1989; Verhoeven, 1991<br>P.Sydney R346a: Coenen, 2006: 82, pl. 14a<br>P.Tübingen 2000: Brunner-Traut and Brunner, 1981: 294, pl. 107; Buroh, 1985; Verhoeven, 1991 |
| Only a few fragments of this Book of the Dead papyrus are known. The most unusual fragment is now in Copenhagen. It is glued onto a piece of wood and placed in a wooden box—obviously to simulate a papyrus scroll. | |

## FORMATS

The bad state of conservation of the majority of Twenty-sixth Dynasty Book of the Dead papyri provides only for a few papyri reliable data concerning layout and format (See Table 5.2).

The longest preserved manuscript is that of Iahtesnakht, measuring 23.57 meters. In regard to its length, it is comparable to the New Kingdom papyrus of Ani (P.London BM EA 10470) (Verhoeven, 1993: 14). The formats of the other manuscripts show that the Book of the Dead papyri of the Twenty-sixth Dynasty had at least a minimum length of 15 meters, but most were around 20–23 meters long, a length that is, of course, due to the number of Book of the Dead spells they contain. The height of the papyri had no uniform format: three main formats were used—smaller ones with 26–27 cm, medium-sized formats of 36 cm, as well as higher formats up to 42 cm.

## MANUSCRIPT DESIGN AND LAYOUT

Besides a more or less fixed sequence of the Book of the Dead spells 1 to 165, the papyri of the Twenty-sixth Dynasty show a fairly homogeneous manuscript design. (For the numbering system, see the "Excursus" section later in the chapter, which discusses the numbering of spells of the Book of the Dead.) In his study on Theban and Memphite Book of the Dead traditions of the Late period, Malcolm Mosher compared the layout of manuscripts dating from the Twenty-fifth Dynasty to the Ptolemaic Period. The majority of the papyri of the Twenty-sixth Dynasty show a specific layout he defined as

Table 5.2: Overview of formats of the Twenty-sixth Dynasty Book of the Dead papyri discussed in this chapter.

| BD Manuscript | Length | Height |
| --- | --- | --- |
| BD of Ankhwahibre | 17 m | 26–27 cm |
| BD of Arptahhep, Maanwahibre | 20.07 m | 42 cm |
| BD of Djedkhi | 14 m (minimum, fragmentary) | 25–26 cm |
| BD of Iahtesnakht | 23.57 m | 25–26 cm |
| BD of Khamhor C | 3.58 m (preserved, fragments) | 34–35 cm |
| BD of Nesikhonsu | 0.42 m (preserved, only a few fragments) | 27 cm |
| BD of Nespasefy, consisting of 4 scrolls: | 15.88 m (preserved) \| 22.48 m (assumed) | 35–36 cm |
| Scroll A | 5.48 m | |
| Scroll B (incomplete) | 4.80 m | |
| Scroll C (lost) | – | |
| Scroll D (incomplete) | 5.60 m | |
| BD of Men | 3.40 m (preserved) | 21 cm |
| BD of Pasherientaihet | 16 m (preserved) \| 22 m (assumed) | 33.5 cm |
| BD of Tasheretenaset | 17.50 m (minimum, fragmentary) | 24–25 cm |
| BD of Pefiuiu | 1.72 m (preserved, only a few fragments) | 34 cm |

"style 2" (Mosher, 1992: 149–52). It consists of three sections that each had a distinct function. From top to bottom, these are title bar, vignette band, and text field.

Nevertheless, a few papyri do have a different layout, such as, for example, the unpublished Book of the Dead papyrus of Ankhefenkhonsu (http://totenbuch.awk.nrw.de/objekt/tm57443), which consists of several scrolls varying in size and layout. Another particular example is the unpublished Book of the Dead of "Men." It was written in columns and shows no vignettes, but may have been used as a master copy (see "Provenance and Owners," later in this chapter).

## Text fields and text distribution

The lower section occupies the largest part of a manuscript by far and contains the text. These text fields are separated not only from the other sections, but also from each other by dividing lines, designed as single or double lines.

If all three elements (title bar, vignette band, and text field) are present, the height of the text fields hardly varies within the papyrus, whereas the full height—except for the title bar—is used for the text field when the vignette band at the top is missing (Fig. 5.1).

# THE BOOK OF THE DEAD PAPYRI IN THE TWENTY-SIXTH DYNASTY 121

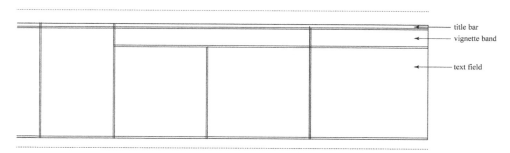

**FIG. 5.1**
The figure shows a schematic drawing of the basic layout (example: The Book of the Dead of Iahtesnakht, Col. 148-152).

Credit Line: Drawing by Svenja A. Gülden.

The width of the text fields in the Book of the Dead of Iahtesnakht (P.Colon. Aeg. 10207), for example, varies slightly in many cases from between 23 centimeters to 25 centimeters (Verhoeven, 1993: 18). The text written in these columns can represent one long spell that covers several columns (example: BD 17/columns 7 to 12), but it can also include several short spells (e.g., BD 100 to 109 [in numerical order]/columns 45 to 47) written as a continuous text, or BD 1 to 15 (in numerical order), where the content correlation is particularly evident (Fig. 5.2). In this case, the vignette positioned above the text clearly marks the correlation of the spells. The titles of the individual spells are marked by the use of red ink.

Elsewhere in this papyrus, the width of the text fields is adapted to the length of the text, such as with BD 145. Here, the structure of the text is reflected in the layout as well. An individual text column with a vignette field above it is provided for each of the guardians of the gates described in the text (Fig. 5.3).

The same kind of layout can be found in other Book of the Dead papyri of that time, for example, the Book of the Dead papyrus of Pasherientaihet. Along with the layout of spell BD 145 (Gasse, 2001: pl. XXV-XXVII), which is designed in the same way as in the Book of the Dead of Iahtesnakht, the spells BD 100–101–102–103–104–106–105–90–107–108–109 (compare Fig. 5.3) are listed in individual columns, each with a vignette field above it. This is a slightly different sequence of spells compared to the Book of the Dead of Iahtesnakht, and apart from this BD 103 and 104 are written in one column (col. 52) (Gasse, 2001: 206–212 and pl. XV–XVI). If the column for the spell is too spacious, if the scribe's script is too small, or if the scribe has shortened the text, then the remaining lower part of the column remains empty. Empty spaces (*spatia*) in Egyptian texts have been studied by Ursula Rössler-Köhler (1985). She defines two types of *spatia*: type A, *spatia* without a text omitted or missing; and type B, *spatia* with a text omitted or missing. Both types have further subtypes. The case above described is a *spatium* caused not by omitted text but by the chosen layout: type A 2 II a (Rössler-Köhler, 1985: 393 and 395).

Figure 5.4 (BD of Iahtesnakht) shows more variations of the previously described basic layout. The names of gods and of Osiris in BD 141/142 are written as lists. The

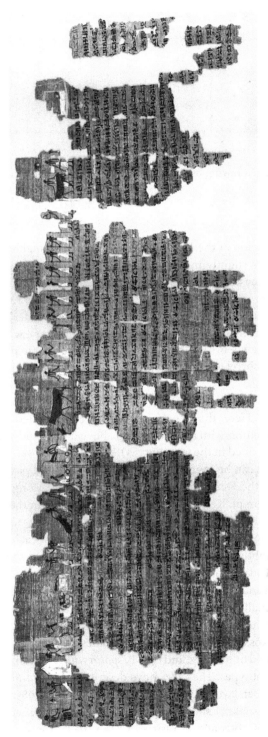

### FIG. 5.2
The Book of the Dead of Iahtesnakht often has text columns of an almost uniform width. Here, the spells BD 1 to 15 (in numerical order, from right to left), with the titles written in red ink.

Credit line: P.Cologne. Aeg. 10207, col. 1-3, https://papyri.uni-koeln.de/stueck/DS_dre28927/img/10207/orig/10207-1.jpg. CC BY 4.0, Institut für Altertumskunde der Universität zu Köln.

**FIG. 5.3**
Book of the Dead of Iahtesnakht spell BD 145. The layout is designed corresponding to the text.

Credit line: P.Cologne. Aeg. 10207, col. 72–84. https://papyri.uni-koeln.de/stueck/DS_die28972/img/10207/orig/10207-25.jpg, CC BY 4.0, Institut für Altertumskunde der Universität zu Köln.

**FIG. 5.4**
Book of the Dead of Iahtesnakht, from right to left: spells BD 141/142 (col. 68) - vignette (col. 69) - 144 (col. 70-71). The deceased is depicted in the gesture of adoration, facing the list with the god's names (BD 141/142).

Credit line: P.Cologne. Aeg. 10207, col. 68-71, https://papyri.uni-koeln.de/stueck/DS_dre28972/img/10207/orig/10207-24.jpg, CC BY 4.0, Institut für Altertumskunde der Universität zu Köln.

*spatia* caused thereby are defined as type A 2 II b: *spatia* in a list (in this case at the end of each line) and without any omitted text (Rössler-Köhler, 1985: 393 and 395). The accompanying vignette—the deceased in the gesture of adoration—is not drawn above the text, but rather in a large vignette following the text and facing the gods' names. Similar to the text layout in this Book of the Dead are the ones in the Book of the Dead papyrus of Pasherientaihet (Gasse, 2001: pl. XXIV), in the Book of the Dead of Tasheretenaset (Munro, 2011: Photo-Tafel 23–24 A), as well as in the Book of the Dead of Ankhwahibre, columns 19 and 18; however, the large vignette to this spell is missing in all of the mentioned examples.

In the Book of the Dead of Iahtesnakht, the text that follows spell BD 141/142 and the accompanying vignette is BD 144. It is also written in a modified layout (see Fig. 5.4). Although the title that is noted above column 70 belongs to the following spell and is thereby in the wrong position, the layout below the title bar is organized in a very different way. A double horizontal line divides the text field into two parts of nearly the same size.

The upper one, in turn, is divided into two areas: on the top are the vignettes with the guardians of the seven gates, whereas the fields below show the associated text. Furthermore, the text and vignettes are structured by double lines, while the subsequent text of BD 144 is written in the text field at the bottom and continues on the next column, which again is set up in a full-height layout. Again, the arrangement of the text and vignette is very similar to that of the papyrus of Pasherientaihet (Gasse, 2001: pl. XXV). In the papyrus of Tasheretenaset (Munro, 2011: Photo-Tafel 25–26), the design is similar, but with the difference that the first part of the spell (vignettes with accompanying text in two registers) covers the full height of the column—except for the title line.

## Vignette band

The vignette band, positioned above the text fields, is used for illustrations that refer to the text and sometimes shows additional aspects of the content. It runs intermittently over the entire length of the papyrus and is defined by a single or double line on the bottom and the top. In some cases, the vignette band is divided by the vertical column separator, particularly when the vignettes are very clearly associated to the text. Occasionally the vertical column separator does not run through the vignette band and, in this case, the opposite effect is achieved, namely placing the emphasis on a close substantive relationship of two (or more) spells (see Figs. 5.2 and 5.7).

In a few cases the vignette band is shortened to a vignette "field," which is then located in the upper-right corner of the text column. Examples are the Book of the Dead of Iahtesnakht (columns 27, 30, and 32; Verhoeven, 1993: 18), the Book of the Dead of Tasheretenaset (Munro, 2011: Photo-Tafel 22 [BD 140]), as well as papyrus P.London BM EA 10558, in BD 41 (see the left-most column of Fig. 5.7).

The text and the corresponding vignettes should be positioned very close to each other, but this is not always the case. As in the anterior periods, vignettes from the

Twenty-sixth Dynasty sometimes feature vignettes that are placed above the "wrong" text, and therefore the direct correlation is lost.

Apart from the previously described arrangement of vignettes in the band above the text, vignettes in a large/full-size format can also be found. An example is the vignette to BD 141/142 (Fig. 5.4), described earlier, but the best-known among these is probably the judgment scene, the vignette to BD 125.

Other vignettes with full-size scenes that cover the entire column are the vignettes to spells BD 15, 110, 142, 148, 149, 151, 152, and 161. In most of these cases the title bar is unaffected, as for example in the papyrus of the Book of the Dead of Ankhwahibre (vignette to BD 110).

## Title bar

The title bar is the third element of the basic layout described. It extends along the entire length of the papyrus. The boundary lines are single or double lines on the top and at the bottom. The vertical column separator can be drawn not only through the vignette band but also through the title line. It then structures the papyrus from the text fields to the vignette band up to the title bar. This can mainly be explained by the content, as shown in the example from the Book of the Dead of Ankhwahibre (Fig. 5.7).

Usually, the title bar contains the title of a spell, while the subsequent text is continued in the text field below the vignette band. If more than one Book of the Dead spell is placed in a text field, only the title of the first spell is written in the title bar, the others are highlighted by the use of red ink in the continuous text (see Fig. 5.7, column 3–4 from right to left). As in the case of the vignettes, titles occasionally can be placed above the "wrong" spell (Verhoeven, 1993: 273, note 4), as shown in the earlier example from the Book of the Dead of Iahtesnakht (Fig. 5.4).

## Lines, auxiliary lines/points

The aforementioned horizontal and vertical lines that structure the layout are drawn in black ink and can be either a single or a double line. Examples of a particularly precise realization are the papyri of Pasherientaihet (Gasse, 2001) and Ankhwahibre. An unusual example of a red dividing line can be observed in the Book of the Dead of Iahtesnakht shown in Figure 5.4; it separates the vignettes of BD 1 (right) and BD 15 (left).

In some manuscripts of this period, guiding lines can be identified that assisted the scribe in writing straight lines. This is particularly clear, for example, in the Book of the Dead of Ankhwahibre, at the end of BD 109. These also provide a clue about the production processes. The guiding lines extend in the following column into the vignette field (V110), apparently without taking into account that the subsequent column is not a text column. To draw accurate guiding lines, the scribes used small auxiliary points (Fig. 5.9).

Auxiliary lines are used not only horizontally but also vertically. On the left and the right of the column lines, they can be found in many manuscripts (though significantly lighter), to ensure a uniform spacing from text to lines.

## Script

The vast majority of the Book of the Dead papyri of the Twenty-sixth Dynasty were written in hieratic script (see chapter of Verhoeven in this volume). This also supports the homogeneous impression one gets from the style of the papyri. The text is executed in black ink. Titles, glosses, and other special terms are rubricated. Special terms within the rubricated parts, however, are written in black. In many manuscripts, more than just one scribe can be distinguished; for example, two scribes wrote the text of the Book of the Dead of Nespasefy. Scribe A wrote scrolls A and B, and scribe B wrote scroll D. In the Book of the Dead of Iahtesnakht, three scribes can be identified, plus another one who added the name of Iahtesnakht (Verhoeven, 2001: 72). A similar case is the Book of the Dead of Tasheretenaset, in which one scribe wrote the BD spells, while another one added the owner's name in the blank spaces (Munro, 2011: 5).

While the main text was written in hieratic script, the captions to the vignettes are very often, but not always, in cursive hieroglyphs (also called "linear hieroglyphic script"; see Parkinson, 2002: 73), as in the vignette to BD 110 in the Book of the Dead of Tasheretenaset (Munro, 2011: Photo-Tafel 20–20A), or the judgment scene in Book of the Dead of Ankhwahibre (Fig. 5.5).

Captions to the vignettes are lacking in the Book of the Dead of Iahtesnakht, with only four exceptions. The name of Iahtesnakht was placed (in hieratic script) above the images of female figures/goddesses (Fig. 5.11), although this was correct in only one case: her depiction in the judgment scene (Fig. 5.13).

There is very little evidence of Book of the Dead papyri dating from the Twenty-sixth Dynasty, in which the main text was written in hieroglyphs. The online database of the Totenbucharchiv shows eight documents, of which only two are relevant. The others can be disregarded because they cannot surely be dated accurately into the Twenty-sixth Dynasty, because they have only hieroglyphic captions for the vignette (like other Book of the Dead papyri where the main text is also written in hieratic), or because they likely belong to the so-called amulet papyri. Although spells BD 100 and 129, including the corresponding vignettes, can be found on two of the papyri, they do not belong to the subject discussed here.

The two relevant papyri are P.Florence 5404 [www.trismegistos.org/text/57431], which is only fragmentarily preserved (Botti, 1947), and P.Paris Louvre N. 3094 [www.trismegistos.org/text/56604]; both correspond significantly to the sequence that is used in the Twenty-sixth Dynasty and are written in cursive hieroglyphs/linear hieroglyphic script.

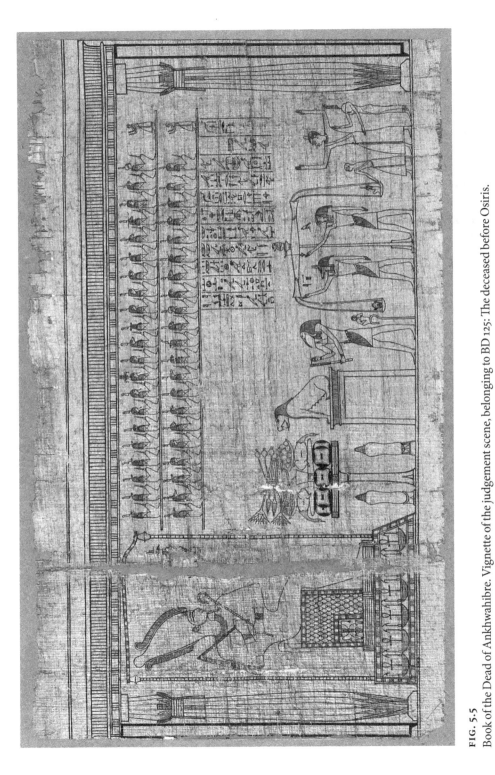

**FIG. 5.5**

Book of the Dead of Ankhwahibre. Vignette of the judgement scene, belonging to BD 125: The deceased before Osiris.

Credit line: P.London BM EA 10558, sheet 18 © Trustees of the British Museum, London.

## Vignettes

Almost all of the Book of the Dead papyri of this time have vignettes, or at least designated fields for the representations. The vignettes can be designed in a polychrome style and may include black outline drawings with occasional "dashes of color," mostly in red.

The color palette in the polychrome vignettes ranges from yellow shades to orange, red, and brown, and from gray, blue, and dark green to black and white (Verhoeven, 1993: 44; Munro, 2011: 48). The preliminary drawing of the polychrome vignettes was mostly done with red contour lines and then the color was applied. This can clearly be seen, for example, in the Book of the Dead of Nesikhonsu in a scene from the vignette belonging to BD 17.

Very similar to the style of vignettes in the Book of the Dead papyrus of Nesikhonsu (polychrome vignettes with red contour lines and a very similar color scheme) is that of the papyrus of Iahtesnakht (Gülden, 2010: 83). Unfortunately, only a few fragments of the papyrus of Nesikhonsu remain, so it cannot be determined whether the stylistic similarities between these two manuscripts were applied elsewhere in the papyrus of Nesikhonsu. Along with the red contour lines and the color design, contour lines in black were occasionally added to some scenes in the papyrus of Iahtesnakht (see Fig. 5.13). Another example of this procedure is attested in the papyrus of Tasheretenaset (Munro, 2011: 49).

The latter has a very close relationship (besides the sequence; see Wegner, this volume) to the papyrus of Ankhwahibre because of the motifs of the vignettes, and it is very likely that the same master copy was used for both (Munro, 2011: 49). Yet the vignettes in the Book of the Dead of Ankhwahibre are not colored, but rather drawn with a black outline. In these cases, red was sometimes used for details in the drawing. Polychrome vignettes, like in the other aforementioned papyri, are not to be found. The papyrus of Pasherientaihet is another example of a vignette design in outline drawing. However, in this case yellow is used for rendering details in addition to red (Gasse, 2001: 13). Either style—both polychrome and black outline drawing—can be applied on the same papyrus, such as on the papyri of Iahtesnakht, Tasheretenaset, or Djedkhi.

Finally, narrow, overlong proportions, especially in the representations of persons, with the deceased usually wearing a calf-length apron, are a typical stylistic element for the vignettes of this time (see, e.g., Figs. 5.6 and 5.13).

## Spell Sequence/Sequences

Earlier manuscripts of the Book of the Dead, those from the New Kingdom and the Third Intermediate Period, often show a large variety and different sequences of spells. For the first time in the textual history of the Book of the Dead, the papyri of the

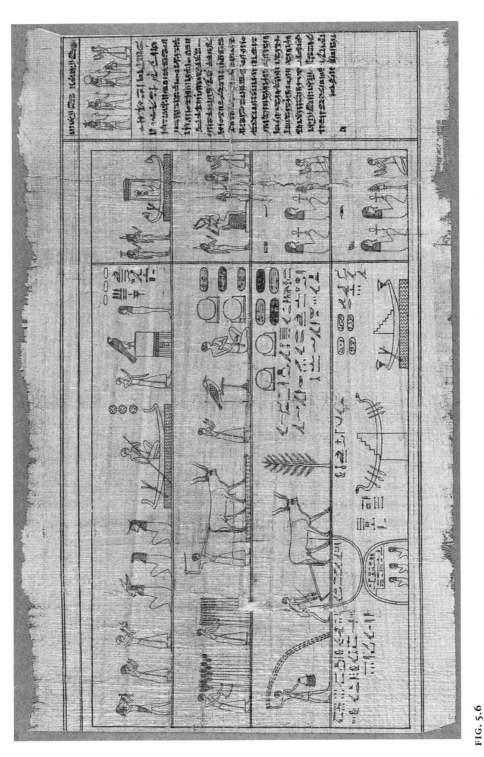

**FIG. 5.6**

The Book of the Dead of Ankhwahibre. The scene (BD V110) shows the deceased working in the Marsh of Offerings.

Credit line: P.London BM EA 10558, sheet 15 © Trustees of the British Museum, London.

**FIG. 5.7**

The Book of the Dead of Ankhwahibre. The layout is structured by double lines in close relation to the text.

Credit line: P.London BM EA 10558, sheet 27 © Trustees of the British Museum, London.

FIG. 5.8
The Book of the Dead of Iahtesnakht. Detail of the vignette band (column 3), where the vignettes of BD 1 (right) and 15 (left) are separated by a red line.

Credit line: P.Cologne. Aeg. 10207, Kol. 3, https://papyri.uni-koeln.de/stueck/DS_d1e289727/img/10207/orig/10207-1.jpg, CC BY 4.0, Institut für Altertumskunde der Universität zu Köln.

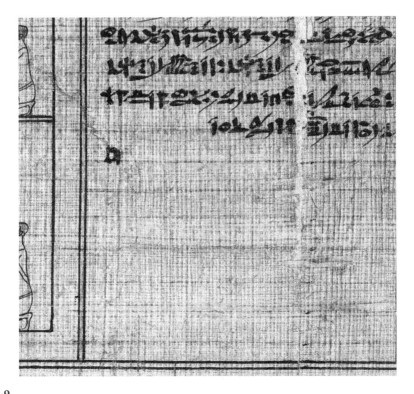

FIG. 5.9
The Book of the Dead of Ankhwahibre. Detail of sheet 15. Auxiliary lines and points.

Credit line: P.London BM EA 10558, sheet 15 © Trustees of the British Museum London.

FIG. 5.10
The Book of the Dead of Nesikhonsu, BD 17. The detail shows the vertical auxiliary lines on the right and the left of the dividing line.

Credit line: P.London UC71075, sheet 1 © Petrie Museum, University College, London.

FIG. 5.11
The Book of the Dead of Iahtesnakht. Detail of the vignette V15. The name of Iahtesnakht is written in hieratic above the goddesses Isis and Nephthys.

Credit line: P.Cologne. Aeg. 10207, Kol. 4, detail https://papyri.uni-koeln.de/stueck/DS_d1e289727/img/10207/orig/10207-2.jpg, CC BY 4.0, Institut für Altertumskunde der Universität zu Köln.

**FIG. 5.12**
The Book of the Dead of Nesikhonsu. The detail of a scene of the vignette of BD 17 (columns X + 2 and X + 3) shows the preliminary drawing in red.

Credit line: P.London UC71075, Kol. X + 2 and X + 3 © Petrie Museum, University College, London.

Twenty-sixth Dynasty follow an approximately fixed spell selection from BD 1 to 165. Apparently, this new sequence of spells—with occasional changes—is a kind of "model" for the sequence of spells in the Ptolemaic Period (Mosher, 2017).

# Excursus: The Numbering of Spells of the Book of the Dead

For the edition of a Book of the Dead published in 1842, Richard Lepsius chose a Ptolemaic papyrus (P.Turin 1791[www.trismegistos.org/text/57201]) of a man named Iufankh because it was by far "the most complete hieroglyphic copy" ("vollständigste hieroglyphische Exemplar"; Lepsius, 1842: 4) he could find at that time. Lepsius recognized that the Book of the Dead is composed of a set of individual spells, most of them beginning with "spell/book of . . . ." By numbering them from 1 to 165, he established a new system that is still in use today. However, he was sometimes inconsistent, for example in assigning individual spell numbers for some of the large-sized vignettes. The vignette to BD 15, for example, was given the number 16, and the vignette to BD 141/142 was assigned the number 143. In other cases, Lepsius subdivided longer spells like the well-known BD 125:

- BD 125a (declarations of innocence before Osiris),
- BD 125b (declarations of innocence before a series of deities),
- BD 125c (address to the deities in the hall and to Osiris), and
- BD 125d (the large-size vignette, the so-called judgment scene).

**FIG. 5.13**
The Book of the Dead of Iahtesnakht. Detail of the vignette of BD 125, the judgement scene. The depiction of the deceased shows that the papyrus was originally designed for a man. The figure of Iahtesnakht and her name written in Hieratic were added later.

Credit line: P.Cologne. Aeg. 10207, column 58, detail, https://papyri.uni-koeln.de/stueck/DS_d1e289727/img/10207/orig/10207-20.jpg, CC BY 4.0, Institut für Altertumskunde der Universität zu Köln.

Other spells, which had been numbered individually by Lepsius, such as BD 141 and 142, actually belong together. Furthermore, some spells, such as BD 64, have both a short and a long version.

Using this Iufankh sequence, some scholars have attempted to find a content-related structure of the Book of the Dead. For instance, Jean-François Champollion divided the text he called "rituel funéraire" into four large sections (Hincks, 1843: 22–23). According to Lepsius' numbering system, these sections cover

- BD 1 to 15,
- BD 17 to 125,
- BD 126 to 161, and
- BD 162 to 165.

FIG. 5.14
The Book of the Dead of Ankhwahibre. Differing sizes of the text fields made it necessary for the scribe to write very compact and in narrow lines.

Credit line: P.London BM EA 10558, sheet 16 © Trustees of the British Museum, London.

Like Champollion, Paul Barguet grouped several Book of the Dead spells together (Barguet, 1967: 34–36, 54–56, 96–101, 168–70, and 232–33):

- BD 1 to 15 (including the vignette)—"La marche vers la nécropole" (The march to the necropolis),
- BD 17 to 63 B—"La sortie au jour. La régénération" (Going out in daylight. The regeneration),
- BD 64 to 129—"La sortie au jour. La transfiguration" (Going out in daylight. The transfiguration),
- BD 130 to 162—"Le monde souterrain" (The underworld), and
- BD 163 to 192—"Les chapitres additionnels" (The additional chapters).

Stephen Quirke also has identified five major subjects in the Book of the Dead, but not based completely on the Iufankh sequence (Quirke, 2013: XIV–XV):

1. physical preservation of the body,
2. nourishing the body,

3. freedom of movement,
4. judgment,
5. transfiguration.

Furthermore, Quirke and Mosher defined smaller thematic groups within the Iufankh sequence (Quirke, 2013: XVII; Mosher, 1992: 153, note 49). This shows that the arrangement of spells in groups according to the Iufankh sequence does not always work well and that some thematic fields can be found in different positions within the Iufankh sequence.

However, there are some Book of the Dead spells that were already arranged in groups in the earliest text witnesses of the Book of the Dead. These are still used in the so-called Saitic sequence. Even the Coffin Texts had characteristic groups of spells, for example the spells of "knowing the powers of places in the afterlife," that have the sequence BD 114–112–113–108–109 (with variants) in the Book of the Dead papyri of the New Kingdom (Lüscher, 2012). This clearly proves that content connections were decisive for the arrangement of spells. The transformation spells (BD 76 to 88, in numerical order) are another example that shows this even more clearly (Mosher, 2016–2018: vol. 4, 432–57 and vol. 5, 29–273). Jan Assmann named this group of spells the "Buch der Verwandlungen," associating the spells with the twelve hours of the day, with BD 76 as an introduction to the other transformation spells (Assmann, 2001: 293; Lüscher, 2006).

Furthermore, there are other spells that were grouped together and that formed new units (Quirke, 2013: XII–XIII). For example, BD 31 to 35 (in numerical order) were intended repel crocodiles or snakes that might harm the embalmed body (Mosher, 2016–2018: vol. 3, 20–125), and BD 107 to 116 (in numerical order) are spells for knowing the *Ba*-souls.

## Provenance and Owners

The provenance of Book of the Dead manuscripts is unknown in many cases. This also applies to the manuscripts of the Twenty-sixth Dynasty. However, in some cases, there are indications that allow for assumptions concerning the origin of a source. A few manuscripts originate from the Memphite region, Herakleopolis Magna, or Abydos, while the majority of the manuscripts of the Twenty-sixth Dynasty come from the Theban area. One can assume that a regular exchange must have taken place between the main manufacturing centers of the Book of the Dead papyri (Verhoeven, 2001: 341). The findings concerning the Book of the Dead papyri of Tasheretenaset and Ankhwahibre discussed earlier in the chapter are significant in this context. The papyri have a strikingly similar sequence and similar motifs in their vignettes. Therefore, they probably shared the same master copy, which must have been transferred from Thebes to Memphis (Munro, 2010). The BD of "Men" was probably such a master copy. Instead of an owner's name "*Wsir mn ms n mnt*" ("Osiris NN born by NN") was inserted; the text was written in columns without any formal structure like the above-described layout. Furthermore, notes such as "first" or "second" may refer to the positioning of vignettes or text in a specific layout (Verhoeven, 2001: 330–31 with note 12), in the way that they were used in later Book of the Dead manuscripts (Kockelmann, 2017: 71, Figs. 5.5 and 5.6).

Due to the presence of the owners' names and titles, a geographical mapping of the Twenty-sixth Dynasty Book of the Dead papyri was possible in some cases. Some individuals who owned Book of the Dead papyri can be associated to the great priestly families in Thebes at that time, for example, Nespasefy, Tasheretenaset, and Djedkhi, who belonged to the Besenmut family (Vittmann, 1978: 3–61; Bohnenkämper, 2015); another example is Khamhor C, who was a member of the Montemhat family (Vittmann, 1978: 34–36; Verhoeven, 2017: 15–21).

## Stock Production or Individual Copy?

Several references indicate that the Book of the Dead papyri of the Twenty-sixth Dynasty were mostly produced in advance and individualized afterward by including the owner's name, title, and genealogical information (see also Verhoeven, this volume). A clear indicator for this is that the space for the owner's name was left blank. In the Book of the Dead of Ankhwahibre, for example, the name was only occasionally inserted. Another example indicating a subsequently added owner's name is the Book of the Dead of Iahtesnakht. Not only can a scribe be identified here who wrote the owner's name in the spaces left blank, but the fact that the text and the vignettes always referred to a man as owner (and not to the lady Iahtesnakht) shows this clearly. This is particularly striking in the vignette of the judgment scene, in which the figure of Iahtesnakht was drawn behind the male figure that originally represented the owner.

Other details also refer to the preproduction of Book of the Dead papyri, such as the post-processing of previously designed layouts, for example. In the Book of the Dead papyrus of Pasherientaihet (Gasse, 2001: pl. XV), it is clearly visible that the double line that separates the text and vignette fields in column 48 has been erased so that the text of BD 99 B can be written as a list.

In some cases, the provided text field was too small and the scribe had to try to fit the text in by shortening it or by writing smaller and in narrower lines. On the other hand, there are examples of large columns with only a short text and the rest of the column left blank (Fig. 5.14).

The lack of vignettes is a further clear reference to the steps required in producing a Book of the Dead papyrus. The Book of the Dead of Nespasefy, for example, shows the vignette band and vignette fields that were provided for the illustrations, but only one single scene of vignette 1 (above col. A1) was drawn in outlines (Verhoeven, 1999: 4, Photo-Tafel 1 and Photo-Tafel 47).

## Summary

The Book of the Dead papyri of the Twenty-sixth Dynasty represent a significant turning point in the Book of the Dead tradition. They show a homogeneous manuscript design and layout, supported by a common choice of script (hieratic). However, variations are possible, especially in the arrangement of text and images, as well as in the design of the vignettes, which may be presented either as polychromatic representations or black outline drawings.

A significant feature of Book of the Dead manuscripts of that time is the selection of the BD spells and the new sequence of spells. Partial sequences that had traditionally been compiled in the papyri of the New Kingdom (or were already present in the Coffin Texts) were integrated into the new sequence. Even though this new sequence of spells, the so-called Saite sequence, was only approximately fixed, with occasional changes in the sequence, it was a kind of "model" for the sequence of spells in the younger tradition of the Book of the Dead papyri.

## Bibliography

Assmann, J. (2001). *Tod und Jenseits im Alten Ägypten* (München: C.H. Beck).

Barguet, P. (1967). *Le livre des morts*. Littératures Anciennes du Proche-Orient (Paris: Cerf).

Bohnenkämper, L. (2015). "Diener von Month und Amun. Zur Tradierung von Priestertiteln in der Bs-n-Mw.t-Familie." In *Weitergabe. Festschrift für Ursula Rößler-Köhler zum 65. Geburtstag*. Göttinger Orientforschungen IV/53, edited by L. D. Morenz and A. El Hawary, 103–35 (Wiesbaden: Harrassowitz).

Botti, G. (1947). "Notizia sui frammenti del Papiro funerario n. 5404 del Museo Archeologico di Firenze." *Aegyptus* 27: 245–52.

Brunner-Traut, E. and Brunner, H. (1981). *Die Ägyptische Sammlung der Universität Tübingen*, 2 vols. (Mainz: Philipp von Zabern).

Buroh, K. (1985). "Totenbuch des Pefiu." In *Hieroglyphenschrift und Totenbuch. Die Papyri der Ägyptischen Sammlung der Universität Tübingen*, Ausstellungskataloge der Universität Tübingen 18, edited by G. Brinkhus, 51–53 (Tübingen: Attempto Verlag).

Coenen, M. (2006). "A Preliminary Survey of the Books of the Dead on Papyrus and Linen in the Nicholson Museum." In *Egyptian Art in the Nicholson Museum, Sydney*, edited by K. N. Sowada and B. G. Ockinga, 81–89 (Sydney: Meditarch Publishing, Southwood Press).

Gasse, A. (2001). *Le livre des morts de Pacherientaichet au Museo Gregoriano Egizio, Monumenti, Musei e Gallerie Pontificie*. Museo Gregoriano Egizio Aegyptiaca Gregoriana 4 (Vatican: Monumenti, Musei e Gallerie Pontificie).

Gülden, S. A. (2007). "Text und Bild im altägyptischen Totenbuch." In Fodor, S. et al. "Varia aegyptiaca: Vom Kosmos altägyptischer Zeichen." In *Kosmos der Zeichen. Schriftbild und Bildformel in Antike und Mittelalter*. Schriften des Lehr- und Forschungszentrums für die antiken Kulturen des Mittelmeerraumes—Centre for Mediterranean Cultures (ZAKMIRA) 5, edited by D. Boschung and H. Hellenkemper, 92–98 (Wiesbaden: Reichert).

Gülden, S. A. (2010). "Fragmente eines Totenbuches des Nesichonsu. P. London UC71075." In *Honi soit qui mal y pense. Festschrift Heinz-Josef Thissen*. Orientalia Lovaniensia Analecta 194, edited by H. Knuf, C. Leitz, and D. von Recklinghausen, 79–84 with plates 23–28 (Leuven: Peeters).

Hincks, E. (1843). *Catalogue of the Egyptian Manuscripts in the Library of Trinity College* (Dublin: Hodges/Figgis).

Kockelmann, H. (2017). "How a Book of the Dead Manuscript was produced." In *Book of the Dead. Becoming God in Ancient Egypt*, Oriental Institute Museum Publictions 39: 67–84, edited by F. Scalf (Chicago: The University of Chicago).

Lepsius, C. R. (1842). *Das Todtenbuch der Ägypter nach dem hieroglyphischen Papyrus in Turin mit einem Vorworte zum ersten Male hrsg. von R. Lepsius* (Leipzig: Georg Wigand).

Lüscher, B. (2006). *Die Verwandlungssprüche (Tb 76–88)*. Totenbuchtexte 2 (Basel: Orientverlag).

Lüscher, B. (2012). *Die Sprüche vom Kennen der Seelen (Tb 107–109, 111–116)*. Totenbuchtexte 8 (Basel: Orientverlag).

Mosher, M. Jr. (1992). "Theban and Memphite Book of the Dead Traditions in the Late Period." *Journal of the American Research Center in Egypt* 29: 143–72, Figs. 1–8.

Mosher, M. Jr. (2016–2018). *The Book of the Dead Saite through Ptolemaic Periods. A Study of Traditions Evident in Versions of Texts and Vignettes*. SPDBStudies 1–6 (Prescot: CreateSpace).

Mosher, M. Jr. (2017). "Transmission of Funerary Literature: Saite through Ptolemaic Periods." In *Book of the Dead. Becoming God in Ancient Egypt*, Oriental Institute Museum Publications 39: 85–96, edited by F. Scalf, 85–96 (Chicago: The University of Chicago).

Munro, I. (1989). "Holzschatulle für einen Papyrus." In *Ägypten. Götter, Gräber und die Kunst. 4000 Jahre Jenseitsglaube, Katalog zur Ausstellung 9. April bis 28. September 1989 im Schlossmuseum, Oberösterreichisches Landesmuseum, Linz*, edited by W. Seipel, 169 no. 135 (Linz: Grosser-Druck).

Munro (2006). "From Nine to One: Scattered Manuscripts Rejoined." In *Totenbuch-Forschungen. Gesammelte Beiträge des 2. Internationalen Totenbuch-Symposiums 2005*. Studien zum Altägyptischen Totenbuch 11: 233–44, Figs. 1–8, edited by B. Backes, I. Munro, and S. Stöhr (Wiesbaden: Harrasowitz).

Munro, I. (2010). "Evidence of a master copy transferred from Thebes to the Memphite area in Dynasty 26." *British Museum Studies in Ancient Egypt and Sudan* 15: 201–24.

Munro I. (2011). *Die Totenbuch-Papyri des Ehepaars Ta-scheret-en Aset und Djed-chi aus der Bes-en-Mut-Familie (26. Dynastie, Zeit des Königs Amasis)*. Handschriften des Altägyptischen Totenbuches 12 (Wiesbaden: Harrassowitz).

Naville, E. (1886). *Das Aegyptische Todtenbuch der XVIII. bis XX. Dynastie, Einleitung* (Berlin: Asher).

Parkinson, R. B. (2002). *Poetry and Culture in the Middle Kingdom Egypt. A Dark Side of Perfection* (London: Continuum).

Posener, G. (1985). *Le Papyrus Vandier*. Bibliothèque Générale 7 (Cairo: IFAO).

Quirke, S. (1993). *Owners of Funerary Papyri in the British Museum*. British Museum Occasional Papers 92 (London: British Museum Press).

Quirke, S. (2013). *Going out in Daylight, prt m hrw, the Ancient Egyptian Book of the Dead, Translation, Sources, Meanings*. Golden House Publications Egyptology 20 (London: Golden House).

Rössler-Köhler, U. (1985). "Zum Problem der Spatien in altägyptischen Texten: Versuch einer Systematik von Spatientypen." *Annales du Service des Antiquités de l'Égypte* 70: 383–408, Pl. 1.

Verhoeven, U. (1991). "'Das einzig bekannte Beispiel seiner Art.' Zu Kopenhagen, Nationalmuseet, AAe5, pTübingen 2000 und pBerlin 3161." In *Ägypten im afro-orientalischen Kontext: Aufsätze zur Archäologie, Geschichte und Sprache eines unbegrenzten Raumes*. Afrikanistische Arbeitspapiere Sondernummer 1991: 405–10 edited by D. Mendel and U. Claudi (Köln: Universität zu Köln).

Verhoeven, U. (1993). *Das saitische Totenbuch der Iahtesnacht, P. Colon. Aeg. 10207*. Papyrologische Texte und Abhandlungen 41 (Bonn: Habelt).

Verhoeven, U. (1998). "Internationales Totenbuch-Puzzle." *Revue d'Égyptologie* 49: 211–32.

Verhoeven, U. (1999). *Das Totenbuch des Monthpriesters Nespasefy aus der Zeit Psammetichs I., pKairo JE 95714 + pAlbany 1900.3.1, pKairo JE 95649, pMarseille91/2/1 (ehem. Slg. Brunner) + pMarseille 291*. Handschriften des Altägyptischen Totenbuches 5 (Wiesbaden: Harrassowitz).

Verhoeven, U. (2001). *Untersuchungen zur späthieratischen Buchschrift*. Orientalia Lovaniensia Analecta 99 (Leuven: Peeters).

Verhoeven, U. (2017). *Das frühsaitische Totenbuch des Monthpriesters Chamhor C*. Unter Mitarbeit von Sandra Sandri. Beiträge zum Alten Ägypten 7 (Basel: Orientverlag).

Vittmann, G. (1978). *Priester und Beamte im Theben der Spätzeit. Genealogische und prosopographische Untersuchungen zum thebanischen Priester- und Beamtentum der 25. Und 26. Dynastie*. Beiträge zur Ägyptologie 1 (Wien: Afro-Pub).

CHAPTER 6

# THE LAST BOOKS OF THE DEAD

FLORENCE ALBERT

During its long textual tradition from the New Kingdom until Roman times, the Book of the Dead underwent significant changes, as described in the previous chapters. But if its structural and stylistic components can be defined until the first half of the Ptolemaic Period, the latest stages of this text corpus's developments are less clear. The plethora of available sources is a good vantage point from which to conduct studies on the late evolutions of the Book of the Dead. However, despite the number of preserved documents, there is little information that allows us to determine their origin or dating in an absolute way. It is thus still hard today to understand how and when the Books of the Dead ceased to be used. The research conducted on the corpus these last few years has nonetheless contributed to highlight the documents stemming from traditions or practices adopted by the corpus from the Twenty-sixth Dynasty to the Roman Period. Analyses centered on the dating of Ptolemaic and Roman copies have also allowed us to establish criteria for comparison. The online publication of the archives of the Book of the Dead Project in 2012 [http://totenbuch.awk.nrw.de] now offers the prospect of making the current situation of the documentation known. These data permit us to define more clearly what the last Books of the Dead are.

## An Overview on the Development of the Book of the Dead from the Late Period

In addition to the elaboration of the Saite recension of the Book of the Dead (Quack, 2009; see Gülden, this volume), the corpus adopts a fairly standardized form at first glance, where texts and vignettes are arranged in sequences that can be found in a large number of manuscripts. The Saite recension constitutes a reference that allows a partial understanding of the local adaptations and the evolution of the Book of the Dead during this time (Mosher, 1992), taking its many variants into account. Possibly set up during the political and cultural reorganization movement that took place in Egypt at the beginning of the Twenty-sixth Dynasty, it was adopted all over the Egyptian territory and most likely remained in use until the Ptolemaic era with 165 spells in a more or less fixed order (see Gülden, this volume). Nevertheless, one manuscript can vary from another in regard to the sequences as well as the selection of the texts. It is not unusual for spells to have been moved or simply not have been copied within the papyri. For example, some manuscripts have only a small number of spells (e.g., the Papyrus of Qeqa: von Falck, 2006). Each of these, however, follows an order according to the logic of the Saite recension of the Book of the Dead and is then referred to as an abbreviated Book of the Dead. The style of the documents also varies, whether in the realization of the vignettes or their location in relation to the text. These textual and stylistic features allow us to distinguish different types of Books of the Dead in use. These are most likely from traditions particular to localities (Thebes, Memphis, Akhmim, Meir, etc.) or even to specific workshops producing funerary documents. Whatever the typologies or the adopted textual selections, these manuscripts characteristically contain spells of the Saite recension. In a way, they may be considered classical Books of the Dead, being a compendium of texts and vignettes necessary to the rebirth and integration of the deceased in the afterlife, according to the religious and theological conceptions defined in the early Twenty-sixth Dynasty and still in use until the Roman Period. From the large bulk of funerary documentation, several exemplary manuscripts of this tradition may be referenced: the papyri P.Colon. Aeg. 10207 (Twenty-sixth Dynasty; Verhoeven, 1993), P.Toronto ROM 910.85.236.1–13 (third century BCE; Munro, 2015), P.Leiden T16 (Ptolemaic Period; Leemans, 1867), or P.Turin 1791 (Ptolemaic Period; Lepsius, 1842) (Fig. 6.1).

Yet, a significant number of Books of the Dead stand out from this recension from the very beginning of the Late Period. These funerary papyri have the same characteristics as the "classical" Books of the Dead: they feature similar spells and vignettes in layouts and styles comparable to those found in the Saite recension, but they also integrate other textual compositions (Backes, 2009: 101–3). The reason for the introduction of new texts into the Books of the Dead can be explained in several ways. First, the burial context and its conditions most likely required and formed the grouping of the different texts that were necessary for the deceased's rebirth on a single manuscript. Such a precondition could be that the deceased was practically and/or financially unable to gather a complete set of funerary equipment (Backes, 2009: 104; Dieleman and Backes, 2015: 7–8). Second, the nature of the texts regularly introduced within these "hybrid" Books of the Dead suggests a change of the ritual practices. For example, the cults of Osiris play a major role in the cultic landscape from the Late Period on. Thus, the priests who participated

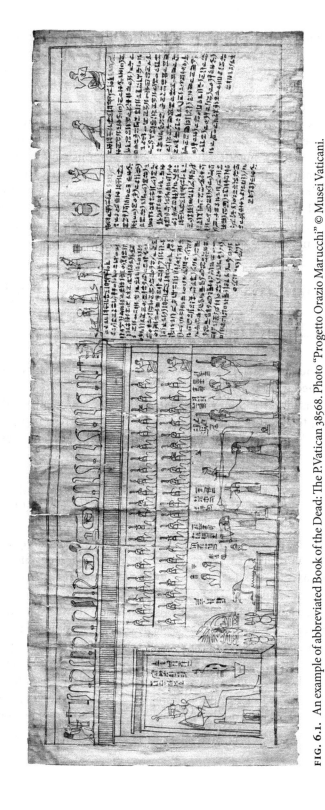

FIG. 6.1. An example of abbreviated Book of the Dead: The P. Vatican 38568. Photo "Progetto Orazio Marucchi" © Musei Vaticani.

in this adapted their funerary equipment according to their ritual experience. The reuse of texts originally intended for ritual use testifies to that (Coulon, 2010: 4–5; Backes, 2015). Consequently, the Books of the Dead adopt developments conditioned both by necessity and by a desire to adapt to social constraints and, at the same time, to religious practices that were in constant flux.

Therefore, if the Book of the Dead is subject to a tradition followed from the beginning of the Late Period—demonstrated by the Saite recension of the corpus—it is no less marked by regular mutations that gradually affect its content. In addition, the socio-religious context of the second half of the first millennium BCE certainly fostered the emergence of a new type of funerary literature. This one coexists, at first, with the Book of the Dead, to which it is complementary, and then seems to have gradually supplanted the corpus during the Ptolemaic Period (see also Kucharek, this volume, and Scalf, this volume).

## The Book of the Dead within the Late Funerary Literature

All throughout the Late Period, new texts appear in the funerary ensembles. They are generally copied from papyri that, like the Book of the Dead, are placed as close as possible to the mummies. Some of these texts have a clearly liturgical origin. They have been readapted to the benefit of priestly families who, during their lifetime, participated in cultic activities performed in temples. This practice of a "transfer" of the liturgical text to the funerary sphere is more and more patent during the Ptolemaic Period. It shows that these texts gradually adopt, in the narrower sense, a funerary function that comes to complement other spells, which had already been used for this purpose a long time before then (Dieleman and Backes, 2015: 8; Backes, 2015).

The development of a new kind of funerary literature particularly popular in the Ptolemaic and Roman Periods certainly ensues from this tendency, illustrated by various funerary compositions, known especially under the names of Books of Traversing Eternity, Books for Breathing, and other related documents (Herbin, 1994, 2008; Smith, 2009b; see also Kucharek, this volume). Probably born at the instigation of specific clergies (Goyon, 1972), these compositions partly situate the future of the deceased in a more concrete cultic reality (Herbin, 1994: 332–64). It shows the new aspirations of the Egyptians in their representation of the quest for the afterlife. This funerary literature seems to appear in the beginning of the second century BCE. First used together with the Book of the Dead—the deceased were equipped with several funerary papyri, or at least with several funerary compositions that could be gathered on a single document—it is assumed that it gradually took over the corpus and replaced it in the second half of the Ptolemaic Period (Coenen, 2001: 71).

To this, various texts taken and/or adapted from rituals practiced within the funerary cults (Smith, 2009b: 210–14) can be added. Many among them are copied on papyri and are mixed with the variety of funerary compositions used. In some manuscripts, which most likely testify to those ritual practices, specific spells are taken from the Book of the Dead and compiled for a prophylactic purpose (Albert, 2017; Albert and Gabolde, 2013; Stünkel, 2015: 407–27). Undoubtedly, their function distinguishes them from the "traditional" copies of the corpus. On the other hand, they show that the texts were not subject to restricted uses. Spells regularly integrated into the Book of the Dead can thus be found in other kinds of funerary manuscripts, and the Books of the Dead could integrate texts that weren't originally part of the corpus. This causes confusion when it comes to classifying and knowing the different categories of funerary texts and manuscripts—if, in fact, the Egyptians ever cared about categorization (Dieleman and Backes, 2015: 6 with n. 34).

Therefore, the Late, Ptolemaic, and Roman Periods are characterized by a diversification of the funerary texts and papyri. Those can be of various origins—liturgical, ritual, or strictly funerary—but whatever their nature, they show the range of methods and adaptations that the Egyptians employed to prepare their dead in the context of inhumation and a specific background of worship. The place taken by the Book of the Dead in this varied documentation is directly dependent on the evolution of funerary practices. If the copies of the corpus seemed to be standardized in the Twenty-sixth Dynasty, they become progressively permeable to other texts and notions that are also logically relevant for the deceased's rebirth. Consequently, there is a polyvalence of the Books of the Dead from the fourth century BCE onward. As has already been said, the moment when the corpus gives way to other funerary compositions of increasing popularity may have occurred in the second century BCE (Coenen, 2001), but motives and texts extracted from the Book of the Dead were still being copied in manuscripts until the Roman Period.

# The Last Books of the Dead: The Issue of Dating Criteria

The issue of dating the sources remains at the center of the problems concerning the last Books of the Dead. The funerary manuscripts can rarely be precisely dated. This prevents us from putting the great majority of the books into a chronology that would allow us to recreate a clear evolution of the corpus. Nevertheless, several studies, in particular those of Jan Quaegebeur (1997), Stephen Quirke (1999), Marc Coenen (2001), and Ursula Verhoeven (2001), have carved out tangible criteria that are currently systematically considered in order to understand the documents of the Ptolemaic and Roman Periods.

Paleography constitutes the most prominent criterion for dating the sources mostly written in hieratic. For example, the third volume of the *Hieratische Paläographie* by Georg Möller, in which he sometimes dates sources of references according to non-absolute criteria (Coenen, 2001: 69), is now complemented by Verhoeven's paleography of late hieratic script. Verhoeven (2001: esp. 23–28) used only dated sources, the latest considered document having been written between 246 and 221 BCE (P.London BM EA 10037). Thus, paleographic comparisons may be undertaken for a period up to the end of the third century BCE. As for the later sources that constitute the heart of the documentation considered in this chapter, however, this method cannot be used as such, since none of the known hieratic and hieroglyphic papyri today is datable in an absolute way (Quaegebeur, 1997: 73; Verhoeven, 2001: 25–28). However, other criteria allow us to put the late documentation into perspective:

- the **epithet of the deceased**, which adopts the female variants "Hathor" and/or "Osiris-Hathor" in some Books of the Dead: even though the recourse to this epithet appears at least once during the Third Intermediate Period (Smith, 2012), this practice seems to be more common in the funerary papyri dated to the end of the Ptolemaic Period and the Roman Period. Although not generalized in the Book of the Dead, it could permit us to attribute the copies that mention this variant to a late tradition of the corpus (Quirke, 1999: 85);
- the **Greek reed pen**, which seems to have been used for writing Theban funerary manuscripts, at least from 50 CE on. Its use is not systematic, however, and it is currently impossible to know when it was first used (Quaegebeur, 1997: 72–77; Quirke, 1999: 85; Tait, 1988);
- the **vignettes**, which show a clumsy, even awkward, picture (figures can be out of proportion, for instance: oblong necks, arms, or legs), that, nevertheless, is teeming with details: these illustrations may be polychrome; some of them are characterized by the use of particular colors (such as pink), which could be specific for the end of the Ptolemaic Period and the Roman Period (Quirke, 1999: 96–97; on the use of pink: Riggs, 2010: 349; Töpfer, 2016: 400);
- the **prosopography**, which allows to determine the position and genealogy of some owners of late funerary manuscripts (Coenen, 2001): this research contributes to matching up different papyri belonging to individuals or family groups that can also be mentioned in other kinds of sources. It is therefore possible to reduce the chronological limits of certain Books of the Dead dated up to now, without a doubt, to the Greco-Roman time.

Taking the whole of these criteria into account enables us to list Books of the Dead that can reasonably be dated to the second half of the Ptolemaic Period, and even to the Roman Period. The several constitutive elements of these documents (spells and vignettes used, sequence of texts, organization and style) present the point of view of the late tradition of the corpus, which can be put in a historical and more precise context.

## ON THE LAST IDENTIFIABLE BOOKS OF THE DEAD

The Books of the Dead following the above-mentioned dating criteria (see Catalogue on pp. 151–56, this chapter) are characterized by their use of spells from the corpus according to a layout that is very close to that of the Saite recension. The texts and vignettes also join a collection related to the one found in most "classical" copies of the corpus, used earlier in the fourth and third centuries BCE. Therefore, we are dealing with papyri that join a continuous tradition. They can be distinguished from earlier traditions of the Book of the Dead on the basis of stylistic considerations and other significant elements of classification included within these late papyri. One of the most typical criteria is the addition in several papyri of extracts or abbreviated versions of the Documents for Breathing (on these texts, see Stadler, 2015). These compositions first appear in the beginning of the second century BCE (Coenen, 2001: 71) and are, together with other related funerary texts, regularly integrated into the funerary equipment as of this date forward. The papyri P.Berlin P 3162, P.Chicago OIM 25489, P.Tübingen 2012, P.Paris Louvre N 3085, P.Paris Louvre N 3125, P.Paris Louvre N 3278, P.Paris Louvre E 3865, and P.Vienna ÄS 3861, which are linked to these late funerary compositions either because they contain some extracts or because their owners owned some copies of them at the same time, can therefore be considered the most trustworthy proof of the developments of the corpus during the second half of the Ptolemaic Period. The publications that have been made of three of these manuscripts (Lejeune, 2006; Töpfer and Müller-Roth, 2011) highlight the precise content of the Book of the Dead spells selected. They either contain quite a large number of variants or give abbreviated versions of the classical spells, which would show that the master copies used had undoubtedly evolved at this time (Lejeune, 2006: 199–201; Töpfer and Müller-Roth, 2011: 71–72). So, these late versions of the spells should be considered references aiming at a more global comparison of the many other Books of the Dead for which a precise dating has not been possible until now (Fig. 6.2).

Textual variations of the spells are also found in the papyri P.London BM EA 10983, P.London BM EA 10671, and P.London BM EA 10098+10844, which, as Stephen Quirke (1999) has suggested, can probably be considered the last known Books of the Dead. These documents were dated into the transitional phase from the Ptolemaic to the Roman Period, according to criteria that go further than the simple stylistic frame (Fig. 6.3).

FIG. 6.2. P.Tübingen 2012. After S. Töpfer, M. Müller-Roth, *Das Ende der Totenbuchtradition und der Übergang zum Buch vom Atmen. Die Totenbücher des Monthemhat (pTübingen 2012) und der Tanedjemet (P.Paris Louvre 3085)*, HAT 13, Wiesbaden, 2011, Fototafel 2.

FIG. 6.3. P.London BM EA 10983. ©Trustees of the British Museum.

It is currently not possible, considering the available and exploitable information, to date other Books of the Dead, beyond a doubt, to a later period. In this sense, the group of funerary documents of Horsaiset, son of Hor and Kaikai, dated into the beginning of the imperial period (around 60 CE; Quirke, 1999: 88–89), as well as those from the tomb of Soter, dated to Trajan's and Hadrian's reigns (Landuyt, 1995; Quirke, 1999: 88), do not include any Books of the Dead. So, if we can reasonably assume that it is at this time that the Books of the Dead, strictly speaking, became obsolete, then motives extracted from the corpus are still copied in many funerary papyri: The judgment scene is regularly included in the Books for Breathing, and, on a larger scale, vignettes and texts extracted from the Book of the Dead are regularly inserted in funerary documents during the Roman Period. For instance, the hieratic papyrus P.Vatican 37481 shows funerary compositions linked with the Osirian cults and the First Book for Breathing, but a judgment scene and texts related to the Book of the Dead are inserted as well: negative confession of BD 125, and mixed texts stemming from BD 26, BD 30, and BD 30A (Gasse, 1993: 79–80, pl. LVI, cat. No.77). The demotic sources also give good evidence for the use of components of the Book of the Dead in the funerary documentation (Smith, 2009a; Quack, 2014). In this respect, P.Paris BN 149, safely dated to 63 CE, contains a demotic translation of BD 125 and 128 and the description of a vignette belonging to BD 148 (Stadler, 2003; Smith, 2009a; Quack, 2014). It offers a strong example of how the Romans' funerary manuscripts refer, at least in part, to the Book of the Dead (Fig. 6.4).

The transitional period during which the late funerary compositions and the Book of the Dead were used at the same time lasted roughly 250 years (from the beginning of the second century BCE until the end of the first century CE). The small number of Books of the Dead known at that time, compared with the Books of Traversing Eternity, the many varieties of Books of Breathing, and other related compositions, gives the impression of a decrease in the popularity of the corpus from and during the second half of the Ptolemaic Period. During this time, private individuals probably adhered to ideas

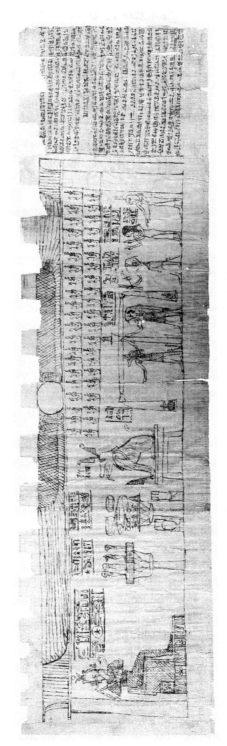

FIG. 6.4. P. Vatican 37481. Photo "Progetto Orazio Marucchi" ©Musei Vaticani.

passed on through the newly established funerary literature. The Book of the Dead may then have been reminiscent of a time-honored tradition with which some individuals wanted to be associated and/or wanted to prove they knew and had access to in an archival way, introducing excerpts or things reminiscent of the corpus in their funerary papyri. This shows that the Book of the Dead remains an important source of reference even after having ceased to be widely used.

## CATALOGUE

*(Credits by Totenbuch-Projekt: Http://Totenbuch.Awk.Nrw.De//)*

### Based on strong dating criteria:

*P.Berlin P. 3162 A+B*

| | |
|---|---|
| Sequence | Abbreviated version of the Book of Breathing: BD 17–26–77–83–159–149–87–85–89 |
| Dating | From the second half of the Ptolemaic Period–Roman Period |
| Criterion | Book of the Dead spells mixed with an abbreviated version of the Book of Breathing |
| Bibliography | Kaplony-Heckel, 1986: No. 87 |

*P.Chicago OIM 25389*

| | |
|---|---|
| Sequence | Book of the Dead spells, Book of Traversing Eternity, Second Book of Breathing. |
| Dating | From the second half of the Ptolemaic Period |
| Criterion | Book of the Dead spells mixed with other late funerary texts |
| Bibliography | Coenen, 1997–2000: 41–48. |

*P.London BM EA 10098 + 10844*

| | |
|---|---|
| Sequence | Adoration Scene: BD 1V–2–3–4–5–6–7–8–9–10/48–11/49–12/120–13/121–14–15V–V15–17V–90–18V–19–21–22–23–24+V17 (on BD 19–24)–25+V18(?)–26+V18(?)–28+V18(?)–30A–64+V25+V26+V27+V28+V?(V29?)+V30+V64–66–31V /// 32V–33[V] /// 39+V? ///? BD 30B?–65–66–68–?–72–73–74–75–78–79–80–81–80–82–83–84–85–86–87–88–89–90–91–92–93–94–95–96–97–98–99/99B–100/129–101–102–103–104–105–106–107–108–109–V110c+ |

| | V110b–111–112–113–114–115–116–117–118–119–122–123/139–124–125A–125B–125C–Judgment Scene–126–127–128+V130–100/129–130–132–133–134–135–136/136A–Title 138+Title 140+138—137–123/139–140–141–142–144V–145V–V143(Part)–146V–147V–190–149V–V148–V150–V151–152V–V161–153–154V–155V–156V–157V–158V–159V–160V–163V–164V–165V–162V + amulet plan: V66–V68–V71–V72–V79–V81–V82–V83–V78–V85–V86–V87–V88–V89–V90–V91–V92–V93–V94–V98–V100/129–V102–V104–V105–V108? (on 109); V115–V117(?)–V119 (on BD 111–125C); VV126–V100/129–V133–V134–V136/136A–V140 (on BD 126–140) |
|---|---|
| Dating | End of Ptolemaic Period–beginning of Roman Period |
| Criterion | Greek reed pen; style of vignettes |
| Bibliography | Quirke, 1999: 83–98 |

## *P.London BM EA 10671*

| Sequence | /// Judgment Scene–V126 /// 130V (?) /// V150–V148–151V–152V |
|---|---|
| Dating | End of Ptolemaic Period to beginning of Roman Period |
| Criterion | Style of vignettes |
| Bibliography | Quirke, 1999: 83–98 |

## *P.London BM EA 10983 + Location unknown [28]*

| Sequence | 146V–/// BD V 148–146V ///–V151–V152–155V–157V–156V–158V /// V148 /// V162 /// |
|---|---|
| Dating | End of Ptolemaic Period–beginning of Roman Period |
| Criterion | Style of vignettes (specific colors); "Hathor" predication |
| Bibliography | Quirke, 1999: 83–98; Müller-Roth and Weber, 2012: 126 |

## *P.Paris Louvre N 3125*

| Sequence | Judgment Scene–BD 1–2–3–4–9–11/49–12/120–18–19–54 (with Title's var.)–125A–125B + abbreviated version of Book of Breathing |
|---|---|
| Dating | First half of first century BCE |
| Criterion | Genealogical information; Book of the Dead mixed with Book of Breathing; Style of vignettes |
| Bibliography | Lejeune, 2006: 197–202 |

## P.Paris Louvre N 3278

| | |
|---|---|
| Sequence | /// Judgment Scene /// BD 132V–104+V102(?)–133+V134–133+V140 (Part)–134+V140 (Part)–134+V133–92+V144(?)–102V–145V–144–145V–V146–125A–125 B–124+V148–100/129+V89–V161—Prayer to Hathor + V162 |
| Dating | First half of first century BCE |
| Criterion | Prosopographical information; the owner owns a Book of Breathing (P.Munich 805). |
| Bibliography | Coenen, 2001: 69–84 |

## P.Paris Louvre N 3085

| | |
|---|---|
| Sequence | V15–15–36–18–19–20–21–23–25–26–27–30–45–54V–44+V?–59+V?–43+V?–80+V? (V87?)–91V–100/129+V?–101V–162V |
| Dating | First century BCE to first century CE |
| Criterion | Comparison with P.Tübingen 2012 (same workshop) |
| Bibliography | Töpfer and Müller-Roth, 2011; Mosher, 1992. |

## P.Paris Louvre E 3865

| | |
|---|---|
| Sequence | BD 68–42–44–47–10/48–11/49–53–54–56–57 + Second Book of Breathing |
| Dating | Second half of Ptolemaic Period to Roman Period. |
| Criterion | Book of the Dead with Second Book of Breathing on the same papyrus |
| Bibliography | Goyon, 1972: 243–285 |

## P.New York, Amherst fragments, group 7 + group 8

| | |
|---|---|
| Sequence | /// BD 11/49 ///? /// |
| Dating | End of Ptolemaic Period, Beginning of Roman Period (50–150 CE?) |
| Criterion | Paleography (Greek reed pen?); comparison with P.Paris Louvre N 3279 |
| Bibliography | Unpublished |

## P.Oslo (without number)

| | |
|---|---|
| Sequence | Judgment Scene–BD 126V–127–128–100/129V–130–18 (?) |
| Dating | End of Ptolemaic Period–beginning of Roman Period |
| Criterion | Vignettes (colors); comparison with P.London BM EA 10983 |
| Bibliography | Unpublished |

*P. St. Gallen*

    Sequence      /// V148–V155–V156–V157–V158 ///

    Dating      End of Ptolemaic Period

    Criterion      Anthroponomy, style

    Bibliography      Chappaz and Poggia, 1996: 47

*P. Tübingen 2012*

    Sequence      V?–BD V15–15B III (g)(c)–18V–19V–21+V57–23+V27?–25+ V?–26+V74?–27V–30A V–46+V?–54+V?–55–44+V?–43V–59VV (Var.)–80+V87–91+V85–100/129+V?–101V–162V + Abbreviated version of Book of Breathing + Royal decree of Osiris Onnophris

    Dating      first century BCE to first century CE

    Criterion      Owner of M. Turin 1873; belongs to a priest's family with Books of the Dead and Books of Breathing; Book of the Dead spells mixed with other late funerary texts

    Bibliography      Töpfer and Müller-Roth, 2011

*P. Vienna KHM ÄS 3861*

    Sequence      Judgment Scene–BD 13/121–14–18V–19V–21V–Title 22+23–25+V27–26V–27+V26–28V–29–30V–Hymn to Hathor+V

    Dating      Second half of first century BCE

    Criterion      Genealogical information; comparison with the Book of Breathing P. Vienna KHM ÄS 10158

    Bibliography      Coenen, 2003: 160–69

## Based on stylistic observations only

*P. Barcelona Palau Rib. 450 + Mannheim REM without. No. [1]*

    Sequence      V145 + other funerary texts and vignettes (BD?)

    Dating      Second half of Ptolemaic Period-beginning Roman Period?

    Criterion      Stylistic

    Bibliography      Unpublished

*P. Berlin P. 14420*

    Sequence      Book of the Dead spells (?)

    Dating      End of Ptolemaic Period or Roman Period

| | |
|---|---|
| Criterion | Paleography, style |
| Bibliography | Kaplony-Heckel, 1986: No. 172 |

*P.Cortona 3184*

| | |
|---|---|
| Sequence | BD 15V + V1, Judgment Scene. |
| Dating | End of Ptolemaic Period |
| Criterion | Style |
| Bibliography | Seeber, 1976: 230, n. 4; Bruschetti et al., 1988: 67, pl. 154–155 |

*P.Geneva MAH D229 + P.Paris Louvre N 3220 D*

| | |
|---|---|
| Sequence | Title 1–BD 1+V1–Title 2–4–5–6–7–8–9–14–15V–V15–17V–18V–19 /// |
| Dating | Second half of Ptolemaic Period? |
| Criterion | Inscription related to Medinet Habu Graffiti; style |
| Bibliography | Devauchelle, 1978 |

*P.Modena Or. 101*

| | |
|---|---|
| Sequence | BD 17–18 /// 23 /// 28 |
| Dating | End of Ptolemaic Period or Roman Period |
| Criterion | Style |
| Bibliography | Biblioteca Estense, Modena, Firenze, 1987, pl. 1 |

*P.New York Amherst 38*

| | |
|---|---|
| Sequence | BD 1 |
| Dating | Second half of Ptolemaic Period to beginning of Roman Period |
| Criterion | Stylistic. |
| Bibliography | Newberry, 1899: 53 |

*P.Vienna ÖNB Aeg. 12012+12008 a-c*

| | |
|---|---|
| Sequence | /// BD 125A–125B–125C–125D–Judgment Scene |
| Dating | second half of Ptolemaic Period-beginning of Roman Period? |
| Criterion | Style of vignettes: part. V125 |
| Bibliography | Unpublished |

*P.Toledo TMA 27.71 (Papyrus Stevens)*

| | |
|---|---|
| Sequence | Late funerary texts, Book of the Dead spells, Judgment Scene |

| | |
|---|---|
| Dating | End of Ptolemaic Period, Roman Period |
| Criterion | Stylistic, mixed textual compositions |
| Bibliography | Unpublished |

## Bibliography

Albert, F. (2017). "Un groupe de papyrus funéraires tardifs." In *Studies in Ancient Egyptian funerary Literature*, Orientalia lovaniensia analecta. Dép. d'étud. orient., univ. cathol. 257, edited by S. Bickel and L. Díaz-Iglesias, 29–43 (Leuven: Peeters).

Albert, F. and Gabolde, M. (2013). "Le papyrus-amulette de Lyon Musée des Beaux-Arts H 2425." *Egypte nilotique et mediterraneenne* 6: 159–68.

Backes, B. (2015). "Gedanken zu Kategorien und Funktionspotentialen funerärer Ritualpapyri." In *Liturgical Texts for Osiris and the Deceased in Late Period and Greco-Roman Egypt. Studi storico-religiosi* 14, edited by B. Backes and J. Dieleman, 15–35 (Wiesbaden: Harrassowitz).

Backes, B. (2009). *Drei Totenpapyri aus einer thebanischen Werkstatt der Spätzeit*. Handschriften zum altägyptischen Totenbuchs 11 (Wiesbaden: Harrassowitz).

Bruschetti, P., Gori Sassoli, M., Guidotti, M. C., and Zamarchi Grassi, P., eds. (1988). *Il Museo dell'Accademia Etrusca di Cortona, Catalogo delle Collezioni* (Cortona: Calosci).

Chappaz, J.-L. and Poggia, S. (1996). Collections égyptiennes de Suisse. Un répertoire géographique. Cahiers de la Société d'égyptologie, Genève 3 (Geneva: Soc. d'Égyptologie).

Coenen, M. (1997–2000). "The Quaritch Papyrus: A Graeco-Roman Funerary Papyrus from Esna." *Jaarbericht van het vooraziat.-egyptisch Genootschap, Ex Oriente Lux* 35/36: 41–48.

Coenen, M. (2001). "On the Demise of the Book of the Dead in Ptolemaic Thebes." *Revue d'egyptologie* 52: 69–84.

Coenen, M. (2003). "The Funerary Papyri of Horos Son of Estneteretten in the Kunsthistorisches Museum in Vienna." *Zanzibar Archaeological Survey* 130: 160–69.

Coulon, L. (2010). "Le culte osirien au Ier millénaire av. J.-C. Une mise en perspective(s)." In *Le Culte d'Osiris au Ier millénaire av. J.-C. Découvertes et travaux récents. Actes de la table ronde internationale tenue à Lyon Maison de l'Orient et de la Méditerranée (université Lumière-Lyon 2) les 8 et 9 juillet 2005*. Bibliothèque d'étude 153, edited by L. Coulon, 1–19 (Cairo: Institut Français d'Archéologie Orientale).

Devauchelle, D. (1978). "À propos du papyrus de Genève D 229." *Enchoria* 8.2: 73–76.

Dieleman, J. and Backes, B. (2015). "Current Trends in the Study of Liturgical Papyri." In *Liturgical Texts for Osiris and the Deceased in Late Period and Greco-Roman Egypt. Studi storico-religiosi* 14, edited by B. Backes and J. Dieleman, 1–13 (Wiesbaden: Harrassowitz).

von Falck, M. (2006). *Das Totenbuch der Qeqa aus der Ptolemäerzeit (pBerlin P. 3003)*. Handschriften zum altägyptischen Totenbuchs 8 (Wiesbaden: Harrassowitz).

Gasse, A. (1993). *Les papyrus hiératiques et hiéroglyphiques du Museo Gregoriano Egizio*. AegGreg 1 (Vatican: Monumenti, Musei e Gallerie Pontificie).

Goyon, J.-Cl. (1972). *Rituels funéraires de l'ancienne Égypte*. Littératures anciennes du Proche-Orient 4 (Paris: Éd. du Cerf).

Herbin, Fr.-R. (1994). *Le Livre de parcourir l'Éternité*. Orientalia lovaniensia analecta 58 (Leuven: Peeters).

Herbin, Fr.-R. (2008). *Books of Breathing and Related Texts*. Catalogue of the Books of the Dead and Other Religious Texts in the British Museum IV (London: British Museum Press).

Kaplony-Heckel, U. (1986). *Ägyptische Handschriften* III, Verzeichnis der orientalischen Handschriften in Deutschland XIX (Wiesbaden: Steiner).

Landuyt, K. van (1995). "The Soter Family: Genealogy and Onomastics." In *Hundred-Gated Thebes*, edited by S. Vleeming, 69–82 (Leiden: Brill).

Leemans, C. (1867). *Papyrus Egyptien Funéraire Hiératique (T.16) du Musée d'Antiquités des Pays-Bas* (Leiden: Brill).

Lejeune, B. (2006). "A Study of pLouvre N. 3125 and the End of the Book of the Dead Tradition." In *Totenbuch-Forschungen. Gesammelte Beiträge des 2. Internationalen Totenbuch-Symposiums 2005*. Studien zum altägyptischen Totenbuch 11, edited by B. Backes, I. Munro, and S. Stöhr, 197–202 (Wiesbaden: Harrassowitz).

Lepsius, R. (1842). *Das Todtenbuch der Ägypter nach dem hieroglyphischen Papyrus in Turin* (Leipzig: Wigand).

Mosher, M. (1992). "Theban and Memphite Book of the Dead Traditions in the Late Period." *Journal of the American Research Center in Egypt* 29: 143–72.

Müller-Roth, M. and Weber, F. (2012). "Pretty Good Privacy." In *Herausgehen am Tage. Gesammelte Schriften zum altägyptischen Totenbuch*. Studien zum altägyptischen Totenbuch 17, edited by R. Lucarelli, M. Müller-Roth, and A. Wüthrich, 113–34 (Wiesbaden: Harrassowitz).

Munro, I. (2015). *The Golden Book of the Dead of Amenemhet (pToronto ROM 910.85.236.1–13)*. Handschriften zum altägyptischen Totenbuchs 14 (Wiesbaden: Harrassowitz).

Newberry, P. E. (1899). *The Amherst Papyri: Being an account of the Egyptian Papyri in the Collection of the Right Hon. Lord Amherst of Hackney, F.S.A., at Didlington Hall, Norfolk* (London: Quaritch).

Quack, J.-Fr. (2009). "Redaktion und Kodifizierung im spätzeitlichen Ägypten. Der Fall des Totenbuches." In *Die Textualisierung der Religion*. Forschungen zum Alten Testament 62, edited by J. Schaper, 11–34 (Tübingen: Mohr Siebeck).

Quack, J.-Fr. (2014), "A New Demotic Translation of (Excerpts of) a Chapter of the Book of the Dead." *Journal of Egyptian Archaeology* 100: 381–93.

Quaegebeur, J. (1997). "Books of Thoth Belongings to Owners of Portraits? On Dating Late Hieratic Funerary Papyri." In *Portraits and Masks. Burial Customs in Roman Egypt*, edited by M. Bierbrier, 72–77 (London: British Museum Press).

Quirke, St. (1999). "The Last Books of the Dead?" In *Studies in Egyptian Antiquities. A Tribute to T.G.H. James*. British Museum Occasional Papers 123, edited by W. V. Davis, 83–88 (London: British Museum Press).

Riggs, Chr. (2010). "Tradition and Innovation in the Burial Practices of Roman Egypt." In *Tradition and Transformation: Egypt under Roman Rule. Proceedings of the International Conference, Hildesheim, Roemer- and Pelizaeus-Museum, 3-6 July 2008*, edited by C. Lembke, M. Minas-Nerpel, and S. Pfeiffer, 343–56 (Leiden: Brill).

Seeber, Chr. (1976). *Untersuchungen zur Darstellung des Totengerichts im Alten Ägypten*. Münchner ägyptologische Studien 35 (München: Deutscher Kunstverlag).

Smith, M. (2009a). "New Extracts from the Book of the Dead in Demotic." In *Actes du IXe congrès international des Études démotiques, Paris, 31 aout–3 Septembre 2005*. Bibliothèque d'étude 147, edited by D. Devauchelle and G. Widmer, 347–59 (Cairo: Institut Français d'Archéologie Orientale).

Smith, M. (2009b). *Traversing Eternity: Texts for the Afterlife from Ptolemaic and Roman Egypt* (Oxford: Oxford University Press).

Stadler, M. A. (2003). *Der Totenpapyrus des Pa-Month (P. Bibl. nat. 149)*, Studien zum altägyptischen Totenbuch 6 (Wiesbaden: Harrassowitz).

Smith, M. (2012). "New References to the Deceased as *Wsir n* NN from the Third Intermediate Period and the Earliest Reference to a Deceased Woman as Ḥ.t- Ḥr NN." *Revue d'egyptologie* 63: 187–96.

Stadler, M. A. (2015). "Prätexte funerärer Rituale. Königsliturgie, Tempelliturgie, Totenliturgie." In *Liturgical Texts for Osiris and the Deceased in Late and Greco-Roman Egypt—Liturgische Texte für Osiris und Verstorbene im spätzeitlichen Ägypten*, Proceedings of the Colloquiums at New York (ISAW), May 6, 2011, and Freudenstadt, 18–21 July 2012, Studi storico-religiosi 14, edited by B. Backes and J. Dieleman, 75–90 (Wiesbaden: Harrassowitz).

Stünkel, I. (2015). "An Amulet Plaque and a Book of the Dead Papyrus from the Metropolitan Museum of Art and some Observations on Gold Amulets." In *Weitergabe. Festschrift für die Ägyptologin Ursula Rößler-Köhler zum 65. Geburtstag*. Göttinger Orientforschungen 53, edited by L. D. Morenz and A. El Hawary, 407–27 (Wiesbaden: Harrassowitz).

Tait, J. W. (1988). "Rush and Reed: The Pens of Egyptian and Greek Scribes." in *Proceedings of the XVIII International Congress of Papyrology. Athens 25–31 May 1986*, edited by B. G. Mandilaras, 477–82 (Athens: The Greek Papyrological Society).

Töpfer, S. (2016). "'Aggressives Rosa'—Zu einer Mumienauflage der spätptolemäisch-frührömischen Epoche aus Achmim (ÄMUL Inv.-Nr. 7810)." *Bulletin de l'Institut francais d'archeologie orientale* 116: 385–410.

Töpfer, S. and Müller-Roth, M. (2011). *Das Ende der Totenbuchtradition und der Übergang zum Buch vom Atmen. Die Totenbücher des Monthemhat (pTübingen 2012) und der Tanedjemet (pLouvre N 3085)*. Handschriften zum altägyptischen Totenbuchs 13 (Wiesbaden: Harrassowitz).

Verhoeven, U. (1993). *Das Saitische Totenbuch der Iahtesnacht. P. Colon. Aeg. 10207* (Bonn: Habelt).

Verhoeven, U. (2001). *Untersuchungen zur Späthieratischen Buchschrift*. Orientalia lovaniensia analecta 99 (Leuven: Peeters).

# PART II

# TYPES OF SOURCES: THE MATERIAL ASPECT OF THE BOOK OF THE DEAD

CHAPTER 7

# WRITING BOOK OF THE DEAD MANUSCRIPTS

*Tasks and Traditions*

URSULA VERHOEVEN

## CHOICE OF MATERIAL AND ORGANIZATION

MANUSCRIPTS with chapters from the Book of the Dead could be made from different materials. Large linen shrouds occur at the beginning of the tradition in the middle of the second millennium BCE, while long, narrow strips of cloth were used as a writing surface for the mummy bandages in the last centuries of the first millennium BCE (Kockelmann, 2008). Ostraca with Book of the Dead texts were used as the master copy for tomb decorations with Book of the Dead texts (Lüscher, 2013). Papyrus was the most common material and was used in different formats, while leather and wood occurred only rarely (see p. 164 and 174, this chapter).

Usually only the recto of the papyri was inscribed with Book of the Dead texts and vignettes (an exception is P.Brooklyn 37.1777E: O'Rourke, 2016: 51). Sometimes the verso shows a single line of thoroughly executed hieroglyphs that give the title and name of the owner within an offering spell (Eighteenth Dynasty; Taylor, 2010: 265, 298).

The re-examination of the joins in the famous papyrus of Ani (Nineteenth Dynasty) showed that the papyrus sheets were not glued together before the BD chapters were written down, and that it was manufactured out of a selection of already finished sections with texts and vignettes. By mistake, some chapters had been redundantly added twice. The borders of the vignettes were redrawn and repainted, and the scribe added text when necessary. It seems that "a continuity of vignettes was more important than text, appearance more important than content" (Leach and Parkinson, 2010: 46).

**FIG. 7.1.** Stock produced Book of the Dead for Tui with empty spaces for his name, from Thebes (c. 1450 BCE). The hieratic page number "24" in the upper right margin is written in the same retrograde direction as the hieroglyphic text columns.

Credit: P.London BM EA 9913.4 (detail). © The Trustees of the British Museum.

In very few cases, an administrative papyrus was reused for a Book of the Dead on the verso (Twenty-first Dynasty; Taylor, 2010: 278), and a papyrus with a narrative text on the recto was reused as a master copy for the Book of the Dead on the verso (Twenty-sixth Dynasty; Verhoeven, 2001: 329–37).

While the numbering of papyrus pages or rolls seems to be rare (Fig. 7.1), mummy bandages show an extensive numbering system, which Kockelmann (2008 II: 147–89) analyzed in detail. In the case of the large papyrus roll of the highest quality belonging to the lady Nesitanebetisheru (P.Greenfield, Twenty-first Dynasty), some sheets have different heights and are sometimes marked with lone red signs of hieroglyphs on the upper and lower margin (ibis, bow, mouth, prisoner) to help the worker who had to assemble the joins (Taylor, 2010: 284–85).

## Producing on Personal Order or on Stock

Usually, a Book of the Dead manuscript was produced after someone ordered a personal copy for themselves or a relative according to their own wishes and possibilities. Furthermore, we find several copies that were pre-produced, leaving space for the name of the future owner (Fig. 7.1, Fig. 7.4).

In cases of such mass-produced papyri, the scribe had to fill all the empty spaces, either with only the name of the beneficiary or together with his or her title(s), proper name, epithets, and genealogy—sometimes up to about 400 times within a single manuscript—using many orthographical variations (e. g. Verhoeven, 1993 I: 3 and 349–51). Alan Shorter (1934: 34) discovered that in the case of the leather manuscript of Neby-mes, the scribe not only inserted the name of the owner in the space after "Osiris," but also erased pronouns of the first person singular or the word for "man," which occurs in the titles of Book of the Dead spells, and replaced them with the name of the owner, Neby-mes. If a woman received a manuscript originally intended for a male owner, some vignettes could also be adapted or changed to reflect a female owner (Fig. 7.2; Verhoeven, 1993 I: 71–72; Töpfer, this volume).

The 20-meter-long Book of the Dead on P.Paris Louvre N 3091, dating from the end of the Twenty-sixth Dynasty, was originally made for a priest called Ar-Ptah-Hep. It was later changed to become the papyrus for "the general Menenwahibre," with different titles and names for the father and another name for the mother. The title, name, and genealogy of the first owner were removed in the initial sections and the spaces were filled with the new owner's information (Verhoeven, 2001: 73–74 with pl. 3). Later in the same papyrus, the passages with the original name were simply struck through (cf. Mosher, 2008: 239, Fig. 1). Whether this is a case of usurpation (Verhoeven, 2001; Wüthrich, 2015: 215) or the man simply changed his name during his lifetime (Quack, 2016: 270) is still to be discussed. Although there are a lot of examples of the mass production of papyri, this custom was not as common for mummy bandages with Book of the Dead texts (Kockelmann, 2008 II: 143–45).

FIG. 7.2. Stock produced Book of the Dead for the lady Iahtesnakht from Herakleopolis magna (c. 600 BCE). In the vignette to BD Spell 15, her name is added to the figures of the goddesses Isis and Nephthys and to the wife of the presupposed male papyrus owner.

Credit line: P.Colon. Aeg. 10207.2 (detail). © Institut für Altertumskunde an der Universität zu Köln; https://papyri.uni-koeln.de/stueck/tm57143.

## Workshops and *Vorlagen*

There must have been workshops where trained scribes and draftsmen prepared Book of the Dead documents on linen, leather, or papyrus using master copies for individual spells or complete sets of spells. Whether these workshops were always directly connected with temples (e.g., the per-ankh "House of Life," cf. e.g., Albert, 2013

I: 152–54; Cancik-Kirschbaum and Kahl, 2018: 112–19) and whether other cities apart from Memphis, Herakleopolis, Akhmim, Abydos, and Thebes also played a major role in the tradition and the use of Book of the Dead papyri is hard to say (for the groups and traditions during the Late Period, cf. Mosher, 2016: 8). We know of only a very few cases of real master copies; for example, the Papyrus Vandier from the end of the Saite Period, of which the verso was used for Book of the Dead spells using *mn* ("so-and-so") instead of a personal name (cf. Verhoeven, 2001: 330–31) or the completely hieratic Book of the Dead on P.London BM EA 10098 + 10844, which was written with a Greek-style split reed, a calamus, as early as the second half of the first century BCE and also used *mn*, but this time in demotic (Quirke, 1999: 91–92).

Several groups of sources seem to be based on the same *Vorlagen*, for example the so-called Deir el-Medina group (Lüscher, 2013, 2015); the twin papyri of Paennestitauy and Gatseshen, the first one dated exactly in the second year of Amenemope (Munro, 2001: 69; Lucarelli, 2006); the group of the priests of Montu in the beginning of the Twenty-sixth Dynasty in Thebes (Verhoeven, 1999, 2017); and the Ptolemaic Akhmim group (Mosher, 2016–2018, Vol. 1: 35–36; Stadler, 2012: 156). At the end of the Twenty-sixth Dynasty, a master copy was transferred from Thebes to Memphis (Munro, 2010, 2011, 2012). Kockelmann (2008 II: 118–23) discussed further examples of workshops where papyrus and/or mummy bandages could have been produced. In the case of three papyri from the fourth century BCE from Thebes, Backes proved that they must have been made in the same workshop, but nevertheless uniquely: different-colored vignettes from the Book of the Dead as well as some traditional Book of the Dead spells were mixed with other funerary texts, and each papyrus displayed its own selection of spells (Backes, 2009: 101–2).

## Scribes Copying and Checking

In a few cases, it is obvious that the owner of a Book of the Dead manuscript was most likely also its writer: the high-quality papyrus of Nebseni (P.London BM EA 9900) dates to the Eighteenth Dynasty, measures 23 66 x 34.3 centimeters, and is written and drawn only with black and red ink (Fig. 7.3). The owner was a "scribe," "draftsman," and "scribe-copyist" (*sẖꜣ sp̱ẖrw*) of several temples in Memphis. The last title indicates that he was responsible for the copying of texts in cursive script on papyri or stelae (Lapp, 2004: 28). Even though the vignettes and the images of the papyrus owner himself are quite elaborate (Lapp, 2004: pl. 96), the scribe made some mistakes because he mixed up the lines he copied from the *Vorlage* (Lapp, 2004: 64–65).

In another case, the bad handwriting, the erroneous text, and the fact that the name is mentioned many times may indicate that the shroud of a man called Siaa ("big man") was not written by a professional scribe, but probably by Si-aa himself (Munro, 1994: 34). Yet, the writer of a late papyrus is supposedly a man called Padimenu, since he is named in a demotic note at the beginning (Kockelmann, 2008 II: 117).

We also know about some scribal practices concerning the Book of the Dead from certain colophons. One very elaborate example is in the papyrus of Yuya (from the time

FIG. 7.3. Book of the Dead of Nebseni from Saqqara (c. 1400 BCE) with cursive hieroglyphic and retrograde writing. Nebseni was "scribe-copyist" and has presumably written his own papyrus. The papyrus case under his seat is named "container of scripts" and the word "script" is written with the hieratic sign.

Credit: P.London BM EA 9900.32 (detail). © The Trustees of the British Museum.

of Amenhotep III) and is positioned at the end of the roll, after the texts of BD 149 and before its vignettes (= BD 150) in the last text columns 971 and 972: "It came (has been finished) from the beginning until the end like it was found <in> the script, copied (sphr. tj), collated (shsf.tj), checked (smtr.tj), and emended (smlḫ.tj) sign by sign, (for?) the god's father Yuya, justified." (cf. Lenzo Marchese, 2004: 369).

In fact, we sometimes find corrections and additions in the manuscripts which show that the copyist himself or another editor checked the texts. Missing passages were inserted between the lines or marked with a small cross or the hieroglyph of the walking legs and added below the column (e.g., Lapp, 1997: pl. 21, line BD 71/8–9: pl. 56, line BD 50/1: pl. 58–59: line BD 153A/32–33; Verhoeven, 2020: 103–108). On the other hand, the scribes marked missing passages in the *Vorlage* with the note *gm wš* "found destroyed."

Since the whole composition of the Book of the Dead was supposed to be a great secret, or at least restricted knowledge of the scribal elite, and was believed to have magical power, some spells include instructions for accurate and secret copying. Three examples can be cited from the Book of the Dead of Nu from the early Eighteenth

Dynasty: in BD 137A the text says (Lapp, 1997: pl. 78, line BD 137A/37–38; cf. also Eyre, 2013: 52; see also the commentary on these colophons by Stadler, 2009: 70–89): "Copy (*sph̲r*) this text as it was found in written form. The prince Djed-ef-hor was the one who found it in a secret box, in the handwriting of the god himself in the temple of Unut, lady of Hermopolis…"

BD 144 warns (Lapp, 1997: pl. 76, line BD 144/49): "You should use this book roll without anybody being allowed to see it." And similarly, BD 148 stipulates (Lapp, 1997: pl. 32, line BD 148/17–18): "Don't use it for anybody except yourself, this book roll of Wennefer." A postscript, which is not attested before the Late Period, is that of BD 161 (Verhoeven, 1993 I: 329; II: 135*): "It is a secret, which the rabble should not know. You should not use it for anybody, even your father or your son, except for yourself, because it is a real secret, not even one of the crowd should know it."

In the New Kingdom, it was usually only a single scribe who wrote a complete Book of the Dead manuscript, whereas the long papyri of later periods show that several scribes took the writing in turns but in different stages. For example, the partly preserved early Saite Book of the Dead of the priest of Montu Khamhor C was written by four scribes (Verhoeven, 2017: 55–66) as well as the nearly 24-meter-long complete text of the papyrus of the lady Iah-tes-nakht from the middle of the Saite Period: three scribes wrote the entire text, and the fourth one was responsible for inserting the names. Here, the first one wrote about 17 meters, the second about 4 meters, starting in the middle of the text of BD 144 and continuing until the end, while the third added only four narrow columns in between with the complete texts of BD 157–160 (Verhoeven, 1993 I: 340–43; paleographical comparison in Verhoeven, 2001: 102–225). Also, the Ptolemaic papyrus of Hor (Munro, 2006), which today consists of 766 hieroglyphic vertical columns, was written by at least four scribes. Only one of the scribes wrote a few longer passages, while the hands usually switched after only four, five, or eight vertical columns, but never within a single spell. These details enable us to distinguish different qualities and characters of the scribes. It is also obvious that near the end, the scribe changed his writing style, becoming nervous and irregular, maybe because he anticipated the end of his work (Munro, 2006: 6–13). The evidence of different scribes is not as clear in the case of mummy bandages; Kockelmann (2008 II: 134–36) mentions only a few unquestionable cases.

There are no general indications for the daily writing quota of the individual scribes or for the time span between the order and the delivery of a Book of the Dead manuscript. If it was ordered just after somebody's death, then the scribe would of course have had to finish it before the funeral. In the Saite hieratic Book of the Dead of Iah-tes-nakht, two cursive hieratic/early demotic notes on the margin of the papyrus give specifications of the day but are presumably written by different hands: above column 10 was written "day 24," while "day 6" is noted above column 17. The name of the month(s) is not mentioned. If it was the sixth day of the next month, the time span was eleven days, but we don't know if the scribe was working every day and always busy with this papyrus or other tasks (Verhoeven, 1993 I: 339, 347).

It is possible in some manuscripts to determine in which intervals the scribe took fresh ink. The analysis of dippings in the Book of the Dead of Khamhor C (Verhoeven, 2017: 64–66) could demonstrate that scribe B had very good, long-lasting ink, while scribes C and D had to dip twice to three times more frequently. Scribe B also tended to dip after words or other semantic units, while the others mostly preferred to dip mechanically at the beginning of a line.

## Layout and Vignettes

The writing traditions of Book of the Dead manuscripts include several features that concern the layout:

- different kinds of lines with a clear hierarchy,
- spaces for headings and postscripts as well as captions,
- varying combinations of vignettes (within the text flow or in a special register),
- large and narrow columns,
- charts for lists of names or places with space-saving layouts to avoid repetitions (e.g., in the lists of body parts),
- spaces at the end of a spell or for structuring a long text (different traditions for hieratic and hieroglyphic texts, and for several purposes [cf. Rössler-Köhler, 1984–1985]),
- and finally, the use of red ink (Fig. 7.4) for special passages of the spells ("spell of...," "another spell...," "to be recited by...," "to be used for...," also for names of dangerous beings like Apophis, etc.). The names of gods and places within rubric passages were always written in black (cf. Allen, 1936, for the Book of the Dead, Posener, 1949, 1951, as a general overview, and further comments in recent Book of the Dead editions). A small papyrus from the Nineteenth Dynasty first shows the use of red ink—for BD 100 as a charm—which was written over with white ink afterward except for the name of Apophis (Taylor, 2010: 47).

Writing down the texts seems to have taken place after marking the papyrus with different lines for the spaces of the headlines, vignettes, spells, and columns, for which Ursula Rössler-Köhler (1990) worked out the ancient system. Sometimes the scribes faced problems because the intended text was too long or too short for the given space. Each scribe reacted differently: by enlarging or minimizing their signs, adding titles or an elaborate genealogy of the owner, using margins, lines, or columns outside the determined space, cutting the text of the spell, or even leaving columns partially empty. If the text was too long for the designated column, a scribe might also use the margins or other empty spaces to continue the text, applying small circles or the sign of the finger to indicate where the misplaced passages belonged (Verhoeven, 1999: photo pl. 11, line 22, photo pl. 17, line 28–29; Quack, 2005; Verhoeven, 2020).

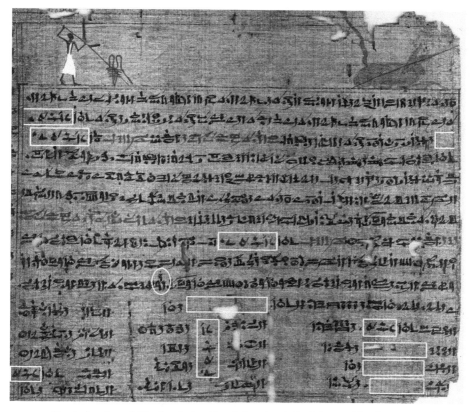

FIG. 7.4. Stock produced Book of the Dead for the lady Iahtesnakht from Herakleopolis magna (c. 600 BCE). The titles of BD spells and recitation remarks are written in red. The names of the owner are added later in the allocated spaces—but not everywhere—within the text and the charts (white rectangles). The white oval marks the addition of a forgotten sign above the line.

Credit line: P.Colon. Aeg. 10207.9 (detail; white lines added by the author). © Institut für Altertumskunde an der Universität zu Köln; https://papyri.uni-koeln.de/stueck/tm57143.

Chloé Ragazzoli (2010) discussed the question of whether the vignettes were always drawn after the text was written. In her example (P.Paris BN 62–88, Twenty-first Dynasty), unusual "marginalia" were added to denote which vignettes were to be added, for instance "falcon" or "the lotus" (Ragazzoli, 2010: 232–33). The variation of combining text lines and vignettes shows a close cooperation between scribe and draftsman. Therefore, it seems clear that vignettes were drafted before the texts (cf. another example in the papyrus of the royal scribe and general Nakht in Fig. 7.5).

In two papyri of Theban priests of Montu from the beginning of the Twenty-sixth Dynasty it is clear that the extensive texts were written first because the spaces for the vignettes are still empty or have only a few preparatory drafts (Verhoeven, 1999: 50; 2017: 37–43). In the Book of the Dead of Kham-hor there is a note inserted

FIG. 7.5. Book of the Dead of Nakht from Thebes (c. 1300 BCE). In the lower right corner, the scribe wrote the last words of his litany to Re (BD Spell 15) on the surface of the colored vignette which was therefore painted first.

Credit line: P.London BM EA 10471.21 (detail). © The Trustees of the British Museum

into an empty space saying "to be made according to this image which is in script" (Verhoeven, 2017: 42). However, splashes of white color from the vignettes that trickled down on to the writing in the nearly contemporary papyrus of Iah-tes-nakht demonstrate that the drawing or at least the coloring was the last step (Verhoeven, 1993: 13–14).

## Scripts and Writing Directions

A history of scripts used for Books of the Dead throughout the ages is still lacking. We find hieratic, more or less cursive hieroglyphic in different directions, and rarely demotic. Sometimes the scripts are mixed within one document, like in the Eighteenth-Dynasty Book of the Dead of Sobek-mose (O'Rourke, 2016: 55: recto cursive hieroglyphs, verso hieratic), and sometimes one person could have both a hieratic and a hieroglyphic Book of the Dead papyrus (Queen Nedjmet, Twenty-first Dynasty).

At the beginning of the redaction of the Book of the Dead, the Theban coffins of Queen Mentuhotep (Geisen, 2004: Thirteenth Dynasty) and Prince Herunefer (Parkinson and Quirke, 1992: Seventeenth Dynasty) seem to be the first "indisputable" sources of this funerary text genre. The Book of the Dead texts are written in hieratic columns without any vignettes on the inner surfaces of the coffins, while the outer surfaces (preserved only on the coffin of Mentu-hotep) are still decorated with hieroglyphic lines of Coffin Texts (Gestermann, 2012). At the beginning of the Eighteenth Dynasty, the leather manuscript BM EA 10281, first used as a *Vorlage* before the name of Neby-mes was inserted for his funeral (Shorter, 1934), was also written in hieratic columns.

Other early sources used single horizontal lines or vertical columns, and some were written with cursive hieroglyphs, which were traditionally used for sacred texts "appropriate for a temple or royal library" (Parkinson and Quirke, 1995: 26). Louise Gestermann (2006: 105) concludes that the written form of the early Book of the Dead texts (i.e., hieratic) was also adopted from the *Vorlagen*, not only the content and sequences of spells.

The cursive or linear hieroglyphs that came into use for Book of the Dead manuscripts during the entire New Kingdom are sometimes called *Totenbuchkursive* (cursive script of the Book of the Dead), which is misleading, since this kind of writing of linear hieroglyphs with ink was used as early as the Fourth Dynasty (cf. Junker, 1940: pl. 3. 10), and extensively in the Coffin Texts of the Middle Kingdom. It was developed as a parallel to hieratic and sculptured hieroglyphs, and its use was not restricted to Book of the Dead texts (Verhoeven, 2015: 38). The cursive hieroglyphs, as used in Book of the Dead manuscripts of the New Kingdom, mostly show variations by the same scribes and include several hieratic signs that were not used consequently, but may have been employed due to issues of space and time (Fig. 7.6; see e.g., lists by Munro, 1987: 254–57, and commentaries and examples by Lüscher, 2008: 4–6; Graefe, 2015). It does not seem to be by chance that the sign for "script," "scribe," and "to write" is mostly written in its hieratic form within cursive hieroglyphic texts or captions (Fig. 7.3; cf. also Lapp, 2014), since the scribes themselves were so familiar with this word.

During the New Kingdom, the hieroglyphic manuscripts with the Book of the Dead were mostly written in retrograde (75 copies from the Eighteenth Dynasty, 36 from the Nineteenth/Twentieth Dynasty), which means that the text starts on the left side and faces the right (usually indicating a reading direction from right to left) and that the reader has to open the book roll at the unusual end (cf. also Goelet, this volume). This opposite, or mirrored, direction in comparison with the normal way of writing and reading was explained as being chosen because the vignette of the funerary procession (BD 1) started on the left (i.e., on the eastern side, according to the Egyptians' view of their land) and included many figures walking toward the right side, i.e., the west, the land of the deceased and the place where the sun set. Michael Chegodaev (1996), who proposed this as a reason, explained it in view of the Egyptians' habit of assuming the

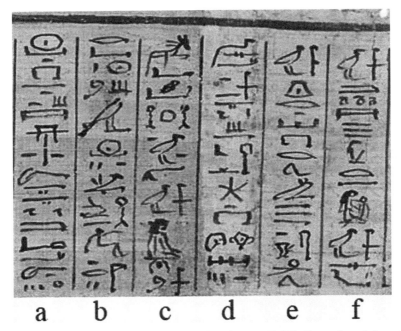

a     b     c     d     e     f

FIG. 7.6. Book of the Dead of Nakht from Thebes (c. 1300 BCE). Examples of the mixture of cursive hieroglyphs, elaborate signs (line c and f: woman giving birth and suckling) and hieratic forms (line b: *pʒ*-bird without phonetic complements).

Credit line: P.London BM EA 10471.21 (detail; letters added by the author).
© The Trustees of the British Museum.

viewing direction of human and animate beings in hieroglyphs and pictures. The "false" direction would not have caused any problems for the users of the papyri because the world of the deceased was conceived as mirror-inverted, and because traveling from west to east was perceived as dangerous. Andrzej Niwiński (1989: 15–17), who was not cited by Chegodaev, made a similar argument. Sometimes we find a change of writing direction within a unit of text, for example, when the text belongs to figures facing each other in a vignette (Fig. 7.7). Such changes could cause mistakes when the text was copied for other layouts, of course (e.g., in P.Leiden T 3, cf. Graefe, 1993).

In addition to the retrograde writing, there are some manuscripts that show the normal orientation and reading direction of signs (from right to left, signs facing right: 11 copies from the Eighteenth Dynasty, 8 from the Nineteenth/Twentieth Dynasty) and others that must be read from left to right and with signs facing left (two copies from the Eighteenth Dynasty; for all numbers see Munro, 1987: 200 and 261–63). A Book of the Dead papyrus with retrograde hieroglyphs in which the scribe used hieratic numbers on top of the sheets also shows how exceptional a retrograde direction was in daily scribal practice (Fig. 7.1; cf. already Parkinson and Quirke, 1995: 40, Fig. 25; Taylor, 2010: 266 with other sections).

The number of hieratic papyri constitutes only about 5 percent of all sources during the New Kingdom according to the Book of the Dead database (http://totenbuch.

FIG. 7.7. Book of the Dead of Nakht from Thebes (c. 1300 BCE). The normal text orientation (lines 1 and 2 belonging to Osiris, lines 3–6 with the beginning of the sun hymn spoken by Nakht) changes in the middle of line 6—including some errors—into retrograde direction, which continues in the following columns.

Credit line: P.London BM EA 10471.21 (detail; numbers added by the author).
© The Trustees of the British Museum.

awk.nrw.de//; there are only 15 hieratic versus 311 hieroglyphic papyri from the New Kingdom).

Beginning with the Twenty-first Dynasty, Book of the Dead papyri are mostly written in hieratic wherein it is impossible to change the direction of writing—it always runs from right to left and, since the Middle Kingdom, in horizontal lines exclusively. Therefore, the vignette of the funerary procession (BD 1) also starts on the right side and the people walk toward the left. Giuseppina Lenzo Marchese (2007a: 1118) proposed reasons for the change of script. She suggested that an accumulation of papyri and quick-to-write texts probably took the place of the absent tomb decoration and that at that time the hieratic script was possibly more easily understood than the elaborate cursive hieroglyphs. For the Third Intermediate Period, Lenzo (2007b: 201–7) stated that hieratic became increasingly more cursive under Pinudjem II, while it was written less cursively and more distinctly and clearly under Psusennes (Pasebakhaennut) III (Lenzo, 2007b: 207).

In the Twenty-fifth to Twenty-sixth dynasties only about 10 percent of the papyri were written in hieroglyphs, while the long papyrus rolls of this period were entirely composed in hieratic (Verhoeven, 2001: 17–19; 1993, 1999, 2017; Munro, 2010, 2011, 2012).

An exceptional case is the Book of the Dead on wood from the burial of a priest called Nekau at Abusir; possibly because of the shortage of papyrus in these times, the scribe used "third-hand" material for writing down the hieratic texts. The wooden pieces were originally parts of a painted box, which were then stuccoed to make apprentice boards. Finally, they were used for the Book of the Dead spells and placed inside the outer coffin of Nekau (Janák and Landgráfová, 2010).

In the Ptolemaic and Roman Periods, approximately a quarter of the papyri were again executed in cursive hieroglyphs; the remaining ones were still in hieratic. As for the mummy bandages of the Thirtieth Dynasty and of the Ptolemaic Period, far less than 10 percent of them use hieroglyphs. Yet, all these numbers are far from definite, mostly due to the problems in dating the sources. Neither is it specified whether the entire text of a hieratic manuscript is written in hieroglyphs or only the captions. In addition, the registered sources are very different in size, ranging from very small fragments to long rolls of about 20–40 meters. In the so-called Akhmim group, dating into the Early Ptolemaic Period, the retrograde writing of hieroglyphs underwent a revival (Mosher, 2016–2018: 35). For the Late and Ptolemaic Periods, a synoptic edition and commentary of a great number of sources is available (Mosher, 2017–2021). The end of the hieratic Book of the Dead tradition is marked by combinations with other funerary texts, like the Book of Breathing (Albert, Scalf, and Kucharek, this volume). During the late Ptolemaic and the Roman Periods, the calamus rather than the reed pen came into use, a custom that may have started in the middle of the second century BCE (Quirke, 1999; Quack, 2015). Nevertheless, a very late pair of manuscripts coming from the same workshop from the time between the first century BCE and the first century CE were written with a reed pen and in hieratic, but by different scribes: one wrote very thoroughly on horizontal auxiliary lines and with linear vignettes, the other rapidly, without lines, yet with colored vignettes (Töpfer and Müller-Roth, 2011: 16–20).

A handful of sources transmit single chapters of the Book of the Dead in demotic together with other texts for the afterlife: these are BD 15A with a hymn to the sun, BD 125 with the negative confession, and BD 171 (Pleyte) belonging to the funerary rituals (for sources and discussion cf. Stadler, 2012: 87–88, 130–33).

The main tendencies in the choice of script can be summarized as follows:

- Thirteenth to beginning of the Eighteenth Dynasty: hieratic without vignettes
- Eighteenth to Twentieth Dynasty: cursive hieroglyphs, retrograde, regularly with vignettes
- Twenty-first to Twenty-second Dynasty: hieratic starting in the second half of the Twenty-first Dynasty, often with hieroglyphic texts in the large vignettes
- Twenty-fifth to Twenty-sixth Dynasty: mostly hieratic
- Thirtieth Dynasty to Ptolemaic Period: papyri mostly hieratic, less hieroglyphic (retrograde in Akhmim); mummy bandages mostly hieratic
- Roman Period: hieratic, only three single spells in demotic

It is still very difficult to date a manuscript based only on the character of the script. Scholars have tried to formulate tendencies; for example, Matthieu Heerma van Voss (1977: 86) has stated that in the beginning of the New Kingdom one finds a robust character, and that later the script became more fluent. The research on the paleography of hieratic and cursive hieroglyphs in manuscripts of the Book of the Dead has intensified during the last two decades. Munro developed criteria for the New Kingdom, especially for hieratic signs within cursive hieroglyphic texts (list in Munro, 1987: 254–57) and for the cursive hieroglyphs themselves (Munro, 1987: Ch. V, 190–97): for example, the position of the arms in the sign of the seated man (Gardiner Sign-list A1: 𓀀) was thought to differ characteristically in the periods before and after Amarna. Further documents indicate that this does not seem to be so significant (Lüscher, 2008: 5). Another criterion could be—in the pre-Amarna period of the Eighteenth Dynasty—that ideograms and determinatives of gods or divine objects and terms are often executed on a larger scale, thus applying a standard according to the higher prominence of these objects (Lüscher, 2008: 6–8).

The painted tomb inscriptions in the Theban tomb of Sennedjem deliver a complete inventory of the cursive hieroglyphs used for Book of the Dead spells as well (Haring, 2006).

For the Third Intermediate Period, we have a detailed analysis of the hieratic script of the Book of the Dead papyri of the Egyptian Museum, Turin (Lenzo Marchese, 2007b), and special contributions about significant forms of Gardiner Sign-list R8 𓊹 here and V28 𓎛 in the late eighth century to the middle of the seventh century BCE (Taylor, 2006: 358 and passim). In addition, some major hieratic sources of the Twenty-sixth Dynasty have been studied entirely (Verhoeven, 2001, 2017: 55–66; Gasse, 2002). For the Ptolemaic period, the cursive hieroglyphs of some papyri have been analyzed (Lüscher, 2000: 6–7; Munro, 2006: 6–13) as well as the hieratic script on the mummy bandages of Hor (Kockelmann, 2008 I: 26–43).

## Conclusion

The search for scribes, their skilled manual work, and their methods of organizing the huge amounts of papyrus sheets and difficult text versions, in combination with detailed vignettes, is very fascinating. Studying their hieratic or cursive hieroglyphic handwriting is like looking over the shoulders of the individuals. The traces of their ink on a linen shroud or a papyrus sheet give us—apart from long-standing traditions—a vivid insight into their different stages of knowledge and beliefs, and even into more personal situations in which they were tired, produced mistakes, or suddenly discovered a solution to optimize their product.

The interest in the material aspects of ancient Egyptian manuscripts has increased since the so-called "material turn" influenced the research topics of the written culture. Therefore, it is no surprise that questions of how to make a Book of the Dead, as well as other papyri, are dealt with in publications of the past ten years, such as Etienne and Pagès-Camagna (2013), Eyre (2013), Kockelmann (2017), Meyer, Ott, and Sauer, eds. (2015), Mosher (2017–2021: Vol. 1: 50–57), Ryholt (2017), and Verhoeven (2016).

## Bibliography

Albert, F. (2013). *Le Livre des Morts d'Aset-Oueret*, 2 vols. (Vatican: Edizioni Musei Vaticani).
Allen, T. G. (1936). "Types of Rubrics in the Egyptian Book of the Dead." *Journal of the American Oriental Society* 56: 145–54.
Backes, B. (2009). *Drei Totenpapyri aus einer thebanischen Werkstatt der Spätzeit*. Handschriften zum altägyptischen Totenbuchs 11 (Wiesbaden: Harrassowitz).
Cancik-Kirschbaum, E. and Kahl, J. (2018). *Erste Philologien. Archäologie einer Disziplin vom Tigris bis zum Nil* (Tübingen: Mohr Siebeck).
Chegodaev, M. A. (1996). "Some Remarks Regarding the so-called "Retrograde" Direction of Writing in the Ancient Egyptian "Book of the Dead." *Discussions in Egyptology* 35: 19–24.
Etienne, M. and Pagès-Camagna, S. (2013). "Illustrer un papyrus." In *L'art du contour. Le dessin dans l'Egypte ancienne*, edited by G. Andreu-Lanoë, 74–79 (Paris: Musée du Louvre).
Eyre, C. (2013). *The Use of Documents in Pharaonic Egypt* (Oxford: University Press).
Gasse, A. (2002). *Un papyrus et son scribe. Le Livre des Morts Vatican—Museo Gregoriano Egizio 48832* (Paris: Cybele).
Geisen, C. (2004). *Die Totentexte des verschollenen Sarges der Königin Mentuhotep aus der 13. Dynastie: Ein Textzeuge aus der Übergangszeit von den Sargtexten zum Totenbuch*. Studien zum altägyptischen Totenbuch 8 (Wiesbaden: Harrassowitz).
Gestermann, L. (2006). "Aufgelesen: Die Anfänge des altägyptischen Totenbuchs." In *Totenbuch-Forschungen: Gesammelte Beiträge des 2. Internationalen Totenbuch-Symposiums 2005*, Studien zum altägyptischen Totenbuch 11, edited by B. Backes, I. Munro, and S. Stöhr, 101–13 (Wiesbaden: Harrassowitz).
Gestermann, L. (2012). "Auf dem Weg zum Totenbuch: Von Tradition und Neuerung." In *Herausgehen am Tage: Gesammelte Schriften zum altägyptischen Totenbuch*. Studien zum altägyptischen Totenbuch 17, edited by R. Lucarelli, M. Müller-Roth, and A. Wüthrich, 67–78 (Wiesbaden: Harrassowitz).
Graefe, E. (1993). "Papyrus Leiden T3 oder: Über das Kopieren von Texten durch altägyptische Schreiber." *Oudheidkundige Mededelingen uit het Rijksmuseum van Oudheden te Leiden* 73: 23–28.
Graefe, E. (2015). "Hieroglyphische, kursivhieroglyphische und hieratische Schriftzeichen in Totentexten." In *Ägyptologische "Binsen"-Weisheiten I–II, Akten zweier Tagungen in Mainz im April 2011 und März 2013*. Abhandlungen der Akademie der Wissenschaften und der Literatur Mainz 14, edited by U. Verhoeven, 119–42 (Stuttgart: Franz Steiner).
Haring, B. J. J. (2006). *The Tomb of Sennedjem (TT1) in Deir El-Medina. Palaeography*. Paléographie Hiéroglyphique 2 (Cairo: Institut Français d'Archéologie Orientale).
Heerma van Voss, M. (1977). "Over het dateren van dodenboeken." *Phoenix* 23: 84–89.
Janák, J. and Landgráfová, R. (2010). "Colourful spells and wooden grid: Nekau's Book of the Dead once more." In *Egypt in Transition: Social and Religious Development of Egypt in the First Millennium BCE. Proceedings of an International Conference, Prague, September 1–4, 2009*, edited by L. Bareš, F. Coppens, and K. Smoláriková, 219–23 (Prague: Czech Institute of Egyptology, Charles University in Prague).

Junker, H. (1940). *Die Mastaba des Kai-em-anch.* Giza IV (Wien und Leipzig: Hölder-Pichler-Tempsky A.G.).

Kockelmann, H. (2008). *Untersuchungen zu den späten Totenbuch-Handschriften auf Mumienbinden,* 2 vols., Studien zum altägyptischen Totenbuch 12 (Wiesbaden: Harrassowitz).

Kockelmann, H. (2017). "How a Book of the Dead Manuscript was Produced." In *Book of the Dead: Becoming God in Ancient Egypt.* Oriental Institute Museum Publications 39, edited by F. Scalf, 67–74 (Chicago: The Oriental Institute).

Lapp, G. (1997). *The Papyrus of Nu (BM EA 10477): With a Ccontribution by T. Schneider.* Catalogue of the Books of the Dead in the British Museum 1 (London: British Museum Press).

Lapp, G. (2004). *The Papyrus of Nebseni (BM EA 9900).* Catalogue of the Books of the Dead in the British Museum 3 (London: British Museum Press).

Lapp, G. (2014). *British Museum Totenbuch-Papyrus Nebamun (BM EA 9964).* Beiträge zum Alten Ägypten 5 (Basel: Orientverlag).

Leach, B. and Parkinson, R. (2010). "Creating Borders: New Insights into Making the Papyrus of Ani." *British Museum Studies in Ancient Egypt and the Sudan* 15: 35–62.

Lenzo Marchese, G. (2004). "Les colophons dans la littérature égyptienne." *Bulletin de l'Institut Français d'Archéologie Orientale* 104(1): 359–76.

Lenzo Marchese, G. (2007a). "Les abrégés hiératiques du Livre des Morts durant la troisième période intermédiaire." In *Proceedings of the Ninth International Congress of Egyptologists,* OLA 150, II, edited by J.-C. Goyon and C. Cardin, 1117–24 (Leuven; Paris; Dudley, MA: Peeters).

Lenzo Marchese, G. (2007b). *Manuscrits hiératiques du Livre des Morts de la troisième période intermédiaire (papyrus de Turin CGT 53001–53013).* Cahiers de la Société d'Égyptologie 8; Catalogo del Museo Egizio di Torino, serie seconda—collezioni 11 (Geneva: Société d'Égyptologie).

Lucarelli, R. (2006). *The Book of the Dead of Gatseshen: Ancient Egyptian Funerary Religion in the 10th century BC.* Egyptologische Uitgaven 21 (Leiden: Nederlands Instituut voor het Nabije Oosten).

Lüscher, B. (2000). *Das Totenbuch des pBerlin P. 10477 aus Achmim (mit Photographien des verwandten pHildesheim 5248).* Handschriften zum altägyptischen Totenbuchs 6 (Wiesbaden: Harrassowitz).

Lüscher, B. (2008). *Der Totenbuch-Papyrus Princeton Pharaonic Roll 5.* Beiträge zum Alten Ägypten 2 (Basel: Orientverlag).

Lüscher, B. (2013). *Die Vorlagen-Ostraka aus dem Grab des Nachtmin (TT 87).* Beiträge zum Alten Ägypten 4 (Basel: Orientverlag).

Lüscher, B. (2015). "Kursivhieroglyphische Ostraka als Textvorlagen: Der (Glücks-)Fall TT 87." In *Ägyptologische "Binsen"-Weisheiten I–II, Akten zweier Tagungen in Mainz im April 2011 und März 2013.* Abhandlungen der Akademie der Wissenschaften und der Literatur Mainz 14, edited by U. Verhoeven, 85–117 (Stuttgart: Franz Steiner).

Meier, Th., Ott, M. R., and Sauer, R., eds. (2015). *Materiale Textkulturen. Konzept—Materialien—Praktiken* (Berlin; München; Boston: de Gruyter).

Mosher, M. Jr. (2008). "Five Versions of Spell 19 from the Late Period Book of the Dead." In *Egypt and Beyond: Essays Presented to Leonard H. Lesko upon his Retirement from the Wilbour Chair of Egyptology at Brown University June 2005,* edited by S. E. Thompson and P. Der Manuelian, 237–60 (Providence, RI: Brown Univ., Dep. of Egyptology and Ancient Western Asian Studies).

Mosher, M. Jr. (2017–2021). *The Book of the Dead Saite through Ptolemaic Periods: A Study of Traditions Evident in Versions of Texts and Vignettes,* Vol. 1–6 and 8–10 to be continued (Prescott, AZ: SPBD Studies, Malcom Mosher Jr.).

Munro, I. (1987). *Untersuchungen zu den Totenbuch-Papyri der 18. Dynastie: Kriterien ihrer Datierung* (London; New York: Kegan Paul International).

Munro, I. (1994). *Die Totenbuch-Handschriften der 18. Dynastie im Ägyptischen Museum Cairo*, 2 vols., Ägyptologische Abhandlungen 54 (Wiesbaden: Harrassowitz).

Munro, I. (2001). *Das Totenbuch des Pa-en-nesti-taui aus der Regierungszeit des Amenemope* (pLondon BM 10064), Handschriften zum altägyptischen Totenbuchs 7 (Wiesbaden: Harrassowitz).

Munro, I. (2006). *Der Totenbuch-Papyrus des Hor aus der frühen Ptolemäerzeit*. Handschriften zum altägyptischen Totenbuchs 9 (Wiesbaden: Harrassowitz).

Munro, I. (2010). "Evidence of a Master Copy Transferred from Thebes to the Memphis Area in Dynasty 26." *British Museum Studies in Ancient Egypt and Sudan* 15: 201–24.

Munro, I. (2011). *Die Totenbuch-Papyri des Ehepaars Ta-scheret-en-Aset und des Djed-chi aus der Bes-en-Mut-Familie* (26. Dynastie, Zeit des Königs Amasis). Handschriften zum altägyptischen Totenbuchs 12 (Wiesbaden: Harrassowitz).

Munro, I. (2012). "Die Fragmente zweier Totenbücher der 26. Dynastie." In *Herausgehen am Tage: Gesammelte Schriften zum altägyptischen Totenbuch*. Studien zum altägyptischen Totenbuch 17, edited by R. Lucarelli, M. Müller-Roth, and A. Wüthrich, 135–52 (Wiesbaden: Harrassowitz).

Niwiński, A. (1989). *Studies on the Illustrated Theban Funerary Papyri of the 11th and 10th Centuries B.C.*, Orbis biblicus et orientalis 86 (Freiburg, CH/Göttingen: Universitätsverlag; Vandenhoek & Ruprecht).

O'Rourke, P. F. (2016). *An Ancient Egyptian Book of the Dead. The Papyrus of Sobekmose* (London: Thames & Hudson).

Parkinson, R. and Quirke, S. (1992). "The Coffin of Prince Herunefer and the Early History of the *Book of the Dead*." In *Studies in Pharaonic Religion and Society in honour of J. Gwyn Griffiths*. Egypt Exploration Society Occasional Publications 8, edited by A. B. Lloyd, 37–51 (London: The Egypt Exploration Society).

Parkinson, R. and Quirke, S. (1995). *Papyrus* (London: British Museum Press).

Posener, G. (1949). "Les signes noirs dans les rubriques." *The Journal of Egyptian Archaeology* 35: 77–81.

Posener, G. (1951). "Sur l'emploi de l'encre rouge dans les manuscrits égyptiens." *The Journal of Egyptian Archaeology* 37: 75–80.

Quack, J. F. (2005). "Positionspräzise Nachträge in spätzeitlichen Handschriften." *Studien zur Altägyptischen Kultur* 33: 343–47.

Quack, J. F. (2015). "Rohrfedertorheiten? Bemerkungen zum römerzeitlichen Hieratisch." In *Ägyptologische "Binsen"-Weisheiten I–II, Akten zweier Tagungen in Mainz im April 2011 und März 2013*. Abhandlungen der Akademie der Wissenschaften und der Literatur Mainz 14, edited by U. Verhoeven, 435–68 (Stuttgart: Franz Steiner).

Quack, J. F. (2016). Rezension zu A. Wüthrich (2015) in: Welt des Orients, 46, 206, 268–78.

Quirke, S. (1999). "The Last Books of the Dead?" *Studies in Egyptian Antiquities. A Tribute to T.G.H. James*. British Museum Occasional Paper 123, edited by W. V. Davies, 83–98 (London: British Museum Press).

Ragazzoli, C. (2010). "The Book of the Dead of Ankhesenaset (P. BNF Egyptien 62–88). Traces of Workshop Production or Scribal Experiments?" *British Museum Studies in Ancient Egypt and the Sudan* 15: 225–48.

Rössler-Köhler, U. (1984–1985). "Zum Problem der Spatien in Altägyptischen Texten: Versuch einer Systematik von Spatientypen." *Annales du Service des Antiquités de l'Égypte* 70: 383–408.

Rössler-Köhler, U. (1990). "Die formale Aufteilung des Papyrus Jumilhac (Louvre E.17110)." *Chronique d'Égypte* 65: 21–40.

Ryholt, K. (2017). "Scribal Habits at the Tebtunis Temple Library: On Materiality, Formal Features, and Palaeography." In *Scribal Repertoires in Egypt from the New Kingdom to the Early Islamic Period*, edited by J. Cromwell and E. Grossmann, 153–83 (Oxford: Oxford University Press).

Shorter, A. (1934). "A Leather Manuscript of the Book of the Dead in the British Museum." *The Journal of Egyptian Archaeology* 20: 33–40.

Stadler, M. A. (2009). *Weiser und Wesir: Studien zu Vorkommen, Rolle und Wesen des Gottes Thot im ägyptischen Totenbuch*. Orientalische Religionen in der Antike 1 (Tübingen: Mohr Siebeck).

Stadler, M. A. (2012). *Einführung in die ägyptische Religion ptolemäisch-römischer Zeit nach den demotischen religiösen Texten*. Einführungen und Quellentexte zur Ägyptologie 7 (Berlin; Münster: Lit).

Taylor, J. H. (2006). "The Sign ⸗ (Gardiner V28) as a Dating Criterion for Funerary Texts of the Third Intermediate Period." In *Totenbuch-Forschungen: Gesammelte Beiträge des 2. Internationalen Totenbuch-Symposiums 2005*. Studien zum altägyptischen Totenbuch 11, edited by B. Backes, I. Munro, and S. Stöhr, Simone, 357–64 (Wiesbaden: Harrassowitz).

Taylor, J. H. (2010). *Ancient Egyptian Book of the Dead: Journey through the afterlife* (London: British Museum Press).

Töpfer, S. and Müller-Roth, M. (2011). *Das Ende der Totenbuchtradition und der Übergang zum Buch vom Atmen*. Handschriften zum altägyptischen Totenbuch 13 (Wiesbaden: Harrassowitz).

Verhoeven, U. (1993). *Das saitische Totenbuch der Iahtesnacht, P. Colon. Aeg 10207*. Papyrologische Texte und Abhandlungen 41/1-3 (Bonn: Habelt).

Verhoeven, U. (1999). *Das Totenbuch des Monthpriesters Nespasefy aus der Zeit Psammetichs I*. Handschriften zum altägyptischen Totenbuch 5 (Wiesbaden: Harrassowitz).

Verhoeven, U. (2001). *Untersuchungen zur späthieratischen Buchschrift*. Orientalia lovaniensia analecta 99 (Leuven: Peeters).

Verhoeven, U. (2015). "Stand und Aufgaben der Erforschung des Hieratischen und der Kursivhieroglyphen." In *Ägyptologische "Binsen"-Weisheiten I-II, Akten zweier Tagungen in Mainz im April 2011 und März 2013*. Abhandlungen der Akademie der Wissenschaften und der Literatur Mainz 14, edited by U. Verhoeven, 23–63 (Stuttgart: Franz Steiner).

Verhoeven, U. (2016). "Von Pyramiden und Papyrusrollen. Gedanken zur Materialität im Alten Ägypten." In *Materialität. Herausforderungen für die Sozial- und Kulturwissenschaften*, edited by H. Kalthoff, T. Cress, and T. Röhl, 289–303 (Paderborn: Wilhelm Fink).

Verhoeven, U. (2017). *Das frühsaitische Totenbuch des Monthpriesters Chamhor C*. Unter Mitarbeit von Sandra Sandri. Beiträge zum Alten Ägypten 7 (Basel: Orientverlag).

Verhoeven, U. (2020). "Paratextual Signs in Egyptian Funerary and Religious Texts from the Saite and Early Ptolemaic Period." In Signes dans les textes. Continuités et ruptures des pratiques scribales en Égypte pharaonique, gréco-romaine et byzantine. Actes du colloque international de Liège (2-4 June 2016). Papyrologica Leodiensia 9, edited by N. Carlig, G. Lescuyer, A. Motte, and N. Sojic, 95–112 (Liège: Presses universitaires de Liège).

Wüthrich, A. (2015). *Édition synoptique et traduction des chapitres supplémentaires du Livre des Morts 162 à 167*. Studien zum altägyptischen Totenbuch 19 (Wiesbaden: Harrassowitz).

http://totenbuch.awk.nrw.de//

http://www.trismegistos.org/index2.php

# CHAPTER 8

# PRODUCTION AND LAYOUT OF NEW KINGDOM BOOK OF THE DEAD PAPYRI

OGDEN GOELET

## THE IDEAL OR CLASSICAL FORM OF BOOK OF THE DEAD IN THE NEW KINGDOM

TODAY, one usually first encounters the Book of the Dead in a museum, displayed proudly as a large and highly prized representative of the Egyptian illustrated book par excellence (Černý, 1952: 25). In fact, much of the Book of the Dead's appeal to the modern museum audience probably lies in its well-ordered presentation—sections clearly demarked, with colorful vignettes that appear well integrated with the text. The Book of the Dead arguably achieved its most ornate form in the New Kingdom, between the Eighteenth and Twentieth Dynasties. These manuscripts might be considered "standard New Kingdom" Books of the Dead. This would be a rather cumbersome term if used often, so we shall instead call them "classical Books of the Dead," with the understanding that the adjective "classical" in this case has no connection with the culture and history of ancient Greece and Rome. The description following here focuses on these classical manuscripts since they presented scribes with the greatest challenges to produce their complex formatting and layout and thereby provide the most useful evidence about the manufacturing and design processes involved. All later forms of the Book of the Dead essentially represented either modifications or revivals of the same. In any case, a particular Book of the Dead, no matter when it was made, might have some standard feature missing or appearing in a variant form. No design feature of the Book of the Dead was absolutely required. An Egyptian scribe wished to produce a Book of the Dead—never *the* Book of the Dead, which, in any event, would be impossible. To describe the classical Books of the Dead, then, is to present an ideal.

To be sure, from the Egyptians' perspective, the Book of the Dead was first and foremost a key religious document in a funerary assemblage. At the same time, as with other funerary equipment, a high-quality roll would also be a mark of the owner's prestige. Several features of a Book of the Dead combined to provide it with the authority of exclusivity and antiquity that would hopefully impress the gods with its owner's worthiness and ritual wisdom. Ironically, some of the most striking exemplars were often products of a system of mass production, in the sense that they were prefabricated and carefully transcribed from master copies in funerary workshops. On close examination, we can see that many papyri were prepared in advance with no specific owner in mind, somewhat in the same manner as standard preprinted legal documents or form letters available in stationery stores today, featuring blank spaces where certain key information may be filled in as needed. We might describe these as stock papyri.

When we examine a given manuscript, we might find a standard feature missing or appearing in a variant form. No physical feature of the Book of the Dead was unique to the genre. In fact, each element of the standard Book of the Dead had, so to speak, a prehistory in earlier scribal practices that included the Coffin Texts (Gestermann, this volume) and some rather mundane bookkeeping. For instance, the visually striking tabular format of the classical Book of the Dead had its origins in the complex layout of some administrative accounts in Old Kingdom administrative documents of the Fourth and Fifth Dynasties from Wadi el-Jarf (Tallet, 2017; Tallet and Marouard, 2017) and Abusir (Posener-Kriéger and de Cenival, 1968: Pls. III–IX; Goelet, 2004). Since scribes had adopted the more convenient horizontal format of writing for nearly all standard documents by the late Middle Kingdom (Parkinson and Quirke, 1995: 38–39), adopting the archaizing columnar format for the Book of the Dead's layout was a strategy to appropriate the prestige of earlier times.

# The Basic Features of a Classical Book of the Dead Manuscript and Its Visual Effect

Motivated by a desire to make a standard Book of the Dead of the New Kingdom an extraordinary document, the scribes adopted many features that deliberately differed from the standard practices of quotidian scribal work. A Book of the Dead, after all, was intended for use in the strange and difficult world of the underworld. It had several characteristic features: sheets of papyrus were still the medium, but the content (and the roll itself) flowed from left to right on the roll, unlike documentary or literary papyrus scrolls that were assembled and inscribed from right to left; the texts of the individual spells or chapters were written mostly in the increasingly archaic Middle Egyptian stage of the language; the goal was to inscribe each spell into a well-delineated rectangle; in most papyri, these rectangles had subsections that contained an illustration, frequently multicolored, known as a vignette; the remaining space in the text field was further subdivided into black-lined vertical columns into which the actual text was written, usually in reverse of the normal writing and reading order; a special form of hieroglyphic writing, the so-called cursive hieroglyphs, was employed instead of the hieratic script used in documents from daily life, thus contributing to the artificial antiquity of the whole; the opening line or title of the text unit was normally marked off from the rest of the text in red ink, followed by the main body of the text in black ink; sometimes a colophon in red ink also appeared at the end of the spell.

This was the general pattern of the classical manuscripts, but in the case of a few select spells, particularly BD 42, 110, 125, and 151, the relationship between text and illustration could become quite complex. Of course, some of these standard features of the classical New Kingdom Books of the Dead were dropped or altered in subsequent eras, in particular the script form, retrograde writing, and columnar format, yet these later papyri can still be recognized and analyzed as variants based on the model just described (Fig. 8.1).

The Book of the Dead offered its owners authoritative information about the next world, but whose authority is seldom specified. There is a largely unspoken message throughout the Book of the Dead, and indeed throughout all Egyptian afterlife literature, that someone—a god, one of the blessed dead, or even a king from the distant past (Thoth and Hermopolis are important in this respect, Stadler, 2009: 74–94)—had been able to convey information about the afterworld to mortals and tell what they would encounter in the beyond, but this is exceptional. It was a document that purported to contain restricted information to negotiate through the hidden world of the gods and the next life. Spells sometimes include appeals to the reader to keep its contents secret or rubricized colophons attesting to the spell's great power (Allen, 1936). The fact that many Egyptians were buried with a Book of the Dead speaks strongly to their belief in its efficacy.

## Assembling a Classical Book of the Dead—The Papyrus Roll as a Metaphor

How was a Book of the Dead assembled? On its face, the initial assembly of a new roll for a Book of the Dead was a repetitive procedure that produced something that differed from its counterparts in more mundane use only in its ultimate orientation. Orientation seems a trivial detail, but it is a difference that establishes a central motif—movement of the deceased and the sun god backward in time toward dawn and "emerging by day." Ideally, a Book of the Dead would be written on fresh, entirely blank papyrus. The fact that a roll had not been previously used immediately made it more expensive and therefore more prestigious. A few palimpsest manuscripts have been found, but these are quite rare (Parkinson and Quirke, 1995: 48; Caminos, 1986: 49–50; Quack, 2006). A large

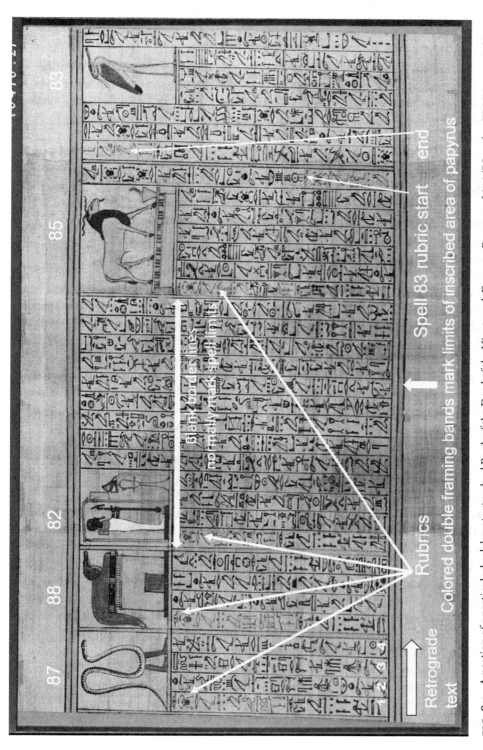

FIG. 8.1. A portion of a particularly elaborate standard Book of the Dead of the Nineteenth Dynasty, Papyrus of Ani (P.London BM EA 10470, sheet 27). Credit line: © The Trustees of the British Museum.

roll of new papyrus could normally be expensive, but the price might be also affected by vagaries such as fluctuation in seasonal availability (Caminos, 1986: 47; Parkinson and Quirke, 1995: 19; Eyre, 2014: 22–27). Another indication of the importance of fresh papyrus was that it was quite exceptional for a Book of the Dead manuscript to continue on the verso side of a roll once the recto had been fully inscribed (Lucarelli, 2010: 265). As much as practicable, the texts and other decoration were written on the inside surfaces of a roll that had the horizontal fibers on top, thus affording an extra degree of protection to the contents.

Since there were no standard lengths or widths for Books of the Dead, features such as a roll's dimensions, the number of spells, and the quality of vignettes were undoubtedly all influenced by what the prospective owner could afford, or more fundamentally, according to what kinds of prefabricated papyri may have been available at the moment. Naturally, the preference was for the larger formats due to their inherently greater prestige (Eyre, 2013: 24).

Whether a roll of papyrus was to be assembled for a Book of the Dead or for normal, secular use such as literary and administrative texts, the process was identical for the initial steps. The roll was created by pasting sheets along their height and with the horizontal fibers facing upward—by common agreement called the recto side—onto the end of the accumulating roll until it had achieved its desired size. The sheets were glued with a flour paste, the whole operation most likely proceeding right (new sheet) over left (previous sheet), and heading rightward, thus following the normal direction of Egyptian secular writing. The completed roll would be configured so that the accumulated blank, rolled papyrus would be to the scribe's right with the left side of the last sheet protruding slightly. There was no need to rewind a new, finished roll. If the roll was intended for normal, secular use, the scribe would now revolve the roll 180° and begin writing. In the case of a roll intended for use as a Book of the Dead, no rotation was needed due to the retrograde direction that the writing would follow (Fig. 8.2). Except for the different writing (and reading) direction of the classical Books of the Dead and secular documents, the manufacturing process and their physical structure were the same. One way of visualizing the situation is to consider why there are no such things as left-handed or right-handed teacups. Once a papyrus roll had been inscribed, however, at that point it would certainly need to be re-rolled, no matter what type it was.

As a precautionary measure, in many cases an extra piece of papyrus was affixed to the front end of the roll that had the phrase *prt m hrw*, "Emerging by Day"—the Egyptian title of the Book of the Dead—written vertically on its verso, thus allowing a person to identify the contents of the roll without unwinding it, while protecting the front end of the roll from the inevitable damage of frequent use. This step, which imitated a standard practice for storage of documents in archives, would be particularly useful in locating a finished roll for copying purposes or a prefabricated roll for its final processing. In the case of rolls prepared as burial goods, the addition of the protective strip is a tacit confirmation of the belief that the roll would be deployed many times as its owner progressed through the afterworld. During the Third Intermediate Period, when burials were

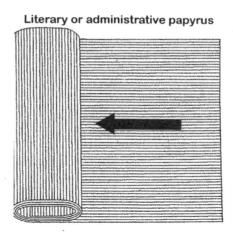

FIG. 8.2. Once manufactured, the reading and writing order on a normal literary document moved from right to left. On a Book of the Dead papyrus, the order was reversed: vignettes and writing progressed from left to right. Illustration by author.

outfitted with a Book of the Dead and an Amduat papyrus, having a readily accessible identification label of this sort would be useful for roll producers and owners alike.

## Retrograde Writing and Narrative Order

The reorientation of the roll toward the left was not the only inversion of normal scribal practice. Although hieroglyphic texts could be written from right to left as well as from left to right depending on which way the characters faced, the normal orientation of hieroglyphic writing had right-facing characters and text running toward the left. However, in the great majority of classical Books of the Dead, the reversed topical and physical motion of the scroll was enhanced by a reversed reading order of the text columns in the spells as well (for a rare exception in the Eighteenth Dynasty, see Munro, 1995a). Although the characters faced rightwards, the leftmost column was the first in the spell, so that one read (and wrote) the columns in a rightward sequence. This practice is known as retrograde writing (Fischer, 1986: 105–30). Occasional horizontal captions in Books of the Dead were retrograde, but these were rather uncommon; it was overwhelmingly associated with columnar format and may have reflected the sun god's reversed movement in time during his underworld journeys (Chegodaev, 1996). As a mode of text presentation, it had a profound influence on the layout of the papyri. As we shall see shortly, retrograde enhanced the relationship between the owner of the roll and his speeches to the gods.

It is not surprising that scribes might find this backward sequence artificial, so sections of text with the normal orientation occur even in the best manuscripts, particularly if

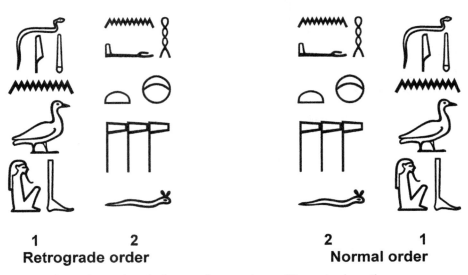

FIG. 8.3. The reading order of columnar-formatted texts. Illustration by author.

the text involved a hymn to a deity or an offering formula. Columnar format was likewise awkward, since by the New Kingdom it was a writing format long discarded in writing letters, administrative documents, and literary texts (Goelet, 2005: 198). Not only is retrograde text one of the most distinctive features of classical Books of the Dead (Niwiński, 1989: 13–17), but it is also one of the most puzzling aspects, particularly because the backward direction of the columns was unnatural and could easily lead a scribe astray in the process of transcribing text from one manuscript to another or onto a different medium, if sizes and formats were appreciably different from each other (Goelet, 2010: esp. 128-30; Graefe, 1993; Mauric-Barberio, 2003; Burkard, 2006; Lapp, 2004: 62–65). Because the scribes sometimes did not understand the meaning and language of the esoteric material, or else they were unfamiliar with the text they were copying, they would be less apt to catch a non sequitur (in the term's most literal sense) in the transition from column to column.

## Vignettes and Ruling: The Mechanics of Book of the Dead Layout in the New Kingdom

Close examination of a few well-illustrated classical Books of the Dead with a magnifying lens can uncover small clues about the procedures used to create these elaborately formatted works. Papyrus of Nu (P.London BM EA 10477) provides a useful model for tracing the practical steps undertaken to produce an inscribed sheet in a Book of the

Dead in this period. The extraordinary regularity of the layout of these papyri signals that straightedges must have played a role in creating these papyri perhaps exceeded only by inks and paints. As the Book of the Dead evolved over centuries of use, the layout of these papyri changed constantly, sometimes radically. The fundamental techniques of graphic design developed for producing Books of the Dead during the New Kingdom and Ramesside Period were applied to its later variations. Virtually every aspect of these papyri later changed (and reverted back): the rolls' physical dimensions and orientation; the script form of their texts; the size of their vignettes; and the general layout of a page. Throughout all these transformations, one feature remained constant: the use of ruling to compartmentalize the text and vignette of individual spells visually as if they were chapters in an anthology of Egyptian afterlife beliefs.

The extensive use of ruled lines, particularly the numerous vertical lines demarking the text columns, immediately impresses observers with the care necessary to rule out a sheet before the text could be inserted and the vignettes drawn. When laying out a new sheet of uninscribed papyrus, however, it was the initial horizontal lines that played the determinative role in the arranging of the scribe's empty canvas, so to speak. These lines formed the borders or outer bands at the top and bottom of the decorated part of the papyrus. The border bands served two purposes: first, they were critical for correct drawing and alignment of the text columns; second, they set off a margin of blank papyrus at the top and bottom of every sheet that provided protection in case the edges of the roll should get abraded or otherwise damaged—a literal margin of safety that also implied an expectation of heavy use in the afterworld. The larger blank space in the middle might usefully be called the text field; this is where the text and illustrations would eventually appear after the initial layout had been completed.

The upper and lower bands of the text field had to run closely parallel to each other so that the vertical columns might be correctly aligned and perpendicular when the time came to draw them. We have no specific information on how accurate collinearity of the border lines was achieved, but occasional small ink dots along the border lines provide important clues. The scribe would place these dots where he thought the ink of the previous line segments had become too faint for his liking or when a new sheet of papyrus was about to be appended (see Figs. 8.4a and 8.4b). After inking small dots directly above each other, the scribe probably began aligning the new border lines with the old ones by first sliding his straightedge a bit backward toward the left, ensuring that the top of the straightedge coincided with the end portions of the faded line. The new horizontal bands would be drawn from or near each small dot, moving toward the right. On papyri where the border bands were thin and the bands' interiors were light-colored or blank, it is easy to observe the ink becoming increasingly dimmer in the rightward direction. More often than not, the corresponding bands at the bottom of the text field would be equally faded in this area. A set of dots would be placed on the bottom line roughly at the same place on a perpendicular line drawn from the dots above, but this is not always the case. These continuation indicators or dots, as they might be described, are often quite difficult to identify on papyri with heavy or brightly colored border bands, probably because the marks would be obliterated as the lines were drawn through them. Bands with bright internal coloring have lines that seem thicker and were possibly re-inked as well

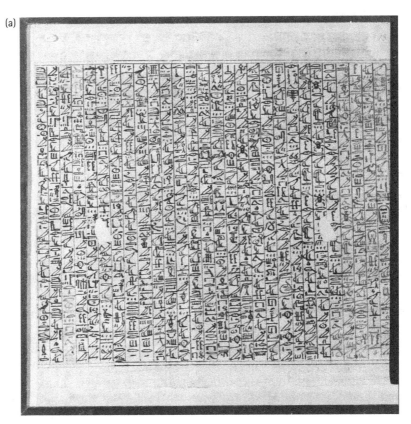

**FIG. 8.4A.** A sheet from the Papyrus of Nu (P.London BM EA 10477, sheet 13) with border bands and vertical ruling. At the top left, the ink of the border band had become too light, so the scribe continued it in fresh ink. Credit line: © The Trustees of the British Museum.

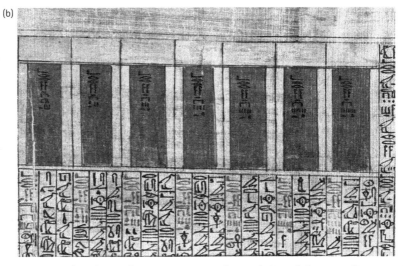

**FIG. 8.4B.** Papyrus of Nu (P.London BM EA 10477, sheet 26). Detail showing alignment dots for the border band above the seventh column from the right. A pair of corresponding dots appears on the bottom frame line, directly below in close perpendicular alignment. Credit line: © The Trustees of the British Museum.

to enhance their more decorative nature. Nevertheless, careful inspection can occasionally reveal the dots' presence. By repeating this process, it would be easy for a scribe to maintain collinearity for the new line segments as needed.

Once the spells for a given sheet in the Book of the Dead roll had been chosen and the border lines drawn, the more detailed planning and layout of a new sheet could begin. The area between the delimiting bands determined the text field—the space available for text and decoration. At this point, knowing which spells and vignettes, if any, were to be used had a fundamental importance in the design and laying out of each sheet in a Book of the Dead papyrus. Once the selection of vignettes, as well as their dimensions and locations—top or bottom, or, rarely, the middle of the text field—had been decided, the layout was pretty much fixed at that stage. Thereafter it would be quite hard to erase several existing vertical column lines to clear out blank space for the insertion of a new vignette. Sheets containing long stretches of text that were uninterrupted by illustrations would be easy to plan because there was no need to provide spaces for vignettes and thereby to adjust the lengths of some text columns. In those sections without illustrations, it was also possible to write one spell after another continuously. A new spell could begin abruptly in the middle of a column, signaled by the switch to red ink and the standard phrase *r3 n* . . . "spell of . ." that introduced the title of the new spell.

The text that appeared under a vignette and in the adjacent columns to its left ideally contained material associated with the current spell. The spell's text ideally began with the leftmost column under the vignette and continued leftwards until it ended with a blank spacer column that ran from the upper border bar to the lower one. In practice, this theoretical ideal was difficult to maintain and frequently ignored. It is not unusual to find the space under and around a vignette shared by other spells. As one can imagine, it must have been quite difficult for a scribe to balance several different objectives simultaneously when estimating how many columns were needed on a sheet.

Vignettes were normally set off from the text by framed rectangles within the text field. These frame lines at the sides of the vignettes were often formed by narrow bands with blank or light monochrome interiors, but sometimes just simple lines sufficed. However, there is such a wide variety of framing styles that it is unwise to generalize about the amount of framing required or where these blank spacers might appear. Depending upon the vignette's position within the text frame, there might be a small framing band at its bottom, or at both its top and bottom. The positioning and number of such separators was dependent on how elaborate the papyrus was overall. When vignettes were adjacent to one another, sometimes these separators were placed at their sides.

As several unfinished papyri indicate, by far the more usual practice was for the text to be inscribed before the vignettes were painted in. In fact, papyri have been found with text inscribed, but spaces for the vignettes left blank or with notations to inform the artist as to what should be inserted (Lucarelli, 2010: 268–69; Parkinson and Quirke, 1995: 56). An important practical consideration was whether drawing the vignette might interfere with inscribing the text or vice versa. Considering that the straightedge used to draw the vertical columns would have to move over the surface of the vignette area, it would probably have been wiser to draw the column lines first to avoid smudging a freshly painted vignette.

After settling on the choice of spells, which vignettes should be used, and how many text columns were needed, then the work of drawing the numerous vertical column lines began, a task that must have been both monotonous and exacting because these lines also had to be evenly spaced and closely parallel. Unfortunately, there is no definite evidence for the instruments that might be employed, but logic and grade school geometry lessons suggest a simple, practical solution of joining or placing two pieces of wood that were each well squared-off to form a right-angled T or L (Fig. 8.5).

First, the ruled portion of the L- or T-square would be carefully aligned along the upper border band, then small, light ink dots would be placed close to each ruler marking, perhaps slightly below the line where marks would not be as visible. Once finished, the column lines could be drawn one by one through the dots down to the lower border line. The dots would not have to be collinear, just evenly spaced in respect to the horizontal axis before each line perpendicular to the border line could be drawn through them. The inking of the column lines moved from top to bottom, as the manner in which the ink faded informs us. Traces of the process involved can be more readily seen when closely inspecting areas under the lower borders of vignettes, as shown in Fig. 8.6. Since the dots were often obscured when the lines were drawn through them, these marks sometimes are detectable only as slight bulges in the column lines. Working continually with the L- or T-square probably was cumbersome. To speed up the process, a scribe might instead place a large group of corresponding alignment dots slightly above the lower borderline, then employ a plain straightedge to draw column lines through the

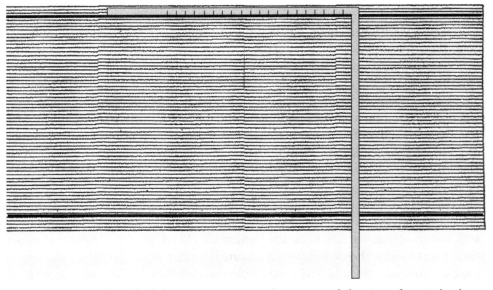

FIG. 8.5. Suggested method for ensuring correct alignment and drawing of vertical column lines. Illustration by author.

FIG. 8.6. Detailed view of the lower edge of a vignette on Papyrus of Nu (P.London BM EA 10477), sheet 22, showing small, barely visible ink dots underneath the vignette's lower border frame. Credit line: © The Trustees of the British Museum.

upper and lower dots. Of course, the quickest way to draw parallel lines would be to dispense with these guide dots altogether and use an adjacent column line as a visual guide.

This process resulted in evenly spaced columns with uniform widths throughout the papyrus, unless the manuscript was a composite created by joining disparate papyri together, as it appears the Papyrus of Ani was assembled (Parkinson and Leach, 2010). The disparity in the size of the text field in some sections combined with the mismatching of the style and coloration of the border bands in other places means that the Papyrus of Ani represents a collection of lengthy groups of prefabricated spells that had been prepared in advance, then joined together to form a very long roll. If it had been a truly collaborative effort, the border bands would have been planned in advance to have a uniform color pattern and the text field would have had a constant size throughout.

## Cursive Hieroglyphs and Calligraphy

What we call hieroglyphs in the proper sense were used for inscriptions on stone, paintings on tomb walls, or incised texts on the sides of wood coffins. The hieroglyphs used in classical Books of the Dead are simplified signs known as cursive hieroglyphs, a somewhat misleading term because these signs often had interior details and could be as nearly as decorative as their fully formed counterparts, but were monochrome and employed a smaller character set. The development and use of this script are more completely described elsewhere in this volume (Verhoeven, this volume; Verhoeven, 2001). To a great extent, inscribing a "classical" Book of the Dead with cursive hieroglyphs was a calligraphic exercise. Cursives were more ornate and time-consuming to draw than hieratic, the script used for the practical, non-funerary documents on papyrus during the New Kingdom (Fischer, 1979: 39–44, with Fig. 8.4), thus making cursives inherently more prestigious and expensive to produce than hieratic texts. Cursive hieroglyphs were confined largely to the Book of the Dead and other arcana (Goelet, 2010). In the Twenty-first Dynasty, when hieratic was adopted as the main script form for the Book of the Dead, this shift brought about a radical change in the layout (see, p. 194, this chapter).

There are some striking features about the way cursives are used in classical Books of the Dead that might escape observers unfamiliar with Egyptian scripts. In a detailed view of the sheet from Papyrus of Nu (see Fig. 8.4a), discussed earlier in this chapter, the text and script in the three columns show several important characteristics found in better-quality classical Books of the Dead. The cursive hieroglyphs have been separately inscribed as individual characters (Fig. 8.7). The characters are fully formed, some with interior detail or solid fill. A few hieroglyphs end with a flourish, but there are no

FIG. 8.7. Comparison of two scripts and writing styles. Left: columns of cursive hieroglyphic text from Papyrus of Nu (P.London BM EA 10477, sheet 13). Right: columns of hieratic text from a Middle Kingdom literary manuscript, *The Tale of Sinuhe* (P.Berlin P 3022 A(1), called "*Sinuhe* B"). Not to scale. Credit line: © The Trustees of the British Museum and Ägyptisches Museum und Papyrussammlung Staatische Museen zu Berlin.

true ligatures linking signs together. The scribe has clearly made a conscious effort to respect the column borders as much as possible. If one examines his work as he moved down the columns, the ink density is noticeably even, indicating that he replenished his brush at every two or three characters. One can sense a conscious effort to respect the column borders as much as possible. The frequent replenishing of the brush and the avoidance of ligaturing leave the impression of a slow, deliberate calligraphic production. Ironically, the impressive appearance of the layout, vignettes, and writing of many of the more splendid Books of the Dead were often not matched by faithful transcription of the text from the original sources (Eyre, 2013: 51).

Though written centuries before the Papyrus of Nu excerpt, the three columns on the right from a Middle Kingdom hieratic literary papyrus, The Tale of Sinuhe, offer a useful

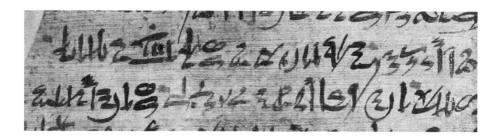

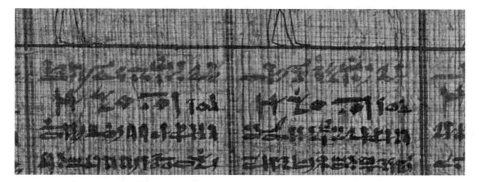

FIG. 8.8. Upper: An excerpt from a late Twentieth Dynasty literary manuscript (P.London BM EA 9994 (P.Lansing), detail of column 4 showing lines of horizontally formatted hieratic in the normal right-to-left direction. It was written rapidly, without lining, yet is neat and fluid. The scribe used ligatures and flourishes frequently; he allowed the ink to fade noticeably before refilling his brush.

Credit line: © The Trustees of the British Museum.

Lower: The top portion of two columns of "Book of the Dead hieratic" from the late Twenty-sixth Dynasty Book of the Dead of Ankhwahibre (P.London BM EA 10558, detail of sheet 25). The columns below the vignettes were narrow and varied in length. The scribe wrote deliberately, using small, compressed characters and refilling his brush frequently to maintain even ink density. The horizontal fibers of the papyrus helped him maintain the baselines. In photographs taken with a raking light, these fine fibers can easily be mistaken for thinly ruled inked lines on the sheet. Due to the sensitivity of the film, the red ink in the first line of each column looks deceptively like fading ink.

Credit line: © The Trustees of the British Museum.

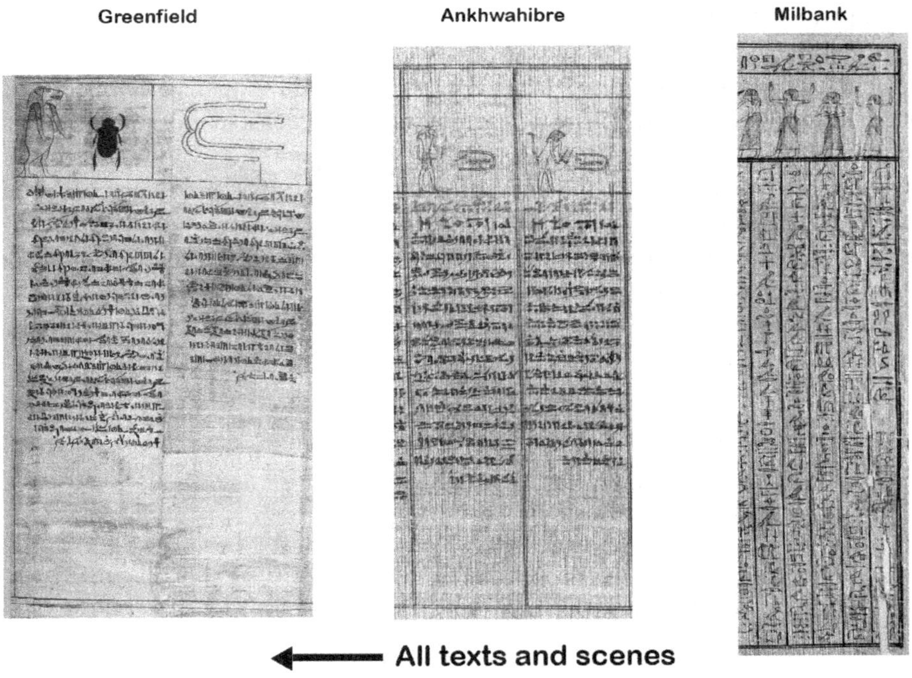

FIG. 8.9. Three examples of the format of post-Ramesside Books of the Dead. (From left to right) P.London BM EA 10554 (P.Greenfield), sheet 55 (late Twenty-first/early Twenty-second Dynasty); BD of Ankhwahibre (P.London BM EA 10558), detail of sheet 25 (late Twenty-sixth Dynasty); P.Chicago OIM E10486A (P.Milbank; Ptolemaic Period). P.Milbank represents a revival of the cursive hieroglyphs and classical format, but the column order moved in the standard right-to-left direction.

Credit line: © The Trustees of the British Museum and the Oriental Institute Museum of the University of Chicago.

comparison by showing a scribe writing quickly (tachygraphy) and free of the strictures imposed by lined columns (description in Parkinson, 2009: 90–102; Goelet, 2015: 199–203). The numerous ligatures and noticeable fading of the ink in several places are the marks of someone who wrote "hastily, but not unthinkingly" (Parkinson, 2009: 111) as he transcribed the tale from a master copy for personal pleasure or practical purposes. The Book of the Dead scribe, by contrast, was deliberately and slowly producing a formal piece of scribal and funerary art, sign by sign. This deliberate calligraphic effect was as important a characteristic of the layout and manufacture as any other feature of a classical Book of the Dead set forth at the beginning of this chapter, and perhaps the most persistent of all.

In the Twenty-first Dynasty, the entire configuration of the Book of the Dead changed dramatically when the script form in the texts switched from cursive hieroglyphs to hieratic. As the script used for everyday documents, hieratic required no specialized skills on the part of the scribes. More importantly, hieratic could be written only from right to left and, by this period, very rarely appeared in columnar format.

Adopting hieratic had several major consequences for the later Books of the Dead (Fig. 8.8). The papyrus rolls now were structurally identical with those used for everyday purposes. The direction of the writing and narrative movement of rolls reverted to the standard right-to-left format. The effect on the visual presentation was even more dramatic—since the fine natural horizontal fibers of the papyrus were on the inner writing surface of the rolls, these fibers provided scribes with what was effectively lined paper. Now, the great majority of lines that needed to be drawn were the border frames for the vignettes. The core motif of travel through the afterworld remained coherent with the physical and narrative structure of the scroll, except that it moved in the familiar right-to-left direction.

Although some exceptional papyri, such as Papyrus Milbank in Fig. 8.9, continued to use the old lined, columnar format, henceforth vertical columns served to separate whole spells rather than individual lines. In sum, the new hieratic tradition considerably simplified the task of preparing and copying manuscripts, but may have had only a marginal effect on the time required to create a high-quality hieratic Book of the Dead.

## Bibliography

Allen, T. G. 1936. "Types of Rubrics in the Egyptian Book of the Dead," *Journal of the American Oriental Society* 56: 145-154.

Andreu, G., editor 2003. *Deir el-Médineh et la Valée des Rois. La vie en Égypte au temps des pharaons du Nouvel Empire. Actes du colloque organisé par le musée du Louvre les 3 et 4 mai 2002* (Paris: Khéops).

Burkard, G. 2006. "Ein früher Beleg der Kemit (O DAN hierat 5)," In *Es werde niedergelegt als Schriftstück. Festschrift für Hartwig Altenmüller zum 65. Geburtstag.* Studien zur Altägyptischen Kultur Beihefte 9, edited by N. Kloth, *et al.*, 37–48 (Hamburg: Buske).

Caminos, R. A. 1986. "Some comments on the reuse of papyrus," In *Papyrus: Structure and Usage*. British Museum Occasional Papers 60, edited by M.L. Bierbrier, 43–61 (London: British Museum).

Caminos, R. A., and H. G. Fischer 1979. *Ancient Egyptian Epigraphy and Palaeography*, 2nd edition (New York: Metropolitan Museum of Art).

Černý, J. 1952. *Paper and Books in Ancient Egypt* (London: H. K. Lewis).

Chegodaev, M. A. 1996. "Some Remarks Regarding the So-called 'Retrograde' Direction of Writing in the Ancient Egyptian 'Book of the Dead,'" *Discussions in Egyptology* 35: 19–24.

Eyre, C. J. 2013. *The Use of Documents in Ancient Egypt*. Oxford Studies in Ancient Documents 1. (Oxford: Oxford University Press).

Fischer, H. G. 1979. "Archaeological Aspects of Epigraphy and Palaeography," In Caminos and Fischer 1979: 29-50.

Fischer, H. G. 1986. *L'écriture et l'art de l'Égypte ancienne. Quatre leçons sur la paléographie et l'épigraphie pharaonique.* (Essais et Conférences Collège de France. Paris).

Goelet, O. 2004. "Accounting Practices and Economic Planning in Ancient Egypt before the Hellenistic Era," In *Creating Economic Order. Record Keeping, Standardization, and the Development of Accounting in the Ancient Near East. International Scholars Conference* on Ancient Near Eastern Economics 4, edited by M. Hudson and C. Wunsch (Bethesda, MD: CDL Press).

Goelet, O. 2015. "The Elements of Format in Middle Kingdom Papyri," In *Joyful in Thebes. Egyptological Studies in Honor of Betsy M. Bryan*, edited by Richard Jasnow and Kathlyn M. Cooney, 197–210 (Atlanta: Lockwood).

Goelet, O. 2010. "Observations on Copying and the Hieroglyphic Tradition in the Production of the Book of the Dead," In *Offerings to the Discerning Eye. An Egyptological Medley in Honor of Jack J. Josephson*. Culture and History of the Ancient Near East 38, edited by S. H. D'Auria, 121-132 (Leiden: Brill).

Graefe, E. 1993. "Papyrus Leiden T3 oder: Über das Kopieren von Texten durch altägyptische Schreiber," *Oudheidkundige Mededelingen uit het Rijksmuseum van Oudheden te Leiden* 73 (1993): 23-28.

Lapp, G. 1997. *The Papyrus of Nu (BM 10477)*. Catalogue of the Books of the Dead in the British Museum I (London: British Museum).

Lapp, G. 2004. *The Papyrus of Nebseni (BM EA 9900)*. Catalogue of the Books of the Dead in the British Museum III (London: British Museum).

Lucarelli, R. 2010. "Making the Book of the Dead," In Taylor 2010b: 264-287.

Mauric-Barberio, F. 2003. "Copie des textes à l'envers dans les tombes royales," In Andreu 2003: 173-194.

Munro, I. 1987. *Untersuchungen zu den Totenbuch-Papyri des 18. Dynastie. Kriterien ihrer Datierung*. Studies in Egyptology (London and New York: Kegan Paul).

Munro, I. 1995a. *Das Totenbuch des Jah-mes (pLouvre E. 11085) aus dem frühen 18. Dynastie*. Handschriften des Altägyptischen Totenbuches 1 (Wiesbaden: Harrassowitz).

Niwinski, A. 1989. *Studies on the Illustrated Theban Funerary Papyri of the 11$^{th}$ and 10$^{th}$ Centuries B.C.* Orbis biblicus et orientalis 86 (Göttingen: Vandenhoek & Ruprecht).

Parkinson, R. B. 2009. *Reading Ancient Egyptian Poetry among other Histories* (Wiley-Blackwell: Malden, MA).

Parkinson, R. B., and S. G. Quirke 1995. *Papyrus*. The Egyptian Bookshelf (Austin: University of Texas Press).

Parkinson, R. B., and B. Leach 2010. "Creating borders, new insights into making the Papyrus of Ani," In *The Book of the Dead- Recent research and new perspectives*. British Museum Studies in Ancient Egypt and Sudan 15, edited by N. Spencer, E. O'Connell, and L. McNamara, 35–62 (London: British Museum).

Posener-Kriéger, P., and J. L. de Cénival 1968. *The Abu Sir Papyri*. Hieratic Papyri in the British Museum. Fifth Series (London: British Museum).

Scalf, F., ed. 2017. *Book of the Dead. Becoming a God in Ancient Egypt*. Oriental Institute Museum Publications 39 (Chicago: Oriental Institute of the University of Chicago).

Stadler, M. A. 2009. *Weiser und Wesir: Studien zu Vorkommen, Rolle und Wesen des Gottes Thot im ägyptischen Totenbuch*. (Tübingen: Mohr Siebeck).

Tallet, P. 2017. *Le « journal de Merer » (papyrus Jarf A et B): Les papyrus de la mer Rouge I*. Mémoires publiés par les membres de l'Institut français d'archéologie orientale du Caire, 136. (Cairo: Institut français d'archéologie orientale).

Tallet, P., and G. Marouard 2017. "Der Hafen des Cheops am Wadi el-Jarf," *Sokar* 35: 14–27.

Taylor, J. H., editor. 2010b. *Journey Through the Afterlife. Ancient Egyptian Book of the Dead*. (Cambridge, MA: Harvard University Press).

Verhoeven, U. 2001. *Untersuchungen zur Späthieratischen Buchschrift*. Orientalia Lovaniensia Analecta 99 (Louvain: Peeters).

CHAPTER 9

# FEMALE OWNERS OF BOOK OF THE DEAD PAPYRI

SUSANNE TÖPFER

ALTHOUGH we know of more copies produced for men than for women, the Book of the Dead was not a funerary composition produced exclusively for the male Egyptian elite. Copies of the Book of the Dead written for or adapted by women are known from the end of the Second Intermediate Period to the Roman Period (Quirke, 1993). As of July 2018, the Totenbucharchiv, the digital database of the Book of the Dead Project of the University of Bonn (http://totenbuch.awk.nrw.de/), registers a total of 2,228 owners for about 2,992 documents with spells of the Book of the Dead; 61.4 percent of these are for men, 22.8 percent are for women, and 15.8 percent are for owners of unspecified gender. Of course, this is only a small sample of the total number of Book of the Dead manuscripts that were produced throughout Egyptian history. The great majority of these have been lost, and there are a number of specimens, especially in private collections, that are not featured in the Bonn database; more will most certainly come to light in future excavations. The aim of this chapter is to present an overview of the known female owners of the Book of the Dead, of their titles and kinship relations, and of the quality and content of their copies, from the beginning to the end of the tradition. However, not all of the approximately 500 copies attested for women (almost half of which are dated to the Ptolemaic Period) can be taken into account; therefore, the discussion in this chapter will be limited to a representative selection of 81 manuscripts. All of the text witnesses are listed in tables at the end of the relevant section; the numbers in square brackets in the text refer to entries in these tables.

## NEW KINGDOM (TABLE 9.1)

Female owners of the Book of the Dead from the beginning of the tradition, that is in the late Seventeenth and early Eighteenth Dynasties, are mainly attested on linen shrouds

(Quirke, 1999: 230; Ockinga, 2006: 185–86; see also Kockelmann, 2008: 9–11). These shrouds are inscribed with multiple spells written in cursive hieroglyphs; some of them are decorated with colored vignettes, such as the shroud of a woman named Iahmes [1] or that of the lady Tany [2], whose owner is depicted in the vignette for BD 100/129. Further depictions of the deceased as part of the "Adoration of Osiris" can be seen on the linen shrouds of the "lady of the house," Resti [3], and the "great nurse of the god's wife," Mahu [4]. The names and titles of four female owners reveal their relation to the Taosid royal family (see Munro, 1988: 5; Dodson and Hilton, 2004: 122–26). For one of these, there is the shroud of Queen Tetisheri [5], "mother of the king" Seqenenre Taa, whose daughter Ahmose, borne by the king's wife, Sitdjehuty, can be attributed as a shroud as well [6]. There is another shroud of a "king's daughter" named Ahmose-Henut-Tjemehu [7], but it is uncertain whether the owner is the daughter of King Seqenenre Taa and his wife Inhapy (Dodson and Hilton, 2004: 124, 126) or of his son, King Ahmose I (PM I: 660). In the first case, one would assume that the shrouds of the two daughters of Seqenenre Taa would have been made in the same workshop, but the writing on the shroud of Ahmose-Henut-Tjemehu is heavily influenced by hieratic. The exact relationship of the "king's daughter," named Amenemwesekhet [8], to the royal family is also unclear (Franco, 1988: 71–82).

Unfortunately, there are no preserved vignettes on the linen shrouds of the members of the royal family. Although the shrouds are preserved in only a fragmentary state, a uniform sequence of the spells can be observed on all of them: BD 124–83–84–85–82–77–86–99–119–7–102–38A–27–14–39–65–116. Another owner of a shroud, remotely connected to the royal family of the Eighteenth Dynasty, was Hatneferet, the mother of Senenmut, who was the tutor of princess Neferure, daughter of Hatshepsut. Hatneferet is one of the rare individuals to have owned texts from the Book of the Dead on three different media: a linen shroud [9] with BD 72–17 and a leather roll [10] with BD 100/129, both written in cursive hieroglyphs, as well as two papyri [11, 12] with a long sequence of BD spells written in hieratic on both the recto and verso.

There is no evidence of linen shrouds inscribed with the Book of the Dead for women (or men) beyond the middle of the Eighteenth Dynasty, the time of Hatshepsut and Thutmose III. The text copies attested for Hatnefert demonstrate the transition from linen to papyrus as writing support for Book of the Dead copies during the Eighteenth Dynasty. Thus, it can be assumed that, around this time, papyrus became more popular as a writing support than the inscribed shrouds (Quirke, 1993: 16; Kockelmann, 2008: 11). The cursive hieroglyphic script continues to be used on papyrus during this time, whereas the hieratic script is rather uncommon for Book of the Dead copies in the early New Kingdom. The two hieratic manuscripts [11, 12] documented for Hatnefert are an exception.

The majority of the Eighteenth-Dynasty Book of the Dead manuscripts written for women are in a rather fragmentary condition [13–18]. Only a few well-preserved papyri are known. Several of the female owners are referred to by the title "lady of the house," while only one held the title of "nurse" [20]. Although some of the owners are not referred to by their titles, or simply by the generic title of "wife," it can be assumed that they were members of higher-ranking families. This is the case for the "lady of the house" Ruyu [19], daughter of the "overseer of all craftsmen of the God's wife," Neferkhawet (TT MMA 729) and the "lady of the house" Rennefer. Given the excellent quality of her papyrus, the "nurse" Amenemopet, called Baki [20], must have been of wealthy origin. The Book of the Dead was made for her personally, rather than as a copy later filled in with her name, as proved by the depiction of the female deceased in the vignettes and the incorporation of both her name and her title in the text. According to Barwik (1997: 334), Amenemopet could have been the wife of Amenemheb called Mahu (TT 85), whose wife was the nurse of the future king Amenhotep II. The fact that she was a nurse makes it clear that she must have been married and had children of her own. It is noteworthy that she is depicted alone in the vignettes of her papyrus, without her husband.

As pointed out by Quirke (1999: 231–33), copies of the Book of the Dead written for women are rare from the mid-Eighteenth Dynasty until the end of the Twentieth Dynasty [21–26]. His suggestion is that in this period women shared their husbands' manuscripts as secondary beneficiaries; they were depicted on the papyri next to their husbands and therefore did not need a copy of their own. This statement might apply to some manuscripts, such as the papyrus of the couple Ptahhotep and Baket [27] from the time of Thutmose IV/Amenhotep III, where the wife is shown next to her husband, or the papyrus of Bary [24], from the Nineteenth–Twentieth Dynasty, where the owner appears next to her husband in an adoration scene. However, one should not generalize this evidence to conclude that women did not need their own papyri. Meryt, the wife of Kha, superintendent of works in the royal necropolis from the reign of Amenhotep II to that of Amenhotep III, had her own Book of the Dead copy [28]. However, this manuscript was not written for Meryt; rather, it was premanufactured, with blank spaces left to be filled in with the future owner's name. Apparently, the manuscript was adapted for Meryt after having originally been intended for her husband, since his name and titles are written in the first column and he is depicted in the vignettes. Kha, however, was buried later with another Book of the Dead (P.Turin Suppl. 8438), also a premanufactured manuscript, which shows Meryt standing next to him only in the opening scene, the adoration of Osiris (Fig. 9.1).

The vast majority of known New Kingdom manuscripts are in a fragmentary condition, and hence the names of the owners are not always preserved. The well-preserved manuscripts dated from the mid-Eighteenth Dynasty until the end of the Twentieth Dynasty include very few specimens belonging to women. This scarcity, however, should not be interpreted as evidence of a "demotion of women" (Quirke, 1999: 232) in the New Kingdom, or at least this demotion was limited to Book of the Dead papyri, but did not extend to the burial assemblage as a whole. For example, the burial equipment of Henutmehyt, dating to the reign of Ramses II (Taylor, 1999: 59–72), features a hieratic copy of BD 100/129 [22] in which the owner is called "lady of the house and chantress of Amenemopet," gilded wooden coffins, a canopic chest including four jars, four shabti boxes with figurines, a set of four magical bricks (which have a connection with BD 151; Theis, 2015: 538–74), and a wooden box containing food offerings. An exceptional Book of the Dead from the Twentieth Dynasty (Andrews, 1978; Quirke, 1993: 17; 1999: 232;

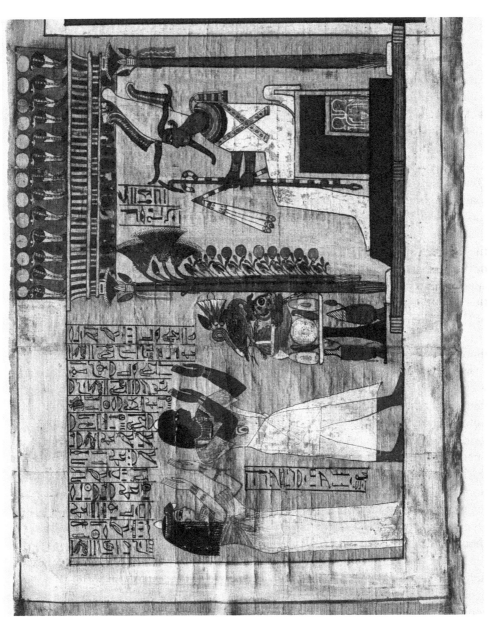

FIG. 9.1. Book of the Dead of Kha (P.Turin Suppl. 8438); © Museo Egizio/ Nicola Dell'Aquila e Federico Taverni.

Taylor, 2010: 71) belongs to the "chantress of Amun," Anhai [25], a woman who was "chief of musicians" in the cult of Osiris, Nebtu, and Khnum. The copy is remarkable not only because it was made specifically for the priestess, who is depicted alone in the vignettes, but also because of the quality of its text and images. This papyrus carries a combination of Book of the Dead spells (BD 15, 146, 110, 125, 82, and 79) and scenes from the Underworld Books, which are a fairly common feature of funerary papyri dating to the Third Intermediate Period (Niwiński, 1989). Finally, the papyrus sheet of Tadimut [26], probably dating to the late Twentieth Dynasty, is inscribed with BD 166 and was used as an amulet, while her funerary equipment included a linen band inscribed with BD 101, which was also used as an amulet (Kockelmann, 2008: 218).

Table 9.1: Overview of female owners during the New Kingdom

| | Inventory No. | Name | Title | Relation | Reference |
|---|---|---|---|---|---|
| 1 | L.Moscow 1027 | Iahmes | - | - | TM 134087 |
| 2 | L.Sydney R 92 | Tany | Lady | - | Ockinga, 2006 |
| 3 | L.London BM EA 73807 | Resti | Lady of the house | - | TM 133688 |
| 4 | L.Hanover 39-64-6623 + L.Berlin P. 10467 | Mahu | Great nurse of the God's wife | Mother: Ipu | TM 133532 |
| 5 | L.Cairo J.E. 96805 | Tetisheri | Queen mother | Son: Seqenenre Taa Granddaughter: Ahmose, see no. [6] Mother: Neferu Father: Tjenna | TM 133677 |
| 6 | L.Turin CGT 63001 = Suppl. 5051 | Ahmose | King's daughter | Mother: Sitdjehuty Father: Seqenenre Taa Grandmother: Tetisheri, see no. [5] | TM 133686 |
| 7 | L.Cairo J.E. 96810 | Ahmose-Henut-Tjemehu | King's daughter | Mother: Inhapy (?) Father: Seqenenre Taa or Ahmose I | TM 133680 |
| 8 | L.Cairo O.A.E. 325+343 | Amenemwesekhet | King's daughter | - | TM 133670 |
| 9 | L.Cairo J.E. 66218 | Hatneferet | Lady of the house | Son: Senenmut | TM 133675 |
| 10 | Leather roll Cairo SN | see no. [9] | see no. [9] | see no. [9] | TM 134276 |
| 11 | P.Cairo TR 25/1/155/6 | see no. [9] | see no. [9] | see no. [9] | TM 134627 |
| 12 | P.Cairo SN (C II) | see no. [9] | see no. [9] | see no. [9] | TM 135561 |

(continued)

**Table 9.1: Continued**

| | | | | | |
|---|---|---|---|---|---|
| 13 | P.Moscow I, 1b, 26 (B) | Henut | Lady of the house | - | TM 134772 |
| 14 | P.Moscow I, 1b, 28 | Mesu | - | - | TM 134766 |
| 15 | P.Bucarest Mss. oriental 376 | Sakhti | Lady of the house | - | TM 134755 |
| 16 | P.TT 65 | Satamen | - | - | TM 134835 |
| 17 | P.London UCL 71001 | Satiah | - | Mother: Sembu | TM 134701 |
| 18 | P.IFAO SN | Tanetnebu | - | Mother: Ahmose Father: Nebsenu | TM 134275 |
| 19 | P.Location unknown [30] (destroyed) | Ruyu | Lady of the house | Mother: Rennefer Father: Neferkhawet | TM 134761 |
| 20 | P.Warsaw 237128 | Amenemopet, called Baki | Nurse | Husband: Amenemheb, called Mahu (?) | TM 134318 |
| 21 | P.London BM EA 9969 = P.Meyrick | Neferetiri | Lady of the house | - | TM 134255 |
| 22 | P.Reading | Henutmehyt | Lady of the house Chantress of Amenemopet | - | TM 134714 |
| 23 | P.Tallin k-542/AM 5877 | Aset | - | - | TM 134676 |
| 24 | P.Barcelona E-615 | Bary | - | - | TM 134752 |
| 25 | P.London BM EA 10472 | Anhai | Chantress of Amun Chief of the musicians | Mother: Nefertiti | TM 134517 |
| 26 | P.Cairo CG 58005 = J.E. 35413 | Tadimut | Chantress of Amun | - | TM 134439 |
| 27 | P.Atlanta MCCM 2004.22.1 et al. | Baket | Lady of the house | Husband: Ptahhotep | TM 133565 |
| 28 | P.Paris BN 826 | Meryt | Lady of the house | Husband: Kha | TM 134305 |

TM = Trismegistos number, stable link to the online tool www.trismegistos.org, which in turn is related to the Totenbuch-Projekt, Bonn http://totenbuch.awk.nrw.de. For references, see Depauw and Gheldof, 2014. This also contains the bibliography of the subsequently mentioned papyri, mummy bandages, and shrouds. It is beyond the scope of this contribution to list the complete bibliography.

## Libyan Period (Table 9.2)

The bulk of the approximately 130 known copies of the Book of the Dead for women from Thebes dating to the Third Intermediate Period (in particular to the Twenty-first and Twenty-second Dynasties) can be explained by the prominent role of women in the leading class during this period, brought about in particular by their Libyan background (Quirke, 1999: 232; Jansen-Winkeln, 2000: 1–20; 2001: 153–82, esp. 161–62; Kitchen, 2015) (see Lenzo in this volume for the BD of the TIP). Probably the best-known papyri of the early Twenty-first Dynasty are those made for Queen Nedjmet, the wife of King (formerly High Priest) Herihor. One [29] is written in hieratic and contains some Book of the Dead spells as well as scenes from the Book of Caverns (for this source see Scalf in this volume). The owner is depicted twice in adoration, bearing the title of "king's mother, who gave birth to the strong bull" and "lady of the Two Lands," but the name of the king is never mentioned. Also referred to as "king's mother" is Nodjemet's mother, Herere. The second papyrus [30] is a pure copy of the Book of the Dead and was written in cursive hieroglyphs. The owner is depicted alone in most of the vignettes, with the exception of the adoration scenes, where she stands next to her second husband Herihor, whose name is written in a cartouche. The second funerary papyrus follows the tradition of the mid-Eighteenth to the Nineteenth Dynasty Book of the Dead copies: the script is hieroglyphic and the woman, even though she is the owner, is depicted standing next to her husband, though she is shown as being taller than him. In contrast, the first papyrus reflects a change occurring around this time: the script is hieratic with the integration of new funerary scenes, and the female owner is depicted alone. A mixture of both traditions can be seen in the Book of the Dead copies of Queen Henttawy [31, 32], daughter of Ramesses XI and spouse of the High Priest Pinudjem I: the writing and layout of the manuscripts conform to those of New Kingdom copies, but the female owner is depicted alone in a prominent position in the vignettes. However, the lone depiction of the female owner is not a total innovation, as it is a feature already known from the linen shrouds of the royal family of the late Seventeenth and early Eighteenth Dynasties and papyri of the first half of the Eighteenth Dynasty.

It becomes thus evident that the existence of Book of the Dead copies for women is correlated with the position of these women in the ruling elite. This is also true of the spouses of the high priests, and of the god's wife of Amun, during the Libyan Period (Graefe, 1981; Koch, 2012). Maatkare, the daughter of Henttawy and High Priest Pinudjem I, was the owner of a Book of the Dead copy [33] similar to that of her mother; Maatkare held the title of "god's wife of Amun." Other female members of priestly families were also connected to the temple cult for Amun through their positions as "great[s] of the harem of Amun-Re," such as the daughters of High Priest Menkheperre, named Henttawy [34] and Gatseshen [35]. The papyrus of Gatseshen is nearly 18 meters long and contains—apart from numerous BD spells—extracts from the Osirian hourly vigils (Stundenwachen; Pries, 2011). As Lucarelli (2006: 256–61) has pointed out,

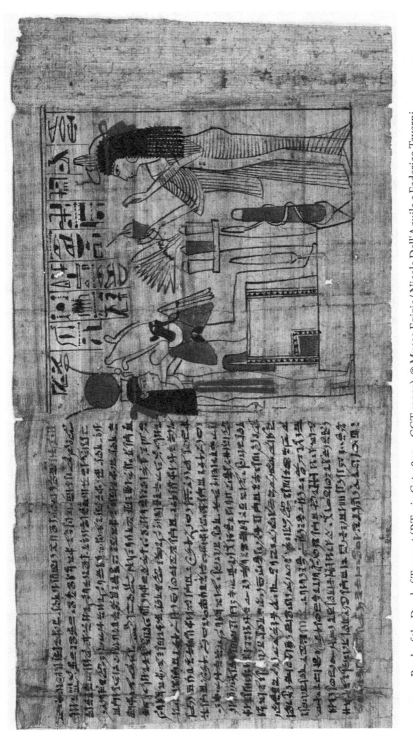

**FIG. 9.2.** Book of the Dead of Tameret (P.Turin Cat. 1849 = CGT 53001); © Museo Egizio/ Nicola Dell'Aquila e Federico Taverni.

the choice of spells can be seen as a reflection of Theban funerary religion during the Twenty-first Dynasty. The increase in importance of the solar religion is demonstrated by the papyri, in which scenes with the adoration of Re-Horakhty are depicted almost as often as the adoration of Osiris. Several vignettes and texts concerning the sun-god can be found in the extraordinary Book of the Dead of Nesitanebetisheru [36], daughter of the High Priest Pinudjem II. The papyrus is exceptional not only because it is the longest known Book of the Dead manuscript (approximately 40m), but also because it contains texts not known from other copies (Taylor, 2010: 307) and mythological scenes mainly known from the Underworld Books.

The Book of the Dead of Nesitanebetisheru is—like the papyrus of Gatseshen—a combination of tradition and innovation. In this context it is noteworthy that there probably exist more papyri from the same Theban workshop as the papyrus of Gatseshen, which seems to have produced copies especially for women (Lucarelli, 2006: 237–47; Ragazzoli, 2010). Among these are copies of Books of the Dead featuring a similar selection of texts and vignettes (showing a female deceased), such as the manuscripts of Ankhesenaset [37] and Neskhonsu [38]—respectively the mother of Nesitanebetisheru [36] and the niece of Gatseshen [35]—those of Nesitabetawi [39] and Asety [40], whose manuscripts are unfinished as the vignettes were not drawn, and a group of papyri including only the adoration of Osiris as a vignette, including those of Tameret [41] (Fig. 9.2), Asty [42], Djedmutiusankh [43], and Djedbastet [44] (for the Turin manuscripts see Lenzo, 2007). Nearly all the female owners of Book of the Dead copies from the Third Intermediate Period are connected to the temple cult of Karnak and therefore bear the titles "chantress of Amun," "great of the harem of Amun-Re" or "great singer of Mut."

All the aforementioned manuscripts were produced specifically for female owners. In this period, only a few Book of the Dead copies are "stock" manuscripts with vignettes depicting a man instead of a woman; their texts, however, are written specifically for the women, whose names and titles they mention. One example is the papyrus for Asetemakhbit [45], which depicts a man adoring Osiris. An exception is the papyrus of Tabakhenkhonsu [46], because both a male and a female deceased are depicted in the vignettes, but in a certain hierarchy: the labor in the field of reeds is carried out by the man, while the woman is sitting in front of the offering tables, sailing in the sun-boat, or praising the gods. The special position of female owners becomes even more apparent when we consider the depiction of the mummy of the deceased and the *ba* in some manuscripts, which are clearly female. This is, for example, the case in the manuscripts of the "chantresses of Amun," Tanetshedkhonsu, [47], Asetemakhbit [48], and Tii [49], as well as that of Queen Nodjemet [30].

After the peak of Book of the Dead copies for women in the time of the Libyan kings of the Twenty-first and Twenty-second Dynasties in Thebes, there is a distinct lack of manuscripts for women from the Twenty-third to Twenty-fifth Dynasties, or at least a lack of datable papyri. Again, troubled times seem to be the reason for a further change in funerary customs (Quirke, 1993: 19; Jansen-Winkeln, 2000: 1–20; 2001: 153–82).

Table 9.2: Overview of female owners during the Libyan Period

| | Inventory No. | Name | Title | Relation | Reference |
|---|---|---|---|---|---|
| 29 | P.London BM EA 10490 | Nedjmet | King's wife Lady of the Two Lands King's mother | Husband: Herihor Mother: Herere | TM 134518 |
| 30 | P.London BM EA 10541+P.Paris Louvre E. 6258 | see no. [29] | see no. [29] | see no. [29] | TM 133525 |
| 31 | P.Cairo CG 40005 = J.E. 95856 | Henttawy | King's wife Lady of the Two Lands King's mother | Father: Ramesses XI Husband: Pinudjem I Daughter: Maatkare, see no. [33] | TM 134430 |
| 32 | P.Cairo J.E. 95887 | see no. [31] | see no. [31] | see no. [31] | TM 134663 |
| 33 | P.Cairo CG 40007 = J.E. 26229 | Maatkare | God's wife of Amun King's daughter | Daughter: Henttawy, see no. [31] Father: Pinudjem I | TM 134431 |
| 34 | P.New York MMA 25.3.29 | Henttawy | Great of the harem of Amun-Re | Mother: Asetemakhbit Father: Menkheperre Sister: Gatseshen, see no. [35] | TM 134562 |
| 35 | P.Cairo J.E. 95838 | Gatseshen | Great of the harem of Amun-Re Chantress of Amun Great singer of Mut | Father: Menkheperre Sister: Henttawy, see no. [34] | TM 134448 |
| 36 | P.London BM EA 10554 = P.Greenfield | Nesitanebetisheru | Great of the harem of Amun-Re | Mother: Neskhonsu, see no. [38] Father: Pinudjem II | TM 134519 |
| 37 | P.Paris BN 62-88 | Ankhesenaset | Chantress of Amun | - | TM 134568 |
| 38 | P.Cairo J.E. 26230 | Neskhonsu | Great of the harem of Amun-Re | Father: Smendes II Husband: Pinudjem II Daughter: Nesitanebisheru, see no. [36] | TM 134444 |
| 39 | P.Paris BN 138-140 + P.Paris Louvre E. 3661 | Nesitabetawi | - | Mother: Tanetditkhonsu | TM 133576 |
| 40 | P.London BM EA 10084 | Asety | Chantress of Amun | - | TM 134511 |
| 41 | P.Turin CGT 53001= Cat. 1849 | Tameret | Chantress of Amun Great singer of Mut | - | TM 134605 |

**Table 9.2: Continued**

| 42 | P.Turin CGT 53007 = Cat. 1851 | Asty | Chantress of Amun | - | TM 134741 |
| 43 | P.Turin CGT 53008 = Cat. 1855 | Djedmutiusankh | Chantress of Amun | - | TM 134609 |
| 44 | P.Turin CGT 53009 = Cat. 1862/2 | Djedbastet | Chantress of Amun | - | TM 134612 |
| 45 | P.Cairo CG 40009 = J.E. 95861 | Asetemakhbit | Chantress of Amun | - | TM 134451 |
| 46 | P.Cairo S.R. VII 10222 | Tabakhenkhonsu | Chantress of Amun | - | TM 134491 |
| 47 | P.London BM EA 9938 | Tanetshedkhonsu | Chantress of Amun | - | TM 134508 |
| 48 | P.London BM EA 9904 | Asetemakhbit | Chantress of Amun | - | TM 134533 |
| 49 | P.New York MMA 25.3.34 | Tii | Chantress of Amun | - | TM 134630 |

## Kushite and Saite Periods (Table 9.3)

The reason for the lack of Book of the Dead copies for women (and also men) from the Twenty-fifth Dynasty is that burials from this time are badly preserved (see the contributions in Pischikova et al., 2014). The (thus far) only known copy for a woman from this period belongs to Tashepenkhonsu, the "noblewoman and musician of Amun-Re" [50]. The dating of the cursive hieroglyphic copy without vignettes is based on the paleography: It is similar to the writing on Tashepenkhonsu's outer coffin (P.Paris Louvre E. 3913), which can be dated to the late Twenty-fifth or early Twenty-sixth Dynasty (Taylor, 2009: 17–23). Tashepenkhonsu was the wife of the Montu-priest Nespasefy II and was therefore a member of one of the highest Theban families of the late Twenty-fifth to Twenty-sixth Dynasties (Vittmann, 1978: 3–61; Kitchen, 2015: 224–30; Töpfer, 2016: 383–87). Another member of the Besenmut family is the "lady of the house," Tawiri, the owner of a "stock" manuscript [51] that had been originally produced for a man: a male deceased is indeed depicted in the vignettes, and there is a spatium for the name of the subsequent owner, with only the determinative of a sitting man having been filled in. Although the number of examples is small, the design of this extensive manuscript seems to be typical for Book of the Dead copies of the Twenty-sixth Dynasty: hieratic script in columns divided by a double bar and delicately colored vignettes. Tawiri was the mother of the Amun-priest Djedkhi (P.Cairo J.E. 95685 et al.), whose wife was Tasheredenaset (Munro, 2011), who also owned a "stock" Book of the Dead manuscript

[52] that is quite similar to that of her husband and mother-in-law [51]. Her name was filled in only in BD 1 without specifying her titles.

Unlike those of the Libyan Period, Book of the Dead copies for women from the Saite Period are mainly "stock" manuscripts, originally produced for a male deceased, like the papyrus of Iahtesnakht [53], probably the best-known example from this time. Here the figure of the female owner was added later behind that of the man in the vignette for BD 125, and her name was added above the figures of Isis and Nephthys and above the wife of the male deceased in the vignette of BD 15. No titles are given, either of the owner or of her parents, which is why nothing can be said about the status of Iahtesnakht; however, considering the high quality of the large manuscript, and especially of the well-preserved colored vignettes, she must have belonged to a wealthy family (Verhoeven, 1993: 3). A rare Book of the Dead copy written exclusively for a woman is the unfinished manuscript of the "musician of Amun-Re," Irtiru [54]. The frames for the spells and vignettes were laid out but the scenes were not added, and five spells (after BD 81) were not written.

The Twenty-sixth Dynasty itself is characterized by the prominence of women of the elite, such as Nitokris and Ankhenesneferibre, playing official roles in the temple cult. However, it should not be forgotten that this was already the case in the Twenty-first, Twenty-second, and Twenty-fifth Dynasties. The fact that female owners of Book of the Dead copies are documented throughout the Nubian and Saite Periods, with some having owned excellent manuscripts, may be explained in light of this female prominence. After the end of the Twenty-sixth Dynasty, Book of the Dead copies are only rarely documented. They become common again during the Thirtieth Dynasty and the early Ptolemaic Period.

Table 9.3: Overview of female owners during the Kushite and Saite Periods

|    | Inventory No. | Name | Title | Relation | Reference |
|----|---------------|------|-------|----------|-----------|
| 50 | P.Moscow I, 1b, 121 | Tashepenkhonsu | Lady of the house Noblewoman Musician of Amun-Re | Husband: Nespasefy II Mother: Aset Father: Iuenfy | TM 112292 |
| 51 | P.Moscow I, 1b, 107+P.Cairo J.E. 95685+95745+95840+95841 | Tawiri | - | Son: Djedkhi | TM 112516 |
| 52 | P.Heidelberg von Portheim-Stiftung (A) et al. | Tasheredenaset | - | Husband: Djedkhi Mother: Namenkhet Father: Besenmut | TM 57043 |
| 53 | P.Colon. Aeg. 10207 | Iahtesnakht | - | Mother: Tadiiw Father: Pasherienaui | TM 57143 |
| 54 | P.Turin Cat. 1842 | Irtiru | Musician of Amun-Re | Father: Horemakhbit | TM 57580 |

# LATE PERIOD TO PTOLEMAIC–ROMAN PERIOD (TABLE 9.4)

The late fifth century BCE sees the beginning of a tradition of copying the Book of the Dead onto mummy bandages (Kockelmann, 2008: 16–23). According to Kockelmann (2008: 289), approximately one-third of the owners are female. Most of the linen copies are written in hieratic; only a few are in hieroglyphic script, such as the bandage of Bastetiirdis [55], which shows a layout resembling the Book of the Dead copies found on papyri such as the manuscript of Kerheb [56]. The hieratic bandages belonging to the members of the Padineith family from Saqqara (Pernigotti, 1985) are well known, for

Table 9.4: Overview of female owners during the Late Period to Ptolemaic–Roman Period

| | Inventory No. | Name | Title | Relation | Reference |
|---|---|---|---|---|---|
| 55 | M.London UC 32381+32382 | Bastetiirdis | - | Mother: Bastetiirdis | TM 114036 |
| 56 | P.Turin Cat. 1814 | Kerheb | - | Mother: Ta(a)mun | TM 57594 |
| 57 | M.Aberdeen ABDUA 84131 et al. | Tasheretentakeri | - | Mother: Tasheketi Son: Padineith | TM 109992 |
| 58 | M.Saqqara R. 306 et al. | Bastetiirdis | - | Mother: Sekhmet | TM 114035 |
| 59 | M.Antwerpen 4943 et al. | Asetemakhbit | Musician of Ptah | Mother: Tanetamun Father: Padiosiris | TM 109626 |
| 60 | M.Uppsala VM MB 37 + 63 | Neferii (?) | - | Mother: Neferetiu | TM 114083 |
| 61 | M.Firenze 5706+ 5707+5709–5714 | Takerheb | - | Mother: Nebetdjenekhit Father: Aapehti | TM 114164 |
| 62 | P.Christchurch EA 1988.73–76 | see no. [61] | see no. [61] | see no. [61] | TM 112313 |
| 63 | P.Turin Cat. 1837 | Tasheretenkhonsu | - | Mother: Tasheretmenu Father: Imhotep | TM 57600 |
| 64 | P.London BM EA 10796 | Tanetaset | - | Mother: Nesnephthys | TM 57276 |
| 65 | P.Turin Cat. 1833 | Taysnakht | - | Mother: Tames | TM 57577 |
| 66 | P.Leiden T 16 | Asetweret | Musician of Amun-Re | Mother: Khonsuirdis | TM 56985 |
| 67 | P.Berlin P. 3158 A–G | Reret | - | Mother: Taditbastet Father: Nakhtpefjabi Son: Padihorpachered Grandchild: Taitem; see no. [68] | TM 57107 |

(continued)

Table 9.4: Continued

| | Inventory No. | Name | Title | Relation | Reference |
|---|---|---|---|---|---|
| 68 | P.Berlin P. 3159 A–D | Taitem | – | Mother: Wedjarenes Father: Padihorpachered Grandmother: Reret, see no. [67] | TM 57108 |
| 69 | P.Turin Cat. 1801 | Asetweret | – | Mother: Tasheretamun | TM 57586 |
| 70 | P.Berlin P. 3008 | Tarudj | – | Mother: Perusis | TM 57089 |
| 71 | P.Leiden T 31 | Tasherettaiihet | – | Mother: Asetweret | TM 56996 |
| 72 | P.Florence 3662 | Arsinoe | – | Mother: Tasherettut | TM 57824 |
| 73 | P.Paris Louvre N. 3083 + P.Paris Louvre N. 3194 A | Asetreshti | – | Mother: Takhibiat | TM 57746 |
| 74 | P.Privat MacGregor | Tarepit | – | Mother: Asetreshti Father: Pakhi | TM 57673 |
| 75 | P.Berlin P. 10477 | Neferetii | – | Mother: Pesedet Father: Neshor | TM 50354 |
| 76 | P.Vatican 38603 | Asetweret | Musician of Amun-Re | Mother: Qiqi | TM 57645 |
| 77 | P.Toulouse 73.1.6 | Tanetimen | Lady of the house Musician of Amun-Re | Mother: Tanetqabeneret | TM 57178 |
| 78 | P.Paris Louvre N. 3063 | Tanetkhebet | Musician of Amun-Re | Mother: Taytef(nu)t Father: Khenemibre | TM 56583 |
| 79 | P.London BM EA 10983 + Private Collection | Beret | – | Mother: Imhotep | TM 57279 |
| 80 | P.Florence 3665+ 3666 + P.Vienna ÄS 3850 | Mutmut | Musician of Amun-Re | Father: Padineferhotep | TM 57738 |
| 81 | P.Paris Louvre N. 3279 | Tawau | Musician of Amun-Re | Mother: Ipetweret | TM 57883 |

example that of Tasheretentakeri [57], the mother of Padineith, and of Padineith's grandmother Bastetiirdis [58]. The female owners are mentioned on the mummy bandages almost entirely without titles, although titles, even priestly ones, are known from other sources (Kockelmann, 2008: 288). An exception are the bandages of Asetemakhbit [59] from Memphis, who is referred to by the title "musician of Ptah," her mother having been a "musician of Sokar." The hieratic handwriting is distinctive, with higher-than-average signs, similar to the handwriting on the mummy bandage of Neferii [60]. The texts on both bandages were most likely copied by the same scribe (Kockelmann, 2008: 121–22).

Late Book of the Dead copies on linen, however, are no substitute for the papyrus specimen, as could already be seen in the case of Hatneferet from the Eighteenth Dynasty [9–12]. The burial assemblage of Takerheb (see for references Töpfer, 2015: 248–49) included—along with the coffin, cartonnage, and hypocephalus—eight mummy bandages with Book of the Dead spells [61], as well as a Book of the Dead papyrus [62]. The papyrus was written, in hieratic, exclusively for the female deceased, who is also depicted in its vignettes. The papyrus of Tasheretenkhonsu [63] is comparable in layout and writing, and both are characterized by high-quality vignettes and texts (Fig. 9.3).

"Stock" manuscripts showing a male deceased, despite belonging to women, are attested on mummy bandages as well as papyri [64]. But when a papyrus was produced exclusively for a female owner, she is pictured in the vignettes without a man in most known examples. One exception is the vignette of the field of reeds, in which the heavy physical work is occasionally executed by men, such as in the papyrus of Taysnakht [65], who is otherwise depicted in nearly all color vignettes as the one who is talking, praising, or offering (Fig. 9.4). In the case of the scene in the large papyrus of Asetweret [66], the figure of the man depicted is instead inscribed with the name of the female owner. Overall, there are more Book of the Dead copies for women on papyrus than on mummy bandages. The dating of the papyri is based mainly on paleographical and stylistic grounds, the majority being dated to the fourth and third centuries BCE. The papyri of Reret [67] and her granddaughter Taitem [68] can be dated to the fourth century BCE. Their papyri are interesting in many regards: they were produced in the same Theban workshop—as was the papyrus of Reret's son and Taitem's father, Padihorpachered (P.Aberdeen ABDUA84023)—and contain other religious texts apart from Book of the Dead spells, such as invocations of and offering formulae to deities (Backes, 2009: 40–56). Similar both in layout and in the style of the cursive hieroglyphic handwriting is the Book of the Dead of Asetweret [69], which is dominated by the scenes of the adoration of Osiris and of the judgment. A noteworthy detail in the weighing scene is that the heart weighs less than the feather.

Papyri with a combination of Book of the Dead spells and other (partly new) funerary compositions for women are documented quite well in this period. There is the Book of the Dead copy of Tarudj [70], written in cursive hieroglyphs, which includes the lamentations of Isis and Nephthys in hieratic; the latter are also found in the papyrus of Tasherettaihet [71]. Several late Ptolemaic papyri contain copies of the Book of the Dead and the Book of Breathing (cf. Albert, Kucharek, and Scalf, this volume). The latter became a distinct funerary composition, as exemplified by the papyri of Arsinoe [72] and Asetreshti [73]. A list of amulets is included in the long Book of the Dead copy of Tarepit [74] from Akhmim, written for her but depicting a male figure in most of the vignettes. Tarepit is pictured only in the central scenes showing the adoration of Osiris and the judgment. Furthermore, a parallel to BD 191, the "*Ba*-Bringer" chapter (Wüthrich and Stöhr, 2013), is contained in the Akhmim papyrus of Neferetii [75] (Lüscher, 1998). The papyrus of the "musician of Amun-Re," Asetweret [76], contains a combination of Book of the Dead spells, glorifications, and scenes from the Ritual of Opening the Mouth (Albert, 2016).

The female title of "musician of Amun-Re" occurs more frequently in Theban copies than the designation "lady of the house," especially in those dating to the late Ptolemaic

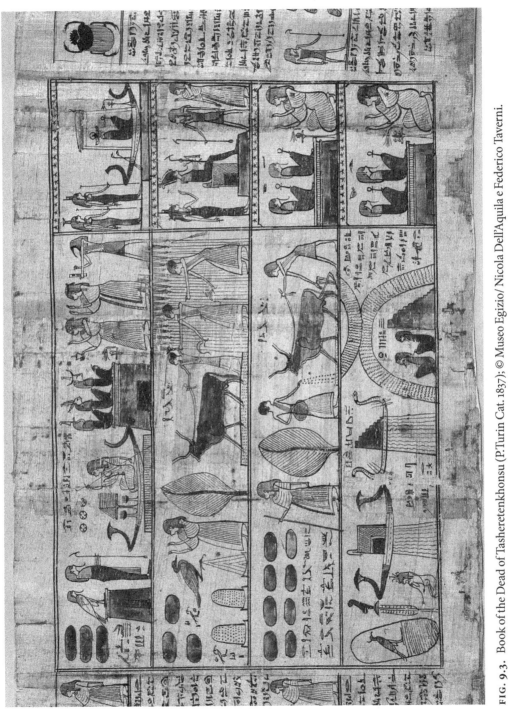

FIG. 9.3. Book of the Dead of Tasheretenkhonsu (P. Turin Cat. 1837); © Museo Egizio / Nicola Dell'Aquila / Federico Taverni.

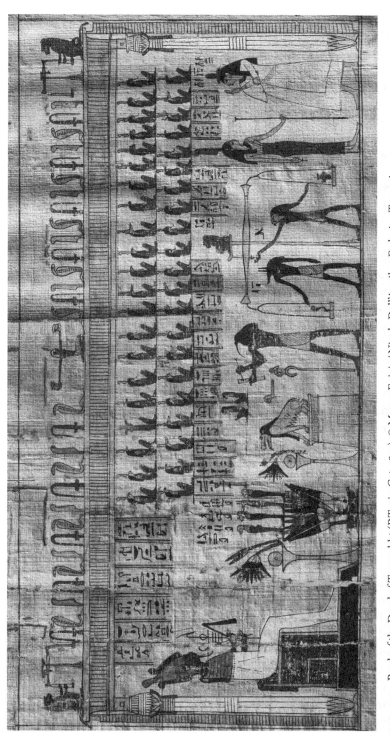

FIG. 9.4. Book of the Dead of Taysnakht (P. Turin Cat. 1833); © Museo Egizio/ Nicola Dell'Aquila e Federico Taverni.

Period. Both titles are mentioned on the papyrus of Tanetimen [77], who is depicted in two vignettes along with her mother, the "lady of the house and musician of Amun-Re," Tanetqabeneret. Many titles are given for Tanetkhebet [78]; besides the titles "lady of the house and musician of Amun-Re," she was also a priestess of Thoth, Khonsu, and Amun-Re. While such an office was usually borne by men, it is clear that the manuscript was produced for Tanetkhebet based on the vignettes, which depict a female deceased, and on the fact that the name and titles are written within the text by the same scribe. Moreover, the determinative of the first mention of the title "priestess" is the sitting woman hieroglyph, and the term "Hathor" follows after the designation "Osiris" preceding the name of the owner. The designation of the beneficiary of the text as "Osiris-Hathor of" illustrates clearly that the owner is female (for the locution, see Smith, 2017: 384–89 with references). The designation of the female deceased as "Hathor," in alternation with "Osiris," can also be seen in the papyrus of Beret [79]. This particular manuscript has red guiding lines for the hieratic script, which are rare and attested in only a few late Ptolemaic to Roman Period papyri (Quack, 2015: 449). The dominant use of the color pink for nearly all figures in the vignette is another striking feature, attested mainly for the late Ptolemaic and Roman Period (see the overview by Töpfer, 2017: 399–400).

The exact dating of manuscripts within the Ptolemaic, and especially the Roman, Periods is difficult. Besides the paleography, the content of the manuscripts also serves as evidence. Papyri primarily consisting of other funerary compositions, such as the Book of Breathing, with very little Book of the Dead material, tend to date to the late Ptolemaic or early Roman Period. An example is the manuscript of the "musician of Amun-Re," Mutmut [80], in which the copy of the Book of Breathing is combined with Book of the Dead scenes such as the adoration of Osiris and the hall of judgment. The text, inscribed for the "musician of Amun-Re," Tawau [81], is based on some Book of the Dead spells (e.g., BD 18, 42, 62, 57, and 59), but forms the composition entitled "The First Letter for Breathing" (Smith, 2009: 499–510). According to both style and paleography, both manuscripts date to the Roman Period (the first or even early second century CE).

# Conclusion

Female owners of the Book of the Dead copies are well documented from the beginning to the end of the textual tradition of this corpus. From the end of the Second Intermediate Period to the Third Intermediate Period, most of the owners are connected with royalty or the ruling elite, while the copies dating from the Saite to the Roman Period belong to members of the priestly community of the temple estates, and mainly to musicians. The most frequent title borne by women is the funerary appellative "lady of the house," which in most cases is the only title, and thus tells us little about the social status of the owner, aside from her legal position as wife. However, it is known that the production of a Book of the Dead papyrus was expensive, and therefore female owners thereof must have belonged to the wealthy upper class by birth, occupation, and/or marriage. The bulk of the manuscripts discussed in this chapter, written or adapted for women, were produced for women of royal status or with prominent positions in temple cult, and bear witness to the influence of political and religious developments on funerary beliefs throughout Egyptian history. Manuscripts for women do not differ significantly in style, content, or quality from those produced for men; moreover, some of the highest-quality copies were inscribed exclusively for women. Ownership of a copy of the Book of the Dead depended on the owner's social and financial position, rather than on gender.

## Bibliography

Albert, F. (2016). *Le livre des morts d'Aset-Ouret.* Aegyptiaca Gregoriana, col. 6 (Vatican: Edizioni Musei Vaticani).

Andrews, C. (1978). "A family for Anhai." *Journal of Egyptian Archaeology* 64: 88–98.

Backes, B. (2009). *Drei Totenpapyri aus einer thebanischen Werkstatt der Spätzeit (pBerlin P. 3158, pBerlin P. 3159, pAberdeen ABDUA 84023).* Handschriften des Altägyptischen Totenbuches, vol. 11 (Wiesbaden: Harrassowitz).

Barwik, M. (1997). "Amenemheb and Amenemopet. New Light on a Papyrus from the National Museum in Warsaw." In *Essays in Honour of Prof. Dr. Jadwiga Lipinska*, vol. 1, edited by J. Aksamit, 331–38 (Warsaw: National Museum in Warsaw).

Depauw, M. and Gheldof, T. (2014) "Trismegistos. An Interdisciplinary Platform for Ancient World Texts and Related Information." In *Theory and Practice of Digital Libraries - TPDL 2013 Selected Workshops (Communications in Computer and Information Science 416)*, edited by Ł. Bolikowski et al., 40–52 (Cham: Springer).

Dodson, A. and Hilton, D. (2004). *The Complete Royal Families of Ancient Egypt* (London: Thames&Hudson).

Franco, I. (1988). "Fragments de "Livres des Morts"-sur toile-découvert dans la vallée des Reines." *Le Bulletin de l'Institut français d'archéologie orientale* 88: 71–82.

Graefe, E. (1981). *Untersuchungen zur Verwaltung und Geschichte der Institution der Gottesgemahlin des Amun vom Beginn des neuen Reiches bis zur Spätzeit.* Ägyptologische Abhandlungen, vol. 37 (Wiesbaden: Harrassowitz).

Jansen-Winkeln, K. (2000). "Die Fremdherrschaft in Ägypten im 1. Jahrtausend v. Chr." *Orientalia* 69: 1–20.

Jansen-Winkeln, K. (2001). "Der thebanische Gottesstaat." *Orientalia* 70: 153–82.

Kitchen, K. A. (2015). *The Third Intermediate Period in Egypt (1100–650 BC)* (Warminster: Aris&Phillips).

Koch, C. (2012). *"Die den Amun mit ihrer Stimme zufriedenstellen"-Gottesgemahlinnen und Musikerinnen im thebanischen Amunstaat von der 22. bis zur 26. Dynastie.* Studien zu den Ritualszenen altägyptischer Tempel, vol. 27 (Dettelbach: Röll).

Kockelmann, H. (2008). *Untersuchungen zu den späten Totenbuch-Handschriften auf Mumienbinden.* Studien des Altägyptischen Totenbuches, vol. 12 (Wiesbaden: Harrassowitz).

Lenzo Marchese, G. (2007). *Manuscrits hiératiques du Livre des Morts de la Troisième Période intermédiaire (Papyrus de Turin CGT 53001-53013)* (Grand-Saconnex: Société d'Égyptologie).

Lucarelli, R. (2006). *The Book of the Dead of Gatseshen. Ancient Egyptian Funerary Religion in the 10th century BC* (Leiden: Nederlands Instituut voor het Nabije Oosten).

Lüscher, B. (1998). *Das Totenbuch pBerlin P. 10477 aus Achmim.* Handschriften des Altägyptischen Totenbuches, vol. 6 (Wiesbaden: Harrassowitz).

Munro, I. (1988). *Untersuchungen zu den Totenbuch-Papyri der 18. Dynastie. Kriterien ihrer Datierung* (London: Kegan Paul).

Munro, I. (2009). *Der Totenbuch-Papyrus der Ta-schep-en-Chonsu aus der späten 25. Dynastie*. Handschriften des Altägyptischen Totenbuches, vol. 10 (Wiesbaden: Harrassowitz).

Munro, I. (2011). *Die Totenbuch-Papyri des Ehepaares Ta-scheret-en-Aset und Djed-chi aus der Bes-en-Mut-Familie*. Handschriften des Altägyptischen Totenbuches, vol. 12 (Wiesbaden: Harrassowitz).

Niwinski, A. (1989). *Studies on the Illustrated Theban Funerary Papyri of the 11th and 10th Centuries B.C.* (Göttingen: Vandenhoeck u. Ruprecht).

Ockinga, B. G. (2006). "The Shroud of Tny, R92: An Early Example of Book of the Dead 100 on Linen." In *Egyptian Art in the Nicholson Museum, Sydney*, edited by K. N. Sowada and B. G. Ockinga, 179–89 (Sydney: Mediterranean Archaeology).

Pernigotti, S. (1985). *Tomba di Boccori. Il "Libro dei morti" su bende di mummia*. Saqqara, vol. II,1 (Pisa: Giardini).

Pischikova, E. et al. (2014). *Thebes in the First Millennium BC* (Newcastle upon Tyne: Cambridge Scholars Publishing).

Pries, A. (2011). *Die Stundenwachen im Osiriskult*. Studien zur spätägyptischen Religion, vol. 2 (Wiesbaden: Harrassowitz).

Quack, J. F. (2015). "Rohrfedertorheiten? Bemerkungen zum römerzeitlichen Hieratisch." In *Ägyptologische "Binsen"-Weisheiten I-II. Neue Forschungen und Methoden der Hieratistik, Akten zweier Tagungen in Mainz im April 2011 und im März 2013*, edited by U. Verhoeven, 435–68 (Stuttgart: Steiner).

Quirke, S. (1993). *Owners of Funerary Papyri in the British Museum* (London: Department of Egyptian Antiquities).

Quirke, S. (1999). "Women in Ancient Egypt: Temple Titles and Funerary Papyri." In *Studies on Ancient Egypt in Honour of H.S. Smith*, edited by A. Leahy and J. Tait, 227–35 (London: Egypt Exploration Society).

Ragazzoli, C. (2010). "The Book of the Dead of Ankhesenaset (P. BNF Egyptien 62–88). Traces of Workshop Production or Scribal Experiments?" *British Museum Studies in Ancient Egypt and Sudan* 15: 225–48.

Smith, M. (2009). *Traversing Eternity. Texts for the Afterlife from Ptolemaic and Roman Egypt* (Oxford: Oxford University Press).

Smith, M. 2017. *Following Osiris: Perspectives on the Osirian Afterlife from Four Millennia*. Oxford: University Press.

Taylor, J. H. (1999). "The Burial Assemblage of Henutmehyt: Inventory, Date and Provenance." In *Studies in Egyptian Antiquities. A tribute to T.G.H. James*, edited by W. V. Davies, 59–72 (London: British Museum).

Taylor, J. H. (2009). Contributions in Munro 2009.

Taylor, J. H. (2010). *Journey through the afterlife. Ancient Egyptian Book of the Dead* (London: British Museum).

Theis, C. (2015). *Magie und Raum. Der magische Schutz auserwählter Räume im alten Ägypten nebst einem Vergleich zu angrenzenden Kulturbereichen*. Orientalische Religionen in der Antike, vol. 13 (Tübingen: Mohr Siebeck).

Töpfer, S. (2015). *Das Balsamierungsritual. Eine (Neu-)Edition der Textkomposition Balsamierungsritual (pBoulaq 3, pLouvre 5158, pDurham 1983.11 + pSt. Petersburg 18128)*. Studien zur spätägyptischen Religion, vol. 13 (Wiesbaden: Harrassowitz).

Töpfer, S. (2016). "Teile des Totenbuches des Anch-ef-en-Chonsu, Sohn des Bes-en-Mut in der Österreichischen Nationalbibliothek (Papyrus Wien Aeg. 12022a+b)." *Studien zur altägyptischen Kultur* 45: 375–88.

Töpfer, S. (2017). "Aggressives Rosa—Zu einer Mumienauflage der spätptolemäisch-frührömischen Epoche aus Achmim (ÄMUL Inv.-Nr. 7810)." *Bulletin de l'Institut francais d'archeologie orientale* 116: 385–410.

Verhoeven, U. (1993). *Das saitische Totenbuch der Iahtesnacht*. P. Colon. Aeg. 10207 (Bonn: Habelt).

Verhoeven, U. (1999). *Das Totenbuch des Monthpriesters Nespasefy aus der Zeit Psammetichs I. pKairo JE 95714+pAlbany 1900.3.1, pKairo JE 95649, pMarseille 91/2/1 (ehem. Slg. Brunner)+pMarseille 291*. Handschriften des Altägyptischen Totenbuches, vol. 5 (Wiesbaden: Harrassowitz).

Vittmann, G. (1978). *Priester und Beamte im Theben der Spätzeit. Genealogische und prosopographische Untersuchungen zum thebanischen Priester- und Beamtentum der 25. und 26. Dynastie* (Wien: Afro-Pub).

Wüthrich, A. and Stöhr, S. (2013). *Ba-Bringer und Schattenabschneider: Untersuchungen zum so genannten Totenbuchkapitel 191 auf Totenbuchpapyri*, Studien des Altägyptischen Totenbuches, vol. 18 (Wiesbaden: Harrassowitz).

CHAPTER 10

# BOOK OF THE DEAD ON TISSUES

*Shrouds and Mummy Bandages*

ANNIE GASSE

As the heir of the Coffin Texts and therefore also of the ancient Pyramid Texts, the Book of the Dead is constituted as a full collection in the Second Intermediate Period.[1] Its oldest testimonials are found on the coffin of Queen Mentuhotep, probably dated in the Thirteenth Dynasty (Geisen, 2004). The texts copied on this object contain a great majority of spells from the Book of the Dead, among which a few spells from the Coffin Texts testify to the incorporation of the texts into the Book of the Dead, even as early as this period (see also Gestermann, this volume).

The first collection of the Book of the Dead on papyrus, as it will be represented during two millenaries, does not appear before the beginning of the Eighteenth Dynasty. Meanwhile, the first versions of what would become the principal funerary text intended to accompany the dead in the netherworld were copied mainly on fabrics.

## SHROUDS

While there are relatively few Books of the Dead on papyrus before the Nineteenth Dynasty, a certain number of shrouds, some of the first of which are dated in the very end of the Seventeenth Dynasty, can already be considered to be a true Book of the Dead. The linen shrouds had been used since the beginning of the history

---

[1] This work benefited from the support of Labex ARCHIMEDE within the program "Investissement d'Avenir," ANR-11-LABX-0032-01.

of the pharaohs, but it was only at the end of the Second Intermediate Period that people began to write texts on them. Today, 44 written shrouds are listed (Müller-Roth, 2008). The most ancient of these shrouds belonged to members of the royal family at the end of the Seventeenth Dynasty (Turin C.G. 63001, 63002, 63003, 63004, 63005). They are large linen pieces intended to wrap almost completely around the dead body. They carry extracts of the Book of the Dead, more precisely BD 149–150, arranged in columns and copied in "retrograde writing" (see Goelet and Verhoeven, this volume). The signs are cursive hieroglyphs and sometimes hieratic ones; hieratic signs may appear among cursive hieroglyphs.

The entirety of the written shrouds belongs to a period ranging from the very end of the Second Intermediate Period (end of the Seventeenth Dynasty) to the reign of Amenhotep III. Most of them can be dated to the beginning of the Eighteenth Dynasty (Fig. 10.1) and, sometimes with more precision, to the reigns of Hatshepsut/Thutmose III or Amenhotep II. One copy from the reign of Thutmose IV/Amenhotep III (New York MMA TT 850; Müller-Roth, 2008: 152) would thus be the most recent one.[2]

These shrouds are always made of linen, whose quality likely depended on the wealth of the deceased or his family. They are different in size, but not a single complete piece has ever survived. The largest ones are among the most ancient pieces, and they can reach from 125 centimeters up to 138 centimeters in length. Soon after this, a much shorter type of mummy shroud appeared; these ranged from 50 centimeters to over one meter in height. They were formatted like the Book of the Dead on papyrus; the text was in cursive or hieratic hieroglyphs, arranged in retrograde columns and topped with a stripe of vignettes. Not all the fragments carry an illustration, but some of them show meticulously drawn vignettes, including a few finely colored ones. The vignettes are arranged at the top of the fabrics, above the text, and sometimes at the bottoms of the columns.[3] They follow the characteristic iconographic canons related to illustrations of the Book of the Dead on papyrus.

Slightly more than three-fifths of those documented are dated more or less precisely between the Seventeenth Dynasty and the beginning of the Eighteenth Dynasty. Two documents are from the reign of Ahmose. In this ensemble, two particular constants can be noted: one sequence dedicated to the spells of transformation (BD 124, 77, 83 to 88, excluding 87) is set in the beginning. BD 124, considered an introduction, allows the deceased to join Osiris's assembly. It has no parallel in the Coffin Texts. This sequence is completed by BD 99B (which has a predecessor in the Coffin Texts), evoking the navigation of the dead in Re's boat.

The ends of some documents frequently consist of three chapters: BD 136B, BD 149, and BD 150 (vignette). The first one, which evolved from a peculiar composition that

---

[2] The fabrics L.Grab TT 360 (Müller-Roth, 2008), dated in the reign of Ramses II, must rather be added to the group of "linen squares," which are a kind of funerary amulet, but do not carry extracts of the Book of the Dead (El-Enany, 2010).

[3] A rare copy (Sydney R92) shows a text written in lines.

FIG. 10.1. Book of the Dead of Kha (Turin Suppl. 8438); © Museo Egizio/ Nicola Dell'Aquila e Federico Taverni.

is part of the Coffin Texts, the so-called Book of the Two Ways (Lesko, 1972; Hermsen, 1991; Rössler-Köhler, 2003; Backes, 2005; Assmann, 2008; Sherbiny, 2017), concerns magic against snakes; the other two, also following the Coffin Texts, describe the topography of the netherworld.

The choice of these spells, still very much steeped in the beliefs expressed in the Coffin Texts, emphasizes two essential points: the ability of the deceased to change into different animals or divine creatures, and his knowledge of the geography of the netherworld, which prevents him from becoming lost among malicious snakes.

The most recent shrouds do not have the same selection. The choice of spells is much more diverse. Chapters that will become essential and among the most popular of the entire history of Book of the Dead appear, such as BD 125 (which includes the final judgment of the dead, or "psychostasy"), BD 30B (on the preservation of the heart, this one having to testify in favor of the deceased), and the very long BD 17 (on the protection that numerous divinities grant the dead against the pitfalls awaiting him in the afterworld). The spells of transformation are still included, although less often, and they are no longer the main focus. A new sequence appears, consisting of BD 22 to 28, granting the dead the conservation of his powers and identity (opening of the mouth, preservation of his name, and magic powers). This group will be of increasing importance in the history of the Book of the Dead; sometimes it is the only one written on the papyri of the Third Intermediate Period. Those preferences expressed by the Egyptians on their funerary shrouds reflect what can be observed on the funerary papyri of the time (Munro, 1987). The shrouds certainly reflect these preferences, even more than the papyri, since they are placed closer to the body. There are significantly fewer inscribed shrouds than papyri in this period. We can therefore assume that people who had a shroud inscribed for themselves or for a loved one were expressing a personal sentiment. It should also be noted that at least one person had both a written shroud and a papyrus carrying the passages of the Book of the Dead in his tomb (Sennefer, from the time of Thutmose III; Strudwick, 2000).

As they are generally incomplete, not all shrouds have preserved the name of their owner. Among the names that are preserved, a considerable number appear to be those of members of the royal families (kings' daughters and sons); the others are names of important civil servants of the central administration and, at least in one case, of a provincial member of the clergy (Gasse, 1983; 2006: 4–5). Most documents whose origin is known (two-thirds in all) were found in Thebes, and only three come from provincial cities.

The use of funerary fabrics with excerpts from the Book of the Dead is attested particularly in Deir el-Bahari; here we also see the use of funerary fabrics without them, such as the squares of linen from Deir el-Medina (El-Enany, 2010), as well as anepigraphic shrouds or shrouds carrying the image of Osiris or another divinity, such as that of Amenhotep I. After Amenhotep III's reign, the use of textiles inscribed with excerpts from the Book of the Dead becomes obsolete.

## Mummy Bandages

The hypothesis of certain authors that the use of inscribed mummy bandages dates back to the New Kingdom cannot be confirmed. The most ancient written mummy bandage could be dated, at the earliest, in the Thirtieth Dynasty (Verhoeven, 2001: 22 and 26; Kockelmann, 2008: II, 17). Indeed, Egyptologists are in agreement on calling the bands of tissue that are more or less long and especially narrow (ca. 10 cm max.) "mummy bandages."

The mummy bandages are always cut out of linen and are, as should be expected, of variable quality. They are mostly taken from large, often reused pieces of fabric. The deceased's kin had the possibility of providing him with fabric taken from slightly used cloth (Bataille, 1939). A famous specimen mentions mummy bandages made from a boat's sail (Goyon and Josset, 1988: 25–27). Once in the hands of the embalming specialists, these stripes of fabrics were prepared, trimmed, and, above all, decorated with texts and vignettes according to both the local customs of the time as well as the choice of the deceased—if he had ever been able to anticipate this event—and the family. The height of the mummy bandages varies roughly between 5 or 6 centimeters and 25 centimeters. The length is also variable; the longest mummy bandages known measure up to 7.70 meters. They are often composed of several pieces of fabrics sewn together, end to end. A numbering, which most probably served as a reference in the scribes' work, appears on some of them in either hieratic or demotic (Kockelmann, 2008: II, 147–85). Sometimes there is only one number, and sometimes there is a more complete indication, for instance "first" or "8th mummy bandage," or even "it is the 10th mummy bandage." In a few cases, the number is noted by mere dots. Currently, the highest number we know is 30. Few written mummy bandages have been found in situ. This shows that they had to be wrapped around the body as closely as possible to reinforce their efficiency.

Most of the texts copied on mummy bandages are written in hieratic; however, hieroglyphs can also be used for this purpose, these being cursive hieroglyphs. They are mainly used in the offering scenes and, more particularly, on the vignettes showing the introduction of the deceased to Osiris (Fig. 10.2).

Hieratic is, therefore, the most frequently used form of writing. The written forms follow the same evolution as the one observed on papyrus, which gives vital clues for dating. In the Roman Period, the signs spread in width, the texts are airier, and horizontal lines are favored. Some copies—still undeciphered—show writing that seems to go back and forth between hieratic and demotic (Vandenbeusch, 2010: 170–71) and is undoubtedly reminiscent of the "pseudo-writing" that is found on some contemporary stelae of "Horus on the crocodiles" (Gasse, 119; Sternberg-e-Hotabi, 1994; 1999: 136–42).

The quality of the copyist's work must be emphasized. The fabrics, which are rather soft and consequently easily stretched, don't generally give a good impression of the original aspects of the documents. Indeed, although the writing is generally simple, the

FIG. 10.2. Book of the Dead of Tameret (P.Turin Cat. 1849 = CGT 53001); © Museo Egizio/ Nicola Dell'Aquila e Federico Taverni.

drawing of the vignettes reveals the artists' excellent skill, necessary to achieve such aesthetic and appealing results on such a difficult writing surface. Apart from some cases (Roccati, 2008), the text is written in black, with no heading, and the vignettes are line drawn, nearly always in black ink. The stylized silhouettes are, most of the time, drawn by a steady hand that allowed itself "whims," making exceptions to the usual canon and thus introducing very lively touches in an ensemble that seems rather stern at first sight (Fig. 10.3).

Like on papyrus, the position of the vignettes is not always in perfect coordination with their corresponding texts (Albert, this volume).

The execution of those pieces was likely difficult, and probably required an installation of which we know nothing yet. To write on the material, the scribe had to maintain a constant tension, which made it more difficult than the process involved in gradually unrolling the papyrus. The text of some mummy bandages is arranged in more or less wide columns, but there are others, very narrow ones, that show a text copied in continuous lines that go on for several meters. Every mummy bandage therefore had to be rolled and unrolled for each line of the text, which requires thorough work and unfailing patience.

Some texts have revealed several terms for designing mummy bandages and shrouds (Vandenbeusch, 2010), but their precise meaning is not yet known. Numerous expressions indicating the various pieces of material used for mummification appear in the texts, in two major compositions in particular: *The Apis Embalming Ritual* (P. Vienna KHM ÄS 3873) (Vos, 1993) and the *Rituel de l'Embaumement* (the Ritual of Embalming; Sauneron, 1952; Töpfer, 2015). The first one, dated in the second century BCE, written mainly in demotic but including some passages in hieratic, gives full details of the mummification of the bull Apis. Five words for mummy bandages and five others for mummy clothes can be noted, although it is not possible to specify either their shape or their precise use. As for the *Rituel de l'embaumement*, written in hieratic in the second century CE, it is dedicated to human mummification; it mentions six terms related to mummy bandages, different from those mentioned in *The Apis Embalming Ritual*. Other texts also give two very frequently used expressions: *wt* (Wb I, 379,4) and *sšd* (Wb IV, 301, 4). As a conclusion, it appears that, besides these two terms, the most frequent designations

FIG. 10.3. Book of the Dead of Tasheretenkhonsu (P.Turin Cat. 1837); © Museo Egizio/ Nicola Dell'Aquila e Federico Taverni.

for mummy bandages are *pyr*, *sḥ.t* and *sbn*, the latest one. It is nevertheless still impossible, in most cases, to determine their precise use or even their size.

If the use of mummy bandages appears around the Thirtieth Dynasty, it especially develops between this period and the second century BCE. Museums and private collections house a large quantity (nearly 1,300 fragments have been listed), which has allowed several specialists to establish more or less elaborated typologies. Albert de Caluwe (1991: XVII–XIX) defined four groups of mummy bandages. Since then, a great number of previously unknown mummy bandages have been published. This enabled Holger Kockelmann (2008: II, 93–115) to establish a more complete classification, grouping the equipment into seven categories. Both authors have founded their typology on the formal features of the bandages of the documents: their dimensions (particularly the height, since the height strictly depends on their state of conservation), the layout of the text, and the illustrations.

Some mummy bandages, among them the most ancient ones, show a disposition similar to the contemporary funerary papyri. One can see an initial scene representing the deceased worshipping Osiris. The text, arranged in fairly wide columns, can be topped with vignettes, and the chapters are usually represented as full-page illustrations, such as BD 125, dedicated to the judgment of the deceased, which occupies the full height of the strip of fabrics. A group of narrow and most often very long mummy bandages bear only a few lines of text: they can be arranged in columns of variable width or go down the whole length of the material, as mentioned above. The vignettes are inserted into the text and are preferably drawn in the upper part of the bandages (Fig. 10.4).

The two mentioned typologies come together to define a last category of mummy bandages, made of little pieces of fabric that were often approximately square and carried only one drawing, sometimes with the name of the deceased. These tissues function as true amulets, as they are linen fragments with only one chapter of the Book of the Dead.

The main motifs of the texts copied on mummy bandages are drawn from the Book of the Dead. However, one can find excerpts of other funerary ritual texts such as the Ceremony of the House, the Ritual of Opening the Mouth, the Documents of Breathing, and so forth (Kockelmann, 2007).

Few complete mummy bandages have been found. Nevertheless, the whole of the documentation allows us to observe some constants in the use of the Book of the Dead. As of the Late Period, the sequence of the chapters copied on mummy bandages is the same as on papyrus (cf. Gülden, this volume). The first chapters (BD 1 to 8), which describe the funerary rites and the arrival at the tomb (Fig. 10.5), are, surprisingly, only minimally represented.

When they do appear, they occupy—logically—the beginning of the strip of fabric, and can be preceded by the scene of the adoration of Osiris, which shows the deceased facing the god as he sits on his throne, sometimes under a canopy. In this scene, the deceased's name and titles may be written in cursive hieroglyphs, even if the rest of the text is in hieratic. Among these chapters, it is often the first one, BD 1, that is copied, in its textual version, and is generally accompanied by an elaborate vignette.

Chapter BD 17, usually flanked by BD 18, is the most frequently copied. Both are generally quite detailed and play a major role on the mummy bandages. They are framed by BD 15 and 19, which also belong to the group of spells related to sunrise. The rebirth of the deceased at dawn is therefore particularly stressed.

The series BD 21 to 30, dedicated to restoring the mouth, heart, and other physical abilities of the deceased as well as providing him or her with magical power, is rarely represented. The same is true for the spells of transformation. Most of the time, they

FIG. 10.4. Book of the Dead of Taysnakht (P.Turin Cat. 1833); © Museo Egizio/ Nicola Dell'Aquila e Federico Taverni.

are represented by only one or two chapters. The access to Re's barque, appearing especially in BD 98 and even more so in BD 99, is one of the most appreciated sequences on papyrus but is not frequently mentioned. The spells dedicated to the netherworld's geography consist of a very extensive group that is present in the majority of the longest mummy bandages and in those that are not entirely preserved.

Texts, as well as vignettes, appear, carrying the names of the doors that provide access to Osiris's kingdom and of the guards watching the doors (BD 144–145; Stadler, 2009: 252–319). BD 149 (Stadler, 2009: 405–13) is sometimes added as a conclusion to this kind of sequence, as was often the case on funerary fabrics at the beginning of the Eighteenth Dynasty.

Mummy bandages rarely contain "supplementary" chapters (Wüthrich, this volume). They are always found at the end of the document. Twice, BD 162 is found at the end of the text sequence. With the protection of the deceased's head, this chapter stresses his assimilation with Re. As the new sun, he can go forth from the netherworld. Some particular versions of BD 163, a spell that assimilates the deceased with Osiris's *ba*, must have been elaborated at Akhmim (Wüthrich, 2010: 129–30). The last formula, BD 164, which puts the dead under the protection of the goddess Mut, who is considered a demiurge, is quoted at least once.

This emphasizes that the Books of the Dead on mummy bandages are quite similar to those copied on the papyri in the same period. The most frequently used spells or groups of spells are often the same. The physically largest ones, those that take up the most space with long texts and important vignettes (BD 1, 17, 144–145, 149–150), were undoubtedly considered the most important from a religious point of view. But some short chapters, such as those of transformation, or BD 99, which ensures the deceased's access to Re's barque, were equally appreciated, even if less often used.

**FIG. 10.5.** Mummy bandage of Djedhor (private collection). Vignette and text of the Chapter 1 of the Book of the Dead. Funerary procession. ©Antonovich.

Even if the Books of the Dead on mummy bandages follow the same evolution as those written on papyri, they cannot be considered their equivalents. It is possible that the mummy bandages were considered even more efficient means to guarantee the deceased's survival in the netherworld, since they were in direct contact with the body. Since the New Kingdom, individuals of the elite and of the clergy owned Books of the Dead either on shrouds and papyri, or on other media such as coffins, shabtis, and so forth. The comparison with the papyri is essential: Both media are similar and are put on or around the mummy. Most of the time, the chapters that are copied onto the material are different. And, although the writings look similar to one another, which shows the validity of the paleographic criteria as far as mummy bandages are concerned, the documents, in most cases, seem to come from different scribes. There may have been specialized scribes or *scriptoria* for papyri on the one hand and for funerary fabrics on the other hand.

Among the roughly 730 mummy bandages (c. 1,300 fragments) listed (Kockelmann, 2008, II: 45–85), it is possible to group some as belonging to the same mummies, allowing us to identify some 300 owners of mummy bandages. Most (more than 180) are men. As was done with papyri, quite a few mummy bandages must have been prepared in advance (cf. Verhoeven, this volume), which explains why some documents have remained anonymous. It is probably also the reason why some women are represented as men on their mummy bandages (cf. Töpfer, this volume).

The titulary is very seldom noted, either for men or for women. Whenever there is a titulary, only one title generally appears. The comparison with the rest of the funerary furniture (shabtis, coffins, and papyri), as long as it is at least partly preserved, allows us to discover and confirm the identity of some well-known persons. The most frequently attested title is by far that of divine father (*it-nṯr*), after that, that of priest (*ḥm-nṯr*), and, far more rarely, that of *sm*-priest. At least six royal scribes are known. Most mummy bandage owners bore religious titles; many of these, not including those just mentioned, appear only once and are often specific titles associated with a specific local member of the clergy. Women's titles are rare; four female musicians (*iḥy.t*) and two *nbt-pr* are attested.

On the documents showing the name of the recipient, the filiation is nearly always indicated, and in almost all the examples, the mother's name is the one noted, very seldom accompanied by a title.

The provenance of only a small number of mummy bandages is known. Among these, the majority come from Lower Egypt: Memphis, Saqqara, and Gurob-Hawara. Middle Egypt and Upper Egypt are both seldom represented. Nevertheless, Thebes comes third after Memphis and Gurob-Hawara. The figures stress the big religious capitals, but it is interesting to note that several provincial towns (Lisht, Herakleopolis Magna, el-Bersha, Akhmim, Qaw el-Kebir, Koptos, etc.) were also the origin of written mummy bandages, which demonstrates their use at least—going from North to South—as far as Thebes. The important role of Lower Egypt reflects the Egyptian political orientation, which was North-centric starting from the Third Intermediate Period, and is in complete contrast with the funerary material of the New Kingdom, which was mainly from Thebes.

## Hypocephali

From the Thirtieth Dynasty until the Ptolemaic Period, BD 162 appears on a particular type of medium, the hypocephalus (Varga, 1998; Vallée, 2007; Wüthrich, 2010: 52–53). Hypocephali are disks composed of several layers of plastered cloth (papyrus, wood, or bronze are very seldom used) that were put under the mummy's head. The center of the disk is occupied by numerous representations: frequently, Re's mother appears in the form of a divine cow (Ihet or Hathor), together with many complex divinities. All around the disk, an extract of BD 162, dedicated to the protection of the head, is written in hieratic, in black ink. Most hypocephali come from the Theban region, or from Akhmim. Through its shape, the disk associates the deceased with the sun and allows him to participate in the rebirth of the divine celestial body (Miatello, 2017).

## Conclusions

The tradition of inscribed and illustrated funerary linen does not only belong to the tradition of the Book of the Dead. It has been stressed that some mummy bandages could include excerpts of other texts. Starting from the Saite period, Demotic becomes the vernacular language, and appears on mummy bandages in the Greco-Roman period.

The text reveals the deceased's name and his filiation, sometimes together with a formula of blessings (Vandenbeusch, 2010: 98), expressing the wish for the *ba* of the deceased to eternally live close to Osiris. Parallel to this, the Greek colonies in Egypt soon adopted many traditions of the old country of the pharaohs. Mummy bandages carrying Greek texts have therefore been found. They provide only the name of the deceased, possibly accompanied by the name of one of his parents, and probably his age. Even if the text no longer belongs to the Book of the Dead, the practice of inscribing mummy bandages is still attested.

A late flourishing of inscribed funerary cloth with Book of the Dead passages can be seen in the painted shrouds of the Greco-Roman period (Cortopassi and Saragoza, 2002; Régen, 2012: 604 with bibliography). These materials were undoubtedly intended to wrap corpses (Régen, 2012: 604–5). The tempera-painted decorations show realistic portraits of the deceased. Most frequently, the deceased stands in front of Osiris and may be guided by Anubis. The iconography is reminiscent of the traditional Egyptian beliefs, transcribed into a highly Hellenized canon (Riggs, 2005; Parlasca, 2011). In some cases, some short excerpts of the Book of the Dead or funerary formulae were copied, often written in very awkward hieroglyphs (e.g., Moorey, 1992; Étienne, 2002) and sometimes in demotic (e.g., Riggs and Stadler, 2003; Vleeming, 2011, 2015). These fabrics, famous for their aspect, from both an aesthetic and an exotic point of view, compared to pharaonic canons, show the vitality of the funerary beliefs of ancient Egypt until very late in the Roman Period.

Whereas the image of the mummy in its wrappings has become a symbol of traditional pharaonic Egypt, the funerary fabrics are a true reflection of the evolution of beliefs concerning the netherworld during the last millenary of Egyptian history. The Book of the

Dead, written on the media described above, provides a link between the most ancient texts (Pyramid Texts, Coffin Texts) and the funerary practices of Hellenistic and Roman Egypt, which were partly Hellenized.

## Bibliography

Albert, F. (2012). "Amulette und funeräre Handschriften, Amulets and funerary manuscripts." In *Grenzen des Totenbuchs. Ägyptische Papyri zwischen Grab und Ritual, Beyond the Book of the Dead. Egyptian Papyri between Tomb and Ritual*, edited by M. Müller-Roth and M. Michael Höveler-Müller, 71–85 (Rahden: Leidorf).

Assmann, J. (2008). "Das Zweiwegebuch, CT 1029–1130." In *Ägyptische Religion. Totenliteratur*, edited by J. Assmann and A. Kucharek, 327–63, 786–811 (Frankfurt; Mainz; Leipzig: Insel).

Backes, B. (2005). *Das altägyptische "Zweiwegebuch." Studien zu den Sargtext-Sprüchen 1029–1130*. Ägyptologische Abhandlungen, 69 (Wiesbaden: Harrassowitz).

Bataille, A. (1939). "Une tombe gréco-romaine de Deir el Médineh." *Bulletin de l'Institut Français d'Archéologie Orientale* 38: 73–107.

De Caluwe, A. (1991). *Un Livre des morts sur bandelette de momie (Bruxelles, Musées royaux d'Art et d'Histoire E. 6179)*. Bibliotheca Aegyptiaca XVIII (Bruxelles: Editions de la Fondation Egyptologique Reine Elisabeth).

Cortopassi, R. and Saragoza, Fl. (2002). "L'évolution des linceuls peints de l'époque pharaonique à l'époque romaine." In *La trame de l'Histoire. Textiles pharaoniques, coptes et islamiques*, edited by M. Dunand and Fl. Saragoza, 36–39 (Paris: Somogy).

El-Enany, Kh. (2010). "Un carré de lin peint au musée de l'Agriculture du Caire (inv. 893)." *Bulletin de l'Institut Français d'Archéologie Orientale* 110: 35–46.

Étienne, M. (2002). "Fragment de linceul peint." In *La trame de l'Histoire. Textiles pharaoniques, coptes et islamiques*, edited by L. Dunand and Fl. Saragoza, 65 (Paris: Somogy).

Gasse, A. (1983). "L'étoffe funéraire de Senhotep." *Bulletin de l'Institut Français d'Archéologie Orientale* 83: 191–96.

Gasse, A. (1991). "La stèle magique égyptienne de Kition-Bamboula," *Report of the Department of Antiquities Cyprus* 1991: 170–71.

Gasse, A. (2006). "Les Livres des morts sur tissu." *Egypte, Afrique & Orient* 43: 3–8.

Geisen, C. (2004). *Die Totentexte des verschollenen Sarges der Königin Mentuhotep aus der 13. Dynastie. Ein Textzeuge aus der Übergangszeit von den Sargtexten zum Totenbuch*. Studien zum Altägyptischen Totenbuch 8 (Wiesbaden: Harrassowitz).

Goyon, J.-Cl. and Josset, P. (1988). *Un corps pour l'éternité. Autopsie d'une momie* (Paris: Le Léopard d'Or).

Hermsen, E. (1991). *Die zwei Wege des Jenseits. Das altägyptische Zweigebuch und seine Topographie* (Orbis biblicus et orientalis 112, Freiburg, Göttingen).

Kockelmann, H. (2007). "It's Not Always Book of the Dead!" *Studia Aegyptiaca* XVIII: 239–61.

Kockelmann, H. (2008). *Untersuchungen zu den späten Totenbuch-Handschriften auf Mumienbinden*. Studien zum Altägyptischen Totenbuch 12 (Wiesbaden: Harrassowitz).

Lesko, L. (1972). *The Ancient Egyptian Book of the Two Ways* (Berkeley: University of California Press).

Miatello, L. (2017). "On Egypt as the Horus Eye." *Göttinger Miszellen*, 252: 97–111.

Moorey, P. R. S. (1992). *Ancient Egypt. Oxford Ashmolean Museum Oxford*, 55 (Oxford: Ashmolean Museum).

Müller-Roth, M. (2008). "Das Leichentuch des Pa-heri-pedjet." *Zeitschrift für Ägyptische Sprache* 135: 149–53.

Munro, I. (1987). *Untersuchungen zu den Totenbuch-Papyri der 18. Dynastie* (London and New York: Kegan Paul).

Parlasca, Kl. (2011). "Ein römisches Leichtuch aus Ägypten in Genf." *Chronique d'Égypte*, LXXXVI, fasc. 171–172, 298–322 (Bruxelles: Brepols).

Régen, I. (2012). "Ombres. Une iconographie singulière du mort sur des « linceuls » d'époque romaine provenant de Saqqâra." In *Et in Aegypto et ad Aegyptum. Recueil d'études dédiées à Jean-Claude Grenier*, vol. IV. Cahiers d'Égypte nilotique et méditerranéenne 5, edited by A. Gasse, Fr. Servajean, and Chr. Thiers, 603–47 (Montpellier: Université Paul Valéry).

Riggs, C. (2005). *The Beautiful Burial in Roman Egypt: Art, Identity, and Funerary Religion* (Oxford: Oxford University Press).

Riggs, C. and Stadler, M. A. (2003). "A Roman Shroud and its Demotic Inscription in the Museum of Fine Arts, Boston." *Journal of the American Research Center in Egypt* 40: 69–87.

Roccati, A. (2008). "A Fragmentary Mummy Bandage Inscribed with Three Isis Spells in the Book of the Dead." In *Egypt and Beyond. Essays Presented to Leonard H. Lesko upon his Retirement from the Wilbour Chair of Egyptology at Brown University June 2005*, edited by St. E. Thompson and P. Der Manuelian, 315–17 (Providence: Brown Univ., Dept. of Egyptology and Ancient Western Asian Studies).

Rössler-Köhler, U. (2003). "Das Eigentliche Zweiwegebuch." *Göttinger Miszellen* 192: 83–98.

Sauneron, S. (1952). *Rituel de l'embaumement. Pap. Boulaq III, Pap. Louvre 5.158* (Le Caire: Imprimerie Nationale).

Sherbiny, W. (2017). *Through Hermopolitan Lenses: Studies on the So-called Book of Two Ways in Ancient Egypt*. Probleme der Ägyptologie, Band 33 (Leiden; Boston: Brill).

Stadler, M. A. (2009). *Weiser und Wesir: Studien zu Vorkommen, Rolle und Wesen des Gottes Thot im ägyptischen Totenbuch*. Orientalische Religionen in der Antike, 1: 252–319 (Tübingen: Mohr Siebeck).

Sternberg-el-Hotabi, H. (1994). "Der Untergang der Hieroglyphenschrift. Schriftverfall und Schrifttod im Ägypten der griechisch-römischen Zeit." *Chronique d'Egypte* 69: 218–54.

Sternberg-el-Hotabi, H. (1999). *Untersuchungen zur Überlieferungsgeschichte der Horusstelen.: Ein Beitrag zur Religionsgeschichte Ägyptens im 1. Jahrtausend v. Chr.*, 2 vols., 136–42 (Ägyptologische Abhandlungen, 62).

Strudwick, N. (2000). "The Tomb of Senneferi at Thebes." *Egyptian Archaeology* 18: 6–8.

Töpfer, S. (2015). *Das Balsamierungsritual. Eine (Neu-)Edition der pLouvre 5158, pDurham 1983.11 + p.St.Petersburg 18128)*. Studien zur Spätägyptischen Religion 13 (Wiesbaden: Harrassowitz).

Vallée, B (2007). "Les Hypocéphales." In Proceedings of the Ninth International Congress of Egyptologists II, edited by J.-Cl. Goyon and Cgr. Chardin, Orientalia Lovaniensia Analecta 150: 1869–1880 (Louvain: Peeters).

Vandenbeusch, M. (2010). *Catalogue des bandelettes de momies. Musée d'art et d'histoire de Genève*. Cahiers de la Société d'Égyptologie 10 (Genève: Société d'Égyptologie).

Varga, E. (1998). *Les hypocéphales*. In Acta Archaeologica Academiae Scientiarum Hungaricae 50: 13–38 (Budapest: AKJournals).

Verhoeven, U. (2001). *Untersuchungen zur späthieratischen Buchschrift*. Orientalia Lovaniensia Analecta 99 (Louvain: Peeters).

Vleeming, S. P. (2011). *Demotic and Greek-Demotic Mummy Labels and other Short Texts Gathered from Many Publications*, 2 vols. Studia Demotica, 9 (Louvain: Peeters).

Vleeming, S. P. (2015). *Demotic Graffiti and Other Short Texts Gathered from Many Publications (short texts III 1201–2350)*. Studia Demotica, 12 (Louvain: Peeters).

Vos, R. L. (1993). *The Apis Embalming Ritual (P. Vindob. 3873)*. Orientalia Lovaniensia Analecta 50 (Louvain: Peeters).

Wüthrich, A. (2010). *Éléments de théologie thébaine: les chapitres supplémentaires du Livre des Morts*. Studien zum Altägyptischen Totenbuch 16 (Wiesbaden: Harrassowitz).

CHAPTER 11

# THE BOOK OF THE DEAD IN TOMBS

SILVIA EINAUDI

## THE NEW KINGDOM

THE Book of the Dead began to appear as part of tomb decoration in the Eighteenth Dynasty, in accordance with the increasing diffusion of this corpus of funerary texts around this time. The earliest attestations so far date to the reign of Hatshepsut, when her chief steward Senenmut had his two tombs inscribed with some Book of the Dead spells. The first one (TT 71), built on the hillside at Sheikh Abd el-Qurna and considered more precisely as a funerary chapel, is badly damaged. Its false door stela, originally located at the rear wall of the axial corridor and now kept in the Ägyptisches Museum, Berlin (inv. 2066), is inscribed with portions of BD 148 and some iconographic elements pertaining to its vignette: the bull with seven cows, as well as four mummiform figures related to the steering oars and the cardinal points (Saleh, 1984: 81–82; Dorman, 1991: 54–55; Roehrig, 2005: 132–33). This spell, which was supposed to ensure the deceased's eternal provisions, was logically located where offerings would have been placed. Senenmut's second tomb (TT 353), to the east of the temple of Hatshepsut at Deir el-Bahari, presents a larger selection of Book of the Dead spells, associated with "funerary liturgies" partly derived from the Pyramid Texts and the Coffin Texts. The northern, southern, and western walls of Chamber A, with the famous astronomical ceiling, are inscribed with BD 110, 136A+B, 137B, 144, 145, 146w, 148, 149, and 150 (Saleh, 1984: 59, 75–78; 82–84, 96–97; Dorman, 1991: 113–38, 168–69; Galán, 2014: 266–67), most of them with their vignettes. These spells mainly provide the deceased with the knowledge of the netherworld: its topography (gates and mounds) and its guardians' names.

Shortly thereafter, further Eighteenth-Dynasty tombs were decorated with Book of the Dead spells, even though the use of this corpus of funerary texts in tombs was still limited, and far less common than on papyri. About thirty attestations are known, especially in the Theban necropolis. With the exception of tombs TT 11 and 82 (cf. *infra*), just a few formulae were inscribed in these monuments, which almost all belong to private individuals and are dated to a time span from the reign of Thutmose III—or from the last years of the joint reign of Hatshepsut and Thutmose III—to the reign of Horemheb. The only evidence for the use of Book of the Dead spells in an Eighteenth-Dynasty royal necropolis is the tomb of King Ay (KV 23), in the West Valley, whose burial chamber is decorated with BD 130 and 144, dealing, respectively, with the deceased's freedom of movement aboard the sun boat and the names of the doorkeepers in the netherworld.

As has already been pointed out (Saleh, 1984: 95), before the reign of Thutmose IV, the Book of the Dead spells were written almost exclusively in the burial chamber, whereas, toward the end of the Eighteenth Dynasty, they also became a component of the decoration of other rooms on the ground level.

In all, about sixty spells are recorded so far in the Eighteenth-Dynasty tombs. The most frequent are BD 59, 110, and 125 (Saleh, 1984: 95–97; Galán, 2014: 267, table 11.2), which reveal the recurring concerns of the ancient Egyptians about the afterlife: having water and breathing air (BD 59), living as a blessed one in the Fields of Reeds, being eternally provided with food offerings (BD 110), and being justified in the Hall of Justice (BD 125). The vignettes are often depicted, while the texts of the relevant spells can be omitted or abbreviated. It is therefore evident that in these cases the scenes were considered more important than the accompanying inscriptions (a kind of *pars pro toto*).

Among the Eighteenth-Dynasty private tombs, the one with by far the richest selection of Book of the Dead spells is that of Djehuty (TT 11), overseer of the treasury and overseer of works during the joint reign of Hatshepsut and Thutmose III, in Dra Abu el-Naga (Galán, 2014: 248; Shirley, 2014: 197). Originally, the burial chamber was completely inscribed with Book of the Dead spells, but those on the eastern and southern walls were lost (except for fragments) when these walls were destroyed in order to enlarge the room (Galán, 2014: 264–65). At least forty-one spells were inscribed (Galán, 2014: 264, Table 11.1; 267, table 11.2; 265, n. 52), written in cursive hieroglyphs with retrograde writing, on the walls as well as on the ceiling. Some of them are accompanied by their vignettes.

So far, this is the earliest large collection of Book of the Dead texts attested in an ancient Egyptian tomb. The set of preserved formulae comprises the so-called transformation spells (BD 78, 86, 81A, 88, 87), allowing the deceased to assume the forms of different beings, and some chapters that would enable him to travel in the solar boat (BD 99B, 119, 7, 102), have magical power and control over his mouth, limbs and heart (BD 22, 23, 24, 25, 26, 28, 27), or avoid dangers (BD 30A, 31, 33, [34, 35], 74, 45, 93, 91, 41, 42). Moreover, the tomb of Djehuty is one of the earliest Book of the Dead compilations that includes the so-called knowing the *bas* (souls) spells (BD 114, 112, 113, 108, 109) and the famous BD 125 on the final judgment (Galán, 2014: 258, 265), all of them painted on the ceiling.

Slightly later comes the second-richest tomb of the Eighteenth Dynasty in terms of Book of the Dead spells. This is the tomb of Amenemhat, scribe, counter of the grain of Amun, and steward of the vizier Useramun (TT 82), dated to the reign of Thutmose III (Davies, 1915). Besides some texts from funerary rituals and eight Pyramid Texts formulae, the walls of the burial chamber are inscribed with 33 BD spells written in cursive hieroglyphs in retrograde direction, displaying "an unattested sequence for most of the composition" (Galán, 2014: 266–67). In this respect, Amenemhat's tomb also shows one of the first attestations of BD 17 and 18, two important and long spells of the corpus, sometimes paired together at the beginning of papyrus scrolls. Their aim was to provide the deceased with a kind of *summa* of the funerary beliefs concerning the afterlife and to guarantee his justification before the gods.

In the Ramesside Period, the presence of the Book of the Dead in tombs rose dramatically, especially in the Nineteenth Dynasty and in a private context: about 130 tombs with BD spells (texts and/or vignettes) have been identified so far all over Egypt (cf. the database of the Totenbuch Projekt). Just like in the Eighteenth Dynasty, the greater part of the attestations come from the Theban necropolis, with a wide selection of spells coming from the workmen's village of Deir el-Medina. Nevertheless, some tombs in other Egyptian necropolises (from the Nile delta down to Assuan) were also decorated with this funerary corpus, primarily the vignette for BD 125, depicting the weighing of the deceased's heart in the presence of Osiris.

In regard to the private Theban tombs, the number of Book of the Dead spells used was higher in the Ramesside period than ever before.

In addition to the formulae already particularly widespread in the Eighteenth Dynasty (BD 59, 110 and 125), new spells became very popular, such as BD 1, to be recited on the day of burial, and the famous BD 17, the two being among the most recurrent chapters in the New Kingdom papyri as well. Since both these spells and their vignettes are very long, only selected portions (or variants) of their texts and/or scenes are often painted on the walls of the tombs. In Deir el-Medina, BD 1 usually consists only of the well-known scene showing the mummy of the deceased on the funerary bed and a priest with a jackal mask, stressing his identification with Anubis, attending to it (Saleh, 1984: 9–11). As for BD 17, some scenes from the frieze of its traditional vignette are frequently depicted, such as the one representing the deceased playing the *senet*-game, the images of the two lions ("Ruti"), the mummy flanked by Isis and Nephthys, and the cat killing the snake, the symbol of Apophis (Saleh, 1984: 14–22).

A couple of other spells that occur regularly in the Ramesside tombs are BD 74, of which the purpose is to help the deceased to leave the underworld and reach the sky, and a short version of BD 146, dealing with some of the gates of the Duat, which the deceased needs to pass, and their guardians, who are armed with knives (Saleh, 1984: 97).

Simultaneously with the increasing diffusion of the Book of the Dead in a private context, a certain number of Book of the Dead spells also became part of the royal tombs' decoration in the Ramesside Period. More than ten tombs in the Valleys of the Kings and Queens have their walls painted with texts and/or vignettes from this corpus. The most frequently recurring spells concern the final judgment (BD 125) and the geography of the underworld, where the deceased meets gods (BD 127) and demons acting as doorkeepers (BD 144, 146).

In this respect, the tomb of Nefertari (QV 66) is quite original: BD 125 is not attested there, while other spells, absent in the contemporary royal tombs, are present, such as BD 17, with the famous scene of Nefertari playing the *senet*-game, and BD 94, a spell for obtaining the palette and water bowl from Thoth, with its vignette showing the queen before the god (Kaper, 2002: 109–26).

Regarding the royal tombs, it is interesting to note that Book of the Dead spells dealing with the physical needs of the deceased (drinking water, breathing air, etc.) or specific dangers from threatening beings (Quirke, 2013: 101–21) are never attested there, contrary to the private monuments. Apparently, pharaohs and members of the royal families were more interested in texts concerning the transfiguration of the deceased in the gods' domain, the divine judgment, the adoration of the gods, and the topography of the Duat, with its mounds, gates, and guardians, of which the dead must know the names: this last subject was closely related to the Books of the Netherworld, so widely diffused in the royal context.

## Third Intermediate Period

Toward the end of the Twentieth Dynasty and in the following Third Intermediate Period (Twenty-first to Twenty-fourth Dynasties), the Book of the Dead generally fell out of use in tomb decoration, with only few funerary monuments in all of Egypt having Book of the Dead spells.

Most of these are in the necropolis of Tanis, where the capital and the royal cemetery had been transferred to at the beginning of the Twenty-first Dynasty, and two of them belonged to pharaohs: Osorkon II and Sheshonq III. Only a very small selection of Book of the Dead spells can be found in these tombs (BD 16, 110, 125, 144, and 151), with BD 125 and its vignette still representing the most common spell (Munro, 2001: 10, 62, 69, 70, 80, 85, 109).

In contrast to this very rare occurrence of Book of the Dead texts in the Third Intermediate Period tombs, probably due to a lack of space on the walls and to general economic restrictions, coffins and, above all, papyri inscribed with BD spells became particularly widespread at that time. The magical power of this corpus of funerary texts was then transferred from the tomb rooms (left undecorated) to these mortuary objects, close to the mummy (Niwiński, 1988, 1989a).

## Late Period

A vigorous revival in the use of the Book of the Dead in tombs took place in the Late Period, especially in the Theban necropolis. This phenomenon is mainly associated with the construction of the so-called temple tombs in the Assasif area, during the Twenty-fifth and Twenty-sixth Dynasties. In fact, walls, pillars, and pilasters of these huge funerary monuments were inscribed with a larger selection of Book of the Dead spells (more than 140 chapters are attested in all) than ever before.

So far, Book of the Dead spells have been found in fourteen Theban tombs (Einaudi, 2012: 14–36). Twelve are in the North Assasif necropolis: Harwa (TT 37), Akhimenru (TT 404), Padiamenope (TT 33), Montuemhat (TT 34), Ibi (TT 36), Pabasa (TT 279), Mutirdis (TT 410), Basa (TT 389), Padihorresnet (TT 196), Ankhhor (TT 414), Sheshonq (TT 27) and Padineith (TT 197). Two are in the South Assasif necropolis: Karabaskeni (TT 391) and Karakhamun (TT 223) (Einaudi, 2021).

In light of the new hypotheses for the chronology of the Twenty-fifth Dynasty and the relevant royal order of succession (Bányai, 2013: 46–129; Payraudeau, 2014: 115–27; Broekman, 2015: 17–31; 2017: 39–52), the earliest of these monuments to be decorated with the Book of the Dead is probably the tomb of Harwa, great steward of Amenirdis I (TT 37), dated between the end of the eighth and the beginning of the seventh century BCE. Other than some formulae (BD 15, 17, and 18) recorded in the hypostyle halls, where other funerary texts are more common (Pyramid Texts and Opening of the Mouth Ritual), eight Book of the Dead spells are inscribed in the court (BD 15 b–c–d, 45, 50, 55, 89, 91, 106, and 154), reflecting, by their placement, a likely division of the court into two sectors: Osirian and solar (Einaudi, 2015: 1641–52; 2017b: 105–12).

The Assasif funerary monuments showing the most extensive use of Book of the Dead spells are the tomb of Karakhamun (TT 223), probably dating to the reign of Shabaqo (beginning of the seventh century BCE), and those of Padiamenope (TT 33) and Montuemhat (TT 34), built between the end of the Twenty-fifth and the beginning of the Twenty-sixth Dynasty (second quarter of the seventh century BCE). Fifty-seven chapters have been identified so far in the two pillared halls of Karakhamun, where texts and vignettes were carved according to a layout that, especially in the first room, gives the impression of a "wallpaper" converted into rock decoration, as if a real papyrus were unrolled without interruption over the walls and pillars (Molinero Polo, 2014b: 131–72; Griffin, 2014: 173–99).

In addition to these spells, BD 125 is painted on the walls of the burial chamber: the formula consists of the vignette showing the deceased entering the Hall of Justice and facing the 42 judges, as well as the scene of the weighing of the heart, while only some parts of the relevant text (including the "negative confession") are written (Molinero Polo, 2014a: 269–93).

As for the slightly later tombs of the lector priest and chief ($ḥry$-$ḥb$ $ḥry$-$dp$) Padiamenope (TT 33) and the mayor of Thebes and fourth priest of Amun, Montuemhat (TT 34), they present the largest collection of Book of the Dead spells known in Egypt. About seventy Book of the Dead spells have been identified in each of the two monuments, where many other funerary texts are also carved on the walls (Pyramid Texts, Coffin Texts, Amduat, Book of the Gates, Book of Caverns, and Opening of the Mouth Ritual). All these corpora are organized thematically in the decorative program of the tombs, according to religious beliefs and the rooms' functions, and they all contributed to guarantee a successful eternal life for the deceased in the netherworld (Einaudi, 2017c: 247–61; Einaudi, forthcoming; Gestermann, Teotino and Wagner, 2021).

Concerning the tomb of Padiamenope (Einaudi, 2017a: 163–68), the largest part of the spells is inscribed in the two pillared halls, and they often follow the sequence that would become "canonical" in the Saite Period Books of the Dead. In the first hall, after the solar spell BD 15 (in the entrance passage) and the introductive BD 1 (on the eastern part of the southern wall), is a long and continuous succession of spells, from BD 17 to 42, of which the main objectives are the preservation of the deceased's body and the control over harmful creatures. In the second pillared hall, BD 117 to 121, among other spells, are carved, which are meant to help the deceased in reaching the "Fields of Reeds" and going forth from there.

Analogous spell sequences are in the second court of the tomb of Montuemhat (BD 21 to 42; BD 54 to 62; BD 79 to 88 [Rosati, 2006: 297–324]) and in the subterranean rooms (BD 117 to 121).

The general arrangement of Book of the Dead spells in these two tombs reflects the destiny of the deceased, passing through steps as he approaches the burial chamber; to be exact, from the entrance of the tomb onwards, the chapters deal successively with the funerary procession, the physical regeneration of the dead, his justification, and the subsequent transfiguration into a blessed spirit in the netherworld, where he is supposed to travel in the solar boat (Fig. 11.1), safely passing through the gates supervised by the guardians.

Even if to a lesser extent, a rich repertoire of texts and vignettes from the Book of the Dead also decorate the Assasif tombs of Pabasa (TT 279; Rosati, 1993: 108, Fig. 2;

FIG. 11.1. Vignette of BD 100 (detail), from the first pillared hall in the tomb of Padiamenope (TT 33). © French Epigraphic Mission in TT 33, photo L. Schmitt.

Einaudi, 2012: 22–24), Padihorresnet (TT 196; Graefe, 2003: I 97–198), Ankhhor (TT 414; Bietak and Reiser-Haslauer, 1978: I 108, Fig. 32), and Sheshonq (TT 27; Roccati, 1976: 233–50; Sist, 1976: 251–55; Rosati, 1993: 107–17; Roccati, 2003: 347–50), all of them great stewards of divine adoratrices in the Twenty-sixth Dynasty. In all instances, the spells are inscribed in the court and, with the exception of Ankhhor, in some of the subterranean rooms as well.

Among the most frequent Book of the Dead spells in these Late Period monuments are BD 15, 45, 50, 55, 57, 59, and 89. As for BD 15, dealing with the adoration of the sun god during his daily travel through the sky and the netherworld, it is generally inscribed near a door or passage, following the New Kingdom tradition that used to place solar hymns at the entrance to the subterranean rooms (Assmann, 1983: XIII–XV). The large diffusion of the other spells clearly shows which conditions were considered the most essential and desirable to become a blessed spirit in the afterlife: not rotting (BD 45), not dying again and forever (BD 50), breathing air and having water available (BD 55, 57, 59), and allowing the *ba* (soul) to rejoin the corpse of the deceased in the tomb (BD 89).

The position of certain Book of the Dead spells is often the same in these tombs. So, BD 45 and 50 are always inscribed one after the other on a pilaster/pillar in the court (Harwa, Pabasa, Padihorresnet, Ankhhor, and Sheshonq), and they are placed opposite of the pilaster/wall decorated with BD 89. As for BD 17, in the five tombs where this long spell is found (Harwa, Karakhamun, Akhimenru, Padiamenope, and Pabasa), it is carved in the (first) pillared hall, on the left wall, sometimes followed by BD 18 (Harwa, Karakhamun, and Padiamenope) (Fig. 11.2). This particular location, close to the entrance to the subterranean part of the monuments, probably reflects the position of both BD 17 and 18 in certain New Kingdom and Third Intermediate Period papyri, where they were written at the beginnings of the scrolls.

The striking analogies observed in the choice and arrangement of some Book of the Dead spells in the Late Period tombs of the Assasif reveal the existence of common decorative models (or "rules") and also testify to the important "pioneering" role that the earliest funerary monuments (Harwa, Karakhamun, and Padiamenope in particular) played in the diffusion of the Book of the Dead during the Twenty-fifth and Twenty-sixth Dynasties.

Moreover, the long and uninterrupted sequences of spells attested in some cases indicate that a methodical revision and reorganization of the texts from the Book of the Dead had certainly begun in the Kushite Period, with the tombs of Karakhamun, Padiamenope, and Montuemhat representing an evident step toward the redaction of the final Saite recension of this corpus of funerary spells.

Even if most of the Late Period tombs decorated with Book of the Dead spells are concentrated in a small area of the Theban necropolis, some other Saite tombs with texts and/or vignettes from this corpus are, nevertheless, also found in Saqqara, Giza, Heliopolis, Bahariya Oasis, and Abusir. Among these monuments, the one with by far the greatest number of spells is the tomb of the vizier Bakenrenef (LS 24), in Saqqara (Buongarzone, 1990: 81–102). More than sixty Book of the Dead spells are inscribed on the walls and pillars of the subterranean rooms, which show a plan and a decorative

FIG. 11.2. Vignette of BD 18 (detail), from the first pillared hall in the tomb of Padiamenope (TT 33). © French Epigraphic Mission in TT 33. Photo: L. Schmitt.

layout similar, in some ways, to the Assasif tombs. This is particularly true for spells BD 17 and 18, written on the left wall of the pillared hall, close to the entrance. Indeed, their position corresponds to the recurring location of both spells in the contemporary monumental tombs at Thebes. It is therefore likely that Bakenrenef himself, or the person(s) in charge of his tomb decoration, saw the iconographic repertoire of the Theban tombs as a model and a source of inspiration.

Contrary to the extensive use of Book of the Dead spells in private tombs, we know of very few royal tombs in the Late Period that were decorated with excerpts and scenes from this religious body of texts. There is, however, the case of the tomb of the Kushite king Tanutamani (664–56 BCE) (Ku. 16), in the necropolis of El-Kurru (modern Sudan; Dunham, 1950: 60, pl. XVIII, XX), whose burial chamber is painted with colorful texts and vignettes from BD 27, 28, and 30. All these spells concern the heart of the deceased: they prevented it from being removed or stolen, and from testifying against its owner during the final judgment.

The tomb of another Kushite king, Aspelta (600–580 BCE), in Nuri (Nu. 8) (modern Sudan; Dunham, 1955: 98–101, Figs. 71–74), also has some Book of the Dead formulae inscribed in the rooms under the pyramid: BD 125 (with the "negative confession" uttered by the deceased) and BD 145, listing the 21 gates of the Duat and their guardians.

Interestingly, the largest selections of Book of the Dead spells in tombs are from the Kushite and Saite Periods, whereas the number of Books of the Dead written on papyri decreased considerably compared to the New Kingdom and the Third Intermediate Period.

The reason for this intense use of the Book of the Dead in Late Period tombs is clearly linked to the so-called archaism, a cultural and artistic phenomenon that manifested itself in the Twenty-fifth to Twenty-sixth Dynasties (Der Manuelian, 1994; Becker, 2012; Morkot, 2003: 79–99; Smoláriková, 2010: 431–40). At that time, ancient funerary texts from earlier stages of Egyptian history, including the Book of the Dead, were widely (re)introduced in the tombs, as can be seen in the tombs of Padiamenope in particular. This monument can be considered a sort of subterranean "library," or "museum" (Traunecker, 2008: 32; 2014: 213–21; 2015: 60–61; Einaudi, 2018: 117–25), where the *summa* of the Egyptian funerary beliefs and corpora were perpetuated. The function of these texts was probably two-fold: they were certainly meant to provide the deceased with knowledge and magic power considered necessary to ensure his transformation into a blessed spirit, but, in some instances, the inscriptions were also read out loud by priests and cultured devotees who visited the tomb during feasts and ceremonies (Assmann, 1973: 26; 2000: 36; 2003: 374; Traunecker, 2018: 126–51).

The important role played in the Twenty-fifth and Twenty-sixth Dynasties by both Osiris and the sun god in funerary beliefs and tomb architecture, including several sources related to the so-called solar-Osirian unity (Niwiński, 1989b: 89–106; Smith, 2017: 271–355), may also have fostered the large diffusion of the Book of the Dead in that period (Einaudi, 2017b: 105–12). The spells of this corpus actually highlight the strong connection between the deceased and these two deities (BD 15, 125, and 142, for instance).

## The Ptolemaic and Roman Periods

After the Twenty-sixth Dynasty, appearances of the Book of the Dead in tombs became more and more rare. Only a few tombs decorated with Book of the Dead spells and/or vignettes are known for the Ptolemaic and Roman Periods, none of them in the Theban area, but in other necropolises located at Atfih, Tuna el-Gebel, Qaw el-Kebir, Akhmim, Hu, and in the oases of Siwa and Dakhleh. In these cases, a limited number of texts, but, above all, only scenes taken from the Book of the Dead are attested, and, among these, the vignette of BD 125 with the weighing of the heart is the most common.

Curiously, despite the fact that the Book of the Dead was rarely used in tombs, the Ptolemaic Period saw a large-scale revival of the Book of the Dead on papyri, especially in the fourth and third centuries BCE, when long scrolls were inscribed with spells arranged according to the Saite recension (Albert, this volume).

As far as the Ptolemaic Period is concerned, the famous tomb of Petosiris (Tuna el-Gebel, fourth century BCE; Lefebvre, 1924: 124, 177–80; Venit, 2016: 5–49) shows a short version of BD 18, with invocations to Thoth and some divine figures from its accompanying vignettes, as well as excerpts from BD 57, for breathing air and having water in the hereafter.

The lost tomb of Atfih, a collective burial from the Ptolemaic Period, had a series of spells painted on the walls of its two rooms. These texts and scenes were especially meant to preserve the body (BD 154), provide eternal food offerings for the deceased (BD 148), and cause the *ba* (soul) to join his mummy, as a guarantee for an eternal rebirth (BD 89 and 191; Daressy, 1902; Stöhr and Wüthrich, 2013: 19–20).

The last tombs decorated with excerpts of the Book of the Dead date back to the Roman period: two of them, belonging to Petubastis and Petosiris (first to second century CE) are in the Dakhleh Oasis. These monuments have the walls of their rock-cut chambers painted with outstanding and colorful scenes, partly inspired by the Book of the Dead vignettes, such as the funerary procession and rites performed for the mummy at the tomb (from BD 1), the tree goddess dispensing water (from BD 59), the *ba*-birds worshipping the sun god (from the so-called BD 16), the deceased adoring the gatekeepers of the netherworld (from BD 144), and the final judgment before Osiris (from BD 125; Whitehouse, 1998: 255, 256; Riggs, 2005: 161–64; Venit, 2016: 157–81). The iconography displays an amazing mixture of styles: funerary compositions belonging to the traditional repertoire are painted side by side with non-Egyptian figures, characterized by Greco-Roman elements. This bicultural aspect shows that ancient funerary beliefs were perpetuated; in particular, the idea of judgment (and, possibly, punishment) in the hereafter, of which the psychostasy scene present in these tombs is the most emblematic symbol, was probably reinforced in that period (Dunand and Zivie-Coche, 2004: 322).

## Conclusion

Even though the diffusion of Book of the Dead spells and vignettes in tombs has been quite irregular and not uniform (the greater part of attestations being concentrated in Thebes, in private necropolises dating to the Ramesside Period and the Twenty-fifth to Twenty-sixth Dynasties), tombs nevertheless certainly played a crucial role in the development of the Book of the Dead and, in particular, in its systematic revision during the Kushite and Saite Periods.

After a first phase, in which the Book is the Dead is still rare and appears almost exclusively in the burial chamber, there is a growing trend toward a larger diffusion of this corpus of funerary texts in tombs, especially in the Nineteenth Dynasty. Spells and vignettes are then also inscribed in other rooms, but the number of formulae attested in each monument is rather limited, with few exceptions. The use of Book of the Dead in tombs increased considerably during the Late Period, in the Assasif necropolis, where high officials close to the Kushite and Saite royal families were buried. In the "temple tombs" of this area, numerous formulae have been carved on the walls, as part of elaborate decorative programs, which also include other ancient corpora of mortuary and ritual texts.

At that time, the first attempts were made, probably by Theban priests, to arrange the spells in a standardized sequence, according to their contents and purposes. The tombs of Karakhamun, Padiamenope, and Montuemhat in particular have so many spells that they seem to reproduce long papyri on their walls, with a succession of formulae that, to a large extent, is already formally fixed.

Compared to the "linearity" of the papyri, the inscription of Book of the Dead spells in the tombs, that is to say in a three-dimensional complex space, allows us to better understand the meaning and aim of these texts, with regard to the funerary beliefs, the rooms' functions, and the rituals meant to be performed for the dead in the different parts of the monuments. In fact, an undeniable link exists between tomb architecture and position of the Book of the Dead spells. These texts had a dual purpose: on the one hand, they accompanied the deceased step by step on his/her way to the burial chamber and, consequently, to his/her new life in the netherworld, the reign of Osiris, but on the other hand, they allowed him/her to leave the tomb every morning and go out into the daylight, in an eternal and cyclical journey in the company of the sun god.

## Bibliography

Assmann, J. (1973). *Grabung im Asasif 1963–1970, II: Das Grab des Basa (Nr. 389) in der thebanischen Nekropole*. Archäologische Veröffentlichungen 6 (Mainz: von Zabern).

Assmann, J. (1983). *Sonnenhymnen in thebanischen Gräbern*. Theben I (Mainz: von Zabern).

Assmann, J. (2000). *Images et rites de la mort dans l'Égypte ancienne: l'apport des liturgies funéraires* (Paris: Cybele).

Assmann, J. (2003). *Mort et au-delà dans l'Égypte ancienne* (Paris: Editions du Rocher).

Bányai, M. (2013). "Ein Vorschlag zur Chronologie der 25. Dynastie in Ägypten." *Journal of Egyptian History* 6: 46–129.

Becker, M. (2012). *Identität und Krise: Erinnerungskulturen im Ägypten der 22. Dynastie*, Studien zur altägyptischen Kultur Beihefte, 13 (Hamburg: Buske).

Bietak, M. and Reiser-Haslauer, E. (1978). *Das Grab des 'Anch-Hor, Obersthofmeister der Gottesgemahlin Nitokris*. Denkschriften der Gesamtakademie / Österreichische Akademie der Wissenschaften 6–7, Vol. I (Vienna: Verlag der Oesterreichischen Akademie der Wissenschaften).

Broekman, G. P. F. (2015). "The Order of Succession Between Shabaka and Shabataka; A Different View on the Chronology of the Twenty-fifth Dynasty." *Gottinger Miszellen* 245: 17–31.

Broekman, G. P. F. (2017). "Suggesting a New Chronology for the Kushite Twenty-fifth Dynasty and Considering the Consequences for the Preceding Libyan Period." In *A True Scribe of Abydos. Essays on First Millennium Egypt in Honour of Anthony Leahy*, edited by C. Jurman, B. Bader, and D.A. Aston, Orientalia lovaniensia analecta 265: 39–52 (Leuven; Paris; Bristol: Peeters).

Buongarzone, R. (1990). "La funzionalità dei testi nel contesto architettonico della tomba di Bakenrenef." *Egitto e Vicino Oriente* XIII: 81–102.

Daressy, G. (1902). "Tombeau ptolémaïque à Atfieh." *Annales du Service des Antiquites de l'Egypte* 3: 160–80.

Davies, N. de Garis. (1915). *The tomb of Amenemhet (No. 82), copied in line and colour by Nina de Garis Davies and with explanatory text by Alan H. Gardiner* (London: Egypt Exploration Fund).

Der Manuelian, P. (1994). *Living in the Past. Studies in Archaism of the Egyptian Twenty-sixth Dynasty*, Studies in Egyptology (London: Kegan Paul International).

Dorman, P. F. (1991). *The Tombs of Senenmut: The Architecture and Decoration of Tombs 71 and 353* (New York: Metropolitan Museum of Art).

Dunand, F. and Zivie-Coche, C. (2004). *Gods and Men in Egypt. 3000 BCE to 395 CE* (Ithaca: Cornell University Press).

Dunham, D. (1950). *The Royal Cemeteries of Kush. El Kurru* (Cambridge, MA: Harvard University Press).

Dunham, D. (1955). *The Royal Cemeteries of Kush. Nuri* (Cambridge, MA: Harvard University Press).

Einaudi, S. (2012). "Le livre des morts dans les tombes monumentales tardives de l'Assasif." *Bulletin de la Société Française d'Egyptologie* 183: 14–36.

Einaudi, S. (2015). "Le Livre des Morts dans la cour de la tombe d'Haroua (TT 37): nouvelles découvertes." In *Proceedings of the Tenth International Congress of Egyptologists: University of the Aegean, Rhodes. 22–29 May 2008*, 2 vols, OLA. Orientalia Lovaniensia Analecta 241, edited by P. Kousoulis and N. Lazaridis, 241: 1641–52 (Leuven: Peeters).

Einaudi, S. (2017a). "The tomb of Padiamenope (TT33) and its role in the "Saite recension" of the Book of the Dead." In *Proceedings First Vatican Coffin Conference 19–22 June 2013*, edited by A. Amenta and H. Guichard, vol. I, 163–68 (Città del Vaticano: Edizioni Musei Vaticani).

Einaudi, S. (2017b). "Aspects solaires et osiriens des tombes monumentales tardives de l'Asasif." In *Burial and Mortuary Practices in Late-Period and Graeco-Roman Egypt. Proceedings of the International Conference held at Museum of Fine Arts, Budapest, 17–19 July 2014*, edited by K. A. Kothay, 105–12 (Budapest: Museum of Fine Arts).

Einaudi, S. (2017c) "Some remarks on three Book of the Dead vignettes in the tomb of Padiamenope (TT 33)." In *Studies in Ancient Egyptian Funerary Literature*, edited by S. Bickel and L. Diaz-Iglesias, *Orientalia lovaniensia analecta* 257: 247–61 (Leuven; Paris; Bristol: Peeters).

Einaudi, S. (2018). "Combination of tradition and innovation in the decorative program of the tomb of Padiamenope (TT 33)." In *Thebes in the First Millennium BC: Art and Archaeology of the Kushite Period and Beyond*, edited by E. Pischikova, J. Budka, and K. Griffin, 117–25 (London: GHP Egyptology).

Einaudi, S. (2021). *La rhétorique des tombes monumentales tardives (XXV$^e$–XXVI$^e$ dynasties). Une vue d'ensemble de leur architecture et de leur programme décoratif*, CENiM 28 (Drémil-Lafage: Éditions Mergoil).

Einaudi (forthcoming). "Le fil rouge qui relie Padiaménopé à Hatchepsout. La formule 607 des Textes des Sarcophages dans la TT33."

Galán, J. M. (2014). "The Inscribed Burial Chamber of Djehuty (TT 11)." In *Creativity and Innovation in the Reign of Hatshepsut*. Studies in Ancient Oriental Civilizations 69, edited by J. M. Galán, B. M. Bryan, and P. F. Dorman, 247–72 (Chicago: Oriental Institute of the University of Chicago).

Gestermann, L., Teotino, C., and Wagner, M. (2021), *Die Grabanlage des Monthemhet (TT 34) I. Der Weg zur Sargkammer (R 44.1 bis R 53)*, 1-4, Studien zur spätägyptischen Religion 31 (Wiesbaden: Harrassowitz Verlag).

Graefe, E. (2003). *Das Grab des Padihorresnet, Obervermögensverwalter der Gottesgemahlin des Amun (Thebanisches Grab Nr. 196)*, I–II. Monumenta aegyptiaca IX (Turnhout: Brepols).

Griffin, K. (2014). "The Book of the Dead from the Second Pillared Hall of the Tomb of Karakhamun: A Preliminary Survey." In *Tombs of the South Asasif Necropolis. Thebes, Karakhamun (TT 223), and Karabasken (TT 391) in the Twenty-fifth Dynasty*, edited by E. Pischikova, 173–99 (Cairo: American University in Cairo Press).

Kaper, O. E. (2002). "Queen Nefertari and the Frog. On an Amphibious Element in the Vignette to BD 94." *Bulletin of the Australian Centre for Egyptology* 13: 109–26.

Lefebvre, G. (1924). *Le Tombeau de Petosiris. Première Partie: Description* (Cairo: IFAO).

Molinero Polo, M. A. (2014a). "The Broad Hall of the Two Maats: Spell BD 125 in Karakhamun's Main Burial Chamber." In *Thebes in the First Millennium BC*, edited by E. Pischikova, J. Budka, and K. Griffin, 269–93 (Newcastle upon Tyne: Cambridge Scholars Publishing).

Molinero Polo, M. A. (2014b). "The Textual Program of Karakhamun's First Pillared Hall." In *Tombs of the South Asasif Necropolis. Thebes, Karakhamun (TT 223), and Karabasken (TT 391) in the Twenty-fifth Dynasty*, edited by E. Pischikova, 131–72 (Cairo: American University in Cairo Press).

Morkot, R. G. (2003). "Archaism and Innovation in Egyptian Art from the New Kingdom to the Twenty-sixth Dynasty." In *Never Had the Like Occurred'. Egypt's View of its Past*, edited by J. Tait, 79–99 (London: Routledge).

Munro, I. (2001). *Spruchvorkommen auf Totenbuch-Textzeugen der Dritten Zwischenzeit*, Studien zum altägyptischen Totenbuch 5 (Wiesbaden: Harrassowitz Verlag).

Niwiński, A. (1988). *21st Dynasty Coffins from Thebes. Chronological and Typological Studies*, THEBEN V (Mainz am Rhein: Verlag Philipp von Zabern).

Niwiński, A. (1989a). *Studies on the Illustrated Theban Funerary Papyri of the 11th and 10th Centuries B.C.*, Orbis biblicus et orientalis 86 (Freiburg: Universitätsverlag).

Niwiński, A. (1989b). "The Solar–Osirian Unity as Principle of the Theology of the 'State of Amun' in Thebes in the 21st Dynasty." *Jaarbericht van het vooraziat.-egyptisch Genootschap, Ex Oriente Lux* 30: 89–106.

Payraudeau, F. (2014). "Retour sur la succession Shabaqo-Shabataqo." *NeHet. Revue numerique d'Egytolologie* 1: 115–27.

Quirke, S. (2013). *Going out in Daylight—prt m hrw, the Ancient Egyptian Book of the Dead, translation, sources, meanings*, GHP Egyptology 20 (London: Golden House).

Riggs, C. (2005). *The Beautiful Burial in Roman Egypt. Art, Identity, and Funerary Religion* (Oxford: Oxford University Press).

Roccati, A. (1976). "Il libro dei Morti di Šešonq." *Oriens antiquus* XV: 233–50.

Roccati, A. (2003). "Totenbuch und Grabarchitektur: der Fall TT 27." In *Es werde niedergelegt als Schriftstück. Festschrift für Hartwig Altenmüller zum 65. Geburtstag*. Studien zur altägyptischen Kultur Beihefte 9, edited by N. Kloth, 347–50 (Hamburg: Buske).

Roehrig, C. H., ed. (2005). *Hatshepsut from Queen to Pharaoh* (New Haven: Metropolitan Museum of Art).

Rosati, G. (1993). "Il libro dei Morti sui pilastri orientali della corte." *Vicino Oriente* IX: 107–17.

Rosati, G. (2006). "Glimpses of the Book of the Dead in the Second Court of the tomb of Montuemhat (TT 34)." In *Totenbuch Forschungen. Gesammelte Beiträge des 2. Internationalen Totenbuch-Symposiums, Bonn 25.–29. September 2005*. Studien zum Altägytischen Totenbuch 11, edited by B. Backes, I. Munro, and S. Stöhr, 297–324 (Wiesbaden: Harrassowitz).

Saleh, M. (1984). *Das Totenbuch in den Thebanischen Beamtengräbern des Neuen Reiches. Texte und Vignetten* (Mainz: von Zabern).

Shirley, J. J. (2014). "The Power of the Elite: The Officials of Hatshepsut's Regency and Coregency." In *Creativity and Innovation in the Reign of Hatshepsut*, Studies in Ancient Oriental Civilizations 69, edited by J. M. Galán, B. M. Bryan, and P. F. Dorman, 173–245 (Chicago: Oriental Institute of the University of Chicago).

Sist, L. (1976). "Le false-porte del cortile," *Oriens antiquus* XV: 251–55.

Smith, M. (2017). *Following Osiris: Perspectives on the Osirian Afterlife from Four Millennia* (Oxford: Oxford University Press).

Smoláriková, K. (2010). "The Phenomenon of Archaism in the Saite Period Funerary Architecture." In *Egypt in Transition. Social and Religious Development of Egypt in the First Millennium BCE*, Proceedings of an International Conference Prague, September 1–4, 2009, edited by L. Bareš, F. Coppens, and K. Smoláriková, 431–40 (Prague: Czech Institute of Egyptology, Faculty of Arts, Charles University in Prague).

Stöhr, S. and Wüthrich, A. (2013). *Ba-Bringer und Schattenabschneider: Untersuchungen zum so genannten Totenbuchkapitel 191 auf Totenbuchpapyri*. Studien zum Altägyptischen Totenbuch 18 (Wiesbaden: Harrassowitz).

Traunecker, C. (2008). "Le palais funéraire de Padiamenope redécouvert (TT 33)." *Egypte, Afrique & Orient* 51: 15–48.

Traunecker, C. (2014). "The 'Funeral Palace' of Padiamenope: Tomb, Place of Pilgrimage, and Library. Current Research." In *Thebes in the First Millenium B.C.*, edited by E. Pischikova, J. Budka, and K. Griffin, 205–34 (Cambridge: Cambridge Scholars Publishing).

Traunecker, C. (2015). "La tombe de Padiamenopé: avancées récentes et lectures nouvelles." In "La Thèbes des morts. La dynamique thébaine dans les idées égyptiennes de l'au-delà." *Egypte nilotique et mediterraneenne* 8, edited by A. Gasse, F. Albert, S. Einaudi, I. Régen, and C. Traunecker, 58–66 (Montpellier).

Traunecker, C. (2018). "Abydenian Pilgrimage, Immortal stars and Theban Liturgies in the Tomb of Padiamenope (TT 33)." In *Thebes in the First Millennium BC: Art and Archaeology of the Kushite Period and Beyond*, edited by E. Pischikova, J. Budka, and K. Griffin, 126–51 (London: GHP Egyptology).

Venit, M. J. (2016). *Visualizing the Afterlife in the Tombs of Graeco-Roman Egypt* (Cambridge: Cambridge University Press).

Whitehouse, H. (1998). "Roman in life, Egyptian in death: The painted tomb of Petosiris in the Dakhleh Oasis." In *Life on the Fringe: Living in the Southern Egyptian Deserts During the Roman and Early Byzantine Periods*, edited by O. E. Kaper, 253–70 (Leiden: Research School CNWS, Leiden University).

CHAPTER 12

# THE BOOK OF THE DEAD IN TEMPLES

HOLGER KOCKELMANN

## A QUESTION OF ANCIENT AND MODERN PERSPECTIVE: EGYPTIAN VERSUS EGYPTOLOGICAL TEXT CLASSIFICATION

THE BD is possibly the best and longest attested corpus of texts and images with which elite burials were equipped. The typical find context of these documents in graves or coffins or within the wrappings of mummies led to their firm if not exclusive association with the funerary sphere, not only of the physical BD manuscripts, but also of their actual contents. Less well-known is the occurrence of several BD texts and vignettes in the reliefs of Egyptian temples. The latter is found supraregionally in major temples (e.g., Medinet Habu, Dendera; see Fig. 12.1) and small sanctuaries (el-Qala, Deir el-Medina, Fig. 12.2) alike. From the perspective of the present state of research, however, the inclusion of the BD in the epigraphic corpus of the temples is a rather marginal phenomenon. Due to its relative rarity, it has only briefly been noted in general accounts or reference works on the BD (e.g., Hornung, 1997: 22). The topic was addressed in more detail for the first time by László Kákosy (1982), who interpreted BD spells on the walls of the temple as a potential indicator of the latter's funerary character, or at least as evidence for the influence of "funerary literature" on its decoration, especially in the Greco-Roman Period. With good reason, this view was put into question in a comprehensive and groundbreaking article by Alexandra von Lieven (2012), who explained the appearance of BD texts and images in the temple rather differently. In her view, it is enrooted in the non(-exclusively)-funerary origin and cultic nature of these spells and their resultant adaptability for the topics and concerns of both the temple decoration and mortuary texts. Unquestionably, von Lieven's approach offers the most promising key to understanding

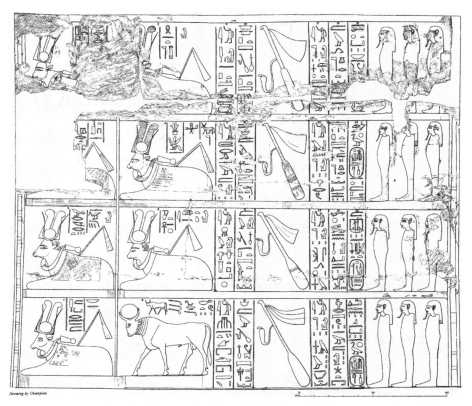

**FIG. 12.1.** Vignette of Book of the Dead spell 148 (*The Epigraphic Survey*, 1963, pl. 474). Courtesy of the Oriental Institute of the University of Chicago.

the interconnection between "Book of the Dead" on the one hand and "temple decoration" on the other.

## THE RELATION BETWEEN THE BD AND THE TEMPLE AS A CHICKEN-OR-EGG DILEMMA

The discussion on the interdependencies between the BD and temple decoration has intensified over the last decade. In the first instance, it centered on the problem of the primary and secondary use of the respective BD spells, either as (ritual) texts for deities and the living or for the deceased. The interference between the two seemingly very different corpora leads us directly into the central and complex problem of text classification, an issue that has not yet been systematically and finally solved in

FIG. 12.2. Judgment Scene ("Weighing of the Heart") in the Ptolemaic Temple of Deir el-Medina as known from Book of the Dead spell 125 (Lepsius 1854, Abth. IV, Blatt 16 [b]).

Egyptology, with respect to either the corpus of temple inscriptions, funerary texts, or literary compositions (Stadler, 2015: 75–76). As has justly been stressed in recent years, the BD is a collection of rather diverse categories of texts, a considerable proportion of which appear to have an originally non-mortuary, or at least not an *exclusively* funerary, background (von Lieven, 2012: 265). This is a characteristic that the BD shares with the two other great "funerary" collections of ancient Egypt. The first of these is the Pyramid Texts, which obviously include numerous ritual texts. The other group is the Coffin Texts, some spells of which seem to have a medico-magical origin (cf. von Lieven, 2017: 345 and 347–48; Dorman, 2017: 32). According to one estimation, more than one-fourth of the spells of the BD may have been used in rites for the living; in the case of certain spells, this is obvious not only from their attestation in non-funerary contexts, but from text-internal evidence (Gee, 2006: 75–81; Barbash, 2017: 81). Some of the BD texts may actually be identified as potential temple rituals (see Gee, 2006: 73–74). If this assumption is accepted, the spells in question would represent particularly clear testimonies for the interconnections between the so-called Book of the Dead and the cult of the temple.

Though the spells known as the "Book of the Dead" as a corpus compiled on a mortuary papyrus and mummy linen or on tomb walls have a purely funerary purpose, the modern denomination of the collection is misleading, as it disguises the true nature and origin of many of the spells and compositions. The scholarly term "Book of the Dead" refers to just one use or context of these texts, but does not indicate the heterogeneous roots and nature of the compilation as a whole. Here, we must thoroughly differentiate between the potential primary and secondary employment of the "spells," some of which can have more than just one "Sitz im Leben." Since the Old Kingdom, the practice of repurposing (Osirian and non-Osirian) ritual texts of the temple for funerary use must have been a fairly widespread custom that can still be seen in Roman times (Smith, 2009: 61–65; Gill, 2015). Text adoption includes cases of non-funerary compositions employed secondarily for mortuary purposes, divine funerary (i.e., Osirian) temple texts for private uses (Smith, 2015: 161–62), and the other way around, the adaptation of funerary texts and images for the temple decoration. A classic case of a text used both in the rituals and decoration of the temple and in mortuary contexts like the BD is the Opening of the Mouth (Cruz-Uribe, 1999). It is also a paradigm for the ongoing debate as to whether certain religious texts were first used in the temple ritual or originally created for a funerary purpose (Quack, 2015). Therefore, the presence of the BD in temples *and* burial contexts is just one of many testimonies for the interdependency of temple and mortuary cult, which is strongly marked by an exchange, adoption, reinterpretation and modification of texts and images as required by the respective context. It seems appropriate to assume an intense reciprocal exchange between temple and funerary cult (cf. Stadler, 2013: 23–25), which also characterizes the textual transmission of the so-called Book of the Dead.

For the ancient Egyptians, there was apparently a much less clear separation between temple and funerary religion. The latter does not form an independent section within Egyptian religion, but is deeply interwoven with temple cult and theology (Assmann, 1989: 149). Both had several key constituents in common such as the solar cycle as a model of continuous regeneration, the offering cult, rites for annihilating and dispelling evil forces, or the aim to inventory and codify sacred topographies and landscapes. Considering their fundamental congruencies and their partially comparable principal concerns, it is not surprising that the funerary and the temple cult make use of similar or even the same religious text compositions to a certain extent. Similar or identical religious and cultic concerns entail the use of similar or identical texts and images.

Instances of spells and iconographical motifs regarded as typical for the BD and attested both in funerary and temple contexts derive from almost the entire time span in which the BD was popular. Interferences between a) the corpus of texts and vignettes found in BD documents and b) the inventory of inscriptions and scenes of the temple decoration are found as early as in the New Kingdom (Abdelrahiem, 2006), in other words, at a relatively early stage in the history of the BD as an established collection of texts in its own right. Hence the phenomenon of an overlap between the repertoires of the epigraphic temple decoration and the BD cannot be ascribed to the aforementioned alleged "funeralization" or marked "mortuary aspect" of late temples, which would have led to an increased incorporation of funerary material in their reliefs (von Lieven, 2012: 249–50). Nevertheless, the presence of "typical" BD texts and images on temple walls would fit well with the temple's quality as an at least partly funerary sphere (Finnestad, 1997: 215–16), especially when employed for the decoration of chapels consecrated to Osiris (von Lieven, 2012: 258). Such Osirian cults became an integral element in the ritual practice of Egyptian temples during the first millennium BCE (Backes and Dieleman, 2015: 2; Coulon, 2010). In turn, the cult for the deceased grew more and more interconnected with the cult of the gods during the last phase of Egyptian religion. Ritual texts from the temple cult were adopted as mortuary texts for the burial of human individuals and in analogy to this appropriation, tombs show similarities with the architecture and decoration of temples (Quack, 2006: 128–32). Elements of the temple reliefs were adapted for the funerary equipment (coffins, cartonnage masks, and mummy shrouds), possibly because the temple was a place and source of regeneration, from which the deceased should profit in the hereafter (Budde, 2011: 368). The underworld with its gates and passages, which the deceased had to pass through in order to unite with Osiris in the "holy of the holiest," was also conceptualized like a temple (cf. Barguet, 1969: 7–17; Assmann, 1989: 149; Stadler, 2009: 277). The objective of this assimilation between burial place and temple was obviously the maximum integration of the deceased in the realm and community of the gods and to guarantee his or her perpetual benefit from the rituals performed for the deities (von Lieven, 2010; Budka, 2016: 175–76). The adaptation of temple texts into funerary literature may signify the transformation of the deceased's status to that of an initiated priest, the proof of his or her priestly knowledge, and, most importantly, the acquisition and exploitation of particularly powerful texts, of which the potential has been approved by the temple cult (see also Stadler, 2013: 25). Most likely, it was this particular effectiveness which induced compilers of the BD to include numerous non-mortuary texts in the corpus at the beginning of its formation in the early New Kingdom. During the next few centuries, the ritual and cultic nature of this material was not forgotten, as is demonstrated by its appearance in Greco-Roman temples (von Lieven, 2012: 267).

# The BD and Temple Decoration: Hoards of Egyptian Religious Ideas

With the diversity of the contents, the compiled "kaleidoscopic" nature rather than being a coherent text, the equal importance of text and vignettes, and with the tendency of having fixed formal arrangements of texts and images ("layouts"), the BD and temple decoration share a number of central characteristics. Due to their complexity and range of subjects, both corpora have been deemed text collections, which are potentially "canonical" for the concepts and ideas of Egyptian religion, as John Gee (2010: 30) has put it: "If any text in ancient Egypt was canonical, it was the Book of the Dead" (for the temple: Anonymous, 2010: 5). This may hold true in a wider sense, if "canonicity" is not defined as an inventory of texts that are strictly the same, but more openly as a loose, but "representative" group of written compositions and images which reflect the central beliefs and topics of Egyptian religion. The BD was not absolutely fixed regarding its inventory of texts and images. Generally, it remained open to modifications and enrichment by supplementary material. At the same time, however, it showed a distinct tendency toward standardization in regard to its content and a number of—more or less fixed—formal conventions. Unlike the Pyramid Texts and Coffin Texts, the BD can justly be called a spell corpus, which shows features of a canonization, at least from the Twenty-sixth Dynasty onward (Quack, 2009a: 14; von Lieven, 2016: 68–69). For the temple decoration, the question of canonicity has yet to be clarified. However, its content is significantly less standardized than that of the Book of the Dead, despite recurrent kinds of texts found in temples of different regions.

Both Book and the Dead manuscripts and temple walls combine texts and images, which are usually closely related to each other. From a merely formal perspective, the text–image distribution in the BD (Luft, 2015: 42) and in the temple decoration follows rather strict rules and conventions (Kockelmann, 2011: 17–45). Both the BD and the layout of a temple wall can be identified as such at once by their characteristic visual appearance; in this respect, they are possibly the most iconic kinds of Egyptian documents. One encounters similar principles of layout, such as the hieroglyphs predominately arranged in columns, which are framed by vertical lines, figures with accompanying texts in large scale vignettes or scenes respectively, and red-yellow horizontal border lines framing the text in New Kingdom BD manuscripts (Munro, 1988: 199–200) and temple scenes alike (Collombert, 2014: 968).

In the Book of the Dead, we can already find a recurrence of certain spell sequences in the New Kingdom, and more clearly, a standardized array of spells from the Twenty-sixth Dynasty onwards ("Saitic recension": Gee, 2010: 26). In the temple, there is a considerable number of standard iconographic elements and conventions of how and where certain categories of texts or scenes should be positioned on the architecture. For example, depictions of "Pharaoh Smiting the Enemies" are found predominantly on the facade of the pylon, while processions of Nile gods, field goddesses, the personified nomes of Egypt and other entities are located in the *soubassements* (dados).

BD documents and temple decoration were subject to similar mechanics of text production, text transmission and editorial processes, which selected material from the same virtual open pool of knowledge (Luft, 2015: 46–47), in which the entire repertoire of Egyptian religious texts and iconography was united. Moreover, the copies of a Book of the Dead, as well as the architectural design and the layout of reliefs of the individual temples were compiled and designed in accordance with individual local or personal requirements, guided by superior rules and norms (Mosher Jr., 1992; Quack, 2009b, 2014). The respective text and image models were the result of a transregional exchange of sources (e.g., Munro, 2010; Winter, 1995).

Formal similarities in layout, related contents, and a comparably organized text compilation could indicate that the creation of BD master copies and the development of drafts of the temple decoration were bound to the same intellectual institution. Also, very specific iconographic details, which are present in both the BD corpus and in the temple decoration, may hint at such a conjoint root (Kockelmann, 2006). This common source, from which the BD documents and the corpus of the temple decoration originated, should be identified with the temple scriptoria ("Houses of Life") and their archives as the principal centers of competence for religious studies. Papyri with collections of BD spells must have been part of these temple libraries. Generally, it is assumed that priests with access to the archives were the responsible redactors of the BD and other funerary compositions (e.g., Cole, 2017: 41 and 46; Scalf, 2017: 142–43). Although we do not know for sure where the "workshops" in which the BD documents were produced in stock or on order were located (Kockelmann, 2008: 117–23; Backes, 2010: 2), it is well conceivable that they were situated at the temple or at least organizationally connected to the "House of Life." This presumption is supported by the fact that temples produced other burial equipment as well, such as shabtis (Edwards, 1971: 120). The latter were not just physically manufactured by the staff of the temple; at the same time, they also seem to have been activated for their task in the hereafter through ritual acts (cf. Menu, 2011: 46), which were the expertise of the priesthood. In analogy to this, one could surmise that creating BD manuscripts for the deceased by ritually competent priestly scribes was not just a technical process of mere text copying, but also ensured the religious effectiveness of these documents. As the temple scriptorium was the most eminent source of religious knowledge, and considering the symbolic role of the temple as a guarantor and provider of regeneration and ritual efficacy par excellence, it is highly likely that the BD documents were manufactured there. The institutional union of temple text scriptorium and BD workshop would have facilitated the migration of "BD" texts and images from one context into the other.

## Examples for the Intersection of the BD and Temple Decoration

It might be going too far to classify the congruency between the BD and texts and images of the temple decoration a widespread phenomenon. At the present state of research, the actual degree at which the "BD" and "temple decoration" overlap is hard to estimate, since interferences are not always obvious and the epigraphic temple text material has not yet been translated and analyzed in its entirety. For the time being, one can only consider evident examples, that is, texts and vignettes that occur frequently and typically in BD documents. Others, like BD 168, which have only been assigned to the BD corpus by modern scholarship, but in reality represent an independent funerary "book" (Quack, 2009a: 20), should be left aside, though they are also attested in the decoration of the Osiris chapels on the roof of the temple of Dendera. If one takes into account only clear and undoubted instances, we would then find less than a dozen BD spells that also occur in the temple decoration. These are: BD 110, 125, 144, 145, 146, 148, and 149 (New Kingdom and Saite recension) plus BD 178 and 182 (found in Pre-Saite BD documents; cf. von Lieven, 2012: 250–53). The spectrum of textual compositions and images that are attested in the BD corpus and have also been incorporated into the temple decoration hence appears to be very limited. The content of most of them (BD 110, 144–6, and 149) is concerned with the topography and inhabitants of transmundane regions (von Lieven, 2012: 254), similar to other "encyclopedic" temple inscriptions recording *res sacrae* and sacred landscapes.

Within the whole quantity of decoration of the individual Pharaonic or Greco-Roman temples, the aforementioned spells accordingly represent a relatively small proportion. Most temples do not preserve more than one or two of these texts or vignettes. The claim that the iconic vignette of BD 125 ("Weighing of the Heart" or "Judgment of the Dead") "appeared ubiquitously both in tombs as well as in temples" (Scalf, 2017: 142) actually applies only to the decoration of tombs (Saleh, 1984: 63–71, 96–97; Seeber, 1976: 16–23). In the temple, the scene is exceptional and solely found in Greco-Roman times. Until recently, the only known example was attested in the Ptolemaic temple at Deir el-Medina (Fig. 12.2; Du Bourguet, 2002: 56–57, and 303, no. 58; see Riggs, 2006: 320). Another adapted version of the judgment scene has recently been discovered on a door lintel from the temples of Philae (Kockelmann, in preparation). Despite its rarity in the non-funerary sources, BD 125 is nonetheless a particularly good and interesting example of the conjunction of the BD and the epigraphic program of temples. Other textual elements of this spell occur in the temple inscriptions, such as the formula "I am pure, I am pure," which is well known from the daily temple liturgy (Gee, 2010: 27). Probably the most intriguing link between the BD and the temple is, however, the "Negative Confession" ("Declaration of Innocence"), which forms the central part of BD 125 (Allen†, 1974: 98–99). Despite skepticism in the past, there is little doubt that this text is another version of a priestly oath, which was probably sworn both on the occasion of the priest's initiation and later when he entered the temple during service. Hence the "Weighing of the Heart" scene in the temple of Deir el-Medina mentioned above does not show the judgment of an anonymous deceased, but the justification of a living priest involved in the temple cult (von Lieven, 2012: 264), possibly during his initiation ceremony, according to Griffiths (cf. Kákosy, 1982: 125). The oath consists of the candidate's declaration that he has not committed certain sins and will not carry out other kinds of offenses in the future. It was first known from Greek papyri, one of which was already published in the 1960s (Schuman, 1960) and was correctly linked to BD 125, which contains very similar affirmations (Merkelbach, 1968a: 13–30; 1968b; 1969; Grieshammer, 1974). The Greek text turned out to be the translation of an Egyptian original, which is part of the priestly prescriptions of the Book of the Temple (Quack, 1997: 297–98; 2000: 8–9). Possible excerpts of the oath alias "Declaration of Innocence" are found as hieroglyphic inscriptions on gates of the temple of Edfu (Fairman, 1958: 91; Gee, 1998: 55–57). The main concern, which the priestly initiation (temple ritual) and the initiation of the deceased ("Weighing of the Heart"/ BD 125) had in common, was ritual purity. The latter qualified the justified to enter the realm of the gods and behold the deity, either in the hereafter or in the sanctuary of the temple (cf. Assmann, 2005: 82; Gee, 2004: 100–101). The "Declaration of Innocence" was a text suitable for ascertaining the individual's purity in both contexts. The temple initiation practice might have provided the model for the *rite de passage* of the deceased in the hereafter, for the transformation of the individual from one state of being into another, from "profane," "not yet transfigured," to "pure, justified, transfigured" (Assmann, 1989: 151; 2005: 135–36, 81–82).

However, whether the "Negative Confession" was the prototype of the oath or vice versa is still a matter of dispute (see Stadler, 2008: 3). The reason why the judgment scene, a.k.a. priestly initiation, is only exceptionally found in the temple reliefs is possibly that the ceremony was arcane knowledge; moreover, the temple decoration concentrates on divine beings rather than on acts that concern human beings.

BD 148 is likely to have been a supraregionally attested element in the epigraphy of the offering hall of the temples; presumably, it only became a component of the BD in a secondary step (Quack, 2007: 216–18). The vignette of BD 148 shows seven sacred cows and their bull and is related to alimentary supply. It seems to be the most frequent text and vignette to be found both in the BD and in temple decoration, attested in at least eight temples, in some of these more than once. In the funerary context, it secures provision for the deceased, while the supply of offerings for the gods und sustenance for the king is its key issue in the context of the temple. At the same time, it is closely related to the sun god and solar circle (von Lieven, 2012: 261; Barbash, 2017: 82). This is another aspect which explains the presence of its vignette and texts in the decoration system of temples that are marked by a solar-Osirian bipolarity (cf. von Lieven, 2012: 255–58).

BD 144 to 146 are a group of texts and vignettes that contain descriptions and depictions of gates and their demonic guardians. These spells are suitable for protecting sacred spaces of various natures, located either in the realm of the dead or in the temple building, to which only the "justified" or "pure" individual may proceed. (Lucarelli, 2010: 86; Stadler, 2009: 252–319) In accordance with their content, they are found at the gates of temples or next to the entrances to chapels (Du Bourguet, 2002: 83, nos. 91–94), especially on doors and passages that lead to Osiris's chambers. Depending on the spell and on the context, the justified individual passing the gate is Horus on the way to his father Osiris (von Lieven, 2012: 259–60), the deceased, or the king as a ritualist represented by a priest. This ritualist simultaneously adopts the role of Thoth (Stadler, 2009: 302–14).

Though the aforementioned texts and images show certain divergences between the BD form and their attestation in the temple decoration, they still preserve enough key elements by which they can immediately be identified as the respective spells. In other cases, the correspondences between the funerary and the temple BD tradition are only approximative. There are indications that texts known as "Book of the Dead" spells were revised and modified to adjust them to the temple context; references to death were exchanged with other phrases of non-funerary context (Barbash, 2017: 82). A prominent non-BD parallel for freely and creatively adapted temple versions of compositions known (also) as funerary texts, is Pyramid Text 600. It occurs in modified forms and excerpts in several New Kingdom and Greco-Roman Egyptian temple ritual scenes that show the offering of the *wesekh*-collar (Graefe, 1991: 129–48). Another case of such an adaptation may be Pyramid Text 269 (Grimm, 1979: 35–46). Examples of similarly fundamentally reworked "Book of the Dead" spells are found in a scene of the "Nile chamber" in the temple of Edfu, of which the inscriptions have apparently been modeled on BD 149 (Baumann, 2012: 15–17), or in a hymn in the temple of Opet at Karnak, which seems to be related to BD 175 (Klotz, 2012: 199).

# Bibliography

Abdelrahiem, M. (2006). "Chapter 144 of the Book of the Dead from the Temple of Ramesses II at Abydos." *Studien zur Altägyptischen Kultur* 34: 1–16.

Allen†, Th. G. (1974). *The Book of the Dead or Going forth by Day. Ideas of the Ancient Egyptians concerning the Hereafter as Expressed in Their Own Terms*. Prepared for Publication by Elizabeth Blaisdell Hauser, Studies in Ancient Oriental Civilization 37 (Chicago: Oriental Institute of the University of Chicago).

Anonymous (2010). "Bibliotheken aus Stein. Ein neues Projekt der Heidelberger Akademie der Wissenschaften." *Göttinger Miszellen* 227: 5–7.

Assmann, J. (1989). "Death and Initiation in the Funerary Religion of Ancient Egypt." Translated by M. Grauer and R. Meyer. In *Religion and Philosophy in Ancient Egypt*, Yale Egyptological Studies 3, edited by Anonymous, 135–59 (New Haven: Yale Egyptological Seminar, Department of Near Eastern Languages and Civilizations, Graduate School).

Assmann, J. (2005). *Death and Salvation in Ancient Egypt*. Translated by David Lorton (Ithaca, NY; London: Cornell University Press).

Backes, B. (2010). "Three Funerary Papyri from Thebes. New Evidence on Scribal and Funerary Practice in the Late Period." *British Museum Studies in Ancient Egypt and Sudan* 15: 1–21.

Backes, B. and Dieleman, J. (2015). "Current Trends in the Study of Liturgical Papyri." In *Liturgical Texts for Osiris and the Deceased in Late Period and Graeco-Roman Egypt/ Liturgische Texte für Osiris und Verstorbene im spätzeitlichen Ägypten*. Proceedings of the Colloquiums at New York (ISAW), 6 May 2011, and Freudenstadt, 18–21 July 2012, Studien zur spätägyptischen Religion 14, edited by B. Backes and J. Dieleman, 1–13 (Wiesbaden: Harrassowitz).

Barbash, Y. (2017). "The Ritual Context of the Book of the Dead." In *Book of the Dead. Becoming God in Ancient Egypt*. With new object photography by Kevin Bryce Lowry, Oriental Institute Museum Publications 39, edited by F. Scalf, 75–84 (Chicago: The Oriental Institute of the University of Chicago).

Barguet, P. (1969). "Essai d'interprétation du Livre des Deux Chemins." *Revue d'Égyptologie* 21: 7–17.

Baumann, S. (2012). "Die Beschreibung der Nilflut in der Nilkammer von Edfu." *Zeitschrift für ägyptische Sprache und Altertumskunde* 139(1): 1–18.

Budde, D. (2011). *Das Götterkind im Tempel, in der Stadt und im Weltgebäude. Eine Studie zu drei Kultobjekten der Hathor von Dendera und zur Theologie der Kindgötter im griechisch-römischen Ägypten*, Münchner Ägyptologische Studien 55 (Darmstadt; Mainz: Philipp von Zabern).

Budka, J. (2016). "Kontinuität und Adaption—zur Einbindung von Ritualhandlungen in die Architektur spätzeitlicher Tempelgräber in Theben (25. Dynastie bis Ptolemäerzeit)." In *Die Variation der Tradition. Modalitäten der Ritualadaption im Alten Ägypten*. Akten des Internationalen Symposiums vom 25.–28. November 2012 in Heidelberg, Orientalia Lovaniensia Analecta 240, edited by A. H. Pries, 171–200 (Leuven; Paris; Bristol, CT: Peeters).

Cole, E. (2017). "Language and Script in the Book of the Dead." In *Book of the Dead. Becoming God in Ancient Egypt*. With new object photography by Kevin Bryce Lowry, Oriental Institute Museum Publications 39, edited by F. Scalf, 41–48 (Chicago: The Oriental Institute of the University of Chicago).

Collombert, Ph. (2014). "Les soubassements des temples au Nouvel Empire." In *Altägyptische Enzyklopädien. Die Soubassements in den Tempeln der griechisch-römischen Zeit*, Soubassementstudien I, vol. 2, Studien zur spätägyptischen Religion 7, edited by A. Rickert and B. Ventker, unter Mitarbeit von E. Jambon, F. Löffler und D. von Recklinghausen, 965–76. Mit Tempelplänen von S. Baumann (Wiesbaden: Harrassowitz).

Coulon, L., ed. (2010). *Le culte d'Osiris au Ier millénaire av. J.-C. Découvertes et travaux récents. Actes de la table ronde internationale tenue à Lyon, Maison de l'Orient et de la Méditerranée (université Lumière-Lyon 2) les 8 et 9 juillet 2005*, Bibliothèque d'étude 153 (Cairo: Institut Français d'Archéologie Orientale).

Cruz-Uribe, E. (1999). "Opening of the Mouth as Temple Ritual." In *Gold of Praise. Studies in Honor of Edward F. Wente*, Studies in Ancient Oriental Civilization 58, edited by E. Teeter and J. A. Larson, 69–73 (Chicago: Oriental Institute of the University of Chicago).

Dorman, P. F. (2017). "The Origins and Early Development of the Book of the Dead." In *Book of the Dead. Becoming God in Ancient Egypt*. With new object photography by Kevin Bryce Lowry, Oriental Institute Museum Publications 39, edited by F. Scalf, 29–40 (Chicago: The Oriental Institute of the University of Chicago).

Du Bourguet, P. (2002). *Le temple de Deir al-Médîna*. Textes édités et indexés par Luc Gabolde, Mémoires publiés par les membres de l'Institut Français d'Archéologie Orientale 121 (Cairo: Institut Français d'Archéologie Orientale).

Edwards, I. E. S. (1971). "A Bill of Sale for a Set of Ushabtis." *Journal of Egyptian Archaeology* 57: 120–24.

The Epigraphic Survey (1963). *Medinet Habu VI: The Temple Proper*, part II: The Re Chapel, The Royal Mortuary Complex, and Adjacent Rooms with Miscellaneous Material from the Pylons, the Forecourts, and the First Hypostyle Hall, Oriental Institute Publications 84 (Chicago: The University of Chicago Press).

Fairman, H. W. (1958). "A Scene of the Offering of Truth in the Temple of Edfu." *Mitteilungen des Deutschen Archäologischen Institutes, Abteilung Kairo* 16: 86–92.

Finnestad, R. B. (1997). "Temples of the Ptolemaic and Roman Periods: Ancient Traditions in New Contexts." In *Temples of Ancient Egypt*, edited by B. E. Shafer, 185–237 (Ithaca, NY; London: Cornell University Press; I.B. Tauris).

Gee, J. L. (1998). *The Requirements of Ritual Purity in Ancient Egypt* (New Haven, CT: Yale Univ., Diss.).

Gee, J. (2004). "Prophets, Initiation and the Egyptian Temple." *Journal of the Society for the Study of Egyptian Antiquities* 31: 97–107.

Gee, J. (2006). "The Use of the Daily Temple Liturgy in the Book of the Dead." In *Totenbuch-Forschungen. Gesammelte Beiträge des 2. Internationalen Totenbuch-Symposiums, Bonn, 25. bis 29. September 2005*, Studien zum altägyptischen Totenbuch 11, edited by B. Backes, I. Munro, and S. Stöhr, 73–86 (Wiesbaden: Harrassowitz).

Gee, J. (2010). "The Book of the Dead as Canon." *British Museum Studies in Ancient Egypt and Sudan* 15: 23–33.

Gill, A.-K. (2015). "The Spells against Enemies in the Papyrus of Pawerem (P. BM EA 10252): A Preliminary Report." In *Liturgical Texts for Osiris and the Deceased in Late Period and Graeco-Roman Egypt/Liturgische Texte für Osiris und Verstorbene im spätzeitlichen Ägypten*. Proceedings of the Colloquiums at New York (ISAW), 6 May 2011, and Freudenstadt, 18–21 July 2012, Studien zur spätägyptischen Religion 14, edited by B. Backes and J. Dieleman, 133–44 (Wiesbaden: Harrassowitz).

Graefe, E. (1991). "Über die Verarbeitung von Pyramidentexten in den späten Tempeln (Nochmals zu Spruch 600 (§1652a–§1656d: Umhängen des Halskragens))." In *Religion und Philosophie im Alten Ägypten. Festgabe für Philippe Derchain zu seinem 65. Geburtstag am 24. Juni 1991*, Orientalia Lovaniensia Analecta 39, edited by U. Verhoeven and E. Graefe, 129–48 (Leuven: Departement Oriëntalistiek; Peeters).

Grieshammer, R. (1974). "Zum 'Sitz im Leben' des negativen Sündenbekenntnisses." In *XVIII. Deutscher Orientalistentag, vom 1. bis 5. Oktober 1972 in Lübeck: Vorträge, Zeitschrift der Deutschen Morgenländischen Gesellschaft*, Supplement 2, edited by W. Voigt, 19–25 (Wiesbaden: Franz Steiner).

Grimm, A. (1979). "Ein Zitat aus den Pyramidentexten in einem ptolemäischen Ritualtext des Horus-Tempels von Edfu. Edfou III, 130.14–15 = Pyr. 376b (Spr. 269). Zur Tradition altägyptischer Texte. Voruntersuchungen zu einer Theorie der Gattungen." *Göttinger Miszellen* 31: 35–46.

Hornung, E. (1997). *Altägyptische Jenseitsbücher. Ein einführender Überblick* (Darmstadt: Wissenschaftliche Buchgesellschaft).

Kákosy, L. (1982). "Temples and Funerary Beliefs in the Graeco-Roman Epoch." In *L'Égyptologie en 1979. Axes prioritaires de recherches*, I, Colloques internationaux du Centre National de la Recherche Scientifique no. 595, edited by Anonymous, 117–27 (Paris: Éditions du Centre National de la Recherche Scientifique).

Klotz, D. (2012). *Caesar in the City of Amun. Egyptian Temple Construction and Theology in Roman Thebes*, Monographies Reine Élisabeth 15 (Turnhout: Brepols).

Kockelmann, H. (2006). "Drei Götter unterm Totenbett. Zu einem ungewöhnlichen Bildmotiv in einer späten Totenbuch-Handschrift." *Revue d'égyptologie* 57: 75–89.

Kockelmann, H. (2008). *Untersuchungen zu den späten Totenbuch-Handschriften auf Mumienbinden*, vol. II: Handbuch zu den Mumienbinden und Leinenamuletten, Studien zum altägyptischen Totenbuch 12 (Wiesbaden: Harrassowitz).

Kockelmann, H. (2011). "Die 'Grammatik' des Tempels. Wie Religion und Kult Architektur und Dekoration bestimmen." In *KultOrte. Mythen, Wissenschaft und Alltag in den Tempeln Ägyptens*, edited by D. von Recklinghausen and M. A. Stadler, 17–45 (Berlin: Manetho).

Kockelmann, H. (in preparation). "Jenseitsgericht und Priesterweihe. Ein singuläres Zeugnis für die Tür als Stätte der Rechtfertigung und Initiation aus der griechisch-römischen Tempelanlage von Philae."

Lepsius, C. R. (1854). *Denkmaeler aus Aegypten und Aethiopien. Nach den Zeichnungen der von Seiner Majestät dem Koenige von Preussen, Friedrich Wilhelm IV., nach diesen Ländern gesendeten und in den Jahren 1842–1845 ausgeführten wissenschaftlichen Expedition, IX: Vierte Abtheilung: Denkmäler aus der Zeit der griechischen und römischen Herrschaft*, Blatt I–XC (Berlin: Nicolaische Buchhandlung).

von Lieven, A. (2010). "Das Verhältnis zwischen Tempel und Grab im griechisch-römischen Ägypten." *Revue d'égyptologie* 61: 91–111.

von Lieven, A. (2012). "Book of the Dead, Book of the Living: BD Spells as Temple Texts." *Journal of Egyptian Archaeology* 98: 249–67.

von Lieven, A. (2016). "Closed Canon vs. Creative Chaos: An In-Depth Look at (Real and Supposed) Mortuary Texts from Ancient Egypt." In *Problems of canonicity and identity formation in ancient Egypt and Mesopotamia*, CNI Publications 43, edited by K. Ryholt and G. Barjamovic, 51–77 (Copenhagen: Museum Tusculanum Press; Department of Cross-Cultural and Regional Studies, University of Copenhagen).

von Lieven, A. (2017). "Originally Non-Funerary Spells from the Coffin Texts: The Example of CT Spell 38." In *Studies in Ancient Egyptian Funerary Literature*, Orientalia Lovaniensia Analecta 257, edited by S. Bickel and L. Díaz-Iglesias, 345–54 (Leuven; Paris; Bristol, CT: Peeters).

Lucarelli, R. (2010). "The Guardian-Demons of the Book of the Dead." *British Museum Studies in Ancient Egypt and Sudan* 15: 85–102.

Luft, D. (2015). "Funerär und liturgisch: Gedanken zur Verbindung von Inhalten, Funktionen und Verwendungsbereichen altägyptischer religiöser Texte." In *Liturgical Texts for Osiris and the Deceased in Late Period and Graeco-Roman Egypt/Liturgische Texte für Osiris und Verstorbene im spätzeitlichen Ägypten*. Proceedings of the Colloquiums at New York (ISAW), 6 May 2011, and Freudenstadt, 18–21 July 2012, Studien zur spätägyptischen Religion 14, edited by B. Backes and J. Dieleman, 37–73 (Wiesbaden: Harrassowitz).

Menu, B. (2011). "Les ouchebtis de Neskhons, entre droit et croyances." *Égypte Nilotique et Méditerranéenne* 4: 39–49.

Merkelbach, R. (1968a). "Ein ägyptischer Priestereid." *Zeitschrift für Papyrologie und Epigraphik* 2: 7–30.

Merkelbach, R. (1968b). "Nachträge zu Band 1 und 2: Priestereid (Band 2, S. 7 ff.)." *Zeitschrift für Papyrologie und Epigraphik* 3: 136.

Merkelbach, R. (1969). "Ein griechisch-ägyptischer Priestereid und Totenbuch." In *Religions en Égypte hellénistique et romaine*. Colloque de Strasbourg, 16–18 mai 1967, Bibliothèque des centers d'études supérieures spécialisés. Travaux du Centre d'études supérieures spécialisé d'histoire des religions de Strasbourg, [edited by Ph. Derchain], 69–73 (Paris: Presses universitaires de France).

Mosher Jr., M. (1992). "Theban and Memphite Book of the Dead Traditions in the Late Period." *Journal of the American Research Center in Egypt* 29: 143–72.

Munro, I. (1988). *Untersuchungen zu den Totenbuch-Papyri der 18. Dynastie. Kriterien ihrer Datierung*, D 7 "Göttinger Philosophische Dissertation" (London; New York: Kegan Paul International).

Munro, I. (2010). "Evidence of a Master Copy Transferred from Thebes to the Memphite Area in Dynasty 26." *British Museum Studies in Ancient Egypt and Sudan* 15: 201–24.

Quack, J. F. (1997). "Ein ägyptisches Handbuch des Tempels und seine griechische Übersetzung." *Zeitschrift für Papyrologie und Epigraphik* 119: 297–300.

Quack, J. F. (2000). "Das Buch vom Tempel und verwandte Texte. Ein Vorbericht." *Archiv für Religionsgeschichte* 2: 1–20.

Quack, J. F. (2006). "Das Grab am Tempeldromos—Neue Deutungen zu einem spätzeitlichen Grabtyp." In *"Von reichlich ägyptischem Verstande." Festschrift für Waltraud Guglielmi zum 65. Geburtstag*, PHILIPPIKA 11, edited by K. Zibelius-Chen and H.-W. Fischer-Elfert, 113–32 (Wiesbaden: Harrassowitz).

Quack, J. F. (2007). "Die Götterliste des Buches vom Tempel und die überregionalen Dekorationsprogramme." In *6. Ägyptologische Tempeltagung: Funktion und Gebrauch altägyptischer Tempelräume*. Leiden, 4.–7. September 2002, Königtum, Staat und Gesellschaft früher Hochkulturen 3.1: Akten der ägyptologischen Tempeltagungen, edited by B. Haring and A. Klug, 213–35 (Wiesbaden: Harrassowitz).

Quack, J. F. (2009a). "Redaktion und Kodifizierung im spätzeitlichen Ägypten: der Fall des Totenbuches." In *Die Textualisierung der Religion*, Forschungen zum Alten Testament 62, edited by J. Schaper, 11–34 (Tübingen: Mohr Siebeck).

Quack, J. F. (2009b). "Die Theologisierung der bürokratischen Norm. Zur Baubeschreibung in Edfu im Vergleich zum Buch vom Tempel." In *7. Ägyptologische Tempeltagung: Structuring Religion*, Leuven, 28. September–1. Oktober 2005, Königtum, Staat und Gesellschaft früher Hochkulturen 3.2: Akten der ägyptologischen Tempeltagungen, edited by R. Preys, 221–29 (Wiesbaden: Harrassowitz).

Quack, J. F. (2014). "Die theoretische Normierung der Soubassement-Dekoration. Erste Ergebnisse der Arbeit an der karbonisierten Handschrift von Tanis." In *Altägyptische Enzyklopädien. Die Soubassements in den Tempeln der griechisch-römischen Zeit*, Soubassementstudien I, vol. 1, Studien zur spätägyptischen Religion 7, edited by A. Rickert and B. Ventker, unter Mitarbeit von E. Jambon, F. Löffler und D. von Recklinghausen. Mit Tempelplänen von S. Baumann, 17–27 (Wiesbaden: Harrassowitz).

Quack, J. F. (2015). "Das *Mundöffnungsritual* als Tempeltext und Funerärtext." In *Liturgical Texts for Osiris and the Deceased in Late Period and Graeco-Roman Egypt/ Liturgische Texte für Osiris und Verstorbene im spätzeitlichen Ägypten*. Proceedings of the Colloquiums at New York (ISAW), 6 May 2011, and Freudenstadt, 18–21 July 2012, Studien zur spätägyptischen Religion 14, edited by B. Backes and J. Dieleman, 145–59 (Wiesbaden: Harrassowitz).

Riggs, Ch. (2006). "Archaism and Artistic Sources in Roman Egypt: The Coffins of the Soter Family and the Temple of Deir el-Medina." *Bulletin de l'Institut Français d'Archéologie Orientale* 106: 315–32.

Saleh, M. (1984). *Das Totenbuch in den Beamtengräbern des Neuen Reiches. Texte und Vignetten*, Archäologische Veröffentlichungen 46 (Mainz: Zabern).

Scalf, F. (2017). "The Death of the Book of the Dead." In *Book of the Dead. Becoming God in Ancient Egypt*. With New Object Photography by Kevin Bryce Lowry, Oriental Institute Museum Publications 39, edited by F. Scalf, 138–47 (Chicago: The Oriental Institute of the University of Chicago).

Schuman, V. B. (1960). "A Second-Century Treatise on Egyptian Priests and Temples." *The Harvard Theological Review* 53: 159–70.

Seeber, Ch. (1976). *Untersuchungen zur Darstellung des Totengerichtes im Alten Ägypten*, Münchner Ägyptologische Studien 35 (Munich; Berlin: Deutscher Kunstverlag).

Smith, M. (2009). *Traversing Eternity. Texts for the Afterlife from Ptolemaic and Roman Egypt* (Oxford: Oxford University Press).

Smith, M. (2015). "Whose Ritual? Osirian Texts and Texts Written for the Deceased in P. BM EA 10209: A Case Study." In *Liturgical Texts for Osiris and the Deceased in Late Period and Graeco-Roman Egypt/Liturgische Texte für Osiris und Verstorbene im spätzeitlichen Ägypten*. Proceedings of the Colloquiums at New York (ISAW), 6 May 2011, and Freudenstadt, 18–21 July 2012, Studien zur spätägyptischen Religion 14, edited by B. Backes and J. Dieleman, 161–77 (Wiesbaden: Harrassowitz).

Stadler, M. A. (2008). "Judgement after Death (Negative Confession)." In *UCLA Encyclopedia of Egyptology. Open version*, edited by J. Dieleman and W. Wendrich, https://escholarship.org/uc/item/07s1t6kj.

Stadler, M. A. (2009). *Weiser und Wesir. Studien zu Vorkommen, Rolle und Wesen des Gottes Thot im ägyptischen Totenbuch*, Orientalische Religionen in der Antike. Ägypten, Israel, Alter Orient 1 (Tübingen: Mohr Siebeck).

Stadler, M. A. (2013). "Von kommunizierenden Röhren. Totenkult und Tempelkult." In *Wege zur Unsterblichkeit. Altägyptischer Totenkult und Jenseitsglaube*, Nilus: Studien zur Kultur Ägyptens und des Vorderen Orients 20, edited by A. Zdiarsky, 19–28 (Vienna: Phoibos).

Stadler, M. A. (2015). "Prätexte funerärer Rituale: Königsliturgie, Tempelliturgie, Totenliturgie." In *Liturgical Texts for Osiris and the Deceased in Late Period and Graeco-Roman Egypt/ Liturgische Texte für Osiris und Verstorbene im spätzeitlichen Ägypten*. Proceedings of the Colloquiums at New York (ISAW), 6 May 2011, and Freudenstadt, 18–21 July 2012, Studien zur spätägyptischen Religion 14, edited by B. Backes and J. Dieleman, 75–90 (Wiesbaden: Harrassowitz).

Winter, E. (1995). "Zeitgleiche Parallelen in verschiedenen Tempeln." In *3. Ägyptologische Tempeltagung, Hamburg, 1.–5. Juni 1994: Systeme und Programme der ägyptischen Tempeldekoration*, Ägypten und Altes Testament 33.1: Akten der ägyptologischen Tempeltagungen, edited by D. Kurth, 305–19 (Wiesbaden: Harrassowitz).

# PART III

# THE BOOK OF THE DEAD'S POSITION IN ANCIENT EGYPTIAN RELIGION

CHAPTER 13

# THE BOOK OF THE DEAD AS A SOURCE FOR THE STUDY OF ANCIENT EGYPTIAN RELIGION

*Methodology, Problems, Prospects*

MARTIN ANDREAS STADLER

## AN EPITOME OF THE ANCIENT EGYPTIAN RELIGION

ALMOST every study on ancient Egyptian religion cites spells or excerpts as evidence from the more or less loose collection of religious texts for which Carl Richard Lepsius established the name *Totenbuch*, or "Book of the Dead" (Lepsius, 1842), a collection that is less homogeneous than such a title might suggest. Some deny that the Book of the Dead is a well-defined collection of spells assembled by the Egyptians themselves and instead stress the corpus's openness (e.g., Quack, 2009b; Gestermann, 2010: 289). It is important in this chapter to keep this problem in mind, perhaps even more so than for other chapters in this handbook, simply for pragmatic reasons. The term "Book of the Dead" is used to refer to a series of spells that occur in tomb inscriptions, funerary papyri, and shrouds, repeatedly in the same combination with other spells (from these so-called spell sequences are established), as well as in temple inscriptions or liturgies. The core of the Book of the Dead goes back to the Coffin Texts of the Middle Kingdom, they themselves being a complement to the Old Kingdom Pyramid Texts (Gestermann, this volume), but new evidence has forced researchers to revise this received wisdom (e.g., Assmann, 2005: 250) and to cast doubt on how, or even whether, it is permissible to distinguish between those latter two corpora (Bickel, 2004; Smith, 2009; Hays, 2011). Such a genealogy has left its traces in the themes and contents of the spells assembled under the heading "Book of the Dead," a remarkable corpus, even if it at times gives a false impression of stability of ancient Egyptian beliefs. The Book of the Dead first appeared in the seventeenth century BCE, underwent an editing process in the eighth and seventh centuries BCE (Gerstermann, this volume), and was quite standardized from then on, remaining in use for some 1,700 years until the first century BCE or even CE (Töpfer and Müller-Roth, 2011; Stadler, 2003; see also Albert and Kucharek, this volume). Thus, the Book of the Dead can guide us through more than two millennia of Egyptian religious history, if we include the Coffin Texts' roots. Its significance as a source is not limited solely to the funerary sphere, which can hardly be isolated from the religious practice, as attested in temples and magical papyri (Rößler-Köhler, 1979: 345–46; Assmann, 1983a; Voss, 1996; Quack, 1999: 13–14). In fact, a series of spells do occur as inscriptions in temples (Kockelmann, this volume), and in many cases funerary spells in general evoke the impression that they are appropriations from temple and royal rituals (Stadler, 2015, 2017). All this has shaped the Egyptological mind and led to a perception of the Book of the Dead as a well-defined corpus, an epitome of the Egyptian belief system, virtually comparable to one of the holy books of the three great monotheistic religions.

Yet this long tradition resulted in a considerable variation in the Egyptians' understanding of the contents. This is hardly surprising. The Book of the Dead provides reasonably homogeneous copies during specific phases of ancient Egyptian history. Even so, no two single manuscripts are identical. Historical changes exerted influence not just on the wording, but also on the contents as a consequence of developments in the language, during which some expressions became obsolete and succeeding generations no longer understood them. Scribes did not shy away from varying and reinterpreting the original, thus creating new religious ideas and changing the contents (cf. e.g., Stadler, 2003). This is a general phenomenon of ancient Egyptian textual transmission (Pries, 2015) that could be termed as "open," but is distinctively more prominent with religious texts (for further examples see Pries, 2013b) because scribes were able to draw upon a wealth of internalized knowledge (Quack, 1994: 19–23; for the Coffin Texts, see also Willems, 2001: 257; Mathieu, 2004: 248). Thus, each period of Egyptian history between about 1700 BCE and 100 CE had its own understanding that calls for studying the Book of the Dead along certain axes of time, the Coffin Texts of the Middle Kingdom as the principal root, the New Kingdom, the Third Intermediate Period, and the Late Period with its so-called Saite recension. Further refining of individual examples is possible (cf. for the Coffin Texts, e.g., Willems, 1996; Meyer-Dietrich, 2006; for the Book of the Dead, e.g., Milde, 1991). Rita Lucarelli (2006) shows how complex such an undertaking can be and how differently some details can be judged by those with a different Egyptological background and point of view (e.g., Pries, 2011: 201 n. 854).

# Resistance to Decryption

Apart from its long tradition, the Book of the Dead has been the focus of more than 150 years of Egyptological study and has become a subject rich in prerequisites for those working in this area. Although we are focusing here on the text of the Book of the Dead, this holds true for the paratextual information accompanying the spells—the vignettes (Mosher, this volume). Almost all full translations taking the Book of the Dead as a coherent corpus (esp. Barguet, 1967; Allen, 1974; Hornung, 1979; Quirke, 2013) differ from each other in more or less significant aspects. This is due to our limited knowledge of the Egyptian language, which allows for—to put it cautiously—alternative interpretations and, due to the basic approach of each translator (Backes, this volume), interpolation of an idealized version from the 3,000 or so manuscripts that have survived, or, more likely, from just a fraction of them. In fact, determined by the available publications of their time, translators were bound to arbitrarily select examples and did not concern themselves too much about the textual tradition and its peculiarities. This is particularly true of Paul Barguet (1967) and Erik Hornung (1979), who—it must be said in defense of these books—tried to make the Book of the Dead available and accessible to a wider audience. Hornung shows a marked tendency toward the *lectio facilior*, i.e., to the version in a certain manuscript that is easier for us to understand nowadays, and then quickly jumping to the next papyrus without further notice if it provides yet another *lectio facilior*. Such an approach ignores the principle that the most difficult reading is the more probable one (*lectio difficilior lectio probabilior*; Vette, 2008). The brief comments in Hornung's appendix cannot counterbalance those deficiencies for a scholarly community for which a hybrid rendering is of limited use. And how much can a non-Egyptologist reader gain from the translation without detailed explanations? Nevertheless, scholars have intensively cited Hornung as the standard reference work.

Five years earlier, an English translation was published that provides information for each spell accompanied by specific examples (Allen, 1974). For spells where Allen drew on different papyri, he even mentions the source for each paragraph. If the Book of the Dead tradition had significantly changed as a result of reinterpretation or if it was unclear to him, he quite often went back to the Coffin Text root and thus presents us with a version of the Coffin Text spell that was incorporated into the Book of the Dead. This conceals the historic development and creates the illusion of an unchangeable religious continuity.

In contrast, those editions of specific later papyri providing a full translation of particular manuscripts (e.g., Allen, 1960; Verhoeven, 1993; O'Rourke, 2016) do not face the difficulties of selection and of establishing a standard version. Rather, they allow for insight into the changes in what certain Egyptians understood and what they reinterpreted. Having said this, a methodological issue raised by the 3,000 or so known examples is addressed: Which papyrus contains the authoritative reading and which reading is faulty? To tackle this problem, some Egyptologists resorted to the method of textual criticism using a form of stemmatics first introduced by Wolfgang Schenkel (1978; see also Luft, 2015a for a description). This kind of textual criticism was developed chiefly in biblical studies and German Classics to establish the correct version of an author's work or the Bible. Particularly in postwar German Egyptology, it dominated the research of the Coffin Texts (e.g., Kahl, 1999; Topmann, 2002; Backes, 2005; Gestermann, 2005), and was applied primarily by Ursula Rößler-Köhler (1979,

1999) to the Book of the Dead, but possibly went unnoticed by some in the anglophone Egyptology world who advocated a "strong dose of textual criticism" (Lesko, 2000: 317). By meticulously analyzing deviations in, ideally, all available examples of a certain text and by establishing a stemma of those examples, stemmatics endeavors to identify corruptions and to reconstruct a hypothetical archetype, i.e., the version that the author created. However, no individual ancient authors are known for Egyptian religious texts, which belong to an open tradition, and thus it is questionable whether recreating an unattested version is sensible because a famous author's individuality cannot be determined, nor can a constitutive religious attitude be reconstructed like in the Bible since it is characteristic for Egyptian religious thinking to develop new ideas by associative speculation and reinterpretation (Stadler, 2009: 43–47; for a criticism of stemmatic textual criticism, see also Pries, 2011: 1–7; Hagen, 2012: 216–17; for an apology, see Backes, 2011; Gestermann, 2017). Such a version claims to come as close as possible to the original, but it actually just represents another example, except this time one created by a modern redactor. If it really once existed, its readings might have quickly lost relevance for the succeeding epochs, which developed their own understanding and interpretation as testified in their copies that have survived. The necessarily limited horizon of the modern editor, who is not a native speaker of the Egyptian language and works only with an accidentally preserved selection of evidence, determines what is considered to be correct or wrong. This is especially true of the process of *divinatio*, which must take into account an author's intention as well as his cultural and historic context. However, if a certain notion and its rare attestation have escaped a scholar's attention—and who dares to boast of knowing all Egyptian religious texts by heart?—she or he might deem a deviation as a corruption or an error and emend it, even though it is actually correct. Yekatarina Barbash (2015), for instance, sees graphic variations as intentional scribal devices, whereas others might consider these mere scribal mistakes despite their use of the neutral term "deviation." In fact, the textual criticism, which is critiqued here and which asserts some objectivity, entails a high degree of subjectivity as even proponents of this method such as Gestermann (2017: esp. 283) concede. Admittedly, all scholarly work is governed by subjectivity. Therefore, this method of textual criticism should be allowed as an alternative because it does have its merits, whereas some kind of new textual criticism adapted to the needs of Egyptology (Pries, 2011) would be the other legitimate and prolific way of dealing with the Book of the Dead (contra Gestermann, 2017: 271 n. 22). Thus, to peruse the Book of the Dead as a source for the study of ancient Egyptian religion requires some fleshing out. The study of its contents is one of the prerequisites for the application of textual criticism, whereas the latter's results might again affect our understanding of the contents. It is with such a system of checks and balances that the Book of the Dead will eventually be decoded.

In any case, students of ancient Egyptian religion in general and of the Book of the Dead in particular must return to the individual manuscript and compare it to as many parallels as possible, and to the precursors in the Coffin Texts or even Pyramid Texts, in order to gain an impression of what the general message of a passage in a Book of the Dead spell might be. For this purpose, various publications are at hand and give an impression of how a Book of the Dead spell as well as the belief system alters over time. These publications document the last approach to understanding the Book of the Dead to be mentioned here: a simple "edition" of the papyri without a translation and a study of its content. Such an "edition"—at best—includes annotations citing variants and commenting on possible mistakes made by the ancient scribe (e.g., Munro, 1994; Lapp, 1997; and the volumes of the series *Handschriften des altägyptischen Totenbuchs*).

## THE MILIEU OF THE BOOK OF THE DEAD: AUTHORS, COPYISTS, CUSTOMERS

Textual criticism is an adequate method for examples that stem from the reproductive phase of a given text's tradition, and generally the Book of the Dead is—like most religious texts with a tendency for reproductivity (Assmann, 1983b: 38, 40)—classified as belonging to the reproductive sphere. However, the sharp distinction between productive and reproductive work in a text, while the latter ultimately leads to an increasing corruption and a decreasing understanding, cannot be maintained in strict linearity. Doubtless, there are phases during which scribes merely copied Book of the Dead papyri to sell them as a commodity (Verhoeven, this volume)—and the combination of religious texts with accounts and other economic notes demonstrate a rather sober attitude toward "holy scriptures" (Quack, 2014). However, even during periods when less care was taken in writing down Book of the Dead papyri, or shortly thereafter, scribes were busy creating or recreating an intelligible body of spells. Generally speaking, those papyri were bought by members of the literate elite, i.e., officials, priestesses, and priests who should have been able to read the texts (cf. Quirke, 1993; Kockelmann, 2008: II 244–87; Albert, 2012; for the latter, see Stadler, 2014: 250). The serious work with the text is attested for individual manuscripts at any time as well as for those of the so-called Saite recension—which is, in fact, rather a late Kushite recension (Lesko, 2000; Munro, 2010: 58): Late Period and Ptolemaic papyri display a higher awareness for grammatical issues and carefulness than some, but not all Ramesside or Third Intermediate Period versions do. Those late copies even testify to an ancient Egyptian philology (for this phenomenon in ancient Egyptian literature in general, see Fischer-Elfert, 1996, Cancik-Kirschbaum and Kahl, 2018) or even textual criticism in noting variants by marking them as $ky \underline{d}d$ (lit. "other speech"). This is the result of Egyptian priestly scholars critically reviewing presumably archival copies. These scribes introduced corrections, emendations, and additions and established a standard version. Of course, such an endeavor is not really productive but rather reproductive, although it is still not evidence for a decay of philological competence.

Such an observation of Egyptian philology strongly hints at the existence of religious archives that preserved master copies. Admittedly, the Book of the Dead was to some extent a commodity, but the Saite recension and its implications point to the Book of the Dead's religious character and it being rooted in a religious corpus from which the Book of the Dead is an excerpt. The Book of the Dead's textual history, as briefly presented in the chapter's beginning, is another reason why the Book of the Dead provides us with insight into the milieu where the spells were created: Egyptian scribes dealing with rituals in the broadest sense who were even members of the House of Life—an institution that in earlier times was associated with both the temple and the king (Eyre, 2013: 311–15, Stadler, 2017a: 35–46). This double association might have facilitated the mobility of concepts, themes, and wordings between the various ritual spheres (temple, tomb, king, magic) (for an example, see Stadler, 2017b).

Rituals also play an important role in medicinal magic, and thus there are parallels to this corpus (Quack, 1999). Headings and colophons of quite a few Book of the Dead spells display a pronounced this-worldly reference, too. For example, the assertion "A truly excellent spell [proved] a million times" (BD 18, 20 [Stadler, 2009: 320–51], 31, 72, 86, 99, 134, 135, 137A [Luft, 2009], 144, 148, 155, 175 [Wüthrich, 2012]) is also well-known from magical and indeed medical spells (e.g., Borghouts, 1978: 45, 49, 55, and passim). "You shall say it over yourself over the bright and early in the morning, (for) it is a great protection. A truly excellent spell (proved) a million times." BD 19 appears like a prescription to consume medicine every morning. In some cases, a Book of the Dead spell does have a decisively magical tone, such as BD 18, an invocation to Thoth, pleading for the god to help the deceased during the judgment. In the Ramesside P.Chester Beatty VIII, a magical papyrus, the composition recurs, but there is a threat against Thoth to betray his misdeeds that is added to the pious hymn: "If you do not listen to what I am saying, I will fall into saying that you ( . . . ) have robbed the offering of the ennead on the day of its feast (in) that night of Concealing the Great ( . . . )." The text returns to an appeasing tone by adding a litany to Thoth. The Third Intermediate Period P.Greenfield (P.London BM EA 10554) follows this very tradition, but it is not a magical papyrus; rather, it is the Book of the Dead papyrus of the priestess Nesitanebetisheru (Stadler, 2009: 343–49)!

Apart from being attested as inscriptions in a temple (Kockelmann, this volume), some colophons indicate an original context within the temple cult. The most illustrative examples are BD 137A, B, and 144. BD 137A seems to be a pastiche combining elements of various other rituals, whereas BD 137B originates in the temple cult of Osiris (Luft, 2009; and 2015b for further examples, e.g., BD 128 and 181). The Saite recension of BD 144 clearly states in the respective colophon: "To be used during the dawn of the Thoth festival." Therefore, it can be connected to festivals celebrating the return of the Dangerous Goddess, an important date in any temple's calendar (Stadler, 2009: 256–63, for the Thoth festival see Medini, 2017). This spell is also an example, among many others in the Book of the Dead, of their importance to members of the Egyptian elite—and it is certainly they alone who could afford to buy a scroll as burial equipment—to document their familiarities with mythology and cultic knowledge, a qualification for entering the realm of Osiris. Thus, the Book of the Dead is a compendium to be used in the afterlife, but at the same time it reflects what a priestess or priest ought to know during his or her lifetime.

Evidence for the formation of individual spells is generally indirect. There is no case of a clear statement saying that a scribe has copied a spell from a scroll in a temple library and incorporated it into the collection of texts that we call the Book of the Dead. Nevertheless, there is a *topos* in Book of the Dead colophons that informs us about how the text was discovered and thus assigning a high authority to it by claiming its *anciennité* (Baines, 2007: 179–201). According to these, King Khufu's son Hordjedef found some spells in the temple of Hermopolis during an inspection campaign around the temples of Egypt in the first half of the twenty-sixth century BCE, and in some versions the colophons maintain that Thoth himself authored the spells. Clearly such information cannot be taken seriously as proof of the actual history of the text, but it still helps us to understand both the Egyptians' concept of their history and how esteemed that particular temple was for the ancient Egyptians (Stadler, 2009: 66–109). The colophon's variation in wording and evocation of significant alternative details also suggest an unhistorical character. For the so-called *chapitres supplémentaires* (Wüthrich, this volume) this is even more evident: the two attested manuscripts of BD 167 (Pleyte) give two different indications. One states that Amenhotep, son of Hapu (early 14th century BCE), found it; the other attributes it to Khaemwaset (13th century BCE), who is supposed to have discovered it with a mummy in the Memphite necropolis (Allen, 1974: 216).

## Prospects: How Fruitful Can a Study of the Book of the Dead Be?

Having said all this, it comes as a surprise and a paradox to find that Egyptologists very rarely use the whole body of the Book of the Dead for a systematic diachronic study of specific topics in ancient Egyptian religion. This calls for an explanation. To understand it, we have to understand what Egyptologists think the Book of the Dead is after all. Is it a ritual text or a collection of spells to accompany funerary rites by recitation, or is it rather a mythological compendium of religious knowledge and thus a book of magic? The answer will have some influence on the potential to use the Book of the Dead as a source for the study of ancient Egyptian religion in general.

For some scholars it is a mythological compendium, despite many references to ritual performance as a context. In this vein, Daniela Luft (2009: 87–90) is puzzled to discover something in the Book of the Dead that she identifies as a ritual text, and, by critically reviewing the tradition of that perspective, aims to maintain it and argues to reconcile her findings with it by postulating a secondary use of liturgical texts in the Book of the Dead. The very same intention seems to lie at the base of her verbose and theoretical article, published six years later without changing things fundamentally (Luft, 2015a). Similarly, Rita Lucarelli (e.g., 2006: 177) suggests the incorporation of ritual texts into the Book of the Dead is a phenomenon from the Third Intermediate Period onwards, implying that this practice is not original to the Book of the Dead. BD 17 (Rößler-Köhler, 1979, 1998, 1999), for instance, does support viewing the Book of the Dead as a wisdom book because it combines mythological statements with explanatory glosses, even though those explanations are still arcane for us. Its title already suggests that it is a summary of the Book of the Dead—the small caps in the following excerpt indicate rubricized text in the original:

"BEGINNING OF THE GLORIFICATIONS (TO BE USED AT) GOING FORTH FROM AND DESCENDING TO THE GOD'S DOMAIN, BECOMING A BLESSED ONE IN THE BEAUTIFUL WEST, BEING IN THE RETINUE OF OSIRIS, BEING SATISFIED WITH THE OFFERING MEALS OF WENNEFER, OF COMING FORTH BY DAY, ASSUMING WHATEVER FORM ONE WILL, PLAYING THE SENET GAME, SITTING IN A PAVILION, GOING FORTH AS A LIVING BA BY N AFTER MOORING. IT IS EFFICACIOUS FOR ONE WHO PERFORMS IT ON EARTH. The words come to pass to the Lord of All:

> (...)
> I am the benu-bird who is in Heliopolis, the examiner of what exists.
>> Who is he?
>> He is Osiris. As for 'what exists': It is his wounds and his corpses—var. (ky ḏd): It is the neheh-eternity and the djet-perpetuity. As for 'neheh-eternity': That is day. As for 'djet-perpetuity': That is night. (...)
> I am the Twin ba who is in the midst of his two children.
>> Who is he?
>> Osiris at entering Mendes. He found Ra's ba there. Then they embraced each other. Then his Twin ba came into being. As for 'his two children': That is Horus who protects his father, and Horus Mekhenti-Irty.—var. (ky ḏd): As for the 'Twin ba': That is Ra's ba, that is Osiris' ba, that is the soul of him who is in Shu, who is in Tefnut, that is the soul of him who is in Mendes. (...)"
> (after Rößler-Köhler, 1979: 157, 158, 161, 212, 214–15, 223)

However, our perception of what constitutes a ritual and what a mythological text is might not concur with the ancient Egyptian classification. In the title of the previously quoted BD 17, the Egyptian term sꜣḫ.w "glorifications" was used, and this refers to a genre of texts to be used ritually (cf. Assmann, 2002: 13–37). Indeed, there are mythological narratives that their original Egyptian title surprisingly terms as "ritual" (nt-ꜥ), i.e., they are to be recited accompanying cultic actions (cf. Quack, 2009a; Luft, 2015b: 49–50). Hymns, too, undoubtedly have a cultic setting and occur in the Book of the Dead as well (e.g., BD 15, cf. Assmann, 1969: 263–332; 1999: 106–7, 111–12, 120–34). Luft's consternation about this might be rooted in her Heidelberg academic socialization, where Assmann (2001: 337–38; 2005: 251–52) declared:

> The Book of the Dead is a book of magic. It contains rituals for domestic use. (...) The Book of the Dead, too, gained three-dimensionality and the power of magical imagination through its images. The mortuary liturgies are mostly excluded from this context. (...) The mortuary liturgies are essentially more accessible to our

comprehension than the mortuary literature. They have the considerable advantage of a ritual context and a textual coherence that seem to be absent from the texts dealing with magical knowledge.

However, it must be admitted that some spells of the Book of the Dead (e.g., BD 64, "the spell for knowing the spells for going forth [by day] in a single spell") are indeed not easily understood and require a high exegetical effort to decode and elucidate them, and this might have led Assmann to his definition. To cope with this perceived predicament, he suggested distinguishing between mortuary and funerary literature. However, upon closer inspection, the system does not work coherently, as it was built up by Assmann in a series of works: he identifies the Book of the Dead as funerary literature and thus still inaccessible to our comprehension, while—according to him—we can, within limitations, understand mortuary liturgies, i.e., texts that are called s₃ḥ.w in Egyptian. Yet, as we have just seen, one of the key spells in the Book of the Dead, BD 17, bears this very word s₃ḥ.w in its title, and BD 17 is undoubtedly a wisdom text. Consequently, the distinction has been rejected with good reason (Baines, 2004: 15 n. 2; Smith, 2009: 209–14) and cannot be expressed properly: Assmann (1990) tried to find a terminological solution in English first (mortuary versus funerary), while in his native German tongue this option is not available. The English differentiation is not understood either, even by native English speakers who translated Assmann's work (2005: 237–52; cf. Stadler, 2012: 128–29) and blurred his original intention. The quote from the English version of Assmann's book given above is a good example of this because what is rendered there as mortuary literature should be "funerary literature" to be in keeping with Assmann (1990).

In fact, Assmann's distinction is the result of a conviction that goes back to some of his earlier Egyptological work and is based on his view that "priestly cult religion and popular religion begin to diverge as the religious discourse becomes a distinct entity within the entire system of cultural communication, becoming a corpus of canonical texts and esoteric knowledge in the hands of few specialists" (Assmann, 2009: 6; first published in German; Assmann, 1983b: 11).

Of course, Assmann's classification and his rationale behind it are a big step forward when compared, for instance, to the verdict by Kurt Sethe (1935–1939; 1962: II 177), who did not hesitate to deem a spell such as BD 5 to be "doubtless nonsense," for, in contrast to Sethe, Assmann does not exclude the possibility that an understanding will be found sometime in the future. BD 5 is a good example of how much lies at the heart of even a short spell that appears enigmatic, if not strange, at first sight and that may confirm Assmann's contention:

"SPELL FOR NOT MAKING A MAN WORK IN THE GOD'S DOMAIN. TO BE SAID BY N:

I am the one who judges the son of the Torpid One,

who came forth from Hermopolis.

I live on the baboon's entrails."

The spell was inherited from the Coffin Texts and was slightly, but significantly, changed in its wording. A Coffin Text version goes as follows:

"This N is the glutton, Torpid One,

who came forth from Nun/who came forth from Hermopolis.

This N, his is every ba.

On the baboon's entrails this N lives."

The high number of variants in individual Book of the Dead papyri testifies to the problems that the Egyptians already had. Thus, the papyrus of Nu (P.London BM EA 10477) changed what was perhaps by that time an enigmatic nomenclature, "the glutton," to "the one who judged" combined with the son of the Torpid One, i.e., referring to Horus and his father Osiris, and evoking the idea of Thoth judging Horus. Most other manuscripts of the Book of the Dead have differing variants, though. The association with Thoth was presumably already present in the Coffin Texts with its reference "who came forth from Wenu (= Hermopolis)." Further hints to Thoth paradoxically come from the last statement, in which the speaker claims to live from the baboon's entrails, as the baboon is Thoth's sacred animal. In fact, the claim to live on the baboon's entrails is all the more surprising because the passage immediately preceding it asserts a connection to Hermopolis, one of the principal cult centers of Thoth, who may be represented as a baboon. It is hard to understand why somebody who claims to be from Hermopolis would be proud to eat the entrails of an animal sacred to Thoth. Since some of the Middle Kingdom coffins from the Hermopolitan necropolis have the same notion, it was apparently acceptable in the Hermopolitan nome. Is this confirmation of the deceased breaking a taboo? I have suggested that it is a relic of early rites performed in royal surroundings (Stadler, 2009: 189–99): During those postulated performances, the baboon symbolized the royal ancestors who were eaten—or, rather, instead of whom baboons were consumed—in a cultic setting to internalize the ancestors' power. Later, figurines of baboons replaced the sacrifice of actual animals. In this early period, Thoth, or rather the ibis god, was more of a royal deity than in later times, and Hermopolis was probably not his original home where the baboon deity Hedj-wer might have had his cult center. Does the spell reveal traces of Thoth's migration to Hermopolis? This would postulate an actual existence of a ritual from the royal context that lost its function and significance and fell out of use, or that votive offerings of ape figurines in early temples (Bussmann, 2009) might be a later adaptation. However, the function and the intentions of those who donated the ape votives are unclear. The same is true of the little clay baboons now on display in the Luxor Museum, which were found in Ramesses XI's tomb (KV 4); they remained unfinished and were reused several times for various purposes. Lacking a proper publication, even their archaeological context is more or less undocumented (cf. Reeves, 1990: 121–23), but it is tempting to interpret them as belonging to the genre speculated here, i.e., as symbols of the ancestors. In any case, in Hermopolis it could have been mythologically reinterpreted by identifying Thoth/ibis as a royal deity and

Hedj-wer/baboon as a royal ancestor and retained some expressiveness. Thus, maybe BD 5 and its precursor in the Coffin Texts are evidence for an etiology of Hermopolis as an outstanding place of Thoth's veneration, encapsulating the memory of Hedj-wer's worship there, and also evidence for the appropriation of formerly exclusively royal texts by Hermopolitan elites. To be sure, such an exegesis is risky because it entails a good deal of speculation and hypothesizing—as the many "maybes," "perhaps," "woulds," and "coulds" in the preceding lines indicate. The lack of securely attested cultic performances, or rather, their metaphorical and enigmatic evidence in Egyptian prehistory, prompts such cautiousness. If there is some truth in the proposed interpretation, Hermopolis's adoption through the ibis god must have taken place during a very early phase, since Thoth is already associated with Hermopolis in the Old Kingdom. Despite, or rather because of, those provisos that appeal to us, Sethe's verdict does not do justice to the spell.

## Conclusions

BD 5 is one of the shortest spells in the Book of the Dead, and its exegesis as it is summarized here has been conducted by looking at it in isolation from the rest of the spells—explaining longer spells can fill entire books (e.g., Borghouts, 2007; Wüthrich and Stöhr, 2013). However, it is integrated into sequences of spells (cf. Weber, this volume) both in the Coffin Texts and the Book of the Dead, and these sequences change over time. Do the surrounding texts in the single manuscripts contribute to an understanding of each other? Is there a certain logic or—to use a problematic and well-worn term (Pries, 2013a)—a grammar of selection and combination behind them? Egyptologists have not dealt with those questions widely, and the sheer amount of texts witnesses, the great variation among them, and the range of manifold attestation contexts of the Book of the Dead seem to be a substantial obstacle. I assume that one would have to study and analyze each example separately. Luckily, there are ancient workshops with their distinct traditions (Verhoeven, this volume) that allow us to pool together a whole series of coffins or papyri so that the results have some validity beyond just one isolated realization.

Within the limited space of this chapter, however, BD 5 exemplifies what is required for using the Book of the Dead as a source for Egyptian religion and what can be gained from such an approach: a sensitivity for textual history helps to understand the process of text formation. Whether a dogmatic application of stemmatic textual criticism is necessary and whether it brings us further than we might be able to go without it is doubtful. The spell's rewording and rewriting show the problems that Egyptian scribes themselves experienced over the course of time. Their reaction is one of emendation and reinterpretation. Diagnosing those approaches allows us to observe the changes and the continuities in the history of ancient Egyptian religion, in the case of some chapters like BD 5, even over the course of more than two millennia. Thus, we learn what held importance for the Egyptians in specific periods, what became obsolete, and what remained relevant over long time spans. In this sense, the Book of the Dead is a valuable guide to Egyptian religion even beyond the funerary sphere.

## Bibliography

Albert, F. (2012). "Quelques observations sur les titulatures attestée dans les Livres des Morts." In *Herausgehen am Tage. Gesammelte Schriften zum altägyptischen Totenbuch*. Studien zum altägyptischen Totenbuch 17, edited by R. Lucarelli, M. Müller-Roth, and A. Wüthrich, 1–66 (Wiesbaden: Harrassowitz).

Allen, T. G. (1960). *The Egyptian Book of the Dead: Documents in the Oriental Institute Museum at the University of Chicago*. Oriental Institute Publications 82 (Chicago: Oriental Institute).

Allen, T. G. (1974). *The Book of the Dead or Going Forth by Day: Ideas of the Ancient Egyptians Concerning the Hereafter as Expressed in Their Own Terms*. Studies in Ancient Oriental Civilization 37 (Chicago: Oriental Institute).

Assmann, J. (1969), *Liturgische Lieder an den Sonnengott: Untersuchungen zur altägyptischen Hymnik, I*. Münchner Ägyptologische Studien 19 (Berlin: Hessling).

Assmann, J. (1983a). "Das Dekorationsprogramm der königlichen Sonnenheiligtümer des Neuen Reiches nach einer Fassung der Spätzeit." *Zeitschrift für Ägyptische Sprache und Altertumskunde* 110: 91–98.

Assmann, J. (1983b). *Re und Amun: Die Krise des polytheistischen Weltbildes im Ägypten der 18.–20. Dynastie*. Orbis Biblicus et Orientalis 51 (Freiburg Schweiz; Göttingen: Universitätsverlag; Vandenhoeck & Ruprecht).

Assmann, J. (1990). "Egyptian Mortuary Liturgies." In *Studies in Egyptology. Presented to Miriam Lichtheim*, 2 vols., edited by S. Israelit-Groll, 1–45 (Jerusalem: Magnes Press).

Assmann, J. (1999). *Ägyptische Hymnen und Gebete*, 2nd ed. (Freiburg Schweiz; Göttingen: Universitätsverlag; Vandenhoeck & Ruprecht).

Assmann, J. (2001). *Tod und Jenseits im Alten Ägypten* (München: C. H. Beck).

Assmann, J. (2002). *Totenliturgien in den Sargtexten des Mittleren Reiches*, with M. Bommas. Supplemente zu den Schriften der Heidelberger Akademie der Wissenschaften Philosophisch-Historische Klasse 14 (Heidelberg: Winter).

Assmann, J. (2005). *Death and Salvation in Ancient Egypt* (Ithaca: Cornell University Press).

Assmann, J. (2009). *Egyptian Solar Religion in the New Kingdom* (London: Routledge).

Backes, B. (2005). *Das altägyptische „Zweiwegebuch." Studien zu den Sargtext-Sprüchen 1029–1130*. Ägyptologische Abhandlungen 69 (Wiesbaden: Harrassowitz).

Backes, B. (2011). "Zur Anwendung der Textkritik in der Ägyptologie. Ziele, Grenzen und Akzeptanz." In *Methodik und Didaktik in der Ägyptologie. Herausforderungen eines kulturwissenschaftlichen Paradigmenwechsels in den Altertumswissenschaften*, edited by A. Verbovsek, B. Backes, and C. Jones, 451–79 (Paderborn: Fink).

Baines, J. (2004). "Modelling Sources, Processes, and Locations of Early Mortuary Texts." In *Textes des Pyramides & Textes des Sarcophages. D'un monde à l'autre*, Actes de la Table Ronde Internationale « Textes des Pyramides Versus Textes des Sarcophages," Institut français d'archéologie orientale, 24–26 septembre 2001. Bibliothèque d'Étude 139, edited by S. Bickel, 15–41 (Le Caire: Institut français d'archéologie orientale).

Baines, J. (2007). *Visual and Written Culture in Ancient Egypt* (Oxford: Oxford University Press).

Barbash, Y. (2015). "Wordplay's Place in Mortuary Liturgies. Scribal Devices in Papyrus W551." In *Liturgical Texts for Osiris and the Deceased in Late and Greco-Roman*

*Egypt—Liturgische Texte für Osiris und Verstorbene im spätzeitlichen Ägypten*, Proceedings of the colloquiums at New York (ISAW), 6 May 2011, and Freudenstadt, 18–21 July 2012. Studien zur spätägyptischen Religion 14, edited by B. Backes and J. Dieleman, 203–15 (Wiesbaden: Harrassowitz).

Barguet, P. (1967). *Le Livre des Morts des anciens Égyptiens* (Paris: Édition du Cerf).

Bickel, S., ed. (2004). *Textes des Pyramides & Textes des Sarcophages: D'un monde à l'autre*, Actes de la Table Ronde Internationale "Textes des Pyramides Versus Textes des Sarcophages," IFAO, 24–26 septembre 2001. Bibliothèque d'Étude 139 (Le Caire: Institut français d'archéologie orientale).

Borghouts, J. F. (1978). *Ancient Egyptian Magical Texts*. Religious Texts Translation Series NISABA 9 (Leiden: E. J. Brill).

Borghouts, J. F. (2007). *Book of the Dead [39]: From Shouting to Structure*. Studien zum altägyptischen Totenbuch 10 (Wiesbaden: Harrassowitz).

Bussmann, R. (2009). *Die Provinztempel Ägyptens von der 0. bis zur 11. Dynastie: Archäologie und Geschichte einer gesellschaftlichen Institution zwischen Residenz und Provinz*. Probleme der Ägyptologie 30 (Leiden; Boston: E. J. Brill).

Cancik-Kirschbaum, E. C., and Kahl, J. (2018), *Erste Philologien* (Tübingen: Mohr Siebeck).

Eyre, C. (2013). *The Use of Documents in Pharaonic Egypt*. Oxford studies in ancient documents (Oxford: Oxford University Press).

Fischer-Elfert, H.-W. (1996). "Die Arbeit am Text. Altägyptische Literaturwerke aus philologischer Perspektive." In *Ancient Egyptian Literature. History and Forms*. Probleme der Ägyptologie 10, edited by A. Loprieno, 499–513 (Leiden: E. J. Brill).

Gestermann, L. (2005). *Die Überlieferung ausgewählter Texte altägyptischer Totenliteratur ("Sargtexte") in spätzeitlichen Grabanlagen*, 2 vols., Ägyptologische Abhandlungen 68 (Wiesbaden: Harrassowitz).

Gestermann, L. (2010). Review of *Weiser und Wesir*, by M. A. Stadler. *Lingua aegyptia. Journ. of Egyptian Stud.* 18: 279–89.

Hagen, F. (2012). *An Ancient Egyptian Literary Text in Context: The Instruction of Ptahhotep*. Orientalia Lovanensia Analecta 218 (Leuven: Peeters).

Gestermann, L. (2017). "Möglichkeiten und Grenzen textkritischen Arbeitens am Beispiel altägyptischer funerärer Texte." In *Studies in Ancient Egyptian Funerary Literature*. Orientalia Lovaniensia Analecta, 257, edited by S. Bickel and L. Díaz-Iglesias, 263–94 (Leuven; Paris; Bristol, CT: Peeters).

Hays, H. M. (2011). "The Death of the Democratisation of the Afterlife." In *Old Kingdom, New Perspectives. Egyptian art and archaeology 2750–2150 BC*, edited by N. Strudwick and H. Strudwick, 115–30 (Oxford; Oakville, CT: Oxbow Books).

Hornung, E. (1979). *Das Totenbuch der Ägypter*. Die Bibliothek der Alten Welt (Zürich: Artemis).

Kahl, J. (1999). *Siut-Theben: Zur Wertschätzung von Traditionen im alten Ägypten*. Probleme der Ägyptologie 13 (Leiden; Boston; Köln: E. J. Brill).

Kockelmann, H. (2008). *Untersuchungen zu den späten Totenbuch-Handschriften auf Mumienbinden*, 3 vols. Studien zum altägyptischen Totenbuch 12 (Wiesbaden: Harrassowitz).

Lapp, G. (1997). *The Papyrus of Nu (BM EA 10477)*. Catalogue of Books of the Dead in the British Museum 1 (London: British Museum).

Lepsius, C. R. (1842). *Das Todtenbuch der Ägypter nach dem hieroglyphischen Papyrus in Turin mit einem Vorworte zum ersten Male* hrsg. von R. Lepsius (Leipzig: Georg Wigand).

Lesko, L. H. (2000). "Nubian Influence on the Later Versions of the Book of the Dead." In *Egyptology at the Dawn of the Twenty-first Century. Proceedings of the Eighth International Congress of Egyptologists*, 3 vols., edited by Z. Hawass, 314–17 (Cairo: American University in Cairo Press).

Lucarelli, R. (2006). *The Book of the Dead of Gatseshen: Ancient Egyptian Funerary Religion in the 10th Century BC*. Egyptologische Uitgaven 21 (Leiden: Nederlands Instituut voor het Nabije Oosten).

Luft, D. C. (2009). *Das Anzünden der Fackel: Untersuchungen zu Spruch 137 des Totenbuches*. Studien zum altägyptischen Totenbuch 15 (Wiesbaden: Harrassowitz).

Luft, D. C. (2015a). "Gedanken zum Erstellen eines Stemmas." In *Weitergabe. Festschrift für die Ägyptologin Ursula Rößler-Köhler zum 65. Geburtstag*. Göttinger Orientforschungen 53, edited by L. D. Morenz and A. El Hawary, 293–300 (Wiesbaden: Harrassowitz).

Luft, D. C. (2015b). "Funerär und liturgisch. Gedanken zur Verbindung von Inhalten, Funktionen und Verwendungsbereichen altägyptischer religiöser Texte." In *Liturgical Texts for Osiris and the Deceased in Late and Greco-Roman Egypt—Liturgische Texte für Osiris und Verstorbene im spätzeitlichen Ägypten*, Proceedings of the colloquiums at New York (ISAW), 6 May 2011, and Freudenstadt, 18–21 July 2012. Studien zur spätägyptischen Religion 14, edited by B. Backes and J. Dieleman, 37–73 (Wiesbaden: Harrassowitz).

Mathieu, B. (2004). "La distinction entre Textes des Pyramides et Textes des Sarcophages est-elle légitime?" In *Textes des Pyramides & Textes des Sarcophages. D'un monde à l'autre*, Actes de la Table Ronde Internationale « Textes des Pyramides Versus Textes des Sarcophages," IFAO, 24–26 septembre 2001. Bibliothèque d'Étude 139, edited by S. Bickel, 247–62 (Le Caire: Institut français d'archéologie orientale).

Medini, L. (2017), "Une oie, du sang et des serpents. Quelques réflexions à propos d'un rite du manuel de Tebtynis." *Bulletin de la Société Française d'Égyptologie*, 198: 20–47.

Meyer-Dietrich, E. (2006). *Senebi und Selbst: Personenkonstituenten zur rituellen Wiedergeburt in einem Frauensarg des Mittleren Reiches*. Orbis Biblicus et Orientalis 216 (Freiburg, Schweiz; Göttingen: Universitätsverlag; Vandenhoeck & Ruprecht).

Milde, H. (1991). *The Vignettes in the Book of the Dead of Neferrenpet*. Egyptologische Uitgaven 7 (Leiden: Nederlands Instituut voor het Nabije Oosten).

Munro, I. (1994). *Die Totenbuch-Handschriften der 18. Dynastie im Ägyptischen Museum Cairo.: Mit einem Beitrag von W. Helck*, 2 vols. Ägyptologische Abhandlungen 54 (Wiesbaden: Harrassowitz).

Munro, I. (2010). "The Evolution of the Book of the Dead." In *Ancient Egyptian Book of the Dead. Journey through the Afterlife*, edited by J. H. Taylor, 54–79 (London: British Museum).

O'Rourke, P. F. (2016). *An Ancient Egyptian Book of the Dead: The Papyrus of Sobekmose* (London; Brooklyn, NY: Thames and Hudson; Brooklyn Museum).

Pries, A. H. (2011). *Die Stundenwachen im Osiriskult: Eine Studie zur Tradition und späten Rezeption von Ritualen im Alten Ägypten*, 2 vols. Studien zur spätägyptischen Religion 2 (Wiesbaden: Harrassowitz).

Pries, A. H. (2013a). "On the Use of a *Grammar of Rituals*. Reflections from an Egyptologist's Point of View." In *Approaching Rituals in Ancient Cultures. Questioni di rito: Rituali come fonte di conoscenza delle religioni e delle concezioni del mondo nelle culture antiche*. Rivista degli Studi Orientali, supplemento 86(2), edited by C. Ambos and L. Verderame, 227–43 (Roma: Fabrizio Serra).

Pries, A. H. (2013b). "Ritualvollzug im Spiegel der überkommenen Tradition, oder: Wie festgelegt war die altägyptische Kultpraxis tatsächlich?" In 9. *Ägyptologische Tempeltagung: Kultabbildung und Kultrealität*. Königtum, Staat und Gesellschaft früher Hochkulturen 34, edited by H. Beinlich, 279–95 (Wiesbaden: Harrassowitz).

Pries, A. H. (2015). "Andere Leser, andere Lehren. Miszellen zum antiken und rezenten Umgang mit der ägyptischen Schrifttradition." *Studien zur altägyptischen Kultur* 44: 301–19.

Quack, J. F. (1994). *Die Lehren des Ani: ein neuägyptischer Weisheitstext in seinem kulturellen Umfeld*. Orbis Biblicus et Orientalis 141 (Fribourg and Göttingen: Universitätsverlag; Vandenhoeck & Ruprecht).

Quack, J. F. (1999). "Magie und Totenbuch. Eine Fallstudie (pEbers 2, 1–6)." *Chronique d'Égypte* 74(7): 5–17.

Quack, J. F. (2009a). "Erzählen als Preisen. Vom Astartepapyrus zu den koptischen Märtyrerakten." In *Erzählen in frühen Hochkulturen I. Der Fall Ägypten*. Ägyptologie und Kulturwissenschaft 1, edited by H. Roeder, 291–312 (München: Wilhelm Fink).

Quack, J. F. (2009b). "Redaktion und Kodifizierung im spätzeitlichen Ägypten. Der Fall des Totenbuches." In *Die Textualisierung der Religion*. Forschungen zum Alten Testament 62, edited by J. Schaper, 11–34 (Tübingen: Mohr Siebeck).

Quack, J. F. (2014). "Totenbuch und Getreideabrechnung. Von der Vereinbarkeit von profanen und religiösen Texten auf einem Schriftträger im Alten Ägypten." In *Erscheinungsformen und Handhabungen Heiliger Schriften*. Materiale Textkulturen 5, edited by D. Luft and J. F. Quack, 111–35 (Berlin: de Gruyter).

Quirke, S. (1993). *Owners of Funerary Papyri in the British Museum* (London: British Museum).

Quirke, S. (2013). *Going out in Daylight: prt m hrw—the Ancient Egyptian Book of the Dead: translation, sources, meanings* (London: Golden House Publications).

Reeves, N. (1990). *Valley of the Kings: The Decline of a Royal Necropolis*. Studies in Egyptology (London: Kegan Paul International).

Rößler-Köhler, U. (1979). *Kapitel 17 des ägyptischen Totenbuches.: Untersuchungen zur Textgeschichte und Funktion eines Textes der altägyptischen Totenliteratur*. Göttinger Orientforschungen 10 (Wiesbaden: Harrassowitz).

Rößler-Köhler, U. (1998). "Sargtextspruch 335 und seine Tradierung." *Göttinger Miszellen* 163: 71–93.

Rößler-Köhler, U. (1999). *Zur Tradierungsgeschichte des Totenbuches zwischen der 17. und 22. Dynastie (Tb 17)*. Studien zum altägyptischen Totenbuch 3 (Wiesbaden: Harrassowitz).

Schenkel, W. (1978). *Das Stemma der altägyptischen Sonnenlitanei*. Göttinger Orientforschungen 6 (Wiesbaden: Harrassowitz).

Sethe, K. (1935–1939; 1962). *Übersetzung und Kommentar zu den altägyptischen Pyramidentexten*, 6 vols. (Glückstadt; Hamburg: Augustin).

Smith, M. (2009). "Democratization of the Afterlife." In *UCLA Encyclopedia of Egyptology*. Open version, edited by J. Dieleman and W. Wendrich, http://escholarship.org/uc/item/70g428wj, accessed March 20, 2015.

Smith, M. (2009). *Traversing Eternity: Texts for the Afterlife from Ptolemaic and Roman Egypt* (Oxford: Oxford University Press).

Stadler, M. A. (2003). *Der Totenpapyrus des Pa-Month (P. Bibl. nat. 149)*. Studien zum altägyptischen Totenbuch 6 (Wiesbaden: Harrassowitz).

Stadler, M. A. (2009). *Weiser und Wesir: Studien zu Vorkommen, Rolle und Wesen des Gottes Thot im ägyptischen Totenbuch*. Orientalische Religionen in der Antike 1 (Tübingen: Mohr Siebeck).

Stadler, M. A. (2012). *Einführung in die ägyptische Religion ptolemäisch-römischer Zeit nach den demotischen religiösen Texten*. Einführungen und Quellentexte zur Ägyptologie 7 (Berlin; Münster: Lit).

Stadler, M. A. (2014). Review of *Herausgehen am Tage*, by R. Lucarelli, M. Müller-Roth, and A. Wüthrich. *Wiener Zeitschrift für die Kunde des Morgenlandes* 104: 250–55.

Stadler, M. A. (2015). "Prätexte funerärer Rituale. Königsliturgie, Tempelliturgie, Totenliturgie." In *Liturgical Texts for Osiris and the Deceased in Late and Greco-Roman Egypt—Liturgische Texte für Osiris und Verstorbene im spätzeitlichen Ägypten*, Proceedings of the colloquiums at New York (ISAW), 6 May 2011, and Freudenstadt, 18–21 July 2012. Studien zur spätägyptischen Religion 14, edited by B. Backes and J. Dieleman, 75–90 (Wiesbaden: Harrassowitz).

Stadler, M. A. (2017a), *Théologie et culte au temple de Soknopaios: Études sur la religion d'un village égyptien pendant l'époque romaine*, Quatre séminaires à l'École pratique des Hautes Études Section des Sciences religieuses, mai-juin 2015 (Paris: Cybèle).

Stadler, M. A. (2017b). "On the Nature of Ancient Egyptian Funerary Rituals." In *Burial and Mortuary Practices in Late Period and Graeco-Roman Egypt*, Proceedings of the International Conference held at the Museum of Fine Arts, Budapest, 17–19 July 2014, edited by K. A. Kóthay, 13–22 (Budapest: MFA).

Töpfer, S. and Müller-Roth, M. (2011). *Das Ende der Totenbuchtradition und der Übergang zum Buch vom Atmen: Die Totenbücher des Monthemhat (pTübingen 2012) und der Tanedjmet (pLouvre N 3085)*. Handschriften des altägyptischen Totenbuchs 13 (Wiesbaden: Harrassowitz).

Topmann, D. (2002). *Die "Abscheu"-Sprüche der altägyptischen Sargtexte*. Göttinger Orientforschungen 39 (Wiesbaden: Harrassowitz).

Verhoeven, U. (1993). *Das saitische Totenbuch der Iahtesnacht. P. Colon. Aeg. 10207*. Papyrologische Texte und Abhandlungen 41 (Bonn: Habelt).

Vette, J. (2008). "Bibelauslegung, historisch-kritische." In *Wissenschaftliches Bibellexikon* edited by M. Bauks, K. Koenen, and S. Alkier, http://www.bibelwissenschaft.de/stichwort/15249/, accessed 20 March, 2015.

Voss, S. (1996). "Ein liturgisch-kosmographischer Zyklus im Re-Bezirk des Totentempels Ramses' III. in Medinet Habu." *Studien zur altägyptischen Kultur* 23: 377–96.

Willems, H. (1996). *The Coffin of Heqata (Cairo JdE 36481): A Case Study of Egyptian Funerary Culture of the Early Middle Kingdom*. Orientalia Lovanensia Analecta 70 (Leuven: Peeters).

Willems, H. (2001). "The Social and Ritual Context of a Mortuary Liturgy of the Middle Kingdom (CT Spell 30–41)." In *Social Aspects of Funerary Culture in the Egyptian Old and Middle Kingdom. Proceedings of the international symposium held at Leiden University 6–7 June, 1996*. Orientalia Lovanensia Analecta 102, edited by H. Willems, 253–372 (Leuven; Paris; Sterling, VA: Peeters).

Wüthrich, A. (2012). "Formule pour ne pas mourir à nouveau." In *Herausgehen am Tage. Gesammelte Schriften zum altägyptischen Totenbuch*. Studien zum altägyptischen Totenbuch 17, edited by R. Lucarelli, M. Müller-Roth, and A. Wüthrich, 143–228 (Wiesbaden: Harrassowitz).

Wüthrich, A. and Stöhr, S. (2013). *Ba-Bringer und Schattenabschneider: Untersuchungen zum so genannten Totenbuchkapitel 191 auf Totenbuchpapyri*. Studien zum altägyptischen Totenbuch 18 (Wiesbaden: Harrassowitz).

# CHAPTER 14

# THE FUNERARY LITERATURE RELATED TO THE BOOK OF THE DEAD

FOY SCALF

## Introduction

For many Egyptologists, treating a composition as one that is related to the Book of the Dead appears self-evident. However, determining the affinity between what is called the "Book of the Dead" and other texts that may be related to it raises questions of scope, content, usage, and origins (Quack, 2009). Furthermore, even to approach the topic requires a definition of what constitutes a "Book of the Dead"—a subject treated elsewhere in this volume. This essay will survey the prolific upsurge in manuscript production attested archaeologically during and after the rise of the Book of the Dead, from the New Kingdom to the Roman Period. Relationships to the corpora of the Pyramid Texts and Coffin Texts, even though they continued to flourish throughout these epochs, will not be investigated. Assumptions about shared content, context, and purpose are also complicated by the intertextuality that is apparent within Egyptian funerary literature, namely between the somewhat arbitrary scholarly classification of ritual texts with a temple setting and those intended for burial with the deceased. Despite these caveats and for the purposes of the subsequent discussion, the material detailed in what follows was judged to be related to the Book of the Dead by the following criteria. It was employed on behalf of deceased individuals to benefit their postmortem existence. Its contents focused on the promotion of the deceased to an elevated afterlife status. It was inscribed primarily on papyrus (but also other media) within textual compendia and interred in the burial. It appeared concurrently in the same manuscript of, or shared intertextual features with, Book of the Dead spells. As this volume is intended to be a comprehensive introduction to the Book of the Dead, focus here will be on the relationship with that text, whether that relationship was direct (for example, in texts derived from the Book of the Dead) or indirect (for example, in texts employed with a common intention).

The Egyptian Book of the Dead was the most dominant collection of funerary compositions from its rise in the late Second Intermediate Period to its eventual disappearance in the late Ptolemaic Period (Coenen, 2001: 70–71). Even at the end of its history the "classic" model of a Book of the Dead on papyrus remained a popular choice for inclusion within elite burials. There are twice as many papyrus copies of the Book of the Dead as there are of the next best attested compositions, which were the Books of Breathing. Its disappearance was surprisingly swift, with few manuscripts securely dated to the Roman Period beyond a handful of vestiges surviving in demotic (Smith, 2009: 389–94; 437–54, 650–62; Stadler, 2012a: 130–33; Quack, 2014b). However, despite being better attested than other compositions, the collection of spells subsumed under our modern term "Book of the Dead" in no way existed within a literary vacuum. A plethora of complementary funerary compositions are attested from throughout the Book of the Dead's 1600-year history, from the Netherworld Books of the New Kingdom to the Demotic "documents of breathing" (šʿ.t n snsn) in the Roman Period. Several important chronological developments occurred during that span, including the proliferation of Amduat papyri (Piankoff, 1957; Niwiński, 1989), an accompanying tendency for the production of single sheet funerary manuscripts that resembled amuletic texts (Dieleman, 2014), and ultimately the replacement of Book of the Dead spells in manuscripts by other texts such as the Books of Breathing (Quirke, 1993). However, it is the fourth century BCE that marks the watershed moment in terms of attested manuscripts documenting new compositions that flourished for the next half-millennium (Backes, 2015: 15–35).

It is clear that the late first millennium BCE witnessed an especially creative period in the production of funerary manuscripts with new compositions relating the Book of the Dead, but questions have been raised about the compositional date of the texts' original creation. Some scholars have argued based on internal linguistic criteria that their date of composition was much earlier than their first appearance in the archaeological record (von Lieven, 2007: 205–57), while other scholars have supported a relatively recent date of composition, referred to as the "positivist" approach, simultaneous with or just prior to their first attestation (Roberson, 2013: 122–28). The following survey will relinquish the debate regarding compositional dates to the technical literature and concentrate on the first appearance of this material in the archaeological record. What we can be sure of is the increased production of such compositions in tandem with the rise of the Book of the Dead papyri in the New Kingdom, already begun in the Eighteenth Dynasty with the Netherworld Books and continuing through the Roman Period with several stretches of intense creative activity.

The proliferation of funerary literature, especially after the fourth century BCE, had several interrelated causes, but one of the primary sources of inspiration was the modification for the benefit of private individuals of material previously designated for use only in temple-based rituals or even in royal contexts (Smith, 2009: 61–65; Stadler, 2015: 75–90). Priestly scribes clearly played an important role in this process (Ritner,

1993: 204–14), as the four papyri from the tomb of the priest Esminis demonstrate, but use of the texts was not restricted to their class alone and quickly became part of the common repertoire (Backes, 2015: 15–35). Sharp distinctions between the categories are often difficult to make due to the fluid employment of religious texts in ancient Egypt and the problem of distinguishing which usage was original and which usage was the secondary adaptation (Feder, 2015; Smith, 2015: 161–77). Even the most fundamental texts, such as the Opening of the Mouth, were clearly exploited for both funerary and temple contexts (Cruz-Uribe, 1999; Quack, 2015: 145–59). Although the original usage may seem obvious in certain cases, there are clear indications that influences flowed both ways between compositions for temple rituals and the individual afterlife (Smith, 2014: 145–55). Ultimately, individuals appropriated temple ritual and liturgical texts in order to share in the ceremonies glorifying gods such as Osiris and to reap the spiritual benefits associated with each ritual act (Barbash, 2011: 29–30).

The modification of such temple texts for individual funerary purposes has inspired discussion about their original intent. Scholarship has centered on a dichotomy established by Jan Assmann consisting of "mortuary texts" (*Totenliturgien*) and "funerary texts" (*Totenliteratur*) (Assmann, 1990: 1–3). According to this dichotomy, "mortuary texts" were meant to be recited during the rites associated with the performance of burial, whether before, during, or after, while "funerary texts" were meant to be interred with the deceased (Assmann and Kucharek, 2008: 625–34; Smith, 2009: 209–14). As heuristic tools, the two contexts can be discussed in separate terms, but such a discussion must take into account the inextricable connections between the varied contexts of such literature within the broad range of cultic practices in ancient Egypt and the appropriate distinctions between usage and content (Luft, 2015: 37–73). The interconnections between the ritual and funerary contexts have proven so pervasive that the ultimate usefulness of these categories has been called into question. Scholars have increasingly sought to diversify and surpass such a taxonomy by reorienting our perspective to these texts and experimenting with their reclassification (Dieleman and Backes, 2015: 5–8). Furthermore, it should be obvious that the Book of the Dead itself consisted of a conglomeration of text types that can hardly be subsumed neatly under our current conceptions of mortuary liturgies and funerary literature (von Lieven, 2012: 249–67; 2016: 51–77). The consolidating feature of all the texts discussed below and what relates them intimately to the Book of the Dead is their ultimate intention within the mortuary sphere as aids, guides, or passports for the deceased individual in their transition to the afterlife where they sought a place within the solar-Osirian cycle among the following of the great god.

The following essay will survey the wealth of compositions related to the Book of the Dead in order to provide a rough sketch on what the material is, how it is related, and why it is important to study alongside the Book of the Dead. It will follow a roughly chronological approach, with the material divided by traditional genres into four sections. No attempt is made here to separate hieroglyphic, hieratic, or demotic texts from each other, as it is the shared content and purpose that bands them together as funerary literature. In the words of Mark Smith, the "time is long past when hieroglyphic and hieratic religious texts of the Greco-Roman Period could be studied to any purpose without taking the demotic evidence into account" (Smith, 2006: 232). The reader should keep in mind the fact that nearly all of these categories are etic, as even the subcategorization of texts as "funerary" within the larger category of "religious," which is assumed to be "natural" in our secondary literature, had no equivalent within ancient Egyptian conceptions. It is likely that our puzzlement at their use of "temple" rituals and "mortuary liturgies" as "funerary literature" would bemuse ancient Egyptian scribes when, as far as can be discerned, they considered the entire range of these works as a single fluid pool to be tapped as needed.

## Books of the Netherworld and Sky

Book of the Dead papyri were the principal medium for the transmission of funerary literature in the New Kingdom for private elite individuals, but the royal mortuary sphere was dominated by the so-called Netherworld Books inscribed upon the walls of their tombs (Hornung, 1999: 26–152). The designation "Netherworld Books" is derived from the texts' focus on the passage through the underworld or sky. Many compositions are subsumed under the designation Books of the Netherworld and Sky, including those known as the Amduat, Book of Caves, Book of Gates, Book of Caverns, Book of the Earth, Book of Nut, Book of the Day, Book of the Night, Book of the Heavenly Cow, and Litany of Re, among others. The best-known and one of the best attested is the Amduat, or "the book of what is in the netherworld" (tꜣ mḏꜣ.t imy.t dwꜣ.t). The first attestations from the Amduat were painted on movable limestone slabs and plaster found in the tombs (KV 20 and KV 38) associated with Tuthmose I and Hatshepsut (Mauric-Barberio, 2001: 315–50). Netherworld compositions became commonly used alongside the Book of the Dead in private tombs, especially in the Third Intermediate Period when individuals incorporated multiple funerary papyri in their burial assemblages. The most common combination was a Book of the Dead papyrus along with an Amduat papyrus (Niwiński, 1989: 213–14). In the Thirtieth Dynasty, these Netherworld Books became popular decoration on sarcophagi produced for a privileged class of patrons (Manassa, 2007). This decorative practice raises the important issue of the transmission medium, as there was a complex interrelationship among texts employed within the mortuary assemblage. While heavy focus has been placed on those compositions inscribed on papyrus, it is important to remember that such texts could be found on virtually any surface, including the linen bandages of the mummy, its coffin and sarcophagus, various figures and containers around the burial chamber, and the walls of the tomb. Within each space, scribes were very cognizant of the religious materials they were designing and often employed unique combinations of texts. Thus, Books of the Netherworld could appear adjacent to Book of the Dead spells on tomb walls as well as on papyri.

Related to the Netherworld Books by granting passage through the realm of the dead was a genre of Divine Decrees that appeared in Late Period Egypt as a popular component in hieroglyphic, hieratic, and demotic texts on stelae, ostraca, and papyri (Manassa, 2007: 414–16). The decrees (*wḏ-ny-sw.t*) were issued to afterlife deities such as Wennefer to recommend the acceptance of the deceased in the underworld among the gods. Elaborate decrees like the Great Decree Issued to the Nome of the Silent Land were clearly produced for use in the temple cult of Osiris to enable rejuvenation of the united solar and chthonic deities, but were adapted by simply inserting the name of the deceased at various points throughout the text (Goyon, 1999; Smith, 2006; Beinlich, 2009; Kucharek, 2010: 275–423). Such decrees had a more restricted scope than the Book of the Dead and other related texts, but they shared the teleology of the Netherworld Books in admittance to and navigation of postmortem pathways.

How closely the Netherworld Books related to the Book of the Dead varies over time, place, and particular composition. Several of the so-called Netherworld Books, such as the Book of Caverns, the Book of Caves, and the Amduat, had superficial similarities to BD 144–147 because of their shared concern with gates or caverns in the underworld. Although designated as BD 168, the Book of Caves is now generally considered an independent composition in its own right that could, however, be combined with others, including Book of the Dead spells, on a single papyrus (Piankoff, 1974). The end of the composition known as the Litany of Re, first attested on the shroud of Thutmose III, can be found incorporated into BD 180 on papyri by the mid- to late Eighteenth Dynasty (Quirke, 2013: 457–60). The Netherworld Books, therefore, provided an important point of transition between the Book of the Dead papyri of the New Kingdom, the Amduat papyri of the Third Intermediate Period, and the decrees of the Late Period. Compositions from the Netherworld Books influenced the development of the Book of the Dead and vice versa, reinforcing the Egyptian predilection for complex intertextuality within its funerary literature traditions and setting the stage for the surge of ingenuity in the middle of the first millennium BCE.

## Glorifications

"Glorifications" (*sꜣḫ.w*), or glorification spells, have been identified based on a loosely shared set of features such as overlapping content and the designation "glorification" (*sꜣḫ*). This term was also employed throughout the Book of Dead, including in the introduction to BD 1: "Beginning of the spells of going forth by day, the praises and glorifications (*sꜣḫ.w*) of going forth and going down in the necropolis." The category of Glorifications takes its name from the modern, if completely arbitrary, classification of four compositions into Glorifications I–IV, otherwise described in the manuscripts as the Book of Glorifying the Spirit (*sꜣḫ.w* I), the Glorification of the Great One (*sꜣḫ.w* II), the Glorification Performed in the Temple of Osiris (*sꜣḫ.w* III), and the Ritual of Glorifying Osiris (*sꜣḫ.w* IV) (Assmann, 2008; Kucharek, 2010: 97–165). References to their performance in the temple of Osiris show their derivation from the library of temple rituals and appropriation for individual use. As the deceased individual was closely linked to Osiris through the designation "Osiris PN," adaptation of Osirian temple rituals is a logical extension of the individual's desire to commune with the god and participate mystically in his ceremonies.

Common to the diverse set of glorification spells were recitations by the lector priests (ḥry-ḥb.t) or important funerary deities such as Isis and Nephthys. Such recitations were meant to ensure resurrection, just as Osiris was resurrected, and to transfigure (sꜣḥ) the deceased into a powerful spirit (ꜣḥ). As such, glorification spells were incorporated into an extensive body of funerary literature. Glorifications (sꜣḥ.w) of the quintessential pair of mourners (Isis and Nephthys) formed the core of the Lamentations of Isis and Nephthys (Kucharek, 2010: 56–96), otherwise known as the Glorifications Performed by the Two Sisters, and the Songs of Isis and Nephthys (Kucharek, 2010: 166–226), otherwise known as the Stanzas of the Festival of the Two Kites. Glorification spells referred to as the "Glorifications of the Two Kites" were further incorporated into the *Stundenwachen*, or Hourly Vigil, a set of rituals in the cult of Osiris based on the division of the day and night into 24 hours that could be found inscribed on temple walls as well as in the tombs of private individuals among the burial assemblage (Pries, 2011). Direct textual references provide the context for Glorifications IV, the Songs of Isis and Nephthys, the Lamentations of Isis and Nephthys, and the Hourly Vigil as the annual Osirian celebrations of the Khoiak festival (fourth month of inundation season). The Ritual of Introducing the Multitude on the Last Day of Tekh, however, is set in the month of Thoth during the festival of drunkenness, yet consists of addresses to Osiris by Isis, Nephthys, and Nut. Isis is also the primary addressor in a demotic composition entitled "Book which Isis Made for Osiris" on P.London BM EA 10507, where she laments and glorifies her deceased brother. Similar glorifications and lamentations associated with the 12 hours of the night were included in a text called the Chapters of Awakening the Ba known from two Roman Period demotic versions on P.London BM EA 10507 and P.Harkness (Smith, 1987; 2005). As the glorifications are so intimately concerned with the transition from death to the state of a powerful spirit, it is not surprising to find them also incorporated into the Liturgy of Opening the Mouth for Breathing inscribed in demotic on four manuscript witnesses from the Roman Period (Smith, 1993).

Although the Osirian context for many of the glorifications is obvious, they were also tied to other festivals such as the Decade Feast of Amenope. This was a weekly celebration carried out every ten days beginning with offerings to the god on the east bank of the Nile in Thebes, from where he traveled to Medinet Habu on the west bank in order to reunite with the divine ancestors as part of a rejuvenation ritual. Like the glorifications, Isis and Nephthys recite the offering formula (*pr.t ḥrw*) for Osiris Wennefer in P.Vienna 3865, a hieratic liturgy associated with the decade feast (Herbin, 1984). References to the decade feast in the Ritual of Embalming (Töpfer, 2015) and in the many texts carrying the designation "book of breathing" suggest partially overlapping contexts for elements of the funerary formulae they contained. Furthermore, elements of the offering formula from the decade feast had been incorporated into the Books of Breathing. The Glorifications, therefore, demonstrate clearly the complex connections between the wide range of Egyptian funerary rituals and attendant literature, from the Hourly Vigil to the Decade Feast, from the Book of the Dead to the Books of Breathing.

# BOOKS OF BREATHING

The term "book of breathing" (šꜥ.t n snsn) is a generic label for funerary literature applied to a wide variety of papyrus manuscripts inscribed with texts in hieratic or demotic, especially common in the Greco-Roman Era (Smith, 1993: 14; Stadler, 2000: 115–16). However, there are three hieratic compositions that contain specific elaborations of the label (Fig. 14.1), each applied with varying consistency (Stadler, 2015: 76–80). These three texts are the Book of Breathing which Isis Made (šꜥ.t n snsn ỉr.n ꜣs.t), the First Book of Breathing (šꜥ.t n snsn mḥ–1.t), and the Second Book of Breathing (šꜥ.t n snsn mḥ–2.t) (Coenen, 1995: 29–38), each of which could be transmitted in an abridged version. Each of these compositions also contained details about the place of interment, with the Book of Breathing which Isis Made placed under the left arm near the chest, the First Book of Breathing placed under the head, and the Second Book of Breathing placed under the feet (Smith, 2009: 466–67; Herbin, 2008a: 1–3). As many of the manuscripts derive from the antiquities market and the archaeological records for those found in situ are often inadequate to determine the original arrangement of funerary materials, it is difficult to conclude whether or not the directions for placement were followed with any uniformity. If the employment of BD 151 on magical bricks is taken as a comparison, we should not expect conformity between the directions found in the text and the manner in which it was prepared for burial (Régen, 2010).

The Book of Breathing which Isis Made could be found on the same papyrus grouped together with Book of the Dead spells or other funerary compositions, but it has not yet been attested in the same manuscript as the First and Second Books of Breathing, which in several witnesses are found together (e.g., P.Berlin P. 3163). One primary difference in the content of these compositions is that the Book of Breathing which Isis Made consists of second person recitations to the Osiris PN by Isis, while the First and Second Books of Breathing consisted of recitations by Osiris PN himself or Hathor PN herself. These three Books of Breathing became increasingly important after the first appearance of the Book of Breathing which Isis Made in the second century BCE. At first, they supplemented Book of the Dead usage, but by the end of the Ptolemaic Period they began to replace that venerated collection. The majority of the manuscript copies of the First and Second Books of Breathing date to the first and second century CE, when they were among the dominant funerary literature employed by several workshops in the Theban area (Coenen, 2000: 97).

The format of papyri carrying Books of Breathing mimicked layouts of certain Book of the Dead traditions, with hieratic texts in columns surmounted by vignettes. At first glance a given manuscript could be mistaken for a Book of the Dead papyrus if attention were not paid to the actual contents. Several vignettes could be positioned

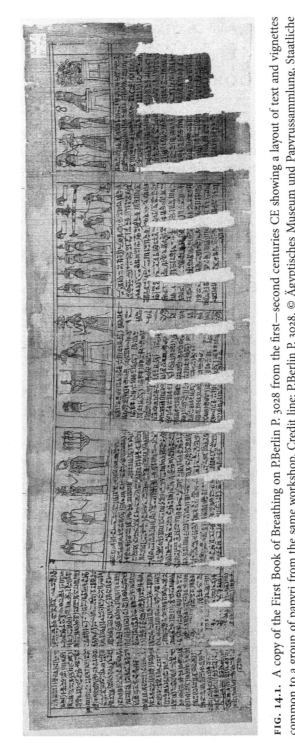

FIG. 14.1. A copy of the First Book of Breathing on P.Berlin P. 3028 from the first–second centuries CE showing a layout of text and vignettes common to a group of papyri from the same workshop. Credit line: P.Berlin P. 3028. © Ägyptisches Museum und Papyrussammlung, Staatliche Museen zu Berlin, Photo by Sandra Steiß.

throughout, as in the Book of Breathing which Isis Made, but the more common format for the First and Second Books of Breathing had connected vignettes running across the tops of the columns. Clearly, the ancient Egyptians of late Ptolemaic and Roman Egypt viewed the Books of Breathing as functionally equivalent to the Book of the Dead, as they transitioned to employing the Books of Breathing in place of the latter. However, the connection between the texts is more intimate than that, and some of these compositions had very close ties with the Book of the Dead. The First Book of Breathing, for example, is clearly derived directly from a running Saite recension sequence of BD spells (BD 18–23, 26–28, 30, 42, and 62) that have been variously compressed, extracted, edited, or cited *verbatim* along with selected supplements (Scalf, 2020). Therefore, not only did the Books of Breathing replace the Book of the Dead in the Roman Period, but in some cases they directly derived from it through a process of exegesis performed on authoritative source material.

Based on their shared content across parallel manuscripts, the three Books of Breathing discussed earlier in the chapter can be kept distinct from the host of other texts labeled as "Books of Breathing" (Smith, 1993: 33). The label "book of breathing" (*šꜥ.t n snsn*) is so ubiquitous in the funerary literature of Greco-Roman Egypt that few categorical distinctions can be made and many of the manuscripts are unique one-offs with few, if any, parallels. Such texts can be found written in hieroglyphic, hieratic, and demotic scripts. For example, an Osirian liturgy inscribed on a demotic papyrus (P.Turin N. 766) from the first or second centuries CE has affinity in content with the "May my name flourish" section of the Second Book of Breathing (Stadler, 1999). On the verso, this text is even labeled as "a document of breathing which goes [lit., comes] under the head" (*šꜥ.t n snsn nty iy ḫr ḏꜣḏꜣ*). In the remarkable "bilingual" hieratic/demotic Rhind Papyri from early Roman Egypt belonging to Monthesouphis and his wife Tanous (Möller, 1913), Thoth is said to make a "document of breathing" for them, a reference to the very papyri themselves.

However, among the diverse group of manuscripts labeled "Books of Breathing" there is a corpus of roughly fifty demotic texts which, while diverse, share elements of a set of recitation formulae (Scalf, 2014; 2015: 212–23). The similarity in content has lead Kim Ryholt (2010: 730) to refer to this composition as the Demotic Book of Breathing (Fig. 14.2), but it should be made clear that there are no direct parallels in content with the Book of Breathing which Isis Made, the First Book of Breathing, or the Second Book of Breathing. The appearance of this set of formulae on coffins, securely dated to the mid-second century CE, indicates that these demotic "Books of Breathing" (*šꜥ.t n snsn*) are among the last funerary texts in the so-called pharaonic tradition, and the volume of the preserved manuscripts (ca. 50 copies) suggests that these papyri were the final chapter in the practice of incorporating inscribed papyri in the burial that began with the Book of the Dead. Despite the variety of available manuscripts, all of these texts function in a similar manner to Book of the Dead papyri—they were buried with the dead to aid the transition between life and death.

Another composition closely related to the Books of Breathing is the Book of Traversing Eternity (*mḏꜣ.t nt sb nḥḥ*), which was among the more popular funerary

FIG. 14.2 A Demotic "document of breathing" papyrus from the first—second centuries CE inscribed with a set of funerary wishes known from ~50 other copies which were used like the Book of the Dead in the Roman Period. Credit line: P.Paris Louvre N 3176 Q, Drawing by Foy Scalf.

compositions known from more than 20 copies. It could even be labeled a "book of breathing" and appear in the same manuscript alongside Books of Breathing, although the geographical and temporal foci of its contexts have been compared to the guides found in the Books of the Netherworld and Sky (Smith, 2009: 396–405). It was transmitted mostly in hieratic, in both long and short versions, but unlike the Books of Breathing, several exemplars derived from outside of the Theban area, including the delta, the Fayum, and Abydos; however, all papyrus copies of the Book of Traversing Eternity have been assigned to Thebes (Herbin, 1994). In P.Paris BN 149 (Stadler,

2003) we find a demotic version of a text that on several occasions is associated with the Book of Traversing Eternity, but that is probably to be considered distinct from it due to the presence of "It is its end" (*pꜣy=f mnq pꜣy*) occurring before it on P.Leiden T 32. The relationship between the Book of Traversing Eternity and the Book of the Dead is clear in P.Paris BN 149, since the initial composition associated with the Book of Traversing Eternity is followed by demotic adaptations of BD 125 and 128. The evidence, therefore, clearly demonstrates the close affiliation between the Books of Breathing, the Book of Traversing Eternity, and the Book of the Dead, each of which served a similar purpose through individual means.

## Conclusions

Although scholars have traditionally focused on the Pyramid Texts/Coffin Texts/Book of the Dead tradition, it could be argued that the most creative and vital period for the production and transmission of funerary literature was from the fourth century BCE to the second century CE. All of the elements for this vigor had appeared in prior periods, but during this half-millennium, funerary literature in ancient Egypt was in extreme flux. New compositions were continuously being written or adapted, including a wide range of unique documents for which there are few parallels (Herbin, 2008b). Although the Egyptian religious "canon" was always an open one, and despite the fact that there are well-represented texts known from multiple copies during this time, it is clear that scribes responsible for maintaining time-honored traditions were seeking to establish new norms by compiling texts, both new and old, into unparalleled sequences. Therefore, "what we see in the richness of variability may be the end of one codified tradition and the beginning of another still in the process of formation" (Scalf, 2014: 61). Perhaps most reflective of this trend and its versatility is the adoption of demotic for funerary literature in the mid-first century BCE. As the Book of the Dead tradition came to an end, the vacuum was filled by a wide variety of new texts, some of which were written in new scripts reflecting a linguistic updating to more contemporary language use.

This chapter should make readily apparent to the reader the great vigor with which scribes composed works of funerary literature during the second half of the first millennium BCE. Numerous new compositions appeared, and the many unique manuscripts demonstrate a renaissance in experimentation and creativity. Among the diverse corpus of funerary literature without neat categorization there is a composition known as the Book of Transformations, attested in a demotic version from the late Ptolemaic Period (P.Paris Louvre E 3452) and two hieratic versions from the Roman Period (P.Berlin P. 3162 and P.Paris Louvre N 3122). The name derives from its delineation of spells for turning into various animal and reptile creatures. These compositions, therefore, have obvious typological similarities to the so-called transformation spells (BD 76–88) of the

Book of the Dead (Lüscher, 2006; Servajean, 2004). However, where the Book of the Dead spells were composed from the first-person perspective, these later compositions were composed in the second (hieratic versions) and third person (demotic version). Furthermore, they were not parallel manuscripts, but rather variant texts based on shared subject matter. Their creation may have been inspired by the Book of the Dead transformation spells, or they may have arisen in tandem out of the same Egyptian religious theology associated with "turning into" (ḫpr m) powerful creatures.

An aspect of this material that may not be readily apparent from the discussion in this chapter is the amount of diversification present in individual manuscript copies. Like copies of the Book of the Dead, which consisted of nearly unique collections of spells and vignettes with virtually no two manuscripts being completely identical, the funerary literature related to the Book of the Dead could be compiled into original anthologies, a feature referred to as the "interchangeability of parts" (Manassa, 2007: 417). For example, the papyrus of Imouthes (P.New York MMA 35.9.21) contained a sequence of compositions including the Great Decree Issued to the Nome of the Silent Land, Glorifications IV, the Revelations of the Mysteries of the Four Balls, the Book of Protecting the Neshmet-Barque, and the Ritual of Introducing the Multitude on the Last Day of Tekh (Goyon, 1999). Likewise, Book of the Dead spells could be mixed together with these newly appropriated compositions, such as on Papyrus Cracow (P.Sękowski), which contained the Book of Glorifying the Spirit, the Book of Breathing in the Necropolis (PT 251–53 and 266), BD 100, BD 175, an unidentified funerary text, and Glorifications I. Thus, as much as scholars may like to think of the Book of the Dead and some of its related texts as "canonical," it is clear the Egyptian funerary canon was always an open one particularly prone to growth and expansion (von Lieven, 2016). As this chapter makes explicit, such growth was particularly prevalent in Late Period Egypt and continued into the second century CE, when a new series of demotic funerary papyri became fashionable and partially replaced usage of the Book of the Dead. These phenomena demonstrate the vitality of religious expression and the scribal tradition responsible for the transmission of funerary literature in ancient Egypt, a vitality that continued to flourish for several centuries and did not die with the Book of the Dead.

## Suggested Reading

The last twenty years have witnessed a particularly productive period in scholarship on Greco-Roman Period manuscripts in hieratic and demotic with many previously unpublished texts appearing. Few synthetic overviews of the material have been published outside of the technical literature, where Goyon (1972, 1974), Burkard (1995: 1–22), Manassa (2007: 411–35), Smith (2009: 1–65 and 209–14), and Stadler (2012b) should be consulted. An accessible introduction to a selection of the source material can be found in the overview of Hornung (1999), whose annotated bibliography is an excellent place to investigate previous scholarship. Scholarship over the last twenty years has focused on the publication of new texts, for which the standard anthology is now Smith (2009), along with the important treatments of Assmann (2005), Assmann (2008), Assmann and Kucharek (2008), Kucharek (2010), and Stadler (2012a). Herbin (2008a) provides a very important catalog of the Books of Breathing and several related compositions from the remarkable collection of the British Museum. A comprehensive treatment of the demotic documents of breathing is the unpublished dissertation of Scalf (2014), which includes an introduction to related funerary literature. The conference proceedings published in Quack (2014a) and Backes and Dieleman (2015) reflect the current state of scholarship concerning the diverse use of cultic texts, mostly from the later periods of Egyptian history.

# Bibliography

Assmann, J. (1990). "Egyptian Mortuary Liturgies." In *Studies in Egyptology Presented to Miriam Lichtheim I*, edited by S. Israelit-Gross, 1–45 (Jerusalem: Magnes Press).
Assmann, J. (2005). *Altägyptische Totenliturgien. Band 2: Totenliturgien und Totensprüche in Grabinschriften des Neuen Reiches* (Heidelberg: Universitätsverlag Winter).
Assmann, J. (2008). *Altägyptische Totenliturgien. Band 3: Osirisliturgien in Papyri der Spätzeit* (Heidelberg: Universitätsverlag Winter).
Assmann, J. and Kucharek, A. (2008). *Ägyptische Religion Totenliteratur* (Frankfurt am Main: Insel Verlag).
Backes, B. and Dieleman, J., eds. (2015). *Liturgical Texts for Osiris and the Deceased in Late Period and Greco-Roman Egypt* (Wiesbaden: Harrassowitz).
Backes, B. (2015). "Gedanken zu Kategorien und Funktionspotentialen funerärer Ritualpapyri." In *Liturgical Texts for Osiris and the Deceased in Late Period and Greco-Roman Egypt*, edited by B. Backes and J. Dieleman, 15–35 (Wiesbaden: Harrassowitz).
Barbash, Y. (2011). *The Mortuary Papyrus of Padikakem: Walters Art Museum 551* (New Haven: Yale Egyptological Seminar).
Beinlich, H. (2009). *Papyrus Tamerit 1: Ein Ritualpapyrus der ägtypsichen Späzeit* (Dettelbach: Verlag J. H. Röll).
Burkard, G. (1995). *Spätzeitliche Osiris-Liturgien im Corpus des Asasif-Papyri* (Wiesbaden: Harrassowitz).
Coenen, M. (1995). "Books of Breathings: More than a Terminological Question?" *Orientalia Lovaniensia Periodica* 26: 29–38.
Coenen, M. (2000). "The Funerary Papyri of the Bodleian Library at Oxford." *Journal of Egyptian Archaeology* 86: 81–98.
Coenen, M. (2001). "On the Demise of the *Book of the Dead* in Ptolemaic Thebes." *Revue d'Égyptologie* 52: 69–84.
Cruz-Uribe, E. (1999). "Opening of the Mouth as Temple Ritual." In *Gold of Praise: Studies on Ancient Egypt in Honor of Edward F. Wente*, edited by E. Teeter and J. Larson, 69–73 (Chicago: Oriental Institute).
Dieleman, J. (2014). "Scribal Routine in Two Demotic Documents for Breathing." In *Gehilfe des Thot: Festschrift für Karl-Theodor Zauzich zu seinem 75. Geburtstag*, edited by S. Lippert, M. Stadler, and U. Jakobeit, 29–42 (Wiesbaden: Harrassowitz).

Dieleman, J. and Backes, B. (2015). "Current Trends in the Study of Liturgical Papyri." In *Liturgical Texts for Osiris and the Deceased in Late Period and Greco-Roman Egypt*, edited by B. Backes and J. Dieleman, 1–13 (Wiesbaden: Harrassowitz).

Feder, F. (2015). "Egyptian Mortuary Liturgies in the Papyri of the Ptolemaic Period." In *Proceedings of the Tenth International Congress of Egyptologists*, edited by P. Kousoulis and N. Lazaridis, 1083–91 (Leuven: Peeters).

Goyon, J.-Cl. (1972). *Rituels funéraires de l'ancienne Égypte* (Paris: Éditions du Cerf).

Goyon, J.-Cl. (1974). "La littérature funéraire tardive." In *Texts et langages de l'Égypte pharaonique*, edited by Institut français d'archéologie orientale, 73–83 (Cairo: Institut français d'archéologie orientale).

Goyon, J.-Cl. (1999). *Le papyrus d'Imouthès, fils de Psintaês, au Metropolitan Museum of Art de New-York (Papyrus MMA 35.9.21)* (New York: Metropolitan Museum of Art).

Herbin, F.-R. (1984). "Une liturgie des rites décadaires de Djeme: Papyrus Vienne 3865." *Revue d'Égyptologie* 35: 105–26, pl. 9.

Herbin, F.-R. (1994). *Le livre de parcourir l'étrnité* (Leuven: Peeters).

Herbin, F.-R. (2008a). *Books of Breathing and Related Texts* (London: British Museum).

Herbin. F.-R. (2008b). "Trois papyrus hiéroglyphiques d'époques romaine." *Revue d'Égyptologie* 59: 125–54.

Hornung, E. (1999). *The Ancient Egyptian Books of the Afterlife* (Ithaca: Cornell University Press).

Kucharek, A. (2010). *Altägyptische Totenliturgien. Band 4: Die Klagelieder von Isis und Nepthys in Texten der griechisch-römischen Zeit* (Heidelberg: Universitätsverlag Winter).

von Lieven, A. (2007). *Grundriss des Laufes der Sterne. Das sogenannte Nutbuch* (Copenhagen: Museum Tusculanum Press).

von Lieven, A. (2012). "Book of the Dead, Book of the Living: BD Spells as Temple Texts." *Journal of Egyptian Archaeology* 98: 249–67.

von Lieven, A. (2016). "Closed Canon vs. Creative Chaos: An In-Depth Look at (Real and Supposed) Mortuary Texts from Ancient Egypt." In *Problems of Canonicity and Identity Formation in Ancient Egypt and Mesopotamia*, edited by K. Ryhot and G. Barjamovic, 51–77 (Copenhagen: Museum Tusculanum Press).

Luft, D. (2015). "Funerär und liturgisch: Gedanken zur Verbindung von Inhalten, Functionen und Verwendungsbereichen altägyptischer religiöser Texte." In *Liturgical Texts for Osiris and the Deceased in Late Period and Greco-Roman Egypt*, edited by B. Backes and J. Dieleman, 37–73 (Wiesbaden: Harrassowitz).

Lüscher, B. (2006). *Die Verwandlungssprüche (Tb 76–88)* (Basel: Orientverlag).

Manassa, C. (2007). *The Late Egyptian Underworld: Sarcophagi and Related Texts from the Nectanebid Period* (Wiesbaden: Harrassowitz).

Mauric-Barberio, F. (2001). "Le premier exemplaire du Livre de l'Amdouat." *Bulletin de l'Institut français d'archéologie orientale* 101: 315–50.

Möller, G. (1913). *Die beiden Totenpapyrus Rhind des Museums zu Edinburg* (Leipzig: J. C. Hinrichs).

Niwiński, A. (1989). *Studies on the Illustrated Theban Funerary Papyri of the 11th and 10th Centuries B.C.* (Freiburg: Vandenhoeck & Ruprecht).

Piankoff, A. (1957). *Mythological Papyri* (New York: Pantheon Books).

Piankoff, A. (1974). *The Wandering of the Soul* (Princeton: Princeton University Press).

Pries, A. (2011). *Die Stundenwachen im Osiriskult, Eine Studie zur Tradition und späten Rezeption von Ritualen im Alten Ägypten* (Wiesbaden: Harrassowitz).

Quack, J. (2009). "Grab und Grabausstattung im späten Ägypten." In *Tod und Jenseits im alten Israel und in seiner Umwelt*, edited by A. Berlejung and B. Janowski, 597–629 (Tübingen: Mohr Siebeck).

Quack, J., ed. (2014a). *Ägyptische Rituale der griechisch-römischen Zeit* (Tübingen: Mohr Siebeck).

Quack, J. (2014b). "A New Demotic Translation of (Excerpts of) a Chapter of the Book of the Dead." *Journal of Egyptian Archaeology* 100: 381–93.

Quack, J. (2015). "Das *Mundöffnungsritual* als Tempeltext und Funerärtext." In *Liturgical Texts for Osiris and the Deceased in Late Period and Greco-Roman Egypt*, edited by B. Backes and J. Dieleman, 145–59 (Wiesbaden: Harrassowitz).

Quirke, S. (1993). *Owners of Funerary Papyri in the British Museum* (London: British Museum).

Quirke, S. (2013). *Going Out in Daylight—prt m hrw. The Ancient Egyptian Book of the Dead: Translation, Sources, Meanings* (London: Golden House Publications).

Régen, I. (2010). "When a Book of the Dead Text Does Not Match Archaeology: The Case of the Protective Magical Bricks (BD 151)." *British Museum Studies in Ancient Egypt and Sudan* 15: 267–78.

Ritner, R. (1993). *The Mechanics of Ancient Egyptian Magical Practice* (Chicago: Oriental Institute).

Roberson, J. (2013). *The Awakening of Osiris and the Transit of the Solar Barques: Royal Apotheosis in a Most Concise Book of the Underworld and Sky* (Fribourg: Academic Press).

Ryholt, K. (2010). "Late Period Literature." In *A Companion to Ancient Egypt*, edited by A. Lloyd, 709–31 (Oxford: Wiley-Blackwell).

Scalf, F. (2014). *Passports to Eternity: Formulaic Demotic Funerary Texts and the Final Phase of Egyptian Funerary Literature in Roman Egypt* (University of Chicago, Ph.D. Diss.).

Scalf, F. (2015). "From the Beginning to the End: How to Generate and Transmit Funerary Texts in Ancient Egypt." *Journal of Ancient Near Eastern Religions* 15: 202–23.

Scalf, F. (2020). "The First Book of Breathing: A New Assessment Based on an Edition of Papyrus FMNH 31324." *Journal of Near Eastern Studies* 79(2): 151–82.

Servajean, F. (2004). *Les formules des transformations du Livre des Morts à la lumière d'une theory de la performativité* (Cairo: Institut Français d'Archéologie Orientale).

Smith, M. (1987). *The Mortuary Texts of Papyrus BM 10507* (London: British Museum).

Smith, M. (1993). *The Liturgy of Opening the Mouth for Breathing* (Oxford: Griffith Institute).

Smith, M. (2005). *Papyrus Harkness (MMA 31.9.7)* (Oxford: Griffith Institute).

Smith, M. (2006). "The Great Decree Issued to the Nome of the Silent Land." *Revue d'Égyptologie* 57: 217–32.

Smith, M. (2009). *Traversing Eternity: Texts for the Afterlife from Ptolemaic and Roman Egypt* (Oxford: Oxford University Press).

Smith, M. (2014). "Bodl. MS. Egypt. a. 3(P) and the Interface between Temple Cult and Cult of the Dead." In *Ägyptische Rituale der griechisch-römischen Zeit*, edited by J. Quack, 145–55 (Tübingen: Mohr Siebeck).

Smith, M. (2015). "Whose Ritual? Osirian Texts and Texts Written for the Deceased in P. BM EA 10209: A Case Study." In *Liturgical Texts for Osiris and the Deceased in Late Period and Greco-Roman Egypt*, edited by B. Backes and J. Dieleman, 161–77 (Wiesbaden: Harrassowitz).

Stadler, M. (1999). "The Funerary Texts of Papyrus Turin N. 766: A Demotic Book of Breathing (Part I)." *Enchoria* 25: 76–110.

Stadler, M. (2000). "The Funerary Texts of Papyrus Turin N. 766: A Demotic Book of Breathing (Part II)." *Enchoria* 26: 110–24.

Stadler, M. (2003). *Der Totenpapyrus des Pa-Month (P. Bibl. nat. 149)* (Wiesbaden: Harrassowitz).

Stadler, M. (2012a). *Einführung in die ägyptische Religion ptolemäisch-römischer Zeit nach den demotischen religiösen Texten* (Berlin: LIT Verlag).

Stadler, M. (2012b). "Funerary Religion." In *The Oxford Handbook of Roman Egypt*, edited by C. Riggs, 383–97 (Oxford: Oxford University Press).

Stadler, M. (2015). "Prätexte funeräre Rituale: Königsliturgie, Tempelliturgie, Totenliturgie." In *Liturgical Texts for Osiris and the Deceased in Late Period and Greco-Roman Egypt*, edited by B. Backes and J. Dieleman, 75–90 (Wiesbaden: Harrassowitz).

Töpfer, S. (2015). *Das Balsamierungsritual: Eine (Neu-)Edition der Textkomposition Balsamierungsritual (pBoulaq 3, pLouvre 5158, pDurham 1983.11 + pSt. Petersburg 18128)* (Wiesbaden: Harrassowitz).

# CHAPTER 15

# THE BOOK OF THE DEAD IN THE PTOLEMAIC AND ROMAN PERIODS AND THE CONTEMPORARY FUNERARY TEXTS

ANDREA KUCHAREK

## THE EMERGENCE OF "NEW" FUNERARY TEXTS IN THE GRECO-ROMAN PERIOD

The Book of the Dead as a self-contained entity, flourishing during the first half of the Ptolemaic Period (Albert, this volume), gradually gave way to a surge of "new" funerary texts that emerged from the second century BCE and dominated the spectrum of Late Ptolemaic and Roman Period funerary texts (Coenen, 2001). None of these texts, including the Book of the Dead, was evenly distributed in terms of geography. The record is of course biased because of the vagaries of both preservation and available information: of the more than 650 Book of the Dead papyri dated to the Ptolemaic Period by the Bonn Totenbuch-Projekt (http://totenbuch.awk.nrw.de//), no fewer than two-thirds are of unknown provenance. Of the roughly 240 remaining papyri, more than 200 are from Thebes, where the corpus originated (Dorman, 2017: 38), 16 are from Saqqara, 12 are from Akhmim, and the rest are scattered throughout Upper and Middle Egypt, the Delta being largely devoid of papyri due to environmental conditions. The two major funerary compositions replacing the Book of the Dead—the Book of Traversing Eternity and the various Books of Breathing—were, in fact, largely restricted to the Theban area (Coenen, 1999b: 70; see Stadler, 2010/2011: 157–60 on the provenance of the texts in Smith, 2009). Of the Book of Traversing Eternity, 21 copies are known at present

(Smith, 2009: 396–97), and the Books of Breathing add up to roughly 120 copies (Smith, 2009: 462, 500, 515). In terms of both geographical impact and absolute numbers, these compositions cannot compare with the Book of the Dead.

The one location apart from Thebes providing sufficient evidence to garner a concept of its late funerary beliefs is Akhmim in Middle Egypt, north of Abydos (Depauw, 2002). Apart from an abundant legacy of funerary objects like coffins (Brech, 2013), stelae (Munro, 1973: 117–55), Ptah-Sokar-Osiris figures (Rindi Nuzzolo, 2017) and mummy labels (Vleeming, 2011: 774 s.v. Panopolis, Panopolite) there is a number of distinctive Book of the Dead copies (Mosher, 2001, 2002; Lüscher, 2000; Einaudi, 2015, 2016). An exclusively Akhmimic composition, the Book of the *Ba*, is appended to two of these papyri (Kucharek, this volume). The unpublished P.Kroch, a compilation of various texts and Book of the Dead vignettes, certainly originated in the region of Akhmim, as indicated by both the style of its vignettes and the emphasis of some sections on the *ba*. This mobile manifestation of the deceased appears to have enjoyed particular interest in the local funerary theology.

Studying Greco-Roman funerary literature, therefore, to a large degree means studying Theban conceptions of the afterlife (cf. Kucharek, 2010: 17 n. 25; Stadler, 2012a: 155), with Akhmim as a second focus. These two places, incidentally, allow a glimpse into regional interconnections as some funerary objects, among them papyri, display features specific to either of these places, a testament to the close relations and exchange between the regions in spite of their own distinct traditions (see p. 300).

## A plethora of sources

In addition to compositions like the Book of Traversing Eternity or the Books of Breathing, extant in multiple copies, there is a considerable number of rare or even unique compositions and compilations for private use, like the demotic P.London BM EA 10507 dating to the first century BCE, again from Akhmim (Smith, 1987; 2009: 245–63; on the date see Stadler, 2010/2011: 155), or P.Harkness, inscribed in 61 CE. The latter, from nearby Qau el-Kebir, comprises a duplicate of one P.London BM EA 10507 text but is otherwise unique (Smith, 2005; 2009: 264–301). The most likely Theban Artémis Liturgical Papyrus (Dieleman, 2015) likewise dates to the early Roman Period; it is a distinctive bricolage apparently customized for the owner but with a partial parallel in the far older Ptolemaic P.Princeton Pharaonic Roll 10 of uncertain origin (Vuilleumier, 2016). P.Parma 183, an early Roman papyrus (Smith, 2009: 535–39), and the somewhat later P.Cairo CG 58009 (Smith, 2009: 526–34), both from Thebes, are remarkable in that they share the title The Book of Entering the God's Domain and Promenading in the Hall of the Two Truths (*mdꜣt nt ꜥḳ r ḥrt-nṯr wnšnš m wsḫt mꜣꜥt*) but have no more than a few phrases in common. The fragmentary P.Barcelona Palau Rib. 450 + Mannheim REM without No. [1], dated to the late Ptolemaic/early Roman Period and of unknown provenance, is largely made up of vignettes with captions, among them a judgment scene and a series of portals as in, for instance, BD 145, but there is an elaborate bier scene as well, without precedent in the Book of the Dead (Sturtewagen, 1991). Three different early Roman Theban compositions united by their purpose are nowadays subsumed under the umbrella term Book of Transformations (Smith, 2009: 610–49), but do not actually share a common title.

The early Ptolemaic P.London BM EA 9916 from Thebes (Kucharek and Coenen, 2021: 101–21, pl. 29; see p. 300) and the Roman Period P.Paris Louvre E 5353 of unknown provenance (ed. Herbin, 2013; see p. 308) are inscribed with excerpts of Osirian liturgies as well as Book of the Dead spells and vignettes. Likewise, the Roman Period P.Turin 1848, apart from remarkable vignettes depicting the weighing of the heart as well as the purification and mourning of the mummy, features seven columns of text of which at least a part is compiled from other sources, among them the Book of Breathing which Isis Made for Her Brother Osiris and several Osirian liturgies (Grewenig, 2014: 256–57; Herbin, 1994: 566). The fragmentary P.Florence PSI inv. I 130 from Tebtynis in the Fayum is dated quite precisely on account of its content, a mortuary ritual for Antinoos, the deified favorite of the emperor Hadrian, who drowned in the Nile in 130 CE (cf. Kucharek, 2019). On a more modest scale, there is, for instance, an early Ptolemaic wooden tablet from Thebes with an idiosyncratic selection and rearrangement of several texts (Kucharek, 2017); the early Roman alabaster tablet New York MMA 55.144.1, perhaps from Hermopolis, with a sequence of apparently unrelated funerary and/or Osirian phrases (Fig. 15.1; Herbin, 2012); and the mummy board London BM EA 35464 of unknown origin (Vittmann, 1990). The demotic P.Turin N. 766 from Thebes,

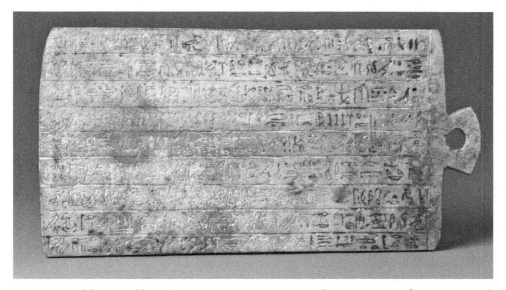

FIG. 15.1. Alabaster tablet MMA 55.144.1, recto. Metropolitan Museum of Art New York Collection Database, Public Domain.

dating to the first century CE, comprises a passage comparable to the Second Book of Breathing (Stadler, 1999, 2000; 2012a: 149–50).

## Osirian rituals adapted for private use

Apart from these more or less genuinely funerary texts, often intermingled with Osirian material, there are a considerable number of papyri inscribed with entire rituals originating in the cult of Osiris and appropriated by private individuals throughout the Greco-Roman Period but predominantly in the early Ptolemaic era (Backes, 2015). Again, most of these originate, with varying degrees of certainty, in Thebes, but there are significant exceptions, the most prominent being P.New York MMA 35.9.21 from Meir (Goyon, 1999). There is a highly abridged version of the first text preserved in this papyrus, the Great Decree (Smith, 2009: 67–95; Kucharek, 2010: 275–423), whose purpose is to install Osiris as sovereign of the netherworld. Contemporary to the extensive Osirian decree, this was edited for private use and for the strictly limited space available on the wooden stelae it was inscribed on (Beinlich, 2009: 11–39; Smith, 2009: 599–606, and 607–9 for an early Roman ostracon from Thebes inscribed with an even shorter version). This is a rare case of an Osirian liturgy adapted for private use not by the usual method of adding the name of the beneficiary—as, for instance, in the Osirian Great Decree of P.New York MMA 35.9.21—but by devising a distinct version. The early Roman demotic P.Berlin P 6750 and P.Berlin P 8765 from Soknopaiou Nesos in the Fayum region feature laments on the death of Osiris and jubilation at the birth of Horus, his son, avenger, and successor (Widmer, 2015).

The position of these texts in relation to the Book of the Dead is variable. It may be complementary, as demonstrated by papyri attached or added to Book of the Dead scrolls or combined with Book of the Dead spells, or dependent, i.e., compositions clearly influenced by Book of the Dead spells or vignettes (like the First and Second Books of Breathing, see Scalf, 2017a: 142–43; this volume). A mutually exclusive attitude ultimately resulted in the demise of the Book of the Dead.

The boundaries of the Book of the Dead corpus had always been fluid, incorporating spells not by conforming to some preconceived standards of form or content but quite pragmatically according to their purpose and desired effect: "Their only common denominator seems to be that they were thought to be useful to the deceased and, therefore, given as a grave good in the sense of a treasure trove of knowledge" (Müller-Roth, 2012: 33); according to Stadler, the basic function of funerary literature is to provide permanent access to the netherworld (Stadler, 2009: 231; also Scalf, this volume). Consequently, a number of spells appear in only a few Book of the Dead papyri, never making it into the core inventory of what would eventually be enshrined in the so-called Saite recension (Gülden, this volume). An early example would be BD 172, probably a private *Stundenwachen* ritual that, starting with a couple of Eighteenth-Dynasty Book of the Dead papyri, is attested in tombs, temples, and Osirian temple cult papyri down to the Roman Period (Kucharek, forthcoming) but never again in a Book of the Dead.

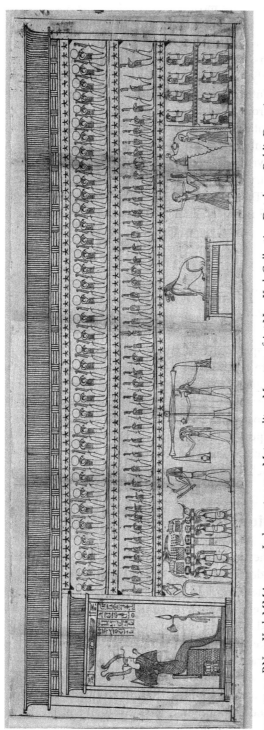

FIG. 15.2. P.New York MMA 35.9.21 Judgment scene. Metropolitan Museum of Art New York Collection Database, Public Domain.

Notwithstanding this elasticity, most Book of the Dead papyri are, generally speaking, instantly recognizable on account of their layout and design (cf. Mosher, 1992; this volume; Goelet, this volume). Hybrid compilations of Book of the Dead spells and other funerary texts that defy easy categorization seem to appear only at a late stage. A prime example would be the early Ptolemaic P.London BM EA 9916 (Kucharek and Coenen, 2021: 101–21, pl. 29; cf. Wüthrich, 2015: 310 pl. 28). Three hieroglyphic text units—two glorification spells taken from Pleyte BD 167 (cf. Wüthrich, this volume), an extract from the Osirian liturgy Lamentations of Isis and Nephthys, and BD 30, the common heart spell—complement a number of mostly straightforward Book of the Dead vignettes. A closer study of the papyrus revealed that it has more in common, in fact, with a select group of contemporary coffins than with papyri, Book of the Dead or otherwise. Moreover, it unites both Theban and Akhmimic features, comparable to the Book of the Dead P.Paris Louvre E 11078 (Einaudi, 2015, 2016). Objects like these exemplify the complex interrelations not only between text genres but across object and geographical borders as well.

## Two Case Studies

Complementing the comprehensive contributions in this volume by Scalf on funerary literature related to the Book of the Dead, and by Albert on the last Books of the Dead, the present chapter comprises two case studies tracing the continuities and modifications that emerge by comparing certain elements of the Book of the Dead with the "new" funerary compositions. The first case study is tied to a formal category, the titles and declarations of purpose according to private and Osirian funerary spells and rituals, the second to a specific topic: the manifold manifestations of the judgment of the dead, best known from spell BD 125 and its accompanying vignette in particular.

### Titles and declarations of purpose: Central tenets

The paraphernalia of funerary culture, like tomb architecture, coffin style, or burial equipment, varied considerably in societal, geographical, and chronological terms. Whether, compared to these more mutable material manifestations of mortuary religion, the underlying afterlife beliefs remained largely untouched through time, or whether they experienced modifications or even rifts is subject to debate, depending on individual perspective and prioritization of elements (Stadler, 2012a: 160–64; 2012b: 390–92; Smith, 2017a: 358–60, 371–72).

The basic needs and expectations of the several aspects representing a deceased person—the stationary body in its coffin and the dynamic soul in its various manifestations (*ka*, *ba*, and *akh*, to name the most eminent ones)—largely persisted. The perishable body required stabilization and protection against decomposition and destruction. *Ka*, *ba*, and *akh* craved sustenance, air, light, free movement, and community: creature comforts of the living person that the deceased desired to retain after death. Other needs were defined by the specific conditions of the afterlife—passing the examination of one's moral conduct on earth in the judgment hall of Osiris, protection against enemies, transformative powers, and community with the gods (Smith, 2009: 1–10). The deceased wished to temporarily return to this world, to reconnect with his erstwhile home and family as well as visit temples and festivals, on occasions when the boundaries between the two worlds became permeable, bridging the divide between the here and the hereafter. All of these needs were addressed and supported by material aids like offerings and burial equipment, and by verbal acts like the recitation of prayers and glorification spells. In order to perpetuate their effectiveness beyond the duration of the active mortuary cult, such recitations were written down and deposited in the tomb, or sometimes even within the coffin, along with funerary literature for the deceased (cf. Smith, 2009: 64; Kucharek, 2015: 236–37).

The enduring nature of these basic tenets is reflected in the continuing use of existing funerary compositions. Numerous spells from the Pyramid Texts and Coffin Texts adorned the walls of Late Period private tombs (Gestermann, 2005), and they make up the bulk of several Osirian liturgies preserved in mostly Ptolemaic papyri (Assmann, 2008: 38–39; 227; 417, 425, 435, 439, 440, 442, 460, 462, 479). These liturgies, in turn, were adopted by private individuals, as complete copies on papyrus but also selectively inscribed on coffins, sarcophagi and other items of tomb equipment (e.g., Assmann, 2008: 38–40; Kucharek, 2017). And, of course, the Book of the Dead remained in use for a considerable period (Albert, this volume; Mosher, 2016ff.; Smith, 2017a: 360).

In condensed form, these central conceptions are enshrined in the titles of funerary text corpora or individual spells, specifying their content or intent in the most concise manner. Some significant corpora, like the Pyramid Texts and Coffin Texts, did not feature an overall title. With others, there was a notable amount of flexibility (or vagueness) regarding the assignment of titles to specific compositions. While there certainly are distinct associations of particular titles to certain texts, allowing for conventional reference, there are numerous individual inventions or overlaps. For instance, the actual title of the Book of the Dead is *prt m hrw* (see Backes, 2009), commonly translated into English as Going Forth by Day or, in a more recent rendering, Going Out in Daylight (Quirke, 2013). However, *prt m hrw*, relating to intent, not content, had already designated a number of spells from the Middle Kingdom on (Schott, 1990: 167–70), and was repeatedly applied to the Book of Traversing Eternity (Smith, 2009: 396) and to other compositions (see p. 290, 291, 292, 295). The Book of the Dead itself never really strayed from Going Forth by Day; it appears to have been the most stable and consistent title of all funerary compositions (cf. Backes, 2009). There were some individual modifications, as in a Book of the Dead papyrus titled Beginning of the Spells of Going Forth by Day which Isis Made for Her Brother Osiris, a hybrid of the default title of the Book of the Dead and one of the recent compositions, the Book of Breathing which Isis Made for Her Brother Osiris. It was hardly by chance that the owner of this particular Book of the Dead was also in possession of a regular Book of Breathing which Isis Made for Her Brother Osiris (P. Vienna KHM 3861 and P. Vienna KHM 10158: Coenen, 2003).

*Prt m hrw*, Going forth by Day (or Going Out in Daylight), emphasizes the desire for free movement, particularly into the world of the living (Müller-Roth, 2012: 29; Scalf, 2017b: 23; dissenting: Quirke, 2013: viii). Considering the frequent application of the title to other funerary spells, the ability to return to the familiar world must have been imperative. As for late funerary compositions, mobility is again featured in the title of the Book of Traversing Eternity: adding a transcending temporal dimension, freedom of movement is again acted out in this world but is now directed toward attending religious festivals, the interfaces with the divine world. Whether Book of Traversing Eternity is indeed the actual title is, however, doubtful, as it never appears where expected, at the very start of the text (Smith, 2009: 396; Quack's arguments regarding the question are as yet unpublished; meanwhile cf. Quack, 2012: 227 n. 14; 2015: 439 n. 30). In that place, one might instead find Going Forth by Day or, to complicate matters further, Book of Breathing, which usually applies to the second major corpus of late funerary texts (Smith, 2009: 396). Another funerary composition, the Liturgy of Opening the Mouth for Breathing, resumes the explicit wish for breath expressed in the various Books of Breathing. These, in their turn, are far from being consistently named: the composition commonly titled Book of Breathing which Isis Made for Her Brother Osiris may on occasion be named Spell of Breathing and Living by Breath in the God's Domain (*rꜣ n snsn ꜥnḫ m ṯꜣw m ḥrt-nṯr*), Another Spell of Going Forth by Day (*kjj rꜣ n prt m hrw*), or The Book of Breathing and Coming Forth by Day (*tꜣ šꜥy snsn ḥnꜥ tꜣ prt m hrw*, Stadler, 2015: 77). On their verso sheets, the First and Second Books of Breathing often feature a title emphasizing the preservation of mummy and tomb; its most extensive version is "Perfect Burial. May it endure over your bones, may it remain over your flesh without decay. May the beautiful West (goddess) extend her arms to receive you by the decree of the lady of the foundations" (Stadler, 2015: 78). Most of these particular interchanges and variations accentuate the utmost importance of the ability to move and breathe—vital signs indicating the reversal of death. The aforementioned Book of Entering the God's Domain and Promenading in the Hall of the Two Truths combines the wish for freedom of movement with the desire to attain the precondition for all other afterlife benefits, justification (see p. 308). The title of the Book of Glorifying the *akh* (Smith, 2009: 455–61; Wagner, 2015) is, in contrast, notable for lacking any reference to the physical capacities of the deceased.

The sheer fact that these "new" texts were created indicates a shift in focus or perception—not abruptly, as the parallel usage of the Book of the Dead and these recent compositions show, but nevertheless slowly superseding previous predilections. For instance, there is a greater particularization of themes without altering the themes themselves (Smith, 2017a: 361). By concentrating in the following on specific explanatory passages, a shift of focus toward the divine sphere becomes visible, modeled on the cult of Osiris.

The titles of spells and ritual texts were occasionally extended or supplemented by passages specifying their purpose and desired effect. Book of the Dead spells also feature these passages, but they were usually added as a "postscript" to the spell proper. These postscripts are often rendered in red ink, introduced by the phrase "Whosoever knows this book/spell . . ." and concluded by a confirmation of their effectiveness. These declaratory passages in general have been variously called "rubrics" (Naville, 1902: 271; Smith, 2017b: 373), "claims" (Allen, 1936: passim), "Funktionsangaben" (Rössler-Köhler, 1979: 321), a "general programme" (Herbin, 2008: 13), a "description of its purpose" (Smith, 2009: 464), and "Wirkungsdeklarationen" (Kucharek, 2010: 314, 522). Regardless of the individual content or structure of the ritual proper, they offer a concise guide to the benefits intended to be reaped by recitation. Such passages first occur with any frequency in the Book of the Dead. In terms of grammar, the majority are sequences of infinitive phrases, setting them apart from the operative text.

More detailed than titles, these passages shed a more conclusive light on the specific afterlife expectations at the time of their composition and the period of their use. In the Book of the Dead, going forth by day, being able to transform, not being hindered passing the gates of the underworld, not dying again, and receiving offerings are the most frequently evoked objectives. Before the New Kingdom, such declarations are very rare, but one Theban copy of a Coffin Text spell, CT 335, titled Going Forth by Day, includes these items in a postscript (Grapow, 1915–1917: 95–96; de Buck, 1951: 326a–j), dating the specific formulation of these wishes back to the Middle Kingdom at the latest (cf. also Quack, 1999: 16, who dates the postscript of BD 72 at least back to the Middle Kingdom as well). CT 335 would later evolve into Book of the Dead spell 17.

This BD 17 is one of the rare Book of the Dead spells that has a declaration of purpose added to its title rather than appended as a postscript. The earliest attestation is dated to the middle of the Eighteenth Dynasty (Lapp, 2006: 2–9; Munro, 1994: 93; see also Grapow, 1915–1917: 96–99). Hardly differing from its New Kingdom predecessor, this is the passage according to the Ptolemaic P.Turin 1791 (Lepsius, 1842: VII; Grapow, 1915–1917: 4–5):

*Title*

Spells of the raisings and glorifications,

(of) going out and descending in the god's domain.

*Declaration of purpose*

Being in the following of Osiris,

being satisfied by the food-offerings of Wennefer,

going forth by day,

making any transformation he desires to perform,

playing the *senet*-game,

being in the *seh*-hall.

The living *ba* of NN is one provided for with the Great Ennead in the west after his landing.

While these passages were retained in the Book of the Dead up to its demise, funerary texts created in the Greco-Roman Period evince a modified perspective. For instance, at the outset of the Book of Traversing Eternity—like the Book of the Dead composed for the benefit of private individuals—there is a short declaration of purpose in the shape of a glorification (cf. Herbin, 1994: 47, 81–84; Smith, 2009: 405). In contrast to the CT 335 and BD 17 declarations, largely reflecting the conditions of earthly existence, the Book of Traversing Eternity's declaration is defined partly by the desire for the inclusion of the several aspects of the deceased into the divine sphere, and partly by the wish for continuity in this world, embodied in the care the living take of the mummy and his enduring memory among the heirs and descendants. The focus has shifted from acts to states of existence:

> May your *ba* live in the sky with Re,
>
> may your *ka* be divine at the forefront of the gods.
>
> May your corpse endure in the *duat* with Osiris,
>
> may your mummy be glorified among the living.
>
> May your heir flourish on earth with Geb,
>
> he who occupies your seat among the living,
>
> while your name endures in the mouths of those who exist by virtue of the Book of Traversing Eternity.

Precursors already existed by the Eighteenth Dynasty. One single copy of the Book of the Dead, P.Paris Louvre N 3074, features postscripts of BD 71 (a spell titled Going Forth by Day) and BD 147 (a spell enabling the deceased to pass the gateways of the underworld). In BD 71, the deceased is promised to dwell with Re and Osiris; however, even the sun god is firmly located on Earth. In BD 147, the deceased is, in a remarkable phrase, guaranteed to be "of one body with Osiris" (Hornung, 1979: 151, 297–98; Budge, 1910: II 13–14, 261; Laan, 1995: 70–71). In contrast to these singular occurrences, the postscript to BD 101, the Spell for Protecting the Barque of Re, is attested from the Eighteenth Dynasty to the Ptolemaic Period. It states that the spell was originally devised by Thoth for Osiris "to cause the sun to rise (var.: rest) upon his corpse," in other words, to be united with the sun god like the corpse of Osiris himself. In other respects, too, the BD 101 postscript emphasizes admission to the divine sphere: to join the followers of Horus, to be in the presence of Sothis, and to have a shrub grown over one's chest by Menqet (Hornung, 1979: 201; Quirke, 2013: 227; Budge, 1910: II 79, 80–81, 82–83).

Several of the Osirian temple rituals mentioned earlier in the chapter, preserved on Greco-Roman Period papyri roughly contemporary with the Book of Traversing Eternity, also have their titles supplemented by a declaration of purpose.

The resemblance between the two is obvious. While for Osiris, the topic of being received into the divine sphere is omitted, as evidently there is no need for him to confirm his divine status, the well-being of his various manifestations and continuity on earth, embodied in his heir, strike the same note. In the so-called Lamentations of Isis and Nephthys, the actual title Invocation of the Glorifications which the Two Sisters Performed pinpoints the function of the ritual, which also constitutes the very first word of the declaration (P.Berlin P 3008, adapted for private use: Smith, 2009: 129; Kucharek, 2010: 56; Kucharek and Coenen, 2021: 149–50, 199–202):

> Glorifying his *ba*,
> stabilizing his corpse,
> making his *ka* jubilant,
> granting breath to the nose of him whose throat is constricted,
> gladdening the hearts of Isis und Nephthys,
> placing Horus on his throne of his father,
> giving life, stability and dominion to the Osiris of Tarudj,
> born of Takhaa, who is called Perses, justified.

The same applies to the closely related, but more elaborate version that precedes the operative text of the liturgy called *sꜣḥw* IV (the Ritual of the Glorification of Osiris in the God's Domain: Smith, 2009: 140; Kucharek, 2010: 97):

> Glorifying his *ba*,
> stabilizing his corpse,
> so that his *ba* shines in the sky,
> so that his corpse endures in the *duat*,
> so that he rejuvenates on the day of the monthly festival
> and his son Horus is established on his throne,
> being in (possession of) his office of eternity.
> Reciting this ritual is effective for Osiris
> and effective for the one who will recite it.
> ...
> This glorification made by Isis and her sister Nephthys
> and her son Horus likewise,
> it is perfomed for Osiris
> so that his *ba* is caused to live in the god's domain daily,
> so that his heart is gladdened

and all his enemies are overthrown.

A third Osirian liturgy adapted for private use, Pleyte BD 168, is simply titled pꜣ ṯs tw, "The (ritual) 'Raise yourself'" [Pleyte, 1881: 138–54; Schott, 1990: 397 (1714); Quirke, 2013: 537]. Its declaration of purpose covers much the same range of objectives as the Lamentations and sꜣḫw IV:

> Adoring his manifestations,
> adoring his shapes(?),
> (thereby)
> erecting his noble mummy,
> raising his *ba*,
> making his heart jubilant
> appeasing his *ka*,
> stabilizing his corpse, the great one of the coffin (?)
> granting breath to the constricted.

One copy of the rare spell BD 182, dating to the Twenty-first Dynasty (P.London BM EA 10010; Budge, 1910: III 101), features a declaration of purpose appended to its title. Like BD 101 (see earlier discussion), BD 182 is said to have been devised by Thoth, and the declarative passages of the two spells are evidently related. The BD 182 declaration of purpose, centering on the revivification and protection of Osiris, is suggestive of an origin as a temple ritual (Stadler, 2009: 234). Its formulation clearly differs from that of the later documents quoted on the preceding pages and may therefore reflect an earlier template:

> Book of stabilizing Osiris,
> (of) granting breath to the weary-hearted through an act of Thoth,
> (of) repelling the enemies of Osiris when he arrives there in his manifestations,
> (of) protecting, sheltering and guarding in the god's domain;
> made by Thoth himself
> so that the sun rests upon his (Osiris's) corpse.

The convergence of the templates of Osirian and individual afterlife objectives in the Greco-Roman Period is underlined by a peculiar hybrid, the declaration of purpose in the Book of Breathing which Isis Made for Her Brother Osiris:

> Beginning of the Book of Breathing which Isis Made for Her Brother Osiris,
> in order to animate his *ba*,
> in order to animate his corpse,

in order to rejuvenate all his limbs again,

in order to unite him with the horizon together with his father Re,

in order to let his *ba* appear in the sky as the disc of the moon,

in order to let him shine as Orion in the womb of the Lower Heaven (*Nnt*),

in order to cause the same to happen to the Osiris of NN.

The title of this composition claims an Osirian origin, but this has been rejected for the lack of any evidence of it having ever been performed in the cult of Osiris (Smith, 2009: 462). Indeed, an Osirian background would be unreconcilable with the composition's emphasis on the judgment of the dead (see p. 309–10): it would be absurd to have Osiris appear before his own court in order to claim innocence and moral purity. His justification, the confirmation of his and his son's sovereignty, was the result of quite another court battle, as recounted, for instance, in the Contendings of Horus and Seth (Simpson, 2003: 91–103; Burkard and Thissen, 2008: 35–47). Therefore, the Book of Breathing which Isis Made for Her Brother Osiris appears as a remarkable case of a private funerary ritual emulating (by way of its title) a cultic one. This, in turn, has been reworked into the Book of the Dead P.Vienna KHM 3861 (see p. 302), whose hybrid title, Beginning of the Spells of Going Forth by Day which Isis Made for Her Brother Osiris, is followed by a declaration of purpose reflecting its mixed origin:

Beginning of the spells of Going Forth by Day which Isis Made for Her Brother Osiris

in order to animate his *ba*,

in order to rejuvenate his mummy,

[in order to (animate?/stabilize?)] his corpse in the god's domain,

in order to cause that he may walk among the living,

(and to) perform the same for the Osiris of NN.

The diachronic survey of statements of purpose from the Middle Kingdom to the Greco-Roman Period indicates a shift toward a greater significance of the transcendent aspects of the afterlife—integration into the divine hierarchies and participation in religious festivals taking precedence over, for instance, receiving offerings. It must be kept in mind, though, that the Book of the Dead spells, including their postscripts, were in use far into the Ptolemaic Period, their ends and purposes continuing to be valid.

The condensed testimony of titles and declarations of purpose provides little evidence for a material alteration in general afterlife conceptions and expectations from Pharaonic to Greco-Roman times. As the CT 335/BD 17 passage exemplifies, earlier conceptions put emphasis on the actions and abilities of the deceased, his sole divine point of reference being Osiris, and were largely concerned with reconstituting a reflection of the deceased's former existence, emphasizing the ability to individually transcend the divide between this world and the next. The Greco-Roman Period texts, on the other hand, reflect a proliferation of transcendency: The deceased communes with a number of deities, most significantly Osiris, Re, and Geb, who preside over the cosmic realms—underworld, sky, and earth—that the several aspects of the deceased—corpse/mummy, *ba*, and *ka*—inhabit. Both spheres merge through the increased desire of the deceased to visit religious festivals on earth, epitomized in the Book of Traversing Eternity.

As Kaper (2000: 124; 2001: 131) observed, the *ba* in particular became more eminent in the Greco-Roman Period than before, as exemplified by the Theban Book of Traversing Eternity and, to a remarkable degree, in the funerary literature from Akhmim (Kucharek, this volume).

## BD 125: Judgment of the Dead

The concept of a moral evaluation after death determining the afterlife of an individual predates the Book of the Dead by a long time; evidence goes back to the Pyramid Texts (Meurer, 2002: 88–93; Grieshammer, 1970: 1–2). The phrase *ȝḫ wsr mȝʿ-ḫrw*, "glorified, powerful, justified," first appears in offering formulas of the later Middle Kingdom (Ilin-Tomich, 2011: 25). In the Second Intermediate Period, the attribute *mȝʿ-ḫrw*, "justified," attached to the name of a deceased person and signaling that he or she had passed judgment, came into widespread use (cf. Kubisch, 2008). Spell 125 of the Book of the Dead, arguably the most eminent spell of the corpus and often associated with or substituted by its iconic vignette, the judgment scene, reflected the central significance of the concept by the early New Kingdom. While the Book of the Dead as a convolute petered out at the end of the Ptolemaic Period (Albert, this volume) and spell BD 125 all but vanishes from the record in the Roman Period, the judgment scene and its derivates remained a staple of funerary iconography into the second and third centuries CE.

Noticeably, the few attestations of spell BD 125 outside the Book of the Dead during and after its declining phase are regularly accompanied by a judgment scene as well (Figs. 15.2 and 15.3). This supports the observation that in ritual scenes, the iconographic element "constitute(s) the constant and canonized element," while the accompanying recitations represent its changeable interpretations (Assmann, 1992: 98–99). A unique demotic composition dating to 63 CE, P.Paris BN 149 (Stadler, 2003, 2018/2019; Smith, 2009: 437–54) comprises a detailed description of the judgment vignette instead of an image. It appears to be based on an earlier, Ptolemaic template, as no scene firmly dated to the Roman Period features either the divine child squatting on a *heqa* scepter or the four sons of Horus upon a lotus flower in front of Osiris as described in P.Paris BN 149. The Roman Period P.Paris Louvre E 5353 comprises a compilation of funerary text passages, among them the title of BD 125, as well as a judgment scene (Herbin, 2013: 261, 263, 264–65, pl. II–IV) with a unique invocation of the devourer (see p. 313).

Several individually composed funerary papyri feature versions of the Book of the Dead judgment scene but lack any vestige of spell 125. The P.Kroch, mentioned earlier in this chapter, includes three Book of the Dead vignettes, among them an elaborate judgment scene (https://blogs.cornell.edu/culconservation/2016/11/17/the-funer

ary-text-of-usir-wer/). The hieratic P.Turin 1848 (see p. 297), most likely dating to the early Roman Period, features a crude judgment scene next to a scene derived from the vignette of BD 1, depicting the rites performed on the mummy before burial.

In contrast to these singular documents, there are more than 30 copies of the Theban Book of Breathing which Isis Made for Her Brother Osiris (attested from the second century BCE to the first century CE) (Smith, 2009: 462). Several of the sixteen paragraphs of the full version (Smith, 2009: 462–65) incorporate material from BD 125. As this Book of Breathing is a "passport" issued by Isis, the first-person utterances of the Book of the Dead spell are transposed to the second and third persons. Immediately following the title and declaration of purpose (see p. 306–7), the deceased is declared to be pure (Smith's §2) in a short BD 125 passage from the conclusion of the address to the deities in the Hall of the Two Truths. The extensive protestation of righteousness preceding this passage in BD 125 is omitted, apart from one section that makes up the first half of §15 of the Book of Breathing which Isis Made for Her Brother Osiris. This is a condensed version of the deceased's virtuous deeds on earth, the phraseology partly lifted from traditional autobiographical texts (cf. Lichtheim's term "moral self-presentation": Lichtheim, 1988: 7; cf. also Assmann, 1996a: 493; 1996b: 141–42):

> O gods who are in the underworld, listen to the voice of NN.
>
> He has come before you with nothing evil attributable to him.
>
> There is no sin charged to him.
>
> There is no witness testifying against him, for he lives on Maat and consumes Maat.
>
> May the gods be pleased with all that he has done.
>
> He gave bread to the hungry, water to the thirsty, and clothing to the naked.
>
> He gave oblations to the gods and invocation offerings to the *akh* spirits.
>
> (P.Paris Louvre N 3284, based on Smith, 2009: 475)

This passage is preceded by a sequence of invocations addressed to a number of divine judges (§14), based on the second negative confession of BD 125 (Hornung, 1979: 236–39; Quirke, 2013: 271–73). Of the 42 invocations in BD 125, the selection chosen was not eclectic; instead, the initial ones were simply copied out in their original order of sequence. While the names of the judges were mostly retained, some of the transgressions were subject to alterations. For instance, of the seven invocations in P.Paris Louvre N 3284, the name of only one judge differs from the BD 125 list. Regarding the transgressions, the discrepancies are more noticeable but mostly concern vocabulary rather than content, the only serious discrepancy being the fifth invocation, where the Book of the Dead's "I have not killed anyone (*smꜣ rmṯ*)" has been downsized to "NN has not disputed (*sḫwn*)."

Numerous copies of the Book of Breathing which Isis Made for Her Brother Osiris feature a full judgment scene as well (e.g., P.London BM EA 9995: Taylor, 2010: 225 no. 111; Herbin, 2008: pl. 24; P.Florence 3666 + P.Vienna KHM 3850: Coenen, 1999a; P.Tübingen

2016: von Recklinghausen, 2007: 166, 174–76 no. 155; Guermeur, 2021: 652, pl. I; in general: Coenen, 1998: 39–41).

The dearth of BD 125 attestations in the Roman Period does not mean that the judgment of the dead as a topic had all but vanished from funerary literature. Rather, it now appeared in various forms in some of the individual compositions from the period: for instance, it pervades much of the Ptolemaic P.Kroch (unpublished). Across the miscellany of texts assembled in this papyrus—glorifications, hymns, a speech by Isis—justification is a major topic, and the "day of judgment" (*hrw n wḏꜥ-mdw*), also called "this perfect day of justification" (*hrw pn nfr n mꜣꜥ-ḫrw*), is repeatedly invoked. In P.Rhind I, the process of introduction, justification, judgment, and reception into the underworld takes up several columns (Assmann and Kucharek, 2008: 601–10, 887–91); and P.Paris Louvre E 3452, a singular late Ptolemaic Book of Transformations, comprises a section modeled on BD 125 without featuring actual parallels (Smith, 2017b). The title shared by two different compositions, Entering the God's Domain and Promenading in the Hall of the Two Truths (see p. 296, this chapter), underlines the prime importance ascribed to judgment.

A vignette derived from the judgment scene but omitting the judgment itself features the presentation of the justified deceased to Osiris (Scalf, 2014: 153–67; cf. Seeber, 1976: 58–62). This is described as an integral part of the judgment scene in P.Paris BN 149 (Stadler, 2003: 20–23, 30; Smith, 2009: 446–47):

> The man [ . . . ], while Anubis holds his hand.
>
> A lotus with two buds, on which are the four sons of Horus.
>
> A chapel in which Osiris is seated upon his throne, with an offering table and a lotus before him.
>
> Isis is behind him, giving praise,
>
> and Nephthys is behind him, giving praise.

This icon heads, for instance, the judgment section of P.Rhind I (Möller, 1913: 22–25, pl. IV; Assmann and Kucharek, 2008: 601–3, Fig. 27) and is added to some of the formulaic demotic funerary papyri studied by Scalf in 2014. It is also featured as part of vignette 3 in the Book of the *Ba* (Kucharek, this volume). As part of full judgment scenes dated to the Greco-Roman Period, it is but rarely depicted; see, for instance, the closely related Roman Period coffins Sydney NMR.344 (Beinlich-Seeber, 2006: pl. 5) and Marseille 260 (Beinlich-Seeber, 1998: 11, Figs. 3, 28, Fig. 7); the Soter family coffins Leiden AMM 8-c/M 75 and London BM EA 6706 (unpublished, cf. Riggs, 2005: 280 no. 76, 281 no. 78), and the Book of the Dead P.Vienna KHM 3861 (Coenen, 2003: pl. XXXVII). The judgment scene in P.Tübingen 2016, a Book of Breathing which Isis Made for Her Brother Osiris, represents something of a "missing link" between the full judgment scene and the presentation scene (Fig. 15.3): to the right, Anubis guides the deceased toward Osiris, enthroned with an offering table and the sons of Horus on a lotus flower, exactly as described in pBN 149.

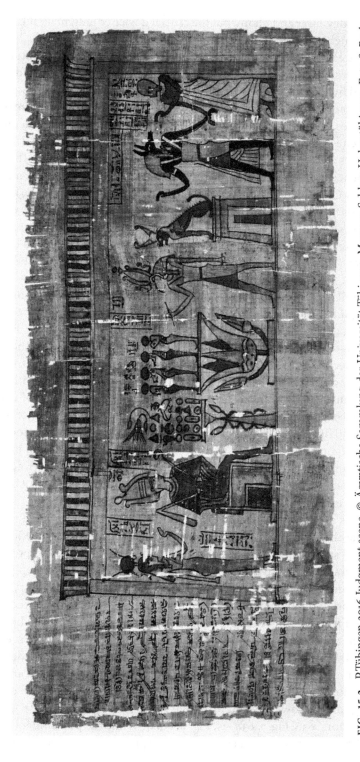

FIG. 15.3. P.Tübingen 2016 Judgment scene. © Ägyptische Sammlung der Universität Tübingen, Museum Schloss Hohentübingen, Foto S. Beck; Ivan Guermeur.

In between are the devourer and Thoth, but the crucial device of judgment, the scales, is absent (von Recklinghausen, 2007: 174–75 no. 155; Guermeur, 2021: 652, pl. I).

In Thebes in the early first century CE, contemporary to the Rhind papyrus, the presentation icon is featured in the lateral vignettes of painted mummy shrouds whose center is occupied by a life-size figure of the deceased (Seeber, 1976: 61–62). Somewhat later, in a further transformation of the scene, mummy shrouds in Saqqara were painted with life-size figures of the deceased flanked by Anubis and Osiris, while elements of the judgment scene—primarily the scales and the devourer—are relegated to small interspersed images (Régen, 2012: see ibid., 621–22, for the range of datings). The provenance of a fragmentary shroud with several judgment vignettes, dating to the middle of the second century CE, is unclear (Griffiths, 1982; Riggs, 2005: 218, 221, Fig. 109). Finally, on painted shrouds from Antinoopolis, dated to the second/third century CE, vignettes depicting the scales remain the only obvious reminder of the judgment. Remarkably, a couple of these scales are off balance, the scale containing the body of the deceased appearing heavier (P.Paris Louvre AF 3027, P.Paris Louvre AF 13042C: Aubert et al., 2008: 218–19 no. 52, 220 no. 53; Régen, 2012: 638, Fig. 10).

As Anubis, in full judgment scenes, may guide the deceased either toward the scales, prior to the weighing of the heart, or, afterward, toward Osiris (Seeber, 1976: 157–58; on Sydney NMR.344 the identical constellation appears in both positions: Beinlich-Seeber, 2006: pl. 5–6, 57), the moment depicted on these shrouds has been the subject of some debate (Seeber, 1976: 61–62; Beinlich-Seeber, 1998: 32–33; Régen, 2012: 616–20). The large scale of the image and the fact that the deceased is literally clothed in it, appears more commensurate with the pivotal significance of the moment of triumph, when Osiris has passed his favorable judgment on the deceased, in accordance with the concept of "resultativity" of the Egyptian mindset (Assmann, 1984: 93–95; 2001). This interpretation is supported by the majority of Ptolemaic and Roman Period judgment scenes as well as by the description of the scene in P.Paris BN 149 (see p. 310), according to which the deceased is introduced to the hall of judgment not by Anubis, but by one or two goddesses representing Maat (cf. Seeber, 1976: 49).

Judgment scenes dated to the Roman Period mostly follow the traditional template, allowing for some change in iconography (Seeber, 1976). The purpose of the judgment scene (as well as of spell BD 125) is to ensure a favorable verdict. While the process is a crisis, a rite of passage, its positive outcome is already established, iconographically as well as in the accompanying spell. A couple of images, both from a funerary context and dated to the early Roman Period, however, infuse the scene with an unprecedented shift in meaning (Fig. 15.4). Both images feature not only the devourer, the hybrid monster that had been a threatening presence almost since the inception of the scene, but also several spindly black human silhouettes, resembling skeletons or the desiccated bodies of a mummy (on these figures see Régen, 2012). In both scenes they are clearly about to be punished, having been transferred to a cauldron in front of the devourer or even dangling from its jaws (Seeber, 1976: 186, 172, Fig. 70; Kurth, 1990: 66, Fig. 24, 67, Fig. 25; Régen, 2012: 636, Fig. 7, 634–35, Fig. 6, 6bis). While the punishment and torture of those who had failed in life had long been explored in great detail in various

FIG. 15.4. Human figures exposed to the devourer in an early Roman Period judgment scene (after von Bissing, 1950: pl. I).

netherworld books (Hornung, 1968), to have it transposed into an environment created to guarantee a positive verdict was unprecedented. It may reflect a "playful," even irreverent attitude toward a hitherto inviolable iconography, a weakening of the established belief. It also addressed a fear that had hardly ever found expression, the threat that one may have to succumb to the devourer after all. Already in the Ramesside Book of the Dead of Ani (P.London BM EA 10470), the Great Ennead claims that the deceased "has no crime or indictment before us, and the devourer shall not be granted power over him" (translation based on Eyre, 1976: 109–10; cf. Seeber, 1976: 171; Herbin, 2013: 282). In a comparable passage in a Roman Period papyrus, the devourer is directly invoked: "Oh great devourer, you shall have no power <over> this *ba* of the Hathor of Hor-ankh, in heaven, on earth, in the *duat* (or) in any place her *ka* wishes to dwell." (P.Paris Louvre E 5353: Herbin, 2013: 264, 281–82, 284, pl. II, III).

In the later Roman Period, the judgment scene was still in use, as shown by the mummy shrouds from Antinoopolis dating as late as the third century CE. This is well after its associated spell had ceased to be employed even in an abbreviated or allusive form in the first century CE. Two iconographical nuclei had emerged by then: The scales as the instrument of judgment became the icon par excellence of the dramatic aspect of the proceedings, with the fate of the deceased literally in the balance even if implicitly conveying a favorable result. In the written evidence, reference to the scales also amounts to a shorthand allusion to judgment: "The god lays the heart on the scales opposite the weight. He knows the impious man and the man of god by his heart." (P.Insinger 5,7–8: Hoffmann and Quack, 2018: 281; translation by Lichtheim, 1992: 141). The second iconographical nucleus, the presentation of the deceased to Osiris, rendered exclusive priority to the desired outcome, giving precedence not to the critical moment but to the triumph of being received into the realm of the gods.

# Conclusion

While the Greco-Roman Period witnessed the emergence of a remarkable number of "new" funerary compositions, these did not immediately take the place of the Book of the Dead but rather superseded it over an extended period of time. The modifications to the afterlife beliefs to be observed during that period comply with this gradual transition. The central needs and expectations remained stable, but their specific expression reflected a perceptible shift of focus: from the actions and abilities of the deceased, aimed at attaining a semblance of life on earth, to an emphasis on the transcendent aspects of the afterlife, as, for instance, acceptance into the divine sphere. The judgment motif, represented in the Book of the Dead by both an extensive spell (BD 125) and an elaborate vignette, remained a staple far into the Roman Period but underwent certain condensations and modifications: It was essentially pared down from its prominent role in the Book of the Dead to selected icons representing the decisive moments of the process, mostly on mummy shrouds. Toward the end, some graphic renderings of the devourer in action may reflect a decline of the significance of the judgment of the dead.

## Bibliography

Allen, T. G. (1936). "Types of Rubrics in the Egyptian Book of the Dead." *Journal of the American Oriental Society* 56: 145–54.

Assmann, J. (1984). *Ägypten. Theologie und Frömmigkeit einer frühen Hochkultur* (Stuttgart: Kohlhammer).

Assmann, J. (1992). "Semiosis and Interpretation in Ancient Egyptian Ritual." In *Interpretation in Religion*. Philosophy and Religion 2, edited by S. Biderman and B. Scharfstein, 87–109 (Leiden: Brill).

Assmann, J. (1996a). *Ägypten. Eine Sinngeschichte* (München: Hanser).

Assmann, J. (1996b). "Erlösung durch Rechtfertigung. Altägyptische Todesvorstellungen." In *Der Tod in den Weltkulturen und Weltreligionen*, edited by C. von Barloewen, 137–60 (München: Diederichs).

Assmann, J. (2001). "Das Ende als Sinngenerator. Zur Kategorie der Resultativität im altägyptischen Denken." In *Sinngeneratoren. Fremd- und Selbstthematisierung in soziologisch-historischer Perspektive*, edited by C. Bohn and H. Willems, 249–62 (Konstanz).

Assmann, J. (2008). *Altägyptische Totenliturgien III. Osirisliturgien in Papyri der Spätzeit*. Supplemente zu den Schriften der Heidelberger Akademie der Wissenschaften, Philosophisch-Historische Klasse 20 (Heidelberg: Universitätsverlag Winter).

Assmann, J. and Kucharek, A. (2008). *Ägyptische Religion. Totenliteratur* (Frankfurt: Verlag der Weltreligionen).

Aubert, M.-F., Cortopassi, R., Nachtergael, G., Amorós, V. A., Détienne, P., Pagès-Camagna, S., and Le Hô, A.-S. (2008). *Portraits funéraires de l'Égypte romaine II. Cartonnages, linceuls et bois* (Paris: Musée du Louvre/Éditions Khéops).

Backes, B. (2009). ""Was zu sagen ist»—zum Gesamttitel des Totenbuchs." In *Ausgestattet mit den Schriften des Thot. Festschrift für Irmtraut Munro zu ihrem 65. Geburtstag*. Studien zum altägyptischen Totenbuch 14, edited by B. Backes, M. Müller-Roth, and S. Stöhr, 5–27 (Wiesbaden: Harrassowitz).

Backes, B. (2015). "Gedanken zu Kategorien und Funktionspotentialen funerärer Ritualpapyri." In *Liturgical Texts for Osiris and the Deceased in Late Period and Greco-Roman Egypt*. Studien zur spätägyptischen Religion 14, edited by B. Backes and J. Dieleman, 15–35 (Wiesbaden: Harrassowitz).

Beinlich, H. (2009). *Papyrus Tamerit 1. Ein Ritualpapyrus der ägyptischen Spätzeit*. Studien zu den Ritualszenen altägyptischer Tempel 7 (Dettelbach: Röll).

Beinlich-Seeber, C. (1998). "Ein römerzeitliches Sargfragment in Marseille." In *Ein ägyptisches Glasperlenspiel. Ägyptologische Beiträge für Erik Hornung aus seinem Schülerkreis*, edited by A. Brodbeck, 9–40 (Berlin: Gebr. Mann).

Beinlich-Seeber, C. (2006). "Painted Judgement Scene on Wood, R344." In *Egyptian Art in the Nicholson Museum, Sydney*, edited by K. N. Sowada and B. G. Ockinga, 27–43 (Sydney: Mediterranean Archaeology).

von Bissing, F. W. (1950). "Tombeaux d'époque romaine à Akhmîm: lettre ouverte au Dr Étienne Drioton." *Annales du Service des Antiquités de l'Égypte* 50: 547–76.

Brech, R. (2013). *Spätägyptische Särge aus Achmim. Eine typologische und chronologische Studie*. Aegyptiaca Hamburgiensa 3 (Gladbeck: PeWe-Verlag).

de Buck, A. (1951). *The Egyptian Coffin Texts IV*. Oriental Institute Publications 67 (Chicago: University Press).

Budge, E. A. W. (1910). *The Chapters of Coming Forth by Day or The Theban Recension of the Book of the Dead I–III*. Books on Egypt and Chaldaea (London: Kegan Paul, Trench, Trübner & Co.).

Burkard, G. and Thissen, H. J. (2008). *Einführung in die altägyptische Literaturgeschichte II. Neues Reich*. Einführungen und Quellentexte zur Ägyptologie 6 (Berlin: Lit).

Coenen, M. (1998). "An Introduction to the Document of Breathing made by Isis." *Revue d'Égyptologie* 49: 37–45.

Coenen, M. (1999a). "A Remarkable Judgement Scene in a Document of Breathing made by Isis: Papyrus Florence 3665 + 3666 and papyrus Vienna 3850." *Orientalia* 68: 98–103.

Coenen, M. (1999b). "The Greco-Roman Mortuary Papyri in the National Museum of Antiquities at Leiden." *Oudheidkundige Mededelingen uit het Rijksmuseum van Oudheden te Leiden* 79: 67–79.

Coenen, M. (2001). "On the Demise of the Book of the Dead in Ptolemaic Thebes." *Revue d'Égyptologie* 52: 69–84.

Coenen, M. (2003). "The Funerary Papyri of Horos son of Estneteretten in the Kunsthistorisches Museum in Vienna." *Zeitschrift für Ägyptische Sprache und Altertumskunde* 130: 160–69.

Depauw, M. (2002). "Late Funerary Material from Akhmim." In *Perspectives on Panopolis. An Egyptian Town from Alexander the Great to the Arab Conquest*. Papyrologica Lugduno-Batava 31, edited by A. Egberts, B. P. Muhs, and J. van der Vliet, 71–81 (Leiden: Brill).

Dieleman, J. (2015). "Scribal Bricolage in the Artemis Liturgical Papyrus." In *Liturgical Texts for Osiris and the Deceased in Late Period and Greco-Roman Egypt*. Studien zur spätägyptischen Religion 14, edited by B. Backes and J. Dieleman, 217–32 (Wiesbaden: Harrassowitz).

Dorman, P. (2017). "The Origins and Early Development of the Book of the Dead." In *Book of the Dead. Becoming God in Ancient Egypt*. Oriental Institute Museum Publications 39, edited by F. Scalf, 29–40 (Chicago: Oriental Institute).

Einaudi, S. (2015). "Le papyrus de Pasenedjemibnakht (Louvre E 11078): Un Livre des Morts de tradition thébaine à Akhmîm." In *Documents de Théologies Thébaines Tardives 3*. Cahiers de l'ENiM 13, edited by C. Thiers, 7–27 (Montpellier: Équipe «Égypte Nilotique et Méditerranéenne»).

Einaudi, S. (2016). "Le Livre des Morts et le travail de rédaction des scribes-copistes: le cas du papyrus Louvre E 11078." *Les Cahiers de l'École du Louvre* 9: 1–10.

Eyre, C. (1976) "Fate, Crocodiles and the Judgement of the Dead." *Studien zur Altägyptischen Kultur* 4: 103–14.

Gestermann, L. (2005). *Die Überlieferung ausgewählter Texte altägyptischer Totenliteratur („Sargtexte") in spätzeitlichen Grabanlagen*. Ägyptologische Abhandlungen 68 (Wiesbaden: Harrassowitz).

Goyon, J.-Cl. (1999). *Le papyrus d'Imouthès, fils de Psintaês, au Metropolitan Museum of Art de New-York (Papyrus MMA 35.9.21)* (New York: Metropolitan Museum of Art).

Grapow, H. (1915–1917). *Urkunden des ägyptischen Altertums, Abt. V. Religiöse Urkunden* (Leipzig: Hinrichs).

Grewenig M. M., ed. (2014). *Ägypten. Götter, Menschen, Pharaonen. Meisterwerke aus dem Museum Egizio Turin* (Heidelberg: Das Wunderhorn).

Grieshammer, R. (1970). *Das Jenseitsgericht in den Sargtexten*. Ägyptologische Abhandlungen 20 (Wiesbaden: Harrassowitz).

Griffiths, J. G. (1982). "Eight Funerary Paintings with Judgement Scenes in the Swansea Wellcome Museum." *Journal of Egyptian Archaeology* 68: 228–52.

Guermeur, I. 2021. "Le Passeport Pour L'au-Delà De Tekhensephônukhos ($Dd$-$Hnsw$-$Iw≡f$-$ʿnḫ$): Un Document De Respiration Qu'a Fait Isis Pour Son Frère Osiris. Le Papyrus Hiératique Tübingen 2016." In *Questionner Le Sphinx: Mélanges Offerts À Christiane Zivie-Coche Par Ses Élèves, Collègues Et Amis*. Bibliothèque d'étude 178, 2 vols., edited by P. Collombert, L. Coulon, I. Guermeur, and C. Thiers, 619–63 (Le Caire: Institut français d'archéologie orientale du Caire).

Herbin, F.-R. (1994). *Le Livre de parcourir l'éternité*. Orientalia Lovaniensia Analecta 58 (Leuven: Peeters).

Herbin, F.-R. (2008). *Books of Breathing and Related Texts*. Catalogue of the Books of the Dead and Other Religious Texts in the British Museum IV (London: British Museum Press).

Herbin, F.-R. (2012). "La tablette hiéroglyphique MMA 55.144.1." *Égypte Nilotique et Méditerranéenne* 5: 286–314.

Herbin, F.-R. (2013). "Le papyrus magico-funéraire Louvre E 5353." *Égypte Nilotique et Méditerranéenne* 6: 257–89.

Hoffmann, F. and Quack, J. F. (2018). *Anthologie der demotischen Literatur*. Einführungen und Quellentexte zur Ägyptologie 4 (Berlin: Lit).

Hornung, E. (1968). *Altägyptische Höllenvorstellungen*. Abhandlungen der Sächsischen Akademie der Wissenschaften zu Leipzig, Philologisch-historische Klasse 59/3 (Berlin: Akademie-Verlag).

Hornung, E. (1979). *Das Totenbuch der Ägypter* (Zurich; Munich: Artemis).

Ilin-Tomich, A. (2011). "Changes in the *Htp-dj-nsw* Formula in the Late Middle Kingdom and the Second Intermediate Period." *Zeitschrift für Ägyptische Sprache und Altertumskunde* 138: 20–34.

Kaper, O. (2000). "Des dieux nouveaux et des conceptions nouvelles." In *Les Empereurs du Nil*, edited by H. Willems and W. Clarysse, 123–26 (Leuven: Peeters).

Kaper, O. (2001). "Review D. Frankfurter (1998). *Religion in Roman Egypt* (Princeton: University Press)." *Bibliotheca Orientalis* 58(1–2): 126–32.

Kubisch, S. (2008). *Lebensbilder der 2. Zwischenzeit. Biographische Inschriften der 13—17. Dynastie*. Sonderschriften des Deutschen Archäologischen Instituts Kairo 34 (Berlin: de Gruyter).

Kucharek, A. (2010). *Die Klagelieder von Isis und Nephthys in Texten der Griechisch-Römischen Zeit*. Supplemente zu den Schriften der Heidelberger Akademie der Wissenschaften, Philosophisch-Historische Klasse 22 (Heidelberg: Universitätsverlag Winter).

Kucharek, A. (2015). "Vignetten und Exzerpte in Osirisliturgien." In *Liturgical Texts for Osiris and the Deceased in Late Period and Greco-Roman Egypt*. Studien zur spätägyptischen Religion 14, edited by B. Backes and J. Dieleman, 233–44 (Wiesbaden: Harrassowitz).

Kucharek, A. (2017). "A Hieratic Tablet from TT 196 Reexamined." In *Illuminating Osiris. Egyptological Studies in Honor of Mark Smith. Material and Visual Culture of Ancient Egypt* 2, edited by R. Jasnow and Gh. Widmer, 197–214 (Atlanta: Lockwood Press).

Kucharek, A. (2019). "Papyrus PSI inv. I 130: A New Egyptian Source on the Cult of Antinoos." *Göttinger Miszellen* 257: 73–84.

Kucharek, A. (forthcoming). "The Various Fates of Book of the Dead Spell 172." In *Tradition et transmissions des rituels égyptiens anciens: continuités et ruptures*. Studien zur spätägyptischen Religion, edited by F. Contardi and A. H. Pries, 71–94 (Wiesbaden: Harrassowitz).

Kucharek, A. and Coenen, M. (2021). *The Carlsberg Papyri 16: The Lamentations of Isis and Nephthys (Invocation of the Glorifications which the Two Sisters Performed)*. Carsten Niebuhr Institute Publications 46 (Copenhagen: Museum Tusculanum Press).

Kurth, D. (1990). *Der Sarg der Teüris. Eine Studie zum Totenglauben im römerzeitlichen Ägypten*. Aegyptiaca Treverensia 6 (Mainz: Philipp von Zabern).

Laan, G. P. (1995). *Niet ten dode opgeschreven. Spreuk 71 uit het Egyptische Dodenboek* (Amsterdam: PhD).

Lapp, G. (2006). *Totenbuch Spruch 17. Synoptische Textausgabe nach Quellen des Neuen Reiches*. Totenbuchtexte 1 (Basel: Orientverlag).

Lepsius, K. R. (1842). *Das Todtenbuch der Ägypter nach dem hieroglyphischen Papyrus in Turin* (Berlin: Wigand).

Lichtheim, M. (1988). *Ancient Egyptian Autobiographies Chiefly of the Middle Kingdom. A Study and an Anthology*. Orbis Biblicus et Orientalis 84 (Fribourg: Universitätsverlag; Göttingen: Vandenhoeck & Ruprecht).

Lichtheim, M. (1992). *Maat in Egyptian Autobiographies and Related Studies*. Orbis Biblicus et Orientalis 120 (Fribourg: Universitätsverlag; Göttingen: Vandenhoeck & Ruprecht).

Lüscher, B. (2000). *Totenbuch pBerlin P. 10477 aus Achmim (mit Photographien des verwandten pHildesheim 5248)*. Handschriften des Altägyptischen Totenbuchs 6 (Wiesbaden: Harrassowitz).

Meurer, G. (2002). *Die Feinde des Königs in den Pyramidentexten*. Orbis Biblicus et Orientalis 189 (Fribourg: Universitätsverlag, Göttingen: Vandenhoeck & Ruprecht).

Möller, G. (1913). *Die beiden Totenpapyrus Rhind des Museums zu Edinburg* (Leipzig: Hinrichs).

Mosher, M. (1992). "Theban and Memphite Book of the Dead Traditions in the Late Period." *Journal of the American Research Center in Egypt* XXIX: 143–72.

Mosher, M. (2001). *The Papyrus of Hor.* Catalogue of the Books of the Dead in the British Museum II (London: British Museum Press).
Mosher, M. (2002). "The Book of the Dead Tradition at Akhmim During the Late Period." In *Perspectives on Panopolis. An Egyptian Town from Alexander the Great to the Arab Conquest.* Papyrologica Lugduno-Batava 31, edited by A. Egberts, B. P. Muhs, and J. van der Vliet, 201–9 (Leiden; Boston; Cologne: Brill).
Mosher, M. (2016ff.). *The Book of the Dead, Saite Through Ptolemaic Periods. A Study of Traditions Evident in Versions of Texts and Vignettes* (Prescott, AZ: SPBD Studies).
Müller-Roth, M. (2012). "Defining the Book of the Dead." In *Grenzen des Totenbuchs. Ägyptische Papyri zwischen Grab und Ritual/Beyond the Book of the Dead. Egyptian Papyri between Tomb and Ritual*, edited by M. Müller-Roth and M. Höveler-Müller, 29–34 (Rahden; Westf.: Marie Leidorf).
Munro, I. (1994). *Die Totenbuch-Handschriften der 18. Dynastie im Ägyptischen Museum Cairo.* Ägyptologische Abhandlungen 54 (Wiesbaden: Harrassowitz).
Munro, P. (1973). *Die spätägyptischen Totenstelen.* Ägyptologische Forschungen 25 (Glückstadt: J.J. Augustin).
Naville, E. (1902). "The Book of the Dead. Chapter CXLVII." *Proceedings of the Society of Biblical Archaeology* 24: 268–71.
Pleyte, W. (1881). *Chapitres supplémentaires du Livre des Morts 162 à 174* (Leiden: Brill).
Quack, J. F. (1999). "Magie und Totenbuch—eine Fallstudie (pEbers 2,1–6)." *Chronique d'Égypte* 74: 5–17.
Quack, J. F. (2012). "Das Dekret des Amun an Isis. Papyrus Kairo CG 58034 + 58028." In *Auf den Spuren des Sobek. Festschrift für Horst Beinlich zum 28. Dezember 2012. Studien zu den Ritualszenen altägyptischer Tempel* 12, edited by J. Hallof, 223–44 (Dettelbach: Röll).
Quack, J. F. (2015). "Rohrfedertorheiten? Bemerkungen zum römerzeitlichen Hieratisch." In *Ägyptologische "Binsen"-Weisheiten I-II. Neue Forschungen und Methoden der Hieratistik.* Akademie der Wissenschaften und der Literatur Mainz, Abhandlungen der Geistes- und sozialwissenschaftlichen Klasse, Einzelveröffentlichung 14, edited by U. Verhoeven, 435–68 (Mainz: Akademie der Wissenschaften und der Literatur; Stuttgart: Franz Steiner).
Quirke, S. (2013). *Going Out in Daylight—prt m hrw. The Ancient Egyptian Book of the Dead. Translation, Sources, Meanings.* GHP Egyptology 20 (London: Golden House Publications).
von Recklinghausen, D. (2007). *Ägyptische Mumien—Unsterblichkeit im Land der Pharaonen* (Stuttgart: Landesmuseum Württemberg; Mainz: Philipp von Zabern).
Régen, I. (2012). "Ombres. Une iconographie singulière du mort sur des «linceuls» d'époque romaine provenant de Saqqâra." In *Et in Aegypto et ad Aegyptum. Recueil d'études dédiées à Jean-Claude Grenier IV.* Cahiers de l'ENiM 5, edited by A. Gasse, F. Servajean, and C. Tiers, 603–47 (Montpellier: Équipe «Égypte Nilotique et Méditerranéenne»).
Riggs, C. (2005). *The Beautiful Burial in Roman Egypt. Art, Identity, and Funerary Religion* (Oxford: University Press).
Rindi Nuzzolo, C. (2017). "Tradition and Transformation. Retracing Ptah-Sokar-Osiris Figures from Akhmim in Museums and Private Collections." In *(Re)productive Traditions in Ancient Egypt. Proceedings of the Conference Held at the University of Liège, 6th—8th February 2013.* Collection Aegyptiaca Leodiensia 10, edited by T. Gillen, 445–74 (Liège: Presses Universitaires).
Rössler-Köhler, U. (1979). *Kapitel 17 des ägyptischen Totenbuches. Untersuchungen zur Textgeschichte und Funktion eines Textes des altägyptischen Totenliteratur.* Göttinger Orientforschungen 10 (Wiesbaden: Harrassowitz).

Scalf, F. (2014). *Passports to Eternity: Formulaic Demotic Funerary Texts and the Final Phase of Egyptian Funerary Literature in Roman Egypt* (Chicago: PhD).

Scalf, F. (2017a). "The Death of the Book of the Dead." In *Book of the Dead. Becoming God in Ancient Egypt*. Oriental Institute Museum Publications 39, edited by F. Scalf, 139–47 (Chicago: Oriental Institute).

Scalf, F. (2017b). "What Is the Book of the Dead?" In *Book of the Dead. Becoming God in Ancient Egypt*. Oriental Institute Museum Publications 39, edited by F. Scalf, 21–27 (Chicago: Oriental Institute).

Schott, S. (1990). *Bücher und Bibliotheken im Alten Ägypten. Verzeichnis der Buch- und Spruchtitel und der Termini technici* (Wiesbaden: Harrassowitz).

Seeber, C. (1976). *Untersuchungen zur Darstellung des Totengerichts im Alten Ägypten*. Münchner Ägyptologische Studien 35 (Munich: Deutscher Kunstverlag).

Simpson, W. K. (2003). *The Literature of Ancient Egypt. An Anthology of Stories, Instructions, Stelae, Autobiographies, and Poetry* (Yale: University Press).

Smith, M. (1987). *The Mortuary Texts of Papyrus BM 10507*. Catalogue of Demotic Papyri in the British Museum III: (London: British Museum Press).

Smith, M. (2005). *Papyrus Harkness (MMA 31.9.7)* (Oxford: Griffith Institute).

Smith, M. (2009). *Traversing Eternity. Texts for the Afterlife from Ptolemaic and Roman Egypt* (Oxford: University Press).

Smith, M. (2017a). *Following Osiris. Perspectives on the Osirian Afterlife from Four Millenia* (Oxford: University Press).

Smith, M. (2017b). "Transformation and Justification: A Unique Adaptation of Book of the Dead Spell 125 in P. Louvre E 3452." In *Essays for the Library of Seshat. Studies Presented to Janet H. Johnson on the Occasion of her 70th Birthday*. Studies in Ancient Oriental Civilization 70, edited by R. K. Ritner, 363–80 (Chicago: Oriental Institute).

Stadler, M. A. (1999). "The Funerary Texts of Papyrus Turin N. 766: A Demotic Book of Breathing (Part I)." *Enchoria* 25: 76–110.

Stadler, M. A. (2000). "The Funerary Texts of Papyrus Turin N. 766: A Demotic Book of Breathing (Part II)." *Enchoria* 26: 110–24.

Stadler, M. A. (2003). *Der Totenpapyrus des Pa-Month (P. Bibl. nat. 149)*. Studien zum altägyptischen Totenbuch 6 (Wiesbaden: Harrassowitz).

Stadler, M. A. (2009). *Weiser und Wesir. Studien zu Vorkommen, Rolle und Wesen des Gottes Thot im ägyptischen Totenbuch*. Orientalische Religionen in der Antike 1 (Tübingen: Mohr Siebeck).

Stadler, M. A. (2010/2011). "Review Smith, Traversing Eternity. Texts for the Afterlife from Ptolemaic and Roman Egypt." *Enchoria* 32: 154–70.

Stadler, M. A. (2012a). *Einführung in die ägyptische Religion ptolemäisch-römischer Zeit nach den demotischen religiösen Texten*. Einführungen und Quellentexte zur Ägyptologie 7 (Berlin: Lit).

Stadler, M. A. (2012b). "Funerary Religion. The Final Phase of an Egyptian Tradition." In *Oxford Handbook of Roman Egypt*, edited by C. Riggs, 383–97 (Oxford: University Press).

Stadler, M. A. (2015). "Prätexte funerärer Rituale: Königsliturgie, Tempelliturgie, Totenliturgie." In *Liturgical Texts for Osiris and the Deceased in Late Period and Greco-Roman Egypt*. Studien zur spätägyptischen Religion 14, edited by B. Backes and J. Dieleman, 75–90 (Wiesbaden: Harrassowitz).

Stadler, M. A. (2018/2019). "Die Korrektur einer Korrektur. Papyrus Bibliothèque nationale 149 I 24 f. und III 7 f." *Enchoria* 36: 211–20.

Sturtewagen, C. (1991). *The Funerary Papyrus Palau Rib. Nr. Inv. 450*. Estudis de Papirologia I Filologia Bíblica 1 (Barcelona: Seminari de Papirologia).

Taylor, J. H., ed. (2010). *Journey through the Afterlife. Ancient Egyptian Book of the Dead* (London: British Museum Press).

Vittmann, G. (1990). "Ein neuer religiöser demotischer Text (Mumienbrett BM 35464)." *Zeitschrift für Ägyptische Sprache und Altertumskunde* 117: 79–88.

Vleeming, S. P. (2011). *Demotic and Greek-Demotic Mummy Labels and Other Short Texts Gathered from Many Publications (Short Texts II 278–1200)*. Studia Demotica 9 (Leuven: Peeters).

Vuilleumier, S. (2016). *Un rituel osirien en faveur de particuliers à l'époque ptolemaïque. Papyrus Princeton Pharaonic Roll 10*. Studien zur spätägyptischen Religion 15 (Wiesbaden: Harrassowitz).

Wagner, M. (2015). "Das Buch zur Verklärung des Ach." In *Liturgical Texts for Osiris and the Deceased in Late Period and Greco-Roman Egypt*. Studien zur spätägyptischen Religion 14, edited by B. Backes and J. Dieleman, 179–202 (Wiesbaden: Harrassowitz).

Widmer, Gh. (2015). *Résurrection d'Osiris—naissance d'Horus. Les papyrus Berlin P. 6750 et Berlin P. 8765*. Ägyptische und orientalische Papyri und Handschriften des Ägyptischen Museums und Papyrussammlung Berlin 3 (Berlin/Boston: de Gruyter).

Wüthrich, A. (2015). *Édition synoptique et traduction des chapitres supplémentaires du Livre des Morts 162 à 167*. Studien zum altägyptischen Totenbuch 19 (Wiesbaden: Harrassowitz).

CHAPTER 16

# THE BOOK OF THE *BA*

ANDREA KUCHAREK

ONLY two copies of this exceptional funerary composition are known, P.Berlin P 10477 (Fig. 16.1) and P.MacGregor (ed. Beinlich, 2000; color images of the entire P.MacGregor in Mosher, 2019). Both are appended to Book of the Dead scrolls from Akhmim, which are closely comparable in other respects, too, suggesting a common source ("Subtradition B": Mosher, 2002: 206). While in P.MacGregor, the Book of the *Ba* follows the Book of the Dead section (Beinlich, 2000: 24), in P.Berlin P 10477 it precedes the Book of the Dead. Beinlich's (2000: 5) claim that this had originally been the *prôtokollon*, the usually blank space serving as a protective cover of the scroll, has been plausibly questioned by von Lieven (2006: 135) on account of its size—the Book of the *Ba* section is 145.7 centimeters wide. Compared to P.MacGregor, P.Berlin P 10477 features a more extensive text and vignettes of superior quality (Beinlich, 2000: 26; the following descriptions are according to P.Berlin P 10477 if not otherwise indicated). The dating of the Akhmim Book of the Dead papyri is subject to debate (cf. Einaudi, 2015: 25–26; Stadler, 2012: 156; Beinlich, 2000: 3 n. 2 explicitly avoids the question of dating). Suggestions range from as late as the first century CE and the late first century BCE down to the third century BCE. Derchain-Urtel (in Lüscher, 2000: 1, 44–45) dates P.Berlin P 10477 epigraphically to the late first century CE. Her methodology is rejected by von Lieven, 2002: 480–81, who doubts the validity of comparing temple text epigraphy with hieroglyphs executed on papyrus, particularly as the comparative material is not from the Akhmim area. She argues that Greco-Roman temples are well known for their idiosyncratic writing systems, and points out that in the one instance in which Derchain-Urtel's argument is based on Akhmim material—the large corpus of stelae— the parallels date to the Ptolemaic Period. Von Lieven concludes that the closer study of late hieroglyphic papyri as well as their vignettes (which are not included in Derchain-Urtel's assessment) is an indispensable precondition for reliably dating the Akhmim papyri. Mosher (2001: 31–36; 2002: 208), argues, on the basis of style and the poor quality of text and vignettes, for the late first century BCE. Discussing the Book of the *Ba* in particular, the presence of some demotic numbers is, in his opinion, further evidence for a late Ptolemaic date (Mosher, 2001: 34 with n. 19). However, demotic numbers already

FIG. 16.1. P.Berlin P 10477 Book of the *Ba* section. © Ägyptisches Museum und Papyrussammlung, Staatliche Museen zu Berlin, Photo by Sandra Steiß.

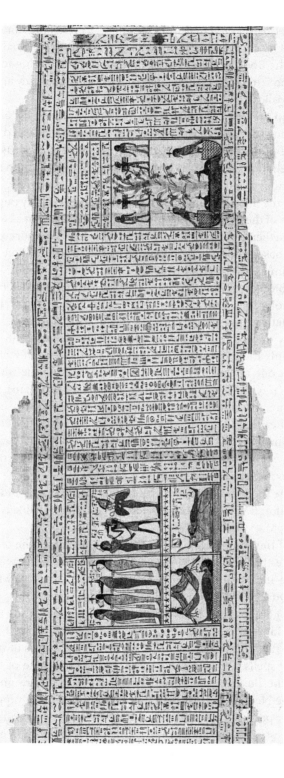

FIG. 16.1. Continued

occur in a most likely early Ptolemaic funerary papyrus from the same region, P.MMA 35.9.21 from Meir (Quack, 2004: 331; Smith, 2009: 90 with n. 112; Kucharek, 2010: 402). Its sister papyrus, the Book of the Dead P.MMA 35.9.20, belonging to the same owner and produced by the same scribe, features the drawing of a mummy annotated with demotic numbers (Mosher, 2020: 465).

De Meulenaere, in a review of Mosher, 2001, bases his much earlier estimate on prosopographical evidence (de Meulenaere, 2002: 493, strongly supported by Kockelmann, 2008: I, 25–26). He points out a number of objects (stelae, a papyrus, and an offering table) that in all likelihood belonged to Hor, the owner of the Akhmim Book of the Dead (P.London BM EA 10479), published by Mosher, and his close family. These objects can be reliably dated to the third century BCE, a date that consequently ought to be valid for the Akhmim Books of the Dead and the appended Books of the *Ba* as well.

In fact, there is further, hitherto unconsidered evidence in support of de Meulenaere's assessment. This is based not on prosopography but on the decoration of some funerary items from Akhmim clearly derived from Book of the *Ba* vignettes. Two Ptah-Sokar-Osiris figures, an object category not attested beyond the Ptolemaic Period (Raven, 1978/79: 291; Rindi Nuzzolo, 2017: 469) feature such vignettes on the top of their pedestals (cf. description of vignettes 1 and 2, p. 327–8). For one of these, formerly in the Lady Meux collection and now on loan to the Basle Museum (Budge, 1896: 86–87, pl. V; Wiese, 1998: 80, no. 99), only Budge's description is available: "a scene in which four souls are standing by a lake, one at each corner, and drinking water." The image on the other figure, Cairo RT 28/3/25/7 (Varga, 1993: 196, Fig. 7; Haslauer, 2012: 210), is obviously quite similar: at each corner of a lake there is a *ba* bird, two of them human-headed, the others falcon- and cobra-headed. They drink from libation vessels positioned on all four sides of the lake. The coffin of the owner of the latter figure, Pahes (Graz, Archäologiemuseum Schloss Eggenberg 23927), also features a Book of the *Ba* vignette, a reclining cow carrying a mummy on its back (Haslauer, 2012: 200, Fig. 14; see vignette 3, p. 327–8). This coffin is dated to the second century BCE by Haslauer (2012: 211), and the closely comparable coffin London BM EA 29582 has been dated to the third/second century BCE (Brech, 2013: 274, 278).

As for the age of the composition itself, the corrupt state of the text in both copies suggests a template that had already deteriorated over an unknown period (Stadler, 2009: 156–57). The inclusion of parts of a Book of the Dead spell may indicate the New Kingdom (Quack, 2001: 209; Stadler, 2009: 156–57; see p. 333, this chapter). Beinlich (2000: 24) argues for a New Kingdom date because of the retrograde orientation of the text. Lines from an offering glorification widely attested as early as the New Kingdom are further evidence for this assessment. Passages of that spell were included in funerary spells well into the Roman Period, but some of the lines inserted into the Book of the *Ba* (see p. 327, this chapter, on Text E) are not known to have been used since the New Kingdom (see Assmann, 2005: 149–77, supplemented by the author's research). Specifically, there are two lines from the very end of the spell (ll. 31 and 32) that are attested several times in the early New Kingdom in extended versions of the spell (Assmann, 2005: 149, 152, 153, 224) and again, as an isolated passage, on an early Nineteenth-Dynasty stela from Deir el-Medina (Bruyère, 1933: 88, pl. XXXVII). The other lines from that spell in the Book of the *Ba*, lines 15–17, are attested up to the Twenty-sixth Dynasty and again on a Roman Period mummy board (Assmann, 2005, 220–21; Vittmann, 1994: 227, 268). Line 15, together with one or more of the preceding lines, is attested on several Ptolemaic and Roman Period objects (Quirke, 2013: 554; Spiegelberg, 1912: 41–42, pl. III/2; Kurth, 1990: 22; 2010: 77–78, 158, 172–74).

Somewhat surprisingly, considering its exclusive provenance from Akhmim, the place does not feature in the text at all. Among the considerable number of toponyms and other topographical identifiers, Abydos, Memphis, and Heliopolis occur most frequently. According to Beinlich (2000: 23), this suggests that the Book of the *Ba* originated in the Memphite-Heliopolitan region; foremost, however, these are places associated with the funerary deities Osiris and (Ptah-)Sokar and funerary motives in general, irrespective of the geographic origin of a specific text.

Due to its striking layout, the Book of the *Ba* is easily distinguishable from the Book of the Dead. The hieroglyphic text is not simply arranged in horizontal and vertical lines but also features lines framing the entire composition as well as one of the vignettes. It has been argued that the layout, similar to the Book of the Fayum and the Book of Nut, suggests a monumental model, such as a ceiling or floor decoration (Quack, 2001: 209). These compositions are not funerary but rather cult-topographical and astronomical (Ryholt, 2005: 148, 153). Whether the Book of the *Ba* was devised for cultic, i.e., Osirian, or funerary purposes is an unresolved question (von Lieven, 2006: 136). However, some of the spells bear evidence of private funerary as opposed to Osirian use (cf. Smith, 2015): for example, Text B includes the phrases "may you fly in the house of Osiris" and "may Osiris come to your voice" (Beinlich, 2000: 42); the initial address of Text D to the deceased is "may Osiris be pleased with you in the god's domain, the Great God, lord of Abydos" (Beinlich, 2000: 54). In Text G, an offering formula, the offerings are granted, in the first place, by "Osiris Khontamenti, the Great God, lord of Abydos." In the absence of parallel versions to any of the texts, it cannot be discounted that these phrases were added at a later stage, though. At any rate, the monumental setting of the Book of the *Ba* would be difficult to imagine in a private funerary context.

The title Book of the *Ba* is an Egyptological makeshift as the text itself is devoid of a title. Rather, it is a compilation of eight spells lacking introductory passages. As the modern title suggests, the purpose of the compilation is to enable the addressee to become a *ba*. This manifestation of the deceased was frequently depicted as a human-headed bird (cf. the vignettes in Figures 16.2–5 this chapter). The bird shape refers to an eminent aspect of the *ba*, its ability to move freely, in contrast to the stationary mummy (see Janák, 2016, in more detail).

The text is notoriously difficult and the translations given below are occasionally tentative (sequence according to Beinlich, 2000; cf. Quack, 2001; 2013: 547–53; for the exact positions of the sections see diagrams in Beinlich, 2000: 10–17):

A) Framing the entire composition: Invocations for the deceased (ll. 1–9). Incipit: "Oh Osiris, Osiris Khontamenti, lord of Abydos...."

This is followed by an extensive litany of diverse manifestations of Osiris and Anubis, as well as several groups of deities associated with either Osirian or Heliopolitan references, for instance "the lords who are in Abydos, the Great Ennead of the Lord of the West, the *ba*s of Heliopolis, the lords of the Great House." By far the largest section of the spell is taken up by an enumeration of mostly Osirian priests, and the final passage of the litany constitutes an all-encompassing summary of those invoked to grant their breath to the papyrus owner: "Every man, every woman, every human being, all *pat*-people, all *rekhyt*-people, all gods and goddesses in the god's domain/necropolis, invoked in each and every of their names." As a result, the papyrus owner is then received into the company of the gods, to be provided for in the "temple of Abydos" and to be established in the "lake(?) of the *ba*s"—probably a reference to vignette 2 (see p. 327–8, this chapter).

B) Between vignettes 1 and 2: Glorification of the deceased, emphasizing his transformation into various birds and animals and the associated ability to reach the sky, the underworld, and places on earth (ll. 9–37), reminiscent of the Book of Traversing Eternity. Incipit: "Oh to you, Osiris of NN, may you come in peace to your place in your house . . ."

As in Text A, Abydos and Heliopolis are repeatedly mentioned, complemented by, for example, Memphis (*Ankh-taui*), Edfu (*wetjes-Hor*), Busiris (or perhaps Mendes), Hermopolis (*Wenu*), and Asyut. A long passage details the funerary rites to be performed by the son of the deceased—enabling him to join the underworld and its denizens by reciting offering formulae and by embalming, wrapping, and anointing the mummy. In accord with its overall theme, the spell ends with the wish that the deceased may follow "the Great God, lord of the ways . . . may you fly up to heaven and unite with the two horizons."

On the intrusive Book of the Dead passage in this spell, see p. 333, this chapter.

C) Framing vignette 2: Invocation of the "*ba*s" to grant the drinking of water (ll. 37–55). Incipit: "Oh *ba*s, rulers of shade, you gods who follow Hebi-khesti . . . ." This spell is marked by a profusion of water-related vocabulary: "Oh those who are in the water of the channel of which a god lives, oh those who are in the lake of the natron house, oh *ba*s who enter into the lakes of the glorified ones . . . oh you who drink from the primeval waters (*nun*) . . . may you cause to live the beautiful *ba* with water, breath and ointment(?) for the Osiris of NN."

D) Between vignettes 2 and 3: Libations and cloth for the deceased granted by Osiris (ll. 55–61). Incipit: "Oh Osiris of NN, may Osiris be pleased with you in the god's domain . . . ." The focus of this short spell is clearly funerary, alluding to the "good burial in the midst of the west" and, particularly, to various kinds of (mummy-)cloth as well as to libations: "May he [Osiris] grant you . . . a libation of water from the hands of his followers, may he grant you cloth in the temple of Abydos, may he grant you . . . a headband in the Great Place; may he grant you water emanating from Elephantine, the water emanating from the hole, the hidden water emanating from the cave of the primeval water."

E) Following vignette 3: A short address to some deities, followed by a glorification of the deceased's *ba* (ll. 62–77). Incipit: "Oh Re, oh Amun . . ."; "Oh you *ba* of the Osiris of NN who breathes above her head as a living *ba* . . .". The spell comprises some verses from a popular offering glorification (ll. 15, 32, 16–17, 31 according to Assmann, 2005: 147–224). It focuses on food and drink but also refers to the other default wishes for breath, light, and community with the gods: "Oh *ba* with great breath in Abydos . . . Re rises for you within his shrine in order to shine his rays for you in the god's domain daily . . . Hesat, she grants you her milk . . . you receive your sustenance at the entrance of the mounds . . . Hathor, she grants you libations and offerings in Heliopolis . . . a good burial in the house of the *duat*, it contains everything."

F) Next to vignette 4: Speech by the *ba* to the deceased, referring to a sycamore tree (ll. 77–86). Incipit: "I am a *ba* who pervades a place . . .". The spell is obviously associated with vignette 4 (see p. 331–2). The *ba* of the deceased wishes to alight on the branches of the sycamore, referring repeatedly to the *ba* as the children of the tree, which is a manifestation of the sky goddess Nut: "Oh whose children go forth in the night to breathe the beautiful air, mother of excellent *bas* . . . oh sycamore of all *bas*."

G) Following vignette 4: Offering formula to Osiris, the sun god, and Ptah (ll. 88–91). Incipit: "An offering that the king gives. Offerings of Osiris Khontamenti, Great God, lord of Abydos . . .". The offering request is quite conventional: "May they (the gods) grant an invocation offering of bread, beer, cattle and fowl, offerings and provisions of all good and pure things, of all sweet and pleasant things on which a god lives."

H) Following text G: Concluding speech to Atum, who is invoked to come to the *ba* of the deceased (ll. 91–93). Incipit: "The going of the *ba*'s breath to every tomb. Come to me, my father Atum, in peace . . .".

All four vignettes feature *ba* birds and water. Vignette 1 (Fig. 16.2) consists of two nearly identical images, arranged at right angles to each other. Each depicts two *ba* birds receiving water from a large libation vase between them. Remarkably, only one of these birds is human-headed; the heads of the others are those of a bird with a thin straight beak (not necessarily an ibis), a cobra, and a falcon. While not exactly matching the transformations mentioned in Text B, the various heads certainly refer to the mutability desired by the deceased's *ba* (Beinlich, 2000: 19–20); the various heads also occur in the vignette on the Ptah-Sokar-Osiris statuette Cairo RT 28/3/25/7 described on p. 324. The caption assigns the four *bas* to the four directions whence they have come (Beinlich, 2000: 71), consistent with the beginning of Text B, "may you come in peace to your place in your house". The return of the migratory *ba* to the stationary mummy in the tomb is a recurring theme in the funerary literature, the best-known example being BD 89, the "Spell for letting the *ba* rest on his corpse," and the so-called BD 191, "Spell for bringing the *ba* to the body" (Schneider, 1994).

Vignette 2 (Fig. 16.3) is closely related to the preceding one, showing four human-headed *ba* birds drinking from a pool (the previously mentioned Ptah-Sokar-Osiris

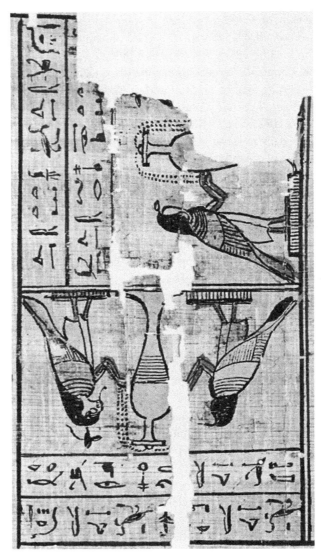

**FIG. 16.2.** P.Berlin P 10477 Book of the *Ba* section, vignette 1. © Ägyptisches Museum und Papyrussammlung, Staatliche Museen zu Berlin, Photo by Sandra Steiß.

statuette Cairo RT 28/3/25/7 features a combination of vignettes 1 and 2: Rindi Nuzzolo, 2017: 453 Fig. 7). The vignette clearly belongs to Text C, which frames it and which is exclusively concerned with the provisioning of water for the deceased; the final line of Text A may also allude to this vignette. The complex vignette 3 (Fig. 16.4) consists of four separate images. The two at the bottom both depict a mummy resting on its back. On the left, Isis and Nephthys, clearly influenced by *ba* bird iconography, hover above it in the shape of human-headed birds. On the right, the mummy rests on the back of a

FIG. 16.3. P.Berlin P 10477 Book of the *Ba* section, vignette 2.© Ägyptisches Museum und Papyrussammlung, Staatliche Museen zu Berlin, Photo by Sandra Steiß.

reclining cow, which the caption describes as "Hathor, mistress of the west, who protects the Osiris of NN." Both images are bordered by a rectangle of water at the bottom and a star-studded sky at the top. The top left image depicts four upright mummies, the sons of Horus, their diverse heads reminiscent of vignette 1. To the right, the deceased is received by Anubis and brought into the presence of Osiris Khontamenti, who grants her protection.

The two images to the left in combination are reminiscent of the unique introductory vignette of the early Roman Period P.Rhind I from Thebes: flanked by Anubis and Thoth, the mummy rests on top of a rectangular body of water; an *udjat*-eye upon it indicates the soundness of the body, and above it stand the four mummiform sons of Horus (Möller, 1913: pl. I; Assmann/Kucharek, 2008: Fig. 24). Perhaps the water alludes to the initial purification of the body in the purification tent before it enters the embalmer's workshop proper. This is also suggestive of a scene on some Late Period coffins from el-Hibe (e.g., Hildesheim 1954: Eggebrecht, 1990: 31). The two images on the left-hand side of the vignette refer to the physical

FIG. 16.4. P.Berlin P 10477 Book of the *Ba* section, vignette 3. © Ägyptisches Museum und Papyrussammlung, Staatliche Museen zu Berlin, Photo by Sandra Steiß.

body in the hall of embalming, the stationary mummy being accompanied by its intestines represented by the sons of Horus. The two images to the right are linked by their captions, which both refer to the west and to protection, the latter with the identical phrase *jrj s3*, "performing protection." They depict the deceased being received by Hathor and Osiris. While Hathor signifies the necropolis, therefore carrying the deceased in her mummy aspect, Osiris receives her as a justified person in the afterlife, depicted as when she was alive. The intermediary stage between the two states, the Judgment of the Dead, the most common theme of the Book of the Dead, is omitted. While Beinlich feels unable to assign a text to the vignette group, I would suggest that Text D, to the immediate left, is associated with it, referring not only to a "good burial" and various kinds of cloth from Osirian places, indicating mummy bandages, but, pointedly, to justification, its sole mention in the entire Book of the

*Ba*. The concluding phrase, "May the *ba* go forth from the god's domain," alludes to freedom of movement as the *ba*-specific attainment achieved through justification.

The central element of the fourth and final vignette (Fig. 16.5) is a tree with numerous human-headed *ba* birds alighting on its branches (*pace* Billing, 2002: 242, who states they "climb up on the branches"). The tree rises from a rectangular body of water flanked by two basket-like containers, also filled with water and with a *ba* bird on top. A jackal reclines on each side of the tree trunk, apparently upon the water. Also flanking the tree but on a raised level are four human figures: two males next to the tree appear to touch or grasp its branches, a gesture that likely indicates veneration and/or protection. Their upper bodies are obscured by four thick horizontal lines, lending them a passing resemblance to anthropomorphous *djed* pillars. Behind each of them, the deceased stands in

FIG. 16.5. P.Berlin P 10477 Book of the *Ba* section, vignette 4. © Ägyptisches Museum und Papyrussammlung, Staatliche Museen zu Berlin, Photo by Sandra Steiß.

a posture of reverence (both papyri were owned by females, but only P.MacGregor correctly depicts women). Such symmetrical compositions with praising and/or protecting figures are well known from Osirian contexts (Kucharek, 2018: 80, Figs. 1, 2). The vignette is obviously associated with the adjacent Text F, which focuses on the mobility of the *ba*, combined with the wish to alight on the branches of the "sycamore of all *bas*." The sky goddess Nut, often evoked as a tree goddess dispensing nourishment, provides for her son Osiris in this aspect: "[His] mother Nut, as a sycamore, protects him and rejuvenates his *ba* in her branches" (Philae temple: Koemoth, 1994: 206). According to the "Khoiak Text," a manual for Osirian mysteries, an annually manufactured Sokar figurine is to rest for several days on a bed of sycamore branches that reflect the womb of his mother, Nut (Koemoth, 1994: 203). The maternal and caring aspect of the tree is a major motif of Text F, invoking it as "mother of the excellent *bas*" who provides shade and breath to her children.

Most elements of the iconography of the vignette—tree, water, *ba* birds—are familiar from Book of the Dead vignettes, from numerous scenes in tombs, and from funerary equipment derived from these. Of the unknown aspects, the *djed* pillar-like men remain a mystery, while jackals reclining on a shrine-like representation of the hall of embalming (*sḥ-nṯr, pr-nfr*) are attested as funerary guardians and are depicted as such, for example in the vignette of BD spell 151 (Lüscher, 1998: 24, 35–37). As the embalming hall is a place of rejuvenation and revivification, the same may apply to the water the tree rises from. While thus unique regarding its specific iconography, the central motif of the vignette and the key issues of the accompanying text are well known from a cluster of Book of the Dead spells whose purpose is to provide the deceased with air and water. Spells 54 to 63 are united by their similar titles, mostly variations of "Spell for breathing air and having power over water" (Quirke, 2013: 135). Vignettes for several of these (see Billing, 2002: 235–38) feature a partly anthropomorphic tree presenting water and often a tray of food offerings to the deceased (Billing, 2002: 231–43). Only one of these spells, BD 59, actually refers to the tree, identifying it as the "sycamore of Nut." Beyond the general theme and the motif of the sycamore tree, neither the Book of the Dead spells nor their vignettes share any specific aspects with Text F and its vignette in the Book of the *Ba*. However, Beinlich (2000: 23) states that numerous offering tables from Akhmim feature sycamores as well as BD spells 58–59. An early Roman painted mummy shroud features a curious vignette that may be conceptually related to the Book of the *Ba* vignette. The deceased presents a mummiform statuette to Osiris, who has risen upon his bier as if enthroned. Between them is a tree with several birds that have alighted on its top branches: a falcon, a human-headed *ba* bird, and a black bird perhaps meant to be a swallow. The corresponding vignette to the right features a tree goddess scene (Moscow I.1a.5763: Kurth, 2010: 16–18). The text framing the shroud comprises an invocation of the deceased to Osiris to let him ascend heavenwards "as a falcon and a goose on the splendid branches in Busiris" (Kurth, 2010: 8–9), reminiscent of Text F of the Book of the *Ba*. The shroud may be from Akhmim, a provenance tentatively proposed by the Bonn Totenbuch Projekt database (totenbuch.awk.nrw.de/objekt/tm134089), while Kurth (2010: 33) sees no evidence indicating a place of origin.

P.Berlin P 10477 and P.MacGregor bear evidence of a link between the Book of the *Ba* and the Book of the Dead sections. In the Book of the *Ba* of P.Berlin P 10477, the final Text H did not entirely cover the remaining space; a passage from BD 17 was inserted, probably to avoid an unsightly blank space (Beinlich, 2000: 17; criticized by von Lieven, 2006: 135). The passage (corresponding to parts of lines 27, 28–29 in section r according to Lepsius, 1842: VIII) differs significantly from its actual BD 17 counterpart in P.Berlin P 10477 (Lüscher, 2000: photo pl. 7, ll. 118, 124) and therefore cannot simply have been copied from one part of the papyrus to the other. In any case, this hint at a connection between the Book of the Dead and the Book of the *Ba* is confirmed by the fact that, conversely, the BD 17 copy in this Book of the Dead features an otherwise unattested passage that fits neatly into the concluding section (not extant in P.MacGregor) of Text B (Beinlich, 2000: 13, 46–49). Rößler-Köhler (in Lüscher, 2000: 42–43) points out another unique intrusive passage in this copy of BD 17, assembled from sections of BD 130, 26, and 27. The most likely Book of the *Ba* passage is seamlessly incorporated into BD 17 (Lüscher, 2000: photo pl. 6, ll. 87–93) between BD 17 sections e and f (Lüscher, 2000: 12, division according to Lepsius, 1842: VII). In terms of both structure and content, the inserted passage is alien to the surrounding BD 17, a spell largely made up of numerous explanatory glosses to statements by the deceased (Quirke, 2013: 52–53; Assmann/Kucharek, 2008: 819–21). In contrast, the intrusive section, like Text B proper, is a sequence of glorifying phrases addressed to the deceased, focusing on transformation and mobility:

> You are a splendid vulture, the White One (Nekhbet) of Nekhen! May you take the shape of a living serpent in Thebes, may you proceed to the cave, may you go forth as a hole-snake . . . may you take the shape of a jackal in the White City, may you follow the Great God in the festival of Sokar, may you traverse that beautiful ground in Ankh-taui (Memphis) . . . may you take the shape of a divine *benu*-bird in the *benben*-house in Heliopolis.

The P.MacGregor Book of the *Ba* also comprises evidence of an affinity with BD 17, if much more concise than P.Berlin P 10477 (Beinlich, 2000: 35 n. 5, 36). The few words appear to have been taken at random from section f (Lepsius, 1842: VII, 9).

These interspersions—BD 17 and otherwise—contradict Beinlich's claim that "therefore, the Book of the *Ba* quite certainly was not projected at the same time as the Book of the Dead for this papyrus"[1] (Beinlich, 2000: 5; see also p. 321). A second, hitherto unnoticed connection between the Book of the Dead and the Book of the *Ba* in the Berlin papyrus is the BD 151 vignette (Fig. 16.6; Lüscher, 2000: photo pl. 18). Of the four *ba* birds exceptionally depicted here, only

---

[1] "Das Ba-Buch ist also keineswegs gleichzeitig mit dem Totenbuch für den Papyrus konzipiert worden."

FIG. 16.6. P.Berlin P 10477 Book of the Dead section, BD 151 vignette. © Ägyptisches Museum und Papyrussammlung, Staatliche Museen zu Berlin, Photo by Sandra Steiß.

two are human-headed; the others feature the heads of a cobra and a thin-beaked bird, respectively, in obvious congruence to vignette 1 of the Book of the *Ba*. While this may be due to the draughtman's whim, with no intrinsic correlation, it is further evidence that both sections of the papyrus, the Book of the *Ba* and the Book of the Dead, were created in one go.

This short account of the Book of the *Ba* certainly demonstrates the need for closer study of this genuinely original creation of the rich and sometimes idiosyncratic funerary culture of Greco-Roman Akhmim. The layout, structure, texts, and vignettes of the Book of the *Ba* provide multiple approaches for analysis, and each of these aspects requires further elucidation. In addition to the composition itself, there is the enigma of its precise relationship with the Book of the Dead, particularly BD 17, of which apparently random snippets are interspersed among the Book of the *Ba* texts. The fact that both copies were not just added to Book of the Dead scrolls but form part of the same papyrus underlines the intimate connection between the two—while the presence of Book of the *Ba* vignettes on other burial objects reflects its impact on the funerary culture of Akhmim in general.

# Bibliography

Assmann, J. (2005). *Altägyptische Totenliturgien II. Totenliturgien und Totensprüche in Grabinschriften des Neuen Reiches*. Supplemente zu den Schriften der Heidelberger Akademie der Wissenschaften, Philosophisch-Historische Klasse 17 (Heidelberg: Universitätsverlag Winter).

Assmann, J. and Kucharek, A. (2008). *Ägyptische Religion. Totenliteratur* (Frankfurt: Verlag der Weltreligionen).

Beinlich, H. (2000). *Das Buch vom Ba*. Studien zum altägyptischen Totenbuch 4 (Wiesbaden: Harrassowitz).

Billing, N. (2002). *Nut. The Goddess of Life in Text and Iconography*. Uppsala Studies in Egyptology 5 (Uppsala: Department of Archaeology and Ancient History).

Brech, R. (2013). *Spätägyptische Särge aus Achmim. Eine typologische und chronologische Studie*. Aegyptiaca Hamburgiensa 3 (Gladbeck: PeWe-Verlag).

Bruyère, B. (1933). *Rapport sur les Fouilles de Deir el Médineh (1930)*. Fouilles de l'Institut français d'archéologie orientale VIII/3 (Cairo: Institut français d'archéologie orientale).

Budge, E. A. W. (1896). *Some Account on the Collection of Egyptian Antiquities in the Possession of Lady Meux* (London: Harrison and Sons).

Eggebrecht, A., ed. (1990). *Suche nach Unsterblichkeit. Totenkult und Unsterblichkeitsglaube im Alten Ägypten* (Mainz: Philipp von Zabern).

Einaudi, S. (2015). "Le papyrus de Pasenedjemibnakht (Louvre E 11078): un Livre des Morts de tradition thébaine à Akhmîm." In *Documents de Théologies Thébaines Tardives 3*. Cahiers de l'ENiM 13, edited by C. Thiers, 7–27 (Montpellier: Équipe "Égypte Nilotique et Méditerranéenne").

Haslauer, G. (2012). "Aegyptiaca im Archäologiemuseum Schloss Eggenberg, Teil 1." *Schild von Steier* 25: 194–223.

Janák, J. (2016). "Ba." In *UCLA Encyclopedia of Egyptology*, edited by J. Dieleman and W. Wendrich (Los Angeles: http://digital2.library.ucla.edu/viewItem.do?ark=21198/zz002k7g85).

Kockelmann, H. (2008). *Untersuchungen zu den späten Totenbuch-Handschriften auf Mumienbinden*. Studien zum altägyptischen Totenbuch 12 (Wiesbaden: Harrassowitz).

Koemoth, P. P. (1994). *Osiris et les arbres. Contribution à l'étude des arbres sacrés de l'Égypte ancienne*. Aegyptiaca Leodiensia 3 (Liège: C.I.P.L.).

Kucharek, A. (2010). *Die Klagelieder von Isis und Nephthys in Texten der Griechisch-Römischen Zeit*. Supplemente zu den Schriften der Heidelberger Akademie der Wissenschaften, Philosophisch-Historische Klasse 22 (Heidelberg: Universitätsverlag Winter).

Kucharek, A. (2018). "Mourning and Lamentation on Coffins." In *Ancient Egyptian Coffins. Craft Traditions and Functionality*. British Museum Publications on Egypt and Sudan 4, edited by J.H. Taylor and M. Vandenbeusch, 77–115 (Leuven: Peeters).

Kurth, D. (1990). *Der Sarg der Teüris. Eine Studie zum Totenglauben im römerzeitlichen Ägypten*. Aegyptiaca Treverensia 6 (Mainz: Philipp von Zabern).

Kurth, D. (2010). *Materialien zum Totenglauben im römerzeitlichen Ägypten* (Hützel: Backe).

Lepsius, K. R. (1842). *Das Todtenbuch der Ägypter nach dem hieroglyphischen Papyrus in Turin* (Berlin: Wigand).

von Lieven, A. (2002). "Review Lüscher, B. (2000)." *Bibliotheca Orientalis* 97: 477–81.

von Lieven, A. (2006). "Review Beinlich, H. (2000)." *Orientalistische Literaturzeitung* 101: 133–37.

Lüscher, B. (1998). *Untersuchungen zu Totenbuch Spruch 151*. Studien zum Altägyptischen Totenbuch 2 (Wiesbaden: Harrassowitz).

Lüscher, B. (2000). *Totenbuch pBerlin P. 10477 aus Achmim (mit Photographien des verwandten pHildesheim 5248)*. Handschriften des Altägyptischen Totenbuchs 6 (Wiesbaden: Harrassowitz).

de Meulenaere, H. (2002). "Review Mosher (2001)." *Bibliotheca Orientalis* 59: 491–93.

Möller, G. (1913). *Die beiden Totenpapyrus Rhind des Museums zu Edinburg* (Leipzig: Hinrichs).

Mosher, M. (2001). *The Papyrus of Hor*. Catalogue of the Books of the Dead in the British Museum II (London: British Museum Press).

Mosher, M. (2002). "The Book of the Dead Tradition at Akhmim During the Late Period." In *Perspectives on Panopolis. An Egyptian Town from Alexander the Great to the Arab Conquest*. Papyrologica Lugduno-Batava 31, edited by A. Egberts, B. P. Muhs, and J. van der Vliet, 201–9 (Leiden; Boston; Cologne: Brill).

Mosher, M. (2019). "Revisiting P. MacGregor." In *The Book of the Dead, Saite Through Ptolemaic Periods. Essays on Books of the Dead and Related Topics*, edited by M. Mosher, 421–54 (Prescott, AZ: SPBD Studies).

Mosher, M. (2020). "A Mystery of Numbers." In *The Book of the Dead, Saite Through Ptolemaic Periods. Essays on Books of the Dead and Related Topics*, edited by M. Mosher, 461–65 (Prescott, AZ: SPBD Studies).

Quack, J. F. (2001). "Review Beinlich (2000)." *Enchoria* 27: 209–11.

Quack, J. F. (2004). "Der pränatale Geschlechtsverkehr von Isis und Osiris sowie eine Notiz zum Alter des Osiris." *Studien zur Altägyptischen Kultur* 32: 327–32.

Quirke, S. (2013). *Going out in Daylight—prt m hrw. The Ancient Egyptian Book of the Dead. Translation, Sources, Meanings*. GHP Egyptology 20 (London: Golden House Publications).

Raven, M. J. (1978/79). "Papyrus-sheaths and Ptah-Sokar-Osiris Statues." *Oudheidkundige Mededelingen uit het Rijksmuseum van Oudheden te Leiden* 59/60: 251–96.

Rindi Nuzzolo, C. (2017). "Tradition and Transformation: Retracing Ptah-Sokar-Osiris Figures from Akhmimin Museums and Private Collections." In *(Re)productive Traditions in Ancient Egypt. Proceedings of the Conference Held at the University of Liège, 6th—8th February 2013*. Collection Aegyptiaca Leodiensia 10, edited by T. Gillen, 445–74 (Liège: Presses Universitaires).

Rößler-Köhler, U. (2000). "Tradierungsgeschichtliche Bemerkungen zum Text von Tb 17 in pBerlin P. 10477 und der Achmimer Gruppe." In *Totenbuch pBerlin P. 10477 aus Achmim (mit Photographien des verwandten pHildesheim 5248)*. Handschriften des Altägyptischen Totenbuchs 6, edited by B. Lüscher, 35–43(Wiesbaden: Harrassowitz).

Ryholt, K. (2005). "On the Contents and Nature of the Tebtunis Temple Library. A Status Report." In *Tebtynis und Soknopaiu Nesos. Leben im römerzeitlichen Fajum*, edited by S. Lippert and M. Schentuleit, 141–70 (Wiesbaden: Harrassowitz).

Schneider, H. D. (1994). "Bringing the *ba* to the Body. A Glorification Spell for Padinekhtnebef." In *Hommages à Jean Leclant IV*. Bibliothèque d'Étude 106/4, edited by C. Berger, G. Clerc, and N. Grimal, 355–62 (Cairo: Institut français d'archéologie orientale).

Smith, M. (2009). *Traversing Eternity. Texts for the Afterlife from Ptolemaic and Roman Egypt* (Oxford: University Press).

Smith, M. (2015). "Whose Ritual? Osirian Texts and Texts Written for the Deceased in P. BM EA 10209: A Case Study." In *Liturgical Texts for Osiris and the Deceased in Late Period and Greco-Roman Egypt*. Studien zur spätägyptischen Religion 14, edited by B. Backes and J. Dieleman, 161–77 (Wiesbaden: Harrassowitz).

Spiegelberg, W. (1912). Hieroglyphisch-demotische Mumienetiketten. *Zeitschrift für Ägyptische Sprache und Altertumskunde* 50: 40–42.

Stadler, M. A. (2009). *Weiser und Wesir. Studien zu Vorkommen, Rolle und Wesen des Gottes Thot im ägyptischen Totenbuch*. Orientalische Religionen in der Antike 1 (Tübingen: Mohr Siebeck).

Stadler, M. A. (2012). *Einführung in die ägyptische Religion ptolemäisch-römischer Zeit nach den demotischen religiösen Texten*. Einführungen und Quellentexte zur Ägyptologie 7 (Berlin: Lit).

Varga, E. (1993). "Recherche généalogique." In *Aegyptus museis rediviva. Miscellanea in honorem Hermanni de Meulenaere*, edited by L. Limme and J. Strybol, 185–96 (Brussels: Musées royaux d'Art et d'Histoire).

Vittmann, G. (1994). "Ein Mumienbrett im Britischen Museum (BM 36502)." In *Zwischen den Beiden Ewigkeiten (Festschrift Thausing)*, edited by M. Bietak, J. Holaubek, H. Mukarovsky, and H. Satzinger, 222–75 (Vienna).

Wiese, A. (1998). *Ägyptische Kunst im Antikenmuseum Basel und Sammlung Ludwig. Neue Leihgaben, Schenkungen und Erwerbungen* (Basle: Antikenmuseum Basel und Sammlung Ludwig).

# PART IV

# PARTICULAR ASPECTS OF THE BOOK OF THE DEAD'S CONTENTS

# CHAPTER 17

# THEMATIC GROUPS AND SEQUENCES OF SPELLS

## FELICITAS WEBER

## INTRODUCTION

MORE than 170 years have passed by since one of the most influential editions of Book of the Dead papyri was published, which started a perpetual study on the Book of the Dead. In 1842, Richard Lepsius decided to use the pattern of P.Turin 1791 as a template and assigned a numeric designation, today known as BD chapter or BD spell, to each visually distinguishable unit. Lepsius (1842: 3–6) identified these BD chapters regardless of any grouping or contextual information or interpretation. His work formed the basis not only for all subsequent studies but also the ongoing identification and numbering of new BD chapters. Until today, this system provides the scholars with a handy reference model applicable to each individual manuscript irrespective of its origin in time and tradition. The 165 chapters of P.Turin 1791 were expanded by Naville (1886) and Pleyte (1881). However, while studying this corpus, one must not forget that this numeric system is merely a convention derived from an individual specimen and not from a master copy or a standard edition in any regard. In fact, every single manuscript contains very individual specifications. Hornung (1979: 23) describes it as a rather loose collection of spells that can be combined in a new order as needed.

On the other hand, within the almost two millennia of BD tradition, developments, emphases, and alterations were naturally conducted, adapting to the preferences of certain time periods, single individuals, and religious evolutions. P.Turin 1791, even though it dates into the Ptolemaic Period, is a fine example of the Book of the Dead tradition of the Saite Period displaying an above-average number of chapters, executed in an elaborately structured manner that combines spells and vignettes. Another excellent example of this period is P.Paris Louvre N 3079, displaying 175 spells and vignettes. A similar extensive manuscript originating in another periods is, for instance, P.London BM EA 10064, dating into the Third Intermediate Period and containing more than 146 BD chapters in combination with additional litanies and formulas (http://totenbuch.awk.nrw.de). In the New Kingdom, a few papyri of exceptional length, such as P.London BM EA 10477 with 134 chapters, P.London BM EA 9900 listing 92 chapters and additional litanies, or P.London BM EA 10470, displaying elaborate texts and vignettes of 70 chapters alongside additional litanies and formulas, represent the early stage of the BD tradition. Later on in the Roman Period, the Book of the Dead recedes in favor of other compositions (Töpfer and Müller-Roth, 2011; Kuckareck, this volume), the Books of Breathing in particular, with individual BD chapters still included. Two examples of this are P.London BM EA 9995, containing five BD chapters combined with the First Book of Breathing, and P.Paris Louvre E. 3865, which includes ten other BD chapters alongside the Second Book of Breathing.

Even though the manufacturer of a BD manuscript would choose a certain number of chapters individually, the composition was not arbitrary but instead followed a certain pattern. One motif would be trailed across various chapters, forming association chains and sequences. These might stand alone or connect to another sequence, but together they formed a motif string that often ran throughout the entire manuscript.

## The Individual Sequences

The key obstacle that scholars face today is the fragmentary condition of the majority of the BD manuscripts, a problem that can be rarely overcome. Studies on the composition of a manuscript are hence always limited to its current integrity. Therefore, every attempt is made to reassemble manuscripts, even though their fragmentary parts might be spread across numerous collections all over the world. The Book of the Dead database at the BD Archive in Bonn compiles information of thousands of Book of the Dead fragments and provides the researcher with the essential data on particular manuscripts or their fragments (http://totenbuch.awk.nrw.de).[*] A prominent example is the manuscript of Tꜣ-Šrt-n-ꜣst, whose fragments are held in seven collections on three continents. It was assembled by Munro (2011) with laborious detail work, and its digital defragmentation now allows studies concerning the composition itself. The completely preserved manuscripts are therefore of immense importance not only for analyzing the original manuscript's sequence, but also for comparative examinations concerning peculiarities related to periods, origin, or even local tradition and individual workshops.

From the very beginning of modern BD research, it was recognized that various themes are addressed in the BD. Jean-François Champollion (1790–1832) tried to accommodate this and divided P.Turin 1791 into three major parts with several levels of subdivisions, which seem to be based on contextual considerations. This approach

---

[*] All statistical information in this chapter concerning the BD, unless otherwise stated, is taken from the Book of the Dead Archive, Bonn, and from its database <http://totenbuch.awk.nrw.de>.

presented some limits not only because there were too many different topics illustrated within one manuscript, but also because of the variety of sequential compositions within other manuscripts.

Based on today's data, it can be stated that several chapters are typically placed together. Such a grouping might be called a partial sequence, a cluster, a group, and so forth. These terms indicate that various chapters placed next to each other contain some contextual connection or a variation of the same motif, and are usually introduced by the ancient Egyptian formula *ky ḏd*, "another saying." The same can be said about the position those clusters are placed in within the sequence of the complete manuscript. Again, typical patterns can be observed, especially for manuscripts dating to the Late Period. It's important to keep in mind that each manuscript is one of a kind and always contains, therefore, individual alterations and preferences.

## THE CHAPTERS OF TRANSFORMATION

One of the most significant partial sequences is the one concerning the ability of the deceased to transform into different shapes (Munro, 1988: 153–55; Lüscher, 2006; Quirke, 2013: 179–204 and 267–68). Up to fifteen chapters may form this cluster throughout all periods, including variations; this number obscures the possibility that the cluster might originate from a fixed unit displaying twelve different shapes (similar to BD 77–88) and a general introduction (BD 76). Jan Assmann (2003: 293) suggests the designation "das Buch der Verwandlungen" (Book of Transformations) for this cluster (Servajean, 2003; Assmann and Kucharek, 2008: 827–32). Its immense importance is mirrored by the fact that the cluster is not only most frequently displayed on manuscripts throughout the entire BD tradition, but also that the texts were typically accompanied by the corresponding depictions, even in those manuscripts with relatively few vignettes. A fine example of this is the manuscript of *Nw* (P.London BM EA 10477), dating to the New Kingdom. It is noticeable that these chapters are the first to display vignettes after a long textual sequence, hence, emphasizing their motifs visually as well.

The theme of taking a different shape points toward a crucial element of the deceased's existence. He, or she, is now able to move freely; an ability that separates humans from gods during their lifetime but connects them after death, adding a divine quality to the deceased. Therefore, it is not surprising that the notion of transformation is already attested in the Pyramid Texts and continues in the Coffin Texts, albeit altered for the appropriate circumstances and desired scope (Assmann and Kucharek, 2008: 632–33; Lüscher, 2006: IX). Alongside their general ability to take *any form desired* (BD 76), the deceased can transform into various birds, such as the *falcon of gold* (BD 77), a *divine falcon* (BD 78), a *bennu-heron* (BD 83 and 124), a *heron* (BD 84), and a *swallow* (BD 86), and into reptiles such as a *snake* (BD 87) or a *crocodile* (BD 88). The latter can also be interpreted as the transformation into the god Sobek, similar to the ability of taking the form of divine beings like the *greatest of the tribunal* (BD 79), a *god, causing the darkness to be light* (BD 80), or the form of *Ptah* (BD 82). The ability to transform into a *lotus-flower* (BD 81 and 81A) and a *living Ba-soul* (BD 85) is likewise essential; both are closely connected with the deceased's identification with creation and eternal existence.

Only a small number of chapters are represented as single copy: BD 81B is labeled with the transformation into the lotus-flower but displays a different content than 81 or 81A, and is only represented in P.Leiden T4, which dates into the Twentieth Dynasty. A chapter for *transforming into a lion* (without BD number) can be found exclusively in P.London UC 71002A, dating into the Eighteenth Dynasty. A third exception is found in TT 290, Nineteenth Dynasty, in direct connection to BD 63, the chapter for *drinking water*, and is headed in the text as *transformation into a Doum-palm*. However, here the emphasis seems to be on the ability to drink water rather than on the actual transformation, even though the motif of the Doum-palm also appears in BD 124 (Lüscher, 2006: X; Saleh, 1984: 32–36 in the context of TT 290). BD 124 itself changes its contextual emphasis over time, and with it, its title and position within the sequences of the manuscripts. In the New Kingdom, it can appear within the order of *chapters of transformation* or those closely related to them (in seven and five cases out of 38, respectively). BD 124 is followed immediately by BD 83 when it opens the cluster, which it does in ten cases. In the Ptolemaic Period, it also neighbors BD 125 and 123. The close connection to BD 83 is obvious due to the similar titles: *taking the form of a bennu-heron* (BD 83) and *taking the form of a benu-bird* (BD 124). P.Cambridge E.2a.1922 exclusively attests another saying closely related to BD 80 and BD 82, addressing the *akh* of the deceased explicitly to *transform into the great god*, and depicting the deceased adoring a god.

This is different in the cases of chapters 81 and 81A. Even though they share the same title, they never appear together on the same manuscript. In fact, chapter 81A is the typical representative for the New Kingdom, while BD 81 is the Ptolemaic version. Regarding the tradition as a whole, BD 85 is the most frequently used chapter, appearing on 229 objects. The *transformation into the Ba-soul* is of essential importance for the deceased to ensure eternal existence in the netherworld, as well as to maintain a continuous connection to the world of the living (Assmann, 2003: 119–31, Assmann and Kucharek, 2008: 640). Often closely connected to this, and of similar frequency, is BD 83, referring to creation. Visually, the vignette links this chapter to BD 84, but the spell also continues the context of divine power. Another frequent chapter, appearing on more than 200 objects, is BD 77 (*falcon of gold*), usually found adjacent to BD 76 as a universal introduction into the cluster, or linked to BD 78, sharing a similar vignette-motif as well as the topic of the divine identification of the deceased (Quirke, 2013: 180 also provides a tableau). However, BD 78 (*divine falcon*) breaks the chapters' typical structural pattern. Often, an elaborate text referring to various religious and mythical themes is depicted containing a dramatic divine dialogue (Quirke, 2013: 183–87; Assmann and Kucharek, 2008: 282–830). The remaining chapters appear more or less frequently and in various orders. Even though after the Saite Recension it often parallels the sequence on P.Turin 1791, it was not randomly chosen in the New Kingdom either, as an overview and detailed compilation on the sequence demonstrate (Munro, 1988: 218–19, "Liste 4"). The chapter arrangement in those early manuscripts clearly shows that internal criteria usually formed the connection in regard to the textual content and visual depiction, placing the individual chapters into a succession following an internal motif string.

# The Chapters of Amulets and Mummification

To ensure the protection of the deceased's body, amulet chapters were included in the BD compositions. Generally attested after the Saite Recension, but also in the early manuscripts, they often form clusters of their own (BD 29–30, 155–162, 166–167). As Munro (2003) states, this might be due to an original "ritual-book for amulets of gold." The term refers to a Late Period manuscript, P.Bonn L 1647, which displays unique texts and vignettes regarding various amulets combined with singular BD chapters. This textual counterpart to the actual amulets placed on the body itself not only intensified their protective power but also ensured their effectiveness. On the manuscript itself, these chapters were often written near the chapters concerning mummification, continuing the motif string of the burial and protection as well as ensuring the integrity and the process of mummification itself. Two aspects of the amulets are usually clearly defined: the exact definition and designation of the object and the material it is made of. The latter especially reveals that the inscribed or depicted versions of amulets resemble the actual objects and were intended as surrogates for the real amulets. Typically, amulets concern the *heart* (BD 29–30), *pillars* (BD 155, 159–160), the *Tjet-knot* (BD 156), the *vulture* (BD 157), the *collar of gold* (BD 158), the *head-rest* (BD 166), and the *udjat-eye* (BD 167), or the image such as the *heavenly cow* (BD 162).

The chapters were clearly intended to be used together with the related amulets, as mentioned in the instructions accompanying BD 28B, namely *a heart of red stone* or, as written in BD 30B, *a scarab of stone*. Additional instructions indicate the manner of exercise as well as the position of the actual amulet on the real body (as in BD 155–159). Some cases (BD 155–156) describe the outcome of the correct execution of rituals. Specific advice is given in BD 162, namely, it "shall not be used by anyone but the deceased himself." Chapter 151, on the other hand, which deals with the mummification in general, also integrates texts that are to be recited over four individualized and personified bricks placed into the four sides of the burial chamber (for the translation of an elaborate example, see Quirke, 2013: 367–75). Other than the rather typical clusters, singular amulet spells are known, such as a manuscript kept in Milan (P.Busca) that displays a large number of amulet chapters, including *a serpent head amulet of carnelian*, from the New Kingdom (Chiappa, 1972). P.Bonn L 1647, dating into the Late Period, may be designated an amulet-book due to its extensive lists of different amulets (Munro, 2003: 46–51; Quirke, 2013: 499).

Amulet chapters appear frequently on manuscripts of all periods. Some clusters are typical for the Ptolemaic Period (BD 155–162), with chapters BD 157–159 occurring almost exclusively on Ptolemaic manuscripts; chapter 166 was apparently popular in the Third Intermediate Period, despite having already being used in the New Kingdom. In general, texts and vignettes are more often coupled (approx. 50%) and were applied by themselves to a significantly lesser extent. Exceptions are BD 161, which has a clear emphasis on the vignette in almost 50 percent of its attestations, and BD 166, where the text is the main focus (89%) and vignettes are never depicted on their own. The clusters were arranged following the motif string for each particular manuscript, therefore connecting the individual amulet chapters in different orders.

# The Chapters of Immanent and Performative Qualities

Closely connected to the amulet chapters are those securing the deceased's powers over his own inner abilities. In the Late Period, they appear in the typical cluster BD 21–30. However, in the New Kingdom, they are often combined with other chapters tying various specific themes together or including additional motifs that are placed elsewhere in later times. Chapter 43, for instance, which is to prevent the deceased's *head being cut off*, is frequently found within chapters concerning the head. Chapters concerning the heart of the deceased are often placed beside each other, and, due to their similar content, in close connection to chapters of mummification and the corresponding amulets. Munro (1988: 155–56) discusses the possibility of the sequence of heart spells, and Assmann defines BD 26–30B as their own group (Assmann and Kucharek, 2008: 823–25).

Even though each period emphasized different chapters, the general importance was recognized in all periods of the BD tradition, as the cluster touches on the fundamental nature of human existence, namely the power over one's own *words* (BD 21–24) and one's own *memory*, which is closely connected with the protection of the *heart* (BD 25–30). A false testimony of the heart, where the memory, as the ancient Egyptians believed, is stored, implies either wrongful memory (hence forgetfulness), wrongful speech, or both, and must be prevented (BD 30A and 30B). All aspects that would not comply with Maat, the cardinal point of ancient Egyptian existence, needed to be omitted (Assmann, 2006: 60–85). It is therefore consequential to place this cluster near the beginning of the entire manuscript, since the chapters are preconditions for the deceased's eternal existence (Munro, 1988: 156). The aspect of rightful speech, the justification of Osiris, and therefore of the deceased, and the anticipation of the judgment are emphasized by the fact that the cluster is placed right behind BD 18–20, in which those motifs are addressed thoroughly (see Lapp, 2009: IX). Manifesting the deceased's abilities over his immanent powers establishes and ensures his successful transition into eternal life.

# The Chapters of Preventing Harm

A vast number of chapters are dedicated to preventing any harm to the deceased, which could befall him in many ways and forms. After the Saite Recension, these chapters form a large cluster of approximately 23 different ones that can be divided into two subclusters. One combines those chapters in which the deceased is protected against actual physical aggressors, mainly crocodiles (BD 31–32), snakes (BD 33–35, 39–40, 41B), or bugs (BD 36). The other is intended to prevent any harm against the deceased's own integrity. Dangers that must be prevented, such as being slaughtered (BD 41–42, 50), having one's head cut off (BD 43), dying/perishing (BD 44–46), and more general threats concerning the deceased's whereabouts (47–49), as well as signs of an inverted world (BD 51–53), are all specified. Regarding the classification of these chapters, scholars follow different approaches. Assmann, for instance, singles out individual motifs such as spells against snakes, the deification of limbs (BD 42), or the permission to enter the region of nourishment (BD 52–53) (Assmann and Kucharek, 2008: 825–26), whereas Quirke divides the text into two sections, BD 31–42, which he calls "repelling aggressors and destructive forces," and chapters 43–53, which he calls "preventing physical loss and reversals of order" (Quirke, 2013: 101–34).

BD 37 and BD 38 feature rather exceptional positions. While BD 38 seems to be misplaced at first glance, since it is titled *living on air*, a motif expected within chapters securing the power over air and water (BD 54–63) (Quirke, 2013: 135), BD 37 does mention the defense against two goddesses, the Merety, often depicted as snakes. To undertake his nocturnal journey, the deceased must overcome the entities by the power of his words. BD 38 continues the theme of traveling forward by means of the right words. Hence, both chapters form a small subunit that fits into the surrounding spells perfectly. This combination is, however, atypical for the New Kingdom. Only five manuscripts are known from this period, all of which include BD 37, pairing with chapters of transformation (BD 87 and 79) and repelling harm (BD 36 and 47).

In comparison to the surrounding chapters, BD 42 is also quite remarkable. It displays several motifs, including a prominent long catalogue of the *deification of limbs* to create a divine body through the power of words. This body cannot be corrupted and, thus, houses the deceased in his external existence (Assmann and Kucharek, 2008: 825; Munro, 1988: 74–76). The theme of the chapter's title, *repelling the slaughter done in Henennesut*, refers to the context of the complete spell but is certainly the reason for its position within other chapters of this nature. Even though the chapter is represented in all periods, the change of vignettes reflects the transition of the motif's emphasis. Whereas the New Kingdom manuscripts depict the deceased repelling a snake, sometimes together with the hieroglyphic sign of the backbone, possibly creating a reference to repelling Apophis, Late Period manuscripts usually focus on the depiction of the deities and, therefore, underscore the aspect of the deification of limbs rather than repelling dangers (Tarasenko, 2009: 248–49). Nevertheless, the text connects with the surrounding chapters on various levels as well. Not only does it refer to the large pantheon of gods, but it also bears a similarity to BD 37 in mentioning the goddess Meret, who can be identified in BD 42 as *gullet* (Guglielmi, 1990: 105–8). Hence, the cluster subtly interweaves several motifs and discloses information in congruence with existing knowledge.

## The Chapters of Securing the Essentials for Existence—the Power over Air and Water

Often closely linked and in the Ptolemaic Period typically succeeding the cluster of chapters of preventing harm are the chapters concerning the essentials for the living: *securing air and water* (BD 54–62) and *preventing harm through water or fire* (BD 63, 63A and 63B). The motif of *living on air* already occurs in BD 38–38B. Whereas BD 38 or 38B can often be found adjacent to chapter 37 from the preceding cluster, emphasizing its repelling nature, BD 38A as well as 38B typically join the motifs associated with *air* (BD 54–59). A chronological development can also be observed here. Chapter 38A is mainly attested throughout the New Kingdom; there are some examples of it from the Third Intermediate Period but only rare evidence for it from the Late Period. BD 38B is represented in all periods, with an emphasis on the Third Intermediate Period. BD 38 can be found on a large number of Late Period (29 examples) and Ptolemaic manuscripts (69 examples) but does not seem to have existed in previous times. Hence, the connection between chapters 55 or 56 and BD 38A or B stems from the same thematic string. Furthermore, it is quite typical for all periods to combine several chapters concerning both air and water. This theme is also displayed in the most commonly used chapter of this cluster, BD 59, attested on more than 300 pieces of evidence, including not only manuscripts but also tomb decorations dating mainly to the New Kingdom and Ptolemaic Period. In this cluster, different chapters can join in variation for individual emphases, but the idea of their being thematically combined can clearly be seen throughout all time periods. Chapter 57, for instance, typically joins in different variations with BD 55, 56, 59, or 58; likewise, BD 59 links BD 60 with BD 57 and 58 to switch the focus to the importance of water. The final chapters of this cluster display a theme typically understood as a general one, whereas, in fact, they represent the crucial meaning of BD compositions: the motif of *going forth into daylight*. This concerns chapters 63, 63A and B in particular, which include the protection from any harm and lead, only consequentially, to the positive result, a successful eternal existence, the *going forth into daylight*.

# The Chapters of Going Forth into Daylight and Knowing the Places

"Beginning of the sayings for going forth into daylight . . ." is not only a typical opening formula for manuscripts but also the theme of numerous chapters, and it appears in various places within the manuscripts (Backes, 2009). The importance of this topic is clear from the fact that the passage *going forth into daylight* has been used to label the entire manuscripts (Quirke, 2013: VIII). Hence, it might be considered the leitmotif of the Book of the Dead, running like a golden thread through each individual composition. The reason for creating a manuscript in the first place, and for providing it to the deceased, was to ensure his or her eternal life and to prevent a second death, the extinction into darkness. The phrase *going out into daylight* accomplishes this intention. Consequently, BD 1 (Tawfik, this volume) not only usually uses the phrase as its title but also presents the theme within.

As a typical opening of numerous manuscripts (attested on 502) throughout all periods, the phrase refers to the transition of the deceased from the world of the living to the realm of the dead. At first glance, however, it seems to correlate with the exact opposite—carrying someone to his grave might rather be associated with "going into the darkness," but the symbolism has to be understood on a different level. Being well prepared, as the justified deceased would be, he or she has already overcome the transitory nature of life through mummification and is about to join the gods on their daily journey. As the sun god Re rises anew every morning, the deceased will now rise with him. The threats of the night are overcome, and the universal order continues—along with the deceased. BD 1 represents this transition quite colorfully in detail, and on two levels: the vignette and the text (Tawfik, 2008; this volume). The former depicts the actual burial ritual in an almost documentary way, presenting what has to be provided in the here and now: necessary preparations, essential goods, mandatory rites, and often the tomb itself are depicted, before the transition into the hereafter can come about. The latter focuses on the divine sphere. It is the first time the deceased is identified as a divine entity and the first time the justification of Osiris is shown. Therefore, it is no surprise to find BD 1 at the very beginning of BD manuscripts, or, in half of its occurrences, right behind a scene of a divine adoration. BD 1 represents the last connection to the world of the living and introduces, almost at the same time, the world of the hereafter, creating a strong connection between both. This chapter equips the deceased in the afterlife: knowledge is preserved, and his or her earthly background is manifested. BD 1 also demonstrates the permeability of the border between the here and the hereafter. At this point, the deceased is associated with both sides: his divine self, possessing the knowledge and executing the rites on the one hand, and, on the other hand, his human side receiving the rites and being buried. The motifs continue in chapters focusing on different themes. BD 2, BD 3, and BD 75 with the motif of *performing rituals* form a typical cluster in the Late and Ptolemaic Periods (134 appearances to only 11 attestations for the New Kingdom and Third Intermediate Period). In addition, BD 1 is often connected to the theme of *entering the house of Osiris* (BD 69, 70, and 172[Pleyte])[1] through themes of possessing *power over enemies* (BD 4, 65, and 179[Naville]), the *identification with the divine* along with the deceased's *identification with Thoth* (BD 4, 65, and 172[Pleyte]) (Stadler, 2009: 134–89), the *going forth into daylight* and *entering god's land* together with the *opening of a chamber and the West* (BD 66–73), or the variations of the general motif of *going in the day* (BD 9, 71, and 74). The theme of *entering the house of Osiris* is a motif strongly connected to BD 146 in which the deceased asks for a safe passage when entering the houses of Osiris, and adoring Re (BD 179[Naville] and 180[Naville]). Depending on the intended emphases, each chapter might develop into a different motif string. BD 64 addresses all aspects of *going forth into daylight* as a more general chapter. It can be displayed in a long or a short version and might be understood, in this context, as an abstract to the notion of eternal life (see Lapp, 2011 and Quirke, 2013: 159–60).

The importance of *going out* or *going in*, the idea of moving forward and being able to pass through, is also found in chapters that thematize it but clearly emphasize other motifs. This can be said for chapters concerning the *Rasetjau* (BD 110, 117, 118, and 119) and *going in and out with* in regard to different places and destinations (BD 12, 13, 122, and 123). These chapters connect tightly to those providing knowledge. It is mandatory to *know the places* and their powers in order to be able to enter, to pass through, and to exit. Thus, BD 107 combines the idea of *entering the underworld by knowing the western bas*. This knowledge regarding the *bas* is also found in BD 108, 109, 111, 112, 113, 114, 115, and 116. The entire cluster appears in 31 manuscripts belonging almost exclusively to the Late and Ptolemaic Periods, except for three examples from the preceding Third Intermediate Period. The vignettes that accompany the texts are often quite similar, each depicting three squatting entities (Munro, 1988: 99–103). The chapters are found throughout all periods as texts, as text and vignette versions, or as sole vignettes, which became extremely popular during the Late and Ptolemaic Periods. The cluster is built within a motif string that combines the context of the cults of Re (BD 115) and Thoth (BD 114) (Stadler, 2009: 392–404), the cult centers of Upper and Lower Egypt (BD 113 and 112), and the two cardinal points crucial for the daily cycle, East and West (BD 109 and 108). Whereas the earlier sources develop the theme from small to broad, the later evidence reverses this. Mainly during the Ptolemaic Period, chapter 110, the formulas of the *Rasetjau* and *going out into daylight* can be found placed within the cluster connecting the motif of BD 109, which already addresses the marshes of offerings together with the knowledge on the Eastern *Bas*, and continues with the knowledge on the Western *bas* in BD 111. In the early manuscripts, BD 110 is found in connection to chapters regarding provision and offerings, clearly demonstrating the shifting emphasis on different motifs over time.

# The Chapters of Encounters in the Netherworld

Knowledge is the key to entering and passing through gateways and landscapes encountered within the netherworld, and to granting the deceased's safe passage. BD

---

[1] For the distinction of BD chapters in Naville and Pleyte versions see Wüthrich, this volume.

FIG. 17.1. BD 146 from papyrus of *Mꜣi-Ḥr-pri*, P.Cairo CG 24095, displaying the amount of eight gates to pass through (sketch by Felicitas Weber).

144 to 150 form clusters in all periods of the BD tradition. A major difference between the early and late examples lies in the repetition of the content. This is first found in P.Greenfield, P.London BM EA 10554, dating to the Third Intermediate Period, displaying all four chapters. This becomes typical for the Ptolemaic Period, whereas the early manuscripts usually pair BD 146 (Fig. 17.1) or 145 with BD 144 or BD 147. The theme of *entering the gates of the Houses of Osiris* and the *Seven Approaches* (Quirke, 2013: 323–25, 350–52) built over Osiris, which must be passed by the deceased, is covered either way. The depictions of the chapters are remarkable: in them we see the personified architectural obstacles and their guarding entities, demons, whom the deceased has to overcome by presenting the correct knowledge, namely their designations, titles, and offerings. Hence, texts and vignettes are typically interwoven by building a stronghold, even a visual one. The chapters' differences lie in the number of obstacles: whereas chapters 144 and 147 give the exact number of seven gates, chapters 145 and 146 provide a variable number that can be extended or abridged as needed to ensure more or less protection (Quirke, 2013: 323–53).

BD 148 continues the motif of providing knowledge on several subjects, presenting eternal provisions and protection against evil, referring to the cycle of rebirth and to *akh* and Re in particular. In contrast to the general custom of representing BD chapters, the vignette of BD 148 is typically displayed in large scale, alone or together with parts of its text. Due to the variation of motifs in BD 148, the motif strings in which the chapter can be embedded are diverse, and more than 330 different possibilities of neighboring spells are attested. However, the most frequently used combinations are BD 147 and 149, which appear in approximately 20 percent of all cases. The manuscript of *Nb-snî*, P.London BM EA 9900 bears one of the most intriguing compositions of the motif string due to the unique layout within two registers (Weber, 2016: 72–73).

Clearly, the emphasis on visual elements is continued in this motif string in BD 149 and 150, which frequently close this unit. These chapters, which typically appear together, describe the topography of the netherworld as 14 or 15 mounds, respectively. Whereas BD 150 contains no text except for the captions to the vignettes, BD 149

FIG. 17.2. BD 149 from Papyrus of Anonymous Owner, P.Paris Louvre N 3073 (sketch by Felicitas Weber).

characteristically depicts its vignettes running as a frieze above the associated texts (Fig. 17.2). The landscape the deceased encounters deep inside the netherworld, and where he finds himself among divine beings, is described as heavily secret and filled with magical powers. He must prove his knowledge, skills, and abilities not only by fighting off Apophis, who swallows the water and sets the barque on dry land, but by overcoming numerous obstacles in regions that even gods may not necessarily have access to. Noteworthy is the connection of vignette motifs to the astronomical ceilings of tombs. BD 149 also represents, to some extent, the final journey of the solar barque toward the sky (Lieven, 2000: 15–16).

However, BD 149 exhibits more than just magical and secret districts. The vignettes, in connection with the texts, string the mounds of the netherworld together like the individual elements of the backbone of the giant snake, Apophis, each representing one stage of the journey, and each possessing its distinct powers and forming specific obstacles intended to stop the solar journey. In the later BD tradition, the mounds become more and more personified (Morenz, 2004) and simultaneously represent places of rejuvenation. As he passes through, the deceased undergoes a similar rejuvenation to that of the sun god on his nightly journey through the body of the regenerating snake, regaining energy and power. The positive result, the defeat of Apophis, is illustrated in the last mound of BD 149, which depicts the Nile's source and its rising waters, ensuring the safe journey of the sun barque and its arrival in the sky as the renewed morning sun (Lucarelli, 2015: 275–91; Weber, 2016: 196–200). Considering this result, it is only logical that BD 149 and 150 were often used as final chapters in many BD manuscripts, especially during the early tradition.

## Scenes of Adoration and the Chapters of Judgment

A fairly autonomous motif is the display of adoration. This theme, directed to a specific divinity and typically represented as a large vignette with a rather short formulaic text, might open the complete BD composition placed even before BD 1, or be integrated within it and hence be assigned a specific BD number, or close the manuscript. Whether or not adoration scenes are placed as the opening or the concluding element, these are an element that notably alludes to the period and provenance of the manuscript (Munro, 1988: 159–61). The god Osiris is the most prominent divinity depicted in the opening adoration scenes of manuscripts across all periods. He can also be found in the closing scenes, but here the sun god Re or another composite divinity appears more frequently. Whereas Re might also appear in the opening scene, his adoration is most popular as a closing scene after the Amarna Period (Niwiński, 1989; Lenzo-Marchese, 2004: 43–62). The adoration of the goddess Hathor as she emerges from the western mountains, BD 186, is exclusively found on manuscripts no earlier than the end of the Ramesside Period and typically as a closing chapter. Even though the chapter might end a manuscript that indeed started with an adoration scene, the counterpart of BD 186 might instead be seen in BD 1, where the deceased is carried to his tomb in the western mountains. Both chapters connect on a meta level, linked through the composition itself, the *pr.t m hrw*, the *going forth into daylight* of the deceased: carried to and placed in his tomb, he evolves into the realm of the gods. Whereas BD 1 depicts the living aspect, BD 186 depicts the divine. A visual example of this metamorphosis can be seen in the manuscript of *Ani*, P.London BM EA 10470, from the Nineteenth Dynasty.

Another prominent adoration scene is found in BD 15, in the hymns either to the rising sun, BD 15A, or to the setting sun, BD 15B (Naville, 1886); both are sometimes illustrated by large vignettes and hence visually recognizable as such. The typical feature of adoration scenes, a large-scale illustration, might be employed to connect, separate, or divide not only motif strings, but whole manuscripts. An example of a perfectly symmetrical partition of a manuscript is that of *Anch-ef-en-Amun*, P.Dresden Aeg. 775, where an adoration of Osiris, whom Isis and Nephthys symmetrically surround, is distinctively placed in the exact center of the manuscript, dividing it visually not only into two different motif strings, but connecting the papyrus at the same time (Weber, 2012). A similar depiction is used in the manuscript of *Setesh-Nakht*, P.New York MMA 35.9.19, as an opening scene, which, remarkably, goes on to display content similar to that found in the Dresden manuscript.

Most significant for the eternal existence of the deceased are the chapters connected to his judgment, BD 125 A to D and typically BD 126 (Munro, 1988: 105–14; Quirke, 2013: 276). Used either individually or as varying clusters, these chapters, in which the deceased must testify not only his adoration of the gods and his appropriate behavior during his lifetime, but also his knowledge of the netherworld, are often used to connect different motifs. This character as a linking element is reflected in its position right within the BD composition. The chapters of judgment are often found closing the ferry themes (BD 99) and leading into the themes of BD 136, where the deceased joins the divine sphere and the sun god Re on his journey. The judgment and BD 125 might also be placed adjacent to the motifs of entering and being within the netherworld (BD 144–150). In addition, BD 125 and the judgment are also featured as stand-alone sequences, closing a manuscript and giving the impression of being the climax of the composition. In particular, the judgment containing the famous scene of weighing the heart might be mistaken for an actual "judgment day," where the fate of the deceased is decided. However, it is quite the opposite: the deceased is not judged here, but his justification is presented and the rightfulness of the life he lived is proven by the weighing of his heart (Janák, this volume) Therefore, it is no surprise to find these chapters not at the beginning of BD manuscripts, as would be expected if the judgment were like an actual trial, deciding the deceased's destiny, but rather within the composition itself, establishing the deceased's participation in the divine daily journey and opening the netherworld for his eternal existence.

## Conclusion

It comes as little surprise that the diversity of BD compositions equals the multitude of BD compositions preserved today. Each example was handmade individually for a specific person and purpose. Master copies were definitely used, but the final composition was still a distinct product developed from the knowledge, thoughts, considerations, hopes, and beliefs of either the manufacturer or the buyer or both. As with any product, contemporary fashion, religious and political parameters, as well as social and individual components influenced each one. Therefore, it is possible to assign dates and provenance to BD compositions by their style, layout, or content. The sequences—the selected BD chapters and their order—are one of those criteria. However, the sequences are more than just a typical or atypical compilation of chapters; rather, the chapters are linked through associative motifs, creating a specific motif string. Those motif strings are numerous and developed into different directions, with variants between each other.

Therefore, certain sequences in a manuscript might display a rather unmethodical order of BD chapters using the BD numbers assigned by Lepsius; nevertheless, the motif may be the linking element. Thus, it is important to focus on the actual conveyed information of the chapter rather than on the modern assigned BD number. This approach changes the notion of sequences known as "typical sequences," as they display effective and powerful associations and, as a result, were frequently used; examples of these "typical sequences" are the so-called chapters of transformation and mummification, of adoration and justification, of ensuring the essentials and knowing the places, of encountering the netherworld and going forth by daylight. Every time that the theme association chains create motif strings, the consequence is the creation of a unique Book of the Dead composition, tailored for one deceased's needs and expectations, and providing him with the essential magic for reaching eternity.

## Bibliography

Assmann, J. (2003). *Tod und Jenseits im Alten Ägypten* (München: C. H. Beck).
Assmann, J. (2006). *Ma'at: Gerechtigkeit und Unsterblichkeit im Alten Ägypten*. 2nd ed. (München: C. H. Beck).
Assmann, J. and Kucharek, A. (2008). *Ägyptische Religion. Totenliteratur* (Frankfurt; M-Leipzig: Suhrkamp; Insel).
Backes, B. (2009). "'Was zu sagen ist'—zum Gesamttitel des Totenbuchs." In *Ausgestattet mit den Schriften des Thot: Festschrift für Irmtraut Munro zu ihrem 65. Geburtstag.*

Studien zum altägyptischen Totenbuch 14, B. Backes, M. Müller-Roth, and S. Stöhr, 5–27 (Wiesbaden: Harrassowitz).

Chiappa, F. (1972). *Il Papiro Busca (circa 1300 a. C.)* (Milano: Edizioni de La ca' grada).

Forman, W. and Quirke, S. (1996). *Hieroglyphs and the Afterlife in Ancient Egypt* (London: British Museum Press).

Guglielmi, W. (1990). *Die Göttin Mr.t: Entstehung und Verehrung einer Personifikation*. Probleme der Ägyptologie 7 (Leiden; New York: E.J. Brill).

Hornung, E. (1979). *Das Totenbuch der Ägypter: Eingeleitet, übersetzt und erläutert* (Düsseldorf; Zürich: Artemis & Winkler).

Lapp, G. (2009). *Totenbuch Sprüche 18, 20. Totenbuchtexte 5* (Basel: Orientverlag).

Lapp, G. (2011). *Die prt-m-hrw-Sprüche (Tb 2, 64–72)*. Totenbuchtexte 7 (Basel: Orientverlag).

Lenzo-Marchese, G. (2004). "La vignette initiale dans les papyrus funéraires de la Troisième Période intermédiaire." *Bulletin de la Société d'Égyptologie Genève (BSÉG)* 26: 43–62.

Lepsius, K. R. (1842). Das Todtenbuch der Ägypter nach dem hieroglyphischen Papyrus in Turin. Leipzig (Neudruck: Osnabrück 1969): Georg Wigand. http://archiv.ub.uni-heidelb erg.de/propylaeumdok/volltexte/2010/467/pdf/lepsius_todtenbuch.pdf.

Lieven, A. von. (2000). *Der Himmel über Esna: Eine Fallstudie zur religiösen Astronomie in Ägypten am Beispiel der kosmologischen Decken- und Architravinschriften im Tempel von Esna*. Ägyptologische Abhandlungen 64 (Wiesbaden: Harrassowitz).

Lucarelli, R. (2015). "The Inhabitants of the Fourteenth Hill in Spell 149 of the Book of the Dead." In *Festschrift für die Ägyptologin Ursula Rößler-Köhler zum 65. Geburtstag*. Göttinger Orientforschungen (GOF) 53, edited by L. D. Morenz and A. el Hawary, 275–91 (Wiesbaden: Harrassowitz).

Lüscher, B. (2006). *Die Verwandlungssprüche (Tb 76–88). Totenbuchtexte 2* (Basel: Orientverlag).

Morenz, L. D. (2004). "Apophis: on the Origin, Name, and Nature of an Ancient Egyptian Anti-God." *Journal of Near Eastern Studies* 63(3): 201–5. https://doi.org/10.1086/424771.

Munro, I. (1988). *Untersuchungen zu den Totenbuch-Papyri der 18. Dynastie: Kriterien ihrer Datierung*. Studies in Egyptology (London; New York: Kegan Paul).

Munro, I. (2003). *Ein Ritualbuch für Goldamulette und Totenbuch des Month-em-hat*. Studien zum altägyptischen Totenbuch 7 (Wiesbaden: Harrassowitz).

Munro, I. (2011). *Die Totenbuch-Papyri des Ehepaars Ta-scheret-en-Aset und Djed-chi aus der Bes-en-Mut-Familie: (26. Dynastie, Zeit des Königs Amasis)*. Handschriften zum Altägyptischen Totembuch (HAT) 12 (Wiesbaden: Harrassowitz).

Naville, É. (1886). *Das aegyptische Todtenbuch der XVIII. bis XX. Dynastie*. 3 vols. (Berlin). http://www.etana.org/sites/default/files/coretexts/14507.pdf.

Niwiński, A. (1989). *Studies on the illustrated Theban funerary papyri of the 11th and 10th century B.C.* Orbis Biblicus et Orientalis (OBO) 86 (Freiburg Schweiz und Göttingen: Vandenhoeck & Ruprecht).

Pleyte, W. (1881). *Chapitres supplémentaires du Livre des Morts 162 à 174: Traduction et Commentaire*, 3 vols. (Leiden: Brill).

Quirke, S. (2013). *Going Out in Daylight—Prt M Hrw: The Ancient Egyptian Book of the Dead*. Golden House Publications Egyptology 20 (London: Golden House Publications).

Saleh, M. (1984). *Das Totenbuch in den thebanischen Beamtengräbern des Neuen Reiches: Texte und Vignetten*. Archäologische Veröffentlichungen. Deutsches Archäologisches Institut, Abteilung Kairo 46 (Mainz am Rhein: Philipp von Zabern).

Servajean, F. (2003). *Les Formules des Transformations du Livre des Morts à la lumière de d'une théorie de la performativité, XVIIIe-XXe dynasties* (Cairo: Institut français d'archéologie orientale).

Stadler, M. A. (2009). *Weiser und Wesir: Studien zu Vorkommen, Rolle und Wesen des Gottes Thot im ägyptischen Totenbuch*. Orientalische Religionen in der Antike—Ägypten, Israel, Alter Orient 1 (Tübingen: Mohr Siebeck).

Tarasenko, M. (2009). "The BD 42 Vignettes During the New Kingdom and Third Intermediate Period." In *Ausgestattet mit den Schriften des Thot: Festschrift für Irmtraut Munro zu ihrem 65. Geburtstag*. Studien zum altägyptischen Totenbuch 14, B. Backes, M. Müller-Roth, and S. Stöhr, 239–65 (Wiesbaden: Harrassowitz).

Tawfik, T. S. (2008). "Die Vignette zu Totenbuch-Kapitel 1 und vergleichbaren Darstellungen in Gräbern." Inaugural-Dissertation Philosophische Fakultät, Rheinische Friedrich-Wilhelms-Universität (Unpublished dissertation).

Töpfer, S. and Müller-Roth, M. (2011). *Das Ende der Totenbuchtradition und der Übergang zum Buch vom Atmen: Die Totenbücher des Monthemhat (pTübingen 2012) und der Tanedjmet (pLouvre N 3085)*. Handschriften zum Altägyptischen Totenbuch 13. (Wiesbaden: Harrassowitz).

Weber, F. (2012). "Der Dresdener Totenbuchpapyrus des Anch-ef-en-Amun." [The Dresden Book of the Dead papyrus of Ankhefenamun]. In *Grenzen Des Totenbuchs: Zwischen Grab Und Ritual [Beyond the Book of the Dead, Egyptian Papyri between Tomb and Ritual]*, edited by M. Müller-Roth and M. Höveler-Müller, 47–70 (Rahden; Westf.: Marie Leidorf GmbH).

Weber, F. (2016). Diegetic Lists in the Early Egyptian "Book of the Dead." A Contextual Analysis of Demonic Entities in Private Second Millennium Manuscripts. Swansea. (Unpublished dissertation).

# CHAPTER 18

# SPELL 1 OF THE BOOK OF THE DEAD AND ITS VIGNETTE

## TAREK SAYED TAWFIK

Book of the Dead chapter 1 (BD 1) is one of the more frequently occurring chapters appearing in the Book of the Dead papyri of all periods. The introductory vignette showing the deceased standing in adoration before the god Osiris often precedes it. A priest must recite the text on the day of the burial. Accordingly, the vignette of BD 1 depicts the funerary procession. The first short versions of this vignette date to the mid-Eighteenth Dynasty from the time of King Thutmose III, but over time, the vignette becomes more and more elaborate; many components and details are added to the funerary procession until it completely dominates the upper part of many Late and Ptolemaic Period papyri.

In contrast to the vignette, the text of BD 1 remains rather consistent with minor changes over the long span of nearly 2000 years. Regional changes in the text are also minimal, while the vignette is attested in clearly different regional editions in Thebes, Memphis, and Akhmim (Mosher, 2001).

BD 1, as text and vignette, appears mainly in BD papyri (Backes et al., 2009: 109–10), but also on linen mummy bandages (Kockelmann, 2008). The funerary procession as it appears in the vignette is also often depicted in the Tombs of the Nobles starting in the New Kingdom. The traditional way of showing the funerary procession in private tombs, especially in the Old Kingdom, is replaced by an actual depiction of the vignette of BD 1. The attestation of the vignette in the tomb of King Tutankhamun is unique.

## The Text of BD 1

Like many of the spells of the Book of the Dead, BD 1 begins with a rubric giving instructions for its use: "Here begin the spells of going forth by day, the praises and recitations for going to and from in the realm of the dead which are beneficial in the beautiful West, and which are to be spoken on the day of burial and of going in after coming out."

The spell then continues with the god Thoth addressing the King of Eternity, the god Osiris, assuring him again and again that he has vindicated him against his foes and that he is one of his companions. Thoth continues to praise Osiris, and then he asks for the excellent soul of the deceased to be allowed near the House of Osiris. The final aim is for the soul of the owner of the Book of the Dead to go into and out of the House of Osiris in peace, meaning that the deceased has successfully passed judgment before Osiris and can freely leave the darkness of the netherworld and go forth into the light of day.

The representative version of BD 1 goes as follows (Allen, 1974: 5–6; Hornung, 1979: 41–45; Faulkner, 1985: 34–35):

> Hail to you, Bull of the West, so says Thoth to the King of Eternity. I am the Great God, the protector. I have fought for you, for I am one of those gods of the tribunal that vindicated Osiris against his foes on that day of judgment. I belong to your company, O Osiris, for I am one of those gods born of Nut, who slew the foes for Osiris and who imprisoned those who rebelled against him.
>
> I belong to your company, O Horus (var. Osiris), I have fought for you and have watched over your name; I am Thoth who vindicated Osiris (var. Horus) against his foes on that day of judgment in the great Mansion of the Noble which is in Heliopolis. I am a Busirite (from Abydos), the son of a Busirite, I was conceived in Busiris (var. Abydos), I was born in Busiris, Busiris is my name, I was with the men who lamented and the women who mourned Osiris on the Shores of Rekhty (the washerman's shores) and who vindicated Osiris against his foes -so they say. O Re, Thoth has vindicated Osiris against his foes-so men say. Thoth has helped me so that I might be with Horus as the protector of the left arm of Osiris who is in Letopolis (ancient *Khem*, modern Ausim in Giza). I go in and out among those who are there on the day of crushing the rebels in Letopolis so that I may be with Horus on the day of the Festival of Osiris; offerings are made on the days of the Sixth-day Festival and the Seventh-day Festival in Heliopolis.
>
> I am a priest in Busiris for the Lion-God in the House of Osiris with those who raise up earth; I am he who sees the mysteries in Rasetjau; I am he who reads the ritual book for the soul in Busiris (var. Mendes); I am the *Sem*-priest at his duties; I am the high priest of Memphis; I am the master craftsman on the day of placing the Barque of Sokar on its sledge; I am he who takes the hoe on the day of breaking up the earth in Heliopolis.
>
> O you who cause the perfected souls to draw near the House of Osiris, may you cause the excellent soul of N (the deceased) to draw near with you to the House of Osiris. May he hear as you hear, may he see as you see, may he stand as you stand, may he sit as you sit.
>
> O you who give bread and beer to the perfected souls in the House of Osiris, may you give bread and beer in all seasons to the soul of N, who is vindicated with all the gods of the Thinite nome, and who is vindicated with you.
>
> O you who open a path and open up roads for the perfected souls in the House of Osiris, open a path for him, open up roads for the soul of N in your company. May he come in freely, may he go out in peace, from the House of Osiris, without

being repelled or turned back. May he go in favor, may he come out loved, may he be vindicated, may his commands be done in the House of Osiris, may he go and speak with you, may he be a spirit with you, may no fault be found in him, for the balance is voided of his misdoings.

BD 1B seldom accompanies or complements BD 1. The former has its own vignette showing Anubis standing at the bier with the deceased, presumably in the burial chamber (ex. P.Berlin P. 3002 a–z). BD 1B, with its vignette, appears especially in the tombs of the workmen in Deir el-Medina (Saleh, 1984). The wording of BD 1B is (Allen, 1974: 6–7; Faulkner, 1985: 35–36) as follows:

Hail to you who are in the sacred desert of the West! N knows you and knows your name; may you save him from those snakes which are in Rasetjau; which live on the flesh of men and gulp down their blood, because N knows you and knows your names.

The First One, Osiris, Lord of All, mysterious of body, gives command, and he puts breath into those frightened ones who are in the midst of the West; what has been commanded for him is the governance of those who exist. May his place within the darkness be opened up for him, may a spirit-shape be given to him in Rasetjau, even to the Lord of Gloom who goes down as the swallower of snakes in the West; his voice is heard but he is not seen. The Great God within Busiris, those who are among the languid ones fear him, they having gone forth with a report to the shambles of the god.

I have come, even I, the vindicated Osiris N, on business of the Lord of All, while Horus has taken possession of his throne and his father has given to him all those honors which are within his father's sacred barque. Horus has come with a report; he goes in so that he may tell what he has seen in Heliopolis. Their great ones on earth wait on him, the scribes who are on their mats magnify him, and it has been given to him the mottled snake in Heliopolis. He has taken possession of the sky, he has inherited the earth, and who shall take this sky and earth from him? He is Re, the eldest of the gods; his mother has suckled him, she has given to him a nurse who is in the horizon.

This spell is to be recited after going to rest in the West, the Tjenenet-shrine having been made content with its lord Osiris when going to and from in the Sacred Barque of Re; his body on his bier shall be reckoned up, and shall endure in the Netherworld, namely that of the deceased N.

# The Vignette of BD 1

## First phase

The development of the vignette of BD 1 can be divided into three phases. First is the early phase, seen on Book of the Dead papyri from the New Kingdom: in this phase the vignette first appears in the Eighteenth Dynasty as a short illustration of the funerary procession showing only the transportation of the mummy. This core scene then develops in the Ramesside Period (Nineteenth/Twentieth Dynasties) into a detailed depiction of the funerary procession heading to the tomb and the last rites preformed for the deceased in front of the mummy. Most components of the vignette that will continue on until the Ptolemaic Period are already established by the end of this early phase. In terms of artistic skill and richness in detail, the vignette of BD 1 of Papyrus Ani (P.London BM EA 10470) can hardly be matched in its excellence (Dondelinger, 1979).

The funerary procession of Ani to his tomb and the opening of the mouth ceremony are described in the following as a superb example for the versions of the vignette of BD 1 from this early phase. The deceased's mummy lies in a shrine on a boat, which oxen draw on a sledge. Figures of the goddesses Nephthys and Isis stand at the head and foot of the mummy. The weeping wife of the deceased kneels to his side. The *Sem*-priest, whom a leopard's skin distinguishes, leads the boat's way by burning incense and sprinkling water, and eight male mourners follow the boat. In the rear, men pull a funeral chest surmounted by a figure of the recumbent jackal Anubis, and carry vases, a couch, a staff, a chair, a palette, and other personal belongings of the deceased. Preceding the oxen drawing the funeral boat are men carrying boxes and plants on yokes. A group of wailing women with uncovered breasts beat at their heads and faces in gestures of grief. Two registers then follow. In the upper register, a cow and her calf are shown. The calf is missing a foreleg, which has been cut off to be used for the funerary rites. In the lower register, there are tables loaded with offerings, and a servant runs to bring a haunch of beef, which is most probably the foreleg of the calf mentioned above.

At the entrance to the tomb, surmounted by a small pyramid, stands a priest with an Anubis mask, supporting the mummy of the deceased, before which kneels the weeping wife. Two priests stand before a table of offerings. One, the *Sem*-priest (still wearing the leopard's skin), holds in his hands a libation vase and a censer; the other holds in his right hand the instrument called a *wer-hekaw* (wr-ḥkꜣ.w, "great of magic"), in the form of a ram-headed serpent, surmounted by an uraeus, and in his left hand, an instrument in the shape of an adze. With these instruments, he is about to perform the opening of the mouth ceremony (for this ritual, see Quack, 2010). On the ground to their side lie further instruments that are to be employed in this ceremony, which will enable the deceased to eat, to drink, and to talk again in his next life after resurrection. They include the *meskhet*, a group of instruments in the form of adzes, and the *pesesh-en-kef*, the libation vases, along with boxes, a bandlet, and a feather. Behind them stands the lector priest, who recites from a papyrus roll (Figs. 18.1 and 18.2).

The vignette of BD 1 on the papyrus of Ani also fulfills all the criteria of narrative analysis according to D. Weber (1998). Some of the main protagonists appear more than once in the scenes. The grieving wife and the *Sem*-priest appear during the funerary procession and again at the opening of the mouth ceremony, showing that the actions are happening one after the other, yet with some of the same people participating. The whole procession heads toward the tomb, where the climax of the action, the opening of the mouth ceremony, takes place. In this way, the seriality of events and the elaboration

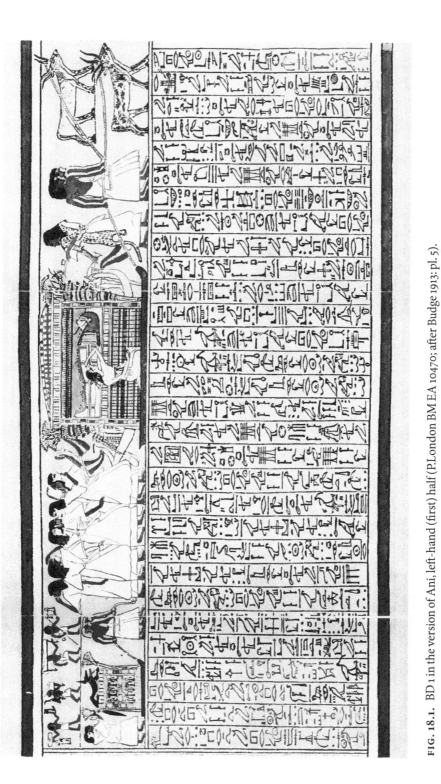

FIG. 18.1. BD 1 in the version of Ani, left-hand (first) half (P.London BM EA 10470; after Budge 1913: pl. 5).

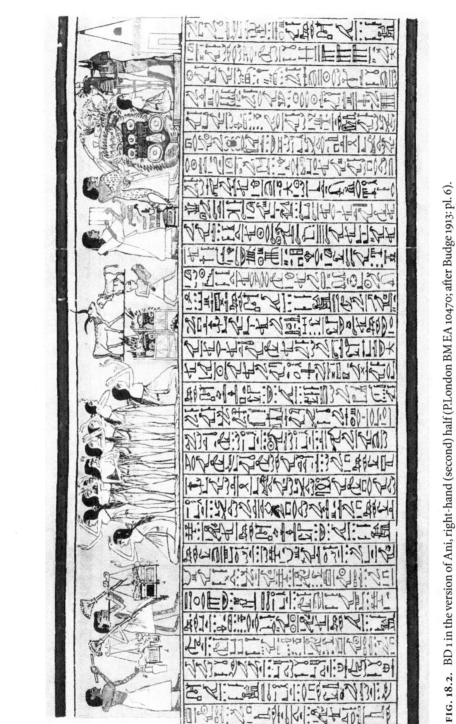

FIG. 18.2. BD 1 in the version of Ani, right-hand (second) half (P.London BM EA 10470; after Budge 1913: pl. 6).

of the narrative are achieved. The vignette depicts events that are not current but are still shown in a sequence of actions that are in a relatively chronological order. The group of female mourners includes women looking toward the funerary procession, and, on the other side, women facing in the opposite direction toward the opening of the mouth ceremony, thereby ingeniously linking the two successive events. The common protagonist during the entire vignette is the weeping widow, clearly recognizable by a band in her hair. She kneels beside the mummy being transported on the sledge; she is the first one of the group of mourning women facing the funerary procession, represented as kneeling; and it is she again who kneels on the other side of the group lamenting and heading toward the opening of the mouth ceremony. Finally, she is seen crying at the feet of her husband's upright standing mummy (El Hawary and Tawfik, 2009).

The facsimiles/drawings of vignettes published in the late nineteenth century, which are often referred to and reproduced (Pierret and Devéria, 1872; Naville, 1886), must be acknowledged as good documentation efforts of their time considering their means, but must be handled with care today as it seems they were made in haste. For this reason, they contain mistakes and omit many interesting details.

The only funerary procession portrayed in a royal tomb is found in the burial chamber of King Tutankhamun in the valley of the Kings (KV 62). On the east wall of the burial chamber, high officials from the reign of King Tutankhamun pull the sledge carrying his mummy in a shrine on a boat. The scene is depicted in exactly the same way as in contemporaneous illustrations of BD 1 for non-royal members of the élite.

The end of the rope that the high officials pull continues on the adjacent northern wall, indicating that the scene continues there. King Aye, Tutankhamun's successor, then performs the opening of the mouth ceremony for Tutankhamun, who is shown as Osiris (Fig. 18.3).

If the position of the main pieces of funerary equipment—they were originally placed in the so-called treasury located directly to the east of the burial chamber—is taken

FIG. 18.3. Tutankhamun's funerary procession (right) and King Aye performing the opening of the mouth ritual (left) in Tutankhamun's burial chamber (© Tarek S. Tawfik).

into consideration, then a three-dimensional continuation of the procession can further complement the depicted part of the funerary procession, resembling in total the way it appears on contemporary papyri. Beneath the aforementioned funerary procession scene on the eastern wall of the burial chamber is the entrance to the treasury. At the time of discovery, the rods used to carry the chest with the recumbent Anubis on it reached into the entranceway, as if to show that this object was directly connected to what was depicted and actually present in the burial chamber. Directly behind Anubis was the gilded head of a cow, presumably representing the "cow and calf scene," followed by the canopic shrine, which is shown on sledges. Comparing this, for instance, to the vignette of BD 1 on the papyrus of Ani, one sees a similar funerary procession composition. It shows the pulling of the sledge with the mummy shrine on a boat and the procession heading toward the opening of the mouth ceremony two-dimensionally, and replaces the rest of the scenes with objects that were actually used during the funeral. They were even placed in the right direction, heading from east to west. The mummy of King Tutankhamun, in its three coffins placed in a stone sarcophagus and surrounded by four gilded shrines, represents the funerary shrine with the mummy after it has reached its final position in the burial chamber.

## Phases two and three: middle and late phases

The middle phase of the vignette's development comprises the rather limited examples surviving from the Third Intermediate Period. Nevertheless, they have their own specific character, as they return to using the first short core scenes of transporting the mummy from the Eighteenth Dynasty.

The late phase includes a substantial number of attestations dating from the Saite/Twenty-sixth Dynasty until the Ptolemaic Period (Mosher, 2016: 96–188). Despite the fact that no complete version of the vignette of BD 1 from the Twenty-sixth Dynasty has survived, the details on the few fragments that are known clearly show that over the course of the Saite Dynasty the scene composition evolves into what remains more or less consistent for the entire late phase.

There are three unusual papyri containing vignettes of BD 1 that most probably date to the fourth century BCE. These are of Theban origin (P.Berlin P. 3158, P.Berlin P. 3159, P.Aberdeen ABDUA 84023) and seem to have been produced in the same workshop (Backes, 2009). The quality of illustration is quite poor, but these versions of the vignette, especially P.Berlin P. 3159, show some unique elements and details; for example, a man pulling the chest for the canopic jars, surmounted by the recumbent jackal Anubis moving in the "wrong direction" (in the opposite way from the rest of the procession); a unique depiction of a squatting god in a boat on a sledge being pulled by a man; the mummy in front of the tomb-stela appearing separately, after an interruption by the vignettes of BD 15 and BD 17; and the mummy being supported by the priest wearing the Anubis mask from the front rather than from behind as usual. Some of these peculiarities remained in later versions of the vignettes of BD 1 from Akhmim.

Throughout the Ptolemaic Period, the funerary procession is depicted in a lengthy and detailed way; this is very similar to how it is depicted on most of the numerous vignettes of BD 1 known from that time.

When discussing the Theban version of the vignette of BD 1, Mosher (2001: 14) divided "the standardized vignette of BD 1 in the Late Period" into fifteen scenes and elements associated with the funerary procession and burial rites. Here, I have applied Mosher's division of scenes and elements to all Late Period and Ptolemaic vignettes of BD 1 regardless of their provenance (Tawfik, 2008: 115–22). Thus, using the well-preserved, long, and detailed version of the vignette of BD 1 of the Turin papyrus (P. Turin 1791), the complete composition of the vignette typical for the Ptolemaic Period can be represented as follows, divided into 16 scenes and sub-scenes for better comprehension and comparison (Fig. 18.4):

1. A group of three mourning men.
2. Two groups of mourning women face each other (in some vignettes with a child among them).
3. A man pulls a funerary chest.
4. A man pulls the chest for the canopic jars, holding the intestines of the deceased, surmounted by the recumbent jackal Anubis.
5. The mummy lies in an open shrine on a boat being pulled by a man. In other versions, the boat can be shown on water or on a vehicle with two, three, or four pairs of wheels. A *ba*-bird with outstretched wings or a winged sun disk can be depicted above the mummy.

   Before and behind the mummy shrine are statuettes of the goddesses Isis and Nephthys with raised arms. In the front of the boat is a standard with a figure of a lion with a human head wearing a double-feather crown on ram horns, and in the back of the boat, a man holds an oar. A *Sem*-priest dressed in a leopard skin burns incense and walks in front of the boat. Sometimes one or two oxen drag the boat, but it can also be a cow that is not drawing, followed by a drover. This cow may wear a double-feather crown with a sun disk between her horns and the *menat*-necklace, both attributes of the goddess Hathor.
6. Several standard-bearers carry different emblems—a standing jackal, an ibis, a sitting falcon, a bull, a vulture, a cushion-like symbol that might be a placenta, a double-feather emblem, and a mummified falcon. The number and order of standards may vary, but normally they are led by one or two standard-bearers with a standing jackal each.
7. Two mourning women. This can also be only one woman or one man, or the number can rise to three, shown behind or next to each other.
8. A man carries boxes on a yoke and another carries a chest with long legs; in a variation, this can be a chest without legs, or there can be two men carrying boxes on yokes.
9. The "cow and calf scene". The cow is sometimes shown wearing a double-feather crown with a sun disk between her horns, the *menat*-necklace, attributed with the *sekhem*-scepter or the *nekhakha*-flail.

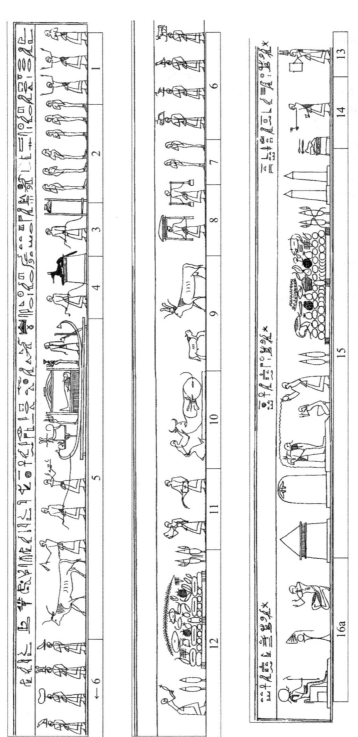

FIG. 18.4. Vignette of BD 1 in the version of Iufankh (P.Turin 1791; drawing after Lepsius, 1842: pl. I–VI, (Leipzig) with additions by Tarek S. Tawfik).

10. A priest slaughters a bovine sacrificial animal, which might be the calf from the preceding scene. In earlier representations of this scene, one foreleg of the calf is cut off and used during the funerary rites.
11. A man carries the foreleg of a calf and a man carries a goose. In a few cases, a tree is also depicted.
12. A heap of offerings lie on a matt topped with a palm leaf. The offerings can also be shown directly on the ground or on a table and can be flanked by two palm leaves. A priest stands to the left of the offerings holding a libation vessel. In other representations, he is depicted pouring water on the offerings or laying down the offerings.
13. A priest recites from a papyrus roll. He wears two feathers on his head, which are affixed by a band that is knotted at the back of his head with the two ends hanging down. In some depictions he wears a leopard skin. A priest holding a long staff can follow him, or a heap of offerings or a chest may precede him. The chest's lid can be open.
14. A priest holds the *wer-hekaw*, an instrument used during the opening of the mouth ritual. This is a tool with a short arm that ends with the head of a ram. He stands in front of a table with further instruments for the opening of the mouth ritual.
15. Two obelisks and a large heap of offerings introduce the next episode: the destination of the procession, the tomb, is represented as a structure with a pyramid topping it and a stela before it, in front of which a priest with a jackal mask (thus embodying Anubis) supports the upright mummy. The grieving widow kneels at the feet of the mummy. In some cases, she wears the throne emblem on her head, assimilating her to the goddess Isis. A priest pours water on the mummy and the priest with the jackal mask. Another obelisk or pair of obelisks also occasionally appear directly in front of the representation of the tomb building.
16. The deceased kneels or stands in front of the enthroned or standing god, Re-Horakhty. Often there is an offering table depicted between the two.

The last scene (16) used to be attributed to BD 15, but it has to be identified as the final scene of the vignette of BD 1 (Tawfik, 2008: 119–26).

This scene (16a) can have other sub-scenes (Figs. 18.5 and 18.6), which include the following: a duplication of adoring Re-Horakhty (16b—not in Figs. 18.5 and 18.6); an adoration to a seated or standing Osiris (16c); the god Thoth standing with a human body and the head of an ibis wearing the Atef crown (16d); the god Anubis with a human body and the head of a jackal (16e) burning incense in front of an upright standing mummy (16f), or following Thoth (16d), or carrying a chest behind the god Horus (16i); the god Ptah-Sokar as an upright standing mummy (16f); Isis and Nephthys (16g) standing behind the mummy (16f); a sitting baboon (16h), who can also be shown raising his hands in adoration in front of the boat (16k); the god Horus with a human body and the head of a falcon wearing the double crown of Upper and Lower Egypt (16i); a mummy opposing a falcon-headed mummy with a sitting baboon and a seated mummy between them (16i); a boat is represented on water with a sun disk in the center of the boat flanked by either Thoth and Isis or Horus and Maat. The deceased is depicted in adoration in front of the boat (16k).

FIG. 18.5. Subscenes of Vignette of BD 1 in the version of Takhebet (P.Paris Louvre N 3063; drawing by Tarek S. Tawfik).

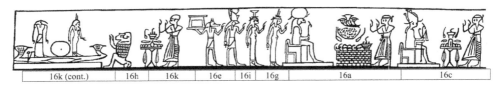

FIG. 18.6. Subscenes of Vignette of BD 1 in the version of Hornedjitef (P.Paris Louvre N 3081; drawing by Tarek S. Tawfik).

Although the vignettes of BD 1 from the Ptolemaic Period cannot yet be dated more accurately within this time span of nearly 300 years, specific regional elements and details have been detected, which allow some papyri to be attributed to Akhmim, Meir (P.New York MMA 35.9.20: Smith, 2006: 217; and on account of many similarities in region-specific details, also P.Chicago OIM 10486 = Papyrus Milbank: Scalf, ed., 2017: 246–54), and Memphis (Jakobeit, 2018).

Most of the Ptolemaic BD papyri belong either to the Theban or the Memphite tradition. Only six BD papyri have so far been attributed with certainty to Akhmim. These papyri are P.Berlin P. 10477 (Lüscher, 2000), P.Hildesheim 5248 (Lüscher, 2000: 47–50, pl. 21–39), P.MacGregor (Mosher, 2001), P.London BM EA 10479 (Mosher, 2001), P.Nesmin, and P.Twt (Frankfurt Liebighaus 1652c; Bayer-Niemeyer et al., 1993: no. 62, 254–85); P.Kopenhagen Carlsberg 201 (unpublished) can probably be added to them. Whether P.Berlin P. 3064A–B can truly be attributed to Akhmim (De Meulenaere, 2002: 492) is doubtful because it shows a unique local tradition which is obvious in both text edition and vignette arrangement (Mosher, 2001: 6–31). The publications that have dealt with these papyri have all commented on the strange reading directions and the sequence of scenes in the vignette of BD 1, and it has been suggested that the unusual retrograde texts on the Akhmim papyri led to the attempt to modify the orientation of the vignette accordingly, which resulted in mistakes, a corrupted sense, and wrong sequences (Lüscher, 2000: 25). However, this might have been an attempt to deal with the problem that occurred during the rituals, because the cemeteries in Akhmim were located on the east bank of the Nile, not on the west bank. The funerary rites before the mummy, which was placed in front of the funerary stela, followed by the adoration to Re-Horakhty, are depicted occurring from right to left, in the opposite direction of the preceding funerary procession, which is heading toward the east. This was meant to reflect that a change of direction toward the west was actually necessary when performing the last rites for the deceased before he entered the west, the realm of the dead (Tawfik, 2015).

The texts and vignette of BD 1 on mummy bandages (Kockelmann, 2008) from the late phase suggest that most of them come from the Memphite area and its surroundings (Gurob, Hawara, Abusir El Melek). The vignette composition and the sequence of scenes are similar to the vignette illustrations on papyri from the same phase.

## BD 1 IN TOMBS

When comparing the vignette of BD 1 on papyri with funerary scenes on the walls of private tombs, especially in Thebes (Settgast, 1985; Barthelmess, 1992), one can notice a continuous mutual influence between both of the carriers of this vignette. The first illustrations of the vignette on papyri seem to have been inspired by tombs of the Old Kingdom and later on from contemporaneous tombs of the Eighteenth Dynasty. This completely changes in the Ramesside Period. Not only does the tomb decoration now imitate the funerary procession as it is depicted in the BD papyri of that time, but the funerary procession scenes in the tombs actually become a representation of the vignette of BD 1. This assumption is supported by observing the workmen's tombs of Deir el-Medina, which are richly decorated with BD vignettes. There, the funerary procession is depicted on the walls of the cult rooms of the tomb's superstructure, as in other Theban tombs of the New Kingdom. The situation is different in the subterranean burial chambers in Deir el-Medina, where vignette 1B depicts a priest with an Anubis mask leaning over the bier and touching the chest of the mummy. This is an illustration of the last rites being performed for the deceased in the actual burial chamber. P.Berlin P 3002 a–z (Munro, 1997) contains both vignettes in the correct order. The funerary possession (vignette of BD 1) is found in the upper part of the papyrus (corresponding to the cult rooms of the tombs), and the priest with the Anubis mask at the bier with the mummy (vignette of BD 1B) appears below the aforementioned vignette and corresponds to the burial chamber. Tomb decorations of the Twenty-fifth and Twenty-sixth Dynasties again return to the vignettes of BD 1 on papyri from the Eighteenth Dynasty for inspiration. At the same time, the contemporaneous vignette of BD 1 on papyri begins to show most of the main components and elements that will prevail all throughout the Late and Ptolemaic Periods. This new edition of the vignette already appears in part in the tomb of Pabasa (TT 279), which dates to the last third of the reign of King Psamtik I from the Twenty-sixth Dynasty (Eigner, 1984: 15). In the slightly later tomb of Padihorresnet (TT 196; Graefe, 2003: 105), the funerary procession scene again exactly resembles the contemporaneous vignette of BD 1 on papyri. Funerary procession scenes in tombs of the Greek and Roman Periods in Egypt are also strongly influenced by the vignettes of BD 1 on papyri. Some of the best-preserved examples are found in the tombs of Petosiris in Tuna el Gebel (Lefebvre, 1924: vol. I, 128), Siamun in the Oasis of Siwa (Lembke, 2003), and Petubastis in the Dakhla Oasis (Osing, 1982: 75).

As for the placement and function of the content of BD 1 and its vignette, it has been stated that the text and the vignette of BD 1 do not much relate to each other (Mosher,

2016: 157). However, they actually complement one another and represent the transitional phase from the world of the living to the realm of the dead.

Starting in the mid-Eighteenth Dynasty, many private tombs in Thebes have sloping passages that connect the cult room in the tomb with the burial chamber, and thus, Osiris becomes involved in the interpretation (Assmann, 1984; Seyfried, 1987). In several tombs from the Ramesside Period, the funerary procession scenes of the vignette of BD 1 are depicted on the wall leading directly to the sloping passage, which represents the transition into the realm of Osiris. This is the point of intersection between the world of the living and the world of the dead. The transportation of the mummy through the sloping passage into the burial chamber was to ensure a safe entry into the realm of Osiris.

The vignette of BD 1 differs from all other vignettes of the Book of the Dead in that its happenings still take place in the world of the living. It is often preceded by the introductory scene showing the deceased in front of Osiris. The funerary procession then portrays the last rites being performed for the deceased in the world of the living before it continues with the happenings in the netherworld leading to successful resurrection of the deceased. Therefore, the vignette of BD 1 is here the link between the domain of the living and the domain of the dead, finally leading to the successful achievement of the main goal: resurrection and the ability to stand in adoration in front of the sun god, Re-Horakhty.

This is best illustrated and summarized in the exceptional vignette of BD 1 of Nebqed (P.Paris Louvre AE/N 3068; Pierret and Devéria, 1872; André-Leicknam and Ziegler, eds., 1982: 288–89), dating to the New Kingdom. At the end of the funerary procession, beneath the tomb representation, a shaft is shown leading down to the burial chamber with the mummy inside. The *ba*-bird, the soul of the deceased, is depicted flying down the shaft. From the ceiling of the burial chamber emerges the resurrected tomb owner, shown in larger scale, holding a staff and facing a large sun disc with its descending rays. A brief accompanying text confirms that he has achieved coming forth by day (Fig. 18.7).

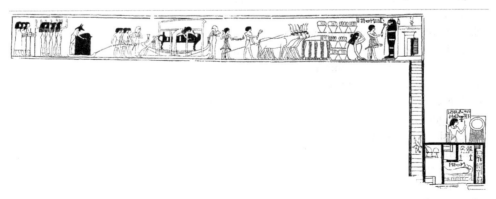

**FIG. 18.7.** Vignette of BD 1 in the version of Nebqed (P.Paris Louvre AE/N 3068; drawing after Pierret and Devéria, 1872, revised and corrected by Tarek S. Tawfik).

## Bibliography

Allen, T. G. (1974). *The Book of the Dead or Going Forth by Day: Ideas of the Ancient Egyptians Concerning the Hereafter as Expressed in Their Own Terms*. Studies in Ancient Oriental Civilization, 37 (Chicago: University of Chicago Press).

André-Leicknam, B., and Ziegler, C., eds. (1982). *Naissance de l'écriture: Cunéiformes et hiéroglyphes*, Galeries nationales du Grand Palais, 7 mai—9 août 1982. 4. éd., rev. et corr. (Paris: Éd. de la Réunion des musées nationaux).

Assmann, J. (1984). "Das Grab mit gewundenem Abstieg: zum Typenwandel des Privat-Felsgrabes im Neuen Reich." *Mitteilungen des deutschen archaologischen Instituts, Abt. Kairo* 40: 277–90.

Backes, B. (2009). *Drei Totenpapyri aus einer thebanischen Werkstatt der Spätzeit: pBerlin P. 3158, pBerlin P. 3159, pAberdeen ABDUA 84023*. Handschriften des altägyptischen Totenbuchs, 11 (Wiesbaden: Harrassowitz).

Backes, B., Gülden, S., Kockelmann, H., et al. (2009). *Bibliographie zum Altägyptischen Totenbuch*. Studien zum altägyptischen Totenbuch, 13; 2nd edn. (Wiesbaden: Harrassowitz).

Barthelmess, P. (1992). *Der Übergang ins Jenseits in den thebanischen Beamtengräbern der Ramessidenzeit*. Studien zur Archäologie und Geschichte Altägyptens, 2 (Heidelberg: Orient-Verlag).

Bayer-Niemeyer, E., Borg, B., Burkard, G., et al. (1993). *Ägyptische Bildwerke, Band III: Skulptur, Malerei, Papyri und Särge*. Liebieghaus—Museum Alter Plastik, Frankfurt am Main, Wissenschaftliche Kataloge (Melsungen: Gutenberg).

Budge, E. A. W. (1913). *The Papyrus of Ani: A Reproduction in Facsimile, with Hieroglyphic Transcript, Translation and Introduction* (London; New York: The Medici Society, Ltd.; G. P. Putnam's Sons).

De Meulenaere, H. (2002). "Rez. zu Mosher, Papyrus of Hor." *Bibliotheca orientalis*, 59: 491–93.

Dondelinger, E. (1979). *Papyrus des Ani: Vollständige Faksimile-Ausgabe im Originalformat des Totenbuches aus dem Besitz des British Museum* (Graz).

Eigner D. (1984). *Die Monumentalen Grabbauten der Spätzeit in der Thebanischen Nekropole* (UÖAI VI, Wien: Verlag der Österreichischen Akademie der Wissenschaften).

El Hawary, A., and Tawfik, T. S. (2009). "Narrative Elemente der Vignette zum 1. Kapitel des altägyptischen Totenbuchs." In *Modi des Erzählens in nicht-abendländischen Texten*. Narratio aliena, 2, edited by S. Conermann, 41–51 (Berlin: EB-Verl.).

Faulkner, R. O. (1985). *The Ancient Egyptian Book of the Dead* (London).

Graefe, E. (2003). *Das Grab des Padihorresnet, Obervermögensverwalter der Gottesgemahlin des Amun (Thebanisches Grab Nr. 196)*, 2 vols., MonAeg IX (Turnhout: Brepols).

Hornung, E. (1979). *Das Totenbuch der Ägypter: Die Bibliothek der Alten Welt, Der Alte Orient* (Zürich: Artemis).

Jakobeit, U. (2018). "Das Totenbuch des Chonsiu. Untersuchungen zur memphitischen Totenbuchredaktion in der ptolemäischen Zeit." Dissertation (Würzburg, Julius-Maximilians-Universität; urn:nbn:de:bvb:20-opus-161035).

Kockelmann, H. (2008). *Untersuchungen zu den späten Totenbuch-Handschriften auf Mumienbinden*, 3 vols. Studien zum altägyptischen Totenbuch, 12 (Wiesbaden: Harrassowitz).

Lefebvre, G. (1924). *Le Tombeau de Petosiris*, 2 vols. (Cairo).

Lembke, K. (2003). *Aus der Oase des Sonnengottes-Das Grab des Siamun in Siwa*. In *Fremdheit-Eigenheit. Ägypten, Griechenland und Rom Austausch und Verständnis*, Städel Jahrbuch 19, P. C. Bol et. al. (Herg.), 363–73 (München).

Lepsius, C. R. (1842). *Das Todtenbuch der Ägypter nach dem hieroglyphischen Papyrus in Turin mit einem Vorworte zum ersten Male herausgegeben* (Leipzig: Georg Wigand).

Lüscher, B. (2000). *Das Totenbuch pBerlin P. 10477 aus Achmim (mit Photographien des verwandten pHildesheim 5248)*. Handschriften des altägyptischen Totenbuchs, 6 (Wiesbaden: Harrassowitz).

Mosher, M. (2001). *The Papyrus of Hor (BM EA 10479) with Papyrus MacGregor: The Late Period Tradition at Akhmim*. Catalogue of Books of the Dead in the British Museum, 2 (London: British Museum Press).

Mosher, M. (2016). *The Book of the Dead, Saite through Ptolemaic Periods: A Study of Traditions Evident in Versions of Texts and Vignettes 1: BD Spells 1–15* (Prescott, AZ: SPBD Studies).

Munro, I. (1997). *Das Totenbuch des Nacht-Amun aus der Ramessidenzeit (pBerlin P. 3002)*. Handschriften des altägyptischen Totenbuchs, 4 (Wiesbaden; Harrassowitz).

Naville, É. (1886). *Das AegyptischeTodtenbuch der XVIII. bis XX. Dynastie ausverschiedenenUrk undenzusammengestellt*, 2 vols. (Berlin: Asher).

Osing J. (1982). *Denkmäler der Oase Dachla aus dem Nachlass von Ahmed Fakhry*, AV 28 (Mainz: Philipp von Zabern).

Pierret, P. and Devéria, T. (1872). *Le papyrus de Neb-qed (exemplaire hiéroglyphique du Livre des Morts) reproduit, décrit et précédé d'une introduction mythologique* (Paris: A. Franck).

Quack, J. F. (2010). "Bilder vom *Mundöffnungsritual*—Mundöffnung an Bildern." In *Bild und Ritual. Visuelle Kulturen in historischer Perspektive*, edited by C. Ambos, P. Rösch, B. Schneidmüller et al., 18–28 (Darmstadt: WBG).

Saleh, M. (1984). *Das Totenbuch in den thebanischen Beamtengräbern des Neuen Reiches. Texte und Vignetten*. Archäologische Veröffentlichungen / Deutsches Archäologisches Institut, Abteilung Kairo, 46 (Mainz: Philipp von Zabern).

Scalf, F. D., ed. (2017). *Book of the Dead: Becoming God in Ancient Egypt*. Oriental Institute Museum Publications, 39 (Chicago: CASEMATE ACADEMIC).

Settgast, J. (1985). *Ägyptisches Museum Berlin* (Mainz: Philipp von Zabern).

Seyfried, K. J. (1987). "Bemerkungen zur Erweiterung der unterirdischen Anlagen einiger Gräber des Neuen Reiches in Theben—Versuch einer Deutung." *Annales du Service des Antiquités de l'Égypte* 71: 229–49.

Smith, M. (2006). "The Great Decree Issued to the Nome of the Silent Land." *Revue d'egyptologie* 57: 217–32.

Tawfik, T. S. (2008). "Die Vignette zu Totenbuch-Kapitel 1 und vergleichbare Darstellungen in Gräbern." Dissertation (Bonn, University of Bonn).

Tawfik, T. S. (2015). "Heading West on the Akhmim Book of the Dead Papyri." In *Weitergabe. Festschrift für die Ägyptologin Ursula Rößler-Köhler zum 65. Geburtstag*. Göttinger Orientforschungen, 53, edited by L. D. Morenz and A. El Hawary, 429–36 (Wiesbaden: Harrassowitz).

Weber, D. (1998). *Erzählliteratur: Schriftwerk, Kunstwerk, Erzählwerk*. UTB für Wissenschaft, 2065 (Göttingen: Vandenhoeck & Ruprecht).

CHAPTER 19

# THE FIELD OF OFFERINGS OR FIELD OF REEDS

## MILAGROS ÁLVAREZ SOSA

Among the set of images and texts that form the Book of the Dead, vignette 110 portrays a place in the hereafter that has been interpreted either as the dwelling place of the Egyptians in their afterlife, or as a transit region where the deceased can enjoy an environment that reminds them of their daily routine when they were still alive, and where they can find nourishment, move freely, and meet the gods. The first literary references to these fields hint at a region called the Field of Reeds and the Field of Offerings.

This place in the hereafter is visualized as a landscape of waterways, ovals representing "towns," islands, and boats for sailing in this place. There the deceased will also meet various deities, among them the Great Ennead and the "heron of plenty" besides providing food for the *akh-* and *ka-*spirits. The deceased is involved in agricultural operations: seeding the earth, plowing, and harvesting. The spell describes what happens in the field: "eating therein, drinking therein, copulating and doing everything that was once done on earth."

The Pyramid Texts provide a first notion of this place, but in a funerary context that lacks any additional illustration. The texts make clear that the Field of Reeds is included in a journey that starts with the death of the king and his ascension into Heaven. Some spells allude to doors in the sky that must be knocked down in order to access this place (PT § 981a–985b; PT § 1132a–1137b; PT § 1408a–1412b). The deceased travels across the sky as Re and then descends into the Field of Reeds. Various references provide a physical description of this region and relate it to flooding; for example, there are mentions of flooded fields, ponds, and winding canals that the deceased crosses by boat.

Among the whole set of texts making up this funerary literature of the Old Kingdom, however, there are only a few references to crops or harvest in these regions (PT § 374b–c, PT § 761, PT § 1748b, PT § 2070a). This scarcity is quite peculiar if we consider the great importance that these activities have in the imagery of the afterlife's fields in later periods.

If the Field of Reeds appears to be a transit region, then the Field of Offerings is defined as a dwelling place for the king. It displays similar features, for example an area submerged in water that is referred to as the Great Flood, but also a place where the king can meet the gods and get in contact with them. It is also a region where other spirits convene, known as *akhw*, and where the king meets his *ka*, another component of a human being that some Egyptologists see as the self, others as human lifeforce, and yet others as an intergenerational entity transferred from father to child. All of them need food, and it is in the Field of Offerings that feeding occurs.

## Its First Representation: Middle Kingdom

The Coffin Texts specify that the Field of Reeds and the Field of Offerings, which are clearly identified as two different places, are located up in the sky. This feature is in continuity with the Old Kingdom, as is the prerogative for the deceased to move freely, which is a constant motif in the funerary texts.

The view of the Field of Reeds as a place of purification, as was conceived in the Pyramid Texts, is rarely attested in the Coffin Texts. In the Middle Kingdom these fields are seen in a new perspective that seems to view them as a destination, a region where food is supplied, and an object of knowledge. In fact, knowing the corresponding spells becomes an essential requisite to move freely in the afterlife, a motif that is only vaguely suggested in the Pyramid Texts.

The first representation of the Field of Offerings appears in the coffins of Deir el-Bersheh, the necropolis of Hermopolis, and the capital of District XV of Upper Egypt. A small number of spells (CT 464–68) from the Coffin Texts provide a description of the Field of Hotep or Field of Offerings, including a sort of map (CT 466). This is the central element of the sequence of four texts that appear in the same order on most of the coffins, and it is located on one side, particularly on the eastern wall (referred to as the front).

The oldest map is most probably on the B6C coffin, dating to the reign of Amenemhat I. This example is not only the oldest, but also bears a version of the map that differs from those of the necropolis of Middle Kingdom Hermopolis at Deir el-Bersheh. In it, the field is distinctive in being composed only of texts, without any dividing lines. Later models represented on other coffins are more similar to each other: B5C, B6C, B9C, B3L, B1L, B1C, and B2P. (For classification of these coffins and their location in the necropolis, see Willems, 1988; for a table showing the inclusion of this sequence in each of the coffins, see Lesko, 1971–1972, Robinson, 2007).

The image of the map seems to represent a specific place. The only iconographic elements clearly established are the water canals, which divide the map; the ovals, which represent the different regions (which must be islands, given the presence of canals); and a ladder and a boat, which are figurative indications of the capacity of the deceased to move on.

The texts are evocative of two different landscapes related to the scenery of the Nile valley: on the one hand are the natural views of marshes, canals, and plants, which are quite ordinary scenes; on the other hand is the symbolic view of the transformation of the human being. This latter aspect, however, is not stressed much, since only one text out of twenty-seven refers to the plot of land that is in possession of the god and that can be plowed and sown by the deceased to get his food. It was Text XIV inside the map which probably inspired the idea of including a scene of agricultural work in the Book of the Dead.

## Vignette Bd 110: New Kingdom

The practice of including a papyrus containing religious literature in the funerary equipment was only introduced in the Eighteenth Dynasty. When looking at the characteristics of the Book of the Dead of this period, one will notice that it is typically long, which means that it could encompass a large number of spells. Although many of them were illustrated, texts were still predominant up until the end of the Eighteenth Dynasty. Despite their high quality, vignettes were in fact still of secondary importance in comparison to later periods.

If we consider the number of papyri catalogued in the Eighteenth Dynasty (Munro, 1988), we can conclude that there are few copies containing vignette 110, which indicates that it was underrepresented in the Book of the Dead of this period. This probably explains why we have only one typology belonging to this period, vignette type A, which shows quite a relative homogeneity in the papyri where it is included (Fig. 19.1). This type is the only one documented during the Eighteenth Dynasty in Thebes and is represented in both tombs and papyri. A significant feature is the inclusion of a purification scene that is unique to this model; it does not appear in any other vignette type. The deceased appears while receiving a libation and an offering, a scene that is reminiscent of the decorative programs of tombs and temples of the New Kingdom.

A thorough understanding of the layout of the vignette is essential for the various studies that can be conducted concerning the iconography of the Book of the Dead. For this reason, it is important to go back to the oldest model. If we examine the vignette carefully, we will notice how the figurative composition follows both an orderly pattern and a conventional structure. The narrative technique is synoptic, combining different snapshots or episodes into a single representation. With the exception of the scenes portraying the sequence of agricultural activities, the registers do not seem to have any chronological organization. As for the time portrayed in the vignette, we are surely confronted with an image of eternity.

Interestingly, one of the papyri of the Eighteenth Dynasty (P.Nebseni, P.London BM EA 9900, Lapp, 2003) shows the vignette juxtaposed with other texts and images related to the field. This somehow allows us to make assumptions on the "order of scenes" (see Fig. 19.1). Since the deceased first meets the gods and hands them the corresponding

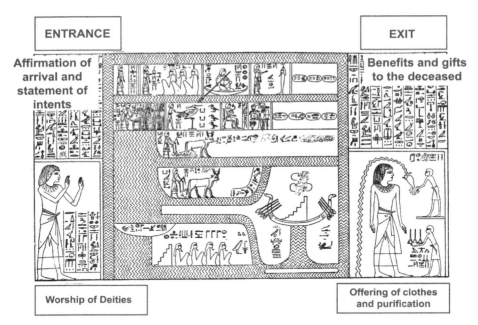

FIG. 19.1. Papyrus P.London BM EA 9900 (Nebseni), Eighteenth Dynasty. Vignette-type A (from Kolpaktchy, 1842).

offering, we may assume that the register must be read from the point where this scene appears. Another scene that might indicate the reading order is the one in which the owner appears alone. The fact that this scene is placed at one end of the vignette and that the deceased is at "rest" and not involved in any action might allow us to identify it as a scene of "arrival to the field". Also, it seems quite logical that the scene representing the deceased on board a boat must precede the one with the ovals that represent lands or places of destination, according to the texts.

The vignette of papyrus Nebseni is flanked by texts and scenes. The text on the left is a statement of his arrival at the field and a notice of intentions, and is completed by the image of the deceased worshipping, facing the vignette with raised arms. Another text related to the Field of Reeds, and mentioning the gifts and benefits to Nebseni, is located on the right-hand side. This text includes a scene of libation and offering to the deceased by two individuals. The fact that this image does not face the vignette is quite significant. We may conclude that there is a scene of "entrance" (left) and a scene of "exit" (right). This assumption, however, does not allow us to infer the order of "reading" as in the case of hieroglyphic texts, namely, by establishing the direction of the iconographic elements as signs. The "key" is to keep the order of the scenes of the first register: arrival, worship of the gods, rowing the boat, and freeing Horus from Seth before reaching the lands (ovals).

It is interesting to note that the first model of vignette type A of the Eighteenth Dynasty bears some similarities to the map of CT 466, and this is peculiar to this group of documents. The common traits are mainly related to the locations of the ovals, scenes, and texts.

If we consider the chronology of the vignettes of this period, it must be noted that the oldest of them is the image represented in the tomb of Senenmut, which dates to the reign of Hatshepsut. Therefore, this is in line with the appearance of the Book of the Dead on papyri. This is particularly interesting since, when comparing the image of Senenmut with vignette 110 of the Eighteenth Dynasty, the characteristics of the image in the tomb seem to be closer to the map of CT 466 than to the vignettes on papyri (Fig. 19.2).

The fact that Senenmut's image is the oldest evidence for this, and that there are no other pictures in tombs or papyri so very similar to the map of the Middle Kingdom, leads us to assume that the type A specimens of this period might have used the master copy created for the Field of Reeds in the Tomb of Senenmut as their model. This hypothesis is supported by the following arguments:

- The location of the ovals and texts in Senenmut's vignette is the same as in the map of the coffins, which allows us to associate it with the funerary literature of the Middle Kingdom (see Fig. 19.2). The later copies of the Book of the Dead bear various changes concerning the location of the ovals and texts in the vignette.
- The connection between Senenmut's tomb and the Coffin Texts is not confined to the vignette only. The text of BD 110, which is illustrated by the picture of the Field of Offerings, is a direct derivation of CT 464, 465, and part of CT 467, which appear around the Field of Hotep in the coffins of Deir el-Bersheh.

It is also interesting to note that references to this region of the hereafter as the Field of Hotep were restricted to the spells of Deir el-Bersheh's coffins until the composition of the

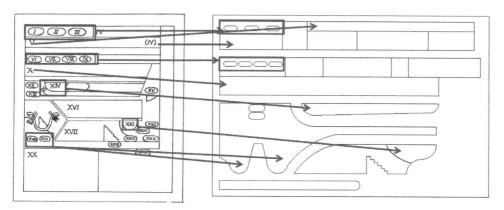

FIG. 19.2. Parallels between the Map of the Coffin B5C belonging to *Ḏḥwty-ḥtp* (Cairo Museum N° JdE 37566) and the vignette of Senenmut's tomb, TT 353 (Eighteenth Dynasty) (from De Buck, 1935–1961).

Book of the Dead. So it is highly significant that this denomination is still retained in the spell associated with Senenmut's vignette and in the third register therein. This reference is lost when the spell is transferred to papyrus in later copies.

## THE VIGNETTE DURING THE NINETEENTH DYNASTY

The post-Amarna and Ramesside Book of the Dead papyri tend to replace texts with vignettes. At the same time, the number of scenes increases while the accuracy of texts declines, that is, the texts tend to disappear, how it can be seen in the papyrus of Iufankh (P.Turin 1791; Lepsius, 1842). The reason for this inversion is apparently to be found in organizational changes within workshops.

A general attitude toward a different form of expression of religious ideas may have followed an evolution that understood the figurative representations as magically more effective than the texts. This iconographic program of the Book of the Dead and the decline of the texts on papyri are important aspects that Niwiński defines by the Latin term *pars pro toto* (Niwiński, 1987–1988), which consists in the use of short versions of the text with the aim of providing the papyri with "all" possible recitations. Of course, all of this resulted in large textual gaps. On the other hand, when a vignette was to be associated with two spells, a text could be added in combination with the image of another spell. In this way, both spells were represented.

The typological study of the vignettes of this period has led to the establishment of a main type, which is called vignette type C. This was the most frequently represented type during the Nineteenth Dynasty, not only in tombs and papyri, but also in other places. Most examples in tombs are from Thebes, but some are also from Sedment. Evidence of this type also appears in the tomb of Pennut in Aniba, or, even before the Nineteenth Dynasty, in a tomb of the Eighteenth Dynasty in Memphis, the tomb of Paatonemheb (Álvarez Sosa, 2010).

The analysis of the models of vignette 110 from the Nineteenth and Twentieth Dynasties allows us to determine a set of typical features that make them different from the vignette's attestations of other periods:

- there is an absence of internal division of the image due to the removal of the vertical lines;
- in most vignettes, the scenes change their location inside the registers, which is in contrast to the fixed locations found in vignette type A;
- the vignette is complemented by an external scene in which the deceased, alone or accompanied by his wife, is depicted in adoration, facing the field;
- new iconographic elements may occur, creating "unique vignettes";

- the drawings are of higher quality and show a preference for iconographic details and application of color;
- new texts are included inside the vignette that are not part of the map of Hotep (CT 466) of the Middle Kingdom; some vignettes may entirely lack them;
- the text of BD 110 has been reduced to a shorter version.

Another aspect to be considered, and that is further accentuated in the vignettes of this period, is that although all of them seem to be modeled on the same master copy, they nevertheless introduce variations that could be due to space limits or personal intervention by the artist.

In contrast to the homogeneity of vignette 110 during the Eighteenth Dynasty, a number of extraordinary and unique specimens characterized by variations in the standard image, and also by greater iconographic complexity, are attested in this period. The inclusion of new scenes inside the Field of Offerings may indicate that some vignettes were accurately redesigned for specific papyri. Another possibility is that scribes or skilled artists were the authors of the higher-quality papyri, where greater care in the design of the images can be noted. The introduction of new scenes thus shows a reworking of the vignette in this period.

## The Vignette During the Twenty-First Dynasty

During this period, the papyri and the decoration of the coffins were an alternative to the lack of funerary texts and representations that previously decorated the tombs (see Lenzo, this volume). Economic problems also led to shorter funerary papyri in the Twenty-first Dynasty, when compared to the New Kingdom papyri. Consequently, the total number of decorated surfaces was much smaller than in earlier times. In this period, the workshops producing the Book of the Dead went back to ancient models. The vignette type A of the Eighteenth Dynasty resurfaces, which shows how, despite the iconographic creativity of this period, old types of vignettes were also consulted.

Highly significant is the resemblance of a vignette from the Twenty-first Dynasty papyrus of Horemakhbit (P.Leiden T6 = AMS 33) to another Eighteenth Dynasty vignette in Senenmut's tomb (TT 353). These common features are not shared with such precision by any other type A specimens either in the Eighteenth or in the Twenty-first Dynasty. The vignette follows exactly the same scheme as the decoration of the tomb, even in the arrangement of its tiniest iconographic details. It is so faithful, in fact, that we can even rely on it to reconstruct a lost text in TT 353: above the boat in its third register, there are two ovals and, near them, an empty space where a text was removed. The vignette of Horemakhbit is the only type A vignette that contains the text *wỉꜣ Rꜥ* "boat of Re."

Another remarkable aspect is related to the gods represented in the last register beside the staircase. In the vignette type A specimens of the Eighteenth Dynasty papyri, the gods are portrayed as figures of regular size forming one of the scenes of the vignette (see Fig. 19.1). In Senenmut's tomb and the papyrus of Horemakhbit, however, they appear very small, almost like hieroglyphs.

Based on the considerable similarities in the features of both models, we could conclude that the Twenty-first Dynasty papyrus might have been copied directly from Senenmut's tomb. Although it is widely known that the New Kingdom tombs were opened in order to be reused in this period (Taylor, 1992), this would, however, be a rash conclusion. It is equally imaginable to assume that the Theban workshop responsible for the decorative program of Senenmut's tomb might have stored or had access to a papyrus copy of the decoration that was used as a model for the Book of the Dead of the Theban priest 400 years later.

The analysis of the formal aspects and content of the vignettes during the period in which this funerary papyrus was used can provide information about the changes to which they were exposed, as well as knowledge concerning to what extent they were based on the spells that accompanied them. Studying the illustrations in their context and comparing them with each other allows us to better understand the way in which the scribes or draftsmen involved in the elaboration of the Book of the Dead papyrus worked with the images and the knowledge they had of it (Álvarez Sosa, 2010).

During the Twenty-first Dynasty, it is evident that Nineteenth Dynasty vignette types were in fact consulted. An outstanding example is vignette 110, represented in P.Greenfield (P.London BM EA 10554) belonging to Nesitanebetisheru, daughter of the High Priest Pinedjem II (Budge, 1912). Interestingly, this model (vignette type I) is also present on a tomb wall of one of the kings of Tanis, Osorkon II, of the Twenty-second Dynasty (Montet, 1947; Lull, 2002). This vignette is based on a model that appeared in the Nineteenth Dynasty. We can notice its transformation through a comparison with the vignette of the papyrus of Ani (P.London BM EA 10470; Budge, 1895, 1913).

The fact that the same type of vignette 110 represented on the papyrus of the daughter of Pinedjem II, buried in the Royal Cachette of Deir el-Bahari (Thebes), can be found in Osorkon II's tomb in Tanis, allows us to consider a Theban origin for the model. The master copy remained in the workshop, thus meaning that either this vignette or a copy of it must have been transferred to the Delta to be placed in Osorkon II's tomb.

During the Twenty-first Dynasty, a number of new iconographic compositions were created, illustrating how the new theological ideas of the period affected the funerary texts. The emergence of new types of vignettes and the fact that some of them were subject to revision and changes allow us to speculate on some sort of "vignette experimentation" on the set of images of the Book of the Dead in this period. The vignettes belonging to this typology, in fact, break the rules of standard representation in most cases (e.g., P.Cairo S.R. VII 10256). These vignettes show a certain degree of autonomous and challenging "reformulation" of the Field of Offerings and its scenes. The fact that the figurative elements of the image are scattered, reduced, or combined with other scenes means that their identification requires a good degree of competence.

Regarding the content, vignette 110 in the Havana papyrus (Álvarez Sosa, Chicuri Lastra, and Morfini, 2017) is an illustrative example of the omission of some otherwise recurrent scenes, and the introduction of new iconographic elements (Fig. 19.3). This includes some common scenes: the seated gods, the boat (although in a different

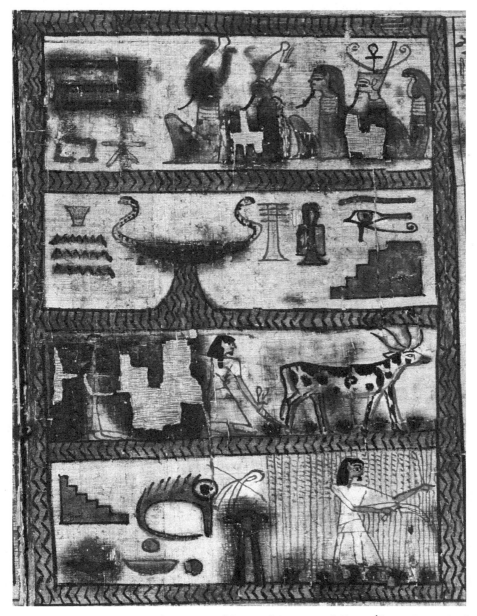

FIG. 19.3. P.Havana MNBA Habana 94–97 (Twenty-first Dynasty) (from Álvarez Sosa, Morfini and Chicuri Lastra, 2015).

register than the usual one), the harvest, and plowing. By contrast, the new iconographic elements produce a sort of "jumble" that is somehow reminiscent of the decoration of the sarcophagi of this period (referred to as "horror vacui," Niwiński, 1981, 2006). Nevertheless, the symbols introduced by the scribe do not seem to be arbitrary. Rather, they appear to be related to access to the field (regions), displacement (stairs), and protection (amulets). All of these are aspects associated with the meaning of the regions of the afterlife.

Although this papyrus is inspired by a well-established model, the work of the scribes and artists on this vignette makes it a unique specimen. We may therefore assume that, particularly on this occasion, the artist enjoyed a certain degree of freedom in selecting the components from the master copy, and was allowed to omit some scenes while introducing new iconographic elements that he considered to be in line with the theme of the image.

With regard to the new versions of the vignettes of the Twenty-first Dynasty, the innovations are probably, on the one hand, essentially due to a change in the layout of the papyri: since these are shorter, they called for a different composition of the vignette.

On the other hand, however, a series of vignettes seems to be the result of the new theological beliefs of this period. This might explain why vignette 110 differs from one papyrus to another. All these variations probably depended on the degree of freedom the scribe could enjoy, and his artistic ability in mastering the elements of the visual system. In conclusion, it can be said that this period witnessed a continuous creative work on the image of the Field of Offerings.

## The Vignette in the Late and Ptolemaic Periods

The largest number of attestations of vignette 110 belong to this later phase. This is the time of the "Saite recension," when a massive revision of this funerary corpus was carried out (see Albert and Gülden, this volume). The typological study of the vignettes of this period allows us to establish two main models, with subtypes. Following the analysis of the models (Álvarez Sosa, 2010), it can be concluded that the vignettes created in this period are not entirely new, but rather are based on master copies from the New Kingdom.

Particularly interesting in these results is that the contextualization of the two main typologies analyzed corresponds to two specific periods: the beginning of the Twenty-sixth Dynasty, which saw the revival of the Book of the Dead, and the Ptolemaic Period. This means that both models perfectly reflect the two chronologies that other scholars associate with a likely process of revision of the Book of the Dead.

The analysis of subtypes shows that both models were subject to a number of revisions, which would imply a great deal of work in workshops copying this funerary book. Based on the study of the vignettes of this period, we can therefore observe the following:

- a higher number of specimens, which might suggest that the Book of the Dead was now accessible to a wider sphere of people;
- a higher number of poor-quality vignettes, coarsely executed compared to other periods;
- vignettes serially produced;
- a greater iconographic elaborateness of the vignettes, with more figurative elements within the field and the incorporation of attached scenes into some vignettes, as in the case of vignette "c." (The numbering of the vignette corresponds to the suggestion given by [Allen, 1960]. The vignette and spell 110 are designated by letters. Text 110 would be "a," the vignette of the field "b," and these new scenes "c.") These scenes may appear attached to the field or in its vicinity. The most common way of finding them will be in the union with vignette 110;
- a considerable number of textual errors;
- decreased textual extent, so that the image may lack recitation of BD 110 and even the relevant legends; this might indicate that a recitation could be easily epitomized and recalled only by the image.

The type referred to as K seems to be the oldest model in this period and the source of several subtypes. This type presents the same number of scenes as in New Kingdom attestations, which would be vignette type C of the Nineteenth Dynasty, reversed and with new scenes added, namely vignette 110c.

Since an example of vignette 110 of this type is attested in Bakenrenef's tomb, we can date this model to the beginning of the Twenty-sixth Dynasty. The dating of Bakenrenef's tomb to the reign of the founder of the Saite Dynasty (Buongarzone, 1990, 1991–1992; Álvarez Sosa, 2010) leads us to assume that this should be one of the first models of vignette 110 created by the scribes of this period. In turn, this would allow us to establish hypotheses concerning the dating of the papyri that include this typology.

The other main vignette type of this period, type L, is more standardized than type K, since only one subtype is identifiable. This type is not only the most complex, but also the most often represented in the Ptolemaic Period.

For the identification of type L and its description, the vignette of Iufankh may serve as a model because its good condition of preservation allows us to properly analyze the iconographic and textual elaborateness of this typology (Fig. 19.4).

With regard to the texts within the image, some of them can be found in vignette 110 of the New Kingdom types, and others are new additions of the Ptolemaic Period.

The standardization of the Book of the Dead in this period probably favored a more frequent reproduction of the vignette. As a rule, the recitations appear in a regular order that already includes BD 110 or its vignette. Also, the lack of the deceased's names and titles in many vignettes is indicative of a sort of serial production. The vignette of Iufankh is an illustrative example in this respect because it contains empty spaces where the name of the owner was to be inserted, between the

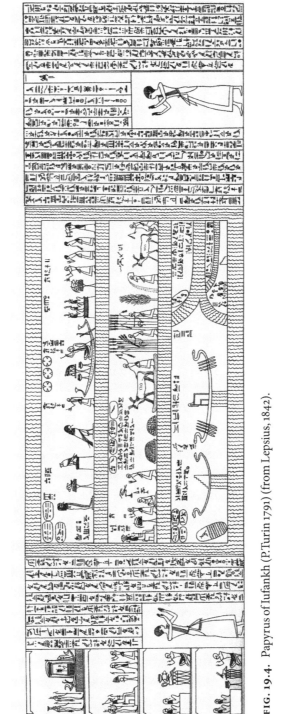

FIG. 19.4. Papyrus of Iufankh (P.Turin 1791) (from Lepsius, 1842).

name of Osiris and his denomination as justified, *mꜣꜥ-ḫrw*. This scribe's lapsus shows that the vignettes were not drawn for a particular deceased, but would instead be individualized with the details of the client when they were included in the whole composition of the papyrus.

## Transmission

The study of the evolution of vignette 110, starting with its origin in the Eighteenth Dynasty and even its precedent in the Coffin Texts, has allowed us to observe the continuity in the workshops' activity regarding this image. When considering the coffins from Deir el-Bersheh, it is evident that the map of the Field of Offerings is documented as an exceptional occurrence. In fact, the number of governors and officials who included it in the decoration of their coffins is regionally restricted and by no means high. This leads us to assume that this image was not of fundamental importance in the beliefs of the hereafter when the vignette was used in the necropolis of Deir el-Bersheh.

In the period between the middle of the Twelfth and the Eighteenth Dynasty, the image somehow disappears. Interestingly, when the Field of Reeds or Field of Offerings resurface as part of the Book of the Dead, it no longer occurs on coffins, as in the Middle Kingdom, but in tombs and on papyri.

Regarding the period in which this image was exported from its place of origin, two hypotheses can be mentioned: it might have appeared in Thebes during the Eighteenth Dynasty, coming directly from the archives where it was kept, or it might have reached Thebes during the Twelfth Dynasty or later, although this remained undocumented until the tomb of Senenmut was built. It cannot be excluded, however, that it might have been present at an even earlier time, but on other supports that have not been preserved. The lack of sources allows us merely to speculate.

During the Twenty-first Dynasty, a curious phenomenon in the transmission of the Book of the Dead is recorded. As a consequence of the disappearance of the private tombs, the spells appear on the coffins as well as being inscribed on papyri as part of the funerary equipment. A study conducted by Niwiński demonstrates how the funerary equipment of the people buried in the cachettes includes the same spells represented in the New Kingdom tombs, or at least in the most popular ones (Niwiński, 2006). The iconographic boom of this period accounts for the massive number of new types of vignettes and points to an increased activity in the workshops involved in the reproduction of this funerary corpus. Furthermore, the vignettes of the Field of Offerings reveal a certain degree of "freedom" in the execution of the images of the Book of the Dead.

The occurrence of the same type of vignette 110 in the tomb of Osorkon II in Tanis and in the papyrus that belonged to the daughter of Pinedjem II and was stored in the Royal Cachette at Deir el-Bahari, allows us to postulate a transfer of the model from Thebes to Tanis (Römer, 1986), thus confirming the importance of the Theban workshops even in a period of crisis, when the kings ceased to be buried in this necropolis. Moreover, the reappearance of type A of the Eighteenth Dynasty and the influence of models of the Nineteenth Dynasty on vignettes of this period, as we have seen, are examples of archival work conducted in this period.

During the Twenty-fifth Dynasty, the Kushite period, a revival of Egyptian culture began (Russman, 2005). In this context, the rediscovery of ancient traditions, including funerary literature, played an important role. Thus, after a period of neglect, the Book of the Dead comes to the fore again. The majority of sources for vignette 110 are dated to the Late and Ptolemaic Periods, which probably means that a greater number of papyri of this funerary book were executed in this period. However, the iconographic study on them reveals that an increasing number of copies of the Book of the Dead did not result in the creation of more types, as in the case of the Twenty-first Dynasty. Our study of the tradition of this spell and vignette leads therefore to the conclusion that there was no mechanical reproduction of the texts or perpetuation of old ideas, but rather a reformulation, both of the texts related to this region of the hereafter and of the image that represented it.

## Appendix: List of Vignettes

### Vignette- type A (Eighteenth Dynasty)

| Papyri/Tombs | Provenance | Current location | Publication |
|---|---|---|---|
| BD of Userhat | Thebes | British Museum, P.London BM EA 10009 + 9962,1 | Munro, 1988; Taylor, 2010 |
| BD of Iuia | Thebes, KV 46 | Egyptian Museum P.Cairo CG 51189 | Davis, 1908; Munro, 1994 |
| BD of Neferubenef | Thebes | Musée du Louvre, P.Louvre N. 3092 (III 93) + P.Montpellier | Ratié, 1968 |
| BD of Nebseni | Memphis | British Museum, P.London BM EA 9900 | Lapp, 2003 |
| TT 353 Senenmut Tomb | Thebes | Deir el-Bahari | Dorman, 1991 |
| TT 57 | Thebes | Sheikh Abd el-Qurna | Unpublished (©Metropolitan Museum of Art, New York) |
| TT C 4 | Thebes | Sheikh Abd el-Qurna | Manniche, 1988 (vignette MSS Wilkinson) |

### Vignette- type A (Twenty-first Dynasty)

| Papyri/Tombs | Provenance | Current location | Publication |
|---|---|---|---|
| BD of Nedjemet | Thebes, TT 320 | Musée du Louvre, P.Louvre E 6258 (= Nedjemet A) / P.London BM EA 10541 | Budge, 1899 |

| | | | |
|---|---|---|---|
| BD of Gatseshen | Thebes, Bab el-Gasus | Egyptian Museum P.Cairo J.E. 95838 (= S.R. IV 936) | Lucarelli, 2006 |
| BD of Nesykhonsu | Thebes, TT 320 | Egyptian Museum P.Cairo, S.R. VII 11573 (=J. 26230, 11485) | Naville, 1912 |
| BD of Horemakhbit | Thebes | Rijksmuseum van Oudheden, P.Leiden T 6 (=AMS 33) | Unpublished |
| BD of Paennestitaui | Thebes (?) | British Museum, P.London BM EA 10064 | Munro, 2001 |

**Vignette- type C (Nineteenth-twentieth Dynasty)**

| Papyri/Tombs | Provenance | Current location | Publication |
|---|---|---|---|
| BD of Ani | Thebes | British Museum, P.London BM EA 10470 | Budge, 1966 Tylor, 2010 |
| BD of Nebqed | Thebes | P.Paris Louvre N 3068 + 3113 | Devéria and Pierret, 1872 |
| P.Cambridge (E.2.1922) | Sedment | Fitzwilliam Museum P.Cambridge E.2. 1922 | online |
| P.London UC 32365 | Sedment | Petrie Museum P.London UC 32365 | online |
| P.Berlin 3002 | ? | Berlin Ägyptisches Museum P.Berlin P. 3002 | Munro, 1997 |
| Tomb of Paatenemheb | Saqqara | Rijksmuseum van Oudheden, Leiden AMt 1–35, AP 52 | Leemans, 1840 |

**New versions of the vignette 110 "unique Type" (Twenty-first Dynasty)**

| Papyri/Tombs | Provenance | Current location | Publication |
|---|---|---|---|
| P.Cairo S.R.VII 10249 | Thebes, Deir el-Bahari Bab el-Gasus | Egyptian Museum P.Cairo S.R.VII 10249 (= T.N.14.7.35.7) | Gesellensetter, 1997 |
| BD of Maatkare | Thebes Deir el-Bahari Cachette Real | Egyptian Museum P.Cairo S.R. IV 980 = J.26229 = 40007 | Naville, 1912 |
| P.Havana | Thebes | Museo Nacional de Bellas Artes, P.Havana MNBA Habana 94–47 | Álvarez Sosa, Chicuri Lastra, and Morfini, 2015 |

| P.Cairo CG 40016 | Thebes, Deir el-Bahari Bab el-Gasus | Egyptian Museum P.Cairo CG 40016(=S.R.VII 10240) | Piankoff and Rambova, 1957: n° 18 |
| P.Cairo S.R. VII 10256 | Thebes, Deir el-Bahari Bab el-Gasus | Egyptian Museum P.Cairo S.R.VII 10256=14.7.35.6 =JE 31986=CG 4884 | Piankoff and Rambova, 1957: n° 71 |

**Vignette type I (Twenty-first Dynasty)**

| Papyri/Tombs | Provenance | Current location | Publication |
|---|---|---|---|
| P.Greenfield | Thebes, TT 320 | British Museum, P.London BM EA 10554 | Budge, 1912; Taylor, 2010 |
| Tomb of Osorkon II | | Tanis | Roulin, 1998; Lull, 2002 |

**Vignette type K (Late and Ptolemaic Periods)**

| Papyri/Tombs | Provenance | Current location | Publication |
|---|---|---|---|
| P.Vaticano 48832 | Memphis | Museo Gregoriano Egizio P.Vatican 48832 =Vaticano 1 (N. 16) | Gasse, 2001 |
| P.Turin 1831 | Thebes | Museo Egizio P.Turin 1831 | Unpublished (©Archivio Fondazione Museo delle Antichità Egizie di Torino) |
| P.London BM EA 10097 | ? | British Museum P.London BM EA 10097/10 | Unpublished |
| P.Cologny Bodmer, CV | Thebes | Bibliotheca Bodmeriana, Fondation Martin Bodmer, P.Cologny Bodmer CV + P.Cincinnati, Art Museum 1947.369 + P.Denver Art Museum 1954.61 | Munro, 2006 |
| P.Turin 1793 | Thebes | Museo Egizio P.Turin 1793 | Unpublished (©Archivio Fondazione Museo delle Antichità Egizie di Torino) |

| | | | |
|---|---|---|---|
| P.Köln 10207 | Abusir el Meleq | Seminar für Ägyptologie P.Köln Aeg.10207 | Verhoeven, 1993 |
| Tomb of Bakenrenef | - | Saqqara | Bresciani, 1993 Wilkinson MSS vii.51–52 |

### Vignette type L (Late and Ptolemaic Periods)

| Papyri/Tombs | Provenance | Current location | Publication |
|---|---|---|---|
| BD of Iufankh | Thebes | Museo Egizio P.Turin 1791 | Lepsius, 1842 |
| P.Turin 1806 | ? | Museo Egizio P.Turin 1806 | Unpublished (©Archivio Fondazione Museo delle Antichità Egizie di Torino) |
| P.Dublin TCL 1662 | Thebes | Trinity College Library, P.Dublin TCL 1662 | Unpublished |
| P.Berlin 3008 | Thebes | Ägyptisches Museum und Papyrussammlung, P.Berlin P. 3008 | Lacovara, D'Auria and Roehrig, 1988 |
| P.New York Amherst 30 | Thebes | Nueva York, Pierpont Morgan Library Amherst 30; P.Paris Louvre N 3129 + E 4890B; P.Krakau, Nationalmuseum XI 1503-06. 1508–11; P.Brüssel MRAH E. 4976 | Unpublished |
| BD of P.Ryerson | ? | Chicago Oriental Institute P.Chicago OIM 9787; P.New York Columbia University Library Inv.784 | Allen, 1960 |
| P.Paris Louvre N. 3089 | ? | Musée du Louvre P.Paris Louvre N 3089 | Unpublished |
| P.Paris Louvre N. 3143 | Thebes | Musée du Louvre P.Paris Louvre N 3143; P.Genf D 229 | Mosher, 1990 |
| P.Paris Louvre N. 3248 | Thebes | Musée du Louvre P.Paris Louvre N 3248 | Mosher, 1990 |

| | | | |
|---|---|---|---|
| P.London BM EA 10034 | Thebes | London British Museum P.London BM EA 10034 + 10705 (3) | Unpublished |
| P.London BM EA 10088 | Thebes | London British Museum P.London BM EA 10088 | Unpublished |
| P.Cologny CIV | Thebes? | Bibliotheca Bodmeriana, Fondation Martin Bodmer, P.Cologny Bodmer CIV | Unpublished |

# Bibliography

Allen, T. G. (1960). *The Egyptian Book of the Dead: Documents in the Oriental Institute Museum at the University of Chicago*. Oriental Institute Publications 82 (Chicago: Oriental Institute).

Álvarez Sosa, M. (2009). "Origen y primera elaboración de la viñeta 110 del Libro de la Salida al Día." *Trabajos de Egiptología / Research Papers on Ancient Egypt* 5 and 6-Actas del III Congreso Ibérico de Egiptología: 49–65.

Álvarez Sosa, M. (2010). *Escribas, talleres y copias maestras. Análisis iconográfico y tipológico de la viñeta del Campo de Juncos. Un modelo para el estudio de la transmisión del Libro de la Salida al Día* (Unpublished PhD thesis, La Laguna University).

Álvarez Sosa, M. M. (2012). "El *Libro De La Salida Al Día* En La Tumba De Senenmut: Una Propuesta De Análisis Iconográfico." In *Novos Trabalhos De Egiptologia Ibérica: IV Congresso Ibérico De Egiptologia - IV Congreso Ibérico De Egiptología*, vol. 1, edited by Luís M. de Araújo and José d. C. Sales, 101–15 (Lisboa: Instituto Oriental e Centro de História da Facultade de Letras da Universidade de Lisboa).

Álvarez Sosa, M., Chicuri Lastra, A., and Morfini, I. (2015). *La Colección Egipcia del Museo de Bellas Artes de la Habana/ The Egyptian Collection of the National Museum of Fine Arts in Havana* (San Cristóbal de La Laguna, Santa Cruz de Tenerife: Ad Aegyptum).

Andrews, C. (1998). *Egyptian Mummies* (London: British Museum Press).

Bresciani, E. (1993). "L'attivitá archeologica in egitto dell'universitá di Pisa nel 1992 e nel 1993." *Egitto e Vicino Oriente* XVI: 1–14.

Buck, A. (1935–1961). *The Egyptian Coffin Texts* (Chicago: University of Chicago Press).

Budge, E. A. W. (1899). *The Book of the Dead: Facsimiles of the papyri of Hunefer, Anhai, Kerasher and Netchement, with Supplementary Text from the Papyrus of Nu* (London: British Museum).

Budge, E. A. W. (1912). *The Greenfield Papyrus in the British Museum* (London: British Museum).

Budge, E. A. W. (1913). *The Book of the Dead. The Papyrus of Ani in the British Museum* (London, 1895); Ernest Alfred Wallis Budge, *The papyrus of Ani: A Reproduction in Facsimile*, edited, with Hieroglyphic Transcript, Translation and Introduction (London and New York: G. P. Putnam's Sons).

Buongarzone, R. (1990). "La Funzionalità Dei Testi Nel Contesto Architettonico Della Tomba Di Bakenrenef." *Egitto e Vicino Oriente* 13: 81–102.

Buongarzone, R. (1991–1992). "Su Alcuni Testi Della Tomba Di Bakenrenef: A Proposito Di Una Redazione Saitica." *Egitto e Vicino Oriente* 14–15: 31–42.

Devéria, T. (1872). *Le papyrus de Neb-qed, exemplaire hiéroglyphique du Livre des Morts* (Paris: A. Franck).

Dorman, P. F. (1991). *The Tombs of Senenmut: The Architecture and Decoration of Tombs 71 and 353* (Metropolitan Museum of Art Publications 24, New York: Metropolitan Museum of Art).

Faulkner, R. O. (1969). *The Ancient Egyptian Pyramid Texts* (Oxford: Clarendon Press).

Gasse, A. (2002). *Le Livre des Morts de Pacherientaihet au Museo Gregoriano Egizio* (Aegyptiaca Gregoriana V, Cité du Vatican: Cybèle).

Gesellensetter, J. (1997). *Das Sechet-Iaru.Untersuchungen zur Vignette des Kapitels 110 im Ägyptischen Totenbuch* (Dissertation Julius-Maximilians-Universität Würzburg, urn:nbn:de:bvb:20-opus-3757).

Kolpaktchy, G. (1954). *Livre des morts des anciens Egyptiens* (Paris: Éditions des Champs-Élysée).

Lacovara, P., D'Auria, S., and Roehrig, C. H. (1988). *Mummies and Magic* (Boston: Museum of Fine Art).

Lepsius, R. (1842). *Das Todtenbuch der Ägypter nach dem hieroglyphischen Papyrus in Turin* (Leipzig: Georg Wigand).

Lesko, L. H. (1971–1972). "The Field of Hetep in Egyptian Coffin Texts." *Journal of the American Research Center in Egypt* 9: 89–101.

Lull, J. (2002). *Las tumbas reales egipcias del Tercer Período Intermedio, dinastías XXI–XXV: tradición y cambios* (Oxford: Archaeopress).

Lapp, G. (2003). *The Papyrus of Nebseny (BM EA 9900)* (Catalogue of the Books of the Dead in the British Museum 3, London: British Museum Press).

Lucarelli, R. (2006). *Book of the Dead of Gatseshen: Ancient Egyptian Funerary Religion of the 10th Century B.C.* (Leiden: Nederlands Instituut voor het Nabije Oosten).

Manniche, L. (1988). *Lost Tombs: A Study of Certain 18th Dynasty Monuments in the Theban Necropolis* (London: Kegan Paul International).

Montet, P. (1947). *La nécropole royale de Tanis I. Les constructions et le Tombeau d'Osorkon II à Tanis* (Paris: Jourde et Allard).

Mosher, M. (1990). *The Ancient Egyptian Book of the Dead in the Late Period: A Study of Revisions Evident in Evolving Vignettes and Possible Chronological and Geographical Implications for Differing Versions of Vignettes* (Berkeley: Doctoral Dissertation from the University of California).

Munro, I. (1988). *Untersuchungen zu den Totenbuch-Papyri der 18. Dynastie. Kriterien ihrer Datierung*. Studies in Egyptology (London; New York: Kegan Paul Internationa).

Munro, I. (1994). *Die Totenbuch-Handschriften der 18. Dynastie in Ägyptischen Museum Cairo. Aegyptologische Abhandlungen 54* (Wiesbaden: Harrassowitz).

Munro, I. (1997). *Das Totenbuch des Nacht-Amun aus der Ramessidenzeit (p Berlin P.3002). Handschriften des Altägyptischen Totenbuches 4* (Wiesbaden: Harrassowitz).

Munro, I. (2001). *Das Totenbuch des Pa-en-nesti-taui aus der Regierungszeit des Amenemope (pLondon BM 10064). Handschriften des Altägyptischen Totenbuches 7* (Wiesbaden: Harrassowitz).

Munro, I. (2006). *Der Totenbuch-Papyrus des Hor aus der frühen Ptolemäerzeit (pCologny Bodmer CV + pCincinnati 1947.369 + pDenver 1954.61). Handschriften des Altägyptischen Totenbuches 9* (Wiesbaden: Harrassowitz).

Naville, E. (1912). *Le Papyrus hiéroglyphique de Kamara et le Papyrus hiératique de Nesikhonsou au Musée du Caire* (Paris).
Niwiński, A. (1981). "Towards the Religious Iconography of the 21st Dynasty." *Göttinger Miszellen* 49: 47–59.
Niwiński, A. (1989). *Studies on the Illustrated Theban Funerary Papyri of the 11th and 10th Centuries B.C.* (Orbis Biblicus et Orientalis 86, Freiburg/Göttingen Universitätsverlag, Vandenhoeck & Ruprecht).
Niwiński, A. (2005). "The Book of the Dead on the Coffins of the 21st Dynasty." In *(Hgg.): Totenbuch-Forschungen. Gesammelte Beiträge des 2. Internationalen Totenbuch-Symposiums. Bonn, 25. bis 29. September 2005. Studien zum altägyptischen Totenbuch SAT 11*, edited by B. Backes, I. Munro, and S. Stöhr, 245–72 (Wiesbaden: Harrassowitz).
Niwiński, A. (2006). "The Book of the Dead on the Coffins of the 21st Dynasty." In *Totenbuch-Forschungen. Gesammelte Beiträge des 2. Internationalen Totenbuch-Symposiums. Studien zum altägyptischen Totenbuch 11*, edited by B. Backes, I. Munro, and S. Stöhr, 251 (Wiesbaden: Harrassowitz).
Niwiński, A. (1987–1988). "The Solar-Osirian Unity as Principle of the Theology of the "State of Amun." Thebes in the 21st Dynasty," *Jaarbericht van het Vooraziatisch-Egyptische Genootschap Ex Oriente Lux* 30: 89–106.
Piankoff, A. and Rambova, N. (1957). *Mythological Papyri (ERT 3)* (New York: Pantheon Books for the Bollingen Foundation).
Ratié, S. (1968). *Le papyrus de Neferoubenef (Louvre III 93)*, Bibliothèque d'Étude 43 (Le Caire).
Robinson, P. (2007). "The Locational Significance of Scatological References in the Coffin Texts." In *Current Research in Egyptology 2006: Proceedings of the Seventh Annual Symposum Which Took Place at the University of Oxford 2006*, edited by Maria Cannata, 146–61 (London: Oxbow Books).
Römer, M. (1986). *Lexikon der Ägyptologie* VI, edited by W. Helck and W. Westendorf, 196–98, s.v. Tanis. (Wiesbaden: Otto Harrassowitz).
Roulin, G. (1998). "Le tombes royales de Tanis: analyse du programme décoratif." In *Tanis. Travaux récents sur le tell Sân el-Hagar*, edited by P. Brissaud and C. Zivie-Coche, 193–276 (Paris).
Russman, E. (2005). "Asspetti del rinascimento kushita." In *L'Enigma di Harwa. Alla Scoperta di un capolaboro del rinascimento egizio*, edited by F. Tiradritti and S. Einaudi, 61–79 (Turin).
Taylor, J. H. (1992). "Aspects of the History of the Valley of the Kings in the Third Intermediate Period." In *After Tutankhamun. Research and Excavations in the Royal Necropolis at Thebes*, edited by C. N. Reeves, 186–206 (London; New York).
Taylor, J. H., ed. (2010). *Journey Through the Afterlife: Ancient Egyptian Book of the Dead* (London: British Museum Press).
Verhoeven, U. (1993). *Das Saitische Totenbuch der Iahtesnacht (P.Colon.Aeg.10207)*. Papyrologische Texte und Aabhandlungen 41, 3 vols. (Bonn: Habelt).
Willems, H. (1988). *Chests of Life. A Study of the Typology and Conceptional Development of Middle Kingdom Standard Class Coffins* (Leiden: Ex Oriente Lux).

# CHAPTER 20

# THE JUDGMENT

## JIŘÍ JANÁK

## Introduction

Due to its intellectual clarity, which coheres with Euro-Atlantic cultural traditions coined by their Jewish, Christian, and Muslim conceptions of eschatology (Griffiths, 1991; Walls, 2007), as well as due to the relatively high number of preserved attestations from ancient Egypt (Munro, 1987; Backes et al., 2009), the scene of the Judgment of the Dead before Osiris represents one of the most iconic images in the modern perception of ancient Egyptian civilization.

According to the ancient Egyptian concept of death and the afterlife, the deceased individuals had to prove their ability and worthiness to become *akhu* (i.e., mighty, powerful, and influential ancestor spirits; Janák, 2013) and thus enter the glorified state of existence in the afterlife (Assmann, 2001). The dead would only be admitted and elevated to this new, transfigured state of being after the embalming, burial, and mortuary rites were performed on and for them (Barta, 1968: 61; Allen, 1994: 27; Assmann, 2001; Friedman, 2001: 7; Smith, 2009: 4; 2017).

The lack of the aforementioned ceremonial preparedness represented a cardinal obstacle to the ritual elevation of the deceased. These obstacles were, however, complemented by threats, challenges, or trials that the deceased had to pass through and overcome during his posthumous journey through the underworld (i.e., the *Duat*), the region in which also the sun traveled by night. The Pyramid Texts, the Coffin Texts, and later the Book of the Dead and Underworld Books, described these obstacles in the underworld vividly as demon creatures, butchers, hunters, cobras, beasts, gates, fiery pits, or places of execution (Zandee, 1960; Hornung, 1991; Lucarelli, 2006, 2010).

By safely passing the challenges, the deceased both proved his worthiness to enter the afterlife and demonstrated special knowledge of divine beings, which enabled him to control the hostile forces (Stadler, 2008). Many of the corporeal, intellectual, and social requirements for the deceased's acceptance among the elite group of the blessed dead did not reflect the person's moral values and integrity, as they were limited to ritual, ceremonial, and material preconditions (Taylor, 2010: 204). A test of the deceased's moral status or an assessment of his character was, however, also incorporated into the evaluation process of his acceptance into the afterlife. Only then did the Egyptian concept of posthumous transfiguration and salvation reach its classical complex form of "moral mummification" and "corporeal justification" (Assmann, 2001: 103; Smith, 2009: 6).

## Two Modes of Judgment

The most elaborate and best-known version of the assessment of the deceased's character, consciousness, and moral values was represented by the so-called Judgment of the Dead before Osiris, the ruler of the dead, and a tribunal of 42 deities. This notion of posthumous judgment (in its developed and pictorially expressed form) is attested in the Book of the Dead of the New Kingdom (BD 30B and 125) for the first time. The idea of a trial or a hearing concerning the misdeeds of a deceased person that took place in the afterlife can, however, be traced back as early as the Fourth and Fifth Dynasties.

Egyptian texts of a different nature, context, and historical period refer to two variants of posthumous judgment: a divine judgment of a dead person, and the judgment of (all) the dead. The first was represented by a juridical hearing regarding a specific trespass of a deceased individual. This type of trial, located in the hereafter, followed the model of hearings before (local) earthly authorities. In the latter form of judgment, all the deceased (not only the denunciated evildoers) were meant to be examined or assessed individually before their acceptance into the afterlife.

## The Divine Judgment

The first of the two aforementioned modes of judgment (a trial over individual wrongdoings) is attested in non-royal tomb inscriptions of the Fourth and Fifth Dynasties that addressed threats to tomb visitors who violated the purity of the tomb (Edel, 1944: 10–11). Later, the so-called Appeals to the Living of the Fifth and Sixth Dynasties developed the idea further by addressing the passers-by with both pleas for offerings and threats against tomb violation; they also present an idealized picture of a just and powerful deceased person (Sainte-Fare Garnot, 1938; Morschauser, 1991; Stadler, 2008: 1–2). These texts mention a violent revenge upon the evildoers, a (posthumous) divine judgment for their misdeeds, and, hence, they may be interpreted as curses or calls for the premature death of the evildoer. Although these tomb inscriptions do explicitly mention a divine trial or a judgment before the Great God (Baines, 1982: 13–28; Quirke, 2001: 173; Stadler, 2008: 1–2; Janák, 2011: 126), they do not allow us to interpret this type of judgment as a test of the deceased's worthiness to enter the afterlife or as an assessment of his character. Rather, they stand for individual punishments or juridical hearings over particular misdeeds. The effects of these trials should take place either in the world of the living (perhaps causing the premature death of wrongdoers) or later in the hereafter (after their natural death), as an excerpt from the tomb inscription and autobiography of Harkhuf (Sixth Dynasty) may exemplify:

> O you who live upon earth,
> who shall pass by this tomb going north or going south,
> who shall say 'a thousand loaves and beer jugs for the owner of the tomb.'
> I shall watch over them in the necropolis.
> I am an excellent equipped spirit (*akh*), a lector-priest who knows his speech.
> As for any man who enters this tomb unclean,
> I shall seize him by the neck like a bird, he will be judged for it by the great god!
> (Urk. I, 122, 9–16; here after Lichtheim, 1975: 24;
> see also Simpson, 2003: 408; Strudwick, 2005: 329)

The conviction that juridical appeals and processes would be available even to the dead and that claims of justice would not cease with the death of the wrongdoer is also evident in the so-called Letters to the Dead (Wente, 1990; O'Donoghue, 1999; Quirke, 2001: 173; Verhoeven, 2003). The living addressed these letters to their deceased ancestors or other influential *akhu* with urgent requests for help in serious matters (Baines, 1987: 87; 1991: 151–61). They often asked the benevolent spirits to take action in their name (sometimes against the malevolent dead), including legal actions before a divine court. But again, these cases represent mere punishments of malevolent spirits rather than underworld examinations of the deceased before their acceptance into the afterlife.

## *Maa-kheru*, the Justified

The latter half of the Old Kingdom saw an introduction and then gradual growth of the cult of Osiris, the god of resurrection and of royal authority in the afterlife (Smith, 2017). Among the many motifs connected to the mythical story of Osiris's death, resurrection, and becoming the ruler of the dead, a concept of a divine trial hinting at the idea of a posthumous justification occurs. After Osiris's death, a conflict between Seth (Osiris's brother and murderer) and Horus (Osiris' son, avenger, and heir) commenced, which was subsequently concluded with the latter's victory and Osiris's deliverance from the unjust state of death (Assmann, 2001: 92; Stadler, 2009: 334–37). After that, both the father and the son become justified, each in his own special way and context. This motif of justification against enemies—both in a battle and before a divine tribunal—and becoming the "true of voice" (*maa-kheru*) (Griffiths, 1960: 57–58) represents the earliest attested step toward the concept of a judgment that differentiated between the justified who, like Osiris, become *akhu* and enter the afterlife, and those who are unjust and unworthy and thus remain dead (*mutu*) (Grieshammer, 1970: 11–45; Roeder, 1996: 19–74; Assmann, 2001: 100–15, 504–18; Quirke, 2001: 173; Taylor, 2010: 215; Smith, 2006, 2017). The BD 18–20, of which the core texts reach back to the mid-Twelfth Dynasty (CT 337–339), witness the rise and importance of the concept of justification of Osiris (and of the deceased) against his enemies (Stadler, 2009: 326–43; Quirke, 2013: 69). In BD 18–20, it is the god Thoth who bears the role of the Justifier of Osiris before the tribunal of Re.

"Thoth! Justifier of Osiris against his enemies,

justify the Osiris N., true of voice,

against his enemies,

in the presence of the tribunal that is with Re,

as the tribunal that is with Osiris,

as the great tribunal that is in Iunu,

on this night of offerings of evening in Iunu,

that night of battle, of active guard of the rebels."

(from BD 18; after Quirke, 2013:70–71)

## The Judgment of (All) the Dead

Apart from allusions to the story of Osiris and the use of the term *maa-kheru*, there are also other references to the second of the two aforementioned modes of posthumous judgment that can be traced back to the First Intermediate Period and the Middle Kingdom. These come mainly from the Coffin Texts (CT 335–39) and refer to an assessment of the deceased's character and to the use of scales (or "the balance of Re on which Maat is raised") during the process of "calculation of differences" (Grieshammer, 1970: 46–70; Roeder, 1996: 19–74; Assmann, 2001; Quirke, 2001: 174–75; Stadler, 2008: 1; Taylor, 2010: 205).

Although the weighing of the heart is not explicitly attested in the Coffin Texts, they refer to scales as the instrument of the examination; other texts refer to the fact that the deceased's heart could bear witness against him (Grieshammer, 1970: 51–55). Similar motifs suggesting a posthumous assessment of the deceased before a divine tribunal most likely occur on the First Intermediate Period stelae of Merer and Intef, and a passage of the *Instructions for Merikara* (Quack, 1992) even evokes the idea of a divine tribunal judging the deceased according to their earthly deeds (Quirke, 2001: 173–74;

Stadler, 2008: 3). The ambiguity and uncertain dating of some of these references (Quack, 2013) do not, however, allow us to interpret them clearly as early evidence of a notion of the judgment of the dead undertaken during the deceased's journey to the afterlife in the underworld.

The earliest attestation of the latter mode of judgment (the judgment of all the dead) occurs explicitly in BD 30 and 125 and in their accompanying illustrations, the so-called vignettes. These two spells are among the most frequently attested elements of the Book of the Dead itself, thus making the scene of the Judgment of the Dead one of the most iconic images of ancient Egyptian religion. Whereas attestations of BD 125, which fully presents the posthumous judgment, do not predate the joint reign of Hatshepsut and Thutmose III, the text of BD 30B has been found on objects (like heart scarabs, coffins, and a gold plaque) dating to as early as the late Middle Kingdom. Since the occurrence of the earliest New Kingdom evidence, both BD 30B and 125 became integral parts of the BD corpus, reappearing regularly on papyri, coffins, mummy bandages, shrouds, and shabti chests until their latest attestation in the latter half of the first century CE (Seeber, 1976; Quirke, 2001: 174; Stadler, 2008: 1–2).

The Judgment of the Dead, as textually and pictorially described in BD 125, takes place in the Hall of the Two Maats—*maat* being the Egyptian concept of the universal order or justice with the goddess Maat as its divine personification (Assmann, 1990). Although the spell does not reveal many details about the exact location and time of the hearing, it might be assumed that the deceased would reach the court hall during his nightly travels through the underworld (Janák, 2003a: 203), since other New Kingdom sources (e.g., the Underworld Books) place the Judgment in the middle of the sun's nightly journey through the *Duat* (Hornung, 1991; Manassa, 2006).

The Hall of the Two Maats (Fig. 20.1) is presented as a broad court where the deceased appears before the supreme authority of the afterlife, the Great God—usually interpreted as Osiris or one of the creator gods, like Atum or Re (Seeber, 1976: 120–36)—and a tribunal of 42 other gods. Two Maat goddesses (usually depicted as female goddesses, identified only by an ostrich feather upon their heads) are sometimes present on the

FIG. 20.1 The Hall of Two Maats (the Judgment scene and the weighing scene var. 1) (drawing after P.Hunefer, Nineteenth Dynasty, P.London BM EA 9901/3 by Lucie Vařeková).

vignette as well: they either witness the trial's process or represent the highest authority of the legal process (as in P.Paris Louvre N 3073). Although the name of the hall itself (esp. the duality of Maats) has not yet been satisfactorily explained (Seeber, 1976: 36–67), it is clearly indicated as the place of justification of the worthy and damnation of the unrighteous, both by the text of BD 125 and by its decoration with living *uraei* (solar cobras) and fire (Munro, 1987: 105–14; Seeber, 1976: 63–67; Quirke, 2001: 175; Taylor, 2010: 205–7). A similar idea of justification by fire (i.e., fiery elimination of wrongdoings and wrongdoers) received a visualization through the Lake of Fire, which represents the main motif of BD 126 but sometimes also forms a part of the vignette to the Judgment of the Dead. A similar motif of the destruction of the enemies of Re by burning frequently occurs in the Underworld Books, particularly in the Amduat and the Book of the Gates (Stadler, 2014).

The Judgment of the Dead vignettes (assigned either to BD 125 or 30B) sometimes show the deceased accompanied or led by a divine entity when entering the court hall. Horus and Anubis occur most often among these attendants in New Kingdom attestations (see Fig. 20.1); later sources also depict Thoth, Maat, Imentet (the goddess of the West), or other beings accompanying the deceased before the divine court of justice (Seeber, 1976: 116–20). BD 125 instructs the deceased on how to enter the Hall of the Two Maats in the proper manner and equips him with knowledge of mystical nature (e.g., knowledge of the names of individual doorway components), which enables him both to enter the Hall and to be accepted by the divine court of justice (consisting of the names of Osiris and the 42 gods), as explained in the introduction to that chapter.

Although the knowledge of divine names and other secrets represents both a strong indication of the deceased's worthiness to enter the afterlife and an equally strong means of gaining respect from the gods, it does not reflect his moral integrity (Taylor, 2010: 204, 212), which, on the other hand, is the theme of the main part of the spell.

> Speech at arrival at this broad hall
> of the Two Goddesses of Maat, shielding NN
> from all forbidden things that he has done,
> and seeing the faces of the gods.
> Words spoken by NN:
> "Hail Great God, lord of the place of Two Goddesses of Maat,
> I have come before you, my lord,
> so that you may bring me to see your perfection.
> I know you, I know your name,
> I know the name of the 42 gods
> who are with you
> in this broad court of the Two Goddesses of Maat,

who live on the guards of evil
and eat their blood
on that day of calculating characters
in the presence of Wennefer."

(from BD 125; after Quirke, 2013: 270)

# The Negative Confession, or the Proclamation of Innocence

After entering the Hall of the Two Maats, the deceased appears before the Great God and the tribunal of 42 deities. There, in a series of statements, he proclaims his innocence of and vindication from specific wrongdoings. The benefits of the afterlife are thus closely linked to a person's past conduct and correct behavior on earth (Taylor, 2010: 204). This denial of crimes, sins, or acts against ritual purity is usually denoted as the "protestation/declaration of innocence" or the "negative confession" by scholars (Stadler, 2008).

The first set of the confessed wrongdoings *not* committed by the deceased consists of 36 declarations of innocence spoken before the Great God and concluded by a repeated affirmation of the deceased's purity. This section of the negative confession is called Part A, according to J. Assmann and A. Kucharek (Assmann and Kucharek, 2008: 835–37).

The second set consists of 42 negative statements (often tabulated graphically). This section (the so-called part Part B) encompasses denials of forbidden, sinful, impure, or blasphemous actions and was to be recited before a tribunal of 42 gods. The deceased was supposed to address each of the divine assessors in turn by their names and local affiliation (cult centers, cosmic spheres, etc.). The "names" of these gods—in the form of unusual epithets or mysterious names revealed only to the worthy—increase the importance of the deceased and indicate his elevated, or even initiated, status.

"O Broad of step who comes from Iunu,
I have done no evil.
O Flame embracer who comes from Kheraha,
I have not robbed.
O Beaked god who comes from Khemenu,
I have not been greedy.
O Swallower of shades who comes from the cavern,
I have not stolen."

(from BD 125; after Quirke, 2013: 271)

The fact that the towns and geographical localities mentioned in Part B are situated in Lower and Middle Egypt might either provide evidence for the period and time of redaction (the so-called Heracleopolitan kingdom of the First Intermediate Period), or present a northern (i.e., Lower and Middle Egyptian) tradition (Quirke, 2001: 175). The number 42 seems to refer to the total number of Lower and Upper Egyptian provinces or districts (the so-called nomes) and thus, to a symbolical judgment or assessment of purity before the country as a whole (Assmann, 2001: 111). However, the actual number of provinces in the time of the first attestation of BD 125 was not 42, but 39. Hence, some scholars seek a different reasoning for the number 42, for example a combination of the symbolic numbers seven and three ($7 \times 3 = 21$), doubled for the Two Lands or the Hall of the Two Maats (Seeber, 1976: 137; Quirke, 2013: 276). However, there is always a possibility that the number might have referred to the completeness of the country regardless of the actual number of the nomes.

The content of the negative confession stays remarkably consistent in different historical periods, varying only in sequence in individual manuscripts (Quirke, 2001: 175; Lapp, 2008; Stadler, 2008: 2). The range of transgressions assessed by the Great God and the tribunal of deities is very wide, reaching from general ethical norms that concur with moral maxims of other cultures (e.g., instructions against doing evil, stealing, killing, lying, adultery, etc.) to more specific crimes against social order and peace (causing hunger, pain, or tears; gossiping; holding back waters of the inundation; committing offenses of a sexual nature, etc.) and committing crimes against personal or temple ritual purity (reducing or stealing offerings or temple property, killing sacred animals, blaspheming). Some scholars, thus, consider the negative confession of Parts A and B a summary of ancient Egyptian ethical standards (e.g., Assmann, 2001: 110–15).

Although these statements are indeed linked to ideas attested in Egyptian wisdom literature (teachings or instructions) and idealized autobiographies (Assmann, 1990; Lichtheim, 1997; Assmann, 2001: 100–115; Quirke, 2001: 175–76; Landgráfová, 2011), they do not follow them in every detail and they do not encompass some of the most important instructions, such as, for instance, respecting one's parents and seniors. The ultimate moral standard that embraced all the norms, both general and specific, was to live in accordance with *maat*, the cosmic, political, and social order of the world (Assmann, 1990). Hence, the speech of the deceased in the Hall of the Two Maats (Part A) begins with an affirmation that he has brought *maat* to the Great God and has removed the evil for him.

In the next section of BD 125 (Part C, according to Assmann and Kucharek, 2008), the deities of the Hall of the Two Maats are described as terrifying beings full of *maat* who live on *maat* and slaughter evildoers. The deceased addresses these gods with yet another assurance of knowing their names and of being a person of no evil, who has never committed crimes and who shall not fall to their slaughter. Further protestations of moral values and of good deeds resemble autobiographical inscriptions attested in tombs of the Old, Middle, and New Kingdoms (Kloth, 2002; Guksch, 1994; Frood, 2007; Kubisch, 2008; Landgráfová, 2011). The speech of the deceased refers to maintaining *maat*, which is similar to the ultimate duty of the king, together with pleasing the gods and the blessed *akhu* with offerings (Assmann, 1970; 1975: 120):

"Hail to you,
who are in this broad hall of the Two Goddesses of Maat,
in whose bodies there is no falsehood,
who live on *maat*, who consume *maat*,
rescue me from Baba
who lives on the entrails of the great,
on this day of the great court.

See I am come before you,
there being no evil of mine, no crime of mine,
no wrong of mine, no witness of mine,
none against whom I have done anything.
I live on *maat*, I consume *maat*,
I have done what men ask and what pleases the gods.
I have pacified the god with what he loves.
I have given bread to the hungry, beer to the thirsty,
clothes to the naked, a ferry to the boatless.
I have offered divine offerings to the gods,
and voice offerings to the blessed dead."
(from BD 125; after Quirke, 2013: 273)

The concluding part of the spell (Part D) presents the deceased in a test of secret knowledge that would enable him to proceed to the Hall of the Two Maats, be accepted by the deities, and win their favor in the process of the assessment of his character. After initial probing questions of mystical nature, the deceased names individual parts (as well as the guardians) of the underworld gates leading to the Hall in order to be introduced there. At the very end of BD 125, the deceased proves that he knows much more: the secret nature and whereabouts of Thoth and Osiris, the two main characters of the Judgment of the Dead.

"Let him approach, they say to me.
Who are you, what is your name, they ask of me.
I am the lower thorn of the papyrus reed,
He who is in his moringa-tree is my name.
I have passed the city north of the moringa.
...
Come then, enter this gate

of this broad hall of the Two Goddesses of Maat.

You have knowledge of us.

We will not let you enter past us,

say the jambs of this door.

You do not say our names.

Your names are plumb-bob of accuracy.

...

I will not open to you,

I will not let you enter past me,

says the keeper of this door.

You do not say my name.

Your name is ox of Geb.

You know us.

Pass by us then."

(from BD 125; after Quirke, 2013: 274–75)

In addition to moral values and secret knowledge, the protestation of innocence stresses correct religious observance, ritual purity, and respect for temple integrity and cultic property. Hence, some researchers have noted that priestly oaths (Gee, 1998: 114; Assmann, 2001: 110–11; Stadler, 2003: 23–24; 2008: 2; Taylor, 2010: 208–9) and parts of the so-called Book of the Temple of the Roman Period (Quack, 1997, 2005) might have been sources of inspiration for the negative confession of the Book of the Dead in both their form and content. These scholars suggested that the negative confession may have originated from a temple initiation rite assessing the purity and worthiness of the initiated priest (Merkelbach, 1969; Assmann, 2001: 110–12). However, it remains unclear whether the Roman evidence represents a late variant of an unattested precursor of a confession-like initiation rite, or whether it is, on the contrary, a very late adaptation of BD 125 (Quirke, 2001: 175–76; Stadler, 2008: 3).

If we consider all the aforementioned aspects of the proclamation of innocence dealing not only with ethical norms and religious piety but also with more practical issues connected to the transfiguration and initiation into divine secrets, a need for the reconsideration of the term "judgment" may arise. The negative confession represents neither an apocalyptic judgment similar to the Last Judgment in Christianity and Islam, nor a simple separation of the blessed and the damned. Rather, it resembles an "assessment of purity" before initiation (into a sacred office) or an "immigration interview" before being accepted as a resident of the afterlife. Maybe the last parallel will prove to be the most fitting one, as the mighty *akhu* represented elite migrants from this life into the next, and even these seemingly permanent residents of the hereafter could be reassessed, judged, expelled, or killed.

# The Weighing Scene

The most important part of the Judgment of the Dead was visually represented by the weighing of the deceased's consciousness or deeds, manifested by the heart, against the order of *maat*. This iconographic motif has been illustrated in detail on vignettes to BD 125 or 30B, occurring in many manuscripts of the Book of the Dead, as well as on Late Period coffins or in the Documents for Breathing of the Roman Period (Seeber, 1976). The text of BD 125 surprisingly refers to the weighing of the heart only in hints. Thus, only vignettes to BD 125 and their captions, together with BD 30A and B, shed some light upon this mysterious process of weighing the deceased's heart. Hence, as the Egyptians considered the heart the seat of the mind, spirit, emotions, decision-making, and consciousness, they connected it with the deeds and assessment of the earthly life of the deceased.

The most common depiction of the Judgment scene shows the deceased's heart on one pan of a scale being weighed against a manifestation of *maat* on the other. The cosmic order of *maat* might have been represented either by its hieroglyph (an ostrich feather) (see Fig. 20.1) or directly, by a figure of the goddess Maat (Fig. 20.2). Although such an image frequently occurs on vignettes to BD 125 or 30B, it also has many variants and significant modifications. For example, the heart could be substituted for an image of the deceased person, as was the case in the Book of the Dead for the Queen Nedjmet (early Twenty-first Dynasty; P.London BM EA 10541) (Fig. 20.3). A more important variant of the scene shows an image of the dead person on one pan of the scales and his heart on the other (as in P.Cairo CG 24095, P.Cairo CG 40004, and P.London BM EA 9900) (Fig. 20.4). The deceased himself is, thus, confronted with his heart as the seat of consciousness and the sum of his earthly deeds.

The latter image visually reflects ideas recorded textually in BD 30A and B of the Book of the Dead, which seek to ensure the heart's loyalty to the deceased in the Judgment of the Dead. The text of these spells presents a plea from the deceased to his heart not to stand as a witness against him and implies that a good result of the trial would be beneficial for all the involved parties (the deceased, the heart, and the divine tribunal). Besides being incorporated into the Book of the Dead manuscripts, BD 30B occurs frequently on heart scarabs—amulets placed over the heart in or on the mummy wrappings (Andrews, 1994: 55–59; Backes et al., 2009: 133–36; Sousa, 2011; Taylor, 2010: 209; Quirke, 2013: 97–100):

> "My *ib*-heart of my mother, my *haty*-heart of my mother,
> my fore-heart of my forms,
> do not stand against me as witness,
> do not oppose me as witness,
> do not oppose me in the tribunal,

FIG. 20.2 The weighing scene var. 2: the heart against the goddess Maat (drawing after P.Anhai, Twentieth Dynasty, P.London BM EA 10472/2 by Lucie Vařeková).

FIG. 20.3 The weighing scene var. 3: the deceased against the goddess Maat (drawing after P.Nedjmet, Twenty-first Dynasty, P.London BM EA 10541 by Lucie Vařeková).

FIG. 20.4 The weighing scene var. 4: the deceased against his heart (drawing after P.Senhetep, Eighteenth Dynasty, P.Cairo CG 40004 by Lucie Vařeková).

FIG. 20.5 The weighing scene var. 5: balancing two stones (drawing after P.Pinudjem I, Twenty-first Dynasty, P.Cairo CG 40006 by Lucie Vařeková).

do not lean against me in the presence of the balance-keeper.

...

Do not say falsehood against me beside the Great god.

See, the decision on you (too) is in play here."

(from BD 30B; after Quirke, 2013: 99–100)

Among the variants of the weighing scene, there are also depictions that replace one or both objects on the pans with stone weights. For instance, two vignettes to BD 30B dated to the Third Intermediate Period (P.Cairo CG 44006 and P.Paris BN 38–45) show two weights (probably made of stone) being weighed against each other (Fig. 20.5), and two other Book of the Dead manuscripts from the Egyptian Museum Cairo (P.Cairo CG 51189 and P.Cairo JE 99881) depict the heart counterbalanced with a stone weight or a stone amulet.

An interesting variant of the scene shows the weighing of the head (Fig. 20.6) or the eyes of the deceased (Fig. 20.7) against the order of *maat* (e.g., P.London BM EA 10013 and P.Berlin P. 3195). These examples may indicate that the return of the person's corporeal integrity and his bodily functions (i.e., the ability to be revived) represented one of the main outcomes of a successful weighing. A minor, but very significant variant (attested in TT 365) shows a heart on one pan of the scales and an *udjat*-eye on the other (Fig. 20.8). The motif of the *udjat*, or the Eye of Horus, which symbolized completeness, intactness, or soundness, will be dealt with later (see p. 414).

A different view on the weighing process is attested in a rather late Story of Setne Khamwas (Setne II) dating to the Roman Period (P.London BM EA 604; Hoffmann and Quack, 2007: 118–37). This story—similar to the New Testament parable of a rich man and Lazarus

FIG. 20.6 The weighing scene var. 6a: the eyes of the deceased against Maat (drawing after P.Hornefer, Twenty-first Dynasty, P.London BM EA 10013 by Lucie Vařeková).

FIG. 20.7 The weighing scene var. 6b: the head of the deceased against the feather of Maat (drawing after P.Taatum, Late Period, P.Berlin P. 3159 by Lucie Vařeková).

FIG. 20.8 The weighing scene var. 7: the heart against the udjat-eye (drawing after TT 365 – Nefermenu, Eighteenth Dynasty, Western Thebes, el-Khokha by Lucie Vařeková).

(Luke 16:19–31)—explains why a poor man of low status would be rewarded with blessings and raised to a high status in the hereafter, whereas a rich man would suffer eternal torments. The message of the story is that such a reversal of fortunes in the afterlife stems from an assessment of earthly deeds in the underworld. Unlike the earlier BD spells, the judging (or weighing) process described in Setne II examines the difference between the good and the bad deeds of the deceased person. Such an assessment had four possible outcomes.

> "He who would be found to have more bad (deeds) than the good (deeds) is handed over to the Devourer belonging to the Lord of the West.
> His *ba* and body is destroyed, and thus she does not allow him to breathe ever again.
> He who would be found to have more good (deeds) than the bad (deeds) is taken in among the gods (and/of?) the Entourage of the Lord of the West, while his *ba* goes to the sky together with the prominent spirits.
> He who would be found to have good (deeds) equal to his bad is taken among the excellent spirits who serve Sokar-Osiris."
> (after Lichtheim, 1980: 140 and Hoffmann and Quack, 2007: 121)

According to some scholars, the Setne story is of a very late date and, thus, may reflect Hellenistic or other religious, philosophic, and apocalyptic influences of the time (Taylor, 2010: 209, 215). According to others, however, the story (although late in its attestation) is still deeply rooted in traditional Egyptian ideas and concepts, and it does

FIG. 20.9 An exceptional weighing scene from the Roman Period (drawing after P.Paris Louvre AF 6493 by Lucie Vařeková).

FIG. 20.10 The weighing scene var. 8: the deceased against a stone(?) (drawing after P.Yuya, Eighteenth Dynasty, Egyptian Museum Cairo, P.Cairo CG 51189 by Lucie Vařeková).

not represent a novelty shaped by external influences (Stadler, 2016). This textual description of the judgment coheres with a few pictorial representations of the weighing dated to the Roman Period (a coffin and a mummy shroud; Paris Louvre AF 6493; Fig. 20.9) (Seeber, 1976: 77; for Demotic variants of BD 125, see Stadler, 2003; Smith, 2009). These images show the deceased weighed against an oval stone weight (Fig. 20.10). The deceased is depicted in a much lower position, which implies that the deceased, who has been found to be justified, is much heavier than the counterweight. This version of a positive result may, however, refer to the idea of balancing the deceased's good deeds against his misdeeds, as in the second Story of Setne Khamwas.

# The Keeper of the Scales and the Scribe of the Gods

Many of the Judgment scenes attested from the New Kingdom sources and subsequent periods of ancient Egyptian history depict one or two deities closely observing the process of weighing in the Hall of the Two Maats. One of them usually performs the role of the Keeper of the Scales (called *iri-mechat* in Egyptian) who would operate the balance, steady the scale pans, and try to make the measurement as precise as possible. The other would attend the weighing as an overseer and a scribe. The jackal-headed god

FIG. 20.11 The weighing from a market scene (drawing after TT 178 - Neferrenpet, Nineteenth Dynasty, Western Thebes, el-Khokha by Lucie Vařeková).

Anubis (either squatting or standing in front of the balance) is most frequently depicted as performing the first task. There are also manuscripts that substitute Anubis with Horus or an anthropomorphic figure simply called the Keeper of the Scales (Seeber, 1976: 154–63). If depicted, the person who oversees the process of weighing and writes down its outcome is Thoth, the lunar god of wisdom, accuracy, and writing (Seeber, 1976: 147–54; Stadler, 2009: 430–39). Importantly, a very similar rendering of weighing appears on market scenes and other images related to daily life depicted in Egyptian tombs. In Neferrenpet's tomb in el-Khokha (TT 178), dated to the reign of Thutmose III (Hofmann, 1995), two men are depicted in the process of weighing (Fig. 20.11). One of them (bearing the title of *iri-mekhat*) is operating the balance in the same way as Anubis does in the Book of the Dead, while the other (captioned as scribe) records the result, similarly to Thoth. Anubis and Thoth themselves play significant roles of justifiers of Osiris and, hence, of the deceased in other Book of the Dead spells (Willems, 1998; Stadler, 2009: 320–51; 435–38; Quirke, 2013: 69–79).

> "Thoth! Justifier of Osiris against his enemies,
>
> justify the Osiris NN against his enemies,
>
> in the presence of the tribunal that is with Re,
>
> as the tribunal that is with Osiris,
>
> as the great tribunal that is in Iunu,
>
> on the night of offerings of evening in Iunu,
>
> that night of battle, of active guard of the rebels. ( … )"
>
> (from BD 18; Quirke, 2013: 70)

## THE DEVOURER AND THE FATES

Following the latter part of the New Kingdom, the scene of the Judgment of the Dead received a new motif: a depiction of a demon or an underworld being called Amemet, Amemait, or Ammut, who is the Devourer (of the Damned). She occurs frequently in post-Amarna manuscripts, but the earliest attestation (the Book of the Dead of Nebqed; P.Paris Louvre N 3068) probably dates to the reign of Amenophis III. This demon—whose image is usually located near the balance or in front of an enthroned Osiris—has a hybrid form corresponding to the description found in the Book of the Dead of Hunefer (P.London BM EA 9901) and in the tomb of Nakhtamon (TT 341): "Her forepart is that of a crocodile, her rear of a hippopotamus, her middle as a lion" (Davies, 1948; see Figs. 20.1 and 20.2). Late depictions of the demon, however, present her in a shape of a large dog (Seeber, 1976: 163–84; Taylor, 2010: 212–14).

FIG. 20.12 Gods and beings connected with birth and fate (Meskhenet, Shai, Renenutet) present at the Judgment (drawing after P.Ani, Nineteenth Dynasty, P.London BM EA 10470/3 by Lucie Vařeková).

Amemet's terrifying appearance shows striking similarities to the iconographic form of the goddess Thoueris, which also combines the features of a hippopotamus, a crocodile, and a lion. The main characteristic of both divine beings is focused on deterring, repelling, and eliminating evil. Thoueris, as a goddess of maternity and childbirth, protected women and newborn children; Amemet, on the other hand, eliminated evildoers and protected the blessed spirits newly born into the afterlife. The similarities between Thoueris and Amemet thus are very fitting in the ancient Egyptian conviction that glorification and resurrection, which would follow a successful judgment, represented both the revival of the deceased and his birth into the afterlife.

Such an interpretation is strengthened by depictions of divine beings connected to personal fate allotted at birth (Meskhenet, Renenutet, and Shai) that in some manuscripts occur as integral components of the Judgment scene (Seeber, 1976: 83–86; Fig. 20.12). Meskhenet is usually depicted as a human-headed birth brick (a special brick used to support women during childbirth), but she may even appear twice (as in the papyrus of Ani; P.London BM EA 10470): as a human-headed brick (probably representing a personal fate) and as a female deity (as the goddess of fate). A depiction of the *ba* of the deceased (his posthumous manifestation, or "soul") sometimes also complements the scene of the Judgment (Seeber, 1976: 106–8).

FIG. 20.13 Resurrection as restoration of organs and senses (drawing after P.Tawedjatra, Twenty-first Dynasty, Egyptian Museum, P.Cairo S.R. VII 11496 by Lucie Vařeková).

## Redemption

After successfully passing through the obstacles of the Judgment of the Dead and being declared true of voice (*maa-kheru*), the deceased could enter the afterlife. Acceptance among the blessed spirits of the afterlife was probably also linked to the deceased's permission to leave the netherworld and come back again as he or she pleased, which was the main theme of the Book of the Dead itself (Coming Out by Day, or Going Out in the Daylight; Backes, 2009; Quirke, 2013: viii). However, in order to overcome the passive state of death and come back to life (albeit in a new form and with higher status), the vindicated person had to be re-equipped with vital organs and senses. The return of the heart, eyes, or mouth (Seeber, 1976: 93–98) represents the main topic of BD 21–29. It is also sometimes mentioned in captions or even in vignettes to BD 125 (P.Paris Louvre E 17401) (Fig. 20.13). Such corporeal redemption metaphysically supplements similar actions undertaken physically during the embalming process or ritually by the Opening of the Mouth (Janák, 2003a: 9–10).

In the Book of the Dead manuscripts from the Third Intermediate Period or later, the vindicated deceased is sometimes pictorially represented as showing gestures of jubilation, being adorned with *maat*-feathers, or supported by the goddess Maat (Seeber, 1976: 98–106, 143–45; Taylor, 2010: 215). The so-called garland of justification or vindication represented an additional sign of the deceased's victory over death and his vindication. Such floral garlands—mentioned in BD 19 and popular in the Late and Ptolemaic Periods (Quirke, 2013: 75–77)—were placed on the mummified body of the deceased to confirm and acknowledge his justification, or used in rituals for the gods of resurrection, Sokar and Osiris (Assmann and Kucharek, 2008: 822).

# The Weight of a Just Heart

Two frequently recurring questions deal with the core idea of the Judgment of the Dead and with its possible liturgical or ritual performance. The first concerns the heaviness or lightness of the heart placed on a pan of the underworld balance, and the second deals with performative or liturgical re-enactments of the judgment itself.

As for the first question, all the known attestations of the Judgment scene recorded in the Book of the Dead, on coffins or tomb walls, present the ideal outcome of the trial. These depictions suggest that the deceased or his heart should be found righteous, literally resting balanced with *maat* without tipping the arms of the scales (as mentioned in P.London BM EA 1008, P.Paris Louvre N 3068, and P.Dresden Aeg. 775). But what would happen if the heart of an impure, unworthy human were to be placed on the scale pan? Would it rise because it was too light, or come down because it was full of misdeeds or sin?

In this respect, the depictions of the balance itself do not provide much information. While some scenes show the two pans in an exact equilibrium, others present one of the pans (regardless of its content) in a lowered position. The plummet (weight) of the scales—as the most important indicator of the result—is always depicted in its proper place without inclining, as captioned in the Book of the Dead versions of P.London BM EA 9904 and P.Cairo CG 40007. The significance of the (heart-shaped) plummet (*tḫ*; Sousa, 2009) is also evident from its careful manipulation and close observation by the keeper of the balance (often Anubis; see Figs. 20.2 and 20.10).

Textual comments on the scene reveal a very significant detail. They describe the pure heart of the righteous deceased as a heart that is full or filled (*mḥ*), complete, intact, or sound (*wḏꜣ*), with nothing missing (Urk. IV, 119, 10–11; Seeber, 1976: 79–80, 111; Schmidt, 2006). The completeness (*wḏꜣ*) of the heart coheres with the aforementioned image of the *udjat*-eye of Horus (*wḏꜣ.t*) which is sometimes represented (or at least mentioned) in the scene of the Judgment of the Dead (Seeber, 1976: 65, 71–75; Manassa, 2006). The idea that the heart of a righteous person should be filled with *maat*, wisdom, duties, gods, or the king, and be free of all things that "make the heart light" found its way into the teachings of Ani and Ptahhotep, and the Story of the Eloquent Peasant (Parkinson, 1997: 54–88; 246–72), as well as into autobiographical inscriptions of the Middle Kingdom (Landgráfová, 2011) and hymns (Assmann, 1975: 188, 191). Moreover, according to the weighing scene described in the P.Northumberland III Verso, a light heart should be supplemented with additional parts in order to rest in ideal equilibrium with *maat* (Fischer-Elfert, 2003; Schmidt, 2006: 254).

If the heart of a just man was considered to be complete and full, one has to interpret unrighteousness, impurity, and misdeeds violating *maat* not as a burden but rather as incompleteness, insufficiency, or damage to the heart (Schmidt, 2006). Thus, the Egyptians most probably considered the imperfect, "sinful" heart to be too light, since it did not have the same value (i.e., weight) as *maat*.

The aforementioned parallels to Egyptian market scenes and other profane depictions of weighing also remind us that the main purpose of this use of balances was to ascertain the right value of the product, not to measure its exact weight. The same holds true for the weighing in the Hall of Two Maats: the heart should be found true or complete and pure, not false and incomplete. In this respect, an interpretation of the heart scarab or the heart amulet (Sousa, 2007, 2011) may be considered. These amulets should be made of green *nḥmf*-stone (lit. "which does not float," or "which sinks"; Andrews, 1994: 56–59) and placed over the heart of the deceased, as stated in BD 30B. Their shape usually combines the features of the scarab beetle, which symbolizes (self-)creation, resurrection, changing of forms, and the eternal cycle (*ḫpr*), with features of the heart that hint at its use during the Judgment of the Dead. But these amulets were most probably tied to a further symbolism, since their shapes—and weight—show striking similarities to stones normally used as ballasts or weights in weighing (Gee, 2009). Moreover, several lunar hymns mention a scarab (the Noble Scarab) that—similarly to P.Northumberland III—bridges the gap in the process of completing the *udjat*-eye (Manassa, 2006: 140). Thus, we may consider that heart scarabs could have represented either heavier substitutes for the heart or additional weights supplementing any possible lacking in the deceased's heart.

The other question often raised by scholars regarding the Judgment of the Dead is based on the Hellenistic interpretation of this ancient Egyptian concept documented by Diodorus Siculus (*Bibliotheca Historica* I 91–93; Murphy, 1985). On the basis of this text, some researchers have proposed that the judgment of the deceased was performed as a drama or as a dramatic/ritual trial at the tomb during burial ceremonies (Merkelbach, 1993; Assmann, 2001: 114). However, such an interpretation of the posthumous judgment might have followed a Hellenistic point of view that reduced a complex Egyptian approach—combining mythical, physical, moral, cosmological, and ritual aspects—to a single semantic component of an earthly ritual (Stadler, 2001; Janák, 2003b; Stadler, 2008: 3; Smith, 2008: 313–16; Quack, 2016; Stadler, 2017: 28, 34–35).

# Conclusion

In order to enter the glorified state of existence in the afterlife and become mighty ancestral spirits (*akhu*), Egyptians had to meet several requirements and fulfill many conditions both during their lives as well as after their departure to the underworld. These conditions ranged from embalming ceremonies and the preparation of a tomb to being acquainted with secret knowledge and upholding ethical norms.

The ancient Egyptian religion and the concept of the afterlife witnessed two different yet still interconnected notions of the judgment of the dead—or rather, of the judgment over a dead person. One was represented by a juridical hearing regarding a specific (earthly or posthumous) trespass of a dead individual, and the other referred to the trial in the underworld of each of the deceased individually, where both their character and ability or worthiness to enter the afterlife would be assessed. It is the latter notion that is usually denoted "the Judgment of the Dead" in both scholarly and popular literature. After its introduction to ancient Egyptian religion, this type of "judgment" held a cardinal position among the obstacles and tests that awaited the deceased in the underworld.

According to the Book of the Dead spells (mainly BD 30B and 125), the Judgment of the Dead or the assessment of the deceased's character should take place in the so-called Hall of the Two Maats before Osiris (or the Great God) and a tribunal of 42 deities. At this divine court the deceased should proclaim his innocence in a series of negative statements. Such ritual denial of crimes, sins, or acts against ritual purity has earned the designation of "proclamation of innocence" or the "negative confession." In BD 125, where the negative confession was both recorded textually and represented in illustrations, it was divided into two major parts. The first set of the confessed wrongdoings not committed by the deceased consisted of 36 declarations of innocence spoken before the Great God, and the second encompassed 42 negative statements recited before a tribunal of 42 gods.

The most important part of the judgment in the underworld before Osiris was visually represented by an image of weighing the deceased's consciousness or deeds (manifested by the heart as the seat of the mind, emotions, and consciousness) against the order of *maat* (represented by the goddess Maat or her emblem, an ostrich feather). This iconographic motif has been illustrated in detail on vignettes to BD 30B and 125. Although every Book of the Dead depiction of the judgment presents the ideal outcome, the heart resting in a perfect equilibrium with *maat*, textual hints hidden in the spells and captions to vignettes reveal clues to understanding the weighing process. There, the heart of a just person was considered to be complete and full, and thus one has to view unrighteousness and misdeeds not as the heart's heavy burden but rather as incompleteness, insufficiency, or damage to the heart. The Egyptians thus most probably considered the heart of an unjust person to be too light, not having the same weight, or value, as *maat*. After successfully passing through the judgment and assessment of character, the deceased was considered justified and vindicated and regained his ability to live by reacquiring his vital organs and senses. This was a corporeal precondition to the final act of redemption—becoming one of the *akhu* (mighty blessed spirits) and entering the divine afterlife.

As the proclamation of innocence and the act of weighing the heart dealt not only with ethical norms and commandments and religious piety, but also with corporeal requirements for the transfiguration and initiation into divine secrets, the underworld trial known as the Judgment of the Dead resembled an assessment of the individual in an immigration interview (before acceptance into the afterlife) rather than a direct precursor of the apocalyptic judgment in Christianity and Islam.

# Acknowledgments

This paper represents the results of a research project of the Charles University research program Q11: Complexity and Resilience. Ancient Egyptian Civilisation in Multidisciplinary and Multicultural Approach. It was also supported by the European Regional Development Fund project "Creativity and Adaptability as Conditions of the Success of Europe in an Interrelated World" (No. CZ.02.1.01/0.0/0.0/16_019/0000734).

# Bibliography

Allen, J. P. (1994). "Reading a Pyramid." In *Homages à Jean Leclant. Volume 1: Études pharaoniques*, edited by C. Berger, 5–28 (Cairo: Institut Français d'Archéologie Orientale).
Andrews, C. (1994). *Amulets of Ancient Egypt* (London: British Museum Press).
Assmann, J. (1970). *Der König als Sonnenpriester. Ein kosmographischer Begleittext zur kultischen Sonnenhymnik in thebanischen Tempeln und Gräbern* (Glückstadt: Augustin).
Assmann, J. (1975). *Ägyptische Hymnen und Gebete* (Zürich; München: Artemis Verlag).
Assmann, J. (1990). *Ma'at. Gerechtigkeit und Unsterblichkeit im Alten Ägypten* (München: C. H. Beck).
Assmann, J. (2001). *Tod und Jenseits im alten Ägypten* (München: C. H. Beck).
Assmann, J. and Kucharek, A. (2008). *Ägyptische Religion. Totenliteratur* (Frankfurt am Main: Verlag der Weltreligionen).
Backes, B. (2009). "Was zu sagen ist—zum Gesamttitel des Totenbuchs." In *Ausgestattet mit dem Schriften des Thot. Festschrift für Irmtraut Munro zu ihrem 65. Geburtstag*. Studien zum Altägyptischen Totenbuch 14, edited by B. Backes, M. Müller, and S. Stöhr, 5–27 (Wiesbaden: Harrassowitz).
Backes, B., et al. (2009). *Bibliographie zum Altägyptischen Totenbuch*, 2nd ed. Studien zum Altägyptischen Totenbuch 13 (Wiesbaden: Harrassowitz).
Baines, J. (1982). "'Greatest God' or Category of Gods?" *Göttinger Miszellen* 67: 13–28.
Baines, J. (1987). "Practical Religion and Piety." *Journal of Egyptian Archaeology* 73: 79–98.
Baines, J. (1991). "Society, Morality, and Religious Practice." In *Religion in Ancient Egypt*, edited by B. E. Shafer, 123–200 (Ithaca: Cornell University Press).
Barta, W. (1968). *Aufbau und Bedeutung der altägyptischen Opferformel* (Glückstadt: Augustin).
Davies, N. de Garis (1948). *Seven private tombs at Kurnah* (London: Egypt Exploration Society).
Edel, E. (1944). "Untersuchungen zur Phraseologie der ägyptischen Inschriften des Alten Reiches." *Mitteilungen des Deutschen Archaeologischen Institus Abteilung Kairo* 13: 1–90.
Fischer-Elfert, H. W. (2003). "Papyrus Northumberland Nr. III: Zeugnis einer Entsakralisierung der Herzenswägung von Totenbuch 125 unter Sethos I." In *Es werde niedergelegt als Schriftstück. Festschrift für Hartwig Altenmüller zum 65. Geburtstag*, edited by N. Kloth, K. Martin, and E. Martin-Pardey, 109–15 (Hamburg: Buske).
Friedman, F. (2001). "Akh." In *Oxford Encyclopedia of Ancient Egypt*, I., edited by D. B. Redford, 47–48 (Oxford: Oxford University Press).
Frood, E. (2007). *Biographical texts from Ramessid Egypt* (Atlanta: Society of Biblical Literature).

Garnot, J. S.-F. (1938). *L'Appel aux vivants dans les textes funéraires égyptiens des origines à la fin de l'Ancien Empire* (Cairo: Institut Français d'Archéologie Orientale).

Gee, J. (1998). *The Requirements of Ritual Purity in Ancient Egypt*. Ph.D. Diss., Yale University.

Gee, J. (2009). "Of Heart Scarabs and Balance Weights? A New Interpretation of Book of the Dead 30B." *Journal of the Society for the Study of Egyptian Antiquities* 30: 1–15.

Grieshammer, R. (1970). *Das Jenseitsgericht in den Sargtexten* (Wiesbaden: Harrassowitz).

Griffiths, J. G. (1960). *The Conflict of Horus and Seth from the Egyptian and Classical Sources* (Liverpool: Liverpool University Press).

Griffith, J. G. (1991). *The Divine Verdict. A Study of Divine Judgment in the Ancient Religions* (Leiden; New York; København; Köln: E. J. Brill).

Guksch, H. (1994). *Königsdienst. Zur Selbstdarstellung der Beamten in der 18. Dynastie* (Heidelberg: Heidelberger Orientverlag).

Hoffmann, F. and Quack, J. F. (2007). *Anthologie der demotischen Literatur*. Einführungen und Quellentexte zur Ägyptologie, 4 (Berlin: Lit).

Hofmann, E. (1995). *Das Grab des Neferrenpet gen. Kenro (TT 178)* (Mainz am Rhein: Zabern).

Hornung, E. (1991). *Die Nachtfahrt der Sonne. Eine altägyptische Beschreibung des Jenseits* (Zürich: Artemis & Winkler).

Janák, J. (2003a). "From Dusk till Dawn." *Archiv Orientální* 71(1): 1–12.

Janák, J. (2003b). "Journey to the Resurrection. Chapter 105 of the Book of the Dead in the New Kingdom." *Studien zur altägyptischen Kultur* 31: 193–210.

Janák, J. (2011). "The Structure of Egyptian Pantheon." In *U4 DU11-GA-NI SÁ MU-NI-IB-DU11. Ancient Near Eastern Studies in Memory of Blahoslav Hruska*, edited by L. Vacín, 119–27 (Dresden: Islet-Verlag).

Janák, J. (2013). "Akh." In *UCLA Encyclopedia of Egyptology*, edited by J. Dieleman and W. Wendrich (Los Angeles: UCLA), http://escholarship.org/uc/item/7255p86v

Kloth, N. (2002). *Die (auto-)biographischen Inschriften des ägyptischen Alten Reiches. Untersuchungen zur Phraseologie und Entwicklung* (Hamburg: Buske).

Kubisch, S. (2008). *Lebensbilder der 2. Zwischenzeit. Biographische Inschriften der 13.–17. Dynastie* (Berlin-New York: Walter de Gruyter).

Lapp, G. (2008). *Synoptische Textausgabe nach Quellen des Neuen Reiches* (Basel: Orientverlag).

Landgráfová, R. (2011). *It is My Good Name that You Should Remember: Egyptian Biographical Texts on Middle Kingdom Stelae* (Praha: Charles University in Prague).

Lichtheim, M. (1975). *Ancient Egyptian Literature, Vol. I: The Old and Middle Kingdoms* (Berkeley; Los Angeles; London: University of California Press).

Lichtheim, M. (1980). *Ancient Egyptian Literature, Vol. III: The Late Period* (Berkeley; Los Angeles; London: University of California Press).

Lichtheim, M. (1997). *Moral Values in Ancient Egypt* (Göttingen: Vandenhoeck & Ruprecht).

Lucarelli, R. (2006). "Demons in the Book of the Dead." In *Totenbuch-Forschungen. Gesammelte Beiträge des 2. Internationalen Totenbuch-Symposiums 2005*. Studien zum altägyptischen Totenbuch 11, edited by B. Backes, I. Munro, and S. Stöhr, 203–12 (Wiesbaden: Harrassowitz).

Lucarelli, R. (2010). "Demons (benevolent and malevolent)." In *UCLA Encyclopedia of Egyptology*, edited by J. Dieleman and W. Wendrich (Los Angeles: UCLA), http://escholarship.org/uc/item/1r72q9vv

Manassa, C. (2006). "The Judgment Hall of Osiris in the Book of Gates." *Revue d'Égyptologie* 57: 109–50.

Merkelbach, R. (1969). "Ein griechisch-ägyptischer Priestereid und das Totenbuch." *Religions en Égypte hellénistique et romaine*, Travaux de centre d'études suprérieures spécialisé d'historie des religions de Strasbourg (Paris): 69–73.
Merkelbach, R. (1993). "Diodor über das Totengericht der Ägypter." *Zeitschrift für ägyptische Sprache und Altertumskunde* 120: 71–84.
Morschauser, S. (1991). *Threat-Formulae in Ancient Egypt: A Study of the History, Structure and Use of Threats and Curses in Ancient Egypt* (Baltimore: Halgo).
Munro, I. (1987). *Untersuchungen zu den Totenbuch-Papyri der 18. Dynastie Kriterien ihrer Datierung* (London; New York: Kegan Paul).
Murphy, E. (1985). *Diodorus Siculus. Diodorus On Egypt*. Translated from the Ancient Greek. Book I of Diodorus Siculus' Historical Library (Jefferson, NC; London: McFarland & Company).
O'Donoghue, M. (1999). "The 'Letters to the Dead' and Ancient Egyptian Religion." *Bulletin of the Australian Centre for Egyptology* 10: 87–104.
Parkinson, R. (1997). *The Tale of Sinuhe and Other Ancient Egyptian Poems, 1940–1640 B.C.* (Oxford: Oxford University Press).
Quack, J. F. (1992). *Studien zur Lehre für Merikare*. Göttinger Orientforschungen 4/23 (Wiesbaden: Harrassowitz).
Quack, J. F. (1997). "Ein ägyptisches Handbuch des Tempels und seine griechische Übersetzung." *Zeitschrift für Papyrologie und Epigraphik* 119: 297–300.
Quack, J. F. (2013). "Irrungen, Wirrungen? Forscherische Ansätze zur Datierung der älteren ägyptischen Literatur." In *Dating Egyptian Literary Texts*. Lingua Aegyptica Studia Monographica, 11, edited by G. Moers, 405–69 (Hamburg: Widmaier Verlag).
Quack, J. F. (2016). "Nochmals zu Balsamierung und Totengericht im großen demotischen Weisheitsbuch." *Enchoria* 34 (2014/2015): 106–18.
Quirke, S. (2001). "Judgment of the Dead." In *The Oxford Encyclopedia of Ancient Egypt*, Vol II, edited by D. B. Redford, 211–14 (Oxford: Oxford University Press).
Quirke, S. (2013). *Going out in Daylight—prt m hrw the Ancient Egyptian* Book of the Dead: *translation, sources, meanings*. GHP Egyptology 20 (London: Golden House).
Roeder, H. (1996). *Mit dem Auge sehen. Studien zur Semantik der Herrschaft in den Toten- und Kulttexten*. Studien zur Archäologie und Geschichte Altägyptens 16 (Heidelberg: Heidelberger Orientverlag).
Schmidt, H. C. (2006). "Gewogen und zu leicht befunden." In *In Pharaos Staat. Festschrift für Rolf Gundlach zum 75. Geburtstag*, edited by D. Bröckelmann and A. Klug, 251–58 (Wiesbaden: Harrassowitz).
Seeber, C. (1976). *Untersuchungen zur Darstellung des Totengerichts im alten Ägypten*. Münchner ägyptologische Studien 35 (München; Berlin: Deutscher Kunstverlag).
Simpson, W. K. (ed.) (2003). *The Literature of Ancient Egypt: An Anthology of Stories, Instructions, Stelae, Autobiographies, and Poetry*, 3rd ed. (New Haven; London: Yale University Press).
Smith, M. (2006). "Osiris NN or Osiris of NN?" In *Totenbuch-Forschungen. Gesammelte Beiträge des 2. Internationalen Totenbuch-Symposiums 2005*. Studien zum altägyptischen Totenbuch 11, edited by B. Backes, I. Munro, and S. Stöhr, 325–38 (Wiesbaden: Harrassowitz).
Smith, M. (2009). *Traversing Eternity: Texts for the Afterlife from Ptolemaic and Roman Egypt* (Oxford: Oxford University Press).
Smith, M. (2017). *Following Osiris: Perspectives on the Osirian Afterlife from Four Millennia* (Oxford: Oxford University Press).

Sousa, R. (2009). "Symbolism and Meaning of the Pendulum Heart Amulets." *Göttinger Miszellen* 221: 69–79.

Sousa, R. (2011). *Heart of Wisdom. Studies on the Heart Amulet in Ancient Egypt* (Oxford: Archaeopress).

Stadler, M. A. (2001). "War eine dramatische Aufführung eines Totengerichtes Teil der ägyptischen Totenriten?" *Studien zur altägyptsiche Kultur* 29: 331–48.

Stadler, M. A. (2003). *Der Totenpapyrus des Pa-Month (P. Bibl. Nat. 149)*. Studien zum Altägyptischen Totenbuch 6 (Wiesbaden: Harrassowitz).

Stadler, M. A. (2008). "Judgment after Death (Negative Confession)." In *UCLA Encyclopedia of Egyptology*, edited by J. Dieleman and W. Wendrich (Los Angeles: UCLA), https://escholarship.org/uc/item/07s1t6kj.pdf

Stadler, M. A. (2009). *Weiser und Wesir: Studien zu Vorkommen, Rolle und Wesen des Gottes Thot im ägyptischen Totenbuch* (Tübingen: Mohr Siebeck).

Stadler, M. A. (2014). "Elysische Gefilde und Orte der Schrecknisse. Die Fahrt des Sonnengottes durch die Unterwelt nach den altägyptischen Unterweltsbüchern." In *Unterwelten. Modelle und Transformationen*. Würzburger Ringvorlesungen, 9, edited by J. Hamm and J. Robert, 6–28 (Würzburg: Könighaus & Neumann).

Stadler, M. A. (2016). "Dioskourides, Titus Flavius Demetrius, Tanaweruow et al., or: How Appealing is an Egyptian Afterlife?" In *Burial Rituals, Ideas of Afterlife, and the Individual in the Hellenistic World and the Roman Empire*. Potsdamer Altertumswissenschaftliche Beiträge, 57, edited by K. Waldner, R. L. Gordon, and W. Spickermann, 151–66 (Wiesbaden: Franz Steiner Verlag).

Stadler, M. A. (2017), "Ägyptenrezeption in der römischen Kaiserzeit" In *Platonismus und spätägyptische Religion. Plutarch und die Ägyptenrezeption in der römischen Kaiserzeit*. Beiträge zur Altertumskunde, 364, edited by M. Erler and M. A. Stadler, 21–42 (Berlin: de Gruyter).

Strudwick, N. (2005). *Texts from the Pyramid Age*. Writings from the Ancient World, 16 (Leiden: E. J. Brill).

Taylor, J. H. (2010). *Journey through the Afterlife: Ancient Egyptian Book of the Dead* (Cambridge, MA: Harvard University Press; London: British Museum Press).

Verhoeven, U. (2003). "Post im Jenseits: Formular und Funktion altägyptischer Briefe an Tote." In *Bote und Brief. Sprachliche Systeme der Informationsübermittlung im Spannungsfeld von Mündlichkeit und Schriftlichkeit*, edited by A. Wagner, 31–51 (Frankfurt am Main: Peter Lang).

Walls, J. L., ed. (2007). *The Oxford Handbook of Eschatology* (New York: Oxford University Press).

Wente, E. F. (1990). *Letters from Ancient Egypt* (Atlanta: Scholars Press).

Willems, H. (1998). "Anubis as a Judge." In *Egyptian Religion: The Last Thousand Years. Studies Dedicated to the Memory of Jan Quaegebeur*, edited by C. Willy, A. Schoors, and H. Willems, I. 719–43 (Leuven: Peeters).

Zandee, J. (1960). *Death as an Enemy according to Ancient Egyptian Conceptions* (Leiden: E. J. Brill).

CHAPTER 21

# GODS AND DEMONS IN THE BOOK OF THE DEAD

RITA LUCARELLI

## The Gods of the Netherworld between Myth and Funerary Religion[*]

SUPERNATURAL beings of different sorts populate all the spells and vignettes of the Book of the Dead, and their high number and variety of names, epithets, and forms may leave us with a sense of bewilderment. It is difficult to detect which are the most important divine entities from which the deceased wishes to obtain favor of or with whom they wish to become assimilated, or which are the demonic beings he fears the most. A few gods are mentioned more often than others, so that we may speak of major and minor gods; however, when a minor deity or spirit is mentioned in one spell or represented only in a vignette, her/his role seems still to be important both for the deceased and in relation to the main gods (such as Re and Osiris) within each spell context. The netherworld of the ancient Egyptians was inhabited by beings whose hierarchy—if there was one—is often unclear. Unlike the divine population in a temple, most of which are generally dedicated to one or a couple of main gods, we cannot always distinguish between major and minor deities when dealing with the divine inhabitants of the ancient Egyptian netherworld. Instead, we can sense a complex, harmonious architecture of divine, demonic, and spiritual entities cooperating alongside each other, through different roles and functions, in order to help the deceased to reach the state of *akh* (glorified spirit) through various stages—some of them challenging and rather dangerous—that will guide her/him toward the final

---

[*] This chapter is a reviewed and updated version of an essay previously published in Scalf, 2014: 127–36. I wish to thank the Oriental Institute at the University of Chicago for granting me the permission to republish this study.

assimilation with the gods. The power of transformation into divine beings and symbols is actually the topic of one of the most attested group of spells of the corpus, the so-called transformation spells (BD 76–88; Servajean, 2003; Smith, 2009: 610–17), where the deceased expresses her/his wish to become a lotus (BD 81A), a god ("the greatest of the tribunal" in BD 79), "a god, causing darkness to be light," Ptah (BD 82), a snake (BD 87), a crocodile (BD 88), or a bird (a falcon in BD 77 and 78, a heron in BD 83 and 84, a *ba*-bird in BD 85, a swallow in BD 86). The theme of transforming into a divine bird, which is the most popular of the group, also reflects the wish for freedom of movement in the netherworld. The word *ḫpr*, "becoming," which occurs in the incipits of these spells ("Spell for becoming...") is expressed by the hieroglyph of the scarab. Here, also a symbol of the sun as Khepri, in its cycle of transformation from night to day. As a matter of fact, these spells are closely related to the solar journey, and the fact that, in the standard versions of the Late Period papyri, they occur in the number of twelve (77 to 88, 76 being an introductory formula for "transforming into any form one wishes to take") mirrors the journey of the sun god during the twelve hours of the day and of the night (Quirke, 2013: 179–80; Weber, this volume).

In the spells of the Book of the Dead, the deceased is called "the Osiris NN" (or "the Osiris of NN," according to other scholars: Smith, 2017); he is, therefore, starting with the beginning of his journey in the Realm of the Dead, a god himself. Osiris, as *Khenty-Imentyw*, "Chief of the Westerners" (the Westerners being the dead souls inhabiting the Beyond, associated with the West/sunset), is clearly a prominent figure in the Book of the Dead, and his name and figure occur almost constantly in the spells; his function as the of god of death and rebirth mingles with that of the sun god Re (also in his forms of Atum/the creator/aged god and Khepri) with whom he unites temporally each night in the syncretistic form of Osiris-Re, the *nṯr ꜥꜣ* (*netjer aʾa*) or "great god." The latter is an epithet that can apply to other gods as well, but when it refers to Osiris and Re in the Book of the Dead and in other funerary compositions such as the Books of the Underworld, it seems to imply more specifically the union of the two gods. This union, however, should always be considered temporary and cyclical rather than implying that the two deities have merged fully into a sort of super-god (Smith, 2017: 330–31). Re and Osiris's main presence in the Book of the Dead is closely connected with and complemented by a number of other gods, some of whom can join Re and Osiris in syncretistic forms as well, such as Amun-Re, Ptah-Sokar-Osiris, and Re-Horakhty. The other gods of the Heliopolitan account of creation, the so-called Ennead, are also widely mentioned, namely the air god Shu and his female counterpart Tefnut, the earth god Geb, the sky goddess Nut, Osiris's brother Seth and his sister Isis (who is also his wife), and Nephthys. Osiris and Isis's son Horus is very often invoked as well in the spells and represented in the vignettes either in his fully falcon form or as an anthropoid god with a falcon head. The mention of the members of the Ennead is generally in relation to the mythological cycle of creation from Heliopolis, which sees Re-Atum as the creator god and Horus as the living king of Egypt after the murder of Osiris by his brother Seth. Thoth plays a prominent, manifold, and highly differentiated role as a funerary god as well, which has been thoroughly analyzed in a monograph by Martin Stadler (2009) and which will be discussed more in detail later in the chapter in relation to the final judgment of the deceased.

## NUT AND THE FEMALE DIVINE PROTECTION OF THE DECEASED

The cosmogonic associations of the primordial gods also influence their representation and mention in the Book of the Dead; being the goddess of the sky, Nut is depicted as mother of the deceased, embracing her/him in a celestial netherworld and protecting her/him during the journey as s/he ascends to the sky. In Spell 136A, it is said that the deceased "sails on it [i.e., the boat] to Nut." In many other incantations, she is mentioned as the mother of the sun god and therefore the deceased is born from her womb, the same as the sun god with whom he assimilates. One of the most popular and beautiful images of the sky goddess, which is also attested on funerary papyri belonging to genres other than the Book of the Dead, is that of Nut arching her body on a prostrate Geb while supported by Shu, occurs on one of the longest scrolls of the Book of the Dead (almost 40 m), the so-called P.Greenfield (P.London BM EA 10554; Fig. 21.1) (Lucarelli, 2017: 129, Fig. 11.2). The role of Nut as mother of the creator sun god and of the deceased, toward whom the other gods move in procession, is expressed at the end of one of the transformation spells mentioned earlier, namely BD 79: " . . . in his (i.e., the sun god/Atum's) beautiful processions to the

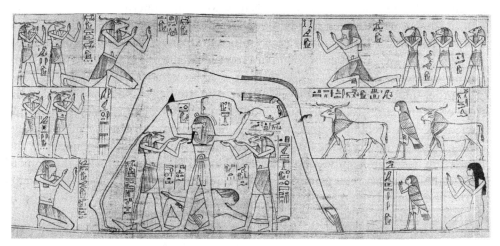

FIG. 21.1. P.Greenfield (P.London BM EA 10554, 87): Nut arching over Geb and Shu supporting her (after Budge 1912, Pls. CVI–CVII).

body of the Lower Sky, he whom his mother Nut has borne" (P.London BM EA 10477, translation in Quirke, 2013: 189). When allusions to the myth of the rebellion of humanity against the old sun god are made, as in BD 175 (Wüthrich, 2012), humans are called "the children of Nut." The title of BD 59, which is particularly widespread in papyri of the Late and Ptolemaic Period, is "Spell for breathing air and having power over water"; its vignette depicts the "sycamore of Nut," which is also invoked in the text as granter of water and air to the deceased. The theme of the tree-goddess is very popular in the Book of the Dead and not only connected to Nut; female goddesses such as Isis, Hathor, the Goddess of the West, and others are also depicted in connection with a tree (Billing, 2004).

The aforementioned BD 175 and 59 have no earlier sources but occur in temple rituals as well (about the possible earlier origin of BD 175 see Stadler, 2009: 371–72). Contrary to that, the text of Spell 79 and many others where Nut and the other gods of the Ennead are mentioned are newer versions of older texts for the protection of the deceased king that are found in the Pyramid Texts of the Old Kingdom, as well as re-editions of spells in the so-called Coffin Texts employed in the Middle Kingdom mainly on coffins of the elite and officials close to the king. The role of these primordial gods toward the deceased does not seem to have changed much; the main difference is that now not only the king (or a very restricted elite, such as in the case of the Coffin Texts) but also a large number of private individuals (elite members of the population—mostly members of priestly families and scribes working in the temples) may try to gain the gods' favor in the netherworld and even attempt to become assimilated with them by possessing a funerary papyrus of the Book of the Dead. A very popular spell, employed in papyri from the Eighteenth Dynasty to the Ptolemaic Period where the gods of the Ennead all occur together, is BD 134, for "glorifying an *akh*-spirit," which includes instructions on how to draw an image of these deities in the solar boat on a bowl; the vignette of this spell indeed represents a number of deities (mostly those of the Ennead) in a boat, and the same image can also be found on pottery bowls used for temple offerings (Taylor, 2010: 48–49). The theme of the solar boat and the deceased traveling in it with the gods is a central motif in texts and vignettes of the Book of the Dead; on one single papyrus, multiple vignettes of the solar boat can be found in a row (where the primordial gods of the myth are the "followers of Re").

Another important female deity is Hathor, who, similar to Nut, can be part of the solar crew and is related to the tree-goddess motif. Her main characteristic in the ancient Egyptian religion is that of goddess of sensuality, love, and female creative power, but, as is also the case for other deities, her role becomes more nuanced and focuses on her relationship with the deceased in the funerary context of the Book of the Dead. In funerary texts (for example, the Books of Breathing) and on monuments of the later periods (and in particular by the end of the Ptolemaic Period and in the Roman Period), it became common practice to refer to the female deceased as "Hathor NN," showing how the importance of this goddess in the funerary cults and literature had grown and how she had become the female counterpart of Osiris (Riggs, 2005: 41–48). It has been also pointed out that the gender distinction between

Osiris NN and Hathor NN may have its origin in the funerary religion of the Middle Kingdom (Riggs and Stadler, 2003). The funerary role of Hathor gains importance starting from the New Kingdom; the frequent representations of the celestial cow of Hathor in the Book of the Dead is a consequence of this increased role as funerary deity, in which she manifests in the form of a cow or of a woman with cow horns and the solar disk on her head. In particular, many Theban papyri of the Ramesside period employ in their closing section the vignette of BD 186, depicting Hathor as a cow and as a manifestation of the Mistress of the West, emerging from the Western mountain within a thicket of papyri, protecting the tomb depicted on her back and welcoming the deceased in the netherworld together with Ipet, the hippopotamus birth goddess. This motif, also popular on coffins of the Third Intermediate Period, includes an important detail, namely the *udjat*-eye of the cow, which symbolizes another main characteristic of Hathor, that of apotropaic goddess, related either to the furious eye of Re or to the eye of Horus. P.Milbank of the Ptolemaic Period closes with BD 162, which is an incantation "for providing heat under the head of the dead" and includes at the end a short colophon with instructions on reciting the spell "over a figure of the heavenly cow (i.e., Ihet) made of fine gold and placed at the throat of the blessed one" (Wüthrich, 2017). The idea of female deities with apotropaic characteristics, which are connected to the eye of the god, is also attested by peculiar amulets where a "dangerous goddess," such as Sakhmet, Neith, Isis, or Tefnut, is depicted on one side of the *udjat*-eye; this sort of amulet is described in Spell 163 of the Book of the Dead as well, as a representation of the solar power (Darnell, 1997). The vignette of BD 163, which is widespread in the late papyri, indeed represents two winged *udjat*-eyes (Fig. 21.2) (Lucarelli, 2017: 130, Fig. 11.3).

Other divine cows, which are related to Hathor and other female cow goddesses in the myth, appear as well in the Book of the Dead. The vignette of Spell 148 is the most representative in this respect, since it depicts the seven celestial cows and their bull as providers of offerings and rebirth for the deceased. They are also a manifestation of the "Seven Hathors," who are mentioned in literary texts as deities of the fate, having the skill to predict the future for the newly born. A heavenly cow with sun disk and Hathor plumes is also depicted in the final vignette of P.Milbank of the Ptolemaic Period (P.Chicago OIM E10486O; Allen, 1960; Scalf, 2017: 300).

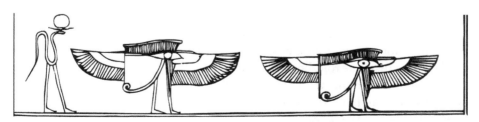

FIG. 21.2. Vignette of Spell 163 (after Lepsius 1842, Pls. LXXVII–LXXVIII).

# Thoth and the Male Deities of the Final Judgment

While female deities may in general be interchangeable in their motherly, protective role toward the deceased, male deities have more individual roles in the Book of the Dead. In the popular scene of the final judgment, which is represented by the vignette of BD 125 (Janák, this volume) and which is also a widespread iconographic motif on coffins from the New Kingdom onwards and on the later Books of Breathing, a few central male deities occur, such as Thoth, Anubis, and the Four Sons of Horus.

The importance of the judgment and in general of trials for the dead in front of divine tribunals (in ancient Egyptian *djadjat*, which is also the topic of BD 18 and 20) is connected to myth as well, in particular to the mythological account of the justification of Osiris (Stadler, 2009: 320–51) and of the Contending of Horus and Seth. The scene of the scale (Seeber, 1976) upon which the heart of the deceased is weighed against the feather of Maat (the symbol of justice and cosmic order, also personified as a goddess) in front of Osiris (or more rarely Re) and of the gods overseeing this crucial moment is also attested very frequently on coffins, mummy bandages, and shrouds; in one isolated case, a temple version of the judgment scene dating to the Ptolemaic Period occurs as well in Deir el-Medina (Thebes; see Kockelmann, this volume). In this scene, Thoth, the ibis- or baboon-god, who is known in general as god of writing and wisdom, takes the specific role of recorder of the verdict and is generally represented as an ibis-headed anthropomorphic god, his human body making it possible to exploit his scribal activity. In general, the anthropomorphic bodies of gods in the Book of the Dead, as well as in other ritual and funerary depictions, denote their "humanness" and ability to interact with humans either living or deceased (Wilkinson, 2008). Indeed, the same concept applies to Anubis, the jackal-headed god who, in the judgment scene, oversees the scale—sometimes accompanied by another god such as Horus. In a less active role, Thoth in his theriomorphic form of baboon can be depicted over the scale as well, as in P.Ryerson of the Ptolemaic Period (P.Chicago OIM E9787F; Scalf, 2017: 230), where two extra, small scales overseen by a baboon are used as decorative motifs to frame the architecture of the "Hall of the Two Truths," where the judgment takes place.

Similar to Thoth and Anubis, the main gods mentioned in the Book of the Dead who appear in mythological accounts and temple scenes and texts have more than one manifestation (mostly animal or hybrid with animal head and human body) and can play more than one role; both Thoth and Anubis, for instance, occur in a number of other spells besides BD 125 and in each of them are characterized according to the context (for a comprehensive analysis of the role of Thoth in the Book of the Dead, see Stadler, 2009). The jackal-headed Anubis, for instance, when he occurs in BD 151 (Lüscher, 1998), takes on the role of embalmer; the vignette of the same spell, whose central scene depicts him overseeing the funerary bed where the deceased's mummy or coffin lies, is another popular motif on funerary objects and in tomb decorations. Anubis was, as a matter of fact, a very old funerary god, protector of the king's burial since the beginning of the Pharaonic Period and with chapels in temples throughout Egypt; he shared the important epithet of "Foremost of the Westerners" (*Khenty-Imentyw*) with the god Osiris, but must be distinguished from another ancient and important funerary jackal god, Wepwawet (literally "The Opener of the Ways"). In the vignette of BD 138, which is a "spell for entering Abydos and being in the following of Osiris," both Anubis and Wepwawet are depicted as jackals on a stand. A series of other jackal-faced gods and demonic beings populate the Book of the Dead as well, showing how popular canids and in particular jackals were as a manifestation of funerary deities.

Returning to our earlier discussion of a "sample" of deities mentioned and depicted in the Book of the Dead, one may already be able to single out a few central features characterizing the divine world of the ancient Egyptian afterlife. First of all, the main deities of the ancient Egyptian pantheon, when acting within a funerary context such as that of the Book of the Dead, recall the mythological accounts in which they play a role. Moreover, they generally have a protective and benevolent function toward the deceased, who seeks physical and spiritual empowerment in order to become an *akh*, a divine, transfigured spirit. Finally, their iconography is rather fixed and "traditional," e. g., Thoth as an ibis or a baboon, Anubis as a jackal god, Sobek as a crocodile, and Ptah as an anthropomorphic god.

A series of supernatural inhabitants of the netherworld, also widely depicted and mentioned in the spells, seem to gravitate around those main divine figures. Sometimes these liminal beings with heads of dangerous animals, such as jackals and crocodiles, are anonymous and depicted together with the main gods. Therefore, they are hardly distinguished from them unless their names are indicated in the captions of the vignettes. This is where the category of the "great gods" actually intermingles with what are called "minor gods," "demons," or "genii," namely different classes of supernatural beings. An example is that of the 42 judges of BD 125, "who hear cases" in front of which the "negative confession" is recited by the deceased and which are also represented in the vignette (Janák, this volume). A few of them are known already from other religious sources and have attested cults in cities, such as Nefertem in Memphis, or have epithets related to other main gods such as "Nosey" of Hermopolis (Thoth) or White of Teeth (Sobek) (Wilkinson, 2008: 84; Stadler, 2003: 119–23). Moreover, Re, Atum, Shu, and Tefnut as well as other primordial gods may be represented among the judges in the vignette, as for instance in the already mentioned papyrus of Ani. The other judges, however, have very specific and otherwise unattested names; these are connected to other places, and each of them is related to a specific sin that the deceased must avoid. Their names are rather frightening (Far-strider, Swallower of Shades, Dangerous One, etc.) and their nature could be defined as "demonic" if we accept the existence of demons in addition to the gods.

# From Gods to Demons

In the ancient Egyptian language, the only general word referring to the category of the divine is *netjer*, represented by the hieroglyph 🚩, which probably depicts a cult flag or wrapped fetish, while the sign of a falcon on a pole 𓅆 or the hieroglyph of the seated god 𓀭 occur as determinatives of divine names (Hornung, 1982: 33–42). *Netjer* is generally translated as "god," and it indicates the main gods mentioned earlier, which occur in the myths, have cult places, and reside in temples (Assmann, 2001: 7–8). However, a crowd of supernatural entities that are not worshipped in temples and do not appear in myths or official cults are present as well in the texts and vignettes of the Book of the Dead. They have various names and epithets according to their physical appearance, their function, or the place where they live within the variegated regions of the Duat. If, on the one hand, they belong to the sphere of the *netjer* because of their superhuman nature, they differ on the other hand from the main gods on the basis of not possessing a universal power. Their sphere of action and range of magical power is limited and circumscribed to a physical space and very specific roles or influences concerning the deceased. An example of this limited power is Amemet, "The Devourer of the Dead," a composite animal being (with a crocodile head, the upper body of a lion, and the lower body of a hippopotamus) who is a constant presence during the final judgment, standing ready to destroy the lives of those who do not pass the judgment; her divine power was therefore related only to retribution in the afterlife. Similarly, the mostly hybrid creatures supervising the gates and doors of the netherworld, which occur in a group of very popular spells of the corpus (BD 144–147), are better defined as guardian demons than as gods; their sphere of action is restricted to the place they guard and it is only there that the deceased will face them and interact with them in order to be allowed to pass through. Stadler (2009: 235–329) suggested that the guardians and their gates in these spells are connected to the myth of the "Dangerous Goddess" (Sakhmet), whom the deceased tries to appease by taking over Thoth's role.

The popularity of these guardians was so widespread that they are depicted and mentioned not only on papyrus but also on coffins, tomb walls, and even temples. In the case of the latter, their status changes from guardians of the afterlife to genii of the temple, but their static function—they cannot leave the place they guard—is the same. The protective function of the guardians is related to the important moment of the vigil of Osiris during the hours of the night, when the mummified body of the god needs protection before rebirth; for this reason, it is not surprising that the spells on the guardian demons and their vignettes are widely employed on coffins in order to protect the mummy (Fig. 21.3) (Lucarelli, 2017: Fig. 11.5). The guardians usually have a hybrid iconography, with an animal head and an anthropomorphic body. The head can represent various sacred animals, from reptiles to birds and mammals, in particular crocodiles, snakes, dogs, rams, bulls, monkeys, and falcons, to name just a few. They are depicted sitting or standing, alone, as a couple, or as triads, while holding attributes that can vary

FIG. 21.3. Coffin of Padiamun (World Museum, Liverpool 53.72D). Courtesy of National Museums Liverpool (World Museum).

from vegetal elements resembling barley—probably a symbol of fertility—to knives or upstanding lizards, corresponding to the hieroglyphic sign ꜥšꜣ, meaning "many." Their iconography may be confusing since, in some cases, it is the same as that of certain main gods, such as the jackal-headed Anubis or the crocodile god Sobek. Their names are what distinguish them from the main gods, although some of those names may also be used as epithets for the gods, such as "the one with many forms," which is also an epithet of the god Amun-Re, or "the one with many faces," which in other religious texts also applies to Osiris and Re.

Unlike the guardians, there are gangs of demons that are rarely depicted and only mentioned through collective names such as the "Murderers," the "Messengers," and the "Wanderers." Their names are very representative of their fear-inducing function as punishers, sent to earth by angry deities, or of their service to a main god such as Osiris, Sakhmet, or Re. These demons are also mentioned widely in spells for everyday magic, where they are especially feared as disease carriers and as messengers of Sakhmet. This shows that the supernatural world and the beliefs in demons and spirits as represented in the Book of the Dead is closely related to the world of the living and to the daily magical practices that the local magicians and the priests in the temple perform in order to heal the living and protect them from unwanted happenings. The spells and vignettes against dangerous, demonic animals in the Book of the Dead should also be seen in relation to the same need for protection; the group of spells 31 to 42 aims at repelling hostile beings and forces and at demonizing certain animals, such as snakes, crocodiles, pigs, and insects, which were also to be warded off in spells of daily magic. The antisnake spells are the most numerous in the group (BD 33, 34, 35, 37, and 39); they are also attested in the oldest magical corpus of the Pyramid Texts of the third millennium BCE (Leitz, 1996) and are widespread in spells for daily magic throughout the New Kingdom and even later. We can consider those snakes and the other animals mentioned in these spells to be "demonic," since they do not inhabit the earth but belong instead to the variegated divine category of the inhabitants of the netherworld. Moreover, when the pig and the donkey are mentioned, as in some variants of BD 36 for the pig and BD 40 for the donkey, the god of chaos, Seth, is meant; when the snake occurs in this kind of spell, the main association is with the giant snake, Apophis. The latter, mentioned in a few spells but more extensively in BD 39 of the Book of the Dead, together with its earlier variant of Rerek (Borghouts, 2007), also occurs in BD 7 of the corpus, where the "spine of Apophis" is also the sandbank that halts the boat of the sun god during its journey. Apophis cannot be considered either a god or a demon, but rather an archetypal enemy of creation that can be compared to primordial monsters, in the same way that dragons and snakes represent chaos and oppose creation in other religions, such as the Babylonian Tiamat or Leviathan of the Hebrew Bible. Apophis has been also seen as a leftover from the creation of Re, namely his umbilical cord (Quack, 2006). He is also represented in the vignette of BD 17, where we see him being fettered with a knife by Atum, who manifests in the form of a wild cat; he can also be seen attacking the solar boat in the scenes of the so-called Book of the Hidden Chamber or the Amduat.

The latter illustrates the journey of the sun god in his boat throughout the 12 hours of the night in the subterranean netherworld, in order to unite with the dead body of Osiris (Scalf, this volume). A series of divine and demonic figures accompany the sun god in his journey, and among them are snake-like creatures, some of them benevolent and related to deities, while others play the role of punishers of the damned souls. Some motifs of the Amduat, which was originally employed to decorate the royal tombs of the New Kingdom, converge in the Book of the Dead and other funerary papyri of the Third Intermediate Period that accompanied the deceased in the coffin.

# The *Akhw*: Transfigured Spirits and Ghosts

Finally, the Book of the Dead spells also contribute to our understanding of another important religious concept, that of "spirit" or "ghost," which also indicates creatures belonging to the sphere of the supernatural. However, they are not independent entities such as the gods and demons; rather, they represent the transfigured status of the living after death. The ancient Egyptian term that indicates these creatures is $₃ḥ$, "akh," represented by the hieroglyph of the crested ibis, whose root has a vast array of meanings, from "being effective, efficacious" to "transfigure" and "glorify" (although those can be also considered as two separate roots, as Jansen-Winkeln, 1996, argues). The similar root *iḫ*, "to be bright," indicates the close connection of the blessed spirits with the sun; BD 130–136, which are all focused on the solar boat, are for "making an *akh* excellent" in assimilation with the sun god. However, in other contexts the *akhw* can be understood as spirits inhabiting the netherworld and even as demons controlled by a main deity, as in the case of a peculiar spell attested in only a few papyri of the Ramesside and Third Intermediate Period, the so-called BD 194 of the Book of the Dead (DuQuesne, 1994); here, Anubis is depicted at the head of seven *akhw* holding snake-wands, which are said to belong to the tribunal and are mentioned in spell 17 as well (Lucarelli, 2006). These demonic *akhw* can even be seen as ghosts when the term is used for ghostly manifestations occurring on earth, as in many Ramesside spells of daily and funerary magic.

Finally, the term *b₃*, "ba," which is similar to *akh*, indicates mainly the transfigured status of the deceased in the afterlife in relation to freedom of movement and is represented by the hieroglyph, the jabiru-bird, and may designate supernatural forces when used in its plural form, *baw*. BD 107–116 are for knowing the *baw* of different places in the netherworld, which are represented as triads of divine figures, probably local gods. The *baw* of the gods also occur in spells of daily magic as rather dangerous forces.

In conclusion, we could say that the world of gods, spirits, and demons in the Book of the Dead is a faithful mirror of how the ancient Egyptians already conceived of and dealt with divine entities during their cultural and religious activities on earth; they believed in an afterlife where the encounters with the supernatural were not an exceptional but rather an ordinary occasion, to be dealt with using the catalogue of spells and vignettes of the Book of the Dead and in general the magical objects included in the funerary equipment of their tombs, their coffins, and their mummies.

## Bibliography

Allen, T. G., ed. (1960). *The Egyptian Book of the Dead: Documents in the Oriental Institute Museum at the University of Chicago.* Oriental Institute Publications 82 (Chicago: The University of Chicago Press).

Assmann, J. (2001). *The Search for God in Ancient Egypt.* Translated by David Lorton (Ithaca: Cornell University Press).

Borghouts, J. F. (2007). *Book of the Dead [39]: From Shouting to Structure.* Studien zum altägyptischen Totenbuch, 10 (Wiesbaden: Harrassowitz).

Billing, N. (2004). "Writing an Image: The Formulation of the Tree Goddess Motif in the Book of the Dead, Ch. 59." *Studien zur Altägyptischen Kultur* 32: 35–50.

Budge, E. A. W. (1912). *The Greenfield Papyrus in the British Museum. The Funerary Papyrus of Princess Nesitanebtashru, Daughter of Painetchem II and Nesi-Khensu, and Priestess of Amen-Ra at Thebes, about B.C. 970* (London: Trustees of the British Museum).

Darnell, J. C. (1997). "The apotropaic goddess in the eye." *Studien zur Altägyptischen Kultur* 24: 35–48.

DuQuesne, T. (1994). *At the Court of Osiris: Book of the Dead Spell 194. A Rare Egyptian Judgment Text Edited and Interpreted with Commentary.* Oxfordshire Communications in Egyptology, 4 (London: Da'th Scholarly Services; Darengo Publications).

Hornung, E. (1982). *Conceptions of God in Ancient Egypt: The One and the Many*. Translated by John Baines (London; Ithaca, NY: Routledge & Kegan Paul; Cornell University Press).

Jansen-Winkeln, K. (1996). "'Horizont' und 'Verklärtheit.' Zur Bedeutung der Wurzel ꜣḫ." *Studien zur Altägyptischen Kultur* 23: 201–15.

Leitz, C. (1996). "Die Schlangensprüche in den Pyramidentexten." *Orientalia* 65(4): 381–427.

Lepsius, C. R. (1842). *Das Todtenbuch der Ägypter nach dem hieroglyphischen Papyrus in Turin*. Leipzig.

Lucarelli, R. (2006). "Demons in the Book of the Dead." In *Totenbuch-Forschungen. Gesammelte Beiträge des 2. Internationalen Totenbuch-Symposiums. Bonn, 25. bis 29 September 2005*, edited by B. Backes, I. Munro, and S. Stöhr, 203–12 (Wiesbaden: Harrassowitz).

Lucarelli, R. (2017). "11. Gods, Spirits, Demons of the Book of the Dead." In *Book of the Dead: Becoming God in Ancient Egypt*. Oriental Institute Museum Publications 39, edited by Foy D. Scalf, 127–36 (Chicago: CASEMATE ACADEMIC).

Quirke, S. (2013). *Going Out in Daylight—prt m hrw: The Ancient Egyptian Book of the Dead; Translation, Sources, Meaning*. GHP Egyptology 20 (London: Golden House Publications).

Lüscher, B. (1998). *Untersuchungen zu Totenbuch Spruch 151*. Studien zum Altägyptischen Totenbuch 2 (Wiesbaden: Harrassowitz).

Riggs, C. (2005). *The Beautiful Burial in Roman Egypt: Art, Identity, and Funerary Religion*. Oxford Studies in Ancient Culture and Representation (Oxford: Oxford University Press).

Riggs, C. and Stadler, M. A. (2003). "A Roman Shroud and its Demotic Inscription in the Museum of Fine Arts, Boston." *Journal of the Research Center in Egypt* 40: 69–87.

Seeber, C. (1976). *Untersuchungen zur Darstellung des Totengerichts im Alten Ägypten*. Münchner Ägyptologische Studien, 35 (Berlin: Deutscher Kunstverlag).

Scalf, F., ed. (2017). *Book of the Dead: Becoming God in Ancient Egypt*. Oriental Institute Museum Publications 39, 127–36 (Chicago: The Oriental Institute).

Servajean, F. (2003). *Les formules des transformations du Livre des morts à la lumière d'une théorie de la performativité: XVIIIe-XXe dynasties*. Bibliothèque d'étude 137 (Le Caire: Institut français d'archéologie orientale).

Smith, M. (2009). *Traversing Eternity: Texts for the Afterlife from Ptolemaic and Roman Egypt* (Oxford: Oxford University Press).

Smith, M. (2017). *Following Osiris: Perspectives on the Osirian Afterlife from Four Millennia* (Oxford; New York: Oxford University Press).

Stadler, M. A. (2003). *Der Totenpapyrus des Pa-Month (P. Bibl. nat. 149)*. Studien zum altägyptischen Totenbuch, 6 (Wiesbaden: Harrassowitz).

Stadler, M. (2009). *Weiser und Wesir: Studien zu Vorkommen, Rolle und Wesen des Gottes Thot im ägyptischen Totenbuch*. Orientalische Religionen in der Antike 1 (Tübingen: Mohr Siebeck).

Taylor, J., ed. (2010). *Journey through the Afterlife: Ancient Egyptian Book of the Dead* (London; Cambridge, MA: British Museum Press; Harvard University Press).

Wilkinson, R. H. (2008). "Anthropomorphic Deities." *UCLA Encyclopedia of Egyptology*, UCLA. http://escholarship.org/uc/item/5s54w4tc

Quack, J. F. (2006). "Apopis, Nabelschnur des Re." *Studien zur Altägyptischen Kultur* 34: 377–79.

Wüthrich, A. (2012). "Formule pour ne pas mourir à nouveau—le chapitre 175 du Livre des Morts." In *Herausgehen am Tage*, Studien zum altägyptischen Totenbuch 17, edited by R. Lucarelli, M. Müller-Roth, and A. Wüthrich, 153–228 (Wiesbaden: Harrassowitz).

Wüthrich, A. (2017). "Vaches divines et Livre des Morts." *Égypte Afrique et Orient* 83: 19–28.

# CHAPTER 22

# THE SO-CALLED *CHAPITRES SUPPLÉMENTAIRES*

ANNIK WÜTHRICH

## The Designation of *chapitres supplémentaires*

In 1881, Willem Pleyte, the curator of the Egyptian collection of the Museum of Leiden at that time, published an ensemble of spells found on papyrus belonging to that museum, to the Louvre, and to the British Museum, which he called *chapitres supplémentaires* (Pleyte, 1881). He numbered these spells according to the publication of the Book of the Dead by Richard Lepsius (1842) from 162 to 174, adding nine new chapters to the corpus. The slightly later publication by Édouard Naville (1886) created a problem of double numbering from BD 166 to 174, since Naville did not take the numbering by Pleyte into account. To justify his decision, he argued that the BD chapters Pleyte published did not exist in the New Kingdom sources. He also left numbers 162 to 165 "free," because they were already known from the Lepsius reference book (Naville, 1886: 14). This confusion has been maintained in some translations of the BD, which mix both sets of spells (for instance Barguet, 1967: 238, who placed the translation of the two spells one after the other without explaining that this is simply an Egyptological convention).

The modern designation of *chapitres supplémentaires* is inspired by the incipit written before BD 163 on some ten papyri from the Twenty-sixth Dynasty to the Ptolemaic Period, which mentions that those spells are "extracted from another roll as an addition to the *Going forth by Day*, which has been found in the temple of Amun-Re, lord of the thrones of the two lands in Tanis, the one who makes live the two lands" (Wüthrich, 2015: 80–81). However, if Pleyte applied his designation to thirteen spells that appear together only on one single Ptolemaic papyrus (P.Paris Louvre N3248, partially published in Wüthrich, 2015), that ancient designation in fact pertains just to spells 163 to 165. As Jean Yoyotte (1977), who wrote the seminal article for the study of those chapters, remarks,

BD 162, 166, and 167 are conceptually, theologically, and linguistically very similar to these three chapters, whereas BD 168 to 174 focus on a completely different topic. The main purpose of these latter texts is to ensure the preservation and the awakening of the mummy, the so-called Osiris Liturgy. We can therefore assume that the *chapitres supplémentaires* in the ancient sense are BD 163 to 165, and we can consider BD 162, 166, and 167 to be closely related.

## The Incipit

The incipit introducing the *chapitres supplémentaires* is very interesting for several reasons. First of all, it presents the notion of a supplement or an addition to the corpus and raises the issue of what exactly a Book of the Dead spell is. It appears, like three of these spells (BD 163, 164, and 165), for the first time on manuscripts dating from the end of the Twenty-fifth Dynasty or the beginning of the Twenty-sixth Dynasty, when the scribes decided to reorganize the corpus to make a standardized version of it, which the Egyptologists describe as the Saite or Late Recension (see Albert and Gülden, this volume). We do not know the exact purpose of this reorganization, but it seems that after that time, a lot of funerary papyri were mass-produced and personalized only by adding the name and title of the owner of the manuscript. Even the vignettes were not always made for the owner of the papyrus, as scrolls of female owners demonstrate, in which the deceased is depicted as a man (see Töpfer and Verhoeven, this volume).

However, during the same time, we can observe the continuation of the practice of text selection, already attested in the Third Intermediate Period. This practice consisted of selecting some texts that might or might not have belonged to the Late Recension, and that could be reworked to allow the deceased to take with him all the knowledge he needed in the afterlife. Therefore, the designation of "addition" means that the scribes considered, at least when these chapters were first being used, that they did not belong to the classical "Going forth by Day," but were instead added to the "classical" corpus to be useful for the survival of the deceased. Nevertheless, it seems that, throughout the whole documentation, the use of the incipit remains marginal and the scribes did not find it difficult to consider those three spells to be part of the Late Recension, or at least that these texts were essential for the deceased. If the three chapters originated from another repertoire, it is worth noting nonetheless that there is no example of a papyrus containing just those three BD chapters. If they are an addition to the classical Book of the Dead, we have no evidence of their prior existence separate from the BD.

BD 162 is associated with these three spells from their very first attestation at the end of the Twenty-fifth Dynasty. However, it originally appears separate from the group in the Twenty-first Dynasty. The theological concepts involved in this chapter are slightly different from the other three spells: the god invoked is not yet clearly defined as Amun, but the different epithets linked to this deity allow us to identify him with the Theban god. This is, one might say, the first step of the evolution of the Theban theology into the

Book of the Dead. On the contrary, Amun is openly named in BD 163 and 165, while in BD 164 the goddess Mut is the main deity of the text. Another difference is the origin of the foreign words. While a proximity to Nubian languages is quite clear in BD 163, 164, and 165, the origin of the unidentified lexemes in BD 162 remains impossible to establish.

The position of the *chapitres supplémentaires* remains unchanged until the end of the use of the Book of the Dead: as a group, they are always inscribed at the end of the "standard" version. Rarely, however, we can find them separately in personalized manuscripts, as it is the case with BD 163 in some papyri coming from Akhmim, although they still appear near the end of the text collection (Mosher, 2001), whereas BD 162 was written, even at the beginning of its use, most frequently as the final text.

Besides the incipit, four of the papyri inscribed with the *chapitres supplémentaires* contain the phrase *iw=f pw*, which is the usual colophon used to indicate the end of a text (Lenzo-Marchese, 2004). On P.Marseille 291 (Verhoeven, 1999), which is one of the oldest attestations of BD 163 to 165, the indication is after BD 161, while on the other three it is after BD 162. The sequence of P.Marseille is 291–colophon–incipit–*chapitres supplémentaires*–163–164–165–162. Here, the function of the incipit is probably to introduce the four spells. In the three other papyri, the sequence is BD 162–colophon–incipit–*chapitres supplémentaires*–163–164–165, which means that the scribes considered the colophon to be the final remark of the Book of the Dead and the three chapters as an actual addition to the corpus. All three of these manuscripts date to the Ptolemaic Period. On the other hand, the colophon is attested after BD 162 on about ten other manuscripts, again dating to the Ptolemaic Period, while it is written only once after the last spell (BD 165) on the Ptolemaic P.London BM EA 10097 (partially published in Wüthrich, 2015). Oddly enough, the colophon is written twice on this papyrus, once again after BD 162. In summary, the colophon indicates that the conclusive spell of the Book of the Dead in the Late Period was BD 162, and that at times it can mark the end of the corpus.

These four spells are thus described as an addition and conclusion to this funerary ensemble. But why do these spells have this status? Overall, we can observe that the spells of the Late Recension are organized in thematic groups, which are in part introduced by a common title, as they came from another repertoire, but this mention of an "addition" is unique.

## The *Chapitres Supplémentaires* as the Final Spells of the Book of the Dead

This, however, does not alone explain their final position. The six BD spells (BD 155–160), which are almost always written before the *chapitres supplémentaires*, are linked to the amulets, whereas the rubrics from BD 162 to 165 all contain instructions for the fabrication of such objects. Above all else, the grouping and the final position of the four spells have to do with their theological and linguistic particularism. The themes of the texts, for instance, can explain their position, especially in the case of BD 162. The goal of this text is "to provide heat under the head of the blessed one in the necropolis." The heat (ḥbs in the very first attestation, and then always bs) will ensure that the deceased will be reborn, that he will pass from a lethargic to a living state. Moreover, this text allows the deceased to assimilate his fate to that of the solar god, who is reborn every day after his nightly journey in the underworld. The position of this text could be explained, therefore, as a final spell in the process of rebirth initiated at the beginning of the Book of the Dead with the inhumation of the deceased into his grave.

# Pseudepigraphic Justification

The mention of Tanis as the place where the texts were found is also unusual. This should not be understood literally, but rather as one of the many examples in Egyptian literature of the use of pseudepigrapha, which can be defined as using a famous reference, person, god, or place, to give a text a more sacral value. As for Tanis, it never had the status of a holy city like Heliopolis or Thebes, even if it is sometimes described as the "Northern Thebes" (Guermeur, 2005: 117–24). However, Tanis must have played as significant a theological role as Thebes or Edfu from the Third Intermediate Period onward. If we take into account that the first mention of this group of texts dates from the end of the Twenty-fifth Dynasty, then we can consider this a clue for the sacralization of the city during or after the reign of the Kushites. Later, in BD 163, we first find another geographical reference that can be related to the contemporary theology: the peak of Napata, the Gebel Barkal, is the place where the god Amun rests, and is also viewed as the southern replica of the temple of Karnak by the Kushites (Wüthrich, 2010: 6–8, 130–37). Another city is mentioned with a reference to Neith of Sais. All these cities bore the name of "Northern" or "Southern" Thebes, whereas this designation for Sais is attested only in the Twenty-fifth Dynasty (Guermeur, 2005: 117–25). Therefore, one can see the *chapitres supplémentaires* as an attempt to reflect the theological reality of the time on a geographical level.

The use of pseudepigrapha in order to give to the text more sacrality is also attested in BD 166 and 167, giving them also the status of annex to the corpus: the incipit of BD 166 mentions that the spell has been found "on the neck of Ramses II [User-Maat-Re] in the necropolis" (in the latest variant of the text "at the time of Ramses II"; for a different analysis of this incipit, see Dahms, Pehal, and Willems, 2014), whereas that of BD 167 names Khaemwaset and Amenhotep, son of Hapu, as the discoverers of the text in the necropolis of Memphis. All references are probably pseudepigraphic and have the purpose of placing the texts under the authority of high dignitaries who were celebrated for their wisdom or perhaps for their encyclopedic knowledge.

## Date of Attestation

The six spells appear late in the history of the Book of the Dead: BD 162 and 166 date from the middle of the Twenty-first Dynasty, BD 163 to 165 are not known before the end of the Twenty-fifth Dynasty, and BD 167 is attested entirely on only two papyri from the Ptolemaic Period.

BD 166 was first inscribed on small pieces of papyrus placed directly on different parts of the mummy, sometimes folded and sometimes rolled up and put into the clothes of the mummy. At the same time, we also find this text on longer papyri.

Likewise, BD 162 appears at the end of the so-called abrégés of the Third Intermediate Period. These are short papyri written mostly in hieratic with an initial illustration, representing the deceased in adoration before one or more deities (usually Osiris or Re-Horakhty). The manuscript also contains a selection of texts or of parts of spells, which were the most important element for survival in the afterlife. As we have already emphasized, BD 162 seems to have been understood at this time as the conclusive spell of this repertoire.

## The Language of the *Chapitres Supplémentaires*

All *chapitres supplémentaires* are composed in a language tinged with Late Egyptian constructions, which is quite unusual for this kind of text. The Book of the Dead belongs to those texts conceived in a language similar to what was thought to be the language of the "first occasion" (*zp-tpy*), i.e., contemporary with the creation of the world. This is the language of the first phase, namely Old and Middle Egyptian. But from the beginning of the New Kingdom, it becomes an artificial one that we call "*égyptien de tradition*," which aims at avoiding any trace of contemporary idioms in order to maintain the world in its initial state. As noted by Pascal Vernus, the imitation of the old language leads to a situation of diglossia, especially when the "gap between this language and the spoken language is so large that the knowledge of the latter does not ensure the understanding of the former" (Vernus, 1996: 557). While most of the spells from the corpus of the Book of the Dead have their origin in the corpus of the Coffin Texts, some of them were elaborated during the New Kingdom or later. Since the *chapitres supplémentaires* are not attested before the middle of the Twenty-first Dynasty, we can suppose that they were conceived during the Ramesside era at the earliest. Like the rest of the corpus, the six spells are a combination of different genres: hymn, prayer, descriptive part, rubric, and so on.

Nevertheless, contrary to the other Book of the Dead spells, we can observe in those chapters Late Egyptian features that do not appear with the same quantity in each part of the texts. BD 166 is clearly the text that is most influenced by Late Egyptian. Its first attestation is very similar to another practice from the same period on small papyri found in the funerary context of the village of Deir el-Medina. Their purpose was to protect their owner against all possible misfortunes, such as serpent or scorpion bites (Edwards, 1960; Fischer-Elfert, 2015). The owner of the papyrus asked the deity through the mediation of a priest for an oracular utterance that would protect him. These papyri were then rolled and placed in a cylinder around his neck (Dielman, 2015). If we compare BD 166 with those texts, we can assume that it was conceived as a funerary counterpart to this magical practice because of their very similar appearance and also because of the content of the text: the gods who are addressed in the first part of the text are defined as "the ones who spread the oracle to the solar disc," while the universal god is invoked in the latter part to confirm that the *ushabtis* will work for the deceased in the underworld as they used to do on earth (Černý, 1942). Just as the topics of the spell and its appearance are very similar, we can observe that the language is also closely related to the style of the amuletic decrees, which show many Late Egyptian features. The incipit of BD 166 is clearly written in Late Egyptian, perhaps to reinforce the impression of authenticity. In this text, like in BD 162, many words belong to the lexicon of the second phase (Late Egyptian, Demotic, and Coptic). The period of attestation of BD 166 is short, and so is that of the practice of the amuletic decrees.

If the Late Egyptian features are particularly evident in BD 166, it is in the rubrics of the other spells that we find most of the younger constructions. They contain the practical information regarding the use of the spell as a magic formula to be inscribed on specific objects, such as images of a golden cow or a mummy bandage. From the New Kingdom onwards, the magical papyri were clearly written in the contemporarily spoken language. It is therefore no surprise to find the same practice in the technical part of the *chapitres supplémentaires*.

In its first attestation, the hymnic part of BD 162 clearly exhibits the use of a Late Egyptian vocabulary, which indicates a recent elaboration of the text, while its later variant was reworked using words that belong to the classical lexicon of the earlier period, probably in order to better adapt it to the holy nature of these kinds of texts. The scribes of the Late Recension of the Book of the Dead rewrote this part of the text in a pure "*égyptien de tradition*," expurgating it of its neologisms. BD 164 and 165 also contain a hymnic part at the beginning of the formula. This is clearly written in "*égyptien de tradition*." In the final section, the instructions regarding the construction of the amulet are composed in Late Egyptian to increase its performativity and efficiency. The last part of this section then contains the assurance about the efficiency of the use of the spell: if the text is correctly recited and the object properly made, then the deceased will survive and receive all the advantages he deserves in the afterlife.

## Foreign Words or Abracadabra?

Another particularity of these texts is the use of words written in syllabic script, which can suggest a foreign origin. The reference to Nubia in three of these texts suggests the Nubian origin of these lexemes (Vernus, 1984). Their identification and translation are still very problematic. Thanks to the signs that are used as determinatives for these lexemes, however, we can conclude that they are either toponyms and theonyms or epithets of gods. None of the attempts that have been undertaken to identify them are entirely convincing (Rilly, 2012; Zibelius-Chen, 2013). The main problem is that the exact language has not been identified. Since spells 163, 164, and 165 mention Nubia, we can assume that these words are from that region. They are probably written in what could be described as Proto-Meroitic language; "Proto" because the Meroitic language was the language of Kush from only the eighth century BCE to the fourth century CE. Georges Posener (1940) and Claude Rilly (2012) have demonstrated that there are already traces of the predecessor of this language in the lists of enemies or of toponyms from the Middle Kingdom. The absence of some vowels that are also missing in later Meroitic is a good clue to the identification of the language. But, as underlined by Rilly, these lexemes are lexical elements "genetically close" to the later Meroitic, and the exact nature of this language is still unknown.

The first attestation, which is certainly a transcription of the language of the Nubians, dates from the Hyksos period (sixteenth century BCE). It is a list of anthroponyms that has the purpose of precisely enumerating the allies or the enemies of the kingdom (Erman, 1911; Vernus, 1984). Thanks to it, we can establish a consonantal inventory of Proto-Meroitic. However, the main question remains: Why did the scribes include Nubian words in at least three spells of the Book of the Dead? The Egyptians' interest in Nubia was not new. The sources demonstrate that most of the kings tried, with greater or lesser success, to establish their hegemony in this region for commercial and strategic purposes. The examples quoted so far had the purpose of identifying the enemy or the dangerous entities that could mean trouble for Egypt. There is nothing similar in the *chapitres supplémentaires*. All these lexemes are connected with Amun or his family, or with toponyms. The recent research on the Meroitic lexicography has allowed us to establish a list of some hundred words that can be translated (Rilly, 2012). In her attempt to decipher the foreign lexemes of the *chapitres supplémentaires*, Zibelius-Chen (2013) has been able to recognize some "generic" words such as "princess" or "to engender." The collection of variants of these lexemes shows that their orthography is far from fixed. With great caution, we can hypothesize that these words are in fact an attempt to imitate the Nubian language with some use of real generic terms. The phenomenon is called *voces magicae* and is very popular in the late magical practice (Dielman, 2005). Knowing the power of the Nubian magic, the scribes tried to compose words that seemed Nubian.

# The Theban Theology in the *Chapitres Supplémentaires*

The inclusion of the Theban theology is probably the most remarkable aspect of these texts. The presence of Amun or Mut in the Book of the Dead is indeed very anecdotic, and this innovation is really an ideological revolution. The geographical and historical background in which the *chapitres supplémentaires* appear is therefore particularly illuminating. The growing influence of the priests of Amun-Re at the end of the New Kingdom made the establishment of a truly theocratic form of government possible (Vernus, 1995; Assmann, 1995; Jansen-Winkeln, 2001); theoretically, each decision was submitted for the approval of the Theban god. Therefore, we can observe an important modification in the perception of the deity. A symptom of this phenomenon could be the increase in sources that show a personal piety, in parallel with a decline of royal authority. From this time on, Amun-Re is perceived as the true king of both gods and men. He is presented as an autogenic and primordial god, superior to the other gods who are born from him, a god of fertility as well as a solar god, who can also be observed in the underworld, as a protector and savior, a lawyer and a judge, transcendent and immanent, and one and many. Jan Assmann (1983: 96–143) defines this theology as a New Solar Theology, which appears in most of the hymns of the second part of the Eighteenth Dynasty and later. The exact starting point of this theological "revolution" has not been definitively established yet (Stadler, 2009, 2010). However, it seems rather clear that the theologians of the post-Amarna Period had rethought some aspects of the solar theology. On the basis of sometimes even older concepts, they developed a new theological discourse that established Amun and his consort Mut as universal deities.

In the *chapitres supplémentaires*, Amun and Mut are characterized as funerary deities, competing with, if not replacing, the sovereign of the afterlife, Osiris. However, the role of Amun and of his companion differs from spell to spell, probably relating to the supposed date of composition, and this reflects the evolution of his theology. In BD 162, the god invoked is not named, but his royal and solar epithets clearly link him to Amun-Re, as mentioned in the so-called credo of the Third Intermediate Period (Meyer, 1928: 503). Those characteristics correspond to the sixteen epithets of the lion god of BD 162. Its first specificity is being a royal deity: "Hail to thou, the *rw*-lion, the powerful one, lofty of plumes, lord of the Upper Egyptian crown, equipped with the scourge." The autogenic and primordial aspect is evoked through the following epithet: "Thou art the lord of the phallus." The god is here defined as a reproductive entity on the one hand, a demiurge because he is the one with the instrument of creation, the phallus; and on the other hand as autogenic, this attribute allowing him to create himself. These two notions are to be found slightly more indirectly in the other element: "Thou art the loudly roaring one in the midst of the Ennead, the great courser, swift of step."

The loud roaring must be linked to the creative act, when the silence before creation is broken by the first scream. Those three epithets can be brought together with the warrior and violent aspects of the deity, as per his leonine nature. In a solar context, they also allude to the god's ability to move rapidly. This ability refers to the idea of proximity and distance, another main characteristic of this god.

At the end of the Ramesside Period, Amun-Re is also often evoked in the context of personal piety. In BD 162 the god is defined as: "( . . . ) Thou art the mighty god, the one who comes to whom has called him, who protects the needy from distress," which matches perfectly well with the idea of a judging god protecting the widow and the orphan.

Finally, and this is probably one of his main particularities, the lion god of BD 162 is omnipotent and hidden, transcendent and immanent, one and many. This can be found in a series of epithets: "Thou art the lord of forms, numerous of colors, who conceals himself in the sound eyes from his children." The first is the essence of Amun-Re himself: he is multiform. The two others symbolize the immanence (the bright side of the divine falcon) and the deity's transcendence (the god stays hidden from his children).

As such, "thou art constant as riser, shiner who has no limit." The god shines in the sky and he is untouchable. His power is infinite, as his sun rays are able to reach the limits of the earth. He is also as unchanging as the solar cycle that is renewed every morning.

In BD 162, his mother is the Ihet-cow. She is identified as the one "who gives birth to the solar god" in all periods of her attestation and is related to the function of demiurge (Wüthrich, 2016). Here, she names the god, but these theonyms are completely impervious to any attempt of translation, except for two trigrams showing the solar and timeless nature of the god. We can conclude that, at the beginning of the Third Intermediate Period, BD 162 was introduced into the Book of the Dead's corpus because it presents the universal form of the deity. Even unnamed, Amun has his habitual attributes in this spell, besides those normally reserved for Osiris as a god of the underworld as well as a fertility god.

The unnamed god of BD 166 is closely also related to Osiris: he is "the mourner" (or "the mourned one," if we follow the proposition of Dahms, Pehal, and Willems, 2014: 409) and "the universal master," victim of a violent death. But his attributes are also very close to those of the solar god of BD 162, a god capable of violence and able to rule over the deceased's fate. This god is invoked to act in conformity with what is usually asked of Osiris in the Book of the Dead. In the final section of BD 166, the deceased pleads that the *ushabti*, i.e., the statuettes who magically worked in his place as his servants (doing his farming, for instance, in the underworld) and were acquired by him on earth, act in his favor. Contrary to the traditional BD 6 inscribed on the *shabti*, which were the substitutes for the deceased or his entourage in the New Kingdom, and again on the *ushabti* from the Twenty-fifth Dynasty onwards, the *ushabti* here are not directly commanded to work in the place of the deceased, but it is the universal master who is asked to order them to act. This change again fits perfectly within the establishment of a theocracy in the Third Intermediate Period. When we compare BD 166 and the decree for Nesikhonsu on the McCullum and Rodgers palettes (Černý, 1942), it appears clear that the *ushabti* are forced to act only through the will of Amun-Re. Therefore, it is not because he has become a justified Osiris that the deceased benefits from the work of the *ushabti*, but rather because Amun-Re has decided so. We can speak here of Amun's "Osirianization" (Wüthrich, 2010: 37–41 and 159–61; Smith, 2017: sp. 498–502).

The development of the theology of the Theban family experienced another crucial phase with the Kushites. In the Book of the Dead, the evolution of Amun and Mut into universal entities with a funerary role is completed. Both Amun (BD 163 and 165) and Mut (BD 164) are clearly identified. They bear their usual attributes as solar and royal deities, as well as some funerary epithets. However, unlike in BD 162, the deceased does not ask here to be identified with the solar god to participate in the solar renaissance. The topics used in these three spells are similar to the usual wishes in the Book of the Dead: physical integrity and recovery of the physical functions, ability to move freely, good reputation, and ability to again be a part of society. All these elements are closely related to the usual content of this corpus, but they are simultaneously very innovative because of the use of the Theban pantheon as a reflection of the theology established by the Kushites.

BD 167 is clearly different from the other spells. It is more of a collection of four texts assembled at an unknown period. As mentioned in its title, these four texts are "writings of the bowl." The first three texts refer to the god Amun, first presented as a bull with the demiurge's and royal attributes, reminiscent of the deity of BD 163 and 165. This bull is then defined in the second part as terrifying and blazing, but also as transcendent. The same motif is used in the third part of the spell, but the god is here referred to with an unidentified theonym. In those three parts, we can find the same attributes and themes as those from BD 163, 164 and 165, and, like the other *chapitres supplémentaires*, it ends with a rubric that indicates the procedure to follow for the fabrication of the amulet.

The topic of the last part is completely different: the deceased is called upon out; then, a series of wishes follow that are very consistent with the usual themes of the Book of the Dead (offerings, freedom to exit and enter the underworld, physical integrity, to be justified, etc.) and the wish to be towed during the Sokar-Festival. This latter ritual is a clear association of the deceased with the rebirth of Osiris, and is followed by some allusions to diverse deities in connection with the funerary rituals.

# Conclusion

The appellation *chapitres supplémentaires* is both an ancient and a modern designation. The ancient Egyptian scribes reworked ancient formulas and also composed new spells during the first millennium BCE that, among other things, reflected the developments of the theological concepts of Amun's religion. Three of them (BD 163, 164, and 165) were defined as an "addition to the *Going forth by Day*"—the Book of the Dead. At the end of the Twenty-fifth Dynasty, those three chapters were integrated into the Book of Dead. From this period on they are always associated with BD 162, the spell that concludes this corpus since its first attestation in the Twenty-first Dynasty.

The modern designation of *chapitres supplémentaires* was adopted by W. Pleyte to describe thirteen spells appearing together on only one papyrus from the Ptolemaic Period (P.Paris Louvre N 3248). J. Yoyotte refined the definition by splitting the *chapitres* into two thematic groups: the first one (BD 162 to 167) regrouped the "Theban spells," while the second one can be considered the "Osirian spells." Because of their conceptual similarities (Theban theology, inclusion of foreign magical words, importance of a Nubian background) and stylistic (inclusion of Late Egyptian features), BD 166 and 167 were added to the "ancient" *chapitres supplémentaires*. These six spells are testimony to the Egyptians' creativity and their capacity to adapt and update an ancient corpus of texts, in order to be in keeping with the contemporaneous theological discourse. They are therefore a very important source for the comprehension of the funerary religion of the Late Period.

# Bibliography

Assmann, J. (1995). *Egyptian Solar Religion in the New Kingdom. Re, Amun and the Crisis of Polytheism* (London; New York: Kegan International).
Černý, J. (1942). "Le caractère des 'Oushebits' d'après les idées du Nouvel Empire." *Bulletin de l'Institut français d'archéologie orientale* 41: 105–33.
Dahms, J.-M. Pehal, M., and Willems, H. (2014). "Ramses II Helps the Dead: An Interpretation of Book of the Dead Supplementary Chapter 166." *Journal of Egyptian Archaeology* 100: 395–420.
Dieleman, J. (2005). *Priests, Tongues, and Rites: The London-Leyde magical Manuscripts and Translation in Egyptian Ritual (100–300 CE)*. Religions in the Graeco-Roman World 153 (Leyde-Boston: Brill).
Dieleman, J. (2015). "The Materiality of Textual Amulets in Ancient Egypt." In *The Materiality of Magic*. Morphomata 20, edited by D. Boschung and J. Bremmer, 23–58 (Paderborn: Fink).
Edwards, I. E. S. (1960). *Hieratic Papyri in the British Museum. Fourth Series: Oracular Amuletic Decrees of the Late New Kingdom Edited, Together with Supplementary Texts in Other Collections* (London: British Museum).
Erman, A. (1911). *Hymnen an das Diadem der Pharaonen* (Berlin: de Gruyter).
Fischer-Elfert, H.-W. (2015). *Magika Hieratika in Berlin, Hannover, Heidelberg und München*. Ägyptische und Orientalische Papyri und Handschriften des Ägyptischen Museums und Papyrussammlung Berlin 2 (Berlin: de Gruyter).
Guermeur, I. (2005). *Les cultes d'Amon hors de Thèbes, Recherches de géographie religieuse*. BEHE sc. hist. et philol. Bibliothèque de l'École des Hautes Études 123 (Turnhout: Brepols).
Jansen-Winkeln, K. (2001). "Der thebanische 'Gottesstaat." *Orientalia* 70: 153–82.
Lenzo-Marchese, G. (2004). "Les colophons dans la littérature égyptienne." *Bulletin de l'Institut français d'archéologie orientale* 104: 359–76.
Lepsius, R. (1842). *Das Todtenbuch der Ägypter nach dem Hieroglyphischen Papyrus in Turin* (Leipzig: Georg Wigand).
Meyer, E. (1928). "Gottesstaat, Militärherrschaft und Ständewesen in Ägypten: zur Geschichte der 21. und 22. Dynastie." *Sitzungsberichte der preussischen Akademie der Wissenschaften* XXVIII: 495–532.
Mosher, M. (2001). *The Papyrus of Hor: Catalogue of the Books of the Dead in the British Museum* II (London: British Museum Press).
Naville, E. (1886). *Das Aegyptische Todtenbuch der XVIII. bis XX. Dynastie aus verschiedenen Urkunden* (Berlin: A. Asher & Co).
Pleyte, W. (1881). *Les chapitres supplémentaires du Livre des Morts 162 à 174 publiés d'après les monuments de Leide, du Louvre et du Musée britannique* (Leiden: Brill).
Posener, G. (1940). *Princes et pays d'Asie. Textes hiératiques sur les figurines d'envoûtement du Moyen Empire* (Bruxelles: Fondation égyptologique Reine Élisabeth).

Rilly, C. (2012). *The Meroitic Language and Writing System: A Linguistic and Philological Introduction* (Cambridge: Cambridge University Press).

Smith, M. (2017). *Following Osiris. Perspectives on the Osirian Afterlife from Four Millennia* (London: Oxford University Press).

Stadler, M. A. (2009). "Spätägyptische Hymnen als Quellen für den interkulturellen Austausch und den Umgang mit dem eigenen Erbe. Drei Fallstudien." In *Orakel und Gebete. Interdisziplinäre Studien zur Sprache der Religion in Ägypten, Vorderasien und Griechenland in hellenistischer Zeit*, Forschungen zum Alten Testament 38, edited by M. Witte and J. F. Diehl, 141–63 (Tübingen: Mohr Siebeck).

Stadler, M. A. (2010). "Metatranszendenztheologie im Alten Ägypten. Pyramidentextspruch 215 und der ramessidische Weltgott." In *Kulte, Priester, Rituale. Beiträge zu Kult und Kultkritik im Alten Testament und Alten Orient. Festschrift für Theodor Seidl zum 65. Geburtstag*, Arbeiten zu Text und Sprache im Alten Testament 89, edited by S. Ernst and M. Häusl, 3–31 (St. Ottilien: EOS Verlag Erzabtei St. Ottilien).

Verhoeven, U. (1999). *Das Totenbuch des Monthpriesters Nepasefy aus der Zeit Psammetichs I.* Handschriften des Altägyptischen Totenbuches 5 (Wiesbaden: Harrassowitz).

Vernus, P. (1984). "Vestiges de langues chamito-sémitiques dans des sources égyptiennes méconnues." In *Current Progress in Afro-Asiatic Linguistics, Papers of the Third International Hamito-Semitic Congress*. Amsterdam Studies in the Theory and History of Linguistic Science, Series IV-current Issues in Linguistics Theory 28, edited by J. Bynon, 477–79 (Amsterdam; Philadelphia: John Benjamins Publishing Company).

Vernus, P. (1995). "La grande mutation idéologique du Nouvel Empire: Une nouvelle théorie du pouvoir politique. Du démiurge face à sa création." *Bulletin de la Société d'égyptologie de Genève* 19: 69–95.

Vernus, P. (1996). "Langue littéraire et diglossie." In *Ancient Egyptian Literature*, Problem der Ägyptologie 10, edited by A. Loprieno, 555–64 (Leiden; New York; Cologne: Brill).

Wüthrich, A. (2011). *Éléments de théologie thébaine: les chapitres supplémentaires du Livre des Morts*. Studien zum Altägyptischen Totenbuch 16 (Wiesbaden: Harrassowitz).

Wüthrich, A. (2015). *Édition synoptique et traduction des chapitres supplémentaires du Livre des Morts 162 à 167*. Studien zu Altägyptischen Totentexten 19 (Wiesbaden: Harrassowitz).

Wüthrich, A. (2016). "Ihet, celle qui engendre le dieu solaire." In *Aere Perennius. Mélanges égyptologiques en l'honneur de Pascal Vernus*. Orientalia Lovaniensia Analecta 242, edited by P. Collombert, D. Lefèvre, S. Pollis, and J. Winand, 895–913 (Leuven; Paris; Bristol: Peeters).

Yoyotte, J. (1977). "Contribution à l'étude du chapitre 162 du Livre des Morts." *Revue d'égyptologie* 29: 194–200.

Zibelius-Chen, K. (2013). *"Nubisches" Sprachmaterial in hieroglyphischen und hieratischen Texten Personennamen, Appellativa, Phrasen vom Neuen Reich bis in die napatanische und meroitische Zeit*. Meroitica 25 (Wiesbaden: Harrassowitz).

CHAPTER 23

# ILLUSTRATIONS IN SAITE THROUGH PTOLEMAIC BOOKS OF THE DEAD

MALCOLM MOSHER

The development of the Book of the Dead out of the earlier Pyramid and Coffin Texts is a complex topic (Gestermann, this volume; see also Dorman, 2017: 29–40), and these texts were not accompanied by illustrations, although the Book of Two Ways (Backes, 2005; Sherbiny, 2017), a subset of the Coffin Texts, was accompanied by a painted roadmap with depictions of various beings who inhabit those regions of the underworld. Painted scenes on coffin panels depicting the deceased as the recipient of funerary offerings on Middle Kingdom coffins are not unknown. For example, on the coffin of Djehutynakht at the Museum of Fine Arts, Boston, the scene served a decorative purpose, but its primary purpose was magical—to ensure that the deceased did indeed enjoy an unlimited supply of offerings for his life after death.

Early Books of the Dead were written on linen shrouds that occasionally included illustrations (Gasse, this volume). With most shrouds from the Seventeenth and early Eighteenth Dynasties surviving only in fragments, one cannot be certain about how many illustrations they might have originally carried. In Cairo J.E. 96810, an early Eighteenth-Dynasty shroud, the texts for a broad range of spells survive, but it appears that only the illustrations for BD 136 and 149 were included (for references to this document and all subsequent documents, see the table at the end of this chapter). Similarly, a portion of New York MMA 22.3.296, a shroud from the early Eighteenth Dynasty, survives intact with the texts of BD 124, 83 to 85, 82, 77, 86, and 99, but without any illustrations. As the Eighteenth Dynasty progressed, however, the use of illustrations in Books of the Dead on both shrouds and papyri increased dramatically. For example, the text of almost every spell on the shroud of Paris Louvre N 3097, attributed to the reign of Amenhotep II, is accompanied by a painted illustration. On papyrus, while the texts of only 18 out of 134 spells were accompanied by illustrations in P.London BM EA 10477, likely from the reign of Thutmose III, surviving portions of the unpublished papyrus for a man named Amenhotep (P.London BM 10489 etc.) from the end of the same reign indicate that most spells were accompanied by illustrations. In P.Cairo CG 51189 from the reign of Amenhotep III, nearly every spell was accompanied by an illustration, and this practice continued through the Twentieth Dynasty and in many documents from the Twenty-first Dynasty (see Milde, 1991, for his study on the illustrations in P.Neferrenpet from the Nineteenth Dynasty, and Niwiński, 1989, for Twenty-first-Dynasty examples). While Books of the Dead on papyri and linen wrappings have been attributed to the interval between the end of the Twenty-first Dynasty and the latter part of the Twenty-fifth Dynasty, they tend to be very short in length and contain only a small number of spells, few of which were accompanied by illustrations. The focus of this chapter is on illustrations found in Saite through Ptolemaic documents. With the rise of the Twenty-sixth Dynasty the Book of the Dead underwent a thorough process of revision that resulted in a mostly standardized set of 165 spells arranged in a standardized sequence by which these spells are numbered today, a revision that has been labeled the *Saite Recension*, but it is possible that the process might have begun during the late Twenty-fifth Dynasty (see Gülden, Albert, this volume). The texts were standardized, albeit with variations, and most spells were accompanied by standardized illustrations. This is not to say that every document going forward included all 165 spells. The style or layout of a papyrus, coupled with its length and height, often dictated how many spells could be included; the smaller the document, the more spells had to be excluded. Similarly, in some Saite documents many spells were unaccompanied by illustrations.

# Components of a Spell and Function of the Illustration

A spell from the Saite Period onward consisted of three components: 1) the title that expressed the purpose of the spell, 2) the text or body of the spell that typically mentioned aspects expressed in the title, often coupled with references to mythological events and ritual activities, and 3) an illustration that was typically a graphic depiction of aspects expressed in the title or a depiction of something else expressed in the body of the spell. To obtain maximum efficacy, all three components for each spell were added to a document, but the illustration had significant magical power of its own, and thus it could represent a spell by itself or even a class of spells. This is particularly evident in documents of short length, where the texts of only a few spells could be included, but the magic of many more spells was delivered by the illustrations. For example, Ptolemaic P.Paris Louvre N 3100 contains only the texts of BD 18 and BD 21 to 27, but the spells for BD 17, 110, 28, 30, 31, 33, 36, 40, 77, 83, 86, 81, 87, 125, 155 to 160, 163–164, and 162 were represented by their illustrations, where each illustration delivered the purpose of the corresponding spell. Where BD 33 to 35, 37, and 39 comprised a class of spells for driving off serpents

FIG. 23.1. Version 1, BD 33, P.Paris Louvre N 3100, representing the entire class of related spells for driving away serpents. © Musée du Louvre, Paris.

FIG. 23.2. Illustrations representing BD 54, first of the class of spells for breathing air and BD 57, first of the class of spells for having water in P.Paris Louvre E 3233. © Musée du Louvre, Paris.

that might attack the deceased in the afterlife, the illustration representing BD 33 could also represent this entire class (Fig. 23.1).

Similarly, BD 54 to 56 represent a critical class of spells for breathing fresh air, and BD 57 to 62 represent a class of spells for having both fresh air to breathe and cool water to drink. In the Ptolemaic P.Paris Louvre E 3233, both classes are represented by two illustrations that deliver the magic of those classes (Fig. 23.2).

Depictions of the deceased in illustrations portray him or her in ideal condition—a young man or woman in the prime of life—because it is in this stage of life that the deceased sought to spend his or her afterlife. Two documents written for women, P.Paris Louvre N 3248 and P.Paris Louvre N 3272, raise a curious circumstance (cf. Töpfer, this volume). In each document, each artist correctly depicted the deceased as a woman throughout (Fig. 23.3), but for the class of spells for driving off dangerous creatures (BD 31–37), a man, not the female figure of the deceased, was depicted spearing the crocodiles and snakes (Fig. 23.4). The title of BD 38 specifies that the spell serves two purposes ("Spell for living on air in the necropolis; It is said in order to drive off two *mrty*-snakes"), the illustration was based on the first part of that title, and the female figure of the deceased is again depicted, here holding up an air-sign (Fig. 23.5), but for the illustrations of BD 39–41 that continue the class for driving off dangerous creatures, a man, not the figure of the deceased, was once again depicted driving off the serpents (Fig. 23.6). This depiction of the man performing the combat was clearly not the result

**FIG. 23.3.** Illustration for BD 30 correctly showing deceased as a woman in P.Paris Louvre N 3248. Paris. © Musée du Louvre, Paris.

**FIG. 23.4.** Illustration for BD 33 depicting a man acting as a surrogate for the deceased in P.Paris Louvre N 3248. © Musée du Louvre, Paris.

**FIG. 23.5.** Illustration for BD 38 correctly showing deceased as a woman in P.Paris Louvre N 3248. © Musée du Louvre, Paris.

**FIG. 23.6.** Illustration for BD 41 depicting a man acting as a surrogate for the deceased in P.Paris Louvre N 3248. © Musée du Louvre, Paris.

of an identical error by the two artists. Rather, it would appear that these two artists thought this dangerous activity was not suitable for a woman, and thus each drew a male to act as a surrogate in performing the combat on behalf of the deceased.

## STYLES AND PAIRING OF ILLUSTRATIONS WITH THEIR TEXTS

New Kingdom illustrations were very often painted with great artistic skill and the use of brilliant colors, examples of which are evident elsewhere in this volume. With Saite documents, several styles of artwork were employed for the illustrations. In some, color was used, and the deceased and gods were depicted with full limbs (Figs. 23.7 and 23.8; see Munro, 2011, for color reproductions in the papyrus for a Tasheretenaset). In others, simple black line drawings were used, though with the occasional use of the color red to depict objects like a sun-disk (e.g., Gasse, 2002: Plate II) or bloody knives, to cite just two examples. The illustrations on P.Paris Louvre N 5450, a Ptolemaic Memphite Book of the Dead based on Saite Books of the Dead, consist entirely of black line drawings (Fig. 23.9), and the Saite document, written for a priest named Djedkhy (P.Budapest etc.), consists of black line drawings for most of the document, but the surviving parts of the illustrations for BD 125 and 145 were painted in color with full limbs.

FIG. 23.7. Illustration for BD 147, with painted scenes and figures with full limbs in P.Paris Louvre N 3091. © Musée du Louvre, Paris.

FIG. 23.8. Illustration for BD 149, with black line drawings and figures with full limbs in P.Paris Louvre N 3091. © Musée du Louvre, Paris.

FIG. 23.9. Illustration for BD 18.1, with black line drawings and figures with full limbs in P.Paris Louvre N 5450. © Musée du Louvre, Paris.

With the Persian victory over the last king of the Twenty-sixth Dynasty, the Book of the Dead appears to have fallen out of use until it was again revived during the Theban Thirtieth Dynasty, and it remained in continuous use down through the Late Ptolemaic Period.

With this revival, one encounters multiple versions of texts as well as illustrations. In the northern center of Memphis, the Saite versions of the texts continued to be used, and the same appears to be true for the illustrations, although one must admit that that not many examples of Saite illustrations have survived. In the south, however, the Saite tradition of texts, illustrations, and sequence served only as the starting point for eleven distinct Theban traditions, beginning with three different pre-Ptolemaic workshops in the Theban area (Mosher, 2016a: 10–37). In the workshop responsible for documents like P.London BM EA 10097 (Mosher, 2016a: 11–12), the Saite tradition continued to be used, but it also appears to have died out by the Ptolemaic Period. The master scribes of the main pre-Ptolemaic workshop, however, significantly revised the texts of most spells as well as many of the illustrations (Mosher, 2016a: 12–15). More significantly, they revised the layout of the documents to what has been labeled Style 1 (Fig. 14; Mosher, 1992). The use of color in the illustrations was dropped in favor of simple black line drawings, again with the occasional use of red, and the rendering of full limbs was often dropped in favor of stick-like limbs for men and gods, a practice that undoubtedly facilitated faster production.

In Saite as well as in Ptolemaic Memphite documents, the layout was formally framed with top and bottom bordering lines, with individual columns delineated from each other by bordering lines, and with space allocated for illustrations also framed, labeled Style 2 (Fig. 23.10; Mosher, 1992). This arrangement put the illustration in primary position, where the title of the spell was given either above the illustration (Fig. 23.11) or below it (Fig. 23.12). Often a single spell was placed in a column, and if the space allocated for the illustration was too wide and the text was short, then usable space below the text of the spell in that column was often left blank, thereby resulting in wasted space. Depending on the length of the papyrus, wasted space like this could result in more spells having to be omitted.

A different style not noted in Mosher (1992) can be found in a different subset of Saite documents, where the same general framing was employed, but the texts were arranged continuously from one spell to the next in broad columns. Where space at

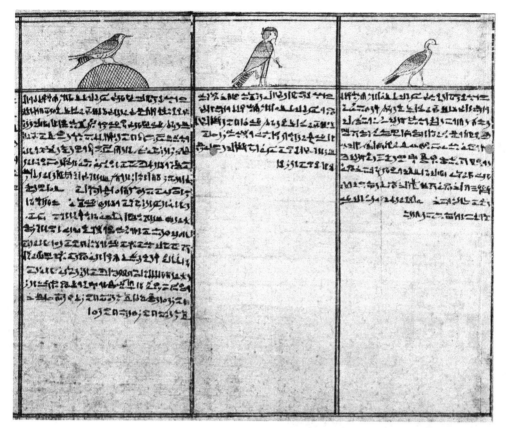

FIG. 23.10. Style 2 with formal framing for the illustrations and the texts for BD 84, 85, and 86, one spell per column in illustrations, in P.Paris Louvre N 3081. © Musée du Louvre, Paris.

the bottom of the column was used up, the remaining text of the spell was continued at the top of the next in the next column, and the illustrations also ran continuously in broadly allocated space at the top of the columns of text, resulting in the illustrations often being only loosely connected to the texts they graphically represented (Fig. 23.13). An example of this style is P.Colon. Aeg 10207, and it is also found in the document for Nespasefy (P.Cairo J.E. 95714), although, curiously, the illustrations were never added in this document except for two scenes from BD 1. This style was also carried forward to a small set of Theban pre-Ptolemaic (e.g., P.London BM EA 10097) and Ptolemaic documents (e.g., P.Turin 1831), and this layout would be best labeled as Style 2A. In P.London BM EA 10097, the lack of a direct connection between the illustrations above and the texts below often led to significant confusion regarding the relationship between specific illustrations and the texts. For example, a string of illustrations that arguably represent BD 21, 92, 24, 105(?), 48(?), 44(?), 28, 30, 28, and 26, an unidentifiable scene of a tomb and a second version of the illustration for BD 28 appear above the texts of BD 22 to 28 and BD 30 (Fig. 23.13).

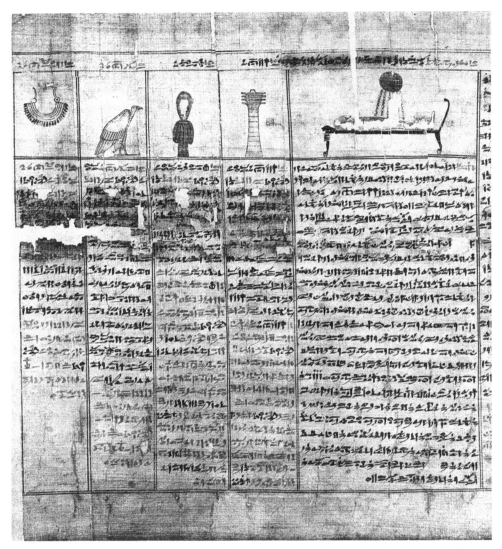

FIG. 23.11. Style 2 with the title of the spell placed above the illustration, body of the spell below in P.Paris Louvre N 3091 for BD 154, 155, 156, 157, and 158. © Musée du Louvre, Paris.

Another curiosity observed in a small set of Saite documents is that, regardless of whether Style 2 or 2A was used, space was allocated for illustrations, but many or most allocated spaces for illustrations were left empty. With the exception of the first scenes of the long illustration for BD 1, all allocated space was left empty in the papyrus for the priest Nespasefy (P.Cairo JE 95714 etc.). Much of the papyrus for the priest Khamhor (P. New York MMA 25.3.212 etc.) is now lost, but most of the allocated space for illustrations in the surviving parts was left empty, although parts of the illustrations for BD 17 and 18 survive. One might be inclined to think that the illustrations were normally entered last and that these two documents were never finished, but P.Colon. Aeg 10207

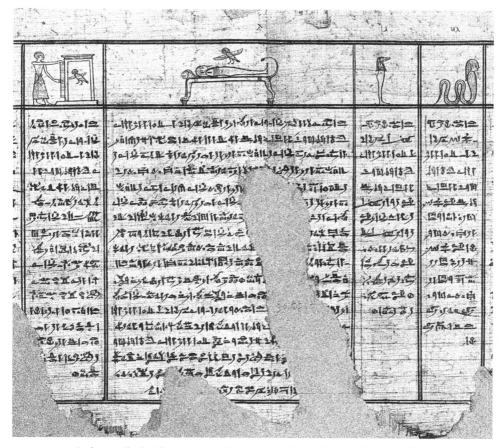

**FIG. 23.12.** Style 2 with the illustration at the top, the title and body of the spell below in P.Paris Louvre N 5450 for BD 87, 88, 89, and 91, with the illustration for BD 92 mistakenly placed above the title and text of BD 91. © Musée du Louvre, Paris.

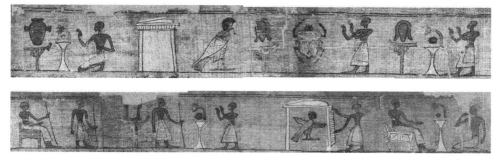

**FIG. 23.13.** Confused string of illustrations with only partial connection to the texts below in P.London BM EA 10097. Courtesy of the Trustees of the British Museum, London.

was completed, and yet the allocated spaces for illustrations above columns 14–19, where the texts of BD 19–30 are located, were left empty, as is column 22, which contained the texts of BD 38 and 39. None of the illustrations for these spells was added. For three Saite documents to have similar situations, one of which was unquestionably completed, some other explanation may account for why the expected illustrations were not entered, although what that explanation might be is uncertain. While the use of illustrations in most Saite documents is well attested, no illustrations were added to the papyrus for the priest Ankhefenkhonsu (P.Cairo CG 40024 etc.), nor was space even allocated for any.

Style 1 (Mosher, 1992), championed by the main pre-Ptolemaic workshop cited above, eliminated the formal bordering, the texts were presented continuously in columns of varying widths, and the illustrations, black-line-drawings, were typically placed directly beside the titles of the spells wherever they happened to occur within a given column (Fig. 23.14; Mosher, 2016a: 12–15). Thus, once again the illustration was directly connected to the title of the spell it represented (Fig. 23.14). This layout became the primary style used by subsequent traditions in Ptolemaic Thebes. One benefit of this style was that it made use of all available space, and it is therefore no surprise that many of these documents contained nearly all 165 spells, although most documents excluded BD 58 and BD 139, and the documents that included those two spells excluded others.

Hybrid variations on this style are known, with one subset consisting of P.Ryerson, P.Turin 1833, and P.Berlin P. 3058 A-I, wherein colored illustrations were arranged at the top like in Saite documents with Style 2, and the texts were arranged similar to Style 2 but without the formal borders (Figs. 23.15–23.17). Only in P.Berlin P. 3058 A-I and P.Ryerson were a few spells with their illustrations presented below spells presented at the top of a column.

Style 3 (Mosher, 1992) used the hieroglyphic script that dictated an entirely different arrangement, but the illustrations were still placed prominently by the title in most cases (Fig. 23.18). This style was used in the third subset of pre-Ptolemaic documents (Mosher, 2016a: 15–16), appears to have fallen out of use by the early Ptolemaic Period, but was revived at least by the second half of the third century BCE. It is in some of the latter documents that many spells were represented only by illustrations (e.g., P.Paris Louvre E 3233 in Mosher, 2016a: 33).

## ORIENTATION OF THE ILLUSTRATIONS

The orientation of figures in the illustrations was an aspect of considerable importance. The primary aim of the Book of the Dead was to enable the deceased to "go forth" from the tomb in order to travel about to a variety of destinations. This notion of *going forth*, an Egyptian expression for attaining life after death, was also graphically depicted. With few exceptions, Saite through Ptolemaic documents were read from right to left, with faces in the hieratic or hieroglyphic script oriented to the right; thus, in reading from right to left one reads into the faces of the characters. Similarly, with few exceptions, the

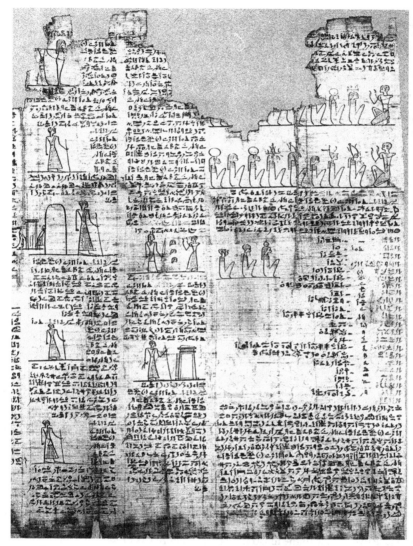

FIG. 23.14. Style 1 in the Theban Ptolemaic P.Paris Louvre N 3089—simple black line drawings and figures with stick-like limbs. © Musée du Louvre, Paris.

figures of deities in the illustrations also faced rightward, and this rightward orientation represented these beings as divine, the state to which the deceased aspired upon revivification. When the deceased was depicted in an illustration in the presence of a deity, that deity was virtually always oriented to the right, occupying the position of status and precedence, and the deceased was oriented to the left, thus facing the deity. When the deceased was depicted in the presence of other mortals, however, his orientation was the same as that of the gods, rightward, which graphically and magically depicted him as already having *gone forth* and thereby having obtained eternal life with the gods. Similarly,

FIG. 23.15. P.Ryerson, with the illustration and text of BD 88 presented below the text of BD 87. Courtesy of the Oriental Institute of the University of Chicago.

in a variety of illustrations, the deceased appears by himself for the same reason. In a small subset of the latter, however, the deceased is depicted with leftward orientation, a graphic depiction for the notion of *entering*, a critical notion that expresses the ability of the deceased to re-enter his tomb when he so chooses. For example, the title of BD 1 reads: Beginning of the spells for going forth by day, raising up the blessed ones in the necropolis, and what is spoken on the day of burial, of entering after going forth. Similarly, the title of BD 12 is" Spell for entering and going forth."

Another interesting example involving orientation can be observed in scenes of conflict against dangerous adversaries, as depicted in Figure 23.4. Here, the orientation

ILLUSTRATIONS IN SAITE THROUGH PTOLEMAIC BOOKS OF THE DEAD 457

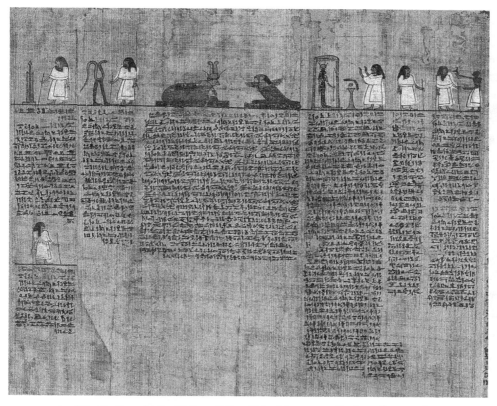

FIG. 23.16. P.Berlin P 3058. Credit line: © Staatliche Museen zu Berlin – Ägyptisches Museum und Papyrussammlung, photo: A. Paasch.

depicts the actual moment of confrontation, with the adversary from the underworld given the position of precedence as a creature to be defeated. The reverse of this, with the deceased given the position of precedence, depicts the moment of triumph or its aftermath (Fig. 23.19).

## Versions of Illustrations

While Books of the Dead in Ptolemaic Memphis nearly always used the same versions of texts and illustrations as those used during the Saite Period, in pre-Ptolemaic and Ptolemaic Thebes eleven different traditions for the Book of the Dead can be observed, most very likely the products of different workshops, where three were pre-Ptolemaic, at least four or five Ptolemaic traditions were in concurrent use around the start of the Ptolemaic Period, and the others evolved later. The master scribes responsible for the main pre-Ptolemaic workshop also worked with the artists to revise many of the

FIG. 23.17. P. Turin 1833. Credit line: Museo Egizio, Turin.

illustrations, and these were used by most subsequent Theban Ptolemaic traditions (Mosher, 2016a, 2016b, 2016c, 2017a, 2018a, 2018b). Thus, for most individual spells at least two versions of illustrations can be observed, where Saite and Ptolemaic Memphite illustrations often differed from Theban pre-Ptolemaic and Ptolemaic versions. A very intriguing situation involves the P.London BM EA 10086 and N3152 Traditions (Mosher, 2009: 124–72; 2016a: 19–21 and 21–22), plus two documents from the N3079 Tradition (Mosher, 2016a: 22–25). For many spells these documents used an entirely different set of illustrations. While the P.London BM EA 10086, N3152, and N3079 Traditions had their own versions of texts for many spells, the P.London BM EA 10086 and N3152 Traditions often shared the same versions of illustrations. Regarding documents P.Paris Louvre N 3079 and P.Paris Louvre N 3144 from the N3079 Tradition, evidence suggests that these two documents were produced later than the others of that tradition, and this indicates that the workshop associated with the N3079 Tradition shifted to a different collection of illustrations toward the end of that tradition's life cycle (Mosher, 2016a: 22–25). Examples of different versions of illustrations in Saite through Ptolemaic documents follow.

FIG. 23.18. Style 3 in P.London BM EA 10017, Courtesy of the Trustees of the British Museum, London.

FIG. 23.19. Moment of triumph depicted in the illustration for BD 31 in P.Paris Louvre N 3144. © Musée du Louvre, Paris.

## VERSIONS OF THE ILLUSTRATION FOR BD 21

The title of BD 21 is "Spell for giving the mouth of a man to him in the necropolis," which refers to the opening of the mouth ritual. In most documents from all traditions, the illustration depicts the deceased, in rightward orientation, sitting on a chair, with a priest, in leftward orientation, holding up an adze in his right hand and offering a cup in his left (Fig. 23.20, and see Mosher, 2016b: 188–90; 193). As stated earlier, the rightward orientation of the deceased magically asserts that he has *gone forth*, and he occupies the position of precedence over the priest who holds the adze associated with the opening of the mouth ritual to revivify the deceased.

Version 2 of this illustration is found in a small and seemingly random subset of Theban Ptolemaic documents (Fig. 23.21; Mosher, 2016b: 191 and 194), where the enthroned figure of Osiris appears on the left, appropriately occupying the position of precedence because he represents the ultimate example of one who died, who was revivified, and who then went forth to rule the West, the realm of the underworld. The identity of the figure on the right is uncertain; he may represent the priest in Version 1, or he could represent the deceased. The purpose of the scene in Version 2 appears to seek the support of Osiris in authorizing the successful completion of the opening of the mouth ritual for the deceased.

## VERSIONS OF THE ILLUSTRATION FOR BD 38

The title of BD 38 was given earlier in this chapter, along with an example of Version 1 of the illustration for this spell (Fig. 23.5 and Fig. 23.22; Mosher, 2016c: 151–52). This version is found in most documents, with a notable exception. The primary elements of Version 1 consist of the deceased holding an *ankh*-sign and an air-sign; the air-sign according with the first part of the title, "Spell for living on air in the necropolis,: while the *ankh*-sign accords with the passage in the text found in all versions where the deceased refers to himself as a

FIG. 23.20. Version 1 of the illustration for BD 21 in P.Paris Louvre N 3079. © Musée du Louvre, Paris.

FIG. 23.21. Version 2 of the illustration for BD 21 in P.Paris Louvre N 3249. © Musée du Louvre, Paris.

living one—*I eat as a living one* (Fig. 23.5; Mosher, 2016c: 151–52 and 154). In Version 2, found in documents from the P.London BM EA 10086 and N3152 Traditions, plus P.Paris Louvre N 3079 and P.Paris Louvre N 3144, the deceased holds up only an air-sign before Osiris, who occupies the position of precedence (Fig. 23.23; Mosher, 2016c: 153–54), although in P.Paris Louvre N 3082 (P.London BM EA 10086 Tradition) and P.Paris Louvre E 3232 (N3152 Tradition) the deceased also holds an *ankh*-sign (Fig. 23.24). Osiris is not mentioned in the text of the spell, but his presence is nevertheless felt because he is the ultimate example of a *living one*, and depicting the deceased holding up the air-sign before Osiris magically asserts that the deceased has obtained approval from Osiris to breathe air and become a *living one*.

## VERSIONS OF THE ILLUSTRATION FOR BD 39

While five versions of the text for BD 39 can be observed, only two versions of the illustration were used (Mosher, 2016c: 155–96). In Version 1 of the illustration, found in Saite, pre-Ptolemaic, and Ptolemaic documents from the Memphite and Theban areas, the deceased is depicted with leftward orientation in the moment of driving off an enormous serpent representing Apophis (Fig. 23.25; Mosher, 2016c: 191–93), the latter being the

**FIG. 23.22.** Version 1 of the illustration for BD 38 in P.Paris Louvre N 3249. Note the *ankh*-sign added later as a correction. © Musée du Louvre, Paris.

**FIG. 23.23.** Version 2 of the illustration for BD 38 in P.Paris Louvre E 7716. © Musée du Louvre, Paris.

**FIG. 23.24.** Version 2 of the illustration for BD 38 in P.Paris Louvre N 3082. © Musée du Louvre, Paris.

**FIG. 23.25.** Version 1 of the illustration for BD 39 in P.Paris Louvre N 3089. © Musée du Louvre, Paris.

FIG. 23.26. Version 2 of the illustration for BD 39 in P.London BM EA 10086. Courtesy of the Trustees of the British Museum, London.

principal adversary cited in the text. A particularly interesting scene can be observed in P.Leiden T 16 (Leemans, 1867: Plate XXVII; Mosher, 2017b: 192), where the artist appears to have been confused about the proper illustration for Version 1; he drew the snake of Version 1, and then above this figure he added a second snake whose head has not been turned back. A legend before the latter reads *ky ḏd* for *variant*. While formal variants introduced by *ky ḏd* are common in the texts of Saite through Ptolemaic Books of the Dead, the scene for BD 39 represents the very rare instance of *ky ḏd* being applied to an illustration. In Version 2, found in documents from the P.London BM EA 10086 and N3152 Traditions as well as in P.Paris Louvre N 3079 and P.Paris Louvre N 3144, the deceased is depicted with rightward orientation, spearing four serpents advancing against him. This scene is not directly based on a specific passage in the text but rather was indirectly based on the passage where the gods of the four cardinal points are mentioned (Fig. 23.26; for the text, see Mosher, 2016c: 165 §3). Accordingly, the scene depicts four serpents advancing against the deceased, each representing a different cardinal point.

## Versions of the Illustration for BD 43

Three versions of the illustration for BD 43 are known. In Version 1 the deceased stands in adoration before an unmarked anthropomorphic deity wearing a short kilt and holding a *was*-scepter symbolizing his power (Fig. 23.27; Mosher, 2016c: 317 and 320–21). The text of the spell begins with an invocation spoken by the deceased to the *Lord of the revered ones*, followed by *I am the great one, son of the Great One*. Accordingly, the deity in the illustration represents either the *lord* or the *Great One*. In Version 2 the deceased stands in adoration before three deities, each wearing a short kilt and holding a *was*-scepter (Fig. 23.28; Mosher, 2016c: 318 and 321). These deities clearly represent the *revered ones*, the only plural reference in the text. In a small subset of Theban Ptolemaic documents, the deceased is depicted a second time, seated on a chair behind the *revered ones* with the orientation of one having successfully *gone forth*, which accords with the passage *I am joined together, I am truthful, I am renewed, and I am youthful* (Fig. 23.29). Version 3 of the illustration is closely tied to the title of the spell: "Spell for not allowing the head of a man to be cut off in the necropolis" (Fig. 23.30; Mosher, 2016c: 319

**FIG. 23.27.** Version 1 of the illustration for BD 43 in P.London BM EA 10086. Courtesy of the Trustees of the British Museum, London.

**FIG. 23.28.** Version 2 of the illustration for BD 43 in P.Paris Louvre N 3151. © Musée du Louvre, Paris.

**FIG. 23.29.** Version 2 of the illustration for BD 43 in P.Paris Louvre N 3090. © Musée du Louvre, Paris.

**FIG. 23.30.** Version 3 of the illustration for BD 43 in P.Paris Louvre N 3143. © Musée du Louvre, Paris.

and 321). Here the deceased stands before a god who holds a knife, with three severed heads depicted between the deceased and this god, the latter doubtless responsible for beheading those unprotected by the magic of BD 43. Interestingly, the severed heads face the deceased, perhaps as a reminder that the fate of the unprotected could befall him without the aid of this spell.

## Illustrations for BD 57

The title of BD 57 in most documents is "Spell for breathing air and having power over water in the necropolis," and the purpose of the spell was to ensure that the deceased had fresh air to breathe and cool water to drink. In most Saite and Ptolemaic Memphite documents the scene magically depicts the deceased as one who has *gone forth*, typically holding an air-sign and receiving cool water from a goddess standing within a sycamore tree who occasionally offers a tray of bread (Fig. 23.31; Mosher 2017a: 164–65 and 170). A similar illustration is found in most pre-Ptolemaic and Ptolemaic Theban documents, but here the sycamore tree, as a divine entity that dispenses the cool water, occupies the position of precedence on the left, and the deceased stands on the right to receive the water (Fig. 23.32). Interestingly, documents from some Theban traditions included a goddess in the tree, while the other Theban traditions excluded her (Fig. 23.33). In Version 3, found in a different subset of documents from various Theban traditions, the illustration is focused entirely on the opening portion of the title and depicts the

FIG. 23.31. Version 1 of the illustration for BD 57 in P.Paris Louvre N 3081. © Musée du Louvre, Paris.

FIG. 23.32. Version 2 of the illustration for BD 57 in P.Paris Louvre N 3089. © Musée du Louvre, Paris.

FIG. 23.33. Version 2 of the illustration for BD 57 in P.Paris Louvre N 3079. © Musée du Louvre, Paris.

FIG. 23.34. Version 3 of the illustration for BD 57 in P.London BM EA 10311. Courtesy of the Trustees of the British Museum, London.

FIG. 23.35. Version 4 of the illustration for BD 57 in P.Paris Louvre N 3082. © Musée du Louvre, Paris.

deceased as having *gone forth* and holding up an air-sign that magically asserts he has fresh air to breathe (Fig. 23.34; Mosher 2017a: 168 and 171–72). Version 4 is found in a subset of documents from the P.London BM EA 10086 and N3152 Traditions, as well as in P.Paris Louvre N 3144, where the deceased, holding an air-sign, appears before Osiris, who occupies the position of precedence, a scene that asserts the same notion as Version 3 but in a different manner (Fig. 23.35; Mosher 2017a: 169 and 172).

FIG. 23.36. Version 1 of the illustration for BD 93 in P.Paris Louvre N 5450. © Musée du Louvre, Paris.

FIG. 23.37. Version 4 of the illustration for BD 93 in P.Paris Louvre N 3129. © Musée du Louvre, Paris.

## Illustrations for BD 93

The title of BD 93 is "Spell for not allowing that a man be ferried to the East in the necropolis." In Version 1, found in Saite and Ptolemaic Memphite documents, the deceased stands on the left as one who has *gone forth* and whose outstretched arm is an apotropaic gesture to send the ferryman back to the East, represented by the sign of the East (Fig. 23.36; Mosher, 2018b: 34–35 and 39). In Version 2, found in pre-Ptolemaic and Ptolemaic Theban documents, the ferryman as a divine entity occupies the position of precedence, and here the deceased bids the backward-looking ferryman to head to the East without him (Fig. 23.37; Mosher, 2018b: 36–38 and 39–40).

## Illustrations for BD 109

As a final example, the title of BD 109 is generally "Spell for knowing the *ba*-souls of the East," but the illustration is based on the last statement in section §3 of the text (Mosher, 2018b: 326), where the eastern *ba*-souls are identified as *Horus of the Horizon, the calf before this god,* and *the morning star.* In Version 1, found in Saite and Ptolemaic Memphite documents, the deceased stands on the right with arms raised in adoration before the figures of Re-Horakhty, a calf, and the morning star (Fig. 23.38; Mosher, 2018b: 346 and 351),

**FIG. 23.38.** Version 1 of the illustration for BD 109 in P.London BM EA 10558. Courtesy of the Trustees of the British Museum, London.

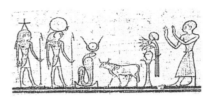

**FIG. 23.39.** Version 1 of the illustration for BD 109 in P.Paris Louvre N 5450. © Musée du Louvre, Paris.

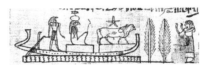

**FIG. 23.40.** Version 4 of the illustration for BD 109 in P.Paris Louvre N 3248. © Musée du Louvre, Paris.

with two Ptolemaic Memphite documents (P.Cairo CG 40029 etc. and P.Paris Louvre N 5450; Mosher, 2016a: 8–9) that came from similar source embellishing the scene further with the addition of a serpent on a mountain sign wearing horns and a sun-disk who clearly represents an unmentioned ally of the sun-god Re (Fig. 23.39). Version 2, found in documents from pre-Ptolemaic and Ptolemaic Theban traditions, is similar but consists of additional elements based on other parts of the text. Here the deceased stands in adoration, in leftward orientation, before two sycamore trees (from §2 of the text: *I know this sycamore of turquoise, in the midst of which Re goes forth*), followed by a pool of water upon which the sun-boat floats, bearing a calf with a star above it, followed by the seated figure of Re-Horakhty, who wears a sail-sign on his head, with some documents also including an additional figure at the rudder (Fig. 23.40; Mosher, 2018b: 347–49 and 351). Regarding the boat and sail, both are directly and indirectly mentioned in the text of §1: " . . . *in the place where Re sails by means of the roaring wind. I am the keeper of reporting in the divine boat.*"

The examples given above represent just a small sampling of different versions of illustrations, and different versions can be observed for most spells used in Saite through Ptolemaic Books of the Dead.

## Multi-scene Illustrations

While most spells are accompanied by a single illustration, a subset of spells were accompanied by illustrations consisting of multiple scenes. For example, BD 1 is accompanied by a sequence of scenes that collectively depict the funerary procession and rites performed at the tomb (Mosher, 2016a: I, 158–88). Similarly, the illustration for BD 17 is the longest and most complex in the collection illustrations, consisting of nearly 40 different scenes to accompany various passages in the text. Spells for BD 144 to 147 and BD 149 are gnostic in nature, providing the names of various gatekeepers, heralds, and others, as well as providing the names of locations the deceased must know in order to pass by on his journey through the underworld (Stadler, 2009: 254–319, 405–13). Each gate or section is accompanied by its own scene (Figs. 23.7 and 23.8).

## Spells without Illustrations

Of the 165 known spells in the normal collection used in Saite through Ptolemaic documents, nearly all were accompanied by a standardized illustration, but a small subset of spells were not given illustrations. The long illustration of BD 1 was normally placed above the texts of BD 1 to 14, and it was followed by one to three scenes associated with the different hymns collectively known as BD 15, followed in turn by a four-register illustration identified by Lepsius as BD 16 (1842: Plate 6). Given this arrangement, there was no space to add illustrations for BD 2 through BD 14 in Style 2 and Style 3 documents, and Theban scribes using Style 1 chose not to alter this practice. It is unclear why BD 22 was not assigned an illustration, although this is not to say that a few documents did not in fact accompany that text with an illustration, but each illustration appears to be the result of a mistake, where a careless scribe had mistakenly allocated space for an illustration thereby forcing the artist to add a scene in order to fill that space rather than leave it empty (Mosher, 2016b: 203–4). The same also applies to BD 29, 62, 111, 123, and 139. In Saite through Ptolemaic documents, BD 69 and 70 were essentially regarded as part of BD 68, and the illustration for BD 68 served all three spells. Similarly, BD 97 was essentially an extension of BD 96 for the period under discussion here; it never had an illustration of its own, and, curiously, BD 96 was also never assigned an illustration. BD 141 and 142, both consisting of litanies of names, were not assigned illustrations, although two small sets of documents accompanied BD 141 with an illustration (Mosher, 2020: 464–65).

## Spells Represented Only by Illustrations

The converse of this is represented by another subset of illustrations that were never accompanied by a title and text. The four-register vertical illustration that separates the text of BD 15i from the start of BD 17, identified by Lepsius as BD 16, has become a controversial issue, with many scholars (e.g., Verhoeven, 1993: 47–48; Budek, 2008) now identifying it as an illustration associated with the text of BD 15 (Fig. 23.41). This topic is complex, and this author has argued that Lepsius was astute in identifying these four scenes as a separate spell consisting only of an illustration that was highly magical by itself (Mosher, 2016b: 1–40); it culminates in scene four in the bottom register, depicting the deceased as one who has successfully *gone forth*, a notion graphically expressed in many spells. A similar arrangement involves the three- or five-register illustration of scenes identified by Lepsius as BD 143, an identification that no one disputes (Fig. 23.42). For a detailed discussion on this interesting and complex illustration, see Mosher, 2020: 547–70.

FIG. 23.41. Illustration for BD 16 in P.London BM EA 10017. Courtesy of the Trustees of the British Museum, London.

FIG. 23.42. Illustration for BD 143 in P.Paris Louvre N 3248. © Musée du Louvre, Paris.

In New Kingdom documents, the text of BD 110 was accompanied by a large illustration of multiple scenes depicting various aspects in the Field of Offerings and the activities performed there by the deceased (Álvarez Sosa, this volume). Curiously, this illustration continued to be used in Saite through Ptolemaic documents, but it often occurs without any accompanying text, particularly in Saite and Ptolemaic Memphite documents, and in this respect, it functioned like the illustrations of BD 16 and 143, all representing magical illustrations that graphically assert that the deceased has successfully *gone forth*.

Yet another arrangement similar to this is the illustration identified by Lepsius as BD 150, a long vertical representation of cryptic shapes that represent different mounds in the underworld (Fig. 23.43). In New Kingdom documents these shapes were typically accompanied by legends that provide names for the mounds, gnostic information to enable the deceased to go past said mounds in his travels through the underworld. Curiously, in Saite documents the names were included, but in Ptolemaic Memphite documents the names were typically omitted, as if knowledge of the shapes of the mounds alone was sufficient. Similarly, in the pre-Ptolemaic P.London BM EA 10097 that was based on a Saite source, the names were included, but in the pre-Ptolemaic P.Turin 1830 from the main pre-Ptolemaic workshop (Mosher,

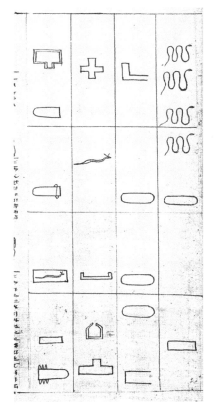

FIG. 23.43. Illustration for BD 150 in P.Paris Louvre N 3129 without the names of the mounds. © Musée du Louvre, Paris.

2016a: 10–15) and in P.London BM EA 9912 from the third pre-Ptolemaic workshop, which produced hieroglyphic documents (Mosher, 2016a: 15–19), the names were omitted. Similarly, in most Ptolemaic Theban documents the names were omitted (Fig. 23.43), although random documents do include the names, indicating that knowledge of the names was not lost (Fig. 23.44). Examples that included the names are P.Milan 1023 from the P.London BM EA 10086 Tradition; P.Paris Louvre N 3079 from the N3079 Tradition; P.London BM EA 10257, P.Paris Louvre N 3089, and P.Paris Louvre N 3248 from the N3089 Tradition; and P.Ryerson from the Ryerson Tradition. Similarly, the multi-scene illustration for BD 151 runs vertically from the top to the bottom (Fig. 23.45), and while Theban pre-Ptolemaic and Ptolemaic traditions

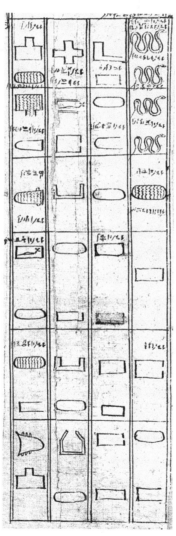

FIG. 23.44. Illustration for BD 150 in P.Paris Louvre N 3079 with the names of the mounds. © Musée du Louvre, Paris.

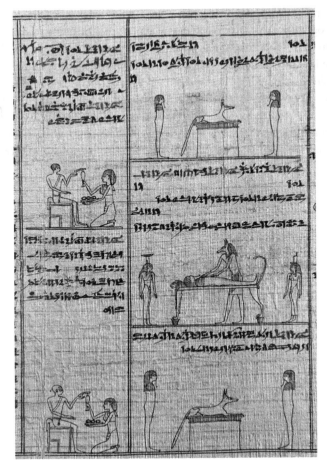

**FIG. 23.45.** Illustration for BD 151 with text in P.London BM EA 10558. Courtesy of the Trustees of the British Museum, London.

included text with the individual scenes (it did not have a title), many Saite and Memphite Ptolemaic documents presented only the illustration, in which, again the scenes magically conveyed the goal of the spell (Fig. 23.46; Mosher, 2018c, 19–74).

## Artistic Creativity and Individuality

With regard to execution of the artwork, where most Ptolemaic artists employed black line drawings, most small illustrations were executed with simplicity for quick but utilitarian function, and this was mostly true for the large illustrations as well, such as those for BD 110 and BD 125. Some artists, however, took the opportunity to utilize their artistic skills by drawing with remarkable detail (Fig. 23.47).

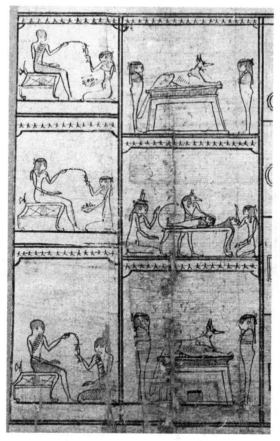

FIG. 23.46. Illustration for BD 151 without text in P.Paris Louvre N 3081. © Musée du Louvre, Paris.

One might ask if the entire set of illustrations was so fixed that no variation or artistic individuality was allowed. In general, it appears that most artists drew only what was expected, perhaps to execute their tasks as quickly as possible. On the other hand, one can observe more than a few examples where individual artists occasionally executed their tasks with what might be called artistic license, and in other instances some artists intelligently embellished a standardized scene based on their knowledge of the text. For example, recall the title of BD 38, discussed earlier in this chapter, which consisted of two parts, a spell for *breathing air* and a spell for *driving off two mrty-snakes*. In the standardized illustrations, the deceased was depicted either holding an air-sign or driving off a snake, but the artists of P.Paris Louvre N 3089 and P.Paris Louvre E 11078 (Mosher, 2016c: 151–54) appear to have considered both parts of the title, and each incorporated an illustration representing both parts, with the artist of P.Paris Louvre E 11078 being more accurate in depicting two snakes (Figs. 23.48 and 23.49).

**FIG. 23.47.** Remarkable detail in small extract from the illustration for BD 125 in P.Paris Louvre N 3084. © Musée du Louvre, Paris.

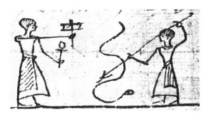

**FIG. 23.48.** Illustration for BD 38 in P.Paris Louvre N 3089 with one *mrty*-snake. © Musée du Louvre, Paris.

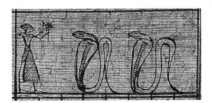

**FIG. 23.49.** Illustration for BD 38 in P.Paris Louvre E 11078 with two *mrty*-snakes. © Musée du Louvre, Paris.

As for artistic creativity or flourish, in Figure 23.50 one can observe the typical illustration for BD 45, although one can observe differing orientations of the figures. In P.London BM EA 10086, the scribe blundered by adding the text of BD 46 out of sequence (BD 43-46-44-45), and this must have confused the artist, who then added the illustration of BD 45 in the allocated space beside the title of BD 46. He then correctly added the illustration of BD 44 beside the text of that spell, and now he was faced with the dilemma of what scene to add near the text of BD 45 because he had already used the correct scene beside the text of BD 46. He appears to have improvised by using a scene from the multi-scene illustration of BD 151 (Figs. 23.45 and 23.51; for the New Kingdom version of this spell and illustration, see Lüscher, 1998; for Saite through Ptolemaic, see Mosher, 2018c).

As stated earlier, BD 62 was one of the spells not assigned an illustration in any of the Saite through Ptolemaic traditions, but the scribe of P.London BM EA 10086 once again erred by mistakenly allocating space for a scene, and the artist must have been aware of the text because he created his own scene that is in full accord with the purpose of the spell—to provide water. Thus we see the goddess Nut standing within the sycamore tree associated with BD 59, dispensing water to both the deceased and her *ba*-soul (Fig. 23.52; Mosher, 2017a: 230).

FIG. 23.50. First instance of the illustration for BD 45 beside the text of BD 46 in P.London BM EA 10086. Courtesy of the Trustees of the British Museum, London.

FIG. 23.51. Second instance of the illustration for BD 45 with the text of BD 45 in P.London BM EA 10086. Courtesy of the Trustees of the British Museum, London.

FIG. 23.52. Improvised illustration for BD 62 in P.London BM EA 10086. Courtesy of the Trustees of the British Museum, London.

FIG. 23.53. Embellishment to the illustration for BD 73 in P.Liverpool 1978.291.264. Credit line: Facsimile rendering by M. Mosher.

FIG. 23.54. Standard illustration for BD 77 in P.London BM EA 10558. Courtesy of the Trustees of the British Museum, London.

A single version of an illustration was used for BD 73; it depicts the deceased, in rightward orientation, holding a staff as one who has *gone forth*. In P.Liverpool 1978.291.264, however, the artist embellished the scene on his own by adding the sign for the West that is, in fact, the destination to which one *goes forth* (Fig. 23.53).

The title of BD 77 is "Spell for making the shape of a falcon of gold," and a single version of illustration was used, depicting a falcon standing on a simple platform with rightward orientation (Fig. 23.54; Mosher, 2017a: 454–57). Where nearly all examples of this scene were executed as black line drawings, the notion of a *falcon of gold* was not conveyed, although in P.London BM EA 10097 the falcon was painted with a yellowish wash that has the appearance of gold (Fig. 23.55). The artist responsible for P.Paris Louvre N 3084 recognized this issue, and he demonstrated intelligent creativity by replacing the simple platform with the hieroglyphic sign for gold (Fig. 23.56). Observe also the small figure of the falcon at the top right, which must have been sketched early on as a reminder of what illustration was to be drawn in the allocated space.

As a final example of artistic embellishment, the single version of the illustration for BD 83 depicts a crested heron with rightward orientation, usually rendered with a minimum of detail (Mosher, 2018a: 182–85). Once again, the artist of P.London BM EA 10086 chose not to use the normal simplistic depiction but instead spent extra time drawing in considerable detail for this small vignette (Fig. 23.57).

As can be seen from the discussion in this chapter, the traditions for Books of the Dead in pre-Ptolemaic and Ptolemaic Thebes were not static with respect to the texts and illustrations, nor were skilled and intelligent individual artists bound by inflexible rules and form.

FIG. 23.55. Standard illustration for BD 77 with falcon painted with a gold wash in P.London BM EA 10097. Courtesy of the Trustees of the British Museum, London.

FIG. 23.56. Embellished illustration for BD 77 with falcon perched on the hieroglyph for gold in P.Paris Louvre N 3084. © Musée du Louvre, Paris.

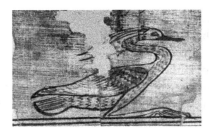

FIG. 23.57. Small embellished illustration for BD 83 in P.London BM EA 10086. Courtesy of the Trustees of the British Museum, London.

# Table of References for Documents

## Eighteenth-Dynasty Documents

P.London BM EA 10477 (Quirke, 1993: 51 #148; Lapp, 1997).
P.London BM 10489 + Amsterdam, Coll. Dortmund 22, + Boston MFA 22.401 + New York MMA 30.8.70 a-b + Newport Redwood Library + Stockholm private collection + Brisbane Queensland Museum (Lapp, 2006, 2008, 2008, 2011, 2017; Lüscher, 2006, 2012, 2016).
P.Cairo CG 51189 (Naville, 1908).
P.Paris Louvre N 3097 (Naville, 1886)
S. Cairo J.E. 96810 (Lapp, 2011; Lüscher, 2006, 2009, 2016).
S. MMA 22.3.296 (Lüscher, 2006, 2009)

## Saite through Ptolemaic Documents

P. Berlin 3058 (Mosher, 2016a, 2016b, 2016c, 2017a, 2018a, 2018b, 2018c, 2020, 2021).
P.London BM EA 9912 (Quirke, 1993: 42 #95; Mosher, 2016a, 2016b, 2016c, 2017a, 2018a, 2018b, 2018c, 2020, 2021)
P.London BM EA 10017 (Quirke, 1993: 35 #49; Mosher, 2016a, 2016b, 2016c, 2017a, 2018a, 2018b, 2018c, 2020, 2021)
P.London BM EA 10086 (Quirke, 1993: 65–65 #258; Mosher, 2016a, 2016b, 2016c, 2017a, 2018a, 2018b, 2018c, 2020, 2021)
P.London BM EA 10097 (Munro, 1973: Plate 51; Quirke, 1993: 52 #158; Mosher, 2016a, 2016b, 2016c, 2017a, 2018a, 2018b, 2018c, 2020, 2021)
P.London BM EA 10257 + P.Paris Louvre N 3255 (Munro, 1973: Plate 51; Quirke, 1993: 52 #158; Mosher, 2016a, 2016b, 2016c, 2017a, 2018a, 2018b, 2018c, 2020, 2021)
P.London BM EA 10311 (Quirke, 1993: 59 #209; Mosher, 2016a, 2016b, 2016c, 2017a, 2018a, 2018b, 2018c, 2020, 2021)

P.London BM EA 10558 (Quirke, 1993: 32 #23; Mosher, 2016a, 2016b, 2016c, 2017a, 2018a, 2018b, 2018c, 2020, 2021)

P.Budapest OSzK Cod. Afr. 2a + P.Cortona 3187 + P.Cairo J.E. 95685 (S.R. IV 615) + P.Cairo J.E. 95690 (S.R. IV 619) + P.Cairo J.E. 95745 (S.R. IV 692) + P.Cairo J.E. 95840 (S.R. IV 938) + P.Cairo J.E. 95841 (S.R. IV 939) + P.Cairo S.R. IV 996 + P.Heidelberg von Portheim-Siftung (B) + P.Moscow I, 1b 152 + P.Uppsala VM MB 160 (Munro, 2011).

P.Cairo CG 40024 + P.Cairo J.E. 95708 + P.Cairo J.E. 95710 + P.Cairo J.E. 95717 + P.Cairo J.E. 95857 (Mosher, 2016a, 2016b, 2016c, 2017a, 2018a, 2018b, 2018c, 2020, 2021).

P.Cairo CG 40029 + P.Cairo J.E. 95653 (S.R. IV 551) + P.Cairo S.R. IV 996 a; (Mosher, 2016a, 2016b, 2016c, 2017a, 2018a, 2018b, 2018c, 2020, 2021)

P.Cairo JE 95714 + Albany 1900.3.1 + P.Cairo JE 95649 + Marseille 91/2/1 + Marseille 291 (Verhoeven, 1999)

P.Colon. Aeg 10207 (Verhoeven, 1993)

P.Leiden T 16 (Leemans, 1867).

P.Liverpool.291.264 (Mosher, 2017a, 2018a, 2018b)

P.Paris Louvre E 3232 (Mosher, 2016a, 2016b, 2016c, 2017a).

P.Paris Louvre E 3233 (Mosher, 1992: 171; Mosher, 2016b, 2017a, 2018a).

P.Paris Louvre E 7716 (Mosher, 2016a, 2016b, 2016c, 2017a, 2018a, 2018b).

P.Paris Louvre E 11078 (Mosher, 2016a, 2016b, 2016c, 2017a, 2018a, 2018b, 2018c, 2020, 2021).

P.Paris Louvre N 3079 (de Rougé, 1861–76; Mosher, 2016a, 2016b, 2016c, 2017a, 2018a, 2018b, 2018c, 2020, 2021)

P.Paris Louvre N 3081 (Mosher, 2016a, 2016b, 2016c, 2017a, 2018a, 2018b, 2018c, 2020, 2021).

P.Paris Louvre N 3082 (de Rougé, 1861–76; Mosher, 2016a, 2016b, 2016c, 2017a, 2018a, 2018b, 2018c, 2020, 2021)

P.Paris Louvre N 3084 (Mosher, 2017a, 2018a, 2018b, 2018c, 2020, 2021).

P.Paris Louvre N 3089 (Mosher, 2016a, 2016b, 2016c, 2017a, 2018a, 2018b, 2018c, 2020, 2021)

P.Paris Louvre N 3090 (Mosher, 2016a, 2016b, 2016c, 2017a, 2018a, 2018b; Quack, 2018).

P.Paris Louvre N 3091 (Mosher, 2016a, 2016b, 2016c, 2017a, 2018a, 2018b, 2018c, 2020, 2021; Quack, 2018).

P.Paris Louvre N 3100 (Mosher, 2016a, 2016b, 2016c, 2017a, 2018a).

P.Paris Louvre N 3129 (Mosher, 2016a, 2016b, 2016c, 2017a, 2018a, 2018b, 2018c, 2020, 2021)

P.Paris Louvre N 3143 (Mosher, 2016a, 2016b, 2016c, 2017a, 2018a, 2018b)

P.Paris Louvre N 3144 (Mosher, 2016a, 2016b, 2016c, 2017a, 2018a, 2018b, 2018c, 2020, 2021).

P.Paris Louvre N 3151 (Mosher, 2016a, 2016b, 2016c, 2017a, 2018a, 2018b, 2018c, 2020, 2021).

P. Paris Louvre N 3248 (Mosher, 2016a, 2016b, 2016c, 2017a, 2018a, 2018b, 2018c, 2020, 2021).

P. Paris Louvre N 3249 (Mosher, 2016a, 2016b, 2016c, 2017a, 2018a, 2018b)

P. Paris Louvre N 5450 (Mosher, 2016a, 2016b, 2016c, 2017a, 2018a, 2018b, 2018c, 2020, 2021).

P. Milan E 1023 + Vatican 38572/3 (Vandoni, 1969; Mosher, 2016a, 2016b, 2016c, 2017a, 2018a, 2018b).

P. MMA 25.3.212 + Ann Arbor KM 81.4.25 + Florence 11912 a-b + MMA 28.3.300 + Providence A 18077 + Toronto ROM 910.85.222; Verhoeven, 2017)

P. Ryerson (Allen, 1960; Scalf, 2017; Mosher, 2017b; Mosher, 2016a, 2016b, 2016c, 2017a, 2018a, 2018b, 2018c, 2020, 2021).

P. Turin 1830 (Mosher, 2016a, 2016b, 2016c, 2017a, 2018a, 2018b, 2018c, 2020, 2021).

P. Turin 1831 (Mosher, 2016a, 2016b, 2016c, 2017a, 2018a, 2018b, 2018c, 2020, 2021).

P. Turin 1833 (Mosher, 2016a, 2016b, 2016c, 2017a, 2018a, 2018b, 2018c, 2020, 2021).

## Bibliography

Allen, T. G. (1960). *The Egyptian Book of the Dead Documents in the Oriental Institute Museum at the University of Chicago*. Oriental Institute Publications 82 (Chicago: Oriental Institute).

Backes, B. (2005). *Das altägyptische "Zweiwegebuch": Studien zu den Sargtextsprüchen 1029–1130*. Ägyptologische Abhandlungen 69 (Wiesbaden: Harrassowitz).

Budek, J. (2008). "Untersuchungen zur Vignette 15 des Altägyptischen Totenbuches während der Spät- und Ptolemäerzeit." *Studien zur Altägyptischen Kultur* 37, 19–48.

Dorman, P. F. (2017). "The Origins and Early Development of the Book of the Dead." In *Book of the Dead: Becoming God in Ancient Egypt*. Oriental Institute Museum Publications 39, edited by Foy D. Scalf, 29–40 (Chicago: CASEMATE ACADEMIC).

Gasse, A. (2002). *Le Livre des Morts de Pacherientaihet au Musei Gregoriano Egizio*. Monumenti, Musei e Gallerie Pontifici (Cittá del Vaticano: Cybèle).

Lapp, G. (1997). *The Papyrus of Nu (BM EA 10477)*. Catalogue of the Books of the Dead in the British Museum I (London: British Museum).

Lapp, G. (2006). *Totenbuch Spruch 17*. Totenbuchtexte 1 (Basel: Orientverlag).

Lapp, G. (2008). *Totenbuch Spruch 125*. Totenbuchtexte 3 (Basel: Orientverlag).

Lapp, G. (2009). *Totenbuch Sprüche (Tb 18, 20)*. Totenbuchtexte 5 (Basel: Orientverlag).

Lapp, G. (2011). *Die Feindabwehrsprüche (Tb 2, 64–72)*. Totenbuchtexte 7 (Basel: Orientverlag).

Lapp, G. (2017). *Die prt-m-hrw-Sprüche (Tb 31–37, 39–42)*. Totenbuchtexte 10 (Basel: Orientverlag).

Leemans, C. (1867). *Papyrus égyptien funéraire hiératique (T. 16) du Musée d'Antiquités des Pays-Bas à Leide*. Monumens Égyptiens du Musée d'Antiquités des Pays-Bas à Leide III (Leiden: Brill).

Lepsius, R. (1842). *Das Todtenbuch der Ägypter nach dem Hieroglyphischen Papyrus in Turin* (Leipzig: Georg Wigand).

Lüscher, B. (1998). *Untersuchungen zu Totenbuch Spruch 151*. Studien zum Altägyptischen Totenbuch 2 (Wiesbaden: Harrassowitz).

Lüscher, B. (2006). *Die Verwandlungssprüche (Tb 76–88)*. Totenbuchtexte 2 (Basel: Orientverlag).

Lüscher, B. (2009). *Die Fährmannsprüche (Tb 98–99)*. Totenbuchtexte 4 (Basel: Orientverlag).

Lüscher, B. (2012). *Die Sprüche vom Kennen der Seelen (Tb 107–109, 111–116)*. Totenbuchtexte 8 (Basel: Orientverlag).

Lüscher, B. (2016). *Die Mund-und Herzsprüche (Tb 21–30)*. Totenbuchtexte 9 (Basel: Orientverlag).

Milde, H. (1991). *The Vignettes in the Book of the Dead of Neferrenpet* (Leiden: Nederlands Instituut Voor Het Nabije Oosten).

Mosher, M. (1992). "Theban and Memphite Book of the Dead Traditions in the Late Period." *Journal of the American Research Center in Egypt* XXIX: 143–72.

Mosher, M. (2009). "An intriguing Theban Book of the Dead tradition in the Late Period." *British Museum Studies of Ancient Egypt and the Sudan* 15: 124–72.

Mosher, M. (2016a). *The Book of the Dead, Saite through Ptolemaic Periods: A Study of Traditions Evident in Versions of Texts and Vignettes 1, BD Spells 1–15* (Prescott: Saite through Ptolemaic Book of the Dead Studies [SPBDStudies]).

Mosher, M. (2016b). *The Book of the Dead, Saite through Ptolemaic Periods: A Study of Traditions Evident in Versions of Texts and Vignettes 2, BD Spells 16, 18–30* (Prescott: Saite through Ptolemaic Book of the Dead Studies [SPBDStudies]).

Mosher, M. (2016c). *The Book of the Dead, Saite through Ptolemaic Periods: A Study of Traditions Evident in Versions of Texts and Vignettes 3, BD Spells 31–49* (Prescott: Saite through Ptolemaic Book of the Dead Studies [SPBDStudies]).

Mosher, M. (2017a). *The Book of the Dead, Saite through Ptolemaic Periods: A Study of Traditions Evident in Versions of Texts and Vignettes 4, BD Spells 50–77* (Prescott: Saite through Ptolemaic Book of the Dead Studies [SPBDStudies]).

Mosher, M. (2017b). "Transmission of Funerary Literature: Saite through Ptolemaic Periods." In *Book of the Dead, Becoming God in Ancient Egypt*. Oriental Institute Museum Publications 39, edited by F. Scalf, 85–96, 201–301 (Chicago: Oriental Institute).

Mosher, M. (2018a). *The Book of the Dead, Saite through Ptolemaic Periods: A Study of Traditions Evident in Versions of Texts and Vignettes 5, BD Spells 78–92* (Prescott: Saite through Ptolemaic Book of the Dead Studies [SPBDStudies]).

Mosher, M. (2018b). *The Book of the Dead, Saite through Ptolemaic Periods: A Study of Traditions Evident in Versions of Texts and Vignettes 6: BD Spells 93–109* (Prescott: Saite through Ptolemaic Book of the Dead Studies [SPBDStudies]).

Mosher, M. (2018c). *The Book of the Dead, Saite through Ptolemaic Periods: A Study of Traditions Evident in Versions of Texts and Vignettes 10: BD Spells 151–165* (Prescott: Saite through Ptolemaic Book of the Dead Studies [SPBDStudies]).

Mosher, M. (2020). *The Book of the Dead, Saite through Ptolemaic Periods: A Study of Traditions Evident in Versions of Texts and Vignettes 8: BD Spells 129–143* (Prescott: Saite through Ptolemaic Book of the Dead Studies [SPBDStudies]).

Mosher, M. (2021). *The Book of the Dead, Saite through Ptolemaic Periods: A Study of Traditions Evident in Versions of Texts and Vignettes 9, Part 1: BD Spells 144–146* (Norwell: Saite through Ptolemaic Book of the Dead Studies [SPBDStudies]).

Mosher, M. (2022a). *The Book of the Dead, Saite through Ptolemaic Periods: A Study of Traditions Evident in Versions of Texts and Vignettes, Volume 9, Part 2: BD Spells 147–148* (Norwell: Saite through Ptolemaic Book of the Dead Studies [SPBDStudies]).

Mosher, M. (2022b). *The Book of the Dead, Saite through Ptolemaic Periods: A Study of Traditions Evident in Versions of Texts and Vignettes, Volume 9, Part 3: BD Spells 149–150* (Norwell: Saite through Ptolemaic Book of the Dead Studies [SPBDStudies]).

Munro, I. (2011). *Die Totenbuch-Papyri des Ehepaars Ts-scheret-en-Aset un Djedchi aus der Bes-en-Mut Familie.* Handschriften des Altägyptischen Totenbuches 12 (Wiesbaden: Harrassowitz).

Munro, P. (1973). *Die Spätägyptischen Totenstelen.* Ägyptische Forschungen 25 (Glückstadt: J. J. Augustin).

Niwiński, A. (1989). *Studies on the Illustrated Theban Funerary Papyri of the 11th and 10th Centuries B.C.* Orbis Biblicus et Orientalis 86 (Göttingen: Universitätsverlag Freiberg Schweiz Vandenhoeck & Rupert).

Naville, É. (1886). *Die Ägyptische Todtenbuch der XVIII. bis XX, Dynastie* (Berlin: Asher).

Naville, É. (1908). *The Funeral Papyrus of Iouiya.* Theodore M Davis' Excavations: Bibân el Molûk (London: Archibald Constable & Co., LTD).

Quack, J. F. (2018). "Psammetich der Eunuch. Wie aus Geschichte Geschichten werden." In *Pérégrinations avec Erhart Graefe. Festschrift zu seinem 75. Geburtstag.* Ägypten und Altes Testament, 87, edited by A. I. Blöbaum, M. Eaton-Krauss, and A. Wüthrich, 475–83 (Münster: Zaphon).

Quirke, S. (1993). *Owners of Funerary Papyri in the British Museum.* British Museum Occasional Papers 92 (London: British Museum).

de Rougé, E. (1861–76). *Rituel Funéraire des anciens Égyptiens: texte complet en écriture hiératique publ. d'après les papyrus du Musée du Louvre et précédé d'une introduction à l'étude du rituel* (Paris: Duprat).

Sherbiny, W. (2017). *Through Hermopolitan Lenses, Studies on the So-called Book of Two Ways in Ancient Egypt.* Probleme Der Agyptologie, 33 (Leiden: Brill).

Stadler, M. (2009). *Weiser und Wesir: Studien zu Vorkommen, Rolle und Wesen des Gottes Thot im ägyptischen Totenbuch.* Orientalische Religionen in der Antike 1 (Tübingen: Mohr Siebeck).

Vandoni, M. (1969). "Due 'Libri dei Morti' Egiziani Conservati Al Civico Museo Archeologico." *Notizie dal Chiostro del Monastero Maggiore*, Fascicle III–IV, 77–85 and Plates I–VII.

Verhoeven, U. (1993). *Das Saitische Totenbuch der Iahtesnacht (P. Colon. Aeg. 10207).* Papyrologische Texte und Abhandlungen 41 (Bonn: Dr. Rudolph Habelt GMBH).

Verhoeven, U. (1999). *Das Totenbuch des Monthpriesters Nespasefy aus der Zeit Psammetichs I. pKairo JE 95714 + pAlbany 1900.3.1, pKairo JE 95649, pMarseille 91/2/1 (ehem. Slg. Brunner) + pMarseille 291.* Handschriften des Altägyptischen Totenbuches 5 (Wiesbaden: Harrassowitz).

PART V

# THE BOOK OF THE DEAD IN MODERN TIMES

# CHAPTER 24

# THE TIME OF THE PIONEERS (SEVENTEENTH TO NINETEENTH CENTURIES)

BARBARA LÜSCHER

## Early Scholars and Key Figures

The early history of scholarly research in the field of the ancient Egyptian Book of the Dead (Lüscher, 2014) is at the same time part of the early history of Egyptology itself (Thompson, 2015), since the decipherer of the Egyptian hieroglyphs, Jean-François Champollion (1790–1832; Fig. 24.1; Lacouture, 1988; Adkins, 2001), and the founding father of German Egyptology, Karl Richard Lepsius (1810–1884; Fig. 24.2; Ebers, 1885; Lepsius, 1933; Freier and Reineke, 1988; Hanus, 2010; Mehlitz, 2011; Lepper and Hafemann, 2012), were among the first main figures. While the former discovered the key that finally unlocked the secrets of the ancient Egyptian script, the latter confirmed and expanded Champollion's theories and thus opened the door to all subsequent scholarly studies on ancient Egyptian culture and texts. It was also Lepsius who introduced the modern title "Todtenbuch" for this heterogeneous compilation of mortuary spells and illustrations—previously called "funerary ritual" by Champollion and known today as the "Book of the Dead".

However, before paying tribute to Champollion's and Lepsius' contributions to the field of the Book of the Dead, a brief look should be taken at the pre-Champollionic and even pre-Napoleonic era and some rare seventeenth- and eighteenth-century sources introduced. Interestingly, the earliest illustrations of ancient Egyptian papyri and mummy bandages were published long before their texts could be deciphered and their real contents and meaning could be understood. For example, volume 3 of Athanasius Kircher's (1602–1680) famous and lavishly illustrated work "Oedipus

**FIG. 24.1.** Jean-François Champollion.

Wikimedia Commons, Public Domain.

**FIG. 24.2.** Karl Richard Lepsius.

Ebers, 1885: Frontispiece.

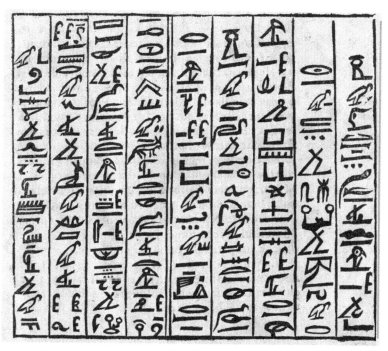

FIG. 24.3. Early facsimile from 1653 of a papyrus fragment (BNF 46).

La Boullaye Le Gouz, 1653: 357.

Aegyptiacus" contains several depictions of Book of the Dead vignettes from a mummy bandage (Kircher, 1654: 421–24; Lüscher, 2018: 9, with Figs. 18–19). Kircher, a German Jesuit as well as a mathematician, physician, and philosopher, was an accomplished polymath of his time and even claimed to have deciphered the hieroglyphic script. While his ideas concerning the Egyptian writing system were misleading, his linking of it with the Coptic language was correct and later proved to be of great importance for Champollion's studies. Another early depiction can be found in a travelogue from 1653 (La Boullaye Le Gouz, 1653) showing the earliest known facsimile of a Book of the Dead papyrus fragment (Fig. 24.3; see Lüscher, 2017; Lüscher, 2018: 6–7 with Figs. 11–12). The illustration mentioned is so accurate that the text can be identified as part of BD 99B, and the present location of the original papyrus fragment can be determined (P.Paris BN 48; see Lüscher, 2017).

Of further interest is a set of early facsimiles of some Ptolemaic mummy bandages, first published by the French scholar and collector Bernard de Montfaucon in 1722 (Montfaucon, 1722: pl. CXL; Fig. 24.4) and 1724 (Montfaucon, 1724: pl. LIV). One part of this had been misunderstood as an ancient Egyptian calendar; a slightly improved rendering can be found in the edition of Anne Claude Philippe de Caylus (1752: pls. XXI–XXV; Fig. 24.5). An even earlier illustration of another part of the same mummy bandages was published in

FIG. 24.4. Early facsimile of a fragment of the mummy bandages of Aberuai.

Montfaucon, 1722: pl. CXL.

1704 (*Journal de Trévoux*: June 1704, illustration to 978; Fig. 24.6). All those fragments belonged to one single document and were found on a female mummy in Saqqara, which was unwrapped in 1698 by the French consul Benoît de Maillet (Maillet, 1735: 275–90). Immediately after discovery, the bandages were cut with scissors and the fragments distributed among the participants of the unwrapping ceremony. Fortunately, several of them have recently been relocated in the collections of the Louvre and the Bibliothèque nationale de France (for their complete history see Lüscher, 2018).

The aforementioned bandages also played an important role in the history of deciphering the hieratic script, which at that time several authors considered to be alphabetic. Champollion—who in his early days had to base his philological studies mainly on unpublished material from private collections and more or less accurate facsimiles in books—studied those fragments and even made his own hand copies (see Lüscher, 2018: pls. 1–12).

From the sixteenth century onwards, so-called curiosity cabinets came into fashion in Europe; these often contained ancient Egyptian objects, among other items, including Books of the Dead. Those private collections were stuffed with exotic items from all over the world and from various fields, like ethnography, geology, archaeology, and the like, and they often formed the core of later museums.

A new and invaluable source on the wonders of Egypt in all its aspects have been and still are the giant volumes of the famous "Description de l'Égypte," which began to be issued from 1809 onwards. It was the outstanding legacy of the scholars and scientists who had accompanied Napoleon's campaign to Egypt in 1798, including—among the thousands of detailed drawings and copper engravings—a reproduction of the famous Rosetta Stone (Description, 1823: pls. 52–54; Parkinson, 1999; Solé and Valbelle, 2001) as

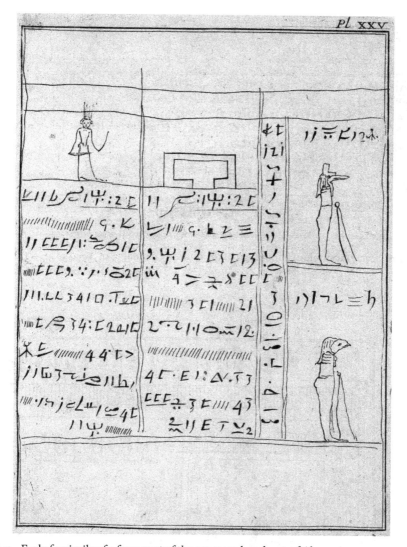

**FIG. 24.5.** Early facsimile of a fragment of the mummy bandages of Aberuai.

Caylus, 1752: pl. XXV.

well as several funerary papyri (Description, 1812: pls. 60–75; see Fig. 24.13; Description, 1823: pls. 44–46). Their documentary legacy thus formed the starting point for the later deciphering of the ancient Egyptian language and script and the emergence of the academic discipline of Egyptology.

In 1842, a Ptolemaic papyrus of a man called Iufankh from the collection of the Turin Museum (P.Turin 1791; Fig. 24.7) was published by Karl Richard Lepsius (Lepsius, 1842) under the designation "Todtenbuch," which from then on became the common

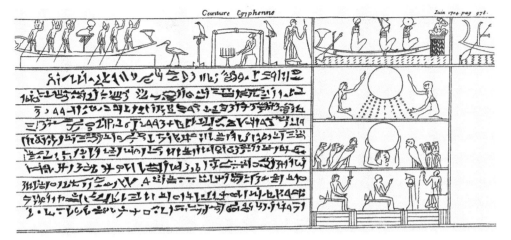

FIG. 24.6. Early facsimile of a fragment of the mummy bandages of Aberuai.

Journal de Trévoux: June 1704, illustration to 978.

FIG. 24.7. Papyrus of Iufankh (P.Turin 1791).

Lepsius, 1842: pl. L.

title for the ancient Egyptian "peret-em-heru," a compilation of funerary spells concerning "Going forth by day(light?)." Lepsius (1810–1884), who led the famous Prussian expedition to Egypt and Nubia between 1842 and 1845, was the founder and pioneer of German Egyptology on the basis of his having confirmed and expanded Champollion's theories. He was also a key figure in early Book of the Dead studies.

In those early days of Egyptology, before the two older religious text corpora of the Pyramid and Coffin texts were known, the Book of the Dead was believed to be the most ancient and most extensive text corpus of the ancient Egyptians and therefore the best source for studying their religion, language, and afterlife conceptions.

The spell sequence in Lepsius' edition of the Turin papyrus still serves as a prototype for our modern numbering system of Book of the Dead spells, although it does not reflect the preferred order of spells of the earlier manuscripts from the so-called Theban Recension of the classical New Kingdom tradition. However, in Lepsius' day, very few papyri were known or published, so he believed that the Turin manuscript with its 165 spells, or "chapters," as he called them, represented a kind of standard edition of the text. It was only years later that he realized the wealth and importance of earlier sources from the New Kingdom, including papyri, linen shrouds, coffins, and tomb walls. This spurred him to produce a new critical Book of the Dead publication, this time not restricted to just one representative manuscript. He presented his project, a full comparative edition, at the Second International Congress of Orientalists in London in 1874. His original plan of including texts from all periods of Egyptian history, however, was ultimately confined to an edition of strictly New Kingdom sources because of the overwhelming amount of material.

The aging Lepsius entrusted his former student (Henri-)Édouard Naville (1844–1926; Fig. 24.8) to carry out this enormous task. Naville, the founder of Swiss Egyptology, is another key figure in early Book of the Dead research (Berchem, 1989; Lüscher, 2010; Lüscher, 2014). After studying in London, Bonn, and Paris, he went to Berlin and became Lepsius' most prominent student, sharing his interest in religious texts. He also conducted several excavation projects on behalf of the newly founded Egypt Exploration Fund, the most important of his archaeological achievements being the excavation and recording of the Deir el-Bahari temples of Mentuhotep Nebhepetre and Queen Hatshepsut. To fulfil his teacher's plan of a complete Book of the Dead edition, Naville spent more than a decade collecting and copying relevant material from all major museums and finally published his three volumes of "Das aegyptische Todtenbuch der XVIII. bis XX. Dynastie" in 1886 (Naville, 1886). It is divided into an introduction with short commentary on each source and spell; a volume of facsimile drawings (skillfully done by his wife Marguerite; see Maurice-Naville et al., 2014); and a volume of synoptic texts. This was to become *the* standard edition for the next 120 years, until the start of a new synoptic edition in the series "Totenbuchtexte (at Orientverlag G. Lapp, Basel)," now based on a much larger set of source documents and including full text versions, rubrics, correct sign orientations, and so forth. In Naville's publication, only one version per spell was given with full text, accompanied by just the main variants from the parallels. As his basic version, he chose one of the finest

FIG. 24.8. Édouard Naville.

© Fondation Naville, Geneva.

and longest specimens from the British Museum's collection, the funerary papyrus of Nebseni (P.London BM EA 9900; Fig. 24.9; Lapp, 2004), an 18th-Dynasty manuscript of Memphite origin. As complementary versions to Nebseni, he made particular use of the Louvre papyri of Mesemnetjer (P.Paris Louvre E.21324) and Neferubenef (P.Paris Louvre N.3092). Many of Naville's handwritten notes, sketches, and facsimiles, together with his extensive correspondence, have been preserved in the archives of the Geneva Library. A selection of his most relevant notes and drawings related to the Book of the Dead was published and discussed in 2014 (Lüscher, 2014).

Other key figures connected with early Book of the Dead publications are the British scholars Samuel Birch (1813–1885), Peter Le Page Renouf (1822–1897; Renouf, 1907), and E. A. Wallis Budge (1857–1934), all of them successive keepers of the Antiquities Department of the British Museum. While all three carried out early translations of the Book of the Dead, Budge is particularly renowned for having acquired an immense number of important objects for the British Museum collection (like the famous Amarna tablets, for example), among them some Book of the Dead manuscripts of the highest quality; examples include the papyri of Ani (P.London BM EA 10470; for a later photographic publication see Dondelinger, 1979), Hunefer (P.London BM EA 9901; Fig. 24.10), Anhai (P.London BM EA 10472), and Nu (P.London BM EA 10477; see also Lapp, 1997), which he published in large facsimiles (for a list of his many editions see Backes, 2009: nos. 75–78, 489–494).

However, outside the United Kingdom, Germany, and Switzerland, some early pioneering work in the field of the Book of the Dead was also being conducted. Regarding France, the names of Emmanuel de Rougé (1811–1872), Paul Pierret (1836–1916), Théodule Devéria (1831–1871), as well as Paul Guieysse and Eugène Lefébure

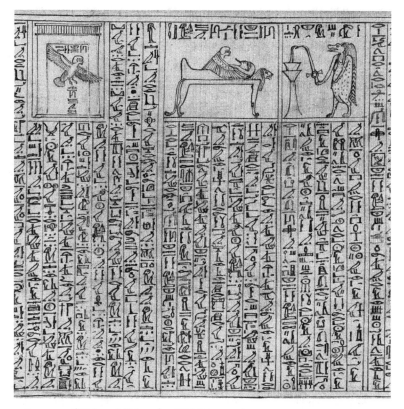

FIG. 24.9. Papyrus of Nebseni (P.London BM EA 9900).

© The Trustees of the British Museum.

(Guieysse and Lefébure, 1877), must be mentioned. The Viscount de Rougé was the direct successor to Champollion's chair of Egyptology in Paris (followed by Paul Pierret) and curator of the Louvre Museum. The title of his publication, "Rituel funéraire des anciens Egyptiens" (Rougé, 1861–1876), used Champollion's early designation of that text corpus. Devéria's facsimile edition of the Louvre papyrus of Nebqed (Devéria and Pierret, 1872; Fig. 24.11) is still the only published source for this beautiful document of the Eighteenth Dynasty. In the Netherlands, Conrad Leemans published a whole series of papyri from the Leiden collection, including the facsimile of the papyrus of Qenna (P.Leiden T2; Leemans, 1882; Fig. 24.12; for more of Leemans' publications, see the list in Backes, 2009: nos. 686–691). As the original papyrus is still unpublished, those early and very accurate facsimiles continue to be an important source to this day. One of the major works of another Dutch Egyptologist, Willem Pleyte (1836–1903), deals with the supplementary chapters of the Book of the Dead, spells 162–74 (Pleyte, 1881).

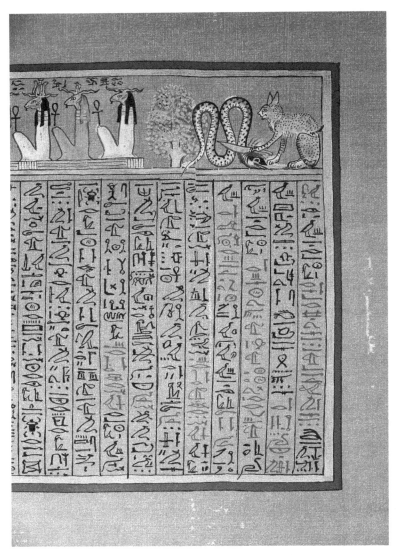

FIG. 24.10. Facsimile of papyrus Hunefer (P.London BM EA 9901).

Budge, 1899: pl. 11.

## First editions

While some very early representations of scenes or texts from the Egyptian Book of the Dead can be found sporadically in books of the seventeenth and eighteenth century, as mentioned on p. 488–91 it was the scientific committee of the Napoleonic campaign in Egypt, with its monumental "Description de l'Égypte," that marks the actual

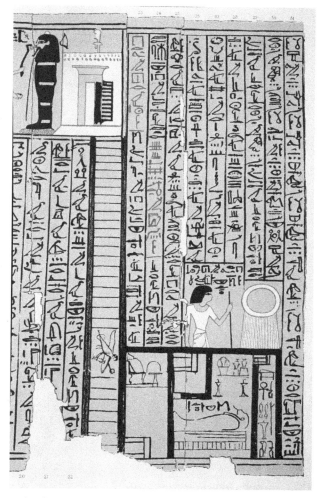

FIG. 24.11. Facsimile of papyrus Nebqed (P.Paris Louvre N. 3068).

Devéria / Pierret, 1872: pl. III.

starting point for the first full publications of Book of the Dead manuscripts, including the reproduction of Jean Marcel Cadet's (1751–1835) facsimile of a complete manuscript from the Ptolemaic Period (P.Paris BN 1–19) (Fig. 24.13; see Cadet, 1805, reproduced in Description, 1812: pls. 72–75). The illustrations in the "Description de l'Égypte" were also used by Champollion for his early philological studies.

In the nineteenth century, with photography still in its infant stages, most early publications were either hand copies or facsimile drawings and therefore of varying quality and reliability. Then, in the early twentieth century, photographic publications became more and more common (e.g., Davis, 1908; Naville, 1912; Naville, 1914; and others). One of the first photographic reproductions was the British Museum

FIG. 24.12. Facsimile of papyrus Qenna (Leiden T2).

Leemans, 1882: pl. VIII.

publication of the papyrus of Nebseni (Nebseni, 1876; Fig. 24.9), which Naville used as the primary text for his comparative edition.

Several articles on Book of the Dead topics can be found in the oldest Egyptological journal, the "Zeitschrift für Ägyptische Sprache und Alterthumskunde," which was established in 1863 by Heinrich Brugsch (1827–1894) and was continued by Karl Richard Lepsius and others.

### First translations

The first complete Book of the Dead translation was in English and published by Samuel Birch in 1867 (in Bunsen, 1867: 123–33). It was based on Lepsius' edition of the

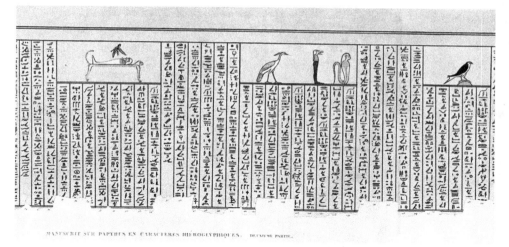

FIG. 24.13. Papyrus Cadet (P.Paris BN 1–19). Description, 1812: pl. 73.

Ptolemaic Turin papyrus of Iufankh, mentioned earlier in this chapter (Lepsius, 1842; Fig. 24.7), as was Paul Pierret's French version from 1882. In 1885, a new translation in French was published by A. Massy (Massy, 1885), based on the New Kingdom papyrus of Nebseni (Fig. 24.9). The first German partial translation of Book of the Dead texts by Heinrich Brugsch appeared in Volume 10 of the aforementioned "Zeitschrift für Ägyptische Sprache und Alterthumskunde" (Brugsch, 1872), but it was not until 1979 that the first complete German translation was released by Erik Hornung (Hornung, 1979).

*First lexica and word indexes*

In 1875, the Norwegian scholar Jens Lieblein (1827–1911) issued the first word index to the Book of the Dead (Lieblein, 1875), again based on the Turin papyrus of Iufankh (Fig. 24.7; for a new index, see Backes, 2005). E. A. Wallis Budge then used the famous British Museum papyrus of Ani (P.London BM EA 10470; Budge, 1890, and several later editions; Fig. 24.14), which he had acquired in Egypt, as the basis for a first hieroglyphic lexicon of the Book of the Dead (Budge, 1911).

The fundamentals and basic tools for today's Book of the Dead studies were thus established by some of the most prolific scholars of the early days of Egyptology and date back to the period before the hieroglyphs themselves had been deciphered. Although many of their editions are now outdated or in need of major corrections, they still form an immense treasure of material and provide interesting insight into the early interpretations of ancient Egyptian religious literature in general. In addition, some of these early facsimiles, as incomplete or inaccurate as they may often be, either are the only remaining source of a particular document or show it in a better state of preservation.

FIG. 24.14. Papyrus of Ani (P.London BM EA 10470).

Budge, 1890: pl. 3.

# Bibliography

Adkins, L. and R. (2001). *The Keys of Egypt: The Race to Read the Hieroglyphs* (London: Harper Collins).

Backes, B. (2005). *Wortindex zum späten Totenbuch (pTurin 1791)*. Unter Mitarbeit von Irmtraut Munro und Simone Stöhr. Studien zum Altägyptischen Totenbuch 9 (Wiesbaden: Harrassowitz).

Backes, B. (2009). *Bibliographie zum Altägyptischen Totenbuch.* 2., erweiterte Auflage. Bearbeitet von Burkhard Backes, Svenja A. Gülden, Holger Kockelmann, Marcus Müller-Roth, Irmtraut Munro und Simone Stöhr. Studien zum Altägyptischen Totenbuch 13 (Wiesbaden: Harrassowitz).

Berchem, D. van (1989). *L'égyptologue genevois Edouard Naville. Années d'études et premiers voyages en Égypte 1862-1870.* (Genève: Journal de Genève and Georg Editeur).

Brugsch, H. (1872). "Das Todtenbuch der alten Ägypter". *Zeitschrift für Ägyptische Sprache und Altertumskunde* 10: 65-72, 129–134.

Budge, E. A. W. (1890). *The Book of the Dead. Facsimile of the Papyrus of Ani* (London: British Museum).

Budge, E. A. W. (1899). *The Book of the Dead. Facsimiles of the Papyri of Hunefer, Anhai, Kerasher and Netchemet with Supplementary Text from the Papyrus of Nu* (London: British Museum).

Budge, E. A. W. (1911). *A Hieroglyphic Vocabulary to the Theban Recension of the Book of the Dead. With an Index to all the English Equivalents of the Egyptian Words.* Books on Egypt and Chaldaea 31 (London: Kegan Paul, Trench Trübner & Co. Ltd.).

Bunsen, C. C. J. Baron, editor (1867). *Egypt's Place in Universal History. An Historical Investigation in Five Books.* Translated from the German by Charles H. Cottrell, with additions by Samuel Birch. Vol. V (London: Longmans, Green).

Cadet, J. M. (1805). *Copie figurée d'un rouleau de papyrus trouvé à Thèbes, dans un tombeau des rois* (Paris: Levrault, Schöll et companie).

Caylus, A.-C.-P. de (1752). *Recueil d'antiquités égyptiennes, étrusques, grècques et romaines.* Vol. 1 (Paris: Desaint & Saillant).

Davis, T. M. (1908). *The Funeral Papyrus of Iouiya. With an Introduction by Edouard Naville* (London: Constable).

Description (1812). *Description de l'Égypte ou Recueil des observations et des recherches qui ont été faites en Égypte pendant l'expédition de l'armée française, publié par les ordres de Sa Majesté l'empereur Napoléon le Grand.* Antiquités, Tome deuxième, planches (Paris: Imprimerie Impériale).

Description (1823). *Description de l'Égypte ou Recueil des observations et des recherches qui ont été faites en Égypte pendant l'expédition de l'armée française.* Seconde édition dédiée au Roi. Antiquités, Tome cinquième (Paris: Panckoucke).

Devéria, T. and Pierret, P. (1872). *Le papyrus de Neb-qed (exemplaire hiéroglyphique du Livre des Morts).* Reproduit, décrit et précédé d'une introduction mythologique (Paris: Franck).

Dondelinger, E. (1979). *Papyrus Ani BM 10.470. Vollständige Faksimile-Ausgabe im Originalformat des Totenbuches aus dem Besitz des British Museum.* Codices Selecti 62. Phototypice Impressi (Graz / Paris: Akademische Druck- und Verlagsanstalt).

Ebers, G. (1885). *Richard Lepsius. Ein Lebensbild* (Leipzig: Engelmann).

Freier, E. and Reineke, W. F., editors (1988). *Karl Richard Lepsius (1810-1884).* Akten der Tagung anlässlich seines 100. Todestages, 10.-12.7.1984 in Halle (Berlin: Akademie Verlag).

Guieysse, P. and Lefébure, E. (1877). *Le papyrus funéraire de Soutimès* (Paris: Leroux).

Hanus, C. (2010). *Wegbereiter der Ägyptologie: Carl Richard Lepsius* (Berlin: Staatliche Museen zu Berlin).

Hornung, E. (1979). *Das Totenbuch der Ägypter* (Zürich / München: Artemis).

Kircher, A. (1654). *Oedipus Aegyptiacus, hoc est Universalis Hieroglyphicae Veterum Doctrinae temporum iniuria abolitae instauratio.* Tomus III (Rom: Mascardi).

La Boullaye Le Gouz, F. (1653). *Les voyages et observations du Sieur de La Boullaye-Le-Gouz gentil-homme angevin, où sont décrites les Religions, Gouvernemens, & situations des Estats & Royaumes d'Italie, Grece, Natolie, Syrie, Palestine, Karamenie, Kaldée, Assyrie, grand Mogol, Bijapour, Indes Orientales des Portugais, Arabie, Egypte, Hollande, grande Bretagne, Irlande, Dannemark, Pologne, Isles & autres lieux d'Europe, Asie & Affrique, où il a séjourné, le tout enrichy de Figures; Et Dedié à l'Eminentissime Cardinal Capponi* (Paris: Clousier).

Lacouture, J. (1988). *Champollion, une vie de lumière* (Paris: Grasset).

Lapp, G. (1997). *The Papyrus of Nu (BM EA 10477).* Catalogue of Books of the Dead in the British Museum I (London: British Museum).

Lapp, G. (2004). *The Papyrus of Nebseni (BM EA 9900).* Catalogue of the Books of the Dead in the British Museum III (London: Britsh Museum).

Leemans, C. (1882). *Aegyptische hiëroglyphische Lijkpapyrus (T. 2) van het Nederlandsche Museum van Oudheden te Leyden* (Leiden: Brill).

Lepper, V. M. and Hafemann, I., editors (2012). *Karl Richard Lepsius. Der Begründer der deutschen Ägyptologie* (Berlin: Kadmos).

Lepsius, B. (1933). *Das Haus Lepsius. Vom geistigen Aufstieg Berlins zur Reichshauptstadt. Nach Tagebüchern und Briefen von Elisabeth und Richard Lepsius* (Berlin: Klinkhardt & Biermann).

Lepsius, R. (1842). *Das Todtenbuch der Ägypter nach dem hieroglyphischen Papyrus in Turin* (Leipzig: Wigand).

Lieblein, J. (1875). *Index alphabétique de tous les mots contenus dans le Livre des Morts publié par R. Lepsius d'après le papyrus de Turin* (Paris: Vieweg).

Lüscher, B. (2010). "In the footsteps of Édouard Naville (1844-1926)." In *British Museum Studies in Ancient Egypt and Sudan* 15: 103–21.

Lüscher, B. (2014). *Auf den Spuren von Édouard Naville. Beiträge und Materialien zur Wissenschaftsgeschichte des Totenbuches.* Totenbuchtexte Supplementa 1 (Basel: Orientverlag).

Lüscher, B. (2017). "Papyrus Paris, Bibliothèque nationale 46: Ein Beitrag zur frühen Rezeptionsgeschichte des Totenbuches." In *Studies in Ancient Egyptian Funerary Literature.* Orientalia Lovaniensia Analecta 257, edited by S. Bickel and L. Díaz-Iglesias, 355–72 (Leuven: Peeters).

Lüscher, B. (2018). *Der sogenannte "Calendrier Égyptien" oder die Mumienbinden der Aberuai (BN 89 + BN 229 / Louvre N. 3059 u.a.). Zur frühen Rezeptionsgeschichte eines späten Totenbuches.* Beiträge zum Alten Ägypten 8 (Basel: Orientverlag).

Maillet, B. de (1735). *Description de l'Égypte, contenant plusieurs remarques curieuses sur la Geographie ancienne et moderne de ce Païs, sur ses Monumens anciens, sur les Mœurs, les Coutumes, & la Religion des Habitans, sur le Gouvernement & le Commerce, sur les Animaux, les Arbres, les Plantes, &c.* Composée sur les Mémoires de M. de Maillet, ancien Consul de France au Caire, par M. l'Abbé le Mascrier (Paris: Genneau et Rollin).

Massy, A. (1885). *Le papyrus de Nebseni. Exemplaire hiéroglyphique du Livre des Morts conservé au British Museum, traduit par A. Massy* (Gand: Waem-Lienders).

Maurice-Naville, D., Naville, L. and Eggly-Naville, C. (2014). *La plume, le pinceau, la prière. L'égyptologue Marguerite Naville (1852-1930). Récit biographique à trois voix* (Genève: La Baconnière).

Mehlitz, H. (2011). *Richard Lepsius. Ägypten und die Ordnung der Wissenschaft* (Berlin: Kadmos).

Montfaucon, B. de (1722). *L'antiquité expliquée et représentée en figures, Tome second, seconde partie: La Religion des Egyptiens, des Arabes, des Syriens, des Perses, des Scythes, des Germains, des Gaulois, des Espagnols, & des Carthaginois* (Paris: Delaulne et al.).

Montfaucon, B. de (1724). *Supplément au livre de l'antiquité expliquée et représentée en figures, Tome second: Le culte des Grecs, des Romains, des Egyptiens, et des Gaulois* (Paris: Delaulne et al.).

Naville, E. (1886). *Das aegyptische Todtenbuch der XVIII. bis XX. Dynastie.* 3 vols. (Berlin: Asher).

Naville, E. (1912). *Papyrus funéraires de la XXIe dynastie. Le Papyrus hiéroglyphique de Kamara et le Papyrus hiératique de Nesikhonsou au Musée du Caire* (Paris: Leroux).

Naville, E. (1914). *Papyrus funéraires de la XXIe dynastie. II. Le Papyrus hiératique de Katseshni au Musée du Caire* (Paris: Leroux).

Nebseni (1876). *Photographs of the Papyrus of Nebseni in the British Museum* (London: British Museum).

Parkinson, R. (1999). *Cracking Codes. The Rosetta Stone and Decipherment* (London: British Museum).

Pierret, P. (1882). *Le Livre des Morts des Anciens Egyptiens. Traduction complète d'après le Papyrus de Turin et les manuscrits du Louvre* (Paris: Leroux).

Pleyte, W. (1881). *Chapitres supplémentaires du Livre des Morts 162 à 174, Traduction et commentaire.* 3 vols. (Leiden: Brill).

Renouf, P. Le Page (1907). *The Life-work of Sir Peter Le Page Renouf. First Series, vol. IV: The Book of the Dead. Translation and Commentary.* Continued and completed by Prof. E. Naville (Paris: Leroux).

Rougé, E. de (1861-1876). *Rituel funéraire des anciens Egyptiens. Texte complet en écriture hiératique publié d'après les papyrus du Musée du Louvre et précédé d'une introduction à l'étude du rituel* (Paris: Duprat).

Solé, R. and Valbelle, D. (2001). *The Rosetta Stone. The Story of the Decoding of Hieroglyphics* (London: Profile Books).

Thompson, J. (2015). *Wonderful Things. A History of Egyptology. Part 1: From Antiquity to 1881. Part 2: The Golden Age: 1881-1914* (Cairo: American University).

CHAPTER 25

# JUST A CATCHY TITLE?

*On the History of Reception of the Egyptian Book of the Dead*

ARIS LEGOWSKI

## THE BEGINNING OF THE RECEPTION OF THE BOOK OF THE DEAD

ANCIENT Egypt has widely caused fascination across different time periods and various cultures. Its reception can be traced back to antiquity and has never ceased since. The most recent modern outbursts of "Egyptomania" took place around key events such as the decipherment of the hieroglyphic script by Jean-François Champollion in 1822 and the discovery of Tutankhamun's tomb a hundred years later by Howard Carter and Lord Carnarvon.

The main difference between the reception of ancient Egypt in general and the Book of the Dead (BD) is that, even before the deciphering of the hieroglyphs, the ancient Egyptian visual culture offered many subjects that were referenced in modern culture. A very prominent example is Wolfgang Amadeus Mozart's *Zauberflöte*, in which Egyptian symbols are frequently included due to their use by the Freemasons' movement (Assmann, 2018). Access to the BD, on the other hand, which was a mainly textual corpus and was handled as a distinct piece of literature, remained limited, which is naturally the case for any textual source that cannot be deciphered. Moreover, while scholars of earlier periods were engaged in studies on monumental hieroglyphs and illustrations, the cursive hieratic script would yet remain inaccessible.

Without the knowledge of the ancient Egyptian language and script, any direct reception of the BD as such is difficult to take place and, thus, be identified. This does not mean that people were unable to deal with the BD as a topic, but rather that the BD could not be referenced directly, since the texts were not accessible until after 1822. Whereas the knowledge of the BD as a textual corpus had been lost, certain singular elements, namely the illustrations, and especially the more attested ones such as the judgment scene (cf., Janák, this volume), which also appear in other Egyptian contexts, could still be referenced and recognized. The manuscripts themselves, when unearthed, may have been perceived as some sort of Egyptian religious text whose exact content was impossible to identify and understand.

The modern history of the reception of the BD is marked by the publication of the Ptolemaic manuscript P.Turin 1791 by Karl Richard Lepsius (1842), as well as the publication of the studies on New Kingdom manuscripts by Édouard Naville (1886). It is worth noting that Champollion had previously worked on BD manuscripts, referring to them as "rituel funéraire," but Lepsius's work stands out. His structuring of the Turin papyrus into numbered chapters paved the way for other scholars to study it, to refer to this collection of spells as one distinct corpus, and to thereby make it available to those outside the realm of Egyptology.

Being able to read the Egyptian texts was also the *conditio sine qua non* before translating the Egyptian title of the manuscripts, r3.w pr.t m hrw, "sayings of going forth in daylight." Understanding the title as a connecting element between the spells facilitated recognizing the affiliation of the numerous BD manuscripts with the very same corpus. While Lepsius stated that the similarity of the images, the vignettes, established the connection between the various manuscripts, it was his choice of the modern title "Todtenbuch der Alten Aegypter" ("Book of the Dead of the Ancient Egyptians") that defined the corpus of spells for the reception as such in times to follow.

This chapter will first elaborate on the role of the title of the BD and then introduce the different forms of reception. The following selection of examples is ordered chronologically, because some cases are based on earlier ones and therefore need to be treated accordingly. This kind of referencing occurs across different genres of art. This chapter will focus on only some of the examples of modern BD reception, though many more works deserve attention for their reception of ancient Egypt, sometimes including BD.

## On the Significance of the Title

The choice of a modern title for the BD corpus has proven to be influential in how it has been perceived and received. It is often not clearly distinguishable whether modern reception simply made use of the title "Book of the Dead." However, the keywords "Egyptian," "book" and "dead" clearly provided a large amount of inspiration.

In addition, the term "Todtenbuch," which Lepsius coined, is not without issue, as it was originally used to refer to a list of deceased people in a certain community. These "Books of the Dead" are official documents usually compiled in a church, monastery, or abbey environment. Later examples include the "Totenbuch der Donauschwaben," in which the names of some 60,000 deceased and missing persons were listed shortly after the end of World War II. Similar lists have been written to preserve the names and information of the deceased of concentration camps (e.g., Morsch, Ley, and

Meyer, 1936–1945). Lepsius applied the term "Todtenbuch" to identify the manuscript as belonging to the deceased ("Todten" in German orthography of that time). He introduced this new title in order to challenge Champollion's definition of the BD as a ritual code (Lepsius, 1842: 1–2) and instead refers to a completely different genre of historical sources. As it is convenient, Lepsius's title has been used ever since, even though attempts have been made to introduce the ancient Egyptian title as a *terminus technicus* (Quirke, 2013).

The study of another important funerary text corpus, the so-called Tibetan Book of the Dead, shows how Lepsius's choice influenced other academic fields This is yet another case of a religious text whose original title is different, in this case Bardo Thodol, or "Liberation Through Hearing During the Intermediate State." The Bardo Thodol was in fact named "Book of the Dead" by its publisher, W. Y. Evans-Wentz, who followed the designation of its Egyptian "counterpart" (Dawa-Samdup and Evans-Wentz, 2000). As for the history of reception, there has been surprisingly little confusion between the Egyptian and the Tibetan "books" despite their having been given similar titles. On the other hand, these two texts, while in the broadest sense sharing the genre of funerary literature, do not to have much in common.

## Forms of Modern BD Reception

The modern reception of the BD can be divided into two phases—without and with awareness of the BD corpus. In this chapter I will refer to the first phase as *unconscious reception*. A good example of this is the so-called Apis-Altar, manufactured by Johann Melchior Dinglinger (Syndram, 1999). A Book of the Dead manuscript had been copied on this altar and its illustrations and texts were used for a baroque piece of art with the only knowledge about the content being that it was of Egyptian origin.

The second phase, *conscious reception* of the BD, occurred only after Lepsius's and Naville's editions of the BD and particularly E. A. Wallis Budge's BD translation with notes from 1898 (Budge, 1898), as well as his other works on the BD (Budge, 1895, 1901), continuing the tradition of calling the *pr.t m hrw* "Book of the Dead." This proved to be quite influential since it allowed a broader public outside of the academic world to become aware of the BD and its content, and inspired some artists who specifically referred to Budge as a source for their works.

Reception, even after Budge's translation, did not always stay truthful to the BD, however. Quite often the mere title in connection to ancient Egypt was enough to evoke ideas that forwent any relation to the BD itself. Whether this happened intentionally, with the user ignoring commonly accessible information, or unintentionally simply due to misunderstanding or misinterpretation, this phenomenon is a form of *misconceived BD reception*. This means that the BD was referred to, but without taking into account the then-known information of its content and meaning, and therefore interpreting it as something completely different.

It is important to keep in mind that the BD is not an independent text. It is well embedded in Egyptian religious beliefs, full of mythological material, and also includes ritual content (Kockelmann and Stadler, this volume). Thus, regarding the modern reception of the BD, its content cannot always be separated from more general Egyptian motifs about the afterlife or the deities and their mythological background. One example of such a phenomenon is the judgment scene, which is typically attributed to the BD but is not at all limited to it. Writer Harry Mulisch's use of the judgment scene analyzed by Müller-Roth is just one of many examples (Müller-Roth, 2010: 581).

## Unconscious BD Reception

The Apis-Altar might be the most prominent example of using BD content and even the template of a manuscript without any specific knowledge of the meaning of the BD. Built in the first half of the eighteenth century, it was purchased by Augustus III, Elector of Saxony, King of Poland as well as Grand Duke of Lithuania, in 1738, five years after the death of his predecessor Friedrich August I, better known as "August der Starke" ("Augustus the Strong"). The latter had virtually transformed the treasuries of his residential palace in Dresden into a museum of the baroque era (Syndram, 1999: 3). The aforementioned artwork had been created by the Jeweller of the Court, Johann Melchior Dinglinger. He had provided the court with several elaborate pieces revolving around other specific themes, and this Egypt-themed "altar" was sold by his heirs to the court after he passed away in 1731.

The altar itself is a composite art piece measuring 128 centimeters in height. It is missing a stand and an obelisk on the top, and thus was originally 195 centimeters high and 102.2 centimeters wide in total. Dinglinger used various gems, metals, and ivory to create a tribute to ancient Egyptian art, copying actual Egyptian artifacts but also including imaginative motifs that were attributed to Egypt in the eighteenth century's perception.

It is possible that a description of this piece of art written by the artist himself existed, which could shed some light on the creation process and the origins of inspiration. It would also be a source for a better understanding of the perception of Egypt during the baroque era, but the whereabouts of this document are unknown (Syndram, 1999: 6). The main source, however, for the motifs of the altar is the work of Benedictine Father Bernhard de Montfaucon, who, in 1719, published ten volumes of copperplate engraving titled "L'antiquité expliquée et représentée en figure." This large folio compendium contains approximately 40,000 images on 1,200 plates. In 1724, five additional volumes were published containing a large number of depictions of ancient Egyptian artifacts. While many existing original objects are shown, there are also a considerable number of images copied from other contemporary publications. These images include imaginative depictions of unknown ancient Egyptian buildings (Syndram, 1999: 21–23).

The second, additional volume shows on plate LIV a facsimile of something described by Montfaucon as "Le Calendrier Egyptien" from the belongings of Abbé Fauvel. It bears depictions and demotic writing. This "calendar" was copied by Dinglinger very precisely onto the middle section of the altar and onto gilded silver plates in the background, even including lacunae of Montfaucon's facsimile. Although the text could not be deciphered at the time, it was depicted accurately. Hence, the sequence of depictions is easily recognizable as BD 149, a part of the BD where the deceased encounters liminal entities and regions of the netherworld (Weber, this volume). The interpretations of the text and depictions vary, and there was the possibility of interpreting the chapter as being related to astrological phenomena, although still not exactly a calendar (Lieven, 2000: 16; passim). The fact that there are 12 vignettes with text could have given the impression of a representation of a calendar, while Montfaucon's plate shows that there were more BD chapters to the right and to the left, probably as part of a longer papyrus. Furthermore, there are additional BD fragments depicted on the plate. Neither the manuscript with BD 149 nor the fragments have been identified with any known BD manuscript; they are, therefore, an important attestation of possibly lost BD manuscripts.

## Conscious BD Reception

The BD experienced a significant boost of attention when Budge published his translations and works on the topic. He was also responsible for numerous acquisitions and exhibitions of BD manuscripts for the British Museum in London. Several non-academic writers are known who were familiar with Budge's works and were influenced by it. Louis Zukofsky (see p. 513), for example, lists Budge's translation of the BD in his card catalogue at the index of "A" (Ahearn, 1983: 136). Conrad Aiken (see p. 511) himself mentions in his notes to "The Coming Forth by Day of Osiris Jones" that he was inspired by Budge's publication and incorporated parts of the text almost unchanged into his poem. The heart-spells and the negative confession are expressed by "the books," which are meant to represent Jones's memories and conscience. Other authors like Ezra Pound or James Joyce (see p. 508–10, 511–12) very clearly refer to the BD too, with Budge also appearing to have been their access point to the material. Nevertheless, it is not always clear whether Egyptian or Egyptian-esque motifs were inspired by the BD alone. General Egyptian religious motifs are used in the works mentioned earlier in this chapter; these are prominent in the BD, but could have been observed in other Egyptian sources as well.

### 1909–1912

The American writer and poet Ezra Pound (1885–1972) wrote two poems that refer directly to ancient Egypt and clearly to the BD (Schmidt, 1971, 2008). One is "De Aegypto," published in 1909 as part of *Personae* (Pound, 1926); the title is vague and was changed from the former "Aegupton," but it is known that Pound had been reading works by Budge, so it can be assumed that he was influenced by the latter's translation of the BD. The poem does not mention any papyrus, tomb, or other textual source itself, but rather uses some motifs that can be understood as direct references to some of the most prominent themes of the BD corpus, as for instance in the following passage opening the poem:

> *I, even I, am he who knoweth the roads*
> *Through the sky, and the wind thereof is my body. (Personae 17)*

Several references to the BD composition can be traced in this poem, but its beginning seems to be a close copy of Budge's translation of BD 78. It mentions the knowledge of the hereafter that is mandatory for a justified deceased, as is often stated throughout the BD, and makes reference to the perception of the BD as a guide for the journey through the netherworld. Knowledge is, of course, one of the most important motifs in the BD, specifically the knowledge of those "roads"; various BD chapters portray regions the deceased is to cross or dwell in. BD 78, which is a spell for transformation into a falcon, touches upon two other central motifs: transformation and freedom of movement. Both motifs are continued by the mention of the flying swallows and maintain the idea of flying freely. The continuation of motifs and the sequences of reoccurring motifs are further explored by Weber (this volume).

The "moon on my forehead" refers to the moon god Thoth, who is most prominently represented in the BD (Stadler, 2009). The identification of the deceased with the divine scribe marks a significant motif in Pound's poem, which corresponds nicely not only with the distinguished role of Thoth but also with the deification of the deceased. The latter then takes his own place among the gods and assumes their identities.

The other BD-related poem Pound created is "The Tomb at Akr Çaar," published in 1912. The title already clarifies the setting of a burial place, immediately providing the reader with the knowledge that the location is connected to the passage into the netherworld. The opening verse reads:

> *I am thy soul, Nikoptis*
> *These five millennia, and thy dead eyes*
> *Moved not, nor ever answer my desire,*
> *And thy light limbs, wherethrough I leapt aflame,*
> *Burn not with me nor any saffron thing. (Personae 56)*

The poem can be understood as being from the perspective of the *ba* of the deceased, Nikoptis. Despite the term "soul" being problematic and ambiguous, it has been and is often used as a translation for the ancient Egyptian "*ba*"-concept. The poem refers to the idea of the *ba* hovering above the deceased's body, as described in the BD on several occasions but most prominently in BD 89 and its vignette. It does not, however, consider the Egyptian idea of the *Ba* flying out of the tomb, returning to the deceased, being transcendent, and living between the netherworld and the physical, mummified body. This idea is best known from the vignette of BD 92, but the principle of the *ba* being able to move freely and unrestricted, and not being imprisoned, is present in various BD chapters, for example 91. Both Pound's poem and the Book of the Dead clearly refer to a wish for the aforementioned freedom of movement.

## 1924

Howard Phillips Lovecraft (1819–1937) invented a whole cosmos of beings from outer space, "The Old Ones," lying dormant (or sometimes not so dormant) underneath the earth's surface, influencing humanity, gathering worshippers, and generally causing terrifying events. Lovecraft is considered by many to be the founder of the horror genre. He liked to refer to mysterious but real, known facts and places, such as the pyramids or ancient Memphis, and to add his own invented historical "facts" and arcane objects. He was fascinated by ancient Egypt and the Oriental world, and thus many of his stories use them as a setting or as background material. Hieroglyphs and pseudo-Egyptian names occur in several instances, but there is no direct mention of the BD (cf., Reinhard, 2008). However, Lovecraft can, in a way, be considered responsible for part of the (flawed) perception of the BD today. As part of his lore, he invented a book he called "Necronomicon ex Mortis," first mentioned in the story "The Hound" (Lovecraft, 1924). It is a grimoire of arcane magic and is sometimes referred to as "The Book of the Dead." In this fictional universe, it is not an Egyptian text but rather a Sumerian one, and a "mad Arab," Abdul Alhazred, supposedly wrote it after having visited ancient places, among them the catacombs underneath the ancient city of Memphis. This Book contains secret wisdom about the gods, namely the old ones, and about how to summon them. A "Book of Thoth" is also mentioned in the *Necronomicon*, but Lovecraft never reveals many details about it in order to keep up the suspense. Allegedly, very few copies of this grimoire were created; one of them currently resides in the British Museum, which also hosts one of the largest BD manuscript collections worldwide. Lovecraft's *Necronomicon*, however, also contains a quote that became somewhat of a motto for his readers: "That is not dead which can eternal lie. And with strange aeons even death may die." Although the words are not from the BD, the vague allusions to it and his commingling of arcane objects and motifs of life, death, and the afterlife may have blurred the understanding of the technical term "Book of the Dead" regarding ancient Egypt. It is no wonder that when the *Necronomicon* became very popular across works of other authors too, it fits well into the trend of occultism at the beginning of the twentieth century.

As another example of how this idea of a "Book of the Dead" occurs in later fiction, the *Necronomicon* appears in the *Living Dead* franchise, which includes films, comics, and other media. In this horror universe, it is also a fictional Sumerian version of the Book of the Dead releasing demonic spirits possessing humans and opening a portal to a world, where undead people reside, the so-called Deadites.

At this point, the term "Book of the Dead" is at least partly understood as an account that enables the resurrection and revival of the dead. By no means does this reflect the true ancient Egyptian function of the composition, which is about entering eternity, following the life cycle of the sun god, and becoming Osiris and part of the divine sphere.

## 1931

The extremely productive American writer Conrad Potter Aiken (1889–1973), who maintained a friendship with Ezra Pound, wrote, among other works with references to ancient cultures, the poem "The Coming forth by Day of Osiris Jones" (Aiken, 1931). The poem is rather episodic and thus structurally reminiscent of the BD, of which the chapters and titles vary in length. Several people, places, and objects, among them an Egyptian obelisk, from the life of Osiris Jones, an "anybody" or everyman character, appear throughout the poem and speak of their relationship to the deceased. "Jones" serves as an everyman's name, as it is one of the most popular surnames in the English language. By putting "Osiris" in front of the person's name, Aiken accurately implemented the Egyptian idea and one omnipresent motif of the BD that everybody bears the name of Osiris in addition to their own in the afterlife. In fact, several passages can be interpreted as more or less inspired by the BD: The episode "Report Made by a Medical Student to Whom Was Assigned for Inspection the Case of Mr. Jones" is an autopsy scene describing the limbs, which can be understood as an allusion to BD 42, of which the theme is the deification of the limbs. Toward the end, actual books are speaking what appears to be inspired by the so-called negative confession represented in BD 125, which consists of a list of the misconducts any ancient Egyptian deceased would distance himself from and deny having ever committed. While the books and their negative confession serve as a representation of Osiris Jones's conscience, the people and objects appearing in the poem are parts of his memories. The BD does not make any reference to the deceased's life on earth, although it mentions his name, title, and family members. The negative confession, though not always listed in the same way, is formulaic rather than an actual testimony of the deceased's individual acts during his lifetime. The source the author used, however, is well established as Aiken himself mentions Budge in his note to the poem.

## 1939

James Joyce's (1882–1941) remarkable book, *Finnegans Wake*, deserves much closer attention than it can receive here, for the simple reason of its complexity. Troy (1976), Rose (1982), and Bishop (1993) have analyzed the BD themes in the *Wake* in detail. It is a significant work that took Joyce 17 years to complete before it was published in 1939, and is regarded as one of his masterpieces. The *Wake* is in a way Joyce's "own Irish book of the dead" (Rose, 1982: 1), and he specifically used the Egyptian source material to express the themes presented in it. The cyclical structure, the highly artificial language, and the countless allusions not only make it a challenge for the reader but offer many opportunities of interpretation. Several studies have been undertaken trying to decipher and analyze Joyce's language, motifs, and narratives. The beginning features the deceased, Irishman Tim Finnegan, who dies by accident, having fallen from a ladder, and is awakened during his wake by the sound of a bottle of whiskey hitting his casket. From there on, the story turns into a journey between life and death with multitudinous related themes.

Death, the process of coming to life again after death, the intermediate state, and the cyclic character of those conditions correspond closely to the Egyptian beliefs regarding the afterlife. Joyce's work and the BD also bear structural similarities. The application of the cyclic structure also found in the BD, in the sense that many motifs re-occur frequently without being redundant, is the most notable structural similarity. Furthermore, both the *Wake* and the BD consist of several single parts that are more or less connected through particular motifs. The characters change names throughout Joyce's story, whereas in the BD deities or other beings are referred to by different epithets or bear more than just one designation. The difficulties of distinguishing between several allusions and different beings in the BD mirrors the challenges readers face when engaging in *Finnegans Wake*. The "main character" of the BD, the deceased, also undergoes a journey starting with his "wake" in both senses, his funerary procession depicted in the vignette of BD 1 and his awakening, the "going forth by day," which is the key idea of the BD. The deceased, like the characters in Joyce's work, while still the same person, is featured in different manifestations, namely his *ba*, *ka*, and heart, and changes forms several times, becoming Osiris and, most importantly, taking the shape of various animals and the identities of other deities. The clearest indication of the kind of source material Joyce was drawing from is, however, the language used in his work. Not only is the *Wake* written in a highly artificial language that is, just like in the BD, full of allusions to various concepts, narratives, and symbolisms, but Joyce also used the authentic ancient Egyptian language, among several other languages, words, and names. In this author's typical style, certain terms are often changed and reformed, but their Egyptian origin often remains recognizable.

The similarities in structure, language, and content make *Finnegans Wake* a fine, if not the densest and most elaborate, example of BD reception. Just as the allusions in both works offer a vast amount of material for interpretation, so both may be regarded as sources for repeated studies to provide new insights with every new approach.

## 1969

The Egyptian movie *The Night of Counting the Years* from 1969, also known as *The Mummy (Al-Mummia)*, directed by Shadi Abdel Salam, tells the story of the Abd el-Rasul clan and the discovery of the Royal Cache, TT 320. The movie begins with a tracking shot over a papyrus with, among others, the texts and vignettes of mourning women from BD 1, the 42 judges of BD 125, the Lake of Fire of BD 126, the amulet chapters (BD 156–160), and the mummification in BD 151. It is, however, clearly a collage of these elements and not an original manuscript, as it also repeats in a loop. The text cited simultaneously to the shot is BD 21, the opening of the mouth, and the passage of BD 25 about the "night of counting the years," which the film's English title references. The words are revealed to be read by scholars around Gaston Maspero in the Museum of Cairo, and the director of the "Service des Antiquités d'Egypte" starts to elaborate on the importance of the deceased's name being known so that their identity will remain intact. This is a somewhat fitting introduction to this story about the problems of tomb robbery and the violation of the deceased's burial place and equipment. BD manuscripts share the same fate as other funerary goods, as they have often been taken from the tombs and sold illegally. Furthermore, the BD was an essential part of the belongings that accompanied the deceased, since it contains knowledge, ensures provision, and grants protection, even if the other funerary equipment was lost.

## 1978

Writer Louis Zukofsky (1904–1978) listed Budge's BD translation in his card catalogue of notes he created for his major work "A" (published 1978) and probes from it at the closing of Chapter 14 (Zukofsky, 1969). The word "Egypt" already occurs at the beginning of the chapter. At the end, the poet actually mentions a manuscript having been obtained, which is said to be a colored facsimile of a papyrus; the Egyptian title "Pert-em-heru," as well as the translation "coming forth by day" are given; and Budge's name appears.

## 1995

In direct reference to Ezra Pound's poem "De Aegypto," Polish composer Zbiginiev Antoni Preisner created an adaptation for musical theater, which was performed and recorded by Telewizja Polska S.A. as a 45-minute-long expression theater piece in 1995. It was directed by Jolanta Ptaszyńska, and, despite its very abstract nature, it uses numerous BD themes. Other than the content, the execution is most striking. The viewer sees in one part, for example, a scene filmed from above. Horizontal register lines are visible, similar to layouts found in some vignettes, such as BD 110, on which several Egyptians are standing, walking, and climbing from one register to another. In this case, the reference to the BD takes the actual material source into account, which could be a papyrus or a tomb wall. Besides creating the illusion of a two-dimensional BD vignette, this scene implements the idea of a journey and especially the concept of permeability in the BD, which is important in regard to the ability of the deceased, or more precisely of his *ba*, to move freely. Additionally, the whole musical-theatrical piece is a very impressive example of a modern approach of the fine arts to perform aspects of the

BD, of which the ritual and liturgical character has often been emphasized (Assmann, 2003: 277); Gee (2006) gives an overview of the liturgical influences in the BD.

The medium of comics may occasionally also present direct and even accurate references to BD themes, as in the case of "Judge Dredd Book of the Dead" (1995). In this futuristic story, the eponymous main character travels to Egypt as part of an exchange program, where he encounters a culture that has returned to certain ancient customs. Most notably, he witnesses a mummification ritual with specific ancient Egyptian details, for example the use of canopic jars. The jars, as well as the sons of Horus, appear throughout the BD both visually and textually. Furthermore, other images and beliefs about the afterlife are mentioned, such as the "fields of Iaru," which appear in BD 110 (Álvarez Sosa, this volume). This example of pop culture shows that, despite the story centering on the mummy/horror/monster cliché, extravagant science fiction stories can still make use of Egyptian and BD themes in an accurate way and somehow stay faithful to the source material.

Other comic books like "Batman: Book of the Dead" (1999) use the modern name of the BD but make no reference to it as a source; instead, they simply use it to advertise an ancient Egypt-themed story. The mention remains ambiguous, since "book" here might refer to the comic volume itself and "dead" might hint at ancient Egypt as a setting of tombs and the idea of the afterlife, but the allusions do not go further than these general ideas.

## 1998

The metal band Nile, which was formed in 1993 and describes their style as "Ithyphallic Metal," are greatly inspired by ancient cultures, mainly Egyptian and Sumerian. Many of their lyrics contain references to or complete passages from ancient texts. As for the Egyptian sources, the musicians often draw inspiration from the Book of Gates and the BD. They also mix these ancient themes with Lovecraftian lore, with the result that it is not always easy for the listener to discern genuine Egyptian source material. A few examples of direct BD references include the following: "The Opening of the Mouth" from the album *Amongst the Catacombs of Nephren-Ka* (1998) cites from the ritual also featured in BD 1 and in the texts of BD 21 and 22; "Chapter for Transforming into a Snake" from the album *Black Seeds of Vengeance* (2000) is named after BD 87, while the lyrics are inspired by BD 88, the BD chapter of transforming into a crocodile; "The Blessed Dead" from the album *In Their Darkened Shrines* (2002) tells the story of the "unblessed," and thus references the idea of being, or in this case not being, mꜣꜥ-ḫrw, justified, in the afterlife. The song also mentions the "Sekhet Aaru," the fields of dwellings or fields of offerings most prominently featured in the text and vignette of BD 110 (Álvarez Sosa, this volume), the "Weighing of the Heart," BD 30, and the judgment scene, including the devourer "Ammitt Who Teareth the Wicked to Pieces." The song interprets the fear of the ancient Egyptians of not becoming justified. In the BD, the deceased's justified status cannot be stressed and mentioned often enough to ensure the proper transition into afterlife.

The Japanese progressive rock band Ars Nova released their album *Reu nu Pert em Hru* in 1998. This is another one of the very few cases in which a direct reference to the actual Egyptian title of the BD is made. The whole album is BD themed, featuring Anubis and *udjat*-eyes on the cover of the Japanese edition, and with some of the song titles being named after BD motifs. Those include BD 125, "The 42 Gods," chapter 110, "Field of Iaru," the judgment scene, "The Judgment of Osiris." and "Ani's Heart and Maat's Feather." The latter indicates the BD manuscript of Ani, P.London BM EA 10470, as the primary source of inspiration. The BD reference, although it stays true to the original source material by quoting the Egyptian title of the BD, is limited to the song names, as the music is instrumental.

## 1999

In the 1999 movie *The Mummy*, directed by Stephen Sommers and featuring what has become one of the classic horror creatures, the Book of the Dead makes a brief but nonetheless important appearance. The film is an adaptation of the 1932 horror classic by Karl Freund and starring Boris Karloff, but apart from its title and the fact that the mummy who is brought back to life is named Imhotep, the movies do not have much in common. Instead, Sommers' take on the mummy theme features elements of both action and comedy. The version of the BD that appears in the movie is a codex-type document with thick, heavy pages, presumably made from metal, and it is supposed to "give life" to the dead. Its counterpart, the "Book of Ra," is said to take life away, in this case the life of the movie's villain, the high priest Imhotep. Despite the book appearing as a codex, the brief view the viewer sees of one specific page reveals that this book's content is actually genuine BD material. The mummification scene of BD 151 is shown to be carved into the metal page, complete with the vignettes showing Anubis taking care of the mummy and the sons of Horus standing in the corners, although it seems that two of them are depicted as rearing cobras. It makes sense that the director refers to mummification and the idea of "giving life" in this movie, although in this case the implementation of "giving life" is quite far from the ancient Egyptian idea of "going forth by day."

## 2006

A notable project by cartoonist and illustrator Rick Griffin (2006) is a short, comic-style story introducing the reader to the BD's judgment scene. It is written and designed from the perspective of the deceased entering the halls of the two Maat goddesses, being guided by the god Anubis. The background shows a facsimile of the BD papyrus of Ani (P.London BM EA 10470, plates 5–7) decorating the walls. Parts of the vignettes of chapters BD 1 and 17 and the texts of BD 1, 17, 21, 22, and 72 are used, although the short story is entirely about BD 30, the judgment. By using original BD material, however, the artist manages to break down the text and the vignette of the judgment scene as it appears in

BD manuscripts and simultaneously merge them together in a new way, literally taking the reader into the BD.

## 2012

The BD has not been absent from the phenomenon of internet memes. In 2012, a very specific entity appearing in the BD found its way into Japanese pop culture. Following an exhibition on ancient Egypt at the Mori Art Museum in Tokyo and the Fukuoka Museum of Art, where P.London BM EA 10554 (P.Greenfield) was displayed, visitors, who had noticed the depiction of Medjed in the vignette of 17 (Cariddi, 2018), developed an interest in the entity. The peculiar image and Medjed's features mentioned in the text of BD 17, namely "shooting from his eyes," inspired people to create all sorts of fan art including drawings, manga, figures, and even pastries. The entity's popularity grew through social media platforms and ultimately appeared several video games. In the mobile game "Soratobu Medjed-niisan," Medjed is seen flying through a maze resembling the inside of a tomb or pyramid; the online game "Puzzle & Dragons" shows a figure named Medjedra, who is described as a guardian of Osiris; and the distinctive entity also appears in the MMORPG (massive multiplayer online role-playing game) "Aura Kingdom" under the name "Nakama"; and in his own animated series, "Kamigami no Ki," Medjed is featured with his "fellow deities" Re, Anubis, and Bastet. There are other similar appearances, which quite impressively show how a minor entity on which not much information is provided by ancient sources has evolved into a deity to be mentioned among other major gods, at least in Japanese pop culture.

While in most adaptations of the Medjed motif the peculiar image and its features appear to be the main reason for its attractiveness, the video game "Persona 5," released in 2016, also makes reference to the BD as a textual source (see Salvador, 2017). The story features a group of hackers calling themselves "Medjed" and giving orders in what might be called a typical BD text style. Their quotes refer to key BD motifs, including the passing of judgment and the elimination of evil, thus merging the name of the entity itself with the overall idea of its source material. In this manner, Medjed might be regarded as a representative for the BD as a whole. It was the peculiar depiction that drew attention in the first place, but the entity does not appear detached from but rather well embedded in its original background and interactions with other entities.

## 2014

Set in Victorian England, another piece of horror fiction makes use of the BD in a rather unusual way in the TV series *Penny Dreadful*. In the first episode, a body is found with hieroglyphs etched beneath its skin. The text is later identified by an Egyptologist as the BD. While the story, which follows classic characters of Victorian horror literature, does not offer any more references to or details on the actual BD, the location of the mentioned BD text is peculiar. The BD in ancient Egypt provided essential knowledge for the deceased and was, therefore, often placed close to the body. BD manuscripts were sometimes wrapped around mummified bodies, and BD content can also frequently be found on mummy wrappings (Kockelmann, 2008). Although BD texts have never been found on human skin, their proximity to the body itself appears to have been integral to the BD's effectiveness.

## 2016

The ancient Egypt–themed fantasy action movie *Gods of Egypt*, released in 2016, is a reimagining of the eponymous gods as counterparts to the popular superhero franchises. It does not have much to offer in terms of faithful historical or mythological aspects, and, to be fair, does not intend to do so, but two details should nevertheless be highlighted regarding the BD. First, there is a scene showing Horus visiting his father Re, on the sun barque, who is eternally battling Apophis. This central Egyptian idea about the circular journey of the sun god also appears in the BD in several instances. The deceased is supposed to join the divine company of the sun god and take part in the battle against Apophis's attacks. The movie tries to highlight the visually intriguing aspects of the scene, as the sun barque is indeed flying through the nocturnal sky, or more precisely through space, orbiting the earth, which is depicted as a disc. This might not represent the exact image the ancient Egyptians held to be true, but it is certainly an interesting take on the sun barque motif from a modern perspective using science fiction elements.

Another scene that implements BD content even more explicitly is one in which the judgment is shown. In this interpretation, an endless line of deceased is passing the judges, who stand at either side of the queue and deliver their verdicts. When a deceased person arrives at an edge, they are either permitted access to the afterlife or thrown into oblivion. The scales with the feather of *maat* are shown, with the major difference to the actual Egyptian beliefs being (Janák, this volume) that, instead of their heart, treasures brought by the deceased are weighed against the feather. It appears that only the wealthy are permitted into the afterlife. Despite this practice being completely non-Egyptian, the visuals in this scene are interesting; for instance, the judges appear to have been mummified and sport Egyptian headwear. The whole scene is dark and very grim, almost black and white, which is the complete opposite of what is shown in BD vignettes featuring the judgment. There, the gods accompany and help the deceased, and often colored depictions show the whole palette available. The fear of not being granted an afterlife by Maat, the judges, and Osiris meant a great deal to ancient Egyptians. The depictions show the successful passing with the deceased rejoicing as their hearts are found even with the symbol of truth and world order. Hence, the scene in the movie completely disregards the idea of the source material and instead displays the idea of a Final Judgment Day—another idea often associated with the BD judgment scene by laymen nowadays. However, the concept of paying off one's sins with treasures does not appear in ancient Egypt but seems to be influenced by the idea of selling one's indulgences in medieval times.

## Conclusion

Allusions to the BD as well as direct references can be found across all forms of art. In some cases, the portrayals are less than true to the source material, and in some cases even misconceived, while in others, the artists demonstrate a thorough preoccupation with its content and character. In any case, it is up to the recipient to decide whether a work inspired by the BD is successful or not in what it tries to accomplish. Clearly, the BD appears to be as present as other well-established motifs from ancient Egypt in its reception, ranging from high literature to the phenomena of Egyptomania. As a final note and nod to the influence of the BD, it should be kept in mind that Egyptomania arguably can hardly be imagined without the discovery of the tomb of Tutankhamun. In fact, Tutankhamun's mask is rarely absent from any visual references to ancient Egypt in general; although its back side is seldom visible, it contains parts of the text of the mummification, BD 151. Therefore, in a way, any depiction or mention of the famous mask is a form of unconscious BD reception.

This chapter has attempted not only to present some of the most important forms of BD reception, like Joyce's *Finnegans Wake*, but also to raise an awareness of less obvious references and those in generally lesser-known genres. Certainly, the BD corpus will continue to appear in new pieces of art of all kinds, offering new ways of approach and thereby influencing the perception of the BD and its motifs of life and death. At this point, the reception of the BD has already developed a life of its own.

## Bibliography

Ahearn, B. (1983). *Zukofsky's "A": An Introduction* (Berkeley; London: University of California Press).
Aiken, C (1931). *The Coming Forth by Day of Osiris Jones* (New York: Scribner).
Assmann, J. (2003). *Tod und Jenseits im Alten Ägypten* (München: C. H. Beck).
Assmann, J. (2018). *Die Zauberflöte: Oper und Mysterium* (München: Hanser, Carl).
Bishop, J. (1993). *Joyce's Book of the Dark: Finnegan's Wake*. Reprint. Mark H Ingraham Prize Ser. (Madison; Chicago: University of Wisconsin Press).
Budge, E. A. T. W. (1895). *The Book of the Dead: The Papyrus of Ani in the British Museum* (London: British Museum).
Budge, E. A. T. W. (1898). *The Book of the Dead, the Chapters of Coming Forth by Day: I: the Egyptian Text in Hieroglyphic Edited from Numerous Papyri, II: an English Translation with Introduction, Notes Etc., III: a Vocabulary in Hieroglyphic to the Theban Recension of the Book of the Dead*, 3 vols. (London: Kegan Paul, Trench, Trübner).

Budge, E. A. T. W. (1901). *The Book of the Dead: An English Translation of the Chapters, Hymns, Etc., of the Theban Recension, with Introduction, Notes, etc*, 3 vols. (London: Keagan Paul, Trench, Trübner).

Cariddi, I. (2018). "Reinventing the Afterlife: The curious Figure of Medjed in the Book of the Dead." In *Proceedings of the Fifth International Congress for Young Egyptologists. Contributions to the Archeology of Egypt, Nubia and the Levant 6*, edited by A. Kalil-bacher and E. Priglinger, 197–205 (Vienna: Austrian Academy of Sciences Press).

Dawa-Samdup, K. and Evans-Wentz, W. Y. (2000). *The Tibetan Book of the Dead, or, The After-Death Experiences on the Bardo Plane: According to Lama Kazi Dawa Samdup's English rendering*, 4th ed. (Oxford: Oxford University Press).

Gee, J. L. (2006). "The Use of the Daily Temple Liturgy in the Book of the Dead." In *Totenbuch-Forschungen: Gesammelte Beiträge des 2. Internationalen Totenbuch-Symposiums Bonn, 25. bis 29. September 2005*. Studien zum Altägyptischen Totenbuch 11, edited by B. Backes, I. Munro, and S. Stöhr, 73–86 (Wiesbaden: Harrassowitz).

Griffin, R. (2006). "Book of the Dead." http://www.deviantart.com/rickgriffin/art/Book-of-the-Dead-cover-32290016.

Joyce, J. (1939). *Finnegans Wake* (London: Faber and Faber).

Kockelmann, H. (2008). *Untersuchungen zu den späten Totenbuch-Hand-schriften auf Mumienbinden, Band I.1–2: Die Mumienbinden und Leinenamulette des memphitischen Priesters Hor; Band II: Handbuch zu den Mumienbinden und Leinenamuletten*. SAT 12 (Wiesbaden: Harrassowitz).

Lepsius, K. R. (1842). *Das Todtenbuch der Ägypter nach dem hieroglyphischen Papyrus in Turin* (Leipzig [Neudruck: Osnabrück 1969]: Georg Wigand).

von Lieven, A. (2000). *Der Himmel über Esna: Eine Fallstudie zur religiösen Astronomie in Ägypten am Beispiel der kosmologischen Decken- und Architravinschriften im Tempel von Esna*. Ägyptologische Abhandlungen 64 (Wiesbaden: Harrassowitz).

Lovecraft, H. P. (1924). "The Hound." *Weird Tales* 3(2): 50–52, 78.

Morsch, G., Ley, A., and Meyer, W. (1936–1945). "Totenbuch KZ Sachsenhausen 1936–1945." Bearbeitet von: Hans Coppi, Frauke Kerstens, Iris Schwarz. http://www.stiftung-bg.de/totenbuch.

Müller-Roth, M. (2010). "'Viele Schriftsteller sind Diebe': Harry Mulisch und Ägypten." In *Honi soit qui mal y pense*. OLA 194, edited by H. Knuf, Chr. Leitz, D. von Recklinghausen, 575–84 (Leuven: Peeters).

Naville, É. (1886). *Das aegyptische Todtenbuch der XVIII. bis XX. Dynastie*, 3 vols. (Berlin: A. Asher & Co.), http://www.etana.org/sites/default/files/coretexts/14507.pdf.

Pound, E. (1926). *Personae: The Collected Poems of Ezra Pound* (London: New Directions).

Quirke, S. (2013). *Going Out in Daylight—Prt M Hrw: The Ancient Egyptian Book of the Dead*. Golden House Publications Egyptology 20 (London: Golden House Publications).

Reinhard, K. (2008). " . . . von den allerbizarrsten Hieroglyphen: Ägyptische Motive bei H.P. Lovecraft." In *Miscellanea in honorem Wolfhart Westendorf*. Göttinger Miszellen Beihefte 3, edited by C. Peust, 83–108 (Göttingen: Seminar für Ägyptologie und Koptologie der Univiversität).

Rose, D. (1982). *Chapters of Coming Forth by Day*. A Wake Newsletter Monograph 6 (Colchester: A Wake Newsletter Press).

Salvador, R. B. (2017). "Medjed: from Ancient Egypt to Japanese Pop Culture." *Journal of Geek Studies* 4(2): 10–20. jgeekstudies.org/2017/08/15/medjed-from-ancient-egypt-to-japanese-pop-culture/.

Schmidt, G. (1971). "De Aegypto: Ezra Pound und das ägyptische Totenbuch." *Arcadia—Internationale Zeitschrift für Literaturwissenschaft / International Journal for Literary Studies* 6(1–3): 297–301.

Schmidt, G. (2008). "Voices from Ancient Egypt? Persona, Text, and Context in 'De Aegypto' and 'The Tomb at Akr Çaar.'" *Quaderni di Palazzo Serra* 15: 56–64.

Stadler, M. A. (2009). *Weiser und Wesir: Studien zu Vorkommen, Rolle und Wesen des Gottes Thot im ägyptischen Totenbuch*. Orientalische Religionen in der Antike—Ägypten, Israel, Alter Orient 1 (Tübingen: Mohr Siebeck).

Syndram, D. (1999). *Die Ägyptenrezeption unter August dem Starken: Der "Apis-Altar" Johann Melchior Dinglingers*. Antike Welt; Sonderband; Zaberns Bildbände zur Archäologie (Mainz: Philipp von Zabern).

Troy, M. L. (1976). *Mummeries of Resurrection: The Cycle of Osiris in Finnegans Wake*. Acta Universitatis Upsaliensis, Studia Anglistica Upsaliensia 26 (Uppsala; Stockholm: Almqvist och Wiksell).

Weber, F. (2016). "Diegetic Lists in the Early Egyptian 'Book of the Dead': A Contextual Analysis of Demonic Entities in Private Second Millennium Manuscripts" (Dissertation, Swansea University).

Zukofsky, L. (1969). *"A" 13–21* (London: Jonathan Cape).

CHAPTER 26

.....................................................................................................

# TRANSLATING THE BOOK OF THE DEAD

.....................................................................................................

BURKHARD BACKES

## Daring Imperfection: Translation in Egyptology

.....................................................................................................

The title of this chapter may appear ambivalent to some readers and, truthfully, it is. Indeed, the following pages only minimally pursue the goal of providing a handy guide to the most important translations of the Book of the Dead (suggested reading at the end of the chapter). Rather, their main intention is to point out the methodological considerations and decisions one must make when being confronted with the task of translating texts from the Book of the Dead. Being aware of these should also help the reader of the Book of the Dead in modern translation to better recognize a translation's peculiarities and thereby enable them to use it on a professional level.

"Translating the Book of the Dead" is certainly not a subject that could be looked at as a separate Egyptological subdiscipline. Any translation of the entire corpus (insofar as this is possible—see the discussion on pp. 534–5), as well as of individual spells, passages, or even short quotes of only one or two sentences, is linked to the progress in the study of the Book of the Dead and to the translator's more general understanding of the Egyptian religious texts. Moreover, the translation of the Book of the Dead reflects issues that one encounters with the translation not only of any Egyptian text but also of texts from other ancient languages that have had to be decoded in the modern age. To the best of my knowledge, the number of Egyptological publications tackling the complex challenge of a sound translation from a systematic point of view is very small, currently not exceeding a handful (Toro-Rueda, 2003: 51–54 on translating metaphors; Hannig, Vomberg, and Witthuhn, 2006; Warnemünde and Hannig, 2007; Warburton, 2007; Blöbaum, 2011); to these, a number of brief statements can be added (some quoted by Blöbaum, 2011; some more are cited on the following pages). This chapter is not meant to fill this long-existing gap, nor does it aim at introducing the reader to translation theories. The publication of two handbooks of Translation Studies within only a few years (Malmkjaer and Windle, 2011; Millán and Bartrina, 2013) illustrates the dimensions of the subject. However, before discussing the points that are specifically relevant to the translation of the Book of the Dead and related texts, a short review on translation issues and some programmatic remarks will be in order.

To begin with, we have to consider briefly what purpose the translation of an Egyptian text can or should fulfill. For one, it must enable fellow Egyptologists to understand the translator's understanding of a given text: how have they identified not only words, but also groups of words (a point stressed by Quirke, 1998: viii), morphology, syntax, and finally the meaning(s) of the entire text and its parts? But ideally, a translation from one language to another should do more: it should create a new text that transports not only the literal meaning of each word, phrase, or sentence, but also the intentions of the original's creator(s). This includes more than "meaning/sense." A good translation also does justice to the register of the original language, to its sound, to its stylistic devices, and so forth. Similar to what Marguerite Yourcenar has demanded concerning the language of historical novels, one could define the good translator's aim as providing "authenticity in tone" (Yourcenar, 1983: 36), in addition to authenticity in meaning. It is well known that even translations from one modern language to another cannot perfectly fulfill this task. Translating always means daring imperfection. It also goes without saying that the case is considerably more difficult for dead languages, especially reconstructed ones such as ancient Egyptian. Therefore, a general statement about the "very amateurish" level of Egyptological translation practice compared to other philological disciplines (Hannig, Vomberg, and Witthuhn, 2006: 67 and 68 with footnote 5) is, in my eyes, an exaggeration. Translations from Egyptian cannot, of course, be compared with those from English, Russian, Japanese, or even Latin and Greek. A comparison with translations from other reconstructed languages, for example Sumerian or Hittite, would probably lead to a more balanced judgment. Moreover, a number of colleagues both living and deceased do or did care about translation beyond correct philological analysis—others obviously don't and did not (see Blöbaum, 2011: 40 with footnote 17). Short remarks here and there indicate that the majority of Egyptologists are not entirely unaware of the problem, whether or not one agrees with their individual conclusions. But it is true that the systematics of translation have so far not found a place in the Egyptological curriculum of any university. A definition of the aims and limitations of a translation must be an early step of the procedure, which, in a discipline like ours, highly depends on the translator's limits of understanding the original text (e.g., Blöbaum, 2011: 43 with footnote 29).

To be aware of these limits is of primary importance. Our knowledge of the Egyptian language, in spite of our capacity to provide translations of virtually every text from ancient Egypt, is and always will be very incomplete (e.g., Quack, 2011a: 539–40 with footnote 31). The same is true for our knowledge of ancient Egyptian culture. This trivial point must be mentioned here first because the resulting limitations are fundamental. As indicated in the preceding paragraph, a fitting translation is more than the result of a thorough philological analysis, but it demands a supplementary working step (Hannig, Vomberg, and Witthuhn, 2006: 68). To be more precise, it is an intercultural act (Blöbaum, 2011: 37 and 42 quoting Warburton, 2007: 264). As a consequence, we often have no secure basis to decide between all theoretically, that is grammatically, possible alternatives. Instead of choosing the translation that "makes the most sense," we are still looking for this "sense"—which is one main reason why our discipline has a right to exist. We would, of course, like to resort to a more detailed set of grammatical rules—specific use of forms or elements of the lexicon—or other evidence, not necessarily textual evidence (cf. Warburton, 2007), that would allow us to make a decision in cases where at first sight several options must be considered. It can indeed be demanded that a thorough textual analysis include such linguistic indices into the argument (cf. Quack, 2011b: 674–75). But often enough, these rules do not seem to have existed; at least they have not yet been identified. The same is true for the material world that surrounds the generation of every "text" and adds to its meaning (see Quirke, 1998: vii–viii).

For the Book of the Dead, several authors have clearly stated the problem of the translator's insufficient knowledge (Allen, 1960: 6; Faulkner, 1972: xv; Hornung, 1979: 17; Verhoeven, 1993: 73; Stadler, 2009: 40–47). Apart from an unknown number of passages that are difficult because of their choice of words and/or unclear mythical allusions, it is not even clear in many cases whether a passage is to be understood as a wish (optative), as an announcement (future), or as a statement (present or perfect). In a number of funerary texts, especially of a later date, the future tense seems to be the preferable option in the majority of cases (cf. Smith, 2009: 53–55; Stadler, 2003: 114–15); this is a compelling invitation to more closely investigate the question for Book of the Dead texts.

This being so, it is clear that the demand for "good" adaptations—translations that do justice to the Egyptian original in the way outlined before—can be fulfilled only to a small extent. A biased approach to each translation process is thus unavoidable. The following three aspects of language and text are probably the most crucial points of reference between which the translator is forced to find an individual compromise:

1. Meaning: What does the text actually say? What is the exact choice of Egyptian words? What are their grammatical forms? There is some danger in choosing too-general terms for translating single words in order to avoid mistakes (Hannig, Vomberg, and Witthuhn, 2006: 69). Additionally, the literal transfer of a grammatical form can sound odd or even be wrong.
2. Grammar: A translation might allow colleagues to guess the structure of the Egyptian sentence. Again, a direct transfer from one language to another bears the danger of a result that does not conform to the written and unwritten rules of the target language.
3. Style, register, ambiance, etc.: These cannot be adumbrated without a certain extent of free adaptation, with the disadvantage that a certain level of guessing is unavoidable.

It is true that the first two approaches, a combination of both, respectively, are still predominant in many publications, especially with German scholars. Their results, albeit impeccable from a purely grammatical point of view, are often not satisfying from an aesthetic perspective. But this is not a question of taste alone (cf. Quack, 2011a: 542–43 with footnote 43; Warburton, 2007: 264). Non-Egyptologist readers in particular can get a misleading impression of the Egyptians' way of expressing themselves when words are translated too literally or when the Egyptian word order and/or word classes are imitated (see also von Recklinghausen, 2012: 309). This aspect is of special relevance here, since the Book of the Dead is definitely among the Egyptian texts that do have a readership beyond the world of academic Egyptology; this is one reason for the existence of the present book. Even if literal translations may be considered helpful by some Egyptologists, more precise information still must be transported by other tools—transcription, commentary notes, interlinear morphemic glossing; these may leave some doubt as to whether staying as close as possible to the Egyptian text is really the best solution. In any case, it is difficult to see how the general public gains any advantage from this practice (Blöbaum, 2011: 41 and 45; Hannig, Vomberg, and Witthuhn, 2006: 67–68). Moreover, a very literal translation almost automatically forces the translator toward imprecisions in the vocabulary and syntax of the language into which the text is translated. As a result, such translations, although seeking a maximum of precision, overinterpret the traceable meaning of the original text to still be termed as "correct." This is not to say that free adaptation cannot obscure the sense of the original, either (e.g., Quack, 2011: 542). Certainly, opinions will always diverge regarding to what extent a smoothly running modern text is possible without straying too far from the original words; for example, the frequent practice of adding verbs in order to translate a preposition idiomatically in different contexts (cf. the critical remarks by Winand, 2013: 338–39). In addition, free adaptations need not sound elegant; rather, they should do justice to the original, which contemporary recipients may not have considered "elegant" at all. However, these obstacles are not reasons to abstain from striving for an elegant translation, especially when we remember that our knowledge and literary competence are too rudimentary in any case to allow for an adaptation that could truly claim to be "free." Often enough, staying close to the original wording is the only possibility translators have as long as they do not attempt to bring in too much of their personal imagination (cf. Parkinson, 1997: xii; Parkinson, 2012: 17–18).

What also must be considered are the connotations of individual words or phrases. Knowledge of them is mandatory to comprehend the entire meaning of the text in question. Therefore, it is clear that no ambitious translation of a text from a culture so remote from ours as ancient Egypt can do without explanations. These might disturb the spontaneous contact between the reader and the text, which a free adaptation intends to provide, but are steps toward a more authentic reception beyond a picturesque impression (Derchain, 1975: 65; cf. Derchain, 1972: 1–2). For the translation itself, such notes do not mean a concurrence with Yourcenar's demand for "authenticity in tone" (see p. 522), but may point to the "basic literary meaning" (Parkinson, 1997: x) by hinting at peculiarities of style, variation in register of language, and the like (cf. Parkinson, 1997: passim, e.g., 161–63, nos. 11, 21, 24; Parkinson, 2012).

As a related matter, the meaningful choice of specific signs should be mentioned; these are widespread in temple inscriptions from Ptolemaic and Roman times, but are also attested elsewhere. The translator might prefer to comment on this in a footnote, as the orthography would not normally have influenced the actual meaning of the spoken text. Particularly in texts that were to be seen and read, it may be preferable to choose a word without direct equivalent in the original (this is frequent) or even to add a word. An explicit example is Philippe Derchain's (2000: 49 with footnote 8) translation "crocodile cruel" in order to take into account the sign of the enemy (Gardiner sign list A14*) as a determinative for "crocodile." In the Book of the Dead, variant spellings of the name of Seth offer some opportunities for the application of this practice: designations of Seth as a "positive" deity (e.g., in BD 60 or 108) may more or less consistently differ from those where he appears as the main enemy of Osiris and/or the deceased. For writings showing weapons on the body or head of Seth—and similarly in the Apophis-snake—one might add a designation of brutal submission, perhaps the word "smitten" or the like. Using parentheses or superscript for such additions seems to be an accurate method to make clear that the words in question, and their corresponding Egyptian signs, were not to be pronounced. For rubrics one could add "beware!" in parentheses, but in such cases a purely graphic indication like italics or small capitals will normally be more adequate, as this approach is virtually identical with the Egyptian one. Whatever solution one chooses, it is important to bear in mind that translating from Egyptian means an intercultural transfer not only between two languages, but also between two writing systems.

Finally, there are practical issues to consider. Normally, a translation, at least in a discipline like Egyptology, does not stand for itself. It can be embedded in a chapter, in which it is meant to illustrate its line of argument, or the other way round: the translation can be the starting point for a chapter, as is the case for a number of spells in Martin Stadler's monograph on the god Thoth in the Book of the Dead (Stadler, 2009). Then the translated text may be accompanied by a commentary of variable scope and intensity; strictly scholarly publications can also provide a transliteration of the hieroglyphic text into the Latin alphabet (including diacritic marks). In my view, a detailed transliteration that also indicates unwritten endings transports more lexical and grammatical information than any close translation and therefore provides room for more freedom in the translation. Also, commentary notes can be used for explaining the chosen translation beyond the lexical and syntactical analysis.

One can conclude that translations for a wider public can and even should differ from those for a purely Egyptological readership (cf. Hannig, Vomberg, and Witthuhn, 2006)—a distinct difference from translations from one modern language to another. But in publications addressed just to fellow Egyptologists, it is of some use to respect, whenever possible, such devices as register of language and style; this can help colleagues to better understand and appreciate the translator's attitude toward the text. One might object that these points can be left to a commentary and that "to engage in poetic license" cannot be a motive when translating Egyptian texts (Warburton, 2007: 264). But there is still some room for making a translated piece of Egyptian poetry sound different when compared with the English (or French or German etc.) rendering of, say, one of Heqanakhte's letters or a spell from the Book of the Dead. Another example is the Tale of Sinuhe, in which the complex narrative structure and large vocabulary differ from real "autobiographies," a difference that should be clear in a translation as well.

I am therefore not convinced that it is really the Egyptian texts themselves that need different translations when addressing "experts" or the wider public; the different readerships can, in my opinion, be better reached by appropriate explanations. It is true that publishers' demands may restrict commentary notes (Hannig, Vomberg, and Witthuhn, 2006: 69 with footnote 6; for an explicit example, see Faulkner, 1985: 7), but this does not diminish their necessity. The most detailed translations of spells of the Book of the Dead for a wider public, in terms of sources and content are, to my knowledge, by Jan Assmann and Andrea Kucharek (2008), Burkhard Backes (2011a), and Stephen Quirke (2013).

# Translating Ancient Egyptian Religious Texts

The points that I have discussed so far are valid for any Egyptian text. Although this is mostly true of the following four points as well, they especially need to be considered when dealing with Middle Egyptian religious texts, among them the Book of the Dead:

1. terms denoting complex concepts
2. Middle Egyptian texts composed or transmitted after the Middle Kingdom
3. complex transmission of text
4. choice and order of spells

## Terms denoting complex concepts

It is well known that a number of Egyptian words, notably from the religious sphere, have no equivalent in any modern language—an issue that belongs to the wider topic of emic and etic perspectives. Among them are such important concepts as those expressed by the short words $k₃$, $b₃$, $₃ḫ$, $m₃ꜥ.t$, and their derivatives. One easy way to deal with this situation is to abstain from a translation and to instead transfer the original word into the modern language. Normally this should be done only when the untranslated terms are explained in a glossary or elsewhere—just one more field of the undeniable need for explanation if the translator aims at allowing, within the limits created due to our fragmentary knowledge, an authentic reception (see discussion in the preceding paragraph). This procedure is probably the best way to transfer the demands of a "systemic" approach; that is, an approach that aims at reconstructing the inherent structures and concepts of a culture (Roeder, 2011a: 748) into a sensible translation. Still, in the practice of translating this approach has its inherent limits. To refrain from translating every important word transporting a complex concept would too often lead to chains of Egyptian words held together by English (or other) words and punctuation. Particularly in translations addressed to a wider public, a high density of untranslated words will likely annoy many readers. It must be left to the individual translator to define what is translated and what is not. Today, for example, few translators will still render *kꜣ* or *bꜣ* with "soul," but most will write "god" instead of *nṯr*/*netjer*, although the concepts behind the two words are far from congruent, in spite of the use of *nṯr* for translating Greek θεός (Roeder, 2011a: 749, footnote 32). As a rule, in order to avoid too many untranslated terms, one should employ a translation if the Egyptian term in question can be rendered by one word that, to our knowledge, transports central elements of its meaning. For instance, for *(s)ꜣḫ* and its derivatives one can work with "(make) effective" or "(en)able" and related words (resp. their equivalents in other languages), which express the basic connotations better than "glorify/-ied" or the German "verklärt," which has been the standard translation of *ꜣḫ*. To solve the dilemma, James P. Allen (2015: esp. 8) renders *sꜣḫ* with the neologism "to akhify," thereby highlighting the close link between "akhs" and "glorification spells." To temper the danger of misinterpretation (e.g., Roeder, 2011a: 758–63, esp. 758–59 on *bꜣ.w*), such standard translations, as well as untranslated Egyptian terms, can be marked in the running text as being included in a glossary where the reader will find information on the Egyptian word together with arguments for the chosen translation(s) and its limits (cf. e.g., the glossaries in Werning, 2011: 475–527 or, explicitly for the general reader, in Smith, 2009: 56, 669–702). Such solutions combine the advantages of a systemic approach with those of a terminological one, in other words, the explanation of a foreign concept using current terminology (cf. Roeder, 2011a: 747). The case is of course different when a chosen term is at the center of a scholarly investigation; in these cases, one will normally abstain from a translation (see, e.g., Roeder, 2011b on *nḏ.tî*).

It is a truism that a word of a given language may not be translated into another using the same word in each instance (from an Egyptological point of view discussed by Stadler, 2016: 521–25). This is especially true for metaphoric expressions; in Egyptian, those including a word for "heart" are certainly the best examples. On the one hand, an equivalent for each of these complex expressions must be found, and, often enough, the nearest parallel in a modern language will have nothing to do with the heart (see Toro-Rueda, 2003: 51–54). On the other hand, the Egyptian expression might be used in a context where the heart matters, referring to the text's subject by use of a pun. The translation would be deprived of this meaningful stylistic device if it did not include a similar, indirect mention of the heart. Still, as shown earlier, a certain level of consistency in the translation of a word or an expression is desirable as well, especially in translations without transcription. The eventual possibilities for dealing with this kind of challenge touch upon the field of "beautiful" or "literary" translation. An Egyptologist, who does not automatically need to be a gifted writer, but who wants to transport all aspects of the Egyptian expression to their readers, must always have the opportunity to add a note where an appropriate translation is not possible. What is required is a clear awareness of the difficult points and imperfections of their own translation.

As for the words mentioned in the four-point list on p. 526, however, a consistent translation is desirable, as these denote complex concepts and thus are often keywords. Therefore, if one decides to translate them, the translation should make clear that two texts, which in other respects might not be similar at all, are both concerned with the same subject—for example, different aspects of the deceased's *ꜣḫ* quality.

A related problem is the identification and appropriate translation of technical terms. As these occur only rarely in the Book of the Dead, most prominently in the catalogues of parts of ships in BD 99, this issue does not need to be treated here beyond Anke Blöbaum's (2011: 42–45) clear-sighted comments.

## Middle Egyptian texts composed or transmitted after the Middle Kingdom

There were certainly general rules about or trends in using Middle Egyptian language in a specific historical period. Nevertheless, especially in the case of transmitted texts composed much earlier, each later version is an individual amalgam of Middle Egyptian and later Egyptian elements. Thus, there is no one single "Late Middle Egyptian," but rather an indefinite number of "égyptien(s) de tradition." Consequently, it is even more difficult, if not impossible, to narrow down the number of alternatives by strictly applying the rules of Middle Egyptian syntax as we would do when reading a literary text from the Middle Kingdom. How can we know which stage of language is relevant when we are trying to identify the grammatical structure of the text? Is a series of sentences all beginning with *iw* to be understood as a sequence of statements, each being a main clause, or are we dealing with a chain of subordinate clauses? Does a *sḏm=f* need to be identified as one of its Middle Egyptian forms, or could it have replaced Middle Egyptian *sḏm.n=f*? And if so, how does this affect our translation? As a matter of fact, *sḏm.n=f* may replace *sḏm=f*, and we have to wonder whether in such cases we should take this as a meaningful variant (e.g., Kockelmann, 2009: 92), as a variant writing of the same form, which it often is (Backes, 2016: 87 with footnote 87), or simply as erroneous.

Another element to consider when translating is the "archaism" (in a very broad sense) that is inherent to Middle Egyptian texts after the Middle Kingdom. One could argue that texts that sounded "old" to the ears of their recipients or even their composers should sound old to the readers of their translations. Not to mention that only those Egyptians with some experience in reading and eventually writing Middle Egyptian were able to understand what we try to render in our translations. But what should such a text look like? We cannot translate Middle Egyptian from the New Kingdom or the Late Period to a medieval Romanic or Germanic language. A pseudo-archaic use of modern language—somewhat similar to what one can hear during "Middle Ages" markets and comparable events—would sound odd if not ridiculous, and, perhaps more to the point, add a completely wrong meaning to the translated text. In any case, such a solution would distract the reader from the content. But what is possible, to my mind, is to indicate the age of the original language by using "old" words here and there so that the readers immediately feel that they are not dealing with a text in "normal" language. In English, one option is to use the old pronouns "thou," "thy," etcetera. These have indeed been used in some translations, mainly earlier ones. This practice has been chosen by Thomas George Allen for translating the Book of the Dead, in order to render the Egyptian personal and possessive pronouns of the second person singular and plural more accurately than is possible when using the ambivalent "you(r)" (Allen, 1974: esp. 4; practiced already in Allen, 1960). We could indicate the archaizing character of an Egyptian text by using the old pronouns in contrast with the translation of a text in (more or less) vernacular language where one would use "you(r)." In the case of German, one can, for example, use the old-fashioned word "Haupt" instead of "Kopf," when the word for "head"/"top" is the old *tp*, not *ḏ3ḏ3*; for texts of the Old and Middle Kingdoms, one would use "Kopf" for *tp*. This practice would also allow the translator to indicate elements of more recent stages of language in the Middle Egyptian text. To use the same example, very few spells, especially in the Late Recension, show *ḏ3ḏ3* and not *tp* for "head"/"top" (see Backes, 2005: 191, listing six instances in BD 31, 64 [twice], 70, and 93 [twice]; two of these are already in the Theban Recension of BD 64 [short] and BD 93).

## Complex transmission of texts: dealing with copies, variants, and archetypes

The Book of the Dead is a prime example of a long-running transmission of a collection of funerary spells. Thousands of copies of Book of the Dead texts have survived, with varying choices and sequences of spells—from long scrolls with the entire sequence of the Late Recension down to one or two *incipit* on a tomb wall. There are multiple challenges resulting from this situation. The first and most fundamental is the question of which basis to choose for the translation of a Book of the Dead spell. Two main options present themselves: selecting one concrete copy of a spell, or reconstructing a text from more than one copy. When choosing the first option, the question arises in which cases the text should be emended. In contributions explicitly dealing with this issue, the trend is toward a minimum of emendations (e.g., Müller, 2011: 345). In practice, this ideal solution is not easy to put into practice, so the portion of Egyptological editions without any emendation of a text is and probably will always be very small. But the issue goes beyond a "yes" or "no" answer to the question of emendation; it is also about the nature of the emendation itself. One can choose among a selected range of copies in which the text runs similarly to that of the translated copy. This approach, which was favored by Allen in his first volume of Book of the Dead translations (Allen, 1960: 4) seems more reasonable than to refer to an "Urtext," as partly done by Christina Geisen (2004) for BD 17, or to older versions such as a forerunner spell in the Coffin Texts. For the Book of the Dead, the second solution has been chosen by Erik Hornung (1979), but only for short passages and as rarely as possible (1979: 16–17). As long as an understandable text can be recognized, there is no reason to replace short or even longer portions of the translated text with an older, presumably "better" version (as done by Assmann, 2008: 405; cf. Backes, 2016: 719–24). Even in the few cases where translation appears to be unfeasible, one does more justice to the text by leaving it untranslated and relegating a translation of the presumed origin to a commentary note.

The two basic solutions discussed here, emending either from close parallels on the or from older versions (including a reconstructed archetype), both produce a "Mischtext," but the first alternative provides a greater chance to come close to what was intended to be written. The combination of a concrete copy with the reconstructed "archetype," often of considerably older date, will in most, if not all cases, result in a text that was never meant to exist. In this practice, two aims are combined: first, presenting the concrete copy at face value, that is, with its peculiarities (which can sometimes be numerous) intact (cf. Gasse, 2002); second, reconstructing a probable original of the preserved copies—but not of the "text" itself, a point that cannot be stressed enough given the frequent misunderstanding of stemmatic reconstructions in Egyptology. The main reason for this is the use of the term "archetype," or of its German equivalent "Urtext," because both suggest a quest for an authored original. It is clear that this cannot be the goal of textual criticism when applied to partly open forms of transmission, as we must assume for ancient Egyptian funerary texts (cf. Backes, 2011b: esp. 463–69). Therefore, when aiming at reconstructing a "correct" or even "original" version instead of choosing a single manuscript as the main basis, it is not sufficient to take a number of copies and choose the "best" option for each passage, each sentence, and each word. This approach, albeit still popular, will again result in a "Mischtext" that was never written by any Egyptian scribe.

As long as stemmata are established for only a minimal number of Book of the Dead spells, the soundest method is to choose one copy as the basis for translation—this is indeed current practice—and to provide reconstructions of lacunae and minimal emendations from those parallels that are supposed to show the lowest level of deviation. Material from other epochs can provide interesting insights in the development of a spell's form and meaning; that is to say, it may be quoted as a deviating parallel, but should not be used as the basis for emendation or restauration (as done by Carrier, 2011b). For the Theban Recension, the famous papyrus of Ani has been the first choice in some editions (Budge, 1898; Barguet, 1962 [mainly based on Budge's hieroglyphic edition]; Faulkner, 1985), but the papyrus of Nu (P.London BM EA 10477) has become the most popular choice as it contains the majority of the Book of the Dead spells of the New Kingdom (*Thesaurus Linguae Aegyptiae*; Carrier, 2009b; Stadler, 2009; Quirke, 2013; cf. also Leitz, 2002). This solution is practical as it saves one from looking for an appropriate textual basis for each spell every time. This is not to say that the papyrus of Nu provides especially "correct" or at least "typical" copies, or, indeed, that it does not; the sheer length of its sequence of spells is in any case atypical.

As already stated, the transmission of the Book of the Dead is so extraordinarily complex that the problem goes beyond what has been outlined in the preceding paragraphs. We are not simply dealing with a supposed original on the one hand and copies showing variants on the other hand. Spells and sequences of spells are not just objects of (almost totally unknown) practices of individual copying; they are also objects of conscious revision. When confronted with a variant, one must thus consider whether it should be better regarded as an individual digression, maybe even a scribe's mistake, rather than a result of redaction, which itself may be based on a comparison of partly erroneous/unintentional variants. This situation results in a third alternative: providing translations not only of ideal texts and individual copies, but also of stages of redaction, including the "archetype." As is well known, two main phases have been defined for the transmission of the Book of the Dead: the "Theban" and the "Saite/Late" Recensions. Both are considered to result from productive textual transmission, but in fact, further lines of traditions, more restricted in time and space, can be identified. The papyrus of Nu dates to the first half of the Eighteenth Dynasty (Thutmose III–Amenhotep II) and does not give any information about how a spell from the Book of the Dead would be read and written during the Ramesside era or the Third Intermediate Period, and the Theban Recension encompasses both periods. To provide translations featuring a specific tradition is certainly of some use here. For example, when writing on funerary practice in Ptolemaic Akhmim, it makes more sense to quote from the local Book of the Dead copies of that period, with their remarkable deviations from papyri of the same period; these seem to be more representative of a standard. When quoting from the Book of the Dead in a Late Period context, it seems much more appropriate to use the Late Recension, an approach recently chosen by the editors of a volume with texts in translation from ancient Israel's neighboring cultures (Backes, 2011a). So far, several single copies from the Late Period have been translated, but to my knowledge, no translation of the Late Recension as such has yet been attempted. Most translations of the late Book of the Dead, published from the mid-1990 onward, are based on one single manuscript, in particular on the papyrus of Iahtesnakht, since this papyrus is available in a full edition including a German translation (Verhoeven, 1993). This papyrus comes from Herakleopolis and probably does not date before the mid-Twenty-sixth Dynasty (Verhoeven, 1993: 12, 369); although it is a very interesting document since it contains variants of spells, it is still not the best model-text to use. With a number of important papyri of the Twenty-sixth Dynasty having been published over the last few years, it is now possible to take one of the earliest as the textual basis, the well-preserved Book of the Dead of Nespasefy (Verhoeven, 1999) being a practicable choice. As long as there is not one stemmatic analysis of the Late Recension of Book of the Dead spells, the only option is to complement or replace the text with passages from other copies of the Twenty-sixth Dynasty where it seems necessary—that is, where the text of papyrus Nespasefy or any other chosen textual basis is lost, or where there is a high probability that it does result from a scribal error (Backes, 2011a: esp. 155–56).

This is not at all meant to say that providing variants that do not help to reconstruct the translated text is of no use. Both specialists and a broader audience can profit from seeing how different one single passage has been interpreted throughout its transmission. The issue of indicating variants, however, goes far beyond the scope of this chapter because it touches on standards for editing texts in Egyptology, which have never been subject to intense discussion beyond some principal statements and mainly practical considerations (cf. Müller, 2011: 365–66; Quack, 2011). The same is true for excerpts from spells that are not fully copied on a manuscript. These are an interesting phenomenon (cf. Kucharek, 2015), and the fact that we do not have the full spell should not influence the translation of the copied passages. In such cases, there is no question concerning the textual basis of the translation, which must of course be the excerpt in question—that is, an individual copy and not an emended text. For eventual reconstructions of the excerpt's more complete master copy, the issues raised are identical with those outlined at the beginning of this sub-chapter.

## Choice and order of spells—more than a practical question

A result of the complex history of transmission of the Book of the Dead is that the translator must consider the choice and order of spells in the publication. As long as a specific copy is translated, there is no difficulty: the order of spells will of course be that of the manuscript, and a concordance will allow the user to find the spells by their modern numbers. Similarly, the issue is trivial for the Late Recension with its standardized sequence, which is close, albeit not identical (cf. Gülden, this volume), to the modern numbering from BD 1 to 165. But how to deal with the varying sequences of the Theban Recension when the aim is to provide a translation of "the" Book of the Dead? Here, too, it is normal to use the modern numbers, a practice introduced as early as the edition of the hieroglyphic texts by Édouard Naville (1886) and Wallis Budge (1898) (with hymns to the sun-god and Osiris being placed in front of the numerical sequence, considering the arrangement in several papyri). Spells BD 1–165 (in the sequence attested before the Late Period) are followed by others not included in the Late Recension (e.g., Hornung, 1979). Several problems arise from this approach. Above all, the result is a "sequence" of BD 1–190 or so, implying the existence of a "corpus" that has never existed in that form—the main reason why the arrangement of spells is more than a practical issue. Each solution has an influence on the reception of the corpus insofar as the relative potentials of feasible alternatives need to be considered.

One alternative might be to choose a longer papyrus as a principal basis and, after representing its sequence, add those spells that are not present in that manuscript. This has been done for a re-edition of Faulkner's translation with reference to the papyrus of Ani (Faulkner and Goelet, 1994). Still, this solution offers just one of hundreds of possible sequences of spells, followed by a random sequence.

For presentations of "the" Book of the Dead (i.e., all spells from both the Theban and Late Recensions), the chronological aspect complicates the matter further because the corpus arranged under such headings is even more distanced from the manifold evidence. Texts separated by some hundreds of years appear as if they belong together—an impression that no explanation can entirely remove. Nonetheless, presumably for the sake of "completeness," this approach appears to be the most widespread and popular one (e.g., Barguet, 1967; Faulkner, 1985; Allen, 1974; Carrier, 2009; Quirke, 2013). An innovative solution is the one in James P. Allen's (2015) translation of the Pyramid Texts, in which he reproduces the sequence of spells in each royal pyramid from the Old Kingdom. For spells appearing in several pyramids, a translation is provided only once, with cross-references for the other instances. This exact structure is not applicable to the Book of the Dead, mainly because the number of copies and the extent of textual variation are much higher; furthermore, the borders of the corpus are less clearly defined. Still, the basic approach of returning to original sequences is attractive, and it is certainly worth trying to adapt it to the requirements of the Book of the Dead corpus. The issue has been addressed in Stephen Quirke's translation, in which he provides the sequence of a number of BD papyri from the New Kingdom with the explicit goal of enabling the reader to virtually read these papyri in the order in which the spells were presented (Quirke, 2013: xvi–xxiii, xxvii–xxviii).

Another solution might be offered by the existence of established text sequences attested in several papyri. These often go together with thematic coherence. Somewhat similar to what Paul Barguet (1986) has done in his translation of the Coffin Texts, some basic groupings could be proposed. These should consist of documented sequences of spells as much as possible, complemented by comparable ones that cannot be integrated into another sequence. It is clear that this approach, too, can do justice to only a part of our evidence, as the length of a sequence and the exact order of spells within were subject to choice and variation. Still, this approach can claim to offer the following advantages: first, it avoids any impression that, for the Theban Recension, the modern numbers are of any value beyond identifying a text, but takes at least a part of the original evidence into account. Second, the thematic aspect in grouping texts is not so far away from Egyptian approaches, because it seems to have played an important role in building up the sequence of the Late Recension (Quack, 2009: 22–25; Backes, 2011a: 153). The chapter on Book of the Dead spells in Jan Assmann and Andrea Kucharek's (2008: 811–55) volume of translated funerary texts takes a thematic grouping into account, but again within the limits of the numerical order. New attempts to acknowledge the mixed approach of original sequences and thematic grouping outlined here will require more research on traditions of sequences and motifs for grouping spells, but they may at least motivate others to work in this field. Besides analyses of the corpus of the Theban Recension, other textual corpora with thematic groupings, such as medical texts, will probably also offer useful points of departure.

For some spells attested only once, it is not clear whether they should really be regarded as having formed a part of the collection "Going Forth by Day," while other texts on papyri qualified as "Book of the Dead" have never received a spell number (cf.

e.g., Quack, 2009: 14). It is certainly helpful to separate such "borderline cases" from a main corpus (as partly done by Quirke, 2013).

## Prospects: Can There Be a Translation of *the* Book of the Dead?

From what has been said in the previous sections of this chapter it is quite clear what a comprehensive presentation of the Book of the Dead in translation should provide. As early as 1960, Allen briefly formulated a vision that is not far from what could be considered to be desirable: "Beyond that [i.e., a translation of the Book of the Dead based on what seems to be the original reading], publication of transliteration and translation side by side, with the successive versions in chronological sequence and an indication of sources of both accepted readings and variants, would be desirable" (Allen, 1960: 2, footnote 7). The main concern is the problem of varying sequences, pointed out above (pp. 529–32). In my opinion, it forces us to distinguish between a translation of the Theban and Late Recensions. From a practical perspective, this is not bad news. The presentation of each can focus on the variants within the same "Recension," while pointing to the text of the other one with its variants for a wider diachronic view.

This vision of a more or less ideal "Annotated Translation of the Book of the Dead (Theban and Late Recensions) in Two Volumes" will certainly not become reality in the near future. Still, even if such a publication would be very welcome, its absence does not mean that the actual state of affairs is particularly problematic. As Ursula Verhoeven (2002: 172) has stated, a large and empty desk is indispensable for serious engagement in Book of the Dead research. Her statement, which was about the necessity of putting a number of folio volumes of papyrus editions side by side when dealing with the text of a spell, may justly be transposed to the field of translations of the Book of the Dead. Compared to the Pyramid Texts or even the Coffin Texts—not to speak of other corpora of Egyptian religious texts—there are a considerable number of translations of the Book of the Dead, and the translators' approaches differ remarkably; this is why the large desk is needed here. The varying perspectives of earlier translators do not simply regard the particular interpretation of each passage, but illustrate how differently even the same interpretation can be expressed in contemporary terms. Advantages and disadvantages of each alternative can be compared in order to find the most appropriate solution for one's own purpose. This point is important because it has become a frequent practice to resign from offering one's own translation in favor of simply quoting from a current translation. For the Book of the Dead, the translations by Faulkner (1985) and Allen (1974) are usually used in English publications (sometimes both as explicitly in Kemp, 2007: xi), their French and German equivalents being those by Barguet (1962) and Hornung (1979). All of these are the work of excellent philologists, but with regard to the inevitable bias of each translation, this practice, which often goes together with reading no more than the translation chosen in advance, should be reduced to a minimum because it raises the individual preferences of one translator to a level of universal validity—which the translator himself has never claimed. What is more, the textual bases of the translations differ considerably (see "Suggested reading").

The complex, but rather comfortable situation in Book of the Dead translation does not mean that no new translations are needed. The potential undertaking outlined at the beginning of this section comes near to what I would, *cum grano salis*, call a translation of "the" Book of the Dead. Still, even such a big project would not lead to a definitive translation: the uncertainties in language and content are simply too numerous. Therefore, each translation of a Book of the Dead spell that is executed with all due accuracy and with awareness of the challenges discussed in this chapter (and some more) will provide a further alternative. By simply relying on another manuscript or by offering some innovative propositions for expressing Egyptian religious thought in a modern language, any serious attempt at "daring imperfection" is worth being taken into consideration.

# Suggested Reading

This section cannot offer hints to further reading on "translating the Book of the Dead" because there are no publications on exactly that issue. What follows instead is a choice of important translations of the Book of the Dead. Some of them are frequently used as a source for quotes from BD spells, others are less popular, but should also be taken into account when looking for translations on a scholarly level. More translations, including less comprehensive ones, can be found in the bibliography by Burkhard Backes et al. (2009: 1–3 and in the lists to each spell); some more recent ones have been mentioned earlier in this chapter. For the first important translations by Le Page Renouf and Naville (1904) and (less precise, but more influential) Wallis Budge (1898), see Hornung (1979: 12–13). The short descriptions provided here aim at highlighting the diversity of the approaches chosen by the translators.

Allen (1960) is an edition of papyri and other Book of the Dead sources in the Oriental Institute Museum of the University of Chicago. Its introduction provides detailed information on each document, including variants such as remarkable spellings or errors. The translations present the spells in numerical order. For each of them, all individual versions of the surviving copies in the Oriental Institute Museum are entirely translated. The notes mostly explain the chosen translation by pointing out the Egyptian spelling. Differences to earlier versions are only occasionally indicated (see also p. 2 with footnote 7).

Barguet (1967) follows a mixed approach. Besides basic information on the transmission and content of the corpus, the introduction divides the sequence of the Late Recension into four large sections. In the translation, each of these is introduced by remarks on its contents and subdivisions. Each spell is translated from the "best" available copy, normally taken from the editions of Budge and less frequently Naville for the Theban Recension, or, for the chapters attested in the Late Recension alone, from Lepsius' edition of the Book of the Dead of Iufaa. Footnotes provide variants, especially in Coffin Texts parallels, and explanations of selected words or motifs. The book's index focuses on divine names and toponyms.

The translation by Faulkner (1972, 1985; various reprints) is based principally on one manuscript, the famous papyrus of Ani of the Nineteenth Dynasty, but translations of most remaining spells of the Theban Recension, up to BD 189, are added in Faulkner (1985), along with some more from the Late Recension. Only the introductory spells are arranged in respect to their order of appearance in Ani's papyrus, as in Budge (1898). They are followed by BD 125 for its connection with the judgment scene, before the numerical order from BD 1 to 189 is used. There is no indication of the spells preserved in the papyrus of Ani or of the sources used for the remaining texts or emendations (cf. Faulkner and Goelet, 1994: 18). Background information is limited to a compact general introduction and short remarks before some important spells, which is explicitly due to the book's intended wider readership (Faulkner, 1985: 7–8).

Allen bases his translation on selected papyri, whereas Faulkner's explicitly addresses the "general reader" (Allen, 1974: 4). Often, a variant of the entire spell or an important part of it, normally from a later period, is added; mixed text is thus avoided. The textual basis for each spell, and occasionally variants of those spells, is indicated in footnotes, but there are very few hints on the content. A concise introduction to the corpus and a detailed table of earlier parallels and indexes of English and Egyptian words in the text are included.

The comparatively long introduction by Hornung (1979) focuses on the early history of modern Book of the Dead reception, the principles and difficulties behind the translation, and the "content" of the Book of the Dead. The translation itself is remarkable for implementing the rules of Egyptian metrics as proposed by Gerhard Fecht (see Hornung, 1979: 17), thus subdividing the texts into "verses." Only spells of the Theban Recension are translated, and although they appear in numerical order, this choice is due to the explicit goal of representing the "form" of the original Book of the Dead from the early Eighteenth Dynasty onwards (Hornung, 1979: 15). Beyond parallel texts (CT and others) and vignettes, the papyri used for each spell are indicated, but it is not clear which of these served as the primary basis. The commentaries to the spells introduce their content, including some hints for further reading, and indicate selected variants. A short glossary of nine untranslated terms and an index are also included.

Verhoeven (1993: 73–339) translates a specific manuscript, the papyrus of Iahtesnakht from the Saite Period, in the context of its edition. The commentary notes are therefore intended to serve as additions to Allen (1974) and Hornung (1979). Variants in a restricted number of representatives of the Theban and Late Recensions are indicated (cf. Verhoeven, 1993: 75–76).

In Faulkner and Goelet (1994), the sequence of spells in Faulkner's translation is adapted to the one in the papyrus of Ani. The remaining spells from the Theban Recension follow in a separate section. Addressed to the general reader are an introduction and the explanations to plates, i.e., to the individual spells and the related vignettes in the papyrus of Ani.

Again, the translation of a papyrus from the Twenty-sixth Dynasty is included in its edition by Annie Gasse (2001: 35–147). As the papyrus is not entirely preserved, some parts of the corpus are missing. The footnotes mostly explain the translations of some difficult passages and individual deviations from the manuscript.

The translations of Book of the Dead spells in the *Thesaurus Linguae Aegyptiae*, most of which was written between 2001 and 2005, are a special case, insofar as the main aim of the lexicographical project is providing not translations, but rather attestations of Egyptian words in their context. Therefore, there is no background explanation beyond information on the textual basis, and the translations are explicitly close to the original wording (cf. http://aaew2.bbaw.de/tla/servlet/S05?d= d001&h=h001). The brief commentaries normally contain explanations or alternative translations. The Egyptian transcription enables the user to check each word for further attestations. The translations are based strictly on one manuscript. With only few exceptions from Book of the Dead tradition, all spells of the Theban Recension are translated from at least one copy, as are the *chapitres supplémentaires*. The Late Recension is represented by the papyrus of Iufaa (P.Turin 1791; Ptolemaic).

Claude Carrier started his series of translations of Book of the Dead texts with a transcription and translation of BD 1–192 (Carrier, 2009a), without the *chapitres supplémentaires*. The introduction recounts on three pages the basic facts about the history and organization of the corpus. It is followed by a list of the sources used, indicating the name of the owner, provenance, date, place of conservation, and edition(s). The translations are based on one manuscript per spell: in most cases the papyrus of Nu, for Late Recension spells the papyrus of Iufankh (Ptolemaic). The few and minor "corrections" taken from other copies are indicated in footnotes. There is also an index of cited documents.

Carrier's translations of individual papyri (Carrier, 2009b, 2010, 2011a, 2011b) start with a very short presentation of the manuscript (collection, date, owner's name and titles). The translations, again accompanied by a transcription, present the spells in their order of appearance on the papyrus, preceded by descriptions of the corresponding vignettes; otherwise, the translations follow the scheme of Carrier (2009a). In Carrier (2011b), New Kingdom sources are used as a basis for emendations of the Ptolemaic papyrus of Iufaa. Schemata showing the repartition of spells and vignettes on the papyrus follow, along with a reproduction of the hieroglyphic text from older publications.

At present, the most recent and most comprehensive translation, also including a transliteration, is Quirke (2013). It consists of all numbered spells, plus others that are attested on Book of the Dead manuscripts but have not been numbered so far. The concise introduction to the structure and history of Book of the Dead papyri and to the main themes of the texts includes a presentation of the sequence of longer papyri preserved from the New Kingdom. For all spells, most New Kingdom copies are indicated, along with the number of copies dated to the Third Intermediate Period and their inclusion into the Late Recension. The order of spells follows the Late Recension, with introductory paragraphs to each of the sequences as defined by Barguet (1962). The translation of each spell is consequently based on one manuscript, possibly from the early New Kingdom; a second attestation is rarely translated. Compact paragraphs on the spell's content and eventual parallels are included.

## Bibliography

Allen, J. P. (2015). *The Ancient Egyptian Pyramid Texts: Translated with an Introduction and Notes*. Writings from the Ancient World 23, 2nd edition (Atlanta: Society of Biblical Literature).

Allen, T. G. (1960). *The Egyptian Book of the Dead Documents in the Oriental Institute Museum at the University of Chicago*. Oriental Institute Publications 82 (Chicago: University of Chicago Press).

Allen, T. G. (1974). *The Book of the Dead or Going Forth by Day: Ideas of the Ancient Egyptians Concerning the Hereafter as Expressed in Their Own Terms*. Studies in Ancient Oriental Civilization 37 (Chicago: University of Chicago Press).

Assmann, J. (2008). *Altägyptische Totenliturgien III: Osirisliturgien in Papyri der Spätzeit*. Supplemente zu den Schriften der Heidelberger Akademie der Wissenschaften. Philosophisch-Historische Klasse 20 (Heidelberg: Winter).

Assmann, J., and Kucharek, A. (2008). *Ägyptische Religion: Totenliteratur* (Frankfurt a.M.: Verlag der Weltreligionen).

Backes, B. (2005). *Wortindex zum späten Totenbuch (pTurin 1791)*. Unter Mitarbeit von Irmtraut Munro und Simone Stöhr. Studien zum Altägyptischen Totenbuch 9 (Wiesbaden: Harrassowitz).

Backes, B. (2011a). "Die späte Rezension des ägyptischen Totenbuchs." In *Grab-, Sarg-, Bau- und Votivinschriften. Texte aus der Umwelt des Alten Testaments, Neue Folge 6*, edited by B. Janowski and D. Schwemer, 144–202 (Gütersloh: Gütersloher Verlagshaus).

Backes, B. (2011b). "Die Textkritik in der Ägyptologie: Ziele, Grenzen und Akzeptanz." In *Methodik und Didaktik in der Ägyptologie: Herausforderungen eines kulturwissenschaftlichen Paradigmenwechsels in den Altertumswissenschaften*. Ägyptologie und Kulturwissenschaft 4, edited by A. Verbovsek, B. Backes, and C. Jones, 451–79 (Munich: Fink).

Backes, B. (2016). *Der "Papyrus Schmitt" (Berlin P. 3057). Ein funeräres Ritualbuch der ägyptischen Spätzeit. Edition und Textkommentar*. Ägyptische und Orientalische Papyri und Handschriften des Ägyptischen Museums und Papyrussammlung Berlin 4 (Berlin: De Gruyter).

Barguet, P. (1967). *Le Livre des morts des anciens Égyptiens*. Littératures anciennes du Proche-Orient 1 (Paris: Éditions du Cerf).

Barguet, P. (1986). *Les textes des sarcophages égyptiens du Moyen Empire. Introduction et traduction*. Littératures anciennes du Proche-Orient 12 (Paris: Editions du Cerf).

Blöbaum, A. I. (2011). "Lost in Translation? Ägyptologie zwischen Text und Übersetzung." In *Lexical Fields, Semantics and Lexicography*. Aegyptiaca Monasteriensia 7, edited by A. I. Blöbaum, K. Butt, and I. Köhler, 39–48 (Aachen: Shaker).

Budge, E. A. W. (1898). *The Book of the Dead: The Chapters of Coming Forth by Day. The Egyptian Text According to the Theban Recension in Hieroglyphic Edited from Numerous Papyri, with a Translation, Vocabulary, etc.* (London: Kegan Paul, Trench, Trübner & Co., Ltd.).

Carrier, C. (2009a). *Le Livre des Morts de l'Égypte ancienne*. Moyen Égyptien. Le Langage et la Culture des Hiéroglyphes. Analyse et Traduction 2 (Paris: Cybèle).

Carrier, C. (2009b). *Le Papyrus de Nouou (BM EA 10477): Traduction / Translittération + transcription hiéroglyphique*. Série des Papyrus du Livre des Morts de l'Égypte Ancienne I. Moyen Égyptien. Le Langage et la Culture des Hiéroglyphes. Analyse et Traduction 3 (Paris: Cybèle).

Carrier, C. (2010). *Le Papyrus d'Any (BM EA 10470). Traduction / Translittération + reproduction du fac-similé*. Série des Papyrus du Livre des Morts de l'Égypte Ancienne II. Moyen Égyptien. Le Langage et la Culture des Hiéroglyphes. Analyse et Traduction 4 (Paris: Cybèle).

Carrier, C. (2011a). *Le Papyrus de Nebseny (BM EA 9900). Traduction / Translittération + reproduction du fac-similé*. Série des Papyrus du Livre des Morts de l'Égypte Ancienne III. Moyen Égyptien. Le Langage et la Culture des Hiéroglyphes. Analyse et Traduction 5 (Paris: Cybèle).

Carrier, C. (2011b). *Le Papyrus de Iouefânkh (Turin, cat. n° 1791). Traduction / Translittération + reproduction du fac-similé de Davis*. Série des Papyrus du Livre des Morts de l'Égypte Ancienne IV. Moyen Égyptien. Le Langage et la Culture des Hiéroglyphes. Analyse et Traduction 6 (Paris: Cybèle).

Derchain, P. (1972). *Hathor quadrifrons: Recherches sur la syntaxe d'un mythe égyptien*. Uitgaven van het Nederlands Historisch-Archaeologisch Instituut te Istanbul 28 (Istanbul: Nederlands Historisch-Archaeologisch Instituut in het Nabije Oosten).

Derchain, P. (1975). "Le lotus, la mandragore et le perséa." *Chronique d'Égypte* 50: 65–86.

Derchain, P. (2000). "Tragédie sur un étang." *Göttinger Miszellen* 176: 47–52.

Faulkner, R. O. (1972). *The Book of the Dead* (New York: Limited Editions Club).

Faulkner, R. O. (1985). *The Ancient Egyptian Book of the Dead*, edited by C. Andrews (London: British Museum Press).

Faulkner, R. O. and Goelet, O. (1994). *The Egyptian Book of the Dead: The Book of Going Forth by Day* (San Francisco: Chronicle Books).

Gasse, A. (2001). *Le Livre des morts de Pacherientaihet*. Aegyptiaca Gregoriana 4 (Vatican City: Monumenti, Musei e Gallerie Pontificie).

Gasse, A. (2002). *Un papyrus et son scribe. Le livre des Morts Vatican Museo Gregoriano Egizio 48832* (Paris: Cybèle).

Geisen, C. (2004). *Die Totentexte des verschollenen Sarges der Königin Mentuhotep aus der 13. Dynastie: Ein Textzeuge aus der Übergangszeit von den Sargtexten zum Totenbuch*. Studien zum Altägyptischen Totenbuch 8 (Wiesbaden: Harrassowitz).

Hannig, R., Vomberg, P., and Witthuhn, O. (2006). "Mit leuchtenden Eingeweiden"—zur Übersetzungstechnik in der Ägyptologie." In *"Von reichlich ägyptischem Verstande." Festschrift für Waltraud Guglielmi zum 65. Geburtstag*. Philippika. Marburger altertumskundliche Abhandlungen 11, edited by K. Zibelius-Chen and H. W. Fischer-Elfert, 67–78 (Wiesbaden: Harrassowitz).

Hornung, E. (1979). *Das Totenbuch der Ägypter* (Zürich; München: Artemis-Verlag).

Kemp, B. (2007). *How to Read the Egyptian Book of the Dead* (London: Granta).

Kockelmann, H. (2009). "Ein neuer funerärer Spruch mit Anrufung der Mumienbinde. Mumienbinde Wien, Österreichische Nationalbibliothek Vindob. Aeg. 8345 und Parallelen." In *Ausgestattet mit den Schriften des Thot: Festschrift für Irmtraut Munro zu ihrem 65. Geburtstag*. Studien zum Altägyptischen Totenbuch 14, edited by B. Backes, M. Müller-Roth, and S. Stöhr, 89–104 (Wiesbaden: Harrassowitz).

Kucharek, A. (2015). "Vignetten und Exzerpte in Osirisliturgien." In *Liturgical Texts for Osiris and the Deceased. Liturgische Texte für Osiris und den Verstorbenen. Proceedings of the Colloquiums at New York (ISAW), 6 May 2011, and Freudenstadt, 18–21 July 2012.*

Studien zur spätägyptischen Religion 14, edited by B. Backes and J. Dieleman, 233–44 (Wiesbaden: Harrassowitz).

Leitz, C., ed. (2002). *Lexikon der ägyptischen Götter und Götterbezeichnungen* I–VII. Orientalia Lovaniensia Analecta 110–116 (Leuven: Peeters).

Lieven, A. von (2007). *Grundriß des Laufes der Sterne: Das sogenannte Nutbuch*. Carlsberg Papyri 8 = CNI Publications 31 (Copenhagen: Museum Tusculanum Press).

Malmkjaer, K. and Windle, K., eds. (2011). *The Oxford Handbook of Translation Studies* (Oxford: Oxford University Press).

Millán, C. and Bartrina, F., eds. (2013). *The Routledge Handbook of Translation Studies* (London; New York: Routledge).

Müller, M. (2011). "Wie historisch ist ein kritischer Text? Fragen zum editionsphilologischen Umgang mit funerären Texten." *Wiener Zeitschrift für die Kunde des Morgenlandes* 101: 343–66.

Parkinson, R. B. (1997). *The Tale of Sinuhe and Other Ancient Egyptian Poems 1940–1640 BC* (Oxford: Oxford University Press).

Parkinson, R. B. (2012). *The Tale of the Eloquent Peasant. A Reader's Commentary*. Lingua Aegyptia. Studia Monographica 10 (Hamburg: Widmaier).

Quack, J. F. (2009). "Redaktion und Kodifizierung im spätzeitlichen Ägypten: Der Fall des Totenbuches." In *Die Textualisierung der Religion*. Forschungen zum Alten Testament 62, edited by J. Schaper, 11–34 (Tübingen: Mohr Siebeck).

Quack, J. F. (2011a). "Textedition, Texterschließung, Textinterpretation." In *Methodik und Didaktik in der Ägyptologie: Herausforderungen eines kulturwissenschaftlichen Paradigmenwechsels in den Altertumswissenschaften*. Ägyptologie und Kulturwissenschaft 4, edited by A. Verbovsek, B. Backes, and C. Jones, 533–49 (Munich: Fink).

Quack, J. F. (2011b). Review of *The Debate between a Man and His Soul: A Masterpiece of Ancient Egyptian Literature*, by J. P. Allen. *Journal of the American Oriental Society* 131: 674–76.

Quirke, S. (1998). "Word and Object: Problems of Translation." In *Lahun Studies*, edited by S. Quirke, vii–viii (Reigate, Surrey: SIA Publ.).

Quirke, S. (2013). *Going out in Daylight: The Egyptian Book of the Dead—Translation, Sources, Meanings*. Golden House Publications Egyptology 20 (London: Golden House Publications).

Recklinghausen, D. von (2012). Review of *Grundriß des Laufes der Sterne: Das sogenannte Nutbuch*, by A. von Lieven. *Journal of Egyptian Archaeology* 98: 307–12.

Renouf, P. Le Page, and Naville, É. (1904). *The Egyptian Book of the Dead: Translation and Commentary* (London: Society of Biblical Archaeology).

Ritter, T. (1995). "Semantische Diskursstrukturen, erläutert am Beispiel des narrativen Texttyps." In *Per aspera ad astra. Wolfgang Schenkel zum neunundfünfzigsten Geburtstag*, edited by L. Gestermann and H. Sternberg-El Hotabi, 123–62 (Kassel: Louise Gestermann).

Roeder, H. (2011a). "Zwischen den Stühlen. Zugangsbeschreibungen zur altägyptischen Religion zwischen Transdisziplinarität und Eigenbegrifflichkeit." In *Methodik und Didaktik in der Ägyptologie: Herausforderungen eines kulturwissenschaftlichen Paradigmenwechsels in den Altertumswissenschaften*. Ägyptologie und Kulturwissenschaft 4, edited by A. Verbovsek, B. Backes, and C. Jones, 739–66 (Munich: Fink).

Roeder, H. (2011b). "Der Nedjti zwischen Kriegszug und Vernichtungsopfer. Potenzielle Räume institutionalisierter Grausamkeit im Alten Ägypten." In *On Cruelty · Sur la cruauté · Über Grausamkeit*. Siegener Beiträge zur Soziologie 11, edited by Trutz von Trotta and J. Rösel, 285–353 (Cologne: Rüdiger Köppe).

Stadler, M. A. (2003). *Der Totenpapyrus des Pa-Month (P. Bibl. nat. 149)*. Studien zum altägyptischen Totenbuch 6 (Wiesbaden: Harrassowitz).

Stadler, M. A. (2009). *Weiser und Wesir: Studien zu Vorkommen, Rolle und Wesen des Gottes Thot im ägyptischen Totenbuch*. Orientalische Religionen in der Antike 1 (Tübingen: Mohr Siebeck).

Stadler, M. A. (2016). "Die Größe der nubischen Katze im Mythos vom Sonnenauge. Zur Semantik von demotisch *qy* 'hoch' oder 'lang.'" In *Sapientia Felicitas. Festschrift für Günter Vittmann zu seinem 64. Geburtstag am 29. Februar 2016*. Cahiers "Égypte Nilotique et Méditerranéenne" 14, edited by S. L. Lippert, M. Schentuleit, and M. A. Stadler, 521–38 (Montpellier: Équipe "Égypte Nilotique et Méditerranéenne").

Toro Rueda, M. I. (2003). *Das Herz in der ägyptischen Literatur des zweiten Jahrtausends v. Chr. Untersuchungen zu Idiomatik und Metaphorik von Ausdrücken mit jb und ḥꜣtj*. (PhD diss., University of Göttingen), http://hdl.handle.net/11858/00-1735-0000-000D-F260-3.

Verhoeven, U. (1993). *Das saitische Totenbuch der Iahtesnacht: P. Colon. Aeg. 10207*. 3 vols. Papyrologische Texte und Abhandlungen 41 (Bonn: Dr. Rudolf Habelt).

Verhoeven, U. (1999). *Das Totenbuch des Monthpriesters Nespasefy aus der Zeit Psammetichs I. pKairo JE 95714+pAlbany 1900.3.1, pKairo JE 95649, pMarseille 91/2/1 (ehem. Slg. Brunner) + pMarseille 291*. Handschriften des Altägyptischen Totenbuches 5 (Wiesbaden: Harrassowitz).

Verhoeven, U. (2002). Review of *Spruchvorkommen auf Totenbuch-Textzeugen der Dritten Zwischenzeit*, by I. Munro, *Das Totenbuch des Pa-en-nesti-taui aus der Regierungszeit des Amenemope (pLondon BM 10064)*, by I. Munro. *Journal of Ancient Near Eastern Religions* 2: 165–72.

Warburton, D. A. (2007). "Texts, Translation, Lexicography, & Society. A Brief Note." *Lingua Aegyptia* 15: 263–79.

Warnemünde, G. and Hannig, R. (2007). "Mit leuchtenden Eingeweiden. Zur Übersetzungstechnik in der Ägyptologie." *Isched. Journal des Ägypten Forum Berlin e.V.* 2007(2): 23–29.

Werning, D. (2011). *Das Höhlenbuch: Textkritische Edition und Textgrammatik II: Textkritische Edition und Übersetzung*. Göttinger Orientforschungen IV. Ägypten 48 (Wiesbaden: Harrassowitz).

Winand, J. (2013). Review of *Das Höhlenbuch: Textkritische Edition und Textgrammatik*, by D. Werning. *Lingua Aegyptia* 21: 329–39.

Yourcenar, M. (1983). "Ton et langage dans le roman historique." In *Le Temps, ce grand sculpteur: essais*, edited by M. Yourcenar, 29–58 (Paris: Gallimard).

# CHAPTER 27

# THE CONSERVATION OF BOOK OF THE DEAD PAPYRI

## MYRIAM KRUTZSCH

Book of the Dead (BD) papyri can be found all over the world, in papyrus collections and in museums of ancient Egyptian art. In most cases they are referred to as "scrolls"; the term is based on their original appearance. Unfortunately, however, because of the poor preservation of most of the papyri, only a few of them can still be considered scrolls; the majority are assemblages of numerous fragments. Both the complete scrolls and the fragments require a sensitive conservatory approach and pose significant challenges to the conservators' skills. It is this chapter's intention to highlight this issue.

## CONDITIONS AT DISCOVERY AND THE STATE OF PRESERVATION

The remaining intact scrolls are usually in very fragile condition. Only with the best efforts is it possible to unroll them, though this is not without risk. Even if successful, the loose and broken fragments must still be placed correctly to re-establish their original positions. The stabilization and fitting pose final problems since the documents are often over 3,000 years old, yet the conservator's aim is to preserve them for future generations.

Difficulties of a totally different nature arise because of procedures conducted more than a hundred years ago. This is especially the case for funerary papyri, the most prominent among them being the numerous BD papyri that are considered to be some of the most popular and belong to the core of any exhibition of Egyptian art. Because of their considerable length, they were often cut into sections for convenience and laminated on to paper, cardboard, textile, or even glass, and sealed across the surface by a cover layer

FIG. 27.1. P.Berlin P 3002 V recto, detail with distortions and pinches. Photo: Myriam Krutzsch.

of glue. As a result, deformation, crushing, and overlapping frequently occurred (Fig. 27.1). The lamination connects the base with the papyrus, but with only one layer of the papyrus fabric, typically the verso. Over the years, frictions occur, causing the upper layer, usually the recto, to separate.

Other problems are caused by papyri in which the inscription on the back side is not covered by lamination but is left open to be visible through a kind of window. In these cases, the verso was often laminated with chiffon silk and subsequently stabilized with varnish (usually cellulose varnish) (Rathgen, 1924). Unfortunately, this kind of varnish becomes unstable with age, turning yellow and hardening, which causes additional breakage (Fig. 27.2).

Occasionally, the front sides—the areas with script and depictions—are also covered with a partial varnish or adhesive coat, which causes those parts to become brittle and results in bits flaking off.

Within the script and illustrations, fissures and chipped spots commonly occur. Carbon-black ink was used for the writing, and, in the colored depictions, the colors white, yellow, red, blue, and green occur (Fuchs, 2006). With the use of green color, copper rust causes so-called ink corrosion (Tintenfraß), leading to voids within the paintings. In some BD papyri, such as P.Berlin P 3058 and P 3059, the yellow was augmented with orpiment (Backes, 2009). Yellow and white in particular are highly thinned out and therefore only sporadically preserved. In some papyri, the paintings are not only colored but are also aureate (P.Havana [P.Hood], P.Kraków MNK IX-752/1-4, P.London BM EA 9940, P.London BM EA 10472).

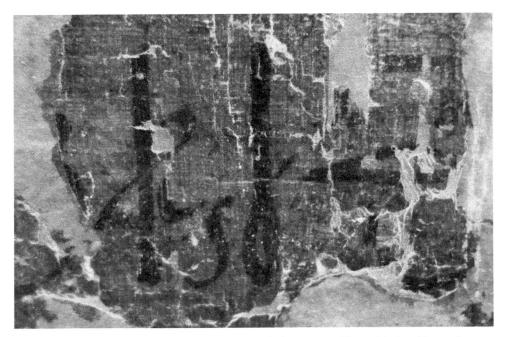

FIG. 27.2. P.Berlin P 3002 A verso, detail with textile lamination. Photo: Myriam Krutzsch.

Hardly any scrolls have an undamaged upper and lower edge; usually, either there are traces of insect damage or the rims are broken because of impact pressure. The broken edges might, however, have occurred for completely different reasons as well. A black crustaceous coating can often be found on the upper and lower rims, especially on BD papyri (Fig. 27.3). This coating looks like a residue of the bitumen with which the scrolls were supposedly sealed. Chemical analyses to confirm this theory have yet to be conducted.

There are some cases in which the scroll was so tightly rolled that the different layers of the papyrus could not be completely separated from each other (Fig. 27.4).

## Procedures of Preservation and Conservation

After the condition of the papyrus is recorded, the conservator must decide which measures are necessary for its preservation. The aim is not to do everything that is possible, but only what is absolutely indispensable. Additionally, all applied methods and means must be reversible.

The beginning of the procedure is the *cleaning*; in regard to papyri, this means dry cleaning with brushes, scalpels, and, for some years now, with a *color shaper (silicon brush)*. Besides the removal of sand, dust, dirt, and plant remains, labels of previous conservators, if possible, are removed. Such labels include the following:

FIG. 27.3. P.Berlin P 3002 W recto, detail with spelled paint coat lamination parts. Photo: Myriam Krutzsch.

FIG. 27.4. P.Berlin P 3134 A recto, detail with overlapped papyrus. Ägyptisches Museum und Papyrussammlung Berlin, SMB, Photo: Sandra Steiß.

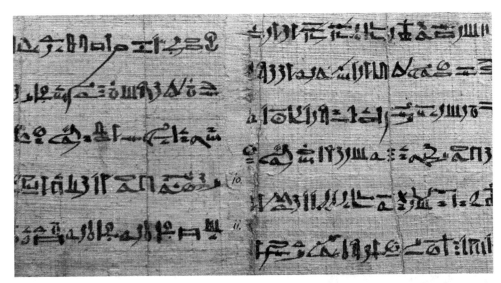

FIG. 27.5. P.Berlin P 3013 B recto, detail with historical ink line numbers. Photo: Myriam Krutzsch.

- accession number or plaque number
- line counts
- marks indicating the end of the sheet (Fig. 27.5).

These labels are applied not only with a pencil but with red crayon or even ink directly on to the papyrus; they may also consist of paper slips glued onto the manuscript. The paper needs to be carefully separated from the papyrus, which in some cases means merely thinning it out. Often, the cleaning is combined with the first fixation of loose fibers.

The removal of labels is followed by the *stabilization* and *affixing* of loose fibers and layers (Fig. 27.6). Additionally, any cracks within the papyrus material, as well as within the script and color, need to be closed. This is performed with Tylose MH 1000 and the finest brushes. In some cases, it is possible to correct and *straighten* small misplaced, crushed, or otherwise deformed parts. Larger creases and deformation can only be corrected after the lamination has been removed, which is only possible when the structure of the papyrus is stable and firm (Menei, 2008: 62–67 and pl. XIV–XVII).

Another possibility is to perform a partial *de-conservation*. The lamination is then removed only from the edges that surround the manuscript as well as from the defective spots (Fig. 27.7). This method allows incorrectly placed fragments to be adjusted (Figs. 27.8a and 27.8b). By doing so, several parts in P.Munich ÄS 808 could be correctly placed in their original positions.

The BD manuscript in the National Museum of Havana, Cuba, exhibits a peculiarity that is usually not attributed to papyri: a retouching of voids. The retouching is used in graphic and painting conservation, following the conservation of missing areas using original material. The individual structure of every papyrus sheet, and therefore of every

FIG. 27.6. P.Munich ÄS 808 recto, detail with loose parts. Photo: Myriam Krutzsch.

papyrus scroll, as well as the lack of ancient blank papyrus material, renders such insertion inadvisable. Modern papyrus fabric is not suitable because of its differences in composition and flexibility in comparison to the ancient material. In the case of the Cuban BD manuscript, a stylized papyrus structure was retouched on a paper lamination.

For the relocation of the Berlin Papyrus Collection in 2012, numerous papyri received temporary emergency protection. During this time, the windowlike openings on the back of BD P.Berlin P 3002 were stabilized with a custom-fitted glass panel. In this way, the continuing mechanical destruction of the hieroglyphic lines underneath the textile lamination on the verso was halted. The next step will be to conserve the 25 pieces of this papyrus and to stabilize it permanently.

## Reconstruction

Once the papyrus has been preserved, the reconstruction of the fragments can begin. Numerous factors are helpful in this process:

a) *material and technique*
   - structure of the fibers, from both the recto and the verso

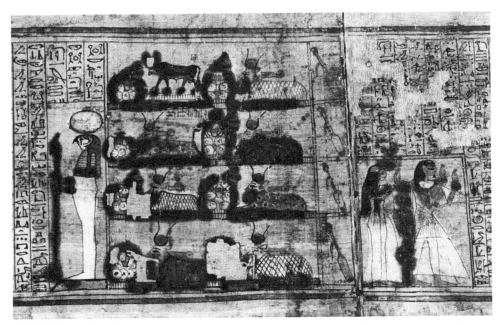

FIG. 27.7. P.Havana P. Hunt recto, detail with retouched hole parts. Photo: David Rodríguez, Museo Nacional de Bellas Artes, La Habana, Cuba.

- form of the fragments
- voids—their form and recurrence
- structure of the scroll, i.e., the layout of the sheets and their joins

b) *inscription and painting*
- Indian ink, ink, and colors
- writing devices and line thickness
- reference lines, arrangement of the texts, preparatory drawings.

If none of these factors is applicable or if joins are poorly identified, collaboration with Egyptologists might be necessary. Concerning the reconstruction of poorly preserved papyri in particular, it becomes obvious that only the collaboration between the expert for the text on the papyrus and the specialist for the material and technique can restore the original condition. In collaboration with an Egyptologist, we reconstructed many fragments and larger sections from a Book of the Dead (Mettlen, 2014). The Egyptologist checked the text and the drawings, and I examined the fibers, sheet structures, and sheet joins.

# Remounting

BD papyri that possess no historical lamination whatsoever are rather rare. Among the approximately 70 BD papyri of the Berlin Papyrus Collection, only two of this kind

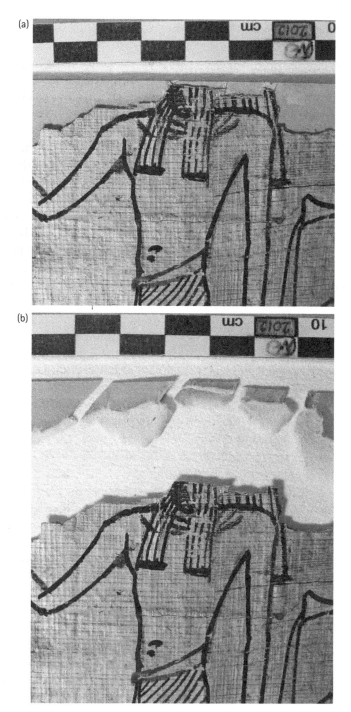

FIG. 27.8. P.Munich ÄS 808 recto, detail from upper margin. (a) State of preservation; and (b) during removal of the card lamination. Photo: Myriam Krutzsch.

can be found: the BD of Nefer-ini (P.Berlin P 10477) and the BD of Pa-di-ash-sedjem (P.Berlin P 10478).

Unfortunately, these two Late Period papyri were cut into manageable parts. After the conservation work, I was able to mount them so that the appearance of an almost complete unit was restored. Depending on the width of the parts, two or three, respectively, are connected with direct joins per frame of approximately 1.5 meters in length. No expansion space was left at the lateral margins, as is commonly the case. In fact, the manuscript concludes at the frame with only 1 millimeter of tolerance. When the frames are placed side by side, the observer's eye closes the narrow gaps between the single frames.

However, numerous papyri possess wedge-shaped gaps, particularly at the frame intersections, which cannot be avoided with this kind of presentation. The attentive observer will notice that those gaps are not voids; rather, they result from the distortion and wrapping of the papyrus, which can be seen in particular on the laminated papyri. This, again, arises from the effects of humidity on the adhesives used during lamination. If those parts were to be joined together in their original position, the result would resemble a Romanesque arch, not only requiring more space but also creating a strange, indistinct picture for the observer.

Generally, papyri are mounted between two glass plates. With regard to the large layout of some papyri, including the BD papyri, this results inevitably in an enormous weight and the problem of handling. To counteract these problems, only the fronts of the frames should be made of glass, with a base of thick, acid-free cardboard.[1] These boards are light and resistant to deformation because of their multilayered structure. Japanese tissue paper is stretched over the cardboard and is attached only on the four edges with methyl cellulose. Then the papyrus is selectively secured at certain points, also with methyl cellulose, and covered with the glass plate. The fixation points are recorded with a photograph to facilitate future disassembling. Finally, the construction is agglutinated by paper tape on all four sides (Fig. 27.9).

The disadvantage of this framing is the covered verso of the papyrus, which is, however, not visible in most cases because of the lamination process. Furthermore, BD papyri are usually inscribed and illustrated on only one side. Exceptions are P.Berlin P 3002 with its hieroglyphic line on the back, as well as some BD fragments at Tokai University in Tokyo, Japan (SK 116-1), which display writing and illustrations on both sides (Figs. 27.10a and 27.10b).

## Storage/Presentation

Three complete BD papyri are found in the permanent exhibition of the Neues Museum Berlin in the "Egyptian Court": the papyrus of Tarudji, called Nai-Nai (P.Berlin P 3008); the papyrus of the Lady of the House Keku (P.Berlin P 3003); and

---

[1] For a long time, we were using a special wood plate (Lightwood).

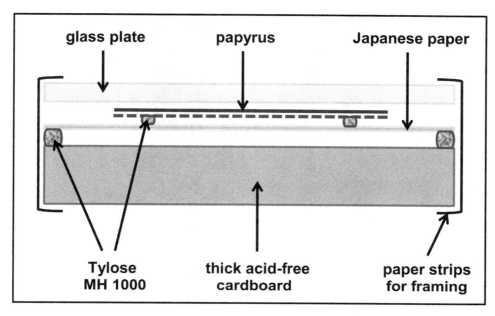

FIG. 27.9. Cross section of the framing. Drawing by Myriam Krutzsch.

the papyrus of the Lady of the House Nefer-ini (P.Berlin P 10477). These papyri are mounted in the described manner between wooden and glass plates, each measuring approximately 1.5 meters in length. The single frames were placed like pearls on a necklace into larger frames installed on the walls. These, as well as all the other objects of the exhibition, now reside in the storage rooms. Since the relocation of the Berlin Papyrus Collection in 2012, all objects are stored in closed cabinets in horizontal compartments. The ones for the larger papyri are constructed to fit a maximum of two frames, one above the other, in order to facilitate handling and therefore to ensure the safety of the objects. The storage rooms, as well as the exhibition rooms, are all air-conditioned accordingly.

## Observations Regarding the Material

Many long-guarded secrets are revealed during the days or often weeks of preservation and conservation of a manuscript; for instance, different structures in the material can be observed with various possible causes:

- method of manufacturing (Pliny the Elder; Bagnall, 2009)
- evidence regarding the date of manufacturing
- characteristics of quality

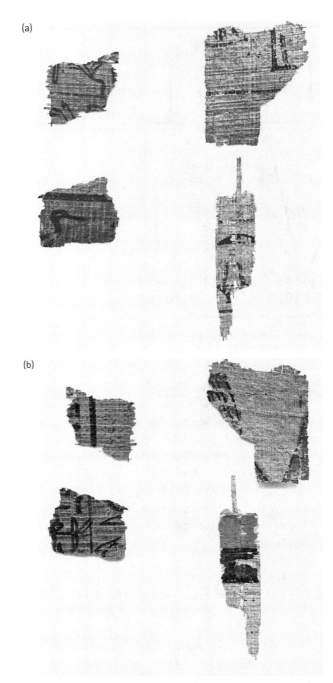

**FIG. 27.10.** P.Tokyo SK 116-1, fragments with text and drawing on both sides. Photo: Kyoko Yamahana, Tokai University Ancient Egypt & Near Eastern Collection.

The structure of the two fiber layers possesses characteristics of quality that can be assigned locally. Initial conclusions can be made with regard to the *method of manufacturing*, which is, however, still not definitely attested. It is hoped that these conclusions will be proven by means of scientific analyses. The amount of the mineral compound can be disclosed and used in future comparisons with soil samples to locate individual sites.

The date of the manuscript's manufacture can be narrowed down by analyzing the writing device, ink, and colors. Another criterion for dating the manuscript is the width of the *papyrus sheet joins* (Krutzsch, 2017). The papyrus sheet joins of the blank scrolls, produced in the papyrus workshops from up to twenty individual sheets, possess either three or four layers (Krutzsch, 2008a, 2012a). By analyzing these joins, it is discernible that the adhesive is often visible in the three-layered joins as a darker strip that contrasts with the hue of the rest of the papyrus. The adhesive used to join two documents often stands out either because the heights of the scrolls differ or because the direction of the overlapping sheets changes (Krutzsch, 2012b).

BD papyri required longer scrolls than were usually manufactured in the papyrus workshops. Therefore, the scribes joined several documents or parts of scrolls together. The manuscript of Ani (P.London BM EA 10470), for instance, is one manuscript with a final length of over 22 meters, composed of three different scrolls. These scribal joins, often made less accurately than those done in the workshops, were skillfully concealed by the scribe using texts or illustrations. In general, the joins played an essential role for the scribe in terms of the arrangement of the columns, as well as influencing the rolling of the scroll.

The analysis and eventual classification of the different types of sheet joins led to the discovery of the different *shapes of sheets*. With regard to the papyri described here, Types II and III are the most common. Type II possesses fibers from the recto at one lateral edge that continue above the verso. Type III exhibits the simplest form, where the recto is level with the verso.

The *proportions* of the individual sheets are 2:1, in regard to the relation of height and width. It is impossible to say whether these were also the original proportions as manufactured in the workshops since it is clear that the scrolls were also trimmed height-wise (Turner, 1978).

What Pliny the Elder describes rather briefly in his *Naturalis Historia* (Book 13, Chs. XXI–XXVI) is gradually revealed to the conservator. Recently, we started scientific analyses using x-ray fluorescence (XRF) devices to complement the observations made so far. XRF devices with a ca. 50 μm interaction spot and M4 and M9 spectrometers made by the Bruker Nano GmbH reveal distributions of characteristic inorganic contaminations, so-called fingerprints that reflect the traces of the place and method of production in addition to those typical for the spots where the papyrus was found. A database of physical features and chemical composition would lead to more precise conclusions regarding dating and origin as well as practices, trade, and circulation of papyrus material.

A collaboration between conservator and Egyptologist may be helpful for more than just the reconstruction of fragmentary objects. More than anything else, the material and technical details may indicate which parts belong together. Furthermore, they may offer important information regarding production dates and the origins of the objects.

## Bibliography

Backes, B. (2009). *Drei Totenpapyri aus einer thebanischen Werkstatt der Spätzeit. (pBerlin P. 3158, pAberdeen ABDUA 84023, pBerlin P. 3159)*. Handschriften des Altägyptischen Totenbuches 11 (Wiesbaden: Harrassowitz).

Donnithorne, A. (1986). "The Conservation of Papyrus in the British Museum." In *Papyrus: Structure and Usage*. British Museum Occasional Papers 60, edited by M. L. Bierbrier, 1–23 (London: British Museum).

Fackelmann, M. (1985). *Restaurierung von Papyrus und anderen Schriftträgern aus Ägypten*. Studia Amstelodamensia ad epigraphicam ius antiquum et papyrologicam pertinentia 24 (Zutphen: Terra Pub. Co.).

Fuchs, R. (2006). "Die Totenbuch-Fragmente der von Portheim-Stiftung Heidelberg. Restaurierung, naturwissenschaftliche Analysen und kulturhistorische Bewertung der Maltechnik." In *Totenbuch-Forschungen. Gesammelte Beiträge des 2. Internationalen Totenbuch-Symposiums Bonn, September 25-29, 2005*. Studien zum altägyptischen Totenbuch 11, edited by B. Backes, I. Munro and S. Stöhr, 35–49 (Wiesbaden: Harrassowitz).

Janis, K. (2006). "Die Konservierung und Restaurierung von Papyrus." In *Totenbuch-Forschungen. Gesammelte Beiträge des 2. Internationalen Totenbuch-Symposiums Bonn, 25. bis 29. September 2005*. Studien zum altägyptischen Totenbuch 11, edited by B. Backes, I. Munro and S. Stöhr, 145–60 (Wiesbaden: Harrassowitz).

Krutzsch, M. (2008a). "Blattklebungen erkennen und dokumentieren." In *Ägypten lesbar machen—die klassische Konservierung/Restaurierung von Papyri und neure Verfahren. Beiträge des 1. Internationalen Workshops der Papyrusrestauratoren. Leipzig, 7.–9. September 2006*. Archiv für Papyrusforschung—Beiheft 24, edited by J. Graf and M. Krutzsch, 93–98 (Berlin; New York: de Gruyter).

Krutzsch, M. (2008b). "Falttechniken an altägyptischen Handschriften." In *Ägypten lesbar machen—die klassische Konservierung/Restaurierung von Papyri und neuere Verfahren. Beiträge des 1. Internationalen Workshops der Papyrusrestauratoren. Leipzig, 7.–9. September 2006*. Archiv für Papyrusforschung—Beiheft 24, edited by J. Graf and M. Krutzsch, 71–83 (Berlin; New York: de Gruyter).

Krutzsch, M. (2012a). "Das Papyrusmaterial im Wandel der antiken Welt." *Archiv fur Papyrusforschung und verwandte Gebiete* 58: 101–8.

Krutzsch, M. (2012b). "Unterweltspapyri unter der Lupe. Mit den Augen des Restaurators." In *Forschung in der Papyrussammlung. Eine Festgabe für das Neue Museum*. Ägyptische und Orientalische Papyri und Handschriften des Ägyptischen Museums und Papyrussammlung Berlin 1, edited by Verena M. Lepper, 483–95 (Berlin: Akademie Verlag).

Krutzsch, M. (2017). "Einzelblatt und Rolle. Zur Anatomie von Papyrushandschriften." In *Ägypten begreifen. Erika Endesfelder in memoriam*. Internet-Beiträge zur Ägyptologie und Sudanarchäologie 19, edited by F. Feder, G. Sperveslage, and F. Steinborn, 213–22 (Berlin, 2017).

Menei, E. (2008). "Fifteen Years of Papyri Conservation at the Louvre: The Influence of Japanese Techniques." In *Ägypten lesbar machen—die klassische Konservierung/ Restaurierung von Papyri und neuere Verfahren. Beiträge des 1. Internationalen Workshops der Papyrusrestauratoren. Leipzig, September 7-9, 2006.* Archiv für Papyrusforschung— Beiheft 24, edited by J. Graf and M. Krutzsch, 62–67 (Berlin; New York: de Gruyter).

Mettlen, J. (2014). *Bearbeitung des Berliner Papyrus 3134 A-I* (Unveröffentlichte Magisterarbeit, Universität Trier).

Rathgen, F. (1924). *Die Konservierung von Altertumsfunden, II. und III. Teil Metalle und Metallegierungen, Organische Stoffe* (Berlin; Leipzig: de Gruyter).

Turner, E. G. (1978). "The Terms Recto and Verso. The Anatomy of the Papyrus Roll." In *Actes du XV$^e$ Congrès International de Papyrologie, Première partie.* Papyrologica Bruxellensia 16, 26–53 (Bruxelles: Fondation Égyptologique Reine Elisabeth).

CHAPTER 28

# THE ART OF FORGERY IN THE MANUSCRIPT CULTURE IN ANTIQUITY*

## RITA LUCARELLI AND MALCOLM CHOAT

THE forging of text had already become a problem in antiquity, on a scale running from the pseudonymous authorship common in all ancient cultures, to the deliberate falsification or invention of official documents such as imperial edicts (Fournet, 2016). In modernity, a steady stream of fakes has emerged since the Renaissance, mimicking—in varying degrees of credibility—texts and artifacts from the all parts of the ancient world (see, e.g., Muscarella, 2000; Lapatin, 2002; Olsson et al., 2015; Jones, 1990). Among Egyptian fakes (for which see in general Wakeling, 1912), textual artifacts on material such as linen, pottery, but above all papyrus, have been a prominent class.

Forged papyri are as old as papyrology; indeed, the first papyrus ever published, by Jean Mabillon in 1681, contained a forged section (Choat, 2019a). With the explosion in the collecting of papyri in the late nineteenth and early twentieth century, fakes became increasingly prevalent, and exist now in every major papyrus collection. Although the forging of papyri in Egypt is less prevalent than it once was, fakes continue to be produced, including recent infamous examples such as the so-called Gospel of Jesus' Wife (Choat, 2019b) and the forging of a considerable number of Dead Sea Scroll-like Fragments (Davis, 2017; Davis, Rabin et al., 2017).

Fake papyri (a term we use in this chapter to cover all ink texts on movable surfaces, including linen) fall into four main categories (Horak, 1991, 2001; Coles and Gallazzi, 1981). (1) "composites" of genuine papyri, parts of different texts put together to give the

---

* This article is a reviewed, enlarged, and updated version of a previous study on the forgeries of the Book of the Dead, which has appeared in *IBAES* XV (see Lucarelli and Müller-Roth, 2014). We wish to thank Martin Fitzenreiter for kindly granting the permission to produce this new version of the study and photos published in his edited volume of *IBAES*; Holger Kockelmann (2020) for sharing his work; and Vanessa Mawby for her assistance in producing the table of forgeries.

appearance of a larger document; (2) papyri in simulated script, nonsensical scribbles which give the passing appearance of being ancient writing; and, finally, (3) papyri in script that closely imitates (with varying degrees of success) genuine ancient scripts and languages. Such forgeries can be new compositions or copies of existing texts. It is the second and third type (in particular the latter) that we deal with here.

# The Forgeries of the Ancient Egyptian Book of the Dead

Compared to the forgery of non-written objects, faking a papyrus or any other written artifact (from cloth to stone) implies that the writing has to look as ancient as the writing support (we leave aside here the chemical composition of the ink or papyrus, which has not been the subject of a sustained study, though see Wagner et al., 2007; Olsson et al., 2015). Therefore, the forger has to be skilled in imitating ancient writing (although some forgers are rather less successful at this than others). In the case of the Book of the Dead, this means for the most part hieroglyphic writing and its cursive variants. Beside the variants in writing, the forger must also decide what kind of material and format (papyrus roll or sheet, or linen fragment) to replicate, since the texts and vignettes of the Book of the Dead can be inscribed on short pieces of papyrus, but also survive on rolls of up to 20 meters. Judging by the confirmed cases of fakes in this genre recognized to this point, forgers generally (though with some notable exceptions) prefer to work on small fragments, no doubt because the amount of text and number of images to copy would be considerably less, but also probably because the small pieces could can easily be made to look "ancient."

A further issue that a forger of the Book of the Dead must keep in mind is the original quality of the manuscripts. In antiquity these varied from beautifully decorated and carefully written specimens—generally destined for the members of the highest elite, such as the High Priests of Amun and their families in Thebes or the high officials close to the royal family in the Ramesside Period and earlier New Kingdom—to poorly executed and somewhat clumsily decorated smaller papyri. The latter may sometimes appear to be forgeries because of the poor quality of their script and images. However, the ancient Egyptians also produced magical papyri for daily use; these contained less regular script and crudely drawn images, but were nevertheless considered to be powerful amulets. Less beautifully produced specimens of the Book of the Dead would also have been considered to be very effective for the deceased's empowerment in the afterlife. The presence of these less aesthetically pleasing fragments of the Book of the Dead in the record, however, allows forgers to mimic them rather than the deluxe full-length rolls, a considerably easier task.

How then do we recognize a forgery of the Book of the Dead? In the first place, we should not assume that the forger always copies from a single original so that the final product may look more authentic. There are cases where forgeries look like they have been made by arranging sections of text and images taken from various manuscripts that are therefore used as model papyri, similar to the way ancient Egyptian scribes proceeded when compiling a new Book of the Dead. In the case of a papyrus kept in Marseille, for instance, extracts from a few spells and vignettes of the Book of the Dead have been curiously matched to motives taken from other funerary compositions such as the Book of Caverns and the Amduat (Meeks, 1993).

Moreover—again similar to the ancient Egyptian models—fake papyri also can have a predominance of text or images; one would assume that the less experienced forger would opt for reproducing more vignettes than texts, since the writing is definitely more difficult to fake than the images. On the other hand, odd images and clumsy sketches are also often seen as a sign of forgery; this is despite the fact that (as mentioned earlier) there are many examples of genuine artifacts used for magical purposes that do not present iconography or writing of outstanding quality. In particular, such odd iconography can be noted in artifacts of the Roman Period, in which we seem to witness individuals who wished to produce magical objects without the help of a trained scribe, artist, or ritualist (see the example of an odd hypocephalus published by Miatello, 2017).

In order to produce a forgery of the Book of the Dead, one should also be able to obtain a suitable medium, namely papyrus or linen fragments: this is in fact not a very difficult task for individuals dealing with antiquities and/or involved in the black market, since papyrus and linen without decoration can be found preserved, providing a blank specimen.

There are currently 26 cases of recognized fakes belonging to the genre of the Book of the Dead, at least on the basis of those collected by the Book of the Dead Project of Bonn University (http://totenbuch.awk.nrw.de/). Most of the cases of forgeries of the Book of the Dead have been detected when private collectors have inquired with scholars about the authenticity and origin of fragments they have purchased; however, occasionally forgeries have also been found in museum collections. Table 28.1 lists those papyri and linen fragments that have been interpreted as forgeries either by the scholars who published them or after inspection on behalf of the team members of the project. The table does not include some of the examples of fakes mentioned in this chapter, which belong to private individuals and collectors who wish to remain anonymous.

# CASE STUDIES OF FORGERIES OF PAPYRI

Among forgeries on papyrus, the easiest type to identify are those where the forgery is an exact (at least in aspiration) copy of an original papyrus, generally a document known by its long-existing publication or exhibition in a major museum. This is the case, for example, with a false funerary papyrus acquired in the Theban region, which is evidently a copy of a published papyrus kept in the Egyptian Museum of Berlin (P.Berlin P. 3127,

## Table 28.1: List of identified forgeries of the Book of the Dead

| Text | TM/TBP | Material | Dimensions | Language | Contents | Bibliography |
|---|---|---|---|---|---|---|
| M. Aberdeen ABDUA 56019 | 134040 | Linen | 8.3cm (h) x 5.8cm (b) | No text (vignette only) | Unidentified BD vignette, depicting a god seated on a throne | Curtis et al., 2005: 56 |
| M. Aberdeen ABDUA 56020 | 134038 | Linen | 7cm (h) x 3.1cm (b) | No text (vignette only) | Unidentified BD vignette, depicting a mummy | Curtis et al., 2005: 56 |
| M. Aberdeen ABDUA 56005 | 134041 | Linen | 7cm (h) x 6.5cm (b) | No text (vignette only) | Line drawing of an unidentified BD vignette, depicting Isis | Curtis et al., 2005: 56 |
| M. Aberdeen ABDUA 56018 | 134044 | Linen | 7.5cm (h) x 7cm (b) | No text (vignette only) | Line drawing of an unidentified BD vignette, depicting an offering table | Curtis et al., 2005: 56 |
| M. Aberdeen ABDUA 56017 | 134045 | Linen | 8cm (h) x 8.7cm (b) | No text (vignette only) | Unidentified BD vignette, depicting a single seated figure | Curtis et al., 2005: 56 |
| M. Aberdeen ABDUA 23246 | 134047 | Linen | 7cm (h) x 13.3cm (b) | No text (vignette only) | BD 83 and an unidentified BD vignette | Curtis et al., 2005: 56; Lucarelli and Müller-Roth, 2014: 42 |
| M. Aberdeen ABDUA 23261 | 134048 | Linen | 7.3cm (h) x 19cm (b) | No text (vignette only) | Unidentified BD vignette, depicting the king and two other figures | Curtis et al., 2005: 56 |
| M. Aberdeen ABDUA 23274 | 134049 | Linen | 7cm (h) x 28cm (b) | No text (vignette only) | BD 76(?), 78, and 50 | Curtis et al., 2005: 56 |
| M. Aberdeen ABDUA 23265 | 134051 | Linen | 7.5cm (h) x 33cm (b) | No text (vignette only) | BD 81, 75, 83, vignette | Curtis et al., 2005: 56 |

*(continued)*

Table 28.1: Continued

| Text | TM/TBP | Material | Dimensions | Language | Contents | Bibliography |
|---|---|---|---|---|---|---|
| M. Aberdeen ABDUA 23262 | 134051 | Linen | 6.2cm (h) x 28cm (b) | No text (vignette only) | Unidentified BD vignette; sequence of deities in a row, including Osiris | Curtis et al., 2005: 56 |
| M. Aberdeen ABDUA 23257 | 134052 | Linen | 8cm (h) x 38cm (b) | No text (vignette only) | Unidentified BD vignette; five figures depicted giving an offering (?) | Curtis et al., 2005: 56 |
| M. Aberdeen ABDUA 84205 + o.Nr. [3] + o.Nr. [4] | 133946 | Linen | Unknown | Hieratic | A cartouche (ABDUA 84205); and 5 unknown texts (o.Nr. [3] + o.Nr. [4]) | Curtis et al., 2005: 56; Kockelmann, 2008: 357 |
| M. Aberdeen ABDUA 56016 | 134036 | Linen | Unknown | No text (vignette only) | Unidentified BD vignette; depicts an adorant | Curtis et al., 2005: 56 |
| M. Aberdeen ABDUA o.Nr. [6] | 134026 | Linen | 25cm (h) x 5.8cm (b) | Hieratic | BD 18a | Curtis et al., 2005: 56 |
| M. Aberdeen ABDUA o.Nr. [2] | 134029 | Linen | 45cm (h) x 6cm (h) | No text (vignette only) | Unidentified BD vignette | Curtis et al., 2005: 56; Lucarelli and Müller-Roth, 2014: 42 |
| M. Aberdeen ABDUA o.Nr [1] | 134028 | Linen | A: 6cm (h) x 38cm (b); B: 6cm (h) x 35cm (b) | No text (vignette only) | BD 18(?), 72–74 | Curtis et al., 2005: 56; Lucarelli and Müller-Roth, 2014: 42 |
| Rylands Hieroglyphic Manuscript 1 | 133813 | Linen | 34cm (h) x 68cm (b) | Hieroglyphic | BD 17 vignette and text | Lucarelli and Müller-Roth, 2014: 43–44; Kockelmann, 2008: 384 (index) |
| Rylands Hieroglyphic Manuscript 2 | 133814 | Linen; beads | 43cm (h) x 37cm (b) | Hieroglyphic | BD 17 vignette and text | Lucarelli and Müller-Roth, 2014: 43–44; Kockelmann, 2008: 384 (index) |

## Table 28.1: Continued

| Text | TM/TBP | Material | Dimensions | Language | Contents | Bibliography |
|---|---|---|---|---|---|---|
| Rylands Hieroglyphic Manuscript 3 | 133811 | Linen | 21.5cm (h) x 32.5cm (b) | Hieratic | BD 17 (vignette) and BD 18 (text) assigned to the name Neshorprê (ns-Hr-pA-rA), as well as two unidentified unrelated scenes | Lucarelli and Müller-Roth, 2014: 43–45; Kockelmann. 2008: 371 (index) |
| Rylands Hieroglyphic Manuscript 4 | 133812 | Linen | 21cm (h) x 54cm (b) | Hieratic | BD 15 and 17, assigned to the name Neshorprê (ns-Hr-pA-rA), as well as an additional figure not present in model. Forger has also filled in lacunae in the cartouche, where model is fragmented | Lucarelli and Müller-Roth, 2014: 43–45; Kockelmann, 2008: 371 (index) |
| P.Privatsammlung Uppsala | 134780 | Papyrus | 14cm (h) x 19cm (b) | "Hieroglyphic" | Nonsensical text with a fragmentary image of a crowned head | *Sotheby's Antiquities* (1988) Nr. 69 |
| P.Marseille 5323 | 134643 | Papyrus | 27cm (h) x 58cm (b) | Hieratic | A motif from the Book of Amduat (126V), written together with BD 149 and presented as a single text | Meeks, 1993: 290–305, pl. 16; Lanzone,1881–1886: pl. 267 |
| TM 134211 | 134211 | linen | 6.8cm (h) x 315cm (b) | Hieroglyphic | BD 17, 30, 64 with various other scenes and an unidentified spell | *Reperti Archeoli* (2008) lot 237 |

(*continued*)

Table 28.1: Continued

| Text | TM/TBP | Material | Dimensions | Language | Contents | Bibliography |
|---|---|---|---|---|---|---|
| M. Vienna 3239 | 114069 | Linen | 11cm (h) x 328cm (b) | Hieroglyphic | Excerpts from BD 17, 30, 64; various scenes depicting different gods and Ennead | Kockelmann, 2008: 382 (index) |
| M. Vienna 3855 | 133916 | Linen | 7.8cm (h) x 92.5cm (b) | Hieroglyphic | Procession of gods | Satzinger, 1994: 36; Kockelmann, 2008: 382 (index) |
| M. Würzburg H2217 | 133836 | Linen | 10.8cm (h) x 279.6 cm (b) | Hieroglyphic (?) | Unidentified BD text | Simon, 1975: 38 |

see Meeks, 1993; for analogous cases among Greek and Coptic forgeries, see Horak, 1991: 97; Askeland, 2015).

The beautifully manufactured Book of the Dead of Hunefer, a "king's scribe" of the Nineteenth Dynasty, kept in the British Museum, has formed the model for a few short papyri, on which Hunefer's section including the final judgment of BD 125 was copied down. These forgeries belonged to a private individual who contacted the Bonn University Book of the Dead Project in 2012 to check the authenticity of the pieces, at which point the identity of the original model could be established. As so often happens when identifying a forgery, however, it was not possible to reconstruct the origin and history of the pieces before they arrived in the hands of the final owner (who wanted to stay anonymous).

Spell 125 of the Book of the Dead, with the popular scene of the final judgment of the deceased (see Janák, this volume), seems to have been one of the favorite compositions to be selected for forgeries on papyrus. Another example has been found on a papyrus fragment found in the Biblioteca Laurentina in Rome (P.Lincei Ieratico I, see Boffula, 2013, in particular p. 87 and Fig. 7). The piece was stuck on a piece of hard paper, and the UV analysis of the papyrus's surface seemed to indicate that the glue used was modern, which may be a sign of forgery (though the practice of gluing genuine papyri on modern cardboard or paper was current in the nineteenth century, see Frösen, 2009: 85–86).

## Case Studies of Forgeries of Mummy Bandages and Linen Fragments

One evident example of forgery of the Book of the Dead on mummy bandages is a set of a fragments from the Marischal Museum in Aberdeen, listed as ABDUA, 56005, 56017,

56018, 56019, 56020, 23246, 23257, 23261, 23262, 23265, 23274, 84205 in the Book of the Dead Project Database (see Table 28.1, p. 559–60; Curtis et al., 2005: 56; Kockelmann, 2008: 8). They present evidently faked vignettes and copies of passages taken from BD 17 and 18. As noted by the publishers of the fragments, the linen used for these faked fragments seems to be ancient, but the occurrence of falsified cartouches in purple pigment are a clear indication of forgery. The use of royal cartouches is widespread in forgeries of ancient Egyptian artifacts since they generally attract the attention of potential buyers and private collectors at auctions; it is, however, very uncommon to find cartouches on Book of the Dead documents, most of which were made for private, non-royal individuals. Moreover, purple ink is not attested in texts of the Book of the Dead, where generally red and black inks are the only ones used (see Verhoeven, this volume).

A similar case of a fake cartouche on a forgery of the Book of the Dead was identified by the team members of the Book of the Dead Project on a linen fragment approximately 30 cm in length, which depicted an embalming scene similar to that in one of the vignettes of BD 151 (Fig. 28.1), which is here accompanied by the depiction of a cartouche of Ramses II. The private collector who was inquiring

FIG. 28.1. Linen Fragment, Private Collection: Vignette of Spell 151 with cartouche (Courtesy Totenbuch Archive, Bonn).

about this object was tricked by the cartouche into thinking that the fragment was perhaps an offering to Pharaoh, not realizing that the hieroglyphs were unreadable and the whole layout of the fragment was not usual for the genre. As is often the case when dealing with specimens from private collections, it is virtually impossible to find out where the forgery was produced and how it then circulated on the market, since private collectors usually do not possess, or are unwilling to provide, such information.

## The mummy bandages of the "Ryland Hieroglyphic Manuscripts"

Mummy bandages inscribed with Book of the Dead spells and vignettes were very common, especially in the Ptolemaic Period (Gasse, this volume), and therefore many of them are also part of Egyptological collections around the world. One of the Book of the Dead Project's team members, Holger Kockelmann, has catalogued most of them in a three-volume publication (Kockelmann, 2008). This research revealed the very interesting case of four fake mummy bandages kept in the John Rylands University Library of Manchester, which had hitherto been considered to be authentic. Through archival research in the library, Kockelmann (2020) has been able to reconstruct something of the history of these mummy bandages, catalogued in the library as "Rylands Hieroglyphic Manuscript 1–4," even though only two of them were written in hieroglyphic, while the other two were in hieratic.

These texts were part of the collection of manuscripts owned by the 26th Earl of Crawford (James Ludovic Lindsay) and purchased by Mrs. Rylands in 1901 to form the foundation of the library created in her late husband's honor (Mazza, 2012; Barker, 1977). Rather than deriving from the large-scale purchases of papyri by the 26th Earl in Egypt in the late nineteenth century (Choat, 2012), these belong to the earliest stratum of the Egyptian manuscripts in the Bibliotheca Lindesiana (on which see in general Barker, 1977). They were purchased by his father, the 25th Earl of Crawford (Alexander Lindsay), who recorded in the library report he compiled near the end of his life "a volume containing fragments of four ancient Egyptian MSS., written in hieroglyphics on cloth." As Kockelmann's investigations have proved, this "volume" is identical with the leather folio containing Rylands Hieroglyphic Manuscripts 1–4, which is still extant in the John Rylands University Library of Manchester; it is also known as the "Atlas contenant des fragments de toiles égyptiennes avec hieroglyphs" (also described, less clearly, as "Fragments Dactylologiques") listed in the catalogue of the van Alstein sale of 1863 (van Alstein, 1863: 384), where the 25th Earl purchased Egyptian manuscripts, including this one (Barker, 1977: 210–11).

Among the four fragments, the one labeled as "Ryl. Hieroglyphic Manuscript 3" (32.5 cm long by 21.5 cm high), belonging to a woman called Neshorprê (*Ns-Ḥr-pꜣ-Rꜥ*) is in a very good state of preservation, and the hieratic text is readable: one wonders is

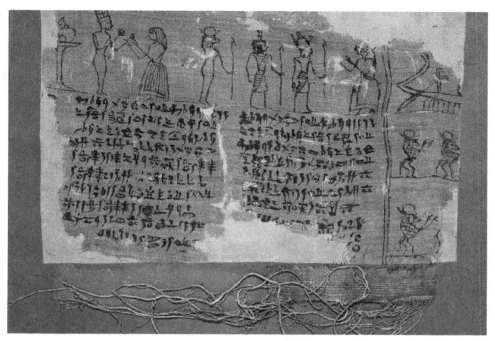

FIG. 28.2. "Rylands Hieroglyphic Manuscript 3" (Courtesy Totenbuch Archive, Bonn).

this proof that forgers could perhaps be trained in writing the cursive Egyptian scripts. Similar to the other three linen fragments, this piece has been pasted onto tissue and glued to a page of red leather for better preservation (Fig. 28.2). It displays part of a very typical and much attested vignette of the Book of Dead, generally associated with BD 15 and representing the boat of the sun god and four baboons worshipping the sun. On the same fragment one can recognize two columns of text (of 10 lines each) from the initial section of spell 18 of the Book of the Dead, with accompanying vignettes in the upper register of the same section, depicting the deceased worshipping Atum, Shu, and Tefnut in one vignette and Min, standing in front of an offering table, in the other. These vignettes are clearly inspired by the composite illustration of BD spell 18, depicting the various divine tribunals mentioned in the text, but with some peculiar variations, such as the presence of the ithyphallic god Min, in an awkward worshipping position with outstretched arms and hands that is not typical of either Min or of other ancient Egyptian gods in ritual scenes. Moreover, the name of the deceased as copied on the fragment, Neshorprê (Ns-Ḥr-pȝ-Rʿ), is the same as found in the other hieratic linen fragment in the group (labeled as Ryl. Hieroglyphic Manuscript 4), which also contains exactly the same text as well as a variation of the vignette of BD spell 15. Since it is unlikely that the same portion of text was written on two different fragments for the same individual, Kockelmann hypothesized that both fragments were copied from the same model papyrus, namely a hieratic Book of the Dead kept in Paris (Bibliothèque nationale/P.Paris BN 93–98) and published in

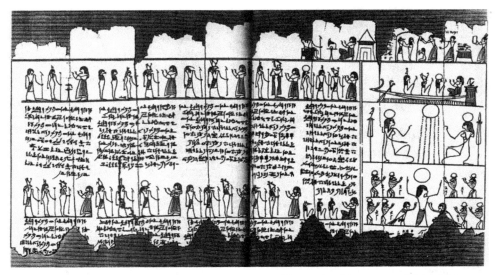

FIG. 28.3. La Description de l'Egypte, Pl. 62: section of facsimile of the papyrus P.Paris BN 63-98.

facsimile in the nineteenth century in *Description de l'Égypte* (Pls. 61–65, in particular Pl. 62; Fig. 28.3). It was very likely the facsimile and not the original papyrus that was used to create the forgeries, which were made as a batch with some variations between them. It is interesting how, in a certain way, the forger behaved like an ancient scribe working in a workshop of prefabricated Book of the Dead scrolls, although he was not changing the owner's name, as an ancient Egyptian scribe had to do in order to personalize each prefabricated piece. Moreover, we should recognize a certain degree of creativity in the forger, who added peculiar elements to the canonical vignette, such as the ithyphallic Min, which never appears in relation to spells of the Book of the Dead.

The existence of forgeries of the Book of the Dead on linen and mummy bandages may also be connected with the phenomenon of "mummymania," which is a subproduct of Egyptomania and the fascination with ancient Egypt in Europe and the Americas in general. Mummies were the main symbol of the mysterious and supernatural magic and curses of the Pharaoh; "mumia," or mummy powder—finely ground bones and other remains—was a renowned drug in sixteenth-century Europe (Dannenfeldt, 1985). Inscribed mummy bandages were therefore likely seen as an equally portentous material, which would justify their presence on the antiquarian market as well.

## Conclusions

It can thus be seen that, far from being uninteresting specimens of modern criminal enterprises, fake fragments of the Book of the Dead actually contribute to our knowledge of the development of attitudes toward ancient Egypt and the discipline of Egyptology in the nineteenth and twentieth centuries, help elucidate aspects of the market for Egyptian antiquities, and—most surprisingly—offer some interesting counterpoints to ancient scribal practice. If they are not as deserving of study as the genuine remains of the Book of the Dead studied elsewhere in this volume, they nevertheless remain worthy of our attention.

## Bibliography

van Alstein, P. L. (1863). *Catalogue des livres et manuscrits formant la bibliothèque de feu Mr. P. Léopold van Alstein*, vol. 1 (Gand: C. Annoot-Braeckman).
Askeland, C. (2015). "A Lycopolitan Forgery of John's Gospel." *New Testament Studies* 61: 314–34.
Barker, N. (1977). *Bibliotheca Lindesiana. The Lives and Collections of Alexander William, 25th Earl of Crawford and 8th Earl of Balcarres, and James Ludovic, 26th Earl of Crawford and 9th Earl of Balcarres* (London: Bernard Quaritch).
Boffula, P. (2013). "Principles of Consolidation and Diagnostic Applied to the Restoration of the Arabic Papyri of Oriental Origin Found in Rome." In *Strategie e programmazione della conservazione e trasmissibilità del patrimonio culturale*, edited by A. Filipović and W. Troiano, 80–87 (Rome: Fidei Signa Edizioni Scientifiche).
Choat, M. (2012). "Lord Crawford's Search for Papyri: On the Origin of the Rylands Papyrus Collection." In *Actes du 26e Congres international de papyrologie. Geneve 16–21 aout 2010*, edited by P. Schubert, 141–47 (Geneva: Droz).
Choat, M. (2019a). "Dating Papyri: Familiarity, Instinct, and Guesswork." *Journal for the Study of the New Testament* 42(1): 58–83.
Choat, M. (2019b). "Forging Antiquities: The Case of Papyrus Fakes." In *The Palgrave Handbook on Art Crime*, edited by S. Hufnagel and D. Chappell (Basingstoke: Palgrave Macmillan) (forthcoming).
Coles R. A. and Gallazzi, C. (1981). "Papyri and Ostraka: Alterations and Counterfeits." In *Scritti in onore di Orsolina* Montevecchi, edited by E. Bresciani, 99–105 (Bologna: Clueb).
Curtis, N. G. W., Kockelmann, H., and Munro, I. (2005). "The Collection of Book of the Dead Manuscripts in Marischal Museum, University of Aberdeen, Scotland. A Comprehensive Overview." *Bulletin de l'Institut français d'archeologie orientale* 105: 49–73.
Dannenfeldt, K. H. (1985). "Egyptian Mumia: The Sixteenth Century Experience and Debate." *The Sixteenth Century Journal* 16: 163–80.
Davis, K. (2017). "Caves of Dispute: Patterns of Correspondence and Suspicion in the Post-2002 'Dead Sea Scrolls' Fragments." *Dead Sea Discoveries* 24(2): 229–70.
Davis, K., Rabin, I., et al. (2017). "Nine Dubious 'Dead Sea Scrolls' Fragments from the Twenty-First Century." *Dead Sea Discoveries* 24(2): 189–228.
Fournet, J.-L. (2016). "Le faux en écriture d'après la documentation papyrologique." In *Académie des inscriptions et belles-lettres. Comptes rendus des séances de l'année 2016*, I (Janvier-Mars), 67–90 (Paris: de Boccard).
Frösén, J. (2009). "Conservation of Ancient Papyrus Materials." In *The Oxford Handbook of Papyrology*, edited by R. S. Bagnall, 79–100 (Oxford: Oxford University Press).
Horak, U. (1991). "Fälschungen auf Papyrus, Pergament, Papier und Ostraka." *Tyche* 6: 91–98.

Horak, U. (2001). "Fälschungen auf Papyrus, Pergament und Papier." In *Kopie und Fälschung*, edited by C. Gastgeber, 51–60 (Graz: Adeva Akademische Druck—und Verlagsanstalt).

Jones, M., ed. (1990). *Fake? The Art of Deception* (Berkeley; Los Angeles: University of California Press).

Kockelmann, H. (2008). *Untersuchungen zu den Späten Totenbuch-Handschriften auf Mumienbinden. II. Handbuch zu den Mumienbinden und Leinenamuletten*. Studien zum Altägyptischen Totenbuch 12.II (Wiesbaden: Harrassowitz).

Kockelmann, H. (2020). "Four Nineteenth-Century *Book of the Dead* Forgeries on Mummy Linen in the John Rylands Library, or: the *Description de l'Égypt* as a Faker's Master Copy." *Bulletin of the John Rylands University Library* 96(1): 1–24.

Lapatin, K. (2002). *Mysteries of the Snake Goddess: Art, Desire, and the Forging of History* (Boston: Houghton Mifflin).

Lanzone, R. V. (1881–1886). *Dizionario di mitologia egizia*, vols. 1–3 (Torino: Doyen).

Mazza, R. (2012). "Graeco-Roman Egypt at Manchester. The Formation of the Rylands Papyri Collection." In *Actes du 26e Congres international de papyrologie. Geneve 16–21 aout 2010*, edited by P. Schubert, 499–507 (Geneva: Droz).

Lucarelli, R. and Müller-Roth, M. (2014). "Fälschungen für die Toten: Gefälschte Papyri des altägyptisches Totenbuch." *IBAES (Internet-Beiträge zur Ägyptologie und Sudanarchäologie)* XV: 41–50.

Meeks, D. (1993). "Deux papyrus funéraires de Marseille (Inv. 292 et 5323). À propos de quelques personnages thébains." In *Ancient Egypt and Kush*, edited by E. G. Karpieskaja and A. A. Kovaljev, 290–305 (Moskow: Gs Korostovtsev).

Miatello, L. (2017). "A Hypocephalus with Odd Iconography and Poor Writing in the Berlin Museum." *Zeitschrift für Ägyptische Sprache und Altertumskunde* 144: 86–97.

Muscarella, O. (2000). *The Lie became Great. The Forgery of Ancient Near Eastern Cultures* (Groningen: Styx).

Olsson, A.-M. B., Calligaro, T. Colinart, S. Dran, J. C., Lövestam, N. E. G. Moignard, B. Orlandi, S., Caldelli, M. L., and Gregori G. L. (2015). "Forgeries and Fakes." In *The Oxford Handbook of Roman Epigraphy*, edited by C. Bruun and J. C. Edmondson, 42–65 (Oxford: Oxford University Press).

Salomon, J. (2001). "Micro-PIXE Analysis of an Ancient Egyptian papyrus: Identification of Pigments Used for the 'Book of the Dead.'" *Nuclear Instruments and Methods in Physics Research Section B: Beam Interactions with Materials and Atoms* 181: 707–14.

Satzinger, H. (1994). *Das Kunsthistorische Museum in Wien: die Ägyptisch-Orientalische Sammlung*. Zaberns Bildbände zur Archäologie 14 (Mainz: Zabern).

Simon, E., ed. (1975). *Führer durch die Antikenabteilung des Martin von Wagner Museums der Universität Würzburg* (Mainz: Philipp von Zabern).

Wagner, B., Donten, M. L., Donten, M., Bulska, E., Jackowska, A., and Sobucki, W. (2007). "Analytical Approach to the Conservation of the Ancient Egyptian Manuscript 'Bakai Book of the Dead': A Case Study." *Microchimica Acta* 159: 101–8.

Wakeling, T. G. (1912). *Forged Egyptian Antiquities* (London: A. & C. Black).

# Index

Aberdeen, Marischal Museum, 562
Abusir, 174, 181, 237
Abusir el-Melek, 369
Abydos, 19, 23, 29, 37, 20–22, 62, 137, 165, 288, 296, 325–27, 358
Adaptation, 524
Address to the deities in the hall and to Osiris, 134
Adhesive, 550
Adoration, 349, 352–53
Adoration of Osiris, 42, 46, 50–51, 198–99, 211, 214
Adoration scene, 39, 151, 199, 203
Aesthetic, 524, 557
Afterlife, 393–95, 438
Ahmose I, 24, 46, 198, 201, 219
Aiken, Conrad Potter, 508, 511
Air, 348
*akh*, 96, 300, 301, 344, 373–74, 393, 395, 396, 400, 402, 415–16, 421, 424, 427, 430–31, 527
Akhenaten, 56
Akhmim, 37, 62, 142, 165, 174, 211, 226–28, 239, 295–96, 300, 308, 321, 324–25, 332, 334, 357, 364, 368, 435, 531
Allen, James P., 533
Allen, Thomas G., 529–30, 534–36
Amarna Period, 353
Amduat, 26, 76, 78, 81–82, 88, 101, 104, 235, 280, 282–83, 398, 430, 558
Amemet, 411–12, 428
Amenemhat I, 374
Amenemhat II, 12, 15
Amenemhat III, 12–13, 15–16, 22
Amenemope, 91–92, 104, 165
Amenhotep I, 83, 221
Amenhotep II, 38–39, 45, 47, 52, 199, 219, 445–46, 531

Amenhotep III, 37, 52, 54, 63, 166, 199, 219, 221, 411, 446
Amenhotep, Coffin Da 6X, 22
Amenhotep, son of Hapu, 269, 436
Ameni, Coffin S 8X, 16
Amenirdis I, 235
Amulet, 201, 345–46, 382, 403, 406, 415, 425, 438
Amulet book, 345
Amulet chapter, 345–46, 513
Amulet heart, 415
Amulet *udjat*, 98
Amun, 77–8, 89, 99, 104, 203, 232, 235, 434–36, 439, 441–42
Amun-Re, 203, 214, 422, 429, 433, 440–41
Aniba, 378
Animal, demonic, 429
Animal, sacred, 428
Ankhenesneferibre, 208
Another saying (*ky ḏd*), 267, 343, 463
Anthroponym, 439
Antinoopolis, 312–13
Anubis, 11–12, 228, 233, 310, 326, 329, 359–60, 364–65, 367, 369, 398, 411, 426–27, 429, 431, 515–16
Anubis mask, 360, 364, 369
Apis, 223
Apis Altar, 506, 507
Apis Embalming Ritual, 223
Apocalypses, 408
Apophis, 168, 233, 347, 352, 430, 461, 517, 525
Apophis, spine of, 430
Apotropaic, 467
Appeal of the Living, 394
Archaism, 528
Archaizing, 529
Archetype, 266, 530–31
Artemis, 296

Aset (P.Moscow I, 1b, 121), 208
Asetemakhbit (P.New York MMA 25.3.29), 206
Asetreshti (P.Privat MacGregor), 210
Asetweret (P.Leiden T 31), 210
Aspelta, 238
Assasif, 234–37, 240
Assasif, tomb no. 729, 36
Assessment of purity, 402
Asyut, 10, 16, 21, 326
Assmann, Jan, 533
Assuan, 233
Aten, 56
Atfih, 239, 240
Atum, 82, 327, 397, 422, 427, 430, 565
Augustus III, Elector of Saxony, King of Poland, Grand Duke of Lithuania, 507
*Aura Kingdom*, 516
Authenic, 524
Authenticity, 438
Authenticity in tone, 522, 524
Autobiography, 400, 414, 526
Autogenic, 440
Awibre Hor, Coffin Da 4C, 13–4
Aye, 363

*ba*, 99, 137, 226, 228, 232, 237, 240, 270, 272, 300–1, 304, 305, 306–8, 313, 325, 326, 327, 331, 332, 408, 412, 431, 509, 510, 512, 513
Bab el-Gusus, Second Cachette, 77, 91
Baba, 401
*ba*-bird, 53, 331–32, 365, 370, 422
Baboon, 272, 367, 426–27
Baboon entrails, 272
*ba*-bringer, 211
Bahariya Oasis, 237
Bakenrenef, 237–38
Balance, 410
Band, Ars Nova, 515
Band, Nile, 514
Bardo Thodol, 506
Barguet, Paul, 533–35, 538
*ba*-soul, 344, 467, 477
Bastet, 516
Bastetiirdis (M.London UC 32381+32382), 209
*Batman: Book of the Dead*, 514

BD 1, 42–43, 50, 53, 68, 97, 119, 121–22, 126, 132, 134–36, 152, 155, 171, 173, 208, 225–26, 233, 236, 240, 283, 309, 349, 352–53, 359–60, 363, 364–65, 368–70, 451–52, 456, 469, 512–15
BD 1 B, 98, 359, 369
BD 1 B vignette, 359
BD 1 I, 97
BD 1 II, 97
BD 1 vignette, 151, 155, 357, 360, 363–64, 367–70, 515
BD 2, 97, 119, 121–22, 134–36, 151–52, 155, 225, 349, 469
BD 3, 97, 119, 121, 122, 134–36, 151–52, 225, 349, 469
BD 4, 119, 121–22, 134–36, 151–52, 155, 225, 350, 469
BD 5, 119, 121–22, 134–36, 151, 155, 225, 271, 273, 469
BD 6, 20, 119, 121–22, 134–36, 151, 155, 225, 441, 469
BD 7, 43, 119, 121–22, 134–36, 151, 155, 198, 225, 232, 430, 469
BD 8, 42–4, 119, 121–22, 134–36, 151, 155, 225, 469
BD 8 B, 27
BD 9, 42, 119, 121–22, 134–36, 151, 155, 152, 469
BD 10, 119, 121–22, 134–36, 469
BD 10/48, 151, 153
BD 11, 119, 121–22, 134–36, 469
BD 11/49, 151–153
BD 12, 119, 121–22, 134–36, 350, 456, 469
BD 12/120, 97, 151–52
BD 13, 17–18, 119, 121–22, 134–36, 350, 469
BD 13/121, 97, 151, 154
BD 14, 42–43, 119, 121–22, 134–136, 151, 154, 155, 198, 469
BD 15, 64, 119, 121–22, 126, 132, 134–136, 153, 164, 170, 201, 208, 225, 235–237, 239, 270, 353, 364, 367, 469, 470, 565
BD 15 A, 174, 353
BD 15 B, 235, 353
BD 15 B III, 98
BD 15 B III (g)(c), 154
BD 15 C, 235
BD 15 D, 235
BD 15 vignette, 151, 153–155

BD 16, 119, 134, 234, 240, 469–70, 472
BD 17, 23, 25, 40, 42, 50, 54, 56, 64, 91, 93, 96, 97, 104, 119, 121, 129, 133–136, 151, 155, 198, 221, 225–26, 233, 235–38, 269–71, 303–4, 307, 333–34, 364, 431, 446, 452, 469–70, 515–16, 530, 563
BD 17 vignette, 151, 155, 430, 515–16, 563
BD 18, 40, 42, 50, 91, 93, 97, 119, 134–36, 152–53, 155, 225, 233, 235–36, 237–39, 268, 287, 346, 396, 411, 426, 446, 452, 563, 565
BD 18 vignette, 151, 154–55, 563, 565
BD 18.1, 450
BD 19, 119, 134–36, 151–53, 155, 225, 236, 268, 287, 346, 396, 413, 454
BD 19 vignette, 154
BD 20, 119, 134–36, 151, 153, 236, 268, 287, 346, 396, 426, 454
BD 21, 50, 119, 134–36, 151, 153–54, 225, 236, 287, 346, 413, 446, 451, 454, 460–61, 513–15
BD 21 vignette, 154
BD 22, 23, 42, 50, 119, 134–36, 151, 154, 221, 225, 232, 236, 287, 346, 413, 446, 451, 454, 469, 514, 515
BD 23, 42, 50, 91, 96, 98, 99, 104, 119, 134–36, 151, 153–55, 221, 225, 232, 236, 287, 346, 413, 446, 451, 454
BD 24, 23, 18, 42, 50, 91, 96, 119, 134–36, 151, 221, 225, 232, 236, 346, 413, 446, 451, 454
BD 25, 23, 42, 50, 91, 96, 119, 134–36, 151, 153–54, 221, 225, 232, 236, 346, 413, 446, 451, 454, 513
BD 25 vignette, 151
BD 26, 23, 42, 50, 91, 96, 119, 134–36, 149, 151, 153–54, 221, 225, 232, 236, 287, 346, 413, 446, 451, 454
BD 26 vignette, 151, 154
BD 27, 42, 43, 50, 91, 96, 119, 134–36, 153, 154, 198, 221, 225, 232, 236, 238, 287, 346, 413, 446, 451, 454
BD 27 vignette, 151, 154
BD 28, 42, 50, 91, 96, 119, 134–36, 151, 155, 221, 225, 232, 236, 238, 287, 346, 413, 446, 451, 454
BD 28 B, 345
BD 28 vignette, 151, 154
BD 29, 50, 119, 134–36, 154, 225, 236, 345, 346, 413, 454, 469
BD 29 vignette, 151

BD 30, 50, 119, 134–36, 153, 149, 225, 236, 238, 287, 345–46, 397, 300, 446, 448, 451, 454, 514, 515
BD 30 A, 23, 42, 149, 151, 232, 346, 403
BD 30 A vignette, 154
BD 30 B, 14, 20, 42–43, 151, 221, 345–46, 394, 406, 415, 416
BD 30 B vignette, 403, 406
BD 30 vignette, 151, 154
BD 31, 23, 42, 50, 119, 134–36, 137, 232, 236, 268, 347, 429, 446, 447
BD 31 vignette, 151
BD 32, 119, 134–37, 236, 347, 429, 447
BD 32 vignette, 151
BD 33, 22, 23, 42, 97, 119, 134–37, 232, 236, 347, 429, 430, 446, 447, 448
BD 33 vignette, 151
BD 34, 27, 42, 119, 134–37, 232, 236, 347, 429–30, 446–47
BD 35, 42, 119, 134–37, 232, 236, 347, 429, 430, 446–47
BD 36, 119, 134–36, 153, 236, 347, 429–30, 446–47
BD 37, 97, 119, 134–36, 236, 347–48, 429–30, 446–47
BD 38, 50, 119, 134–36, 236, 347–48, 429, 447, 448, 454, 460, 462, 475–76
BD 38 A, 17, 43, 97, 198, 348
BD 38 B, 97, 348
BD 39, 43, 119, 134–36, 151, 198, 236, 347, 429–30, 446–47, 454, 461–63
BD 40, 50, 119, 134–36, 236, 347, 429–30, 446, 447
BD 41, 42, 119, 134–36, 232, 236, 347, 429, 447–48
BD 41 B, 91, 347
BD 42, 119, 134–36, 153, 182, 232, 236, 287, 347–48, 429, 511
BD 43, 23, 42, 119, 134–36, 153, 346–47, 463–65, 477
BD 43 vignette, 154
BD 44, 15, 119, 134–36, 153–54, 347, 451, 477
BD 45, 27, 42, 119, 134–36, 153, 232, 235, 237, 347, 477
BD 46, 119, 134–36, 154, 347, 477
BD 47, 18, 119, 134–36, 153, 347
BD 48, 119, 134–36, 451, 489

BD 49, 119, 134–36
BD 50, 119, 134–36, 166, 235, 237
BD 51, 119, 134–36, 347
BD 52, 17, 119, 134–36, 347
BD 53, 119, 134–36, 153, 347
BD 54, 50, 97, 119, 134–36, 152–54, 236, 332, 347–48, 447
BD 54 vignette, 153
BD 55, 23, 42, 50, 97, 119, 134–36, 154, 235, 236–37, 332, 347–48, 447
BD 56, 17, 23, 42, 50, 97, 119, 134–36, 153, 236, 332, 347–48, 447
BD 57, 50, 97, 119, 134–36, 153, 236–37, 240, 332, 347–48, 447, 465–66
BD 57 vignette, 154
BD 58, 97, 119, 134–36, 236, 332, 347–48, 447, 454
BD 59, 119, 134–36, 153, 232–33, 236–37, 240, 332, 347–48, 424, 447, 477
BD 59 vignette, 154, 424
BD 60, 119, 134–36, 236, 332, 347–48, 447, 525
BD 61, 42, 119, 134–36, 236, 332, 347–48, 447
BD 62, 23, 27, 42, 119, 134–36, 236, 287, 332, 347–48, 447, 469, 477–78
BD 63, 50, 119, 134–36, 332, 344, 347–48
BD 63 A, 42, 348
BD 63 B, 43–44, 52, 348
BD 64, 43–44, 97, 119, 134–36, 151, 271, 350
BD 64 L vignette, 42–44
BD 64 S vignette, 42–44
BD 64 vignette, 151
BD 65, 43, 97, 119, 134–36, 151, 198, 350
BD 66, 119, 134–36, 151
BD 66 vignette, 152
BD 67, 42, 119, 134–36
BD 68, 24, 42, 69, 97, 119, 134–36, 151, 153, 469
BD 68 vignette, 152
BD 69, 24, 42, 97, 119, 134–36, 350, 469
BD 70, 42, 97, 119, 134–36, 350, 469
BD 71, 18, 36, 42–43, 45, 119, 134–136, 166, 304
BD 71 vignette, 152
BD 72, 26, 42, 97, 119, 134–36, 151, 198, 268, 303, 515
BD 72 vignette, 152
BD 73, 119, 134–36, 151, 478
BD 74, 42, 119, 134–36, 151, 232–33
BD 74 vignette, 154

BD 75, 119, 134–36, 151, 349
BD 76, 27, 50, 119, 134–37, 289, 343–44, 422
BD 77, 42–43, 50, 119, 134–37, 151, 198, 219, 289, 343–44, 422, 445–46, 478–79
BD 78, 50, 68, 119, 134–37, 151, 232, 289, 343–44, 422, 509
BD 78 vignette, 152
BD 79, 18, 50, 119, 134–37, 151, 201, 236, 289, 343–44, 347, 422–24
BD 79 vignette, 152
BD 80, 43–44, 50, 119, 134–37, 151, 153–54, 236, 289, 343–44, 422
BD 81, 50, 119, 134–37, 151, 208, 236, 289, 343–44, 422, 446
BD 81 A, 232, 344, 422
BD 81 B, 344
BD 81 vignette, 152
BD 82, 42–43, 50, 119, 134–37, 151, 198, 201, 236, 289, 343–44, 422, 445
BD 82 vignette, 152
BD 83, 24, 40, 43, 50, 119, 134–37, 151, 198, 219, 236, 289, 343–44, 422, 445–46, 479, 480
BD 83 vignette, 152, 479
BD 84, 24, 40, 43, 50, 119, 134–37, 151, 198, 219, 236, 289, 343, 422, 445, 451
BD 85, 24, 40, 43, 50, 119, 134–37, 151, 198, 219, 236, 289, 343–44, 422, 445, 451
BD 85 vignette, 152, 154
BD 86, 17, 43, 50, 53–54, 119, 134–37, 151, 198, 219, 232, 236, 268, 289, 343, 422, 445–46, 451
BD 86 vignette, 152
BD 87, 50, 119, 134–37, 151, 219, 232, 236, 289, 343, 347, 422, 446, 453, 456, 514
BD 87 vignette, 152–54
BD 88, 50, 119, 134–37, 151, 219, 232, 236, 289, 343, 422, 453, 456, 514
BD 88 vignette, 152
BD 89, 119, 134, 135–36, 151, 235, 237, 327, 453, 509
BD 89 vignette, 153, 509
BD 90, 119, 121, 134–36, 151
BD 90 vignette, 152
BD 91, 42, 43, 119, 134–36, 151, 154, 232, 235, 453, 510
BD 91 vignette, 152, 153
BD 92, 42, 97, 119, 134–36, 151, 153, 451, 453, 510

# INDEX

BD 92 vignette, 152
BD 93, 42, 119, 134, 135, 136, 151, 232, 467
BD 93 vignette, 152
BD 94, 43–44, 119, 134, 135, 136, 151, 233
BD 94 vignette, 152
BD 95, 42, 119, 134, 135, 136, 151
BD 96, 119, 134–36, 151, 469
BD 97, 119, 134–36, 151, 469
BD 98, 97, 119, 134–36, 151, 226
BD 98 vignette, 152
BD 99, 84, 119, 134–36, 151, 198, 226, 353, 445, 528
BD 99 B, 43, 97, 138, 151, 219, 232, 268, 489
BD 100, 43, 50, 56, 97–8, 119, 121, 127, 134–36, 168, 236, 290
BD 100/129, 151–54, 198–99
BD 100/129 vignette, 152, 153
BD 101, 97–98, 121, 119, 134–36, 151, 201, 304, 306
BD 101 vignette, 153–54
BD 102, 43, 50, 119, 121, 134–36, 151, 198, 232
BD 102 vignette, 152–53
BD 103, 119, 121, 134–36, 151
BD 104, 119, 121, 134–36, 151, 153
BD 104 vignette, 152
BD 105, 42, 119, 121, 134–36, 151, 451
BD 105 vignette, 152
BD 106, 42–43, 119, 121, 134–36, 151, 235
BD 107, 119, 121, 134–37, 151, 350, 431
BD 108, 50, 119, 121, 134–37, 151, 232, 350, 431, 525
BD 108 vignette, 152
BD 109, 50, 119, 121, 126, 134–37, 151–52, 232, 350, 431, 467–68
BD 110, 65, 84, 86, 102, 119, 126–27, 134–137, 182, 201, 231–34, 251, 350, 377, 379, 383, 431, 446, 472, 474, 513–15
BD 110 B vignette, 152
BD 110 C vignette, 151
BD 110 vignette, 373, 375–83, 385, 513
BD 111, 50, 119, 134–37, 152, 350, 431, 469
BD 112, 50, 119, 134–37, 152, 232, 350, 431
BD 113, 50, 119, 134–37, 152, 232, 350, 431
BD 114, 50, 119, 134–37, 152, 232, 350, 431
BD 115, 50, 119, 134–37, 152, 350, 431
BD 115 vignette, 152
BD 116, 43, 50, 119, 134–37, 152, 198, 350, 431

BD 117, 119, 134–37, 152, 236, 350
BD 117 vignette, 152
BD 118, 119, 134–36, 152, 236, 350
BD 42–43, 119, 134–36, 152, 198, 236, 232, 350
BD 119 vignette, 152
BD 120, 119, 134–36, 152, 236
BD 121, 17–18, 119, 134–36, 152, 236
BD 122, 18, 42, 119, 134, 135, 136, 152, 350
BD 123, 97, 119, 134–36, 152, 344, 350, 469
BD 123/139, 152
BD 124, 24, 40, 43, 50, 119, 134–36, 152–53, 198, 219, 343–44, 445
BD 125, 27, 84, 86, 104, 119, 126, 134–36, 149, 152, 174, 182, 201, 208, 221, 224, 232–35, 238–40, 245, 251–52, 289, 300, 308–310, 312, 314, 344, 353, 394, 397–402, 410, 416, 426–27, 446, 449, 474, 476, 511, 513, 515, 562
BD 125 A, 134, 152–53, 155, 353
BD 125 B, 101, 134, 152–53, 155, 353
BD 125 C, 134, 152, 155, 353
BD 125 D, 134, 155, 353
BD 125 D vignette, 134
BD 125 vignette, 155, 403, 413
BD 126, 84, 119, 134–36, 152, 353, 398, 513
BD 126 vignette, 152–53
BD 127, 119, 134–36, 152–53, 233
BD 128, 119, 134–36, 152–53, 149, 268, 289
BD 129, 127, 134–36
BD 130, 50, 91, 97, 98, 119, 134–36, 152–53, 232, 333, 431
BD 130 vignette, 152
BD 131, 50, 119, 134–36, 152, 431
BD 132, 43–44, 50, 97, 119, 134–36, 152, 431
BD 132 vignette, 153
BD 133, 48, 50, 97–98, 119, 134–36, 152–53, 431
BD 133 vignette, 152–53
BD 134, 50, 91, 98, 119, 134–36, 152–53, 268, 424, 431
BD 134 I, 97
BD 134 II, 97
BD 134 vignette, 152–53, 424
BD 135, 50, 98, 119, 134–36, 152, 268, 431
BD 136, 50, 119, 134–36, 152, 353, 431, 445
BD 136 A, 42–3, 50, 91, 98, 231, 423
BD 136 A I, 97
BD 136 A II, 97
BD 136 A III, 97

# 574 INDEX

BD 136 B, 41–43, 50, 97, 219
BD 136/136A, 45, 152
BD 137, 41, 119, 134–36, 152
BD 137 A, 98, 167, 268
BD 137 B, 98, 231, 268
BD 138, 41, 97, 119, 134–36, 152, 427
BD 139, 41, 119, 134–36, 152, 454, 469
BD 140, 41, 119, 134–36, 152
BD 140 vignette, 152–53
BD 141, 41, 119, 134–36, 152, 469
BD 141/142, 121, 124–26, 134,
BD 142, 41, 119, 126, 134–36, 152, 239, 469
BD 143, 41, 119, 134–36, 470–72
BD 143 vignette, 152
BD 144, 41–43, 119, 125, 134–36, 153, 167, 226, 231–34, 240, 251, 253, 268, 283, 351, 428, 469
BD 144 vignette, 152–53
BD 145, 41, 119, 121, 123, 134–36, 226, 231, 238, 251, 253, 283, 351, 428, 449, 469
BD 145 vignette, 152–54
BD 146, 41, 119, 134–36, 201, 233, 251, 253, 283, 351, 428, 469
BD 146 vignette, 152–53
BD 146 W, 231
BD 147, 41, 43, 119, 134–36, 283, 304, 428, 449, 469
BD 147 vignette, 152
BD 148, 41, 65, 84, 98, 119, 126, 134–36, 149, 167, 231, 240, 246, 251, 253, 268, 351
BD 148 vignette, 152–54, 425
BD 149, 22, 24–25, 41–43, 45, 50, 65, 84, 119, 126, 134–36, 151, 166, 219, 226, 231, 251, 253, 351–52, 445, 449, 469, 508
BD 149 vignette, 152, 219, 352, 508
BD 150, 41, 43, 45, 50, 65, 119, 134–36, 166, 219, 226, 231, 351, 472–73
BD 150 vignette, 50, 152
BD 151, 14, 27, 119, 126, 134–36, 182, 234, 285, 332, 345, 426, 470, 473–75, 477, 515
BD 151 A, 68
BD 151 vignette, 152, 333–34, 426, 563
BD 152, 126, 134–36
BD 152 vignette, 152
BD 153, 15, 119, 134–36, 152
BD 153 A, 166
BD 153 B, 15

BD 154, 119, 134–36, 235, 240, 452
BD 154 vignette, 152
BD 155, 98, 119, 134–36, 268, 345–46, 435, 446, 452
BD 155 vignette, 152, 154
BD 156, 98, 119, 134–36, 345, 346, 435, 446, 452, 513
BD 156 vignette, 152, 154
BD 157, 119, 134–36, 167, 345–46, 435, 446, 452, 513
BD 157 vignette, 152, 154
BD 158, 119, 134–36, 167, 345–46, 435, 446, 452, 513
BD 158 vignette, 152, 154
BD 159, 119, 134–36, 151, 167, 345–46, 435, 446, 513
BD 159 vignette, 152
BD 160, 119, 134–36, 167, 345–46, 435, 446, 513
BD 160 vignette, 152
BD 161, 119, 126, 134–36, 167, 345, 435
BD 161 vignette, 152, 153, 346
BD 162, 96, 99, 119, 134–36, 226, 228, 345–46, 425, 434–37, 440–42, 446
BD 162 (Pleyte), 495
BD 162 vignette, 152–54
BD 163, 119, 134–36, 226, 425, 433–37, 439, 441–42, 446
BD 163 (Pleyte), 495
BD 163 vignette, 152
BD 164, 119, 134–36, 226, 433–35, 437–39, 441–42, 446
BD 164 (Pleyte), 495
BD 164 vignette, 152
BD 165, 119, 134–36, 433–35, 437–39, 441, 442
BD 165 (Pleyte), 495
BD 165 vignette, 152
BD 166, 68, 98, 100, 104, 136, 201, 345–46, 434, 436–38, 441, 442, 443
BD 166 (Pleyte), 495
BD 167, 136, 269, 345, 434–37, 442–43
BD 167 (Pleyte), 300, 495
BD 168, 136, 251, 283, 434
BD 168 (Pleyte), 306, 495
BD 169, 27, 136, 434
BD 169 (Pleyte), 495
BD 170, 136, 434
BD 170 (Pleyte), 495

BD 171, 37, 136, 174, 434
BD 171 (Pleyte), 495
BD 172, 27, 136, 298, 434
BD 172 (Pleyte), 350, 495
BD 173, 136, 434
BD 173 (Pleyte), 495
BD 174, 136, 434
BD 174 (Pleyte), 495
BD 175, 136, 253, 268, 290, 424
BD 176, 136
BD 177, 136
BD 178, 136, 251
BD 179, 136, 350
BD 180, 96–98, 104, 136, 283, 350
BD 181, 97, 136, 268
BD 182, 136, 251, 306
BD 183, 136
BD 184, 136
BD 185, 136
BD 186, 65, 136, 353, 425
BD 187, 97, 136
BD 188, 136
BD 189, 536
BD 190, 98, 136, 152
BD 191, 136, 211, 327
BD 192, 136
BD 194, 431
BD 195, 86
Beast, 393
Becoming (*ḫpr*), 422
Beginning of the Spells of Going Forth by Day which Isis Made for Her Brother Osiris, 301, 307
Being, demonic, 427
Being, divine, 422
Being, hostile, 429
Being, liminal, 427
Being, supernatural, 421, 427
Being, underworld, 411
*benben*-house, 333
Beni Hasan, 15
Bennu heron, 343–44
*benu*-bird, 270, 333
Berlin, Egyptian Museum, 558
Besenmut, 138
Besenmut (P.Heidelberg von Portheim-Stiftung A), 207–8

*bia*-metal, 98
Bibliotheca Lindesiana, 564
Birch, Samuel, 494, 498
Bird, divine, 422
Black Seeds of Vengeance (2000), 514
Bonn, Totenbuch-Projekt, 295
Book of *Ba*, 296, 310, 321, 324–25, 328–34
Book of Breathing, 144, 149, 151–52, 154, 174, 211, 214, 280, 284–85, 295–96, 309, 342, 403, 424, 426
Book of Breathing and Coming Forth by Day, 302
Book of Breathing in the Necropolis, 290
Book of Breathing which Isis Made, 285, 287
Book of Breathing which Isis Made for Her Brother Osiris, 297, 301–2, 306–7, 309–10
Book of Breathing which Isis Made for Osiris, 284
Book of Breathing, First, 149, 285–87, 302
Book of Breathing, Second, 151, 153, 285, 287, 298, 302, 342
Book of Caverns, 89, 203, 235, 282–83, 558
Book of Caves, 282–83
Book of Day, 282
Book of Dead, Tibetan, 506
Book of Earth, 101
Book of Entering the God's Domain and Promenading in the Hall of the Two Truths, 296, 302, 310
Book of Fayum, 325
Book of Gates, 78, 235, 398, 514
Book of Glorifying the *akh*, 302
Book of Glorifying the Spirit, 283, 290
Book of Heavenly Cow, 282
Book of Hidden Chamber, 430
Book of Netherworld, 234, 280, 282, 313
Book of Netherworld and Sky, 288
Book of Night, 282
Book of Nut, 282, 325
Book of Protecting the *Neshmet*-Bark, 290
*Book of Ra*, 515
Book of Temple, 252, 402
Book of Thot, 510
Book of Transformation, 289, 297, 310, 343
Book of Traversing Eternity, 144, 149, 151, 287–88, 295, –96, 301–2, 304, 308
Book of Two Ways, 11, 221, 445

Book of Underworld, 422
Book, ramesside, 378
Breathing air, 232, 240
Breathing fresh air, 447
Brick, 345
Brick, birth, 412
Brick, magical, 199
Brugsch, Heinrich, 498–99
Brush, 546
Buau, Coffin of (T 9C), 9
Budge, E. A. Wallis, 494, 499, 506, 508–9, 511, 513, 532, 535–36
Bug, 347
Bull, 365
Burial, 357, 393
Burial chamber, 359
Burial ritual, 349
Busiris, 326, 332, 358–59
Butcher, 393

Cadet, Jean Marcel, 497
Calf, 360
Canid, 427
Canopic jar, 365, 514
Canopic shrine, 364
Cardboard acid-free, 550
Cardinal point, 350
Carrier, Claude, 537
Carter, Howard, 504
Cartouche, 203
Cat, wild, 430
Caylus, Anne Claude Philippe de, 489
Cellulose varnish, 543
Ceremony of the House, 225
Champollion, Jean-François, 342, 487–90, 493, 495, 497, 504–506
Chantress of Amenemopet, 202
Chantress of Amun, 201, 202, 205–7
*Chapitres supplémentaire*, 100, 433–40, 442, 443, 537
*Chapter for Transforming into a Snake*, 514
Chapter of Awakening the *Ba*, 284
Chapter, supplementary, 104, 495
Chief of musicians, 201–2
Childbirth, 412
Children of Nut, 424

Christianity, 402
Cluster, 343
Cobra, 327, 393, 398
Codex, 515
Coffin B 3–4Bo, 10
Coffin B 6–7Bo, 10
Coffin BH 1–2Liv, 15
Coffin BH 15
Coffin BH 1Br, 15
Coffin BH 4C, 15
Coffin BH 4C, Netjeruhotep, 15
Coffin Cairo Museum J.E. 37566, 377
Coffin Da 1–4C, 14
Coffin Da 1C, Sathathormeret, 13
Coffin Da 2–4X, 14
Coffin Da 2C, Nubheteptikhered, 13–14
Coffin Da 2X, It, 13
Coffin Da 3C, Satsobek, 13
Coffin Da 3X, Khenmet, 13
Coffin Da 4C, Awibre Hor, 13–14
Coffin Da 4X, Itweret, 13
Coffin Da 5X, Keminub, 13–4
Coffin Da 6X, Amenhotep, 22
Coffin Graz Archäologiemueseum Schloss Eggenberg 23927, Pahes, 324
Coffin L 1–2Li, Sesenebenef, 16, 23, 28,
Coffin L 1Li, 15, 18
Coffin L 2Li, 14
Coffin L 2-Li, 18
Coffin Leiden AMM 8-c/M 75, 310
Coffin Liverpool 53.72D, Padiamun, 429
Coffin London BM EA 29582, 324
Coffin London BM EA 29997, Herunefer, 40, 171
Coffin London BM EA 6706, 310
Coffin M 2NY, 14
Coffin Marseille 260, 310
Coffin Munich SSÄK ÄS 7163, Satdjehuti, 26, 40, 43, 45
Coffin S 8X, Ameni, 16
Coffin Senebhenaf, 23
Coffin Sydney NMR. 344, 310, 312
Coffin T 1C, Horhetep, 9
Coffin T 1L, Imau, 9
Coffin T 2C, 9
Coffin T 2NY, Meketre, 9
Coffin T 3Be, 14

Coffin T 4L, Mentuhotep, 22–25, 29, 39–40, 42, 65, 171, 218
Coffin T 9C, Buau, 9
Coffin Texts, 9, 10–12, 15, 16–17, 19, 21, 23–24, 26–30, 39–40, 46, 66, 137, 139, 181, 218–19, 221, 229, 231, 235, 247, 250, 263–66, 272–73, 279, 289, 301, 343, 374, 377, 385, 393, 424, 437, 445, 493, 530, 533–34
CT 20, 27
CT 21, 27
CT 22, 27
CT 23, 27
CT 24, 27
CT 25, 27
CT 30, 18
CT 31, 18
CT 32, 18
CT 33, 18
CT 34, 18
CT 35, 18
CT 36, 18
CT 37, 18
CT 75, 27
CT 76, 27
CT 77, 27
CT 78, 27
CT 79, 27
CT 80, 27
CT 81, 27
CT 82, 27
CT 83, 27
CT 135, 40
CT 154, 42, 66
CT 155, 66
CT 179, 17
CT 222, 17
CT 224, 21
CT 225, 24
CT 243, 15
CT 283/296, 17
CT 306, 18
CT 307, 15
CT 308, 15
CT 335, 23, 26, 396, 303–4, 307
CT 336, 396
CT 337, 396
CT 338, 396
CT 339, 396
CT 340, 15, 17, 18
CT 349, 21
CT 352, 17
CT 362, 23, 42
CT 369, 22
CT 370, 22
CT 372, 23, 42
CT 373, 23, 42
CT 395, 18
CT 402, 18
CT 437, 17
CT 464, 374, 377
CT 465, 374, 377
CT 466, 374, 376–77, 379
CT 467, 374, 377
CT 468, 374
CT 472, 20
CT 475, 15
CT 490, 21
CT 491, 21
CT 499, 21
CT 531, 14, 27
CT 552, 18
CT 607, 18
CT 691, 18
CT 777, 21, 23, 30
CT 778, 21, 23, 30
CT 779, 21, 23, 30
CT 780, 21, 23, 30
CT 781, 21, 23, 30
CT 782, 21, 23, 30
CT 783, 21, 23, 30
CT 784, 21, 23, 30
CT 785, 21, 23, 30
CT 786, 15
CT 787, 15
CT 788, 14, 15
CT 792, 17
CT 794, 15
CT 800, 15
CT 803, 17
CT 828, 21
CT 829, 21
CT 830, 21
CT 831, 21
CT 898, 15

CT 899, 15
CT 900, 15
CT 901, 15
Collar of gold, 345
Colophon, 435
Color, 543, 553
Color shaper, silicon brush, 544
Comic, 514
Concept, complex, 526
Connotation, 524
Conservation, 542–54
Conservatory approach, 542
Contending of Horus and Seth, 307, 426
Cool water to drink, 447
Copper rust, 543
Coptic, 438, 489
Corporeal integrity, 406
Corporeal justification, 394
Corpse, 304–6, 308
Cow, 360
Cow and calf scene, 364, 365
Cow, celestial, 425
Cow, golden, 438
Crayon, red, 546
Creation, 422, 437, 440
Creator, 422
Creator sun god, 423
Creature, hybrid, 428
Crime, 400
Crocodile, 343, 347, 411–12, 427–28
Cult, official, 428
Curiosity cabinet, 490
Cursive hieroglyphs, 24–5, 84

Dahshur, 12–16, 29
Dakhleh Oasis, 239–40
*De Aegypto*, 508, 513
Dead Sea Scroll, 556
Dead, blessed, 393
Decade Feast, 284–85
Decade Feast of Amenope, 284
Declaration of Innocence, 134, 252
De-conservation, 546
Decree for Nesikhonsu, 441
Decree, amuletic, 438

Decree, divine, 282
Decree, great, 298
Decree, royal of Osiris Onnophris, 154
Defragmentation, digital, 342
Deification of limbs, 347
Deir el-Bahari, 77, 84, 89, 92–93, 221, 231, 380, 385, 493
Deir el-Bersheh, 10, 16, 20–22, 374, 385
Deir el-Medina, 63, 66, 72, 221, 233, 245, 247, 252, 325, 359, 369, 426, 438
Delta, 295
Demiurge, 440–42
Demon, 233, 393, 411, 421, 427–31
Demotic, 280, 438
Dendera, temple, 245, 251
Description de l'Égypte, 490, 497
Determinative, 439
Devéria, Théodule, 494, 495
Devourer, 312–13, 408, 411, 428
Diglossia, 437
Dinglinger, Johann Melchior, 506–8
Diod. I 91–93, 415
District, 400
Divine Father (*it-nṯr*), 227
Djedefhor, 167
*djed*-pillar, 331–32
Djehuty, 23, 39
*djet*-eternity, 270
Documents of Breathing, 147, 225, *see also* Books of Breathing
Documents of Breathing, demotic, 280, 288, *see also* Books of Breathing
Dog, 411
Doorkeeper, 232–33
Doum-palm, 344
Dra Abu el-Naga, 232
Dra Abu-el-Naga, tomb A 6, 36
Dra Abu-el-Naga, tomb A 7, 36–8
Draftsman, 380
Dresden, 507
Duality of Maats, 398
*Duat*, 233, 304–5, 313, 393, 397, 428
*Duat*, 21 gates of, 238
Dynastie, Fifth, 394
Dynastie, Fourth, 394
Dynastie, Sixth, 394, 395

Dynasty, Thirtieth, 450
Dynasty, Twenty-first, 379, 380

Edfu, temple of, 252, 326, 436
Effectiveness, 303
Efficient *akh*-spirit (*3ḫ iḳr*), 27
Egypt Exploration Fund, 493
Egyptian poetry, 526
*Égyptien de tradition*, 437–38, 528
*Egyptomania*, 504, 518
El-Bersha, 227
Elephantine, 62
El-Hagara, 12
El-Hibe, 329
El-Kuru, 238
El-Lahun, 12
Eloquent Peasant, story of, 414
El-Qala, 245
Embalmer, 426
Embalming, 27, 393, 413
Emendation, 529
Empty spaces, 121
Enemy, 439
Enemy, archetypal, 430
Ennead, 12, 422, 424, 440
Ennead, great, 373
*Entering*, 456
Epigraphy, 321
Epithet, 399, 439, 441
Esminis, 281
Eye of Horus, 406, 425
Eye of Re (of the Sun), 425

Falcon, 327, 332, 343–44, 365, 422
Falcon of gold, 478–79
False door, 231
Faulkner, Raymond O., 532, 534, 536
Fauvel, Abbé, 508
Fayum, 288, 297–98
Fecht, Gerhard, 536
Female musician (*iḥy.t*), 227
Ferry, 353
Ferry boat, 11
Ferryman, 467
Fiber, loose, 546
Field of Hotep, 374

Field of Offerings, 86, 373–74, 377, 379–80, 382, 385, 472
Field of Reeds (of Iaru), 232, 236, 373–74, 376, 377, 385, 514–15
Fiery pit, 393
*Finnegans Wake*, 511
Fire, 348
First Intermediate Period, 396, 400
Flood, great, 374
Fragment, 542
Framing, 550–51
Freedom of movement, 509
Freemason, 504
Freund, Karl, 515
Friedrich August I, August der Starke, 507

Garland of justification or vindication, 399, 413
Gasse, Annie, 537
Gate, 231, 234, 236, 249, 252–53, 393
Gatekeeper, 240
Geb, 14, 304, 308, 402, 422–23
Gebel Barkal, 436
Geisen, Christina, 530
General, 169
Genii, 427–28
Genre, horror, 510
Ghost, 430
Giza, 237
Glass plate, 550
Glorification of the Great One, 283
Glorification Performed in the Temple of Osiris, 283
Glorifications / Glorification spell (*s3ḥ.w*), 98, 211, 270, 283–84, 304, 412
Glorifications I, 290
Glorifications IV, 290, 305–6
Glorifications Performed by the Two Sisters, 284
God, 428
God, creator, 397
God, great, 394, 397, 399–400, 416
God, lion, 440
God, major, 421
God, minor, 421, 427
God, primordinal, 423–24, 427, 440
God, solar, 441
God, super, 422

God, universal, 438
God's wife of Amun, 206
Goddess in the tree, 465
Goddess of the Birth, Ipet, 425
Goddess of the West, Imentet, 398, 424
Goddess, apotropaic, 425
Goddess, birth, 425
Goddess, dangerous, 268, 425, 428
Goddess, sky, 423
Goddess, tree, 424
*Gods of Egypt*, 517
Going forth by day(light), 493
Going forth into daylight, motif of, 348, 350
Going in and out with, 350
Going out into daylight, 349
*Gone forth*, 455, 460, 463, 465–67, 470, 472, 478
Goose, 54, 332
Gospel of Jesus, 556
Great Decree Issued to the Nome of the Silent Land, 283, 290
Great nurse of the god's wife, 198, 201
Great of the harem of Amun-Re, 205–6
Great singer of Mut, 205–6
Griffin, Rick, 515
Grimoire, 510
Group, 343
Guardian, 231, 233–34, 236, 238, 253, 401, 428, 429
Guardians of the Gate, 121
Guieysse, Paul, 494
Gurob, 369
Gurob-Hawara, 227

Hall of judgment, 214
Hall of justice, 232, 235
Hall of Two Maats, 397–401, 410, 415–16
Hall of Two Truths, 309, 426
Harkhuf, autobiography of, 395
Hathor, 46, 146, 152, 214, 228, 327, 329–30, 353, 365, 424–25
Hathor NN, 424–25, 285
Hathor, Hymn, 154
Hathor, Prayer to, 153
Hatshepsut, 26–29, 46, 50, 198, 219, 231–32, 282, 377, 397, 493
Havana, National Museum of Fine Arts, 546
Hawara, 12, 369

Head-rest, 345
Heart, 345–46, 403, 405, 414–15
Hedj-wer, 272–73
Heliopolis, 12, 237, 270, 325–27, 333, 358–59, 422, 436
Henuttauy, 84
Heqanakhte, letters, 526
*heqa*-scepter, 308
Heracleopolitan Kingdom, 400
Herakleopolis, 165, 531
Herakleopolis Magna, 137, 164, 169, 227
Herere (P.London BM EA 10490), 203, 206
Herihor, 203, 206
Hermopolis, 167, 182, 269, 271–73, 326, 374, 427
Heron, 343
Hesat, 327
Hettites, 522
Hierakonpolis, 22
Hieratic, 24–25, 76, 78, 88–91, 104
High Priest of Amun, 77
High Priest of Ptah, 78, 101
Hippopotamus, 411–12, 425, 428
Hordjedef, 269
Horemakhbit (P.Turin Cat. 1842), 208
Horemheb, 232
Horhetep, Coffin T 1C, 9
Hornung, Erik, 499, 530, 534–36
Horror vacui, 382
Horsaiset, son of Hor and Kaikai, 149
Horus, 11, 253, 272, 304–5, 358–59, 367, 376, 395, 398, 411, 422, 426, 514, 517
Horus, Sons of, 12, 308, 310, 330, 426
Hourly vigil (*Stundenwachen*), 27, 203, 284–85, 298
House of Life, 250–51, 268
House of Osiris, 11
Hu, 239
Humidity, 550
Hunter, 393
Hyksos Period, 439
Hymn, 414
Hymn, lunar, 415
Hypocephalus, 211, 228

Ibis, 272, 327, 365, 426–27
Ihet, 228, 425

INDEX 581

Ihet-cow, 441
Imau, Coffin T 1L, 9
Imhotep, 515
*In Their Darkened Shrines* (2000), 514
Incipit, 326–27
Influence, hellenistic, 408
Inhabitant, supernatural, 427
Inhumation, 436
Initiated, 402
Ink, 543, 546, 548, 553, 557
Ink corrosion (Tintenfraß), 543
Instructions, *see* wisdom literature
*Instructions for Merikara*, 396
Intercultural act, 523
Intertextuality, 279
Invocation of the Glorifications which the Two Sisters Performed, 305
Isis, 82, 164, 208, 233, 284–85, 305, 310, 328, 353, 360, 365, 367, 422, 424–25
Islam, 402
It, Coffin Da 2X, 13
*Ithyphallic Metal*, 514
Itjitawy, 10
Itweret, Coffin Da 4X, 13

Jabiru-bird, 431
Jackal, 331–32, 360, 364–65, 426–27, 429
Japanese tissue paper, 550
Journey of the sun god, 422, 430
Journey, nightly, 436
Journey, nocturnal, 347
Joyce, James, 508, 511–12, 518
*Judge Dredd Book of the Dead*, 514
Judges, 42, 427
Judges, divine, 309
Judgment, 137, 211, 268, 310–12, 346, 352–53, 394, 396–97, 400, 402, 410, 412, 426, 428, 514, 517, 562
Judgment hall of Osiris, 301
Judgment of the Dead, 84, 252, 307, 308, 330, 393–94, 397–98, 401, 403, 411, 413–16
Judgment of the Dead vignette, 398
Judgment, apocalyptic, 402
Judgment, final, 221, 232, 238, 240
Judgment, scene, 127, 134–35, 138, 149, 152–55, 247, 252–53, 505, 515

Justification, 302, 395, 398, 413, 426
Justification by fire, 398

*ka*, 300–1, 304–6, 308, 313, 373, 374, 512
Karloff, Boris, 515
Karnak, 77, 93, 99, 205, 253, 436
Keeper of the Scale, 410
Keminub, Coffin Da 5X, 13–4
Kha, 56, 199, 202
Khaemwaset, 269, 436
Khenmet, Coffin Da 3X, 13
*Khenty-Imentyw*, 422, 427
Khepri, 422
Khnum, 201
Khoiak festival, 284
Khoiak text, 332
Khonsu, 214
Khufu, 269
King's daughter, 198, 201
King's mother, 206
King's wife, 206
Kircher, Athanasius, 487, 489
Knive, 429
Knowledge, 349–50, 352, 434, 436, 509
Knowledge, secret, 401–2
Kom el-Hisn, 13
Koptos, 227
Kucharek, Andrea, 533
Kush, 439
Kushites, 436, 441
KV 23, tomb of Ay, 232
KV 34, 36
KV 36, 39
KV 4, tomb of Ramses XI, 272
KV 46, 36, 64

Lady of the house, 198, 201–2, 207–8, 210–11, 214, 227
Lady of the Two Lands, 206
Lake of Fire, 398
Lamentation of Isis and Nephthys, 211, 284, 300, 305
Lamination, 542–43, 545–47, 550
Language, spoken, 438
Late Egyptian, 437–38, 443
Late Middle Egyptian, 528

Late Period, 346–50, 357, 365, 369, 382, 403, 413, 422, 424, 435, 443, 531–32
Layout, 325
Le Page Renouf, Peter, 494, 535
Leather Berlin P. 3131, 46
Leather London BM EA 10281, 38, 42, 46, 48, 171
Leemans, Conrad, 495
Lefébure, Eugène, 494
Leopard skin, 360, 365
Lepsius, Karl Richard, 341, 353, 433, 469, 470, 472, 487–88, 491, 493, 498, 505–6, 536
Letopolis, 358
Letters of the Dead, 395
Libation, 375
Libya, 89
Lieblein, Jens, 499
Lindsay, Alexander, 25th Earl of Crawford, 564
Lindsay, James L., 26th Earl of Crawford, 564
Lion, 54, 411–12, 428
Lisht, 10, 14–16, 227
Litany of Re, 46, 76, 78, 82, 104, 110, 282–83
Litany of Sun, 26, 82
Liturgy, funerary, 27, 231
Liturgy, mortuary, 282
Liturgy, Osirian, 287, 301, 434
Living on air, 347
Lizard, 429
London BM EA 29997 (Coffin of Herunefer), 40, 171
London, British Museum, 494, 508, 510
Lord Carnarvon, 504
Lord of All, 359
Lotusflower, 344
Lovecraft, 514
Lovecraft, Howard Phillips, 510
Lower Egypt, 400
Lower Heaven, 307
Lower Sky, 424
Luke 16:19–31, 408
Luxor, 272

Maat (goddess), 346, 367, 397–98, 401–7, 416, 426, 515, 517
*maat*, concept, 397, 400–1, 403, 406, 414, 416

Maatkare, daughter of Pinedjem I, 84
Magic, 429–31, 438, 439, 441–42, 445, 447, 461, 558
Magic, arcane, 510
Magic, Nubian, 439
Maillet, Benoît de, 490
Manchester, John Rylands University Library, 564
Manga, 516
Manufacturing, 551, 553
Masaharta, 105
Maspero, Gaston, 513
Massy, Adam, 499
Master copy, 137
Maternity, 412
McCullum and Rodgers palettes, 441
Medinet Habu, 155, 245, 284
Medjed, 516
Meir, 14–5, 142, 298, 368
Meketre, Coffin T 2NY, 9
Mekhenti-Irty, 270
Memory, 346
Memphis, 9, 20, 37, 62, 78, 95, 101, 137, 142, 165, 210, 227, 325–26, 333, 357, 368, 378, 427, 436, 449–50, 457, 461, 465, 467–68, 472, 474, 494, 510
*menat*-necklace, 365
Mendes, 270, 326, 358
Menkheperre, high priest, 82, 88–9, 91, 95, 103, 105
Menqet, 304
Mentuhotep II, 9–10, 493
Mentuhotep, Coffin T 4L, 22–25, 29, 39–40, 42, 65, 171, 218
Meret (goddess), 348
Merety (goddesses), 347
Meroitic, 439
Meroitic lexicography, 439
Meskhenet, 412
*meskhet*, 360
Metaphoric, 527
Methyl cellulose, 550
Middle Egypt, 295–96, 400
Middle Egyptian, 437, 528
Middle Kingdom, 374, 377, 396
Min, 565
Mirgissa, 15

*Mischtext*, 530
Misstress of the West, 425
Monster, primordinal, 430
Montemhat, 138
Montfaucon, Bernhard de, 507–8
Monthesouphis, 287
Montu, 169
Moon, 307, 509
Mother of the king, 198
Mounds, 231, 234
Mounds of the netherworld, 352
Mozart, Wolfgang Amadeus, 504
*mrty*-snake, 447, 476
Mulisch, Harry, 507
Mummification, 18, 345–46, 349
Mummification, moral, 394
Mummification, ritual, 514
Mummy, 304, 308
Mummy bandage, 357, 369, 426, 438, 489
M.Aberdeen ABDUA 84131 et. al., Tasheretentakeri, 209–10
M.Aberuai, 490, 491, 492
M.Antwerpen 4943 et. al., Asetemakhbit, 209–10
M.Djedhor, 226
M.Firenze 5706+5707+5709–5714, Takerheb, 209, 211
M.Hor, 175
M.London UC 32381+32382, Bastetiirdis, 209
M.Saqqara R. 306 et. al., Bastetiirdis, 209–10
M.Uppsala VM MB 37+63, Neferii (?), 209–10
Mummy bandage, fake, 564
Mummy board London BM EA 35464, 297
Mummy linen of Ahmose, 26
Mummy wrapping, 403
Mummy, transportation, 360
Mummymania, 565
Musician of Amun-Re, 207–11, 214
Musician of Ptah, 209–10
Musician of Sokar, 210
Mut, 226, 435, 439–41

Name, collective, 429
Name, mysterious, 399
Napata, 436
Napoleon, Bonaparte, 490, 496

Naville, Édouard, 341, 433, 493–94, 497, 505–6, 532, 535–36
Nebtu, 201
Necropolis, 330, 436
Nedjmet, mother of Pinedjem I, 84
Nefertem, 427
Neferure, daughter of Hatshepsut, 198
Negative confession, 149, 235, 238, 252–53, 309, 399–400, 402, 416, 427
*neheh*-eternity, 270
Neith, 425, 436
Nekau, 174
*nekhakha*-flail, 365
Nekhbet, 333
Nekhen, 333
Neologism, 438, 527
Nephthys, 82, 164, 208, 233, 284, 305, 310, 328, 353, 360, 365, 367, 422
Nespasefy II, Priest of Montu, 207, 208
Netherworld, 424, 431
Netherworld, celestial, 423
Netjeruhotep, Coffin BH 4C, 15
New Kingdom, 344, 347–49, 357, 359, 375, 379–80, 382, 493
New Testament, 406
Night sky, 11
Nile delta, 233
Nile source, 352
Nitokris, 208
Noblewoman, 207–8
Nome, 400
Nubheteptikhered, Coffin Da 2C, 13–4
Nubia, 438–39, 443
Nubian, 435, 439
Nun, 272
Nuri, 238
Nut, 17–18, 284, 327, 332, 422–24, 477

Offering, 375, 394, 425
Offering cult, 248
Offering formula, 47, 284, 325
Offering ritual, 18, 95
Offering spell, 18
Old Egyptian, 437
Old Kingdom, 357, 374
Opening of the Mouth, 99, 221, 248, 281, 413

Opening of the Mouth for Breathing, liturgy, 284, 302
Opening of the mouth, ritual, 99, 211, 225, 235, 360, 363, 367
Opening the face of the deceased (wn-ḥr), 14
Opet, temple, 253
Oracle, 438
Oracular utterance, 438
Order, cosmic, 403
Order, social, 400
Orion, 307
Orpiment, 543
Osirianization, 441
Osiris, 11, 19, 22, 46, 56, 77, 82–3, 95, 104, 121, 137, 142, 163, 173, 201, 205, 214, 219, 222, 224–26, 228, 233, 239–41, 248–49, 251, 253, 268, 270, 272, 281, 283–84, 304–8, 310, 312, 325–27, 330, 332, 346, 349, 352–53, 358–59, 363, 367, 370, 385, 393–97, 401, 411, 413, 416, 421–22, 426–27, 429, 437, 440–42, 460–61, 466, 511, 517, 525, 532
Osiris Khontamenti, 329
Osiris NN, 284–85, 422, 425
Osiris Wennefer, 284
Osiris, cult of, 307
Osiris, mystery, 332
Osiris, spell, 442
Osiris, vigil, 428
Osiris-Hathor, 146, 214
Osiris-Re, 67, 422
Osorkon II, 78, 95, 234, 380
Ostrakon Paris Louvre AF 230, 66
Ostrakon Paris Louvre E 22394, 66
Ostrich feather, 397, 403, 416
Overseer of all craftsmen of the God's wife, 199

P.Aberdeen ABDUA 84023, P.Padihorpachered, 209–11, 364
P.Amenemhet, P.Private collection, 38, 47–48, 52
P.Amenemopet,/P.Bakai, P.Warsaw 237128, 199, 202
P.Amenhotep, P.Berlin P. 3005, 81
P.Amenhotep, P.London BM EA 10489, 36–38, 47, 446
P.Anchefenamun, P.Dresden Aeg. 775, 353, 414

P.Anhai, P.London BM EA 10472, 201–2, 404, 494, 543
P.Ani, P.London BM EA 10470, 64, 119, 161, 183, 191, 313, 342, 353, 360–62, 364, 380, 387, 412, 427, 494, 499–500, 515, 530, 532, 536, 553
P.Ankhefenkhonsu, P.Cairo CG 40024, 120, 454
P.Ankhesenaset, P.Paris BnF 62–88, 91, 169, 205–6
P.Ankhesenmut, P.Cairo S.R. VII 10255, 68, 69
P.Ankhwahibre, P.London BM EA 10558, 117, 120, 125–32, 136, 138, 193–94, 468, 474, 478
P.Ann Arbor 2725, 97
P.Arptahhep/P.Menenwahibre, P.Paris Louvre N 3091, 117, 120, 163, 449, 452
P.Arsinoe, P.Florence 3662, 210–11
P.Aset, P.Tallin k-542/AM 5877, 202
P.Asetemakhbit (wife of Pinedjem II), P.Cairo S.R. IV 525 = J.E. 2622, 97
P.Asetemakhbit, P.Cairo CG 40009 = J.E. 95861, 205, 207
P.Asetemakhbit, P.London BM EA 9904, 205, 207, 414
P.Asetreshti, P.Paris Louvre N 3083+Paris Louvre N. 3194 A, 210–11
P.Asety, P.London BM EA 10084, 91, 205–6
P.Assisi Biblioteca Comunale 351+ Budapest National Library Cod. Afr. 2a-b+ Heidelberg P Hier. 566+Heidelberg Portheim-Stiftung A+Jerusalem Bible Lands Museum H 376+Cairo J.E. 95685 (S.R. IV 615)+J.E. 95745 (S.R. IV 692)+J.E. 95840 (S.R. IV 938)+J.E. 95841 (S.R. IV 939)+J.E. 95864 (S.R. IV 964)+New York without no., P.Tasheretenaset, 118, 120, 125, 127, 129, 138
P.Asty, P.Turin Cat. 1851 = CGT 53007, 97, 205, 207
P.Atlanta MCCM 2004.22.1, P.Baket, 199, 202
P.Bakai/P.Amenemopet, P.Warsaw 237128, 199, 202
P.Baket, P.Atlanta MCCM 2004.22.1, 199, 202
P.Barcelona E-615, P.Bary, 199, 202
P.Barcelona Paul Rib. 450+Mannheim REM without no. [1], 154, 296
P.Bary, P.Barcelona E-615, 199, 202

P.Beret, P.London BM EA 10983+Private Collection, 147, 149, 152–53, 210, 214
P.Berlin P. 10477, P.Nefertii, 210, 211, 321–22, 328–31, 333–34, 368, 550–51
P.Berlin P. 10478, P.Padiashsedjem, 550
P.Berlin P. 14420, 154
P.Berlin P. 15778, P.Ramose, 69
P.Berlin P. 3002, P.Nakhtamun, 64, 359, 369, 387, 543, 547, 544–45, 550
P.Berlin P. 3003, P.Keku, 550
P.Berlin P. 3005, P.Amenhotep, 81
P.Berlin P. 3008, P.Tarudj, 210–11, 305, 389, 550
P.Berlin P. 3010, P.Nespaasobek, 99, 105
P.Berlin P. 3013, 546
P.Berlin P. 3022 A(1), Tale of Sinuhe (Sinuhe B), 192
P.Berlin P. 3028, 286
P.Berlin P. 3058, 454, 457, 543
P.Berlin P. 3059, 543
P.Berlin P. 3064 A–B, 368
P.Berlin P. 3120, 97
P.Berlin P. 3127, 562
P.Berlin P. 3132, 36
P.Berlin P. 3134, 545
P.Berlin P. 3158, P.Reret, 209–11, 364
P.Berlin P. 3159 A–D, P.Taitem, 209–11
P.Berlin P. 3161+Kopenhagen Aae 5+Sydney R346a+Tübingen 2000, P.Pefiuiu, 119–20
P.Berlin P. 3162, 147, 151, 289
P.Berlin P. 3195, P.Taatum, 364, 406, 407
P.Berlin P. 6750, 298
P.Berlin P. 8765, 298
P.Bonn L 1647, 345
P.Brüssel E 5043, P.Neferrenpet, 67–69, 71, 446
P.Brüssel MRAH E. 4976, 389
P.Brüssel MRAH without no., 38, 48
P.Bucharest Mss. oriental 376, P.Sakhti, 202
P.Budapest+Heidelberg von Portheim-Stiftung B+Cairo J.E. 95685 (S.R. IV 615)+ J.E. 95690 (S.R. IV 619)+J.E. 95745 (S.R. IV 692)+J.E. 95840 (S.R. IV 938)+J.E. 95841 (S.R. IV 939)+S.R. IV 996+Uppsala VBM 160, P.Djedkhy, 117, 120, 129, 138, 207–8, 449
P.Busca, 345
P.Cairo CG 24095, P.Maiherperi, 36, 64, 351, 403

P.Cairo CG 25095, 39
P.Cairo CG 40002, 37, 46, 48
P.Cairo CG 40003, 38
P.Cairo CG 40004, P.Senhetep, 403, 405
P.Cairo CG 40009 = J.E. 95861, P.Asetemakhbit, 205, 207
P.Cairo CG 40016, 388
P.Cairo CG 40024, P.Ankhefenkhonsu, 120, 454
P.Cairo CG 40029, 468
P.Cairo CG 44006, 406
P.Cairo CG 51189, P.Yuya, 36–7, 47–8, 52, 54, 165–66, 386, 406, 409, 446
P.Cairo CG 58005 = J.E. 35413, P.Tadimut, 201–2
P.Cairo CG 58009, 296
P.Cairo IFAO without no., 36, 202
P.Cairo J.E. 95575, 36, 44
P.Cairo J.E. 95714 (S.R. IV 647)+JE 95649 (S.R. IV 547)+Albany 1900.3.1+Marseille 91/2/1+291, P.Nespasefy, 117–18, 120, 127, 138, 451–52, 531
P.Cairo J.E. 95834, 47
P.Cairo J.E. 99881, 406
P.Cairo S.R. IV 11494, 84
P.Cairo S.R. IV 525 = J.E. 2622, P.Asetemakhbit (wife of Pinedjem II), 97
P.Cairo S.R. IV 526 = J.E. 51948, P.Henuttawy (daughter of Pinedjem I), 88, 105
P.Cairo S.R. IV 527 = J.E. 51949, P.Henuttawy (daughter of Pinedjem I), 88, 105
P.Cairo S.R. IV 549, 91
P.Cairo S.R. IV 650 = J.E. 95716, 98
P.Cairo S.R. IV 936 = J.E. 95838, P.Gatseshen, 91–92, 95, 96–7, 165, 203, 205, 206, 387
P.Cairo S.R. IV 953, 97
P.Cairo S.R. IV 954, 98
P.Cairo S.R. IV 955 = J.E. 95856 = CG 40005 = P.Boulaq 22, P.Henttawy (wife of Pinedjem I), 203, 206
P.Cairo S.R. IV 959, P.Maatkare (daughter of Pinedjem II), 96
P.Cairo S.R. IV 961, 97
P.Cairo S.R. IV 967 = J.E. 95866, P.Menkheperre (grandson of Menkheperre), 97
P.Cairo S.R. IV 980 = J.E. 26229 = CG 40007, P.Maatkare, 105, 203, 206, 387, 414

P.Cairo S.R. IV 981, 91
P.Cairo S.R. IV 992 = J.E. 95887 = P.Boulaq 23, P.Henttawy (wife of Pinedjem I), 105, 203, 206
P.Cairo S.R. IV 999 = CG 40027, 98
P.Cairo S.R. VII 10222, P.Tabakhenkhonsu, 84, 205, 207
P.Cairo S.R. VII 10249, 387
P.Cairo S.R. VII 10255, P.Ankhesenmut, 68, 69
P.Cairo S.R. VII 10256, P.Heruben (granddaughter of Menkheperre), 86, 380, 388
P.Cairo S.R. VII 10267, 97
P.Cairo S.R. VII 11488 = CG 40006, P.Pinedjem I, 105, 406
P.Cairo S.R. VII 11496, P.Tawedjatra, 86, 413
P.Cairo S.R. VII 11573 = S.R. VII 11485 = J.E. 26230, P.Nesikhonsu, 91, 205–6, 387
P.Cairo SN (CII), P.Hatneferet, 201, 211
P.Cairo TN 25/1/55/6, 36–38, 42, 46, 48, 56
P.Cairo TR 25/1/155/6, P.Haneferet, 201–11
P.Cambridge E. 2.1922, P.Ramose, 62, 344, 387
P.Chester Beatty VIII, 268
P.Chicago OIM 10486, P.Milbank, 194, 368, 425
P.Chicago OIM 25389, 151
P.Chicago OIM 25489, 147
P.Chicago OIM 5750, 62
P.Chicago OIM E 9787+New York Columbia University Library Inv. 784, P.Ryerson, 389, 426, 454, 456, 473
P.Christchurch EA 1988.73–76, P.Takerheb, 209, 211
P.Cologne Aeg. 10207, P.Iahtesnakht, 117, 119–27, 129, 132–33, 135, 138, 142, 164, 167, 169–70, 208, 389, 451–52, 531, 536
P.Cologny Bodmer CIV, 390
P.Cologny Bodmer CV+Cincinnati Art Museum 1947.369+Denver Art Museum 1954.61, P.Hor, 167, 388
P.Cortona 3184, 155
P.Cracow, P.Sekowski, 290
P.Djedbastet, P.Turin Cat. 1862/2 = CGT 53009, 205, 207
P.Djedkhy, P.Budapest+Heidelberg von Portheim-Stiftung B+Cairo J.E. 95685 (S.R. IV 615)+J.E. 95690 (S.R. IV 619)+ J.E. 95745 (S.R. IV 692)+J.E. 95840 (S.R. IV 938)+J.E. 95841 (S.R. IV 939)+S.R. IV 996+Uppsala VBM 160, 117, 120, 129, 138, 207, 208, 449
P.Djedmutiusankh, P.Turin Cat. 1855 = CGT 53008, 205, 207
P.Dresden Aeg. 775, P.Anchefenamun, 353, 414
P.Dublin TCL 1662, 389
P.Edinburgh 1956.315, 36–37, 42–43, 48
P.Florence 3660, 37
P.Florence 3660 A, P.Senemnetjer, 62
P.Florence 3662, P.Arsinoe, 210–11
P.Florence 3665+3666+Vienna KHM 3850, P.Mutmut, 210, 214, 309
P.Florence 5404, 127
P.Florence PSI inv. I 130, 297
P.Gatseshen, P.Cairo S.R. IV 936 = J.E. 95838, 91–92, 95–97, 165, 203, 205–6, 387
P.Gatseshen, P.New York MMA 25.3.31, 79, 80
P.Geneva MAH D 229+Paris Louvre N 3220 D, 155
P.Greenfield, P.London BM EA 10554, P.Nesitanebetisheru, 93–96, 100–1, 103, 163, 194, 205–6, 268, 351, 380, 388, 423, 516
P.Hamm 2236, 97
P.Haneferet, P.Cairo TR 25/1/155/6, 201–11
P.Hannover KM 1970.37, 37, 50
P.Harkness, 284, 296
P.Hatneferet, P.Cairo SN (CII), 201, 211
P.Hatnofret (mother of Senenmut), P.Paris Louvre E 11085, 38, 42, 45, 48, 65
P.Havana MNBA Habana 94–97, P.Hunt, 381, 387, 543, 548
P.Heidelberg von Portheim-Stiftung A, P.Tasheredenaset, 207, 208
P.Henttawy (wife of Pinedjem I), P.Cairo S.R. IV 955 = J.E. 95856 = CG 40005 = P.Boulaq 22, 203, 206
P.Henttawy (wife of Pinedjem I), P.Cairo S.R. IV 992 = J.E. 95887 = P.Boulaq 23, 105, 203, 206
P.Henttawy, P.New York MMA 25.3.29, 95, 203, 206
P.Henut, P.Moscow I, 1b, 26 (B), 202
P.Henutmehyt, P.Reading, 199, 202
P.Henuttawy (daughter of Pinedjem I), P.Cairo S.R. IV 526 = J.E. 51948, 88, 105
P.Henuttawy (daughter of Pinedjem I), P.Cairo S.R. IV 527 = J.E. 51949, 88, 105

P.Heruben (granddaughter of Menkheperre), P.Cairo S.R. VII 10256, 86, 380, 388
P.Hildesheim 5248, 368
P.Hood, 543
P.Hor, P.Cologny Bodmer CV+Cincinnati Art Museum 1947.369+Denver Art Museum 1954.61, 167, 388
P.Horemakhbit, P.Leiden T 6 = AMS 33, 379, 380, 387
P.Hornedjitef, P.Paris Louvre N 3081, 165, 368, 451, 465, 475
P.Hornefer, P.London BM EA 10013, 406, 407
P.Hunefer, P.London BM EA 9901, 64, 397, 411, 494, 496, 562
P.Hunt, P.Havana MNBA Habana 94-97, 381, 387, 543, 548
P.Iahtesnakht, P.Cologne Aeg. 10207, 117, 119-27, 129, 132-33, 135, 138, 142, 164, 167, 169, 170, 208, 389, 451-52, 531, 536
P.Imouthes, P.New York MMA 35.9.21, 290, 298, 324
P.Insinger 5, 7-8, 313
P.Irtiru, P.Turin Cat. 1842, 208
P.Iufankh, P.Turin 1791, 134, 137, 142, 303, 341-42, 344, 365-66, 378, 383-84, 389, 491-92, 498-99, 505, 537
P.Kaunas Tt-12848, 69
P.Keku, P.Berlin P. 3003, 550
P.Kerheb, P.Turin Cat. 1814, 209
P.Kha, P.Turin S 8438, 36-7, 54, 200, 220
P.Khamhor C, P.New York MMA 25.3.212+Ann Arbor 81.4.25+Florence 11912a-b+Providence A 18077+Toronto 910.85.222+Unknown, private collection of H. Carter (lost), 117, 120, 138, 167-69, 452
P.Khnumemheb, P.London UC 32365, 62, 387
P.Kopenhagen Carlsberg 201, 368
P.Krakau Nationalmuseum XI 1503-06, 1508-11, 389
P.Kraków MNK IX-752/1-4, 543
P.Kroch, 296, 308, 310
P.Lansing, P.London BM EA 9994, 193
P.Leiden AMt 1-35, AP 52, 387
P.Leiden T 16, P.Asetweret, 209, 211, 463
P.Leiden T 2, P.Qenna, 495
P.Leiden T 3, 172
P.Leiden T 31, P.Tasherettaihet, 210-11
P.Leiden T 32, 289
P.Leiden T 4, 344
P.Leiden T 6 = AMS 33, P.Horemakhbit, 379-80, 387
P.Lille 139, P.Men, 118, 120
P.Lincei Ieratico I, 562
P.Liverpool 1978.291.264, 478
P.London BM EA 10007, P.Pashebmutwebkhet, 88
P.London BM EA 10009+9962,1, 37, 46, 48, 54, 65, 386
P.London BM EA 10010, 306
P.London BM EA 10013, P.Hornefer, 406, 407
P.London BM EA 10017, 459, 470
P.London BM EA 10020, 84
P.London BM EA 10031, 97
P.London BM EA 10034+10705 (3), 390
P.London BM EA 10063, P.Padiamenet, 83
P.London BM EA 10064, P.Paennestitauy, 91, 95-7, 165, 341, 387
P.London BM EA 1008, 414
P.London BM EA 10084, P.Asety, 91, 205, 206
P.London BM EA 10086, 463-64, 473, 477-80
P.London BM EA 10086 and Paris Louvre N 3152, Tradition of, 458, 461, 466
P.London BM EA 10086, P.Paris Louvre N 3152 and P.Paris Louvre N 3079, Tradition of, 458
P.London BM EA 10088, 390
P.London BM EA 10097, 388, 435, 450-51, 453, 472, 479
P.London BM EA 10098+10844, 147, 151, 165
P.London BM EA 10203, 97
P.London BM EA 10257, 473
P.London BM EA 10311, 466
P.London BM EA 10312, 97
P.London BM EA 10466-7, 65
P.London BM EA 10470, P.Ani, 64, 119, 161, 183, 191, 313, 342, 353, 360-62, 364, 380, 387, 412, 427, 494, 499, 500, 515, 530, 532, 536, 553
P.London BM EA 10471+10473, P.Nakht, 46, 64, 169-70, 172
P.London BM EA 10472, P.Anhai, 201-2, 404, 494, 543
P.London BM EA 10477, P.Nu, 37, 42, 44, 46, 48, 64, 166, 186, 188, 191-93, 272, 342-43, 424, 445, 494, 530-31

P.London BM EA 10479, 324, 368
P.London BM EA 10489, P.Amenhotep, 36–38, 47, 446
P.London BM EA 10490, P.Nedjmet, 89, 90, 100, 105, 171, 203, 206
P.London BM EA 10507, 284, 296
P.London BM EA 10541+Paris Louvre E. 6258, P.Nedjmet, 84–85, 89, 105, 171, 205–6, 386, 403, 405
P.London BM EA 10554, P.Greenfield, P.Nesitanebetisheru, 93–96, 100–1, 103, 163, 194, 205–6, 268, 351, 380, 388, 423, 516
P.London BM EA 10558, P.Ankhwahibre, 117, 120, 125–32, 136, 138, 193–94, 468, 474, 478
P.London BM EA 10671, 147, 152
P.London BM EA 10738, 38, 48
P.London BM EA 10793, P.Pinedjem II, 92–96
P.London BM EA 10796, P.Tanetaset, 209
P.London BM EA 10983+Private Collection, P.Beret, 147, 149, 152–53, 210, 214
P.London BM EA 10988, 98,
P.London BM EA 29997, 40
P.London BM EA 604, 406
P.London BM EA 73806, 64
P.London BM EA 73808, 64
P.London BM EA 74125, 38, 47, 48
P.London BM EA 9900, P.Nebseny, 36–37, 48, 62, 64, 165–66, 342, 351, 375–76, 386, 403, 494–95, 498–99
P.London BM EA 9901, P.Hunefer, 64, 397, 411, 494, 496, 562
P.London BM EA 9903, 84
P.London BM EA 9904, P.Asetemakhbit, 205, 207, 414
P.London BM EA 9905, 38, 47, 50
P.London BM EA 9912, 473
P.London BM EA 9913+79431+Bologna KS 3168+Moscow I, 1b,122, P.Tui, 37, 44, 47–48, 162
P.London BM EA 9916, 297, 300
P.London BM EA 9918, 86
P.London BM EA 9919, P.Tentosorkon, 86–87
P.London BM EA 9938, P.Tanetshedkhonsu, 205, 207
P.London BM EA 9940, 543
P.London BM EA 9950, 38, 47–48, 50
P.London BM EA 9955, P.Pashed, 69, 309, 342

P.London BM EA 9964, 44, 48, 56
P.London BM EA 9968, 38, 47–48
P.London BM EA 9969, P.Neferetiri, 202
P.London BM EA 9988, P.Shemes, 46, 64–65
P.London BM EA 9994, P.Lansing, 193
P.London UC 32365, P.Khnumemheb, 62, 387
P.London UC 71001, P.Satiah, 202
P.London UC 71002, 54–55, 62, 344
P.London UC 71004, 47
P.London UC 71075, P.Nesikhonsu, 117, 120, 129, 133–34
P.Los Angeles 83.AI.46.3, 38, 48
P.Maatkare (daughter of Pinedjem II), P.Cairo S.R. IV 959, 96
P.Maatkare, P.Cairo S.R. IV 980 = J.E. 26229 = CG 40007, 105, 203, 206, 387, 414
P.MacGregor, 321, 332–33, 368
P.Maiherperi, P.Cairo CG 24095, 36, 64, 351, 403
P.Marseille 291, 435
P.Men, P.Lille 139, 118, 120
P.Menenwahibre/P.Arptahhep, P.Paris Louvre N 3091, 117, 120, 163, 449, 452
P.Menkheperraseneb, 36
P.Menkheperre (grandson of Menkheperre), P.Cairo S.R. IV 967 = J.E. 95866, 97
P.Meryt, P.Paris BnF 826, 36–37, 199, 202
P.Mesemnetjer, P.Paris Louvre E 21324, 37, 42–43, 47–48, 64, 494
P.Mesu, P.Moscow I, 1b, 28, 202
P.Milan 1023, 473
P.Milbank, P.Chicago OIM 10486, 194, 368, 425
P.Modena Or. 101, 155
P.Moscow I, 1b, 107+Cairo J.E. 95685+95745+ 95840+95841, P.Tawiri, 207–8
P.Moscow I, 1b, 121, P.Tashepenkhonsu, 207–8
P.Moscow I, 1b, 146+132, 38, 48
P.Moscow I, 1b, 26 (B), P.Henut, 202
P.Moscow I, 1b, 28, P.Mesu, 202
P.Munich ÄS 808, 546–47, 549
P.Mutmut, P.Florence 3665+3666+Vienna KHM 3850, 210, 214, 309
P.Nakht, P.London BM EA 10471+10473, 46, 64, 169, 170, 172
P.Nakhtamun, P.Berlin P. 3002, 64, 359, 369, 387, 543–45, 547, 550
P.Nakhtmin, 36, 37
P.Nauny, P.New York MMA 30.3.31, 105

P.Nauny, P.New York MMA 30.3.32, 105
P.Nebqed, P.Paris Louvre N 3068+3113, 53, 370, 387, 411, 414, 495, 497
P.Nebseny, P.London BM EA 9900, 36–37, 48, 62, 64, 165–66, 342, 351, 375–76, 386, 403, 494–95, 498–99
P.Nedjmet, P.London BM EA 10490, 89–90, 100, 105, 171, 203–6
P.Nedjmet, P.London BM EA 10541+Paris Louvre E 6258, 84–5, 89, 105, 171, 205–6, 386, 403, 405
P.Neferetiri, P.London BM EA 9969, 202
P.Neferkhaut, 36, 38, 48
P.Neferrenpet, P.Brüssel E 5043, 67–69, 71, 446
P.Nefertii, P.Berlin P. 10477, 210–11, 321–22, 328–31, 333–34, 368, 550, 551
P.Neferubenef, P.Paris Louvre N 3092 (III 93)+ Montpellier, 38, 47, 386, 494
P.Nesikhonsu, P.Cairo S.R. VII 11573 = S.R. VII 11485 = J.E. 26230, 91, 205–6, 387
P.Nesikhonsu, P.London UC 71075, 117, 120, 129, 133–34
P.Nesikhonsupakhered, P.Paris Louvre E 31856, 96
P.Nesitabetawi, P.Paris BnF 138–140+Paris Louvre E 3661, 50, 91, 205–6
P.Nesitanebetisheru, P.London BM EA 10554 = P.Greenfield, 93–96, 100–1, 103, 163, 194, 205–6, 268, 351, 380, 388, 423, 516
P.Nesmin, 368
P.Nespaasobek, P.Berlin P. 3010, 99, 105
P.Nespasefy, P.Cairo J.E. 95714 (S.R. IV 647)+ JE 95649 (S.R. IV 547)+Albany 1900.3.1+ Marseille 91/2/1+291, 117–18, 120, 127, 138, 451–52, 531
P.Neuchâtel Eg. 429, 69
P.New York Amherst 30, 389
P.New York Amherst 38, 155
P.New York Amherst fragments, group 7 + group 8, 153
P.New York Br.M. 37.1777 E, 38–39, 42, 44, 46–8, 161
P.New York MMA 25.3.212+Ann Arbor 81.4.25+Florence 11912a–b+Providence A 18077+Toronto 910.85.222+Unknown, private collection of H. Carter (lost), P. Khamhor C, 117, 120, 138, 167, 168, 169, 452

P.New York MMA 25.3.29, P.Henttawy, 95, 203, 206
P.New York MMA 25.3.31, P.Gatseshen, 79, 80
P.New York MMA 25.3.32, 98
P.New York MMA 25.3.34, P.Tii, 205, 207
P.New York MMA 30.3.31, P.Nauny, 105
P.New York MMA 30.3.32, P.Nauny, 105
P.New York MMA 35.9.19, P.Seteshnakht, 353, 368
P.New York MMA 35.9.20, 299, 324
P.New York MMA 35.9.21, P.Imouthes, 290, 298, 324
P.New York MMA without no., 37, 38
P.Northumberland III, 414, 415
P.Nu, P.London BM EA 10477, 37, 42, 44, 46, 48, 64, 166, 186, 188, 191–93, 272, 342–43, 424, 445, 494, 530–31
P.Oslo (without no.), 153
P.Padiamenet, P.London BM EA 10063, 83
P.Padiashsedjem, P.Berlin P. 10478, 550
P.Padihorpachered, P.Aberdeen ABDUA 84023, 209–11, 364
P.Paennestitauy, P.London BM EA 10064, 91, 95–97, 165, 341, 387
P.Paris BnF 1–19, 497, 499
P.Paris BnF 138–140+Paris Louvre E 3661, P. Nesitabetawi, 50, 91, 205–6
P.Paris BnF 149, 288–89, 308, 310, 312
P.Paris BnF 38–45, 406
P.Paris BnF 62–88, P.Ankhesenaset, 91, 169, 205–6
P.Paris BnF 63–98, 565
P.Paris BnF 826, P.Meryt, 36, 37, 199, 202
P.Paris BnF 93–98, 565
P.Paris Louvre AF 13042 C, 312
P.Paris Louvre AF 3027, 312
P.Paris Louvre AF 6493, 409–10
P.Paris Louvre E 11078, 300, 475–76
P.Paris Louvre E 11085, P.Hatnofret (mother of Senenmut), 38, 42, 45, 48, 65
P.Paris Louvre E 17401, 413
P.Paris Louvre E 21324, P.Mesemnetjer, 37, 42–43, 47–8, 64, 494
P.Paris Louvre E 31856, P.Nesikhonsupakhered, 96
P.Paris Louvre E 3232, 461
P.Paris Louvre E 3233, 447, 454

P.Paris Louvre E 3452, 289, 310
P.Paris Louvre E 3865, 147, 153, 342
P.Paris Louvre E 5353, 297, 308, 313
P.Paris Louvre E 7716, 462
P.Paris Louvre L 3087, 51
P.Paris Louvre N 3063, P.Tanetkhebet, 210, 214, 368
P.Paris Louvre N 3068+3113, P.Nebqed, 53, 370, 387, 411, 414, 495, 497
P.Paris Louvre N 3073, 38, 47–8, 50, 352, 398
P.Paris Louvre N 3074, 52, 304
P.Paris Louvre N 3079, 51, 341, 458, 461, 463, 466, 473
P.Paris Louvre N 3079, Tradition of, 458, 461, 473
P.Paris Louvre N 3081, P.Hornedjitef, 165, 368, 451, 465, 475
P.Paris Louvre N 3082, 461–62, 466
P.Paris Louvre N 3083+Paris Louvre N. 3194 A, P.Asetreshti, 210–11
P.Paris Louvre N 3084, 476, 479
P.Paris Louvre N 3085, 147, 153
P.Paris Louvre N 3089, 389, 455, 462, 465, 473, 475–76
P.Paris Louvre N 3090, 464
P.Paris Louvre N 3091, P.Arptahhep/P.Menenwahibre, 117, 120, 163, 449, 452
P.Paris Louvre N 3092 (III 93)+Montpellier, P.Neferubenef, 38, 47, 386, 494
P.Paris Louvre N 3094, 127
P.Paris Louvre N 3100, 446–47
P.Paris Louvre N 3122, 289
P.Paris Louvre N 3125, 147, 152
P.Paris Louvre N 3129+E 4890B+Krakau Nationalmuseum XI 1503-06.1508-11+Brüssel MRAH E. 4976, 389, 467, 472
P.Paris Louvre N 3143+Geneva D 229, 389, 464
P.Paris Louvre N 3144, 458, 460–61, 463, 466
P.Paris Louvre N 3151, 464
P.Paris Louvre N 3152, Tradition of, 461
P.Paris Louvre N 3248, 389, 433, 442, 447–48, 468, 471, 473
P.Paris Louvre N 3249, 461–62
P.Paris Louvre N 3272, 447
P.Paris Louvre N 3278, 147, 153
P.Paris Louvre N 3279, P.Tawau, 153, 210, 214
P.Paris Louvre N 3284, 309

P.Paris Louvre N 3292, 86
P.Paris Louvre N 5450, 449–50, 453, 467, 468
P.Paris Louvre N. 3279, 210
P.Parma 183, 296
P.Pashebmutwebkhet, P.London BM EA 10007, 88
P.Pashed, P.London BM EA 9955, 69, 309, 342
P.Pasherientaihet, P.Vatican 48832, 118, 120–21, 125–26, 129, 138, 388
P.Pefiuiu, P.Berlin P. 3161+Kopenhagen Aae 5+Sydney R346a+Tübingen 2000, 119–20
P.Pinedjem I, P.Cairo S.R. VII 11488 = CG 40006, 105, 406
P.Pinedjem II, P.London BM EA 10793, 92–96
P.Princeton Pharaonic Roll 10, 296
P.Princeton Pharaonic Roll 2, 69, 71
P.Princeton Pharaonic Roll 5, 54
P.Privat MacGregor, P.Tarepit, 210–11
P.Private collection, P.Amenemhet, 38, 47–48, 52
P.Qenna, P.Leiden T 2, 495
P.Qeqa, 142
P.Ramose, P.Berlin P. 15778, 69
P.Ramose, P.Cambridge E. 2.1922, 62, 344, 387
P.Reading, P.Henutmehyt, 199, 202
P.Reret, P.Berlin P. 3158, 209–11, 364
P.Rhind I, 310, 329
P.Ruiu, 36, 38, 48, 199, 202
P.Ryerson, P.Chicago OIM E 9787+New York Columbia University Library Inv. 784, 389, 426, 454, 456, 473
P.Rylands Hieroglyphic Manuscript 1–4, 564–65
P.Sakhti, P.Bucharest Mss. oriental 376, 202
P.Satamen, P.TT 65, 202
P.Satiah, P.London UCL 71001, 202
P.Sekowski, P.Cracow, 290
P.Senemnetjer, P.Florence 3660 A, 62
P.Senhetep, P.Cairo CG 40004, 403, 405
P.Senneferi, 36
P.Setesh-Nakht, P.New York MMA 35.9.19, 353, 368
P.Shemes, P.London BM EA 9988, 46, 64–65
P.Sobekmose, 170
P.St. Gallen, 154
P.St. Petersburg 18586, 38, 47
P.Taatum, P.Berlin P. 3195, 364, 406–7

P.Tabakhenkhonsu, P.Cairo S.R. VII 10222, 84, 205, 207
P.Tadimut, P.Cairo CG 58005 = J.E. 35413, 201–2
P.Taitem, P.Berlin P. 3159 A–D, 209–11
P.Takerheb, P.Christchurch EA 1988.73–76, 209, 211
P.Tallin k-542/AM 5877, P.Aset, 202
P.Tameret, P.Turin Cat. 1849 = CGT 53001, 204–6, 223
P.Tanetaset, P.London BM EA 10796, 209
P.Tanetimen, P.Toulouse 73.1.6, 210, 214
P.Tanetkhebet, P.Paris Louvre N 3063, 210, 214, 368
P.Tanetshedkhonsu, P.London BM EA 9938, 205, 207
P.Tarepit, P.Privat MacGregor, 210–11
P.Tarudj, P.Berlin P. 3008, 210–11, 305, 389, 550
P.Tashepenkhonsu, P.Moscow I, 1b, 121, 207–8
P.Tasheredenaset, P.Heidelberg von Portheim-Stiftung A, 207–8
P.Tasheretenaset, P.Assisi Biblioteca Comunale 351+ Budapest National Library Cod. Afr. 2a-b+Heidelberg P Hier. 566+Heidelberg Portheim-Stiftung A+Jerusalem Bible Lands Museum H 376+Cairo J.E. 95685 (S.R. IV 615)+J.E. 95745 (S.R. IV 692)+J.E. 95840 (S.R. IV 938)+J.E. 95841 (S.R. IV 939)+J.E. 95864 (S.R. IV 964)+New York without no., 118, 120, 125, 127, 129, 138
P.Tasheretenkhonsu, P.Turin Cat. 1837, 209, 211–12, 224
P.Tasherettaikhet, P.Leiden T 31, 210–11
P.Tawau, P.Paris Louvre N 3279, 153, 210, 214
P.Tawedjatra, P.Cairo S.R. VII 11496, 86, 413
P.Tawiri, P.Moscow I, 1b, 107+Cairo J.E. 95685+95745+95840+95841, 207–8
P.Taysnakht, P.Turin Cat. 1833, 209, 211, 213, 225, 454, 458
P.Tentosorkon, P.London BM EA 9919, 86–87
P.Tii, P.New York MMA 25.3.34, 205, 207
P.Tokyo SK 116–1, 550, 552
P.Toronto ROM 910.85.236.1–13, 142
P.Toulouse 73.1.6, P.Tanetimen, 210, 214
P.TT 65, P.Satamen, 202
P.TT 79, 38, 47

P.TT 87, 38, 47
P.TT 99, 37–8
P.TT 99, 47
P.Tübingen 2012, 147–48, 153, 154
P.Tübingen 2016, 309–11
P.Tübingen ÄS 2003 a–k, 37, 44
P.Tui, P.London BM EA 9913+79431+Bologna KS 3168+Moscow I, 1b,122, 37, 44, 47–48, 162
P.Turin 1791, P.Iufankh, 134, 137, 142, 303, 341–42, 344, 365–66, 378, 383–84, 389, 491–92, 498–99, 505, 537
P.Turin 1793, 388
P.Turin 1806, 389
P.Turin 1830, 472
P.Turin 1831, 388, 451
P.Turin 1848, 297, 309
P.Turin 1873, 154
P.Turin Cat. 1801, P.Asetweret, 210–11
P.Turin Cat. 1814, P.Kerheb, 209
P.Turin Cat. 1833, P.Taysnakht, 209, 211, 213, 225, 454, 458
P.Turin Cat. 1837, P.Tasheretenkhonsu, 209, 211–12, 224
P.Turin Cat. 1842, P.Irtiru, 208
P.Turin Cat. 1849 = CGT 53001, P.Tameret, 204–6, 223
P.Turin Cat. 1851 = CGT 53007, P.Asty, 97, 205, 207
P.Turin Cat. 1855 = CGT 53008, P.Djedmutiusankh, 205, 207
P.Turin Cat. 1862/2 = CGT 53009, P.Djedbastet, 205, 207
P.Turin CGT 53010, 97
P.Turin CGT 53012, 98
P.Turin N 766, 287, 297
P.Turin S 8438, P.Kha, 36–37, 54, 200, 220
P.Twt, 368
P.Vandier, 165
P.Vatican 37481, 149–50
P.Vatican 38568, 143
P.Vatican 38603, P.Asetweret, 210–11
P.Vatican 48832, P.Pasherientaihet, 118, 120–21, 125–26, 129, 138, 388
P.Vienna KHM ÄS 10158, 154, 302
P.Vienna KHM ÄS 3861, 147, 302, 307, 310
P.Vienna KHM ÄS 3865, 284

P. Vienna ÖN Aeg. 10.994–10.997, 50
P. Vienna ÖNB Aeg. 12.012+12.008 a–c, 155
P. Warsaw 21884, 37, 47
P. Warsaw 237128, P. Amenemopet,/P. Bakai, 199, 202
P. Yuya, P. Cairo CG 51189, 36–37, 47–48, 52, 54, 165–66, 386, 406, 409, 446
Padiamun, Coffin Liverpool 53.72D, 429
Padimenu, scribe, 165–68
Pahes, Coffin Graz Archäologiemuseum Schloss Eggenberg 23927, 324
Pakhi (P. Privat MacGregor), 210
Pantheon, theban, 442
Papyri, magical, 557
Papyri, stock, 181
Papyrus sheer joins, 553
Papyrus, liturgical, 296
Paris, Louvre Museum, 495
*Pars pro toto*, 378
Peace, social, 400
Pencil, 546
*Penny Dreadful*, 516
Personal Piety, 440
*Peseshenkef*, 360
Petosiris, 369
Phallus, 440
Philae, 252, 332
Philology, 267
Pierret, Paul, 494–95, 499
Pinedjem I, 84, 88–89, 105, 110, 203, 206
Pinedjem II, 79, 89, 91, 93, 95–96, 98, 100, 104, 110, 173, 205–6, 380, 385
Pleyte, Willem, 341, 433, 442, 495
Pliny the Elder, 551, 553
Pop culture, 514
Post-Amarna Period, 378, 440
Pound, Ezra, 508, 509, 511, 513
Preisner, Zbiginiev Antoni, 513
Presentation, 550
Priest (ḥm-nṯr), 227
Priest (sm), 227, 358, 360, 365
Priest of Montu, 165
Priestly oaths, 402
Procession, funeral, 357, 360, 363–65, 368–70
Proclamation of innocence, 416
Productive and reproductive, 267
Property, cultic, 402

Proportion, 553
Protestation, 399, 402
Proto-Meroitic, 439
Province, 400
Prussian expedition to Egypt and Nubia, 493
Psametik I, 369
Pseudepigrapha, 436
Psusennes I, 104, 105
Psusennes II, 96
Psusennes III (Pasebakhaennut), 97, 173
Psychostasy, 221, 240
Ptah, 344, 422, 427
Ptah-Sokar, 325, 367
Ptah-Sokar-Osiris, 422
Ptah-Sokar-Osiris statuette, 324
Ptah-Sokar-Osiris statuette, Cairo RT 28/3/25/7, 324, 327–28
Ptaszynska, Jolanta, 513
Ptolemaic Period, 346, 348–51, 357, 360, 364–65, 368–69, 382–83, 413, 424, 426, 433, 435, 446, 450, 454–55, 457–58, 491, 497, 531, 564
Purification scene, 375
*Puzzle & Dragons*, 516
Pyramid Texts, 9–10, 14, 21, 26–27, 39, 46, 66, 218, 229, 231–32, 235, 247, 250, 263, 266, 279, 289, 301, 308, 343, 373–74, 393, 424, 430, 445, 493, 533–34
§ 217, 18
§ 218, 18
§ 219, 18
§ 251, 290
§ 252, 290
§ 253, 290
§ 266, 290
§ 269, 253
§ 374b–c, 373
§ 600, 253
§ 761, 373
§ 981a–985b, 373
§ 1132a–1137b, 373
§ 1408a–1412b, 373
§ 1748b, 373
§ 2070a, 373

Qaw el-Kebir, 22, 227, 239
Queen mother, 201

Quirke, Stephen, 533, 537
QV 66, tomb of Nefertari, 67, 233

Ramesside Period, 360, 369, 437, 440
Ramses II, 67, 199, 219, 436
Ramses XI, 203, 206
*Rasetjau*, 350, 358–59
Re, 19, 29, 170, 219, 226, 228, 270, 304, 307–8, 327, 349–50, 353, 359, 396–98, 421–23, 426–27, 429–30, 468, 516–17, 532
Re, followers of, 424
Realm of the dead, 349
Rebellion of humanity, 424
Rebirth, 425, 436
Recension, 493
Recension, Kushite, 267
Recension, Late, 434, 438, 529, 531–34, 536
Recension, Saite, 50, 61, 77, 96–98, 141–42, 267, 344–45, 347, 382, 434, 446, 531
Recension, Theban, 61–62, 530–31, 533–34, 536
Reception of BD, 506
Reconstruction, 547–48
Register, 523
Register of language, 522
Re-Horakhty, 82, 83, 205, 367–68, 370, 422, 437, 467, 468
Re-Horakhty-Atum, 104
Rejuvenation, 352
Remounting, 548
Renaissance, 556
Renenutet, 412
Rennefer, 199, 202
Reproductive entity, 440
Reproductivity, 267
Rerek, 430
Residue of bitumen, 544
Resurrection, 412
Retouching of void, 546
Retrograde, 24–25, 45, 50, 171, 184, 219, 232
*Reu nu Pert em Hru*, 515
Revelations of the Mysteries of the Four Balls, 290
Revenge, violent, 394
Rifeh, 14, 37, 62
Rite, funerary, 368
Rite, initiation, 402
Rite, mortuary, 393

Rite, temple initiation, 402
Ritual code, 506
Ritual elevation, 393
Ritual for Antinoos, 297
Ritual of Embalming, 223, 284
Ritual of Glorifying Osiris, 283
Ritual of Horus of the Night, 23
Ritual of Introducing the Multitude on the Last Day of Tekh, 284, 290
Ritual of the Glorification of Osiris in the God's Domain, 305
Ritual performance, 414
Ritual purity, 402
Ritual-book for amulets of gold, 345
Roadmap, painted, 445
Roman Period, 402, 424
Rome, Biblioteca Laurentina, 562
Rosetta Stone, 490
Rougé, Emmanuel de, 494–95
Royal Cache, 512
Royal Cachette, 77, 84, 89, 92, 93, 105, 380, 385
Royal scribe, 169
Rubric, 303, 357, 438
Ruti, 233
*rw*-lion, 440

Sacrality, 436
Sais, 436
Saite Period, 137, 139, 341, 446, 449–50, 454, 536
Sakhmet, 425, 428, 429
Salam, Shadi Abdel, 512
Salvation, 394
Sandbank, 430
Saqqara, 12, 66, 166, 209, 227, 237, 295, 312, 490
Sarcophagus of Pashed, 68
Sarcophagus of Senenmut, 27
Sarcophagus shrine of Khonsu, 68
Sarcophagus T 3C, 9
Satdjehuti Satibu, Coffin Munich SSÄK ÄS 7163, 26, 40, 43, 45
Sathathormeret, Coffin Da 1C, 13
Satsobek, Coffin Da 3C, 13
Scale, 396, 403, 410, 414, 426, 517
Scarab, 345
Scarab, beetle, 415
Scarab, heart, 20, 403, 415

Scorpion bite, 438
Scribe, 165–68, 380
Scrolls, 542
Secret, divine, 402
Sedment, 37, 62, 378
*sekhem*-scepter, 365
Sekhet Aaru, 514
Sekhmet, 209
Selfcreation, 415
Senebhenaf, Coffin, 23
Senenmut, 37
Senenmut (L.Cairo J.E. 66218), 198, 201, 231, 377
*senet*-game, 233, 270
Sennefer, 221
Senwosret, 12
Senwosret II, 13
Senwosret III, 13, 15
Seqenenre Taa (Shroud Cairo J.E. 96805), 198, 201
Sequence, 343, 435, 477, 532–34
Serpent, 446, 463
Service des Antiquités d'Egypte, 513
Sesenebenef, Coffin L 1–2Li, 16, 23, 28
Seth, 376, 395, 422, 430, 525
Setne II, 406, 408
Seven, 400
Seven celestial cows, 425
Seven Hathors, 425
Shabaqo, 235
*shabti*, 29, 438, 441
*shabti*-boxes, 199
Shai, 412
Sheikh Abd el-Qurna, 231
Sheshonq, 95
Sheshonq III, 78, 234
Shroud, linen, 426, 445, 493
    L.Berlin 10476+Hanover Dartmouth College 39–64–6623, 41, 43, 45
    L.Cairo CG 40001 = J.E.26203+Boston MFA 60.1472, 36–38, 47–48
    L.Cairo CG 96804, 41, 45, 48
    L.Cairo CG 96807+Norwich 1921.37.50, 38, 41, 43, 45, 47
    L.Cairo IFAO, 38, 47
    L.Cairo IFAO, Senhotep, 62
    L.Cairo J.E. 33984, 49
    L.Cairo J.E. 66218, Hatneferet, 38, 45–47, 198, 201, 211
    L.Cairo J.E. 96805, Tetisheri, 37, 40–41, 43, 45, 198, 201
    L.Cairo J.E. 96806, 38, 41, 43, 45, 47
    L.Cairo J.E. 96810, Ahmose-Henut-Tjemehu, 40–45, 48, 198, 201, 445
    L.Cairo O.A.E. 325+343, Amenemwesekhet, 40–41, 198, 201
    L.Hanover 39–64–6623+Berlin P. 10467, Mahu, 198, 201
    L.Inyotef, 40
    L.London BM EA 7036, 43
    L.London BM EA 73669, 43
    L.London BM EA 73807, 43
    L.London BM EA 73807, Resti, 41, 198, 201
    L.London Horniman Museum 26.106, 9260 i–ii, Itenem, 62
    L.Moscow 1027, Iahmes, 41, 45, 198, 201
    L.Munich, 38, 41, 45, 47
    L.New York MMA 20.3.201, 43
    L.New York MMA 22.3.296, 43, 445
    L.New York MMA TT 850, 219
    L.New York MMA without no., Senimen, 37, 45
    L.Paris Louvre N 3097, 445
    L.Senneferi, 36
    L.Siaa, 165
    L.Sydney R 92, Tany, 42, 198, 201, 219
    L.Thutmose III, 283
    L.TT 65, Senhotep, 43
    L.TT 99, 37–8, 41–2, 45, 47
    L.Turin CGT 63001 = Suppl. 5051, Ahmose, 37–38, 40–31, 43, 45, 47, 198, 201, 219
    L.Turin CGT 63002+63003+Uppsala without no., 40–43, 45, 219
    L.Turin CGT 63004, 41, 45, 219
    L.Turin CGT 63005, 41, 43, 45, 48, 219
    L.Turin CGT 63006, 45
    L.Wellcome Collection Swansea W 869, Hepi, 62
Shu, 270, 422–23, 427, 565
Siamon, 91, 93
Siamun, 369
Sinuhe, Tale of, 193, 526
Siwa Oasis, 239, 369
Sledge, 363

Smendes II, 206
Snake, 343, 347
Sobek, 343, 427, 429
Sokar, 333, 358, 413
Sokar festival, 442
Sokar figurine, 332
Sokar-Osiris, 408
Soknopaiou Nesos, 298
Solar boat, 424, 430, 436
Solar crew, 424
Solar cycle, 248
Solar disk, 425, 438
Solar-Osirian cycle, 281
Solar-Osirian unity, 239
Solar-Osiris / Osiris, solar, 253
Sommers, Stephen, 515
Songs of Isis and Nephthys, 284
*Soratobu Medjed-niisan*, 516
Sothis, 304
Soul, 358
Spell for Knowing the Souls of the Sacred Places, 50
Spell for Protecting the Bark of Re, 304
Spell of Breathing and Living by Breath in the God's Domain, 302
Spell, Theban, 442
Spirit, 421, 427, 430–31
Spirit, glorified, 421
Stabilization, 546
Standard, ethical, 400
Stanzas of the Festival of the Two Kites, 284
Status, initiated, 399
Stela, 231
Stela, Horus on the crocodiles, 222
Stela, London BM EA 305, Neferabu, 69–70
Stela, Museo Archeologico di Torino Suppl. 6148bis, Hui, 68–9
Storage, 550
Style, 523
Sudan, 238
Sumer, 510, 514, 522
Sun, 422
Sun barque, 50, 517
Sun disk, 449, 468
Sun god, *see* Re
Suns nightly journey, 397

Supernatural, 428
Swallow, 54
Sycomore, 332, 424, 468
Sycomore of all *bas*, 332
Sycomore of Nut, 332
Syllabic script, 438
Syncretistic, 422

Tablet, New York MMA 55.144.1, 297
Tanis, 78, 95, 100–2, 234, 380, 385, 433, 436
Tanous, wife of Monthesouphis, 287
Tanutamani, 238
Teaching of Ani, 414
Teaching of Ptahhotep, 414
Teachings, *see* wisdom literature
Tefnut, 270, 422, 425, 427, 565
Temple, 421, 428
Temple integrity, 402
Temple offering, 424
Temple ritual, 424
Temple ritual purity, 400
Testimony, false, 346
Textual criticism, 265, 266, 530
*The Blessed Dead*, 514
*The Coming forth by Day of Osiris Jones*, 511
The First Letter for Breathing, 214, *see also* Books of Breathing; Documents of Breathing
*The Mummy*, 515
*The Night of Counting the Years*, 512
The Old Ones, 510
*The Opening of the Mouth*, 514
Theban Tombs,
Thebes, 9–10, 14–15, 20–21, 24, 29, 37, 40, 62, 66, 67, 76–78, 101, 142, 162, 165, 172–73, 203, 205, 207, 211, 221, 227–28, 231, 233, 235, 238, 240–41, 284–85, 288, 295–97, 300, 303, 309, 312, 329, 333, 357, 365, 368–70, 378, 380, 385, 425, 426, 434, 436, 440, 450, 454–55, 457–58, 461, 463, 465, 467, 469, 473, 479, 493, 557, 558
Theocracy, 441
Theology, new solar, 440
Theology, solar, 440
Theology, theban, 434, 439, 441–42
Theonym, 439

# INDEX

*Thesaurus Linguae Aegyptia*, 537
Third Intermediate Period, 341, 349, 350, 351, 364
Thoth, 182, 214, 239, 253, 268–69, 272, 273, 304, 306, 312, 329, 350, 358, 367, 396, 398, 401, 411, 422, 426, 427, 428, 509, 525
Thoueris, 412
Threat against tomb violation, 394
Thutmose I, 282
Thutmose III, 24–29, 38–39, 41, 45–46, 48, 50, 53, 198, 219, 221, 232, 357, 397, 411, 445, 531
Thutmose IV, 38, 47, 199, 219, 232
Title, 325
Tjenna (Shroud Cairo J.E. 96805), 201
Tomb of Amenemhat, 232
Tomb of Ankhefamum, 100
Tomb of Ankheseamun, 101
Tomb of Bakenrenef, 383
Tomb of Khesuwer, 13
Tomb of Khonsuheb, 100
Tomb of Nefertari, 67, 233
Tomb of Osorkon II, 101–2, 385
Tomb of Paatonemheb, 378, 387
Tomb of Pennut, 378
Tomb of Petosiris, 239–40
Tomb of Petubastis, 240
Tomb of Sheshonq, 101
Tomb of Sheshonq III, 100–1
Tomb of Soter, 149
Topography, 251
Topography of the netherworld, 221
Toponym, 439
*Totenbuch*, 505
*Totenliteratur*, 281
*Totenliturgie*, 27, 281
Transcendent, 441
Transfiguration, 137, 393, 394, 402
Transfiguration spell, 18
Transformation, 187, 327, 343–44, 347, 375, 421, 509
Transformation spells, 24, 26, 40, 50, 54–5, 66, 137, 221, 225, 232, 290, 422
Transgression, 400
Translation, 521–38
Translation Studies, 522
Transliteration, 525
Trial, 426

Tribunal, divine, 394–400, 403, 411, 414, 426
True of voice (*mꜣꜥ-ḥrw*), 396, 413
TT C 4, 386
TT MMA 729, tomb of Neferkhawet, 199
TT 1, tomb of Sennedjem, 67–70, 175
TT 3, 67, 69
TT 5, tomb of Neferabu, 69–70
TT 8, 36, 37
TT 11, tomb of Djehuty, 66, 231–32
TT 27, tomb of Sheshonq, 235, 237
TT 33, tomb of Padiamenope, 235–39, 241
TT 34, tomb of Montuemhat, 235–37, 241
TT 36, tomb of Ibi, 235
TT 37, tomb of Harwa, 235, 237
TT 57, 386
TT 60, MMA 60, 77–78, 88, 95, 105
TT 61, 26, 36–7, 56
TT 65, 36
TT 71, tomb of Senenmut, 27, 36, 231
TT 79, 36
TT 82, 36, 46, 66, 231–32
TT 85, tomb of Amenemheb Called Mahu, 199, 202
TT 87, tomb of Nakhtmin, 36–37, 66
TT 96 B, tomb of Sennefer, 66,
TT 99, tomb of Senneferi, 36, 56
TT 131, 36, 56
TT 178, tomb of Neferrenpet, 410–11
TT 196, tomb of Padihorresnet, 235, 237, 369
TT 197, tomb of Padineith, 235
TT 218, tomb of Amunnakht, 67–68
TT 219, 67
TT 223, tomb of Karakhamun, 235, 237, 241
TT 240, 9
TT 252, 36
TT 265, 67
TT 279, tomb of Pabasa, 235–37, 369
TT 290, tomb of Irynefer, 67, 68, 344
TT 319, 9
TT 320, 512
TT 335, tomb of Nakhtamun, 67
TT 336, tomb of Neferrenpet, 67
TT 341, tomb of Nakhtamon, 411
TT 353, tomb of Senenmut, 27, 36, 46, 66, 231, 377, 379–80, 385–86
TT 358, MMA 65, 77, 105
TT 360, 219

TT 365, tomb of Nefermenu, 406, 408
TT 389, tomb of Basa, 235
TT 391, tomb of Karabaskeni, 235
TT 404, tomb of Akhimenru, 235, 237
TT 410, tomb of Mutirdis, 235
TT 414, tomb of Ankhhor, 235, 237
Tuna el-Gebel, 239, 369
Turquoise, 468
Tutankhamun, 56, 357, 363–64
Twelve, number of, 422
Tylose MH 1000, 546

*udjat*-eye (*wḏꜣ.t*), 11, 16, 18, 329, 345, 406, 408, 415, 425
Umbilical cord, 430
Underworld, 11, 393, 436
Underworld Book, 393, 397–98
Underworld Gate, 401
Union, 422
Union of Re and Osiris, 97
Union, Solar and Osirian, 104
Unut, 167
Unwrapping ceremony, 490
Upper Egypt, 295
Ureaus, 398
Urk. I, 122, 9–16, 395
Urk. IV, 119, 10–11, 414
Urtext, 530
*Ushabti, see shabti*

Valley of the Kings, 67, 233
Valley of the Queens, 24–25, 67, 233

Values, moral, 400
Variant, 463
Verhoeven, Ursula, 534, 536
Vignette, 345, 350–51, 421–22, 427–28, 434, 489, 505, 512, 517, 564
Vocabulary, 438
Voces magicae, 439
Vulture, 345, 365

Wadi el-Jarf, 181
*was*-scepter, 463
Water, 348
Weighing, 408, 410–11, 416
Weighing of the Heart, 235, 245, 252, 396, 403
Weighing scene, 404–9
Wennefer, 167, 270, 283, 399
*Wenu* (Hermopolis), 272
Wepwawet, 427
*wer-hekaw*-instrument, 360, 367
*wesekh*-collar, 253
White City, 333
Wife, 556
Wisdom literature, 400
Words, untranslated, 527
World, inverted, 347

X-Ray fluorescence (XRF), 553

Yourcenar, Marguerite, 522, 524

*Zauberflöte*, 504
Zukofsky, Louis, 508, 513